Introduction to
Clinical Psychology

McGraw-Hill Series in Psychology

CONSULTING EDITOR
Norman Garmezy

Adams Human Memory
Berlyne Conflict, Arousal, and Curiosity
Bernstein and Nietzel Introduction to Clinical Psychology
Blum Psychoanalytic Theories of Personality
Bock Multivariate Statistical Methods in Behavioral Research
Brown The Motivation of Behavior
Campbell, Dunnette, Lawler, and Weick Managerial Behavior, Performance, and Effectiveness
Crites Vocational Psychology
D'Amato Experimental Psychology: Methodology, Psychophysics, and Learning
Dollard and Miller Personality and Psychotherapy
Ferguson Statistical Analysis in Psychology and Education
Fodor, Bever, and Garrett The Psychology of Language: An Introduction to Psycholinguistics and Generative Grammar
Forgus and Melamed Perception: A Cognitive-Stage Approach
Franks Behavior Therapy: Appraisal and Status
Gilmer and Deci Industrial and Organizational Psychology
Guilford Psychometric Methods
Guilford The Nature of Human Intelligence
Guilford and Fruchter Fundamental Statistics in Psychology and Education
Guion Personnel Testing
Hetherington and Parke Child Psychology: A Contemporary Viewpoint
Hirsh The Measurement of Hearing
Hjelle and Ziegler Personality Theories: Basic Assumptions, Research, and Applications
Horowitz Elements of Statistics for Psychology and Education
Hulse, Egeth, and Deese The Psychology of Learning
Hurlock Adolescent Development
Hurlock Child Development
Hurlock Developmental Psychology
Krech, Crutchfield, and Ballachey Individual in Society
Lakin Interpersonal Encounter: Theory and Practice in Sensitivity Training
Lawler Pay and Organizational Effectiveness: A Psychological View
Lazarus, A. Behavior Therapy and Beyond
Lazarus, R. Patterns of Adjustment
Lewin A Dynamic Theory of Personality
Maher Principles of Psychopathology

Marascuilo   Statistical Methods for Behavioral Science Research
Marx and Hillix   Systems and Theories in Psychology
Miller   Language and Communication
Morgan   Physiological Psychology
Mulaik   The Foundations of Factor Analysis
Novick and Jackson   Statistical Methods for Educational and Psychological Research
Nunnally   Introduction to Statistics for Psychology and Education
Nunnally   Psychometric Theory
Overall and Klett   Applied Multivariate Analysis
Porter, Lawler, and Hackman   Behavior in Organizations
Robinson and Robinson   The Mentally Retarded Child
Rosenthal   Genetic Theory and Abnormal Behavior
Ross   Psychological Disorders of Children: A Behavioral Approach to Theory,
   Research, and Therapy
Shaw   Group Dynamics: The Psychology of Small Group Behavior
Shaw and Costanzo   Theories of Social Psychology
Shaw and Wright   Scales for the Measurement of Attitudes
Sidowski   Experimental Methods and Instrumentation in Psychology
Siegel   Nonparametric Statistics for the Behavioral Sciences
Spencer and Kass   Perspectives in Child Psychology
Stagner   Psychology of Personality
Steers and Porter   Motivation and Work Behavior
Vinacke   The Psychology of Thinking
Winer   Statistical Principles in Experimental Design

Introduction to Clinical Psychology

Douglas A. Bernstein

Professor of Psychology
University of Illinois, Urbana–Champaign

Michael T. Nietzel

Associate Professor of Psychology
University of Kentucky

McGraw-Hill Book Company

New York St. Louis San Francisco Auckland Bogotá Hamburg Johannesburg
London Madrid Mexico Montreal New Delhi Panama Paris
São Paulo Singapore Sydney Tokyo Toronto

This book was set in Times Roman by Black Dot, Inc. (ECU).
The editors were Richard R. Wright, Rhona Robbin, and Barry Benjamin;
the production supervisor was John Mancia.
The drawings were done by Danmark & Michaels, Inc.
The cover was designed by Jean King.
R. R. Donnelley & Sons Company was printer and binder.

INTRODUCTION TO CLINICAL PSYCHOLOGY

1 2 3 4 5 6 7 8 9 0 D O D O 8 9 8 7 6 5 4 3 2 1 0

Library of Congress Cataloging in Publication Data

Bernstein, Douglas A
  Introduction to clinical psychology.

  (McGraw-Hill series in psychology)
  Bibliography: p.
  Includes index.
  1. Clinical psychology. 2. Psychotherapy.
3. Personality assessment. I. Nietzel,
Michael T., joint author. II. Title.
[DNLM: 1. Psychology, Clinical. WM105 B53li]
RC467.B47   157′.9   79-18427
ISBN 0-07-005016-3

To Our Parents

Saul and Eleanor Bernstein
Myrle and Verle Nietzel

Contents

1
BASIC CONCEPTS

2
LEARNING ABOUT PEOPLE

3
HELPING PEOPLE CHANGE

4

THE PROFESSION OF CLINICAL PSYCHOLOGY

Preface

In the past, introductory courses in clinical psychology were taught at the graduate level only. This meant that many students committed themselves to graduate training in this field before they really had a chance to get a clear picture of what clinical psychology is, where it came from, and where it seems to be going. In recent years, however, more and more colleges and universities have added an introductory course in clinical psychology to their *undergraduate* curricula. We think this makes very good sense, but we have noticed in our own courses that because most, if not all, clinical textbooks are written primarily for graduate students, many undergraduates find them inappropriate to their background and level of interest. After all, not every undergraduate who takes a course in clinical psychology plans to become a clinical psychologist. And those who do may not yet be ready for the detail and intensity contained in many "graduate-student-only" texts.

With these points in mind, we decided to create a book which contains material appropriate for graduate-level introductory clinical psychology courses but, at the same time, is written with the undergraduate audience in mind. We wanted to present clinical psychology in a way that undergraduate students would find stimulating, whether or not they are psychology majors and whether or not they end up choosing clinical psychology as a career.

In doing so, we tried to accomplish three main goals. The first was to present material on the history, scope, functions, and future of clinical psychology in enough detail to meet scholarly standards without becoming preoccupied with minutiae. Our second goal was to remain as theoretically neutral as we could (in spite of our social-learning orientation) by highlighting psychodynamic, phenomenological, and social-learning perspectives on clinical assessment, treatment, and research. Third, we tried to write in a style that reflects who we are and how we teach: We like being clinical psychologists, and we enjoy teaching both undergraduate and graduate students. Some aspects of our task were less exciting than others but, overall, we had a good time writing this book. We hope you have a good time reading it. Your comments and suggestions are welcome and we hope to hear from you.

Douglas A. Bernstein
Michael T. Nietzel

Acknowledgments

I wish to thank a number of people who have been instrumental in moving this book from a general idea to a finished manuscript. Dana Finney, Barbara Swain, and Donna Wolanski provided excellent library research and reference cataloging services. Marsha Healy, Phyllis Jones, Jan Palumbo, and Nesbit Siems were all extraordinarily helpful in typing various drafts of the manuscript. In addition, Ms. Siems almost single-handedly completed the task of corresponding with publishers and other copyright holders to obtain permission to reproduce many of the figures and tables scattered throughout the book. Finally I wish to thank Vickie Fash, who not only typed early drafts of several chapters but provided much needed encouragement when the prospect of a completed manuscript seemed all too remote.

Douglas A. Bernstein

I am very grateful to Juris Berzins, Stu Fisher, Geri Cole, and Thomas House for their critical reading of several parts of the manuscript and for their many valuable suggestions on how to improve it. I owe special thanks to Ruth McKee, who devoted many hours of patience and skill to the final preparation of the manuscript. The work was made considerably easier by her many talents, not the least of which is a fine editorial eye that I have learned to trust.

Michael T. Nietzel

Part One

Basic Concepts

Chapter 1

The Field of Clinical Psychology

There are now approximately 20,000 students pursuing doctoral degrees in psychology at scores of universities in the United States and Canada, and the largest single group of them (about 33 percent) is studying clinical psychology. At the master's level, clinical psychology programs are also among the most popular in the field. The relative attractiveness and desirability of graduate work in clinical psychology are further illustrated by the fact that, while the ratio of applicants to admissions in nonclinical areas of psychology is about 10 to 1, twenty applications are commonly received each year for every available opening in clinical training programs. At the most prestigious institutions, this ratio may be as high as 100 to 1 (APA, 1975). It is not surprising, therefore, to hear the suggestion in recent years that getting into graduate school in psychology, and particularly in clinical psychology, may be more difficult than gaining admission to medical school (Nyman, 1973).

The appeal of clinical psychology is reflected in membership patterns of the American Psychological Association (APA), the national organization of psychologists in the United States. A recent survey (Cuca, 1975a) showed that 36 percent of all APA members list clinical psychology as their major field. As was the case with doctoral students, this represents the largest single interest area in psychology. It is also worth noting that 25 percent of those identifying themselves with clinical psychology were not originally trained as clinicians, but "transferred in" after graduate training in other areas of psychology.

Obviously then, clinical psychology is an immensely popular educational and occupational field these days, a fact which is rather remarkable considering that it is only about 75 years old and did not really begin to develop markedly until after World War II (see Chapter 2). What accounts for this phenomenon? What is it that a clinical psychologist does that makes so many people want to become one? Or, to put it more generally, what is clinical psychology? As we shall see, the answer to this question is neither simple nor easy (if it were, this book would probably be only about fifteen pages long), but in this chapter and in those which follow, we shall attempt to describe the field in a way which we hope will allow you to draw your own conclusions. In the process, we shall look at the history, current status, and future of the field, its areas of uniqueness and its overlap and relations with other fields, the training and activities of its members, the factors which unite it and the problems and issues which threaten to divide it.

SOME ATTEMPTS AT DEFINITION

It would be convenient at this point to provide a nice, clean, commonly accepted, and easily remembered definition of clinical psychology from which the rest of the material in this book would logically flow. Unfortunately, no such definition exists. The problem is that the field has been growing so rapidly and expanding in so many different directions in recent years that any attempt to capture it descriptively in a sentence or two is bound to be too vague or too narrow and, in any case, soon outdated. As one writer put it, "The field has not stood still long enough to let anyone get a good look at it" (Hoch, 1962, p. 5). A major consequence of this state of affairs is considerable though perfectly understandable confusion in the public mind over what clinical psychology is all about. The same problem exists to a certain extent among clinical psychologists themselves: "We are running in so many directions and we are doing so many things, that we may fall into the danger of not knowing who we are as a profession" (L'Abate, 1964, p. 2). Indeed, articles entitled "What is clinical psychology?" appear often in clinical journals and newsletters, reflecting a continuous process of self-examination within the field. In spite of this apparent confusion, there are a set of factors pervading most definitions of clinical psychology which, taken together, provide a workable outline of the discipline and of what clinical psychologists do.

Box 1-1 presents a sampling of definitions from which these factors may be abstracted and reveals, first, that clinical psychology is a subdivision or specialty within the larger discipline of psychology. This means that clinical psychologists, like all other psychologists, are primarily concerned with the study and understanding of *behavior*. Unlike some other psychologists, however, clinicians are concerned almost entirely with *human behavior*. This is not to say that clinical psychologists never work with lower animals; it simply means that clinicians are ultimately oriented toward humans and that they study animals

Box 1-1   Some Definitions of Clinical Psychology

1 The specialty of clinical psychology may be defined as that branch of psychology which deals with the search for and application of psychological principles aimed at understanding the uniqueness of the individual client or patient, reducing his personal distress, and helping him to function more meaningfully and effectively. (Goldenberg, 1973, p. 1)

2 Broadly stated, clinical psychology is the field of application of psychological principles that is primarily concerned with the psychological adjustment of individuals. (Rotter, 1971, p. 1)

3 Clinical psychology is concerned with understanding and improving human function. . . . As a clinical field it is dedicated to improving the lot of individuals in distress, using the best knowledge and techniques available, while striving through research to increase the knowledge and sharpen the techniques needed for improved intervention in the future. (Korchin, 1976, p. 3)

4 Clinical psychology is concerned with the psychological adjustment problems of the individual—more specifically, with the determination and evaluation of capacities and characteristics relating to adjustment and the study and application of psychological techniques for improving adjustment. (Shakow, 1969, p. 14)

5 [Clinical psychology] is the application of psychological principles and techniques to the problems of an individual. The body of knowledge on which it is based stems from the findings of psychology, personality theory, psychiatry, psychoanalysis, and anthropology. (Watson, 1951, p. 5)

mainly when the use of human subjects is impractical, inconvenient, or unsafe and when the behavior of animals can provide a reasonable analogue to human functioning, thereby illuminating general behavioral principles and relationships which are relevant at the human level. Their interest in human behavior does not, however, set clinicians apart from other (e.g., social) psychologists whose activities and interests also center upon humans.

Neither does the fact that, as shown in Box 1-1, clinical psychologists do *research* on human behavior. The same can be said of many other, nonclinical psychologists. Clinical psychology attempts to *apply* the knowledge and principles gained from research in a practical way, but this alone does not make the field unique; other specialties, such as industrial and educational psychology, are noted for their applied orientation.

Further attention to Box 1-1 will disclose another aspect of the clinical field: *assessment* of the abilities and characteristics of individual human beings. In a sense, this category of clinical functioning is a type of research. The clinician collects information which will later be analyzed and used to support conclusions about the person observed, but while such information might indeed be collected from large groups as part of a clinical research project, it is far more frequently employed by the clinician as a means of understanding the particular individual at hand. Thus, one aspect of the definition of clinical psychology includes the assessment or measurement of individual abilities and personal characteristics. However, though many people assume that testing and clinical psychology are synonymous, many nonclinicians (e.g., psychometricians, personality researchers, and industrial psychologists) administer and score tests of various kinds. Assessment activities alone cannot fully define clinical psychology or account for its distinctiveness.

Our definitional smorgasbord suggests yet another important characteristic of clinical psychology which fills in a bit more of the picture: contemporary clinicians are deeply involved in *helping* people who are psychologically distressed. The therapeutic sphere of activity is the most recently evolved aspect of the field (see Chapter 2), but it clearly rivals the assessment function in the general public's stereotyped image of the clinical psychologist. Nevertheless, providing psychological assistance or therapy of some kind is hardly unique to clinical psychology. Many other professionals, including psychiatrists, social workers, counselors, nurses, educators, and the clergy engage to varying degrees in activities which directly or tangentially include interventions aimed at the alleviation of psychological problems. Clinical treatment thus joins the other functions we have discussed as an aspect of but not the whole truth about clinical psychology.

Where does all this leave us? So far we have a portrait of clinical psychology as a subarea of psychology. It applies psychological knowledge (as do other subareas), and its members are among those who generate research about human behavior, engage in individual assessment, and provide various forms of psychological assistance. When viewed in this way, clinical psychology looks about as distinctive as the members of a crowd scene in a Godzilla movie. However, there *is* a defining characteristic which, though not immediately obvious, distinguishes clinical psychology from the other branches of psychology. This is what has been called the *clinical attitude* or the *clinical approach,* that distinctive orientation of clinical psychologists toward combining knowledge generated by clinical and other research with their own efforts at individual assessment in order to understand and help a particular person. Indeed, the very word "clinical" is derived from the Greek for "bed" or "pertaining to a bed" and, as is the case in clinical medicine, reflects the clinician's concern for helping distressed persons on an individual basis.

Within psychology, the clinical attitude sets clinicians apart from all other psychologists, including those who seek to learn about the nature and causes of distressing psychological problems (e.g., experimental psychopathologists). The interests of these colleagues, though clearly related to those of clinical psychology, usually tend to be rather abstract in that they involve a search for principles and relationships that apply to human behavior problems on a general, or *nomothetic,* level. Clinical psychologists are attentive to, grateful for, and often participate in research of this kind, but they are more often concerned with how general principles and relationships shape lives and problems on an individual, or *idiographic,* level as well as with the potential value of abstract research for guiding the treatment of individuals.

The clinical attitude is distinctive with respect to the helping professions outside psychology as well. As already mentioned, psychiatrists, social workers, and others assist people in psychological distress, but their fields are not traditionally noted for research into or systematic assessment of the problematic behaviors and conditions they seek to alleviate. Their involvement with a given case is more likely to focus upon administration of treatment procedures themselves.

The nature of the clinical attitude and the ways in which it contrasts with other, related approaches are most clearly visible with respect to a given case. For example, in reading a description of the problematic behaviors of a person just admitted to a mental institution, the psychopathologist is likely to search for clues to or confirmation of psychological relationships which might explain the "disorder," while the psychiatrist (a medical doctor who specializes in psychological problems) might weigh the potential benefits of psychological, medical, or combined treatment. The clinical psychologist, however, would probably plan a strategy for further assessment of the nature of the problem and (depending upon the outcome of the assessment process) develop a set of intervention tactics for dealing with the person's distress. The research evidence which guides the clinical psychologist in these pursuits (and which also aids other helping professions) often comes from the work of fellow clinical psychologists.

So it is not the research, the individual assessment, the treatment, or any of the other activities in which we shall see clinicians participate which makes their field unique. Rather, it is the clinical attitude, the idea of not only learning about behavior (particularly problematic behavior) but also doing something about it that is "indigenous to clinical psychology" (Wyatt, 1968, p. 235). Though not every clinician is engaged in all these activities, it is this combination *within a single discipline* of research, assessment, and intervention, all aimed at understanding human behavior and distress in psychological terms, and all oriented toward dealing with that behavior and distress on an individual basis, which provides the shape and substance of clinical psychology.

CLINICAL PSYCHOLOGISTS AT WORK

Now that we have outlined the nature of clinical psychology, it becomes somewhat easier to begin considering in more specific terms the range of things which clinical psychologists do, the variety of places in which they are found, and the array of clients and problems with which they work. In doing so, it is important to keep in mind that no matter how many examples of clinical activities, work settings, clients, and problems are included in our survey, it is always possible to find others which were left out. On the other hand, our coverage will be so broad that it is unlikely that any given clinical psychologist will be associated with all the functions, locations, clients, and problems listed. Thus, the material presented below is neither exhaustive of all the specifics of clinicians' work nor descriptive of how all clinicians spend their time.

Let us look first at some isolated examples of clinical activities, settings, clients, and problems; later, we shall see how these dimensions combine for individual clinicians.

The Activities of Clinical Psychologists

At a party several years ago, after having pleaded guilty to being a clinical psychologist, one of us was asked, "Is it true that you can read minds?" The answer to this question was an emphatic "No," but the very fact that it was asked highlights the uncertainty and mistaken ideas that many people have about clinical psychologists. The popular stereotypes of the clinician as a psychotherapist or a mental tester are, like most stereotypes, only partly accurate at best. The research activity of clinical psychologists is, as already mentioned, a vital though underpublicized aspect of the field and, in addition, clinicians often engage in teaching, consultation, and administrative functions which are even less well known. Thus, it is probably fair to say that 99 percent of all clinical psychologists spend their working lives engaged in some combination of six activities: *assessment, treatment, research, teaching, consultation,* and *administration.*

Assessment   The assessment activities of clinical psychologists involve the collection of information about people: their behavior, their problems, their unique characteristics, their abilities, their intellectual functioning, and the like. The uses made of clinical assessment data vary greatly. The information gathered may be employed by the clinician or others to arrive at diagnostic labels for problematic behavior, to assist in guiding a client toward an optimal vocational choice, to facilitate selection of maximally competent job candidates, to describe a client's personality characteristics, to guide selection of psychological or other treatment techniques, to aid in making legal decisions regarding the commitment of individuals to various types of institutions, to provide a more complete picture of a client's behavior problems, to screen potential participants in a psychological research project, to establish pretreatment "base-line" levels of behavior against which to measure posttreatment improvement, and for literally hundreds of other purposes. The means through which clinical assessment data can be collected are varied enough to make a complete listing impossible, but, in spite of their diversity, most clinical assessment devices fall into one of three main categories: *tests, interviews,* and *observation.*

Tests usually involve asking for responses to a set of standard stimuli which may be presented "live," in oral or written form, in photographs or motion pictures, or on audio or video tape recordings. Interviews are conversations in which the interviewee provides information in response to the interviewer's systematic or informal exploration of relevant topics. Observation involves, obviously, watching in some way how the client deals with some naturalistic or contrived life situation. The behavior observed may be overt and visible or may include physiological activity accessible only through the use of specialized measurement and recording equipment.

Tests, interviews, and observations are not always totally separate and independent means of assessment. For example, a clinician may observe the nonverbal behavior of a client during a testing session or an interview in order to estimate the client's level of discomfort in certain types of social situations. Further, a test may be embedded in the context of an interview, as when the client is asked to provide specific information whose accuracy provides clues to "reality contact." Various modes are also combined in assessment *batteries* and *multiple assessment* strategies. Here, information necessary for the clinician's work is collected through a series of procedures, sometimes including simply a variety of tests, but often encompassing a more diverse combination of tests, interviews, and observations which may focus not only on the client but also upon "significant others" who can provide additional, relevant information.

Treatment   This function of the clinical psychologist involves helping people solve various kinds of distressing psychological problems. The intervention may be called psychotherapy, behavior modification, psychological counseling, or other names, depending upon the orientation of the clinician, and may involve many combinations of clients and therapists. Though one-to-one treatment has been traditional, it is now common for a single psychologist to deal with groups of clients who may be independent of one another or related in some way (e.g., family members, coworkers, hospital ward residents). Sometimes, two or more clinicians work as a team to deal with the problems of an individual, couple, or group. The emphasis of treatment may be upon alleviating the distress and/or problematic behavior of one or more troubled individuals, or may vary to include prevention of psychological problems before they appear by altering the institutions, the social or environmental situation, or the behavioral skills of persons "at risk" (e.g., teenage parents) or of an entire community (see Chapter 12).

Treatment by a clinical psychologist may be on an "outpatient" basis

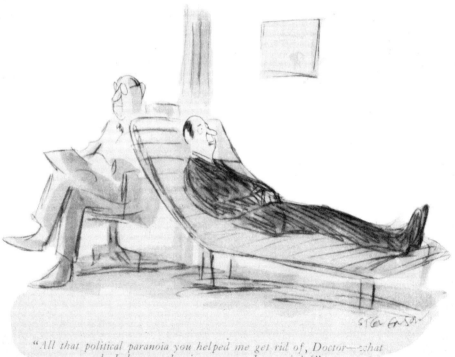

"All that political paranoia you helped me get rid of, Doctor—what do I do now that it turns out I was right?"

(where the client or clients live in the community) or may be part of the services offered to residents ("inpatients") of an institution. It may be as brief as one session or extend over a period of several years. Treatment sessions consist of anything from client (or therapist) monologues to painstaking construction of new behavioral skills to episodes of intense emotional drama, and may range from highly structured to totally spontaneous interactions. The goals of clinician and client may be quite limited (as when a solution to a specific situational problem is sought), very ambitious (as when a complete analysis and reconstruction of the client's personality is planned), or may fall somewhere between these extremes. In approaching these goals, one or more of dozens of differing theoretical principles and technical procedures thought to be central to the appearance and alleviation of human problems may be invoked. The therapy enterprise may be conducted free of charge, on a sliding scale based upon client income, or in return for apparently astronomical payment and may, in given cases, result in anything from worsening of client problems to no change to vast improvement.

Research Clinical psychologists are, by training and by tradition, research-oriented. Their activity in the research sphere makes them notable among all other helping professions, and some would assert that it is in this area that clinicians make their greatest contribution. In the realm of psychotherapy, for example, theory and practice were once based mainly upon case study evidence, subjective impressions of treatment efficacy, and rather poorly designed research. Paul (1969a) noted that this "prescientific" era in the history of psychotherapy research has now evolved into an "experimental" era in which the quality of research has increased greatly. This development is due in large measure to the work of clinical psychologists. The Joint Commission on Mental Illness and Health (1961) alluded to clinicians' research expertise when, after referring to the rather dismal state of earlier mental health research, it noted that "emphasis today is placed increasingly on sophisticated research designs, on highly specialized techniques and instruments, and on complex statistical procedures for data analysis. Psychologists are likely to have had the requisite training and experience for this type of research and this fact helps to account for their prominent position in this field" (p. 199). Indeed, the extent of clinical psychologists' involvement in research is impressive. It has been estimated that over 50 percent of the research grants awarded by the National Institute of Mental Health (NIMH) go to psychologists (Joint Commission on Mental Illness and Health, 1961). Many of these are the clinicians whose research reports appear in the pages of dozens of psychological journals every month.

The targets of clinical research are extremely varied. Brown's (1972) list of areas commonly investigated by clinicians included psychopharmacology, developmental problems, geriatrics, test construction and validation, personality diagnosis and adjustment, psychoanalytic theory, therapeutic processes, brain damage and mental retardation, psychotic, neurotic, and psychosomatic behavior disorders, and marriage and family problems. To these we might add topics such as the outcome of various forms of psychological treatment, the design, methodology, and analysis of experiments, the means through which therapeutically derived benefits may be made broader and more durable, the value and training of nonprofessionals as therapeutic agents, and so on (see Woods, 1976). A journal called *Psychological Abstracts* contains summaries of clinical and other psychological research; a glance at a few issues published over the last several years will provide even more impressive documentation of the diversity and intensity of the clinician's involvement in research.

Clinical investigations vary greatly with respect to their setting and scope. Some are conducted in the controlled, artificial confines of a laboratory while others are run in the more naturalistic but often chaotic and uncontrollable circumstances of the "real world." Some projects are carried out by clinicians who are aided by paid research assistants and clerical personnel and supported by funds from NIMH or other governmental or private sources, but a great deal of research is generated by clinicians whose budgets are virtually nil and who depend upon volunteer help and their own ability to "scrounge" for space, equipment, subjects, and other necessities.

Teaching A considerable portion of many clinical psychologists' time is spent in educational activities. Especially for those who hold full- or part-time academic positions at colleges or universities, this takes the form of conducting regular graduate or undergraduate courses in such areas as personality, abnormal psychology, introductory clinical psychology, psychotherapy (or behavior modification or some other label for clinical intervention), interviewing, psychological testing, research design, clinical assessment, and the like. The teaching techniques involved are those with which all students are familiar: lectures, discussion sessions, demonstrations, lab sessions, field trips, and other standard offerings. Like other teachers, clinical psychologists may also employ aids such as videotapes, computer-based or other types of programmed instruction, and motion pictures.[1] Personalized, student-paced instructional procedures (Keller, 1966) may even be used.

The amount of teaching a clinician does in a college or university depends, in part, upon its size and orientation. In a two-person psychology department at a small college, the teaching load is a lot heavier than would be the case at a large university department with a staff of fifty. In general, the range is from two to five courses per term.

Clinicians often conduct specialized graduate seminars on various advanced topics and frequently supervise the work of graduate students who are learning assessment and therapy skills in the context of practicum courses. Supervision of a practicum is a rather special kind of teaching which combines the use of published research evidence and other didactic material with the clinician's own

---

[1]These may be documentaries or features. In our own abnormal psychology courses, lectures and discussions are often supplemented by evening showings of relevant full-length motion pictures such as *Three Faces of Eve, The Days of Wine and Roses,* and *Dr. Strangelove.*

experience to guide students' application of the theory and techniques of assessment and treatment to actual clients. Details of practicum teaching vary from clinician to clinician, but, in general, they involve a model in which the student sees a client on a regular basis and, between assessment or treatment sessions, also meets with the supervisor (the client is normally aware of the student's status and of the existence and participation of the supervisor). Conversations between student and supervisor regarding the case and its progress may occur on an individual basis or, in order to better share experiences, may be part of a meeting with a small group of practicum students, all of whom recognize and maintain the confidentiality of any material discussed whether relevant to their own clients or to those of others (see Chapter 13). Practicum supervision may be based entirely upon oral reports and/or assessment data provided by the student therapist or may be supplemented by comments from those who have unobtrusively observed a session or by audio or video tape recordings (all made with client consent).

The clinician's teaching task is particularly difficult and delicate in practica since a balance must be struck between directing the student and allowing for independence. The therapist-in-training may feel stifled if supervision is too heavy-handed and prescriptive, but, at the same time, the supervisor is ultimately responsible for the case and thus cannot allow the student to make serious errors which would be detrimental to client welfare. It is no wonder that, in such circumstances, students and clinicians sometimes find practicum supervision problematic (Barnat, 1973; Gelinas, 1976; Potash, 1974; Rioch, Coulter, & Weinberger, 1976).

A good deal of teaching is also done by clinical psychologists who supervise students' research efforts (Seeman, 1973). The level of work varies from undergraduate independent study or honors thesis projects to graduate research for a master's or doctoral degree. Usually, this kind of teaching begins when a student comes to the supervisor with a rather vaguely defined research topic and asks for help, advice, and a list of relevant readings. In addition to providing the reading list, most research supervisors try to help the student learn to frame appropriate research questions, apply basic principles of research design in answering those questions, and use various specific "tricks of the trade" relevant to the problem at hand. These tasks often require considerable teaching skill if the supervisor is to avoid giving the student so much guidance and direction that the latter really becomes an assistant who, instead of wrestling with and learning from research problems, merely carries out orders (note the parallel to practicum supervision). The problem of assisting the student to modify grandiose or otherwise unanswerable research questions (like "What makes people act crazy sometimes?") into more specific and manageable hypotheses is a particularly knotty one.

Often, research and practicum supervision include teaching communication skills, particularly writing. This usually takes the form of reading, commenting on, and rereading students' efforts to describe their research, assessment data, or practicum cases. Like other aspects of supervision, this kind of teaching is usually done in the context of intensive individual or small group interactions and can be a very rewarding experience. It is satisfying to observe and participate in the development, through practice and evaluative feedback, of a student's writing skills. As one might imagine, however, this educational enterprise can in some cases become rather gruesome; it is not much fun to read the eighth unclear draft of a paper on something like "eye movement during electroconvulsive shock" or "dance therapy for geriatrics."

Not all of the teaching done by clinical psychologists is for academic credit. Much of it involves providing in-service (i.e., on-the-job) training, through didactic or practicum courses, to psychological, medical, or other interns, as well as to social workers, nurses, institutional aides, ministers, police officers, suicide prevention and other "hotline" personnel, prison guards, teachers, administrators, business executives, day-care workers, lawyers, probation officers, dentists, and many other groups whose vocational skills might be enhanced by increased psychological sophistication.

Some clinical psychologists feel that they also do a lot of teaching in the context of therapy. This is particularly true of those who adopt a social-learning approach to treatment (see Chapter 10), but it also applies to other clinicians as well, since at least part of therapy usually involves helping people to learn new and more adaptive ways of behaving. Thus, though the degree and explicitness of overlap between the teaching and therapeutic functions in clinical psychology may vary, the fact of that overlap is worth keeping in mind.

One last point about clinical psychologists as teachers: they are often not formally trained for the job. The same might be said, of course, about other psychologists (and many other Ph.D.'s, for that matter), but the lack of attention to teaching skill in clinical training programs is especially unfortunate because educational activities are so often an integral part of clinicians' work, whether or not they hold academic jobs. This significant omission is due, in part at least, to the fact that clinical training time is so precious that it is mostly taken up with attention to research, assessment, and treatment functions. Graduate work on teaching skills, when present at all in clinical programs, is usually restricted to a single (often elective) seminar or is embodied in a requirement that each student teach, or assist in teaching, at least one psychology course. The result is that, too often, the brand new clinical psychologist faces the first class, audience, seminar, or practicum group with very little preparation and a great deal of trepidation.

Consultation   It has been said that an expert consultant is an ordinary person away from home. The truth of this old saw is immaterial here, but it is true that clinical psychologists often temporarily leave "home" (i.e., their regular jobs) to provide help and advice to various types of organizations about a wide variety of problems. In doing so, there is frequently an opportunity to combine aspects of the research, assessment, treatment, and teaching functions already discussed. Perhaps this is why some clinicians find consultation satisfying and lucrative enough that they engage in it full time, either as individuals or as part of psychological consulting firms. Organizations which are the recipients of consultants' expertise range in size and scope from one-person medical practices or small staffs of geriatric units to huge government agencies and multinational corporations.[2] The consultant may also work with neighborhood associations, walk-in treatment centers, and other community-based organizations which are now so much a part of our culture (see Chapter 12).

Rather than attempting to catalog all of the specific consulting activities in which a clinical psychologist might engage, let us look at some basic dimensions of the consulting function. The first of these is the *orientation* or *goal* of the consultation. When consulting is *case*-oriented, the clinician is expected to focus attention on a case (or cases) and either deal with it directly and personally or offer advice as to how it might be handled. An example would be providing assessment or treatment services for a "problem case" referred by a fellow clinician or encountered in some kind of clinical facility. Periodic discussions with executive or staff members of a mental health agency, medical facility, penal institution, business concern, industrial plant, or other organization about handling specific problems with patients, clients, employees, or inmates provide another instance of *case* consultation. A significant advantage of this second type of case-oriented work is that the impact of the clinician's expertise is greatly increased by being shared with several persons who subsequently benefit more individuals than the consultant, working alone, could ever hope to see (e.g., Tharp & Wetzel, 1969).

The other major type of consultation is *program-* or *administration-* oriented, and it focuses not upon case-level problems but upon those aspects of organizational function or structure which are causing trouble. For example, the clinician may be asked to help reorganize the way in which a mental health clinic or a company personnel office operates so as to streamline procedures, eliminate conflict among staff members, and reduce complaints from clients. In another instance, the consultant's assignment might be to come up with a plan for systematically evaluating the adequacy of services provided by an alcoholism rehabilitation center or home for delinquent children. Another type of program-oriented consultation is exemplified by the situation in which a particular executive or administrator seeks help from the clinician in making plans and decisions about an organization and its programs. Here, the consultant may assist in the development of new procedures for screening candidates for various jobs within the organization, help set up guidelines or criteria for identifying promotable personnel, or reduce staff turnover rates by increasing administrators' awareness of the psychological impact of their decisions upon employees.

In addition to the orientation or goal of the consultation, a second major dimension of clinical consulting work is *locus of responsibility*. In some cases,

---

[2]When consulting with business or industry, the role of the clinical psychologist and that of the industrial psychologist may be closely related. We shall focus, however, upon those aspects of the clinical consultant's activities which are most clearly based upon clinical psychology.

responsibility for solution to an organization's problem is transferred to the consultant, as when a county mental health clinic contracts for the psychological assessment of all suspected cases of brain damage among new clients. Here, as in other instances where the consultant "takes over" all or part of a case, responsibility for its disposition or resolution rests with the clinician; giving some advice and then going home is not appropriate. More commonly, however, the responsibility for problem resolution remains with the organization served. A clinician may, for example, participate in decisions about which executive should be promoted, which criminal should be granted probation, or which treatment approach would be of greatest benefit to a client, but if the executive leaves for Rio with company funds, the criminal continues to assault livestock, or the client gets worse instead of better, the consultant is not held culpable. The clinician gave the advice, but the ultimate burden of responsibility remained with the company, court, or clinic.

"Try as we might, sir, our team of management consultants has been unable to find a single fault in the manner in which you conduct your business. Everything you do is a hundred per cent right. Keep it up! That will be eleven thousand dollars."

A third major consulting dimension involves *functions*. Many of these are implied by the material already presented, but they are worth listing here as well. A partial account of what a consultant could do for an organization might include education (e.g., teaching specific skills, presenting theoretical material, familiarizing staff with relevant reading materials or other resources), advice (e.g., about cases, personnel matters, or programs), direct service (e.g., assessment, treatment, and evaluative or other research), and reduction of intraorganizational conflict (e.g., helping staff members communicate and get along better with one another; eliminating sources of trouble by altering organizational structure, procedure, or personnel assignments).

Successful fulfillment of the consulting function is not always easy. The clinician must be constantly aware of his or her role as an outsider and of the implications of that role. The consultant's presence might easily be resented and resisted by rank and file personnel if they see it as a threat to their jobs or an evaluation of their competency engineered by top level administrators. There are other difficulties as well. Interpersonal feuds and rivalries may color and distort the information that the consultant gets about the nature of a problem. Consultants make great scapegoats, and they should recognize the possibility that consulting advice may be used by managers or administrators in a fashion consistent with preconceived problem-solving ideas which, if unpopular after implementation, can always be blamed on "that damned psychologist." (For further reading on the organizational consulting process, see Argyris, 1964; Bennis, 1966; Caplan, 1970; and Dunnette, 1976.)

Administration This function involves the management or day-to-day running of an organization, and, if you were to ask a sample of clinical psychologists to name their least-preferred activity, it would probably be among the top candidates. The reasons given would probably include (among others) aversion to paperwork, lack of interest in routine details of business, budget, and other organizational matters, impatience with complaints from and conflicts among staff members and employees, reluctance to deal with the time-consuming and often acrimonious process of hiring and firing, and the uncertainty and frustration which sometimes attend dealings with other administrators. Nevertheless, clinical psychologists do find themselves in administrative roles, and sometimes it is by choice. In some organizations, clinical psychologists may be asked to take on administrative jobs because of the sensitivity, interpersonal skill, evaluative research expertise, and organizational abilities associated with their field. Having a clinician as administrator is, to some ways of thinking, like employing a full-time consultant who not only gives advice, but follows and takes responsibility for it. Whatever the circumstances, many clinicians find it satisfying to help guide an organization toward reaching its goals and improving its services.

Examples of the primarily administrative posts sometimes held by clinical psychologists include: head of a university psychology department, director of a

*"All right, now! If we will all return to our seats,
the meeting will resume."*

graduate training program in clinical psychology, director of a student counseling center, head of a consulting firm or testing center, superintendent of a school system, chief psychologist at a hospital or clinic, director of a hospital outpatient service, director of a community mental health center, and director of training and evaluation at a Veterans Administration (VA) hospital. People in such positions are normally expected to do things like coordinate staff activities, plan and arrange teaching assignments, allocate financial resources, develop and implement organizational policy, write reports to other administrative units (as well as to local, state, and federal agencies), chair meetings, write proposals for grant support, plan the use and development of physical facilities, entertain visiting dignitaries, represent the organization at meetings and to the public, mediate intraorganizational conflicts, hire secretaries, make decisions regarding staff promotions and salary increases, and delegate responsibility to other individuals and committees.

Members of the committees that an administrator creates may also be clinicians and thus become part-time participants in the administrative function. A clinician may chair or serve on committees which search for a new staff member (or administrator), advise the top administrator, choose next year's graduate or undergraduate students, evaluate the services provided by the organization, develop plans for a new building, or collect information on staff morale. Sometimes these committees are temporary while others are of a "standing" or permanent nature and involve a continuing commitment by chairperson and members.

The clinical psychologist's background and experience can be assets in the administrative role, but they may be a two-edged sword. Referring to the survey responses of a group of psychologists and administrators, Sundberg, Tyler, and Taplin (1973, p. 428) point out that the psychologist-administrator has the advantage of "sensitivity to individual differences, awareness of social and psychological forces, objectivity and skill in communication, selection, and evaluation." These same qualities were also seen as causing problems such as "a tendency to overanalyze workers, conflicts between helping and controlling roles, an overemphasis on empirical data as a basis for decisions, and the lack of certain essential management skills."

If there is little preparation in clinical training programs for the clinician's teaching function, there is even less for the administrative role. Clinical psychologists may make good administrators, but their success is more likely a function of personal characteristics and relevant work experience than of anything they learn in graduate school.

Distribution of Clinical Functions

As noted earlier, not all clinical psychologists engage in each of the six functions we have discussed. Some spend nearly all their time at one type of task while others "spread themselves around." To many clinicians, the potential for distributing their time among several functions is one of the most attractive aspects of their field, and the data from several surveys conducted over the last 20 years provide some idea of the pattern of involvement which results. Unfortunately, each survey asked about clinical functions in a somewhat

Table 1-1   Distribution of Clinical Functions

Function	Kelly (1961)*	Goldschmid et al. (1969)†	Cuca (1975a)‡	Garfield & Kurtz (1976)§
Assessment	50%	34%	49%	9.8%
Treatment	54%			31.8%
Research	25%	12%	8%	10.8%
Teaching	25%	15%	14%	24.3%
Consultation		3%	Included in assessment	5.2%
Administration	5%	6%	13%	13.2%
Other		Not included	1%	4.8%

*Expressed as percentage of 1024 clinicians who spend at least "some time" in each function.
†Expressed as percentage of 241 clinicians who spend one-third or more of their time in each function.
‡Expressed as percentage of 8447 respondents engaged in each function. Figures do not total 100% because of no response from some clinicians.
§Expressed as percentage of time devoted to each function by 855 clinicians.

different way, but the variety of a given clinician's work is still discernible (see Table 1-1).

Garfield and Kurtz (1976) and Kelly (1961) reported that over 50 percent of the clinicians they surveyed held two jobs and that some of them held three or more. Further, the majority of those who have only one job still participate in a variety of functions within it (Goldschmid, Stein, Weissman, & Sorrels, 1969). It is easy to see in Table 1-2 that clinicians tend to spend more time in service of various kinds than in research. Indeed, Garfield and Kurtz (1976) found that 58.7 percent of their survey respondents identified themselves primarily as clinical practitioners, while only 4.7 percent called themselves researchers. Though a larger proportion of clinicians actually spend at least some time in research activity, data like these have caused concern in the field over what some see as an erosion of the traditionally strong research contributions of clinical psychologists. Within the service functions, there has been a noticeable trend over the years toward involvement in treatment and a corresponding movement away from assessment activities (Garfield and Kurtz, 1976; Kelly, 1961). Some reasons for this shift will be discussed in later chapters.

Work Settings for Clinical Psychology

There was a time when virtually all clinical psychologists worked in a single type of facility: child clinics or guidance centers. However, the historical forces which once made this true have shifted (see Chapters 2 and 12), and now, like the concentric circles which appear when a pebble hits a pond, the settings in which clinicians function are continuously expanding in all directions. The great variety of clinical work settings has already been alluded to in previous sections, but it is

Table 1-2 Percentage of Clinicians Employed in Various Work Settings

Type	Kelly (1961) (N=1024)	Goldschmid et al. (1969) (N=241)	Cuca (1975a) (N=8447)	Garfield & Kurtz (1976) (N=855)
Academic	20%	17%	38%	29%
Direct service*	50%	28%	†	35%
Research	‡	‡	†	‡
Community agency	‡	16%	†	†
Schools	3%	‡	†	†
Private practice	17%	28%	†	23.3%
Industry	3%	‡	†	†
Military	1.5%	‡	†	†
Other	5.5%	11%	61%	12.7%

*Includes hospitals, clinics, medical schools, mental health centers, etc.
†Included under "other."
‡Not included.

now time to become more explicit and to present some data on the distribution of clinicians among those settings.

Clinical psychologists are now found in college and university psychology departments, public and private medical and psychiatric hospitals, city, county, and private mental health clinics, community mental health centers, student health and counseling centers, medical schools, the military, university psychological clinics, child treatment centers, public and private schools, institutions for the mentally retarded, prisons, juvenile offender facilities, business and industrial firms, probation departments, rehabilitation centers for the handicapped, nursing homes and other geriatric facilities, orphanages, alcoholism treatment centers, and many other places. Further, a significant number of clinicians function independently in full- or part-time private practice conducted mainly in their own offices. Determination of just how many clinical psychologists are employed in each type of setting is virtually impossible, partly because new jobs are evolving all the time (Woods, 1976), but the surveys summarized earlier have addressed the question. Their results are summarized in Table 1-2 in terms of broad types of employment rather than highly specific locations. As before, there are some problems in combining the data from these surveys; in this case because each of them used a different system for categorizing work settings. Still, it is clear that direct service facilities (e.g., hospitals and clinics) are among the most common places of employment for clinical psychologists (this is particularly true if the figures for direct service and community agencies are combined), followed by academic institutions, then private practice.

Since we already have seen that most clinicians spend their time in at least two activities, it is of interest to note that, when all functions are considered, about 70 percent of survey respondents participate to some extent in direct service settings, 40 percent work at least part time in colleges and universities, and about 50 percent maintain some sort of private practice (Garfield and Kurtz, 1976; Kelly, 1961).[3] With this kind of functional diversity and employment flexibility, it is no wonder that clinical psychologists continue to find jobs even when the placement picture becomes grim for other psychologists (Cuca, 1975b).

Clients and Problems

Clinical psychologists serve everyone. Though most of them work with adults (Kelly, 1961), all age groups from infants to the elderly make up their clientele. The types of persons seen by the clinician cut across age lines to include groups such as the mentally retarded, the physically handicapped, or residents of mental or other hospitals. The clinical contact may be voluntarily arranged by the client

---

[3]This percentage is on the rise (Gottfredson and Dyer, 1978), a fact which is probably due, in part at least, to the financial rewards involved. Two surveys (Boneau, 1974; Gottfredson and Dyer, 1978) showed that income for full-time private practitioners ranged from about $18,000 to over $55,000 (median: $32,000), while psychologists working in other settings earned from about $14,000 to $35,000 (median: $25,500).

(or the client's family), prescribed by a court or other legal agency, or occur more or less accidentally as a function of the clinician's entry into the client's hospital ward, school, or community.

In any case, having already considered the kinds of problems the clinician deals with as teacher, researcher, consultant, and administrator, one should also be aware of the kinds of problems she or he faces in the assessment and treatment areas. Client complaints are often very complex and frequently stem from a combination of biological, psychological, and social factors, with the result that the clinical psychologist does not always work independently. A given case is sometimes referred to other professionals (e.g., a psychiatrist or social worker) or may be dealt with through formation of an assessment and treatment team composed of experts from several related helping professions.

Depending upon training, special interests, level of experience, and location, the clinician encounters a wide range of problems including marital discord, alcoholism, learning disorders, speech disturbances, dissatisfaction with sexual orientation or function, juvenile delinquency, depression, nail-biting, vocational troubles, anxiety, drug abuse, toilet-training, psychosomatic illness, disrupted family relations, overeating, criminal behavior, and bed-wetting. This list could go on indefinitely, but you get the idea. Within the limits imposed by their areas of expertise, clinical psychologists may work (individually or with other professionals) on almost any kind of human behavior problem imaginable.

"Now, just what seems to be the problem?"

If a client presents a rather unique complaint (e.g., tooth grinding, habitual vomiting, sleepwalking, chronic coughing, inflammatory scratching, highway hypnosis, fear of balloons), requisite assessment and treatment procedures are often "custom-made"; cases are seldom abandoned a priori as long as the psychologist believes that it falls within his or her professional realm.

Work Schedules and Specific Illustrations

Let us now pull together what we have been saying about clinical functions, settings, clients, and problems by considering some examples of how and where various clinicians actually spend their time.

A Professor's Day   All six clinical functions often appear in the life of a clinical psychologist employed by a university, so it may be of interest to examine a day in that life. The schedule presented in Box 1-2 is really a composite of things the professor-clinician may do over the course of a month, and many small details (phone calls and other interruptions) have been left out. Of course, if every day were like the example in Box 1-2, the psychologist in question would probably survive for about a week. Nevertheless, some days *are* like this one, and the clinician may wonder if there was undue haste in rejecting the family grain and·feed business.

Box 1-2   A Composite Schedule for the Academic Clinician

7:30– 7:45	Breakfast
8:00– 8:30	Arrive at office; begin reviewing manuscript received as consulting editor for a clinical journal
8:30– 8:50	Look over lecture notes for abnormal psychology class
9:00– 9:50	Teach abnormal psychology class
9:50–10:15	Discuss lecture material and related topics with students
10:20–10:30	Read mail
10:30–11:30	Attend meeting of the graduate admissions committee
11:30–12:00	Confer with graduate student on dissertation research project
12:00– 1:00	Lunch
1:00– 2:00	Office hour (discuss course material with undergraduates in abnormal; if no one shows up, read journals)
2:00– 2:30	Meet with research assistant to discuss plans for experiment to be run next week
2:30– 2:45	As chairperson of the department's undergraduate curriculum committee, review new course proposals to be discussed at next meeting
2:45– 3:00	Talk to director of the county mental health clinic about the possibility of consulting with him on program evaluation
3:00– 4:00	Listen to tape recording of practicum student's interview with a new client
4:00– 6:00	Group practicum supervision
6:00– 7:00	Dinner
7:00– 7:30	Score psychological test given to a client earlier in the week
7:30– 8:30	Interview with client
8:30– 8:45	Write up interview notes
8:45–10:00	Work on draft of article reporting just-completed research project

The Work of Other Clinicians Harrower (1961) asked seventy clinical psychologists in New York City to provide a sketch of their day or week. Some of their responses, presented in edited form below, give a clear picture of the endless variety of clinical work outside of academics (Harrower, 1965, pp. 1449–1454):

1   I spend about eight hours a week with a private agency where I give seminars for fellows in psychology and trainees in psychiatry and social work. I also test infants several hours a week for two adoption agencies. The balance of my time is given over to private work in diagnosis and therapy.

2   Two afternoons and one evening a week are devoted to community clinic work. In one clinic I conduct group psychotherapy. In the other I coordinate and supervise a group psychotherapy program. At least six to eight hours a week are devoted to teaching at a local university. Three afternoons and three mornings a week are spent in my private office practicing both individual and group therapy.

3   My private practice is exclusively assessment-oriented, and when self-referred patients are seen it is with the understanding that they will be referred to a therapist if indicated. I see an average of six patients a week. Three-quarters of my week are devoted to teaching and training activities (six hours of lectures and seminars with psychologists and psychiatric residents and fellows). Outside activities include consultation work with the VA, public speaking, and participation in community activities by serving on boards and committees.

4   My supervisory position at the hospital with which I have been associated all of my professional career occupies most of the midweek day hours. I devote about fifteen hours weekly to therapy and occasional consultation—in private practice.

5   Most of my work involves long-term psychotherapy. My work day, Monday through Friday, is from nine to six, with some variation. One evening is devoted to teaching a graduate course in psychology, and one evening to attending a therapy group. I am at the college, doing counseling and administrative work about four hours each day, and see patients for about the same average amount of time.

6   Two days weekly are spent as consultant (tests, interviews, analysis of personnel files) to two large community agencies; one is spent in research with an alcoholic-vocational project; the remaining time goes to whatever diagnostic work, interviewing and counseling come up.

7   Seeing patients takes up some forty hours per week. Of these, about forty percent are spent with children and adolescents, the remainder with adults. Administrative and research activities at a clinic take up some fifteen to twenty additional hours.

8   Half-time consultant to the United Epilepsy Association as director of program (administration and planning public education and community service programs in epilepsy). Private practice limited to psychotherapy.

9   The basic work week involves about twenty hours of therapy and ten to twenty hours a week of testing, evaluation and report writing. Approximately five hours a week of consultation—usually with parents about diagnostic studies of children or adolescents. About five hours a week to research and consultation to outside agencies. Approximately twelve hours a week in a public clinic. Other time

is spent pursuing a research interest in delinquency psychotherapy and in helping to develop a training institute in this field.

   10   Administration and supervision of psychology department at a hospital; individual assessment and therapy consultations; lead two therapy seminars; consultation and writing in relation to two research projects; average of four to five therapy patients four evenings a week in private office; administration of clinical psychology teaching program for medical students; lecture one hour per week to psychiatric residents.

   11   Director and clinical psychologist of mental retardation diagnostic clinic. About 20 percent of time in assessment, 10 percent in parent counseling, 70 percent in administration and supervision. Also about ten hours per week in private practice (assessment and therapy).

   12   Three full days, Saturday mornings, and two late evenings per week are spent seeing patients. Remainder of time is devoted to directing a research project of which I am principal investigator. Occasional consulting at clinics and home for disturbed children.

   13   I see about thirty patients a week for from one to two hours each, for marriage counseling. In addition, I teach one or more classes a week on preparation for marriage, and conduct seminars for ministers and adult community leaders in marital counseling techniques and sex education.

   14   Three mornings a week are currently devoted to work in two private schools. In one, I serve as "coordinator" of the interdisciplinary guidance department, in another as consultant to teachers and parents about childrens' problems. Remainder of time is devoted to therapy with adults.

The combination of clients, settings, and clinical functions represented in these examples comes about partly as a function of each clinical psychologist's interests and expertise and partly through the influence of larger social factors. For example, a clinician could not work in a community mental health center or VA hospital unless legislation had been passed creating such settings. Similarly, much clinical research depends upon grants from federal agencies like NIMH, whose existence depends upon continued congressional appropriations. Participation in various clinical functions or work with certain types of clients is legitimized by the perceptions of other professions and the general public. If no one saw the clinician as capable of doing effective therapy or of testing adults, that function and class of clients would soon disappear from the field. Thus, the current state and future development of clinical psychology depends in large measure upon the society in which it is embedded. The history of clinical psychology, which is the subject of the next chapter, illustrates this point well.

Chapter 2

The Background of Clinical Psychology

To anyone born in the United States since World War II, the existence of clinical psychology as an academic subject, a science, and a profession is as common-place as plastic or television. Consequently, it is easy to assume the field has always existed. Such an assumption would be false, however, since the clinical psychology described in Chapter 1 is as much a child of the postwar era as plastic wrap or roof antennae. The field is young, and, like a confused adolescent, it is filled with concern and conflict over what it should be and what it should do as it continues to develop. Clinical psychology is also old in the sense that its roots extend back to periods before the field was ever named and to prewar years when it appeared only in embryonic or infantile form.

So in spite of present appearances, clinical psychology did not long ago spring "fully grown from the forehead of Mars" (Hunt, 1956, p. 79) any more than a client seeking help from a clinician begins to exist at the moment of their meeting. And, just as full understanding of clients' problems is easier when their social, cultural, educational, and vocational background is available, it is far easier to understand the current dimensions, new developments, and critical issues in clinical psychology when its historical background is reviewed. The goal of this chapter is to provide that review by first looking at the factors which were most influential in the formal birth of clinical psychology in 1896, and then

Box 2-1   Some Significant Dates and Events in the History of Clinical Psychology

1879   Wilhelm Wundt establishes first formal psychology laboratory at the University of Leipzig.
1885   Sir Francis Galton establishes first mental testing center at the South Kensington Museum, London.
1890   James McKeen Cattell coins term "mental test."
1892   American Psychological Association (APA) founded (first president: G. Stanley Hall).
1895   Breuer and Freud publish *Studies in Hysteria*.
1896   Lightner Witmer founds first psychological clinic, University of Pennsylvania.
1905   Binet-Simon intelligence scale published in France.
        Freud publishes *Three Essays on the Theory of Sexuality*.
1907   First clinical journal, *Psychological Clinic*, founded by Witmer.
1908   First clinical internship offered at Vineland Training School.
1909   William Healy founds first child guidance center, the Juvenile Psychopathic Institute, Chicago.
        National Committee for Mental Hygiene founded.
        Freud lectures at Clark University.
1910   Goddard's English translation of the 1908 revision of the Binet-Simon intelligence scale published.
1912   J. B. Watson publishes *Psychology as a Behaviorist Views It*.
1916   Terman's Stanford-Binet intelligence test published.
1917   Clinicians break away from APA to form American Association of Clinical Psychology (AACP).
1919   AACP rejoins APA as its Clinical Section.
1920   Watson and Rayner demonstrate that a child's fear can be learned.
1921   James McKeen Cattell forms Psychological Corporation.
1924   David Levy introduces Rorschach Inkblot Test to America.
        Mary Cover Jones employs learning principles to remove children's fears.
1931   Clinical Section of APA appoints committee on training standards.
1935   Murray's Thematic Apperception Test (TAT) published.
1936   First clinical text, *Clinical Psychology*, published by Louttit.
1937   Clinical Section of APA breaks away to form American Association for Applied Psychology (AAAP).
1938   First Buros *Mental Measurement Yearbook* published.
1939   Wechsler-Bellevue Intelligence Test published.
1942   Carl Rogers publishes *Counseling and Psychotherapy*.
1943   Minnesota Multiphasic Personality Inventory (MMPI) published.
1945   AAAP rejoins APA.
1946   Veterans Administration and National Institute of Mental Health begin support for training of clinical psychologists.
1947   American Board of Examiners in Professional Psychology organized.
1949   Boulder, Colorado conference on training in clinical psychology convenes.
1953   APA *Ethical Standards for Psychologists* published.
1956   Stanford Training Conference.
1958   Miami Training Conference.
        Joseph Wolpe publishes *Psychotherapy by Reciprocal Inhibition*.
1965   Chicago Training Conference.
1973   Vail, Colorado Training Conference.

Table 2-1 Some Growth Dimensions in Clinical Psychology

Year	APA membership	APA clinical division membership*	APA-approved training programs†	Clinical programs receiving federal funds	State laws recognizing psychologists
1892	31				
1900	100				
1910	222				
1918	375				
1930	1100				
1940	3000				
1947	4661	787	22	19	2
1951	8554	1289	38	40	5
1953	10903	1450	41	43	7
1955	13475	1711	43	46	9
1957	15545	1907	47	49	13
1959	17448	2269	56	53	14
1961	18948	2466	60	59	17
1963	20989	2740	61	58	24
1966	24473	3048	68	73	30
1970	29446	3662	73	78	42
1973	35254	3870	83	70	46
1976	42028	4159	101	78	47
1977	44650	4313	103	81	50
1978	46891	4337	103	83	50

*Note that many psychologists in APA who engage in clinical functions may not be members of this division.
†These are all at the doctoral level.

following the growth of the new field to the present. Many of the details mentioned here are drawn from Reisman (1966) and Watson (1953) to which the interested reader should turn for more intensive historical coverage.

Box 2-1 provides a general chronology of events, and Table 2-1 gives a preview of relevant growth dimensions.

THE ROOTS OF CLINICAL PSYCHOLOGY

Why do clinical psychologists do so much assessment? How did the clinical research function develop? What delayed the popularity of clinical psychology until after World War II? What accounts for the relatively small number of clinicians in full-time private practice?

In order to answer questions like these, and, in fact, to really make sense of modern clinical psychology, one must be aware of three sets of social and historical factors which initially shaped the field and which continue to influence it in varying degrees to this day. They include: (1) the use of scientific methods by psychology in general, (2) the development of interest in human individual differences, and (3) the ways in which human behavior disorders have been viewed and dealt with over the years. The last two of these factors had a profound effect upon *what* clinical psychologists would (and would not) do while the first dictated *how* they were to do it.

The Research Tradition in Psychology

It would be beyond the scope of this chapter to attempt to trace the history of psychology and, in any case, the task has already been admirably accomplished (e.g., Boring, 1950; Hilgard, 1978; Watson, 1963). The main feature of that history to be focused on here is that, from its nineteenth century beginnings in the psychophysics of Fechner and Weber, the experimental physiology of Helmholtz, and the work of the first "real" psychologist, Wilhelm Wundt, psychology sought to establish itself as a *science* which employed in its investigations the methods and procedures of natural sciences like biology and physics. Though the roots of psychology were partly in philosophy, and though many early psychologists were preoccupied with such philosophical questions as the relationship between mind and body, the discipline was determined to approach these and other questions about human behavior by conducting *research* which employed as its methods those powerful tools of science, observation and experiment. Thus, the early history of psychology, which began "officially" in Wundt's psychological laboratory at the University of Leipzig in 1879, is primarily the history of *experimental* psychology.

By the time clinical psychology began to emerge, some 17 years after the founding of Wundt's laboratory, the experimental research tradition in psychology was well established. Psychology laboratories had been set up at major universities in Europe and the United States and early psychologists were busy with experiments on sensation, perception, memory, association, emotion, reaction time, and many other aspects of human behavior. It was only natural then that the first clinicians, already trained as psychologists to think in scientific terms and skillfully use laboratory methods, would apply similar approaches to clinical problems. Their success in doing so often varied, but the research tradition they brought to their work took root and grew in the new field until clinical psychologists attained universal recognition among the helping professions as experts at gathering and evaluating new knowledge about clinical aspects of human behavior and behavior change.

The research tradition in psychology has always prompted clinicians to focus experimental investigations upon the adequacy and value of their own work. From the beginning, clinical psychologists used laboratory methods to evaluate what they were doing, and the results of this research sometimes caused shifts in the popularity and perceived usefulness of various clinical activities. The tendency of clinicians to engage in self-evaluation has even extended to their investigative methods; like other psychologists, they often do research on how well they are doing research

To some, the scientific orientation and skill which forms the basis of clinicians' continuing reputation for research expertise is also the strongest link between clinical psychology and psychology itself. The question of whether this link should be maintained, intensified, or deemphasized in the training and daily activities of clinical psychologists has been one of the liveliest issues in the field. We shall consider this point in more detail later.

In short, the research tradition in experimental psychology has been a strong shaper of clinical psychology. It has provided a methodology for approaching clinical subject matter, engendered empirical evaluation of clinical functions, and acted as a point of contention which keeps clinicians engaged in the healthy process of self-examination.

Attention to Individual Differences

Because clinical psychology is based upon interest in the individual, it could not appear as a discipline until differences among human beings began to be widely recognized and formally measured. There would be little impetus for learning about individual cases in a world where everyone is thought to be about the same, and though today it is "natural" to assume that each person is to a certain extent unique and certainly different from others in interests, abilities, intelligence, and personality, this assumption is really rather new.

Of course, differences among people have always been noticed and sometimes assessed. In his *Republic,* Plato pointed out that people should do work for which they are best suited and suggested specifically that prospective soldiers be tested for military ability prior to their acceptance in the army. Fascinating historical accounts by DuBois (1970) and McReynolds (1975) include references to Pythagoras (sixth century B.C.) selecting members of his brotherhood on the basis of such things as facial characteristics, apparent intelligence, and emotionality and to the 4000-year-old Chinese system of ability testing for prospective government employees. Awareness of the existence and potential importance of individual characteristics continued over the ensuing centuries, but it was not until the early 1800s that the idea of paying close, systematic attention to subtle psychological differences really caught on. Until then, people were still thought of as falling into a few rather broad categories such as male-female, good-evil, sane-insane, wise-foolish, peasant-aristocrat.

The earliest developments in the scientific measurement of differences among individuals came from two rather unlikely sources: astronomy and anatomy. The astronomical story goes as follows. In 1796, Nevil Maskelyne was Astronomer Royal at the Greenwich (England) Observatory. He had an assistant named Kinnebrook whose recordings of the moment at which various stars and planets crossed a certain point in the sky differed from those of his employer by the small but significant amount of five- to eight-tenths of a second. Power structures were much the same then as they are today so Maskelyne assumed that his readings were correct and that Kinnebrook was in error. Result: Kinnebrook lost his job.

This incident would have escaped further notice but for the fact that it was mentioned in a history of Greenwich Observatory published in 1816 and drew the attention of F. W. Bessel, an astronomer at the University of Königsberg (Germany) observatory. Bessel wondered whether Kinnebrook's "error" might reflect something about the characteristics of various observers, and, during the next several years, he compared his own observations with those of other experienced astronomers. Bessel found that discrepancies appeared regularly and that the size of the differences depended upon the person with whom he compared notes. The differences or errors associated with each individual observer became known as the "personal equation" since it allowed for correction of calculations based upon personal characteristics. Bessel's work led to later research by psychologists on the speed of and individual differences in reaction time.

The second early source of interest in variations among individuals was the study of phrenology, first promoted in Europe by the anatomist Franz Gall and his pupil, Johann Spurzheim, at the beginning of the nineteenth century. Later, Spurzheim and two Scottish followers, George and Andrew Combe, promoted this "science" in America. As a child in Germany, Gall thought he saw a relationship between the shape of his schoolmates' heads and their mental characteristics. This idea later became the basis for phrenology, which assumes (1) that each area of the brain is associated with a different faculty or function (like self-esteem, language, or reverence), (2) that the better developed each of these areas is, the more strongly that faculty or function will manifest itself in behavior, and (3) that the pattern of over- or underdevelopment of each faculty will be reflected in corresponding bumps or depressions in the skull.

Though Gall's theory was partly correct (the brain does play the major role in determining behavior and its functions are to a certain extent localized), it was mostly fallacious; the conclusions he drew from it and the procedures he used to test it were scorned by the scientists of his day. Nevertheless, Gall went around Europe, locating and measuring the bumps on peoples' heads. He began with prisoners and mental patients whose behavioral characteristics seemed well established (he thought the "acquisitiveness" bump was especially strong among pickpockets) but later, under Spurzheim's influence, phrenology was applied to more respectable segments of society, and an elaborate map of the brain which showed the thirty seven "powers" or "organs" of the mind was developed (Figure 2-1).

The importance for clinical psychology of the now discredited field of phrenology lies not in its value or lack of value, but in its orientation toward assessment of individual characteristics. Its systematic approach and crude taxonomy or classification of human traits made phrenology remarkable (McReynolds, 1975). Gall, Spurzheim, and later phrenologists specialized in "feeling" heads and then providing the owners with a profile of mental makeup. This process may be the origin of the expression "having your head examined" and certainly anticipated one of the purposes (though not the procedures) of assessment in clinical psychology.

In spite of the ultimate demise of phrenology, the ancient idea of measuring individual mental or behavioral characteristics and tendencies through physical dimensions did not immediately disappear. It survived in the 1876 work of Cesare Lombroso, an Italian psychiatrist who correlated facial features and criminal behavior, and in the twentieth century body-type systems of Ernst

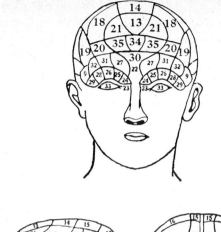

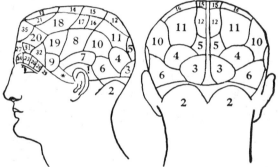

Figure 2-1 Spurzheim's phrenological map. *(From Edwin G. Boring,* A History of Experimental Psychology, *2d ed., copyright 1950, p. 55. Reprinted by permission of Prentice-Hall, Inc., Englewood Cliffs, New Jersey.)*

AFFECTIVE FACULTIES		INTELLECTUAL FACULTIES	
Propensities	Sentiments	Perceptive	Reflective
? Desire to live	10 Cautiousness	22 Individuality	34 Comparison
* Alimentiveness	11 Approbativeness	23 Configuration	35 Causality
1 Destructiveness	12 Self-Esteem	24 Size	
2 Amativeness	13 Benevolence	25 Weight and	
3 Philoprogenitiveness	14 Reverence	Resistance	
4 Adhesiveness	15 Firmness	26 Coloring	
5 Inhibitiveness	16 Conscientiousness	27 Locality	
6 Combativeness	17 Hope	28 Order	
7 Secretiveness	18 Marvelousness	29 Calculation	
8 Acquisitiveness	19 Ideality	30 Evenutality	
9 Constructiveness	20 Mirthfulness	31 Time	
	21 Imitation	32 Tune	
		33 Language	

Kretschmer and William Sheldon. Today, these approaches are not taken seriously by scientists, but they remain a part of our folklore.

The Kinnebrook incident and the rise of phrenology did much to focus attention on the potential importance of individual differences and their measurement, but it was not until later in the nineteenth century that the kinds of procedures which were to form the foundation of clinical psychology's assessment function began to appear. These procedures differed from those seen so far in that, rather than measuring existing physical dimensions or observing differences in performance among a few highly selected individuals, they consisted of systematically collecting *samples of behavior* from relatively large groups of individuals responding to standard sets of stimuli. Such behavior samples were first used to make general statements about individual mental characteristics and later, as statistical sophistication increased, to establish group norms against which a person could be quantitatively evaluated. By 1890, these procedures had been named *mental tests,* but the story of their origin begins some thirty years earlier.

In 1859, Charles Darwin published his momentous work, *The Origin of Species,* in which the importance of two ideas was underscored: (1) variation of individual characteristics within and between species (including humans), and (2) natural selection based in part upon those characteristics. Darwin's cousin, Sir Francis Galton was fascinated by these ideas. Galton was a wealthy English gentleman-scientist with a varied educational background who, though never holding an academic appointment, made scientific contributions in many fields. He studied medicine and mathematics and then worked in areas as diverse as statistics, meteorology, electricity, geography, and fingerprint identification. His interest for us, however, lies in his efforts to explore Darwin's ideas as they apply to the inheritance of individual differences.

Galton was particularly concerned with showing that eminence ran in families (the results of his work in this area were published in an 1869 book entitled *Hereditary Genius*) and he soon realized that, in order to explore human mental characteristics, one must have a systematic and scientific means of measuring them. So for about 20 years, Galton spent part of his time inventing a wide variety of behavior sampling procedures designed to assess many aspects of human functioning. Much of this work was reported in *Inquiries into Human Faculty and Its Development* (1883), a fascinating volume which earned Galton credit for invention of the *test.*[1]

Galton's tests were aimed at measuring the relatively fixed capacities, structures, and functions which he thought comprised the mind. Many of these tests focused on sensorimotor capacity. For example, Galton sought to discriminate high from low intelligence on the basis of individuals' ability to make fine discriminations among objects of differing weight and among varying intensities of heat, cold, and pain. Galton also sought to measure individual differences in vividness of mental imagery and, for this purpose, he invented the questionnaire (see Box 2-2).

Galton's interests extended to variations in associative processes, so he

[1]Strictly speaking, this is not justified since the oral and written tests used by the Chinese to select civil service employees and public officials preceded Galton by thousands of years. Civil service tests based on the Chinese system were already in use in England, France, Germany, and the United States by 1883. Perhaps it is more accurate to say that Galton invented the mental test, though he did not call it that.

Box 2-2   A Sample from Galton's Questionnaire

Think of some definite object—suppose it is your breakfast-table as you sat down to it this morning—and consider carefully the picture that rises before your mind's eye.

1   Illumination—Is the image dim or fairly clear? Is its brightness comparable to that of the actual scene?

2   Definition—Are all the objects pretty well defined at the same time, or is the place of sharpest definition at any one moment more contracted than it is in a real scene?

3   Colouring—Are the colours of the china, of the toast, bread-crust, mustard, meat, parsley, or whatever may have been on the table, quite distinct and natural?

Source: Galton, 1883, in Dennis, 1948, p.279.

developed the word association test to explore this phenomenon. This was long before similar tests were introduced for clinical purposes. Galton first used this test on himself by writing a variety of words on separate sheets of paper, later revealing them one by one, and recording the latency and content of his associations to them.

In order to collect large amounts of data on individual differences in both mental and physical characteristics, Galton set up a laboratory in London where, for a small fee, members of the general public could take a battery of tests and receive a copy of their results (Watson, 1963). This operation comprised the world's first *mental* testing center[2] and it appeared as part of the health exhibition in the 1884 International Exhibition (an early World's Fair) before finally moving to London's South Kensington Museum in 1885. Galton's center remained in operation for six years, during which time 9337 persons were tested (Reisman, 1966).

The few psychologists in existence at this time remained occupied with laboratory research on general principles of human behavior, but by the late 1880s some of them began to show interest in the measurement of individual differences in mental functioning. The person usually credited with merging individual mental measurement with the new science of psychology is James McKeen Cattell, an American who in 1886 took his doctorate in psychology under Wundt in Leipzig. Cattell's interest in the application of psychological methods to the study of individual differences, already evident in his doctoral dissertation on individual variation in reaction time, was intensified by his contact with Galton while lecturing at Cambridge University in 1887. That interest continued for the rest of his life. In 1888, Cattell founded the third psychological laboratory in the United States[3] and by 1890 he had coined the term "mental test" in a paper entitled "Mental Tests and Measurements." Reisman (1966, p. 29) describes Cattell's orientation: "Through the use of mental tests, Cattell predicted, it would be possible to discover the constancy of

[2]The world's first organized *human* testing centers appeared in China in the fourteenth century (DuBois, 1970).

[3]For those keeping score, the first two were set up by William James at Harvard in 1879 and G. Stanley Hall at Johns Hopkins in 1883.

Photo 2-1 James McKeen Cattell (1860–1944). *(From Scientific Monthly, 1929, vol. 28, p. 25. Reprinted by permission of the American Association for the Advancement of Science.)*

mental processes, their interdependence, and their variation under different circumstances. He foresaw *practical applications* of the tests in the selection of people for training and as indicators of disease" (emphasis added). This recognition of the applied potential of mental tests clearly foreshadowed the emergence of clinical psychology.

His experience in Wundt's laboratory taught Cattell that "psychology cannot attain the certainty and exactness of the physical sciences unless it rests on a foundation of experiment and measurement" (Cattell, 1890, in Dennis, 1948, p. 347), so one of his first tasks was to construct a standard battery of mental tests for use by all researchers interested in individual differences. The ten tests he chose reflected Cattell's orientation (inherited from Wundt and Galton) toward using sensorimotor functioning as an index of mental capacity:

1   Dynamometer pressure exerted
2   Rate of movement (time to move an arm a certain distance)
3   Sensation areas (two-point discrimination threshold)
4   Pressure causing pain (hard rubber point against the skin)
5   Least noticeable difference in weight perceived
6   Reaction time for sound
7   Time taken to name colors
8   Bisection of a 50-cm line
9   Judgment of ten seconds time
10 Number of letters repeated on one hearing

Cattell also collected less systematic information from subjects about personal traits such as dreams, diseases, preferences, recreational activities, and future plans (Shaffer and Lazarus, 1952).

Though this particular ten-test battery was never widely adopted, there was no shortage of researchers working on similar Galton-Cattell–style mental measures. For example, at the University of Wisconsin in 1890, Joseph Jastrow assessed mental functioning through tests of vision, color preference, hearing, pain sensitivity, reaction time, memory, and imagery. In 1891, Franz Boas of Clark University employed simple sensorimotor tests to assess children's "intellectual acuteness." At Yale in 1894, J. A. Gilbert found that rate of tapping and judgment of distances discriminated between children labeled "bright" and "dull" by their teachers.

In spite of their popularity, mental tests of the sensorimotor variety were not without detractors who pointed out the less-than-spectacular correlations between test results and anything else (e.g., Sharp, 1899; Wissler, 1901; both cited in Reisman, 1966). By this time, however, an alternative approach to testing had evolved from several quarters. In 1891, Hugo Münsterberg, a psychologist at the University of Freiburg (Germany), constructed a set of fourteen tests to be used in assessing children's mental ability. These tests went beyond Galton-Cattell tasks to include more complex functions like reading, classification of objects, and mathematical operations. When Münsterberg became director of the Harvard University Psychology Laboratory in 1892, he brought the notion of complex mental tests with him.

The German psychiatrist Emil Kraepelin (originator of an early classification system for behavior disorders) was also a designer of tests aimed at more complex mental functions. In 1895, Kraepelin suggested that mental tests be based upon: "(1) the ability to be influenced by practice, (2) the persistence of practice effects, (3) general memory, (4) special memory, (5) fatigability, (6) recovery from fatigue, (7) depth of sleep, (8) concentration of attention against distraction, and (9) adaptability to do effective work under distraction" (Shaffer and Lazarus, 1952, p. 13).

Finally, and perhaps most important, a French lawyer and scientist who had studied medicine and was interested in psychology began in 1895 to develop measures of complex mental ability in normal and defective children. His name was Alfred Binet and much of his involvement in this kind of testing grew out of the recognition growing throughout the nineteenth century that retarded children (who had been distinguished from "psychotics" only as late as 1838) might be helped to a certain extent if they could be identified and given special educational attention.[4] By 1896, Binet and his colleague, Victor Henri, had described a battery of tests which measured not just "simple part processes" such as space judgment, motor skill, muscular effort and memory, but also comprehension, attention, suggestibility, aesthetic appreciation, and moral values.

Thus, by 1896, psychology was not only deeply involved in the measurement of individual differences in mental functioning; it also hosted two partially overlapping approaches to the task: (1) the Cattell-Galton sensorimotor tests aimed at assessing relatively fixed mental *structures,* and (2) the instruments of Binet and others which emphasized complex mental *functions.* Each of these approaches was important to the development of clinical psychology, the former because it fostered the appearance of the first psychological clinic and the latter because it provided a mental test which was to give the new field its first clear identity.

The rest of this part of the story must wait, however, until we examine a third major influence on clinical psychology: changing views of behavior disorder and its treatment.

Conceptions of Behavior Disorder

From the beginning of recorded history, human beings have been faced with the problem of how to explain and deal with behavior which is inappropriate, unusual, bizarre, unexpected, disturbing, or apparently irrational. Reviews of the explanations and procedures which have appeared and disappeared over the centuries to handle this problem make stimulating reading (e.g., Davison and Neale, 1974; Sarason, 1976; Ullmann and Krasner, 1975; Zilboorg and Henry,

---

[4]The famous "Wild Boy of Aveyron" who, though severely retarded, showed some progress under the care of Jean Itard must have impressed Binet. This case, originally reported in 1801–1807, is dramatized in François Truffaut's sensitive film, *The Wild Child.*

1941), but, rather than attempting to cover that material in detail here, we shall merely outline the historical progression of ideas about behavior disorder in order to show how they have influenced the stature and social role of various professions, including clinical psychology.

The earliest conceptions of disordered behavior involved supernatural agents. Persons who acted "crazy" were thought by primitive groups to be possessed by demons or spirits and treatment often involved various forms of exorcism (possibly including *trephining,* or boring small holes in the skull to provide evil spirits with an exit).[5] In Greece before Hippocrates, these ideas continued in somewhat revised form: disordered behavior was attributed to the influence of one or more of the gods. "There was prophetic madness whose patron god was Apollo, ritual madness whose patron god was Dionysus, poetic madness inspired by the Muses, and erotic madness inspired by Aphrodite and Eros" (Ullmann and Krasner, 1975, p. 121). Even in early cultures which practiced monotheism, God was seen as a possible source of behavior problems. In the Old Testament, for example, we are told that "the Lord shall smite thee with madness, and blindness, and astonishment of heart" (Deuteronomy 28:28).

As long as supernatural approaches to behavior disorders were prevalent, philosophy and religion were dominant in explaining and dealing with them. Sometimes, the practitioners in these fields came from the ranks of the "disturbed." In Greece, persons displaying certain kinds of behavior disorders were seen as particularly well suited to helping others and were legitimized as priests or priestesses. Similarly, more primitive groups often identified as shamans, or healers, those who had themselves been possessed or influenced by supernatural beings.

The force of demonological and heavenly explanations of behavior disorders was still strong when, in about the fourth century B.C., the Greek physician Hippocrates began to suggest that these aberrations were due to natural causes and processes. For example, Hippocrates said that the "sacred disease" (now known as epilepsy) was in "no way more divine, nor more sacred than other diseases, but has a natural cause from which it originates like other affectations" (quoted in Zilboorg and Henry, 1941, p. 44). Further, he argued that behavior disorders, like other behaviors, are a function of the bodily distribution of four basic fluids, or humors: blood, black bile, yellow bile, and phlegm. This theory, which is generally acknowledged as the first medical model of behavioral problems, paved the way for the concept of mental illness and legitimized the involvement of the medical profession in its treatment. From Hippocrates until the fall of Rome in 476, physicians and their elaborated medical models provided the dominant approach to behavior disorders.

Then, during the Middle Ages, all this was swept away as the spirit of those

---

[5]This idea still survives in many primitive cultures today, and, lest we become overly smug, we must remind ourselves that it also flavors the views of Western society as well. The popularity of the film *The Exorcist,* the tenets of certain fundamentalist religions, and scattered reports of modern-day beatings and other antidevil procedures (*Time,* 1969) all point to the tenaciousness of demonological notions.

times returned demonological explanations of behavior problems to prominence. The church became the primary social and legal institution in Europe,
and religious personnel again took over responsibility for understanding and
dealing with unusual behavior. Physicians were still respected members of
society, of course, but they were to confine their ministrations to physical
illnesses only. Many medical men solved this problem by becoming priests. "By
the thirteenth century . . . nearly all physicians were also members of the
clergy" (Ullmann and Krasner, 1975, p. 124).

The church began by treating the "insane" humanely and attempting to
exorcise resident spirits. For example, Zilboorg and Henry (1941, p. 131–32)
quote from a tenth-century invocation designed to alleviate hysteria, which was
then believed to be a female disorder caused by a wandering uterus under
demonic control:

> O womb, womb, womb, cylindrical womb, red womb, white womb, fleshy womb,
> bleeding womb, large womb, neufredic womb, bloated womb, O demoniacal
> one! . . . I conjure thee, O womb, in the name of the Holy Trinity to come back to
> the place from which thou shouldst neither move nor turn away . . . and to return,
> without anger, to the place where the Lord has put thee originally. . . . I conjure
> thee not to harm that maid of God, N., not to occupy her head, throat, neck, chest,
> ears, teeth, eyes, nostrils, shoulderblades, arms, hands, heart, stomach, spleen,
> kidneys, back, sides, joints, navel, intestines, bladder, thighs, shins, heels, nails, but
> to lie down quietly in the place which God chose for thee, so that this maid of God
> N. be restored to health.

Later, however, the Church's gloves came off and it was "no more Mr. Nice
Guy." Those who showed or were even suspected of showing deviant behavior
began to be treated as heretics who were (perhaps not unwillingly) possessed by
and under the control of the Devil. Great care was taken by physician-priests to
"diagnose" such cases by looking for signs of the devil (*stigmata diaboli*) on the
skin (Spanos, 1978). Similarly damning evidence of demon-possession was
provided by "dead spots" or local anesthesias which were disclosed by pricking
the body with sharp instruments. Once a "diagnosis" of possession was made
(and it usually was), "treatment" began. This consisted of torture to produce
confession of heresy and, in many cases, burning at the stake. One did not have
to exhibit radical deviance to receive such treatment, but those who did were
particularly likely candidates for it.

This sort of thing went on in varying forms in Europe and, later, in America
until the eighteenth century (the last recorded formal execution of an American
"witch" was in Salem, Massachusetts, in 1692; a "witch" was decapitated in
Switzerland as late as 1782).

However, long before these atrocities finally ended, the demonological
model of disorder was being questioned by some physicians and scholars, and
treatment of deviant individuals gradually began to take the form of confinement in newly established hospitals and asylums such as London's St. Mary of
Bethlehem (organized in 1547 and referred to by locals in contracted form as

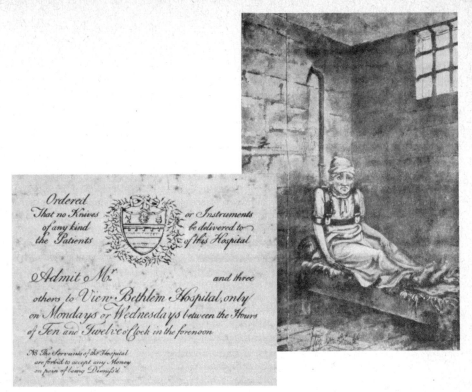

Figure 2-2 The inhumane treatment of the hospitalized "insane" did not deter tourists from buying tickets to gawk at them. *(Reprinted by permission of Hoffman-LaRoche, Inc., Nutley, New Jersey.)*

"bedlam"). The hospital movement grew and saved many lives, but it did not necessarily make them worth living. Even though it was pretty well agreed among eighteenth century scholars that the "insane" were suffering from mental illness (not possession), the medical profession, which was now back in charge of the problem, had little to offer in the way of treatment. And since the general public was not entirely convinced that a devil or two was not lurking among mental patients, the "insane" became little more than prisoners. They lived under abominable conditions and received mainly custodial care. Treatment of their behavior disorders came from doctors who thought of mental illness as resulting from brain damage of some kind or from an overabundance of blood in the brain (an idea borrowed from Hippocrates). At St. Mary of Bethlehem, "a physician would visit once a year to prescribe treatment: bleeding of all patients in April, purges and 'vomits' of surviving patients in May, and once again bleeding all patients in October. At smaller private institutions, . . . a physician might visit once in ten years to prescribe a regime of treatment for the next decade. As a continuing feature of institutionalization, patients were chained to posts in dungeons, whipped, beaten, ridiculed, and fed only the coarsest of slops" (Reisman, 1966, p. 10).

Thanks to the efforts of European and American reformers of the

eighteenth and early nineteenth century (Philippe Pinel, William Tuke, Benjamin Rush, and Eli Todd), this picture changed in the direction of vastly
improved living conditions and far more humane treatment efforts aimed at
actually improving patient behavior (see Chapter 12). Pinel ushered in an era of
"moral treatment" with the following comment: "It is my conviction that these
mentally ill are intractable only because they are deprived of fresh air and
liberty" (quoted in Ullmann and Krasner, 1975, p. 135). Thus began a new
awareness of the possibility that deviates from society's norms could be helped,
rather than simply hidden. Physicians were to retain their treatment responsibilities, however, and for apparently good reason.

Late in the nineteenth century, syphilis was identified as the organic cause
of general paresis, a deteriorative brain syndrome which had once been treated
as a form of insanity. This event did much to bolster the view that all behavior
disorder was organically based and that other disease entities awaited discovery
by doctors. The notion that there could be "no twisted thought without a twisted
molecule" (Gerard, 1956, quoted in Abood, 1960), along with the well-
intentioned crusading of Dorothea Dix which enlarged, proliferated, and
emphasized the medical aspects of mental hospitals in the United States,
hastened the decline of small-scale (but effective) "moral treatment" centers.
These factors also solidified the status of behavior disorder as illness, and further
established medical doctors as the only legitimate agents for its treatment.

The search by doctors for organic causes and physical treatment of mental
illness was to lead some of them in a new direction, however, and would result in
what Zilboorg and Henry (1941) called a "psychiatric revolution." It started
when a few French physicians of the mid-nineteenth century began to explore
the phenomenon which Franz Anton Mesmer had called "animal magnetism"
and which James Braid, an English surgeon, later termed "hypnotism."
Research and demonstrations on the relationship between hypnosis and
behavior disorders (particularly hysteria) by Jean-Martin Charcot, Hippolyte
Bernheim, and Pierre Janet sparked interest in and controversy over the
possibility that mental illness might be at least partially psychological in nature
and thus might respond to psychological as opposed to organic treatment.

The issue attracted the attention of a young Viennese neurologist named
Sigmund Freud who, by 1896, had proposed the first stage of a theory which saw
behavior disorders like hysteria not as the result of fixed organic conditions, but
as a consequence of the dynamic struggle of the human mind to satisfy
instinctual (mainly sexual) desires which begin in infancy while, at the same
time, coping with the social rules, demands, and restrictions of the outside
world. Initial articulation of his theory brought a reaction from Freud's medical
colleagues that was less than enthusiastic. Suggesting that innocent babies are
the repository of base sexual and aggressive instincts was not only revolutionary,
it was unthinkable. One doctor called Freud's idea "a scientific fairy tale"
(Krafft-Ebing, quoted in Reisman, 1966, p. 41). Nevertheless, the idea grew to
become a comprehensive theory of the dynamic nature of behavior and behavior
disorder, and it ultimately redirected the entire course of psychiatry (see
Chapter 9).

Freud's view was to profoundly shape the thinking of clinical psychology as well, but in 1896 its effects on the new field were slight, first because the theory was really only a controversial idea at the start and, second, because it dealt with the problem of mental illness and therefore remained within the province of the medical profession. The newly emerging clinician laid no claim to a treatment function at this time, but we shall see that dynamic approaches to behavior pioneered by Freud and his followers shaped the activities of clinical psychologists in other areas and, when the time came, provided the foundation for their involvement in therapy.

THE DEVELOPMENT OF CLINICAL PSYCHOLOGY

Birth: 1896–1917

We have now examined the three main roots of clinical psychology, and it should be clear that, by the end of the nineteenth century, the ground had been prepared for its appearance. Psychology itself had been identified as a science, and some of its members had begun to apply scientific methods to the study of individual differences. Further, the dynamic approach to behavior disorder was ready to burst forth in psychiatry, opening up vast new areas of subject matter for psychologists interested in understanding deviance.

It was in this historical context that the first recognized clinical psychologist appeared. He was an American named Lightner Witmer (no kidding!). As an undergraduate at the University of Pennsylvania, Witmer had studied under James McKeen Cattell and, upon graduating in 1888, followed in his famous teacher's footsteps by working on his Ph.D. in psychology with Wundt at the University of Leipzig. Witmer completed his doctorate in 1892 and was appointed director of the University of Pennsylvania psychology laboratory

Photo 2-2 Lightner Witmer (1867–1956). *(Courtesy of George Eastman House. Reproduced by permission.)*

which had been vacated when, that same year, Cattell moved to Columbia University.

From this point, the story goes that in March of 1896 a schoolteacher named Margaret Maguire asked Witmer if he could do anything to help one of her students who was a "chronic bad speller." Witmer had himself done some teaching while still an undergraduate and his interest in helping schoolchildren prompted him to "take the case." In doing so, Witmer became the first clinical psychologist and began an enterprise which became the world's first psychological clinic. The willingness of a psychologist to work with a child's scholastic problem may not now seem significant enough to mark the founding of a clinic and a profession, but remember that, until this point, psychology had dealt with people only to study their behavior in general, not to become concerned about them as individuals. Witmer's decision was as unusual then as would be an attempt by a modern astronomer to determine the "best" orbit for the moon in order to alter its path.

The approach taken by Witmer from the beginning was to assess the nature of the child's problem and then facilitate administration of appropriate remedial procedures. In the first case, for example, it was found that Ms. Maguire's bad speller had a vision problem. Witmer saw to it that glasses were fitted and that the child received tutoring. A child with a speech disorder provided Witmer's second case, and it was handled by bringing in a speech teacher.

Though not all that Witmer did was to be equally influential later, there are several immediately apparent aspects of his new clinic which came to characterize subsequent clinical work for a long time.

1   The clients were children. This was natural since Witmer had been offering a course on child psychology and had attracted the attention of teachers concerned about their students.
2   Recommendations for helping clients were preceded by some kind of diagnostic assessment.
3   Witmer did not attempt to work alone. His use of other experts initiated what came to be known as the "team approach" whereby members of various professions consult and collaborate on a given case.
4   There was a clear interest in preventing future problems through early diagnosis and remediation.[6]

At the 1896 meeting of the 4-year-old American Psychological Association, Witmer formally disclosed to his colleagues that he had founded a new kind of psychology and described its approach. His friend Joseph Collins was there and later recounted the scene as follows:

[Witmer said] that clinical psychology is derived from the results of an examination of many human beings, one at a time, and that the analytic method of discriminating

[6]Emphasis on this notion has fluctuated considerably over the years since 1896 and is currently quite strong (see Chapter 12).

mental abilities and defects develops an ordered classification of observed behavior, by means of postanalytic generalizations. He put forth the claim that the psychological clinic is an institution for social and public service, for original research, and for the instruction of students in psychological orthogenics which includes vocational, educational, correctional, hygienic, industrial, and social guidance. The only reaction he got from his audience was a slight elevation of the eyebrows on the part of a few of the older members. (Quoted in Brotemarkle, 1947, p. 65)

The lead-balloon reception accorded Witmer's talk was based on four factors which are summarized by Reisman:

For *one,* the majority of psychologists considered themselves scientists and probably did not regard the role described by Witmer as appropriate for them. *Two,* even if they had considered his suggestions admirable, few psychologists were prepared by training or experience to perform the functions he proposed. *Three,* they were not about to jeopardize their identification as scientists, which was tenuous enough in those early years, by plunging their profession into what they felt were premature applications. *Four,* aside from any prevalent skeptical and conservative attitude, Witmer had an unfortunate talent for antagonizing his colleagues. (1966, p. 46)

Objections two and four were to be only temporary (clinical training would evolve and Witmer would die), but the others were more substantive and provided the first clue that a conflict between psychology as a science and psychology as an applied profession was in the offing. As noted earlier, this issue is at least as active today as it was in 1896.

In spite of objections, Witmer continued his work and expanded his clinic. He hired a full-time social worker and engaged consulting physicians and other specialists to help him deal with the increasing case load, which at first consisted mainly of "slow" or retarded children. Later, the clinic began to deal with other kinds of cases: speech disorders, sensory problems, and learning disabilities. Consistent with his orthogenic (preventive guidance) orientation, Witmer also worked with "normal" and intellectually superior children, providing guidance and advice to parents and teachers.

In 1897, the new clinic inaugurated its training function by offering a 4-week summer course in child psychology. It consisted of case presentations, instruction in Galton-Cattell–style diagnostic testing, and demonstrations of remedial techniques. By 1900, three children per day were being seen and the clinic staff grew to include a director (Witmer), an assistant director, five doctoral-level mental testers, a social worker, and three assistant social workers. Under Witmer's influence, the University of Pennsylvania began offering formal courses in clinical psychology during the 1904–1905 academic year. Witmer took two more important steps in 1907. He set up a residential school associated with his clinic for training retarded children, and he founded and edited the first clinical journal, *The Psychological Clinic.* By 1909, over 450 cases had been handled in Witmer's facilities, and clinical psychology was on its way.

Ironically, however, the influence of Witmer's clinic and school and journal and training courses was really not terribly strong as the new profession grew. You might say that Witmer got clinical psychology rolling but had little to do with steering it. Probably the main reason for this is that, as Watson (1953, p. 79) put it, "Witmer turned his back on almost all that was to predominate in the later days of clinical psychology and became of historical significance only."

The things he turned his back on began to appear in the first decade of the twentieth century and were of immense significance. These included, first, the introduction into the United States of Alfred Binet's new intelligence test, the Binet-Simon Scale. Like Binet's earlier tests, this instrument dealt with complex mental processes rather than the fixed mental structures with which Witmer was mainly concerned. Binet and Simon had developed their test in response to a request from the Minister of Public Education in France for an instrument to identify school children whose mental abilities were too low to include them in regular classes. The Binet-Simon seemed to be effective in this regard and, in spite of Binet's warning that it did not provide a wholly objective measure of intelligence, gained wide attention. Henry H. Goddard of the Vineland (New Jersey) Training School heard about the Binet-Simon Scale while in Europe in 1908 and brought it home for use in assessing the intelligence of "feebleminded" children in the clinic he had set up two years earlier.

The popularity of Goddard's translation of the Binet-Simon Scale and Lewis Terman's 1916 American revision of it (known as the Stanford-Binet) grew so rapidly in the United States that they overshadowed virtually all other tests of intelligence, including, of course, those used by Witmer in Philadelphia. The Binet scales provided a focus for clinical assessment activities which, until 1910, had been rather diffuse and disorganized.[7] All over the country, new university psychological clinics (more than twenty of them by 1914) and institutions for the retarded were adopting the Binet approach while deemphasizing Witmer's "old-fashioned" (and often unimpressive) methods. Witmer clung to his original strategies, however, and was eventually left behind.

Another early-twentieth-century development with which Witmer had little to do was the clinical assessment of adults. This began in the psychology laboratories which had been established at several mental hospitals (e.g., in Massachusetts at McLean, Worcester State, and Boston Psychopathic, and in Washington, D.C., at St. Elizabeth) and was designed to aid psychiatrists in diagnosing and planning treatment in cases of brain damage and other problems. After 1907, psychological examination of all mental patients in some hospitals became a matter of routine, and similar assessments began in prisons to assist staff in identifying disturbed convicts or planning rehabilitation programs (Rotter, 1971). This work sparked psychologists' interest in (and research on) adults displaying severe disorders, and while the adult patient population later became central to clinical psychology, Witmer was never oriented toward it.

[7]An attempt by the APA in 1895 to set up a standard battery of mental and physical tests had, like Cattell's earlier effort, fizzled. The result was that individual psychologists had been on their own in terms of development of assessment batteries and that the staff of institutions for the retarded had had to depend on intelligence "data" like posture or the look in a patient's eyes.

Third, and perhaps most important, Witmer did not join other clinically oriented psychologists in adopting the Freudian approach to behavior and behavior disorder which was beginning to gain strength in psychiatry. Clinical psychology became acquainted with that approach through close association with psychiatry in the mental hospital laboratories and also through child guidance clinics which, though often run by psychiatrists, routinely employed psychologists.

The child guidance movement in America was stimulated in part by the newly organized National Committee for Mental Hygiene, a group founded by a former mental patient, Clifford Beers, and supported by Harvard psychologist William James and Adolf Meyer, the country's most prominent psychiatrist. With funds from philanthropist Henry Phipps, the Committee (which ultimately became the National Association for Mental Health) worked to improve treatment of the mentally ill and prevent psychological disorders before they occurred. Guidance clinics for children were very much in line with this sort of thinking, particularly the preventive aspect. The first of them was founded in Chicago in 1909 by an English-born psychiatrist named William Healy.

Like Witmer, Healy worked with children, employed a team approach (he had a full-time psychologist and consulting social workers), and emphasized prevention, but otherwise his orientation was quite different. For one thing, instead of dealing mainly with children whose problems were retardation, learning disabilities, or other education difficulties, Healy focused on cases of child misbehavior which had required the attention of school authorities, the police, or the courts. In addition, Healy's clinic operated on the assumption that juvenile offenders were suffering from some form of mental illness which, if treated properly, could be prevented from causing more serious problems later. Finally, because Freud's ideas had impressed Healy when he studied in Europe during the 1906–1907 academic year, they strongly influenced the tone of his Chicago clinic (first called the Juvenile Psychopathic Institute and, later, the Institute for Juvenile Research). For example, Healy diagnosed one of his first juveniles as an hysteric whose antisocial behavior was caused by unconscious guilt feelings.

This dynamic, affective, motivational approach was vastly discrepant with that of Witmer, and it received a huge boost in popularity and influence among psychiatrists and psychologists alike when, in the same year that Healy opened his clinic, G. Stanley Hall, a psychologist, arranged for Sigmund Freud and two of his followers, Carl Jung and Sandor Ferenczi, to speak at the twentieth anniversary celebration of Clark University in Worcester, Massachusetts. This event and the lectures associated with it "sold" psychoanalysis to American psychologists. Freud's theory was compatible with their interest in the way the mind deals with its environment (the functionalism of William James and G. Stanley Hall) as opposed to what it is made of (the structuralism of Wundt): "In the United States, there was little patience for a psychology which either dissects into minute detail the structures of the mind or for one which speculates philosophically about its ultimate nature" (Korchin, 1976, p. 42).

The newly established *Journal of Abnormal Psychology* became the major American source of psychoanalytic writing, and it has been suggested that it was "the psychologists and not psychiatrists alone, as is commonly supposed, who offered the first support to psychoanalysis in the United States" (Watson, 1953, p. 77). One of the results of this excitement over Freud was that psychological and child guidance clinics would sooner or later follow Healy's model, not Witmer's. This fact, coupled with the spreading use of Binet intelligence tests, put Witmer and his approach somewhat in the background. His educational focus and structural orientation kept him involved with activities and clients which have since become more strongly associated with school psychologists, vocational counselors, speech therapists, and remedial teachers than with clinical psychologists.

The various trends which Witmer ignored were, in fact, trends and thus did not result in overnight shifts of emphasis and procedure within clinical psychology. The field grew rather slowly even after it adopted the Binet-Simon Scales and was for a long time identified primarily with the testing of retarded, emotionally disturbed, delinquent, and academically problematic children in clinics and guidance centers. This professional image had become clear enough in 1913 to attract critics who argued that clinicians spent too much time in diagnostic work with hopeless cases and that they were not sufficiently psychoanalytic in orientation. At the same time, schools and other institutions which dealt with children were desperately searching for clinical psychologists to do the vast amount of testing which was fast becoming fashionable.[8]

As may be imagined, the need for clinicians' services outweighed the effects of their critics, and the field continued its slow advance during the 1910–1917 period. Its practitioners gave a lot of established tests, constructed a lot of new ones, and conducted evaluative research on the reliability and validity of them all. Most of the new instruments which appeared at this time were aimed at measuring intelligence, but a few began to focus on the assessment of personality through word associations or questionnaire items (see Chapter 6).

Training for clinical psychology was still a problem. A few internships were available at places like the Vineland Training School, and courses in intelligence testing and related subjects were taught here and there, but nothing was formalized and virtually anyone could use the title of clinical psychologist. The science-conscious APA was of little help in this regard. It took no official notice of the problems of the new field within its ranks except to pass a 1915 resolution discouraging the use of mental tests by unqualified persons and then to appoint a committee to consider what "unqualified" meant.

Here was another indication of the rift within psychology between "scientists" and "professionals," and this time there was a temporary rebellion.

---

[8]There were no officially sanctioned clinical training programs at this time, so creatures called clinical psychologists were in very short supply. As a result, many schoolteachers and principals undertook the testing function themselves. The outcome was often rather distressing: "In one school system, almost half the children tested by one teacher were classified as feebleminded, an incident which, though extreme, was not unique" (Reisman, 1966, p. 128).

A group of disgruntled clinicians agreed that they could best advance the interests of their new profession by forming a separate organization so, in December of 1917, the American Association of Clinical Psychologists (AACP) was established. This step did not help much, and, after being promised that the APA would give more consideration to professional issues and problems, the AACP rejoined the APA as its clinical section in 1919.

Between the Wars: 1918–1941

During this infighting, another series of battles called World War I was going on. The main effects of the war for clinical psychology were to focus the field's attention upon assessment of nonhospitalized adults (as opposed to mental patients and children) and, in turn, to expand the number and variety of tests available for such assessment.

When America became involved in World War I, there was an urgent need to classify very large numbers of adult men in terms of their intellectual prowess and psychological stability. No techniques existed to do this, so the Army asked Robert Yerkes (then APA president) to head a committee of assessment-oriented experimental psychologists who were asked to develop appropriate measures.[9] The work of this group resulted in the Army Alpha and Army Beta intelligence tests which could be administered to groups of literate or nonliterate adults. To help detect behavior disorders among the recruits, Yerkes's committee presented the Army with Robert Woodworth's Psychoneurotic Inventory (when actually given to soldiers, it was more politely titled "Personal Data Sheet"; see Yerkes, 1921 in Dennis, 1948). Soon, psychologists of all kinds were being taught by the Army to administer tests and by 1918, they had evaluated nearly 2 million men in group or individual contexts.

After the war, clinical psychologists were still primarily involved with the assessment of children, but they began to find increased employment opportunities as testers in adult-oriented facilities as well. During the postwar years, clinicians were also broadening their horizons by using a wider variety of intelligence tests for children and adults and by adding to their measures of personality, interests, specific abilities, emotions, and traits. They developed many of these tests themselves, while adopting others from the psychoanalytically oriented psychiatrists of Europe. Some of the more familiar instruments of this period include the Seashore Musical Ability Test (1919), Jung's Word Association Test (1919), the Rorschach Inkblot Test (1921), the Miller Analogies Test (1926), the Goodenough Draw-A-Man Test (1926), the Strong Vocational Interest Test (1927), the Thematic Apperception Test (TAT: 1935), the Bender-Gestalt Test (1938), and the Weschler-Bellevue Intelligence Scale (1939).

So many psychological tests appeared (over 500 by 1940) that a *Mental Measurements Yearbook* was needed to catalogue them (Buros, 1938), and the

---

[9]The group included Henry Goddard of the Vineland School, Guy M. Whipple, publisher of a 1910 *Manual of Mental and Physical Tests,* and Lewis Terman, father of the Stanford-Binet Scales.

development, administration and evaluation of these instruments continued to stimulate clinicians' assessment and research functions. Testing also provided financial benefits. For example, in 1921 Cattell formed the Psychological Corporation to sell tests and provide consultation and research to business and industry. "Tests were becoming big business and psychologists were pleasantly torn between delight at their success and objecting to the extent of their commercialization" (Reisman, 1966, p. 181). Clinical and other psychologists of this period were also beginning to engage in research and theorizing on such clinically relevant topics as the nature of personality, the source of human intelligence (i.e., heredity or environment), the causes of behavior disorders, the nature and application of hypnosis, and the relationship between learning principles and deviance.

By the mid-1930s there were fifty psychological clinics and at least a dozen child guidance clinics in the United States. Clinical psychologists in these and other settings "perceived themselves as dealing with educational, not psychiatric problems, but this distinction was growing increasingly difficult to maintain" (Reisman, 1966, pp. 176–77). Slowly, clinicians began to add a treatment function to their already familiar assessment, training, and research roles and by the late thirties a few had even gone into private practice. This new sphere of activity developed through the circumstances in which clinicians worked, the nature of their instruments, and their desire for higher status.

The therapeutic function focussed initially on children and was a natural outgrowth of clinicians' continuing involvement in diagnostic and remedial work which, especially in dynamically oriented child guidance clinics, took on clear treatment overtones by dealing with parent-child relationships. It also stemmed from the increased prestige associated with clinicians' use of personality tests, especially projectives such as the Rorschach and the TAT. These somewhat mysterious techniques provided a common language for communication between diagnostician (psychologist) and therapist (psychiatrist) with respect to child and adult patients and thus increased the clinician's association with treatment (Wyatt, 1968). Engaging in treatment also allowed clinical psychologists to obtain better-paying, more responsible jobs, to be less dependent on testing as a means of dealing with people, and generally to become involved with the "whole patient."

Even though its settings, clients, and functions were beginning to expand, clinical psychology was not a fully recognized profession in the 1930s. By the beginning of World War II, there were still no official training programs for clinicians. Few of them held Ph.D.'s, some had M.A.'s, and many had B.A.'s or less. To get a job as a clinical psychologist (i.e., a mental tester), all one really needed was a few courses in testing, abnormal psychology, and maybe child development, along with an "interest in people." This was causing great public confusion over what clinical psychologists were: "A person who called himself a 'clinical psychologist' might be someone of great eminence, highly qualified academically and with 20 or 30 years of practical experience . . . or he might be a student just graduated from the University, without any kind of relevant experience, capable only of grinding out Binet IQ's without even an adequate understanding of their relevance to the clinical problem presented" (Eysenck, 1950, quoted in Watson, 1953, p. 96).

Clinicians felt frustrated by this situation because, while they did not like their second-class reputation as mental testers, they were receiving little help from their university colleagues or the APA in upgrading that image through encouragement for standardized training programs or official certification. Continuing discomfort on the part of academic psychologists over the appropriateness of "applied" psychology, combined with the cost of clinical training, led to a "slow, dragging response" (Reisman, 1966) by university psychology departments to requests for graduate programs in clinical psychology.

Similarly, many clinicians felt that, in spite of previous promises, the APA was still not supportive of them. Although at various times during the twenties and thirties the organization had appointed committees on clinical training (and had even set up a short-lived certification program), its involvement appeared half-hearted. For example, in 1935 the APA Committee on Standards of Training in Clinical Psychology suggested that a Ph.D. plus one year of supervised experience was necessary to qualify a person as a clinical psychologist, but after issuing its report the committee disbanded and little came of its efforts.

The discontent of clinical and other nonacademic psychologists erupted in 1937, and they again broke away from APA to form a separate organization, this time called the American Association of Applied Psychology (AAAP). It contained divisions of consulting, clinical, educational, and industrial psychology and remained on its own for eight years before rejoining APA.

So, by the end of the 1930s, all the ingredients for the modern field of clinical psychology had been assembled: Its six functions (assessment, treatment, research, teaching, consultation, and administration) had appeared, and though not all of them thrived, clinical psychology had expanded beyond its original clinics into hospitals, prisons, and other settings. It was working with adults as well as children, and it was strongly motivated to stand on its own. Only the support of its parent discipline and the society it served was still needed and this came, in spades, as the result of World War II.

The Postwar Explosion

As had been the case in World War I, America's entry into World War II necessitated mass testing of military personnel on intelligence, ability, and personality dimensions, and again a committee of psychologists was formed to help with the task. Because psychometric (mental measurement) and clinical sophistication had increased greatly since the time of the Yerkes committee, this new group of psychologists produced a correspondingly wider range of military-oriented tests, including the Army General Classification Test (a group intelligence instrument), a psychiatric screening questionnaire called the Personal Inventory, brief measures of intelligence, short forms of the Rorschach and the TAT, and several kinds of ability tests for selection of officers, pilots, and the like.[10]

The magnitude of psychology's involvement in World War II was far greater than it had been in World War I, For example, about 1500 psychologists (nearly 25 percent of those available) served in World War II, and Reisman (1966) reports that, in 1944 alone, over 60 million psychological tests were given to 20 million soldiers and civilians. In addition to giving tests, psychologists were asked to conduct interviews, write psychological reports, and, because of the overwhelming case load of psychological casualties, perform psychoanalytically oriented therapy. For those who had been clinicians before the war, military life meant an opportunity to consolidate and expand their clinical functions, but such individuals were a minority. Most wartime psychologists had been oriented to academic settings and basic research and, for them, the Army's desperate need for applied psychological services meant taking on clinical responsibilities for the first time.

To their surprise and sometimes to their delight, these converted clinicians found that they were able to handle their new jobs remarkably well, and many of them began to like the work. Authorities in the military and civilian establishment were impressed: "The fact that psychologists could take adequate case histories, contribute to the personality evaluation and diagnosis of the patient, help plan research studies, and effectively handle many types of patients in individual and group therapy, demonstrated that here was a professional group that had not been fully utilized in the past" (Garfield, 1974, p. 9). Soon, psychologists became commissioned military officers, just like physicians. By the end of the war, many clinicians were "hooked" on therapy with adults, and former experimentalists became enamored of clinical functions. Their wartime testing and therapeutic activities had brought psychologists increasing public attention and prestige, and "all of a sudden there was a mass exodus from the laboratories out into the world of applied psychology" (Hathaway, 1958, p. 242).

This widespread awakening of interest in clinical work might have come to nothing if there had not been so much of it to do. The war left over 40,000 men in VA neuropsychiatric hospitals and there were just not enough clinical psychologists and psychiatrists available to deal adequately with assessment and treatment tasks. Where the APA and university psychology departments had vacillated over the status, education, and roles of clinicians, the needs of the VA prompted clear and immediate action. In a 1946 VA circular, clinical psychology was defined as a profession which engaged in diagnosis, treatment, and research relating to adult disorders and described clinicians as holders of the Ph.D. More

---

[10]Some of the latter techniques included behavioral measures which required candidates to perform various tasks under conditions of frustration and stress. Such "real life" observation has since become an increasingly popular clinical assessment strategy (see Chapter 7).

important, the VA said it needed 4700 of these individuals to fill lucrative, high-prestige jobs and that it would help pay for clinical training. Hathaway (1958, p. 107) said, "This document, more than any other single thing, has served to guide the development of clinical psychology."

Here was the support that clinical psychology had been waiting for. Early in 1946, the chief medical director of the VA met with representatives of major universities to ask them to start formal clinical training programs and by that fall, 200 graduate students became VA clinical trainees at twenty two institutions (Peck & Ash, 1964). By 1951, the VA had become the largest single employer of psychologists in the United States. Thus, "[It] was not the science and profession of psychology itself, but World War II and its attendant manpower problems, that virtually revolutionized the training and scope of clinical work in psychology" (Garfield, 1974, p. 8).

With this in mind, it is easy to see why not all of the psychology departments which began clinical training programs after the war were equally enthusiastic about doing so. Those faculty members who were sympathetic to or involved in clinical work saw governmental support as a boon, while others, strongly devoted to psychology as a pure science, objected to the intrusion of professionally oriented training which, to their way of thinking, was begun merely because the government (first through the VA and then through the United States Public Health Service, USPHS) was willing to pay for it. Shakow (1965) characterized this as a conflict between the "virgins" and the "prostitutes." Whatever one calls it, it was a continuation of the same "science versus profession" issue which had been brewing ever since 1896; now, however, the fight had moved within the walls of the "ivory tower" and thus caused far greater concern than ever before.

Nevertheless, the VA and USPHS went ahead with their funding plans and turned to the APA for guidance as to which university clinical programs merited federal support. Accordingly, an initial evaluation of existing programs was provided by a Committee on Graduate and Professional Training in 1947 (Kelly, 1961). Later that year, a more extensive report came from David Shakow's Committee on Training in Clinical Psychology, a group which had been appointed by the APA to (1) recommend the content of clinical programs, (2) set up training standards to be followed by universities and internship facilities providing such training, and (3) report on current programs (Shakow, 1978 presents details of the history and composition of this committee).

This "Shakow report" was meant only to provide training guidelines, but since it was so intimately tied up with the dispensation of federal money to individual students (through stipends) and whole departments (through training grants), the "guidelines" were adopted as policy "and soon became the 'bible' of all departments of psychology desirous of having their programs evaluated and reported on favorably by the APA" (Kelly, 1961, p. 110). Shakow felt that this reaction tended to prematurely crystallize the nature of clinical training and that, had things gone a bit more slowly and carefully, the resulting programs might have been better.

As it was, however, the Shakow report laid the groundwork for later controversy over how clinicians should be trained, an issue which related directly to the science-profession problem. The recommendations which are of greatest contemporary importance include the following (APA, 1947):

1   That clinical psychologists should be trained first as psychologists (i.e., as scientists) and second as practicing professionals.
2   That clinical training should be as rigorous as that given to nonclinicians and thus consist of a four-year doctorate including a year of supervised clinical internship experience.
3   That clinical training should focus on the "holy trinity" (assessment, research, and treatment) by offering courses in general psychology, psychodynamics, assessment techniques, research methods, and therapy (see Shakow, 1978 for a succinct summary of the full report).

Thus began "what later came to be recognized as something of an educational experiment: the training of persons both as scientists and as practitioners, not in a separate professional school [as is the case in medicine or law], but in the graduate schools of our universities" (Kelly, 1961, p. 112). This experiment continued with the support of the APA, the federal government, internship facilities, and the universities. Two years after the Shakow report appeared, a national conference on clinical training at Boulder, Colorado, formally adopted its recommendations. In addition, resolutions were passed at that meeting which led to creation of an Education and Training Board within the APA to evaluate and publish lists of accredited doctoral-level clinical programs and related internship settings.

The scientist-professional training package described in the Shakow report and adopted at Boulder in 1949 came to be known, naturally enough, as the "Boulder model" and set the dominant pattern for clinical training during at least the next twenty five years. Nevertheless, not everyone in the field was enthusiastic about it, and though its official APA status was reaffirmed at subsequent training conferences in 1955, 1958, 1962, 1965, and 1973, discontent remained. In Chapter 13 we shall consider the details of these conferences and the modifications which have been suggested to update the Boulder model. Suffice it to say here that psychologists strongly committed to professional practice felt that the model emphasizes research training at the expense of preparation for applied clinical work, while more academically oriented psychological scientists failed to see the need for so much emphasis on application. One sarcastic delegate to the Boulder conference, referring to the relatively unimpressive results then available from clinical research on psychotherapy, remarked: "therapy is an undefined technique which is applied to unspecified problems with non-predictable outcomes. For this technique we recommend rigorous training" (Lehner, 1952).

In spite of such problems, government support of university-based Boulder model training resulted in the explosive growth of clinical psychology. By 1948, there were twenty-two APA-approved clinical training programs, and more were on the way: sixty by 1962, seventy two by 1969, eighty three by 1973, and over a hundred at present. The number of clinicians grew as well, and the nature of their work diversified until it reached the proportions outlined in Chapter 1. Postwar personality and intelligence assessment mushroomed following intro- duction of new tests like the Minnesota Multiphasic Personality Inventory (MMPI), new scoring procedures for projectives like the Rorschach, and new adult intelligence scales. The clinician's treatment function, now recognized by the government and by the public, blossomed as well. Three times as many clinical psychologists engaged in therapy after the war as before it, and the emphasis was swinging toward work with adults rather than children (Andrews & Dreese, 1948). Further, the clinician in private practice became a more common phenomenon as practitioners sought to pattern themselves after physicians.

Legal recognition of clinical psychology as a profession was growing as well. In the postwar years, more and more state governments passed laws providing for licensure or certification of qualified clinicians, and the APA set up an independent certification group called The American Board of Examiners in Professional Psychology (ABEPP; now the American Board of Professional Psychology) to identify those individuals who had attained particularly high levels of clinical experience and expertise. The APA also developed a code of ethics governing the behavior of all its members but focusing particularly on those engaged in applied activities. These and other aspects of clinical psychology as a profession are discussed more fully in Chapter 13.

Like everything else in the field, clinical research also expanded after World War II and produced some disturbingly negative conclusions on the usefulness of some personality tests (see, e.g., Magaret, 1952), the value of clinicians' diagnostic judgments when compared to statistically based decisions (Meehl, 1954), and the effectiveness of traditional (i.e., mainly Freudian) forms of psychotherapy (Eysenck, 1952). Such research had a lot to do with the subsequent shift away from standard clinical assessment noted in Chapter 1 and with the development of many new treatment approaches, including those of Carl Rogers and Joseph Wolpe.

By the mid-1970s, almost everything which could have been said about clinical psychology before World War II had changed, at least in degree. The role of the clinical psychologist before the war was that of a diagnostician whose clients were usually children. When psychiatry allowed clinicians to do treat- ment, it was aimed at "curing mental illness" through application of psychoana- lytically oriented techniques in one-to-one sessions. Since 1945, the functions, settings, and clients presented in Chapter 1 have evolved and brought with them both a rejuvenated recognition of the importance of preventive as well as ameliorative treatment interventions and a much wider range of theoretical approaches and practical tools for dealing with the problems of assessing and altering human behavior. We shall consider each of these facets of today's clinical psychology in subsequent chapters.

For now, however, let us recognize that though the field has advanced in spectacular fashion on many fronts during the last 40 years, neither its development nor its self-examination has been completed. Garfield (1966, p. 353) notes that clinicians appear to be either a "particularly introspective, soul-searching and self-critical group" or one that is chronically dissatisfied. Whichever is the case, conferences on training continue, and the pages of clinical journals are filled with articles reflecting ideas about and concern over where the profession is going. The issues to which clinical psychologists devote so much journal space and convention time include meeting society's needs for psychological service, the role and value of clinical assessment and psychotherapy, the problems and prospects of private practice, the prevention of psychological problems, and ways of providing relevant services to segments of the population (such as the poor) which do not usually receive them.

Above all, clinicians focus on the scientist-professional issue. In dozens of speeches and papers each year, the debate continues: How can the clinician be a scientifically minded, data-oriented psychologist who waits for carefully validated evidence before making a recommendation or proceeding with treatment and, at the same time, function as a "front-line" practitioner who often must take immediate action in order to help distressed people with pressing and often complex problems about which little or no guiding laboratory knowledge may be available? Some observers feel that the scientific and professional roles are basically incompatible and that one must choose one or the other. Accordingly, many clinical students become totally subjective, intuitive practitioners to whom "data" is a nasty word, while others work as full-time researchers in hopes of generating laboratory findings that will someday make clinical practice scientific.

This "either-or" polarization may have rather unfortunate consequences. It often isolates the practitioner from research evidence which may be useful in applied work, and it may place the researcher in a laboratory which is so artificial that results apply only to other laboratory settings or similar situations where some of the most interesting and important clinical problems may not appear. Such extreme reactions to the scientist-professional issue are often viewed with alarm, since their cumulative result could be a reduction in the mutual stimulation between clinic and laboratory which most careful thinkers in the field consider to be vital to the future of clinical psychology.

Thus, in spite of suggestions which would formalize the distinction between the scientific and applied aspects of psychology (through totally separate training programs, for example), a difficult though potentially more fruitful alternative has remained attractive. This involves steering a moderate course which seeks to avoid exclusive identification as scientist *or* professional, and which attempts to generate, utilize, and respect both scientific knowledge and clinically derived experience so that they may nourish rather than compete with one another.

If the past is any indicator of the future, one might be accurate in guessing that those who take varying positions on the scientist-professional issue will remain in contact and in contention.[11] To a great extent, this conflict is the inevitable result of differing points of view. Those who see clinical psychology as an art and have little use for laboratory approaches to it are often lined up on one side of the question, while those who discount the value of subjective judgment and other apparently nonscientific aspects of clinical work are commonly found on the other. Less predictable are the positions of individuals who conceptualize clinical psychology as a field which at present has certain artistic characteristics, a firm scientific base, and a growing capability to exploit both.

This variety in the orientation of individual clinicians is, in part, a consequence of the breadth of their field and is by no means confined to the scientist-professional question. As the size and stature of clinical psychology have grown, concern over the immediate problem of self-preservation has decreased, leaving the field less conservative and more tolerant of divergent ideas, not only about clinical roles and training, but about more basic issues like the development of human behavior problems and the means through which they can best be alleviated. Our task in the next chapter is to review the most influential of these ideas and illustrate their importance for the day-to-day functioning of the individual clinician.

[11]Those interested in absorbing in more detail the flavor of the arguments to date will enjoy readings such as Albee (1970, 1975), Cook (1965), Garfield, (1966), Hathaway (1958), Korman (1976), Mayman (1964), Rabin (1974), Shakow (1969, 1975), and Tryon (1963). A column by Perloff (1978) which puts the "scientists" and the "professionals" in the roles of Egyptians and Israelis provides a humorous look at the conflict.

Chapter 3

Models of Clinical Psychology

To fully appreciate the dimensions of an object one must look at it from several angles; this is why sculpture is often displayed in a place which allows the viewer to walk around it. Events are also subject to multiple interpretations, depending on point of view. When more than one person observes a single incident, be it a football play, an automobile accident, a social interaction, or whatever, there are likely to be differing versions recounted by each witness which reflect his or her vantage point and interpretation of what happened. This phenomenon is so reliable that instructors often stage sudden and unusual classroom events (such as the attempted "murder" of the professor by a "disgruntled former student") in order to demonstrate the inevitable variability in observer recollection.

Listening to differing accounts of the same occurrence based upon varying points of view can sometimes be confusing, but may also be illuminating in the sense that, as with a statue, one is allowed to examine all the angles. And though the "absolute truth" about an event, a relationship, or a person may not necessarily be revealed, there is at least the assurance that potentially important material has not been totally overlooked. Filmmakers have long recognized the value of the multiple viewpoint approach for deepening the analysis of human behavior: Kurosawa's *Rashomon*[1] and Orson Welles's *Citizen Kane* provide excellent examples of the understanding which can come from collecting several editions of the "same" story.

As mentioned in Chapter 1 and as will be illustrated in the next four chapters, clinical psychologists usually adopt a similar strategy in seeking various kinds of assessment information about a client from multiple sources. In this regard, clinicians share procedural characteristics with competent private detectives, congressional committees, investigative reporters, and others who are interested in trying to comprehend a given subject fully. The same open and comprehensive orientation can be of great value to the beginning student of clinical psychology, since the field is a lot like a statue or a mugging: There are many ways to look at it, each of which reveals some aspects and obscures others. The whole picture cannot emerge unless one is familiar with the variety of viewpoints which are available.

The purpose of this chapter is to examine three of the most prominent of these points of view: the psychodynamic, social-learning, and phenomenological models of clinical psychology. They are referred to as *models* because they provide descriptions on a miniature scale of the ways in which various thinkers have approached human behavior in general and clinical psychology in particular. Each model has something to say about how behavior develops and becomes problematic, and they have all exerted clear influences on the assessment, treatment, and research styles of their adherents.

For example, if one's model of or approach to clinical psychology were based upon the assumption that all human behavior is primarily determined by the foods that people eat, that assumption would probably lead to statements about how diet affects behavioral development through infancy, childhood, adolescence, adulthood, and old age (e.g., "mushy foods produce mushy thinking and uncoordinated behavior in infants and the elderly, while increasingly solid food and mature, stabilized eating habits result in clear thought processes and maximally efficient overt behavior"). Further, a dietary model might suggest hypotheses about the appearance of disordered behavior in which, say, excesses of carbohydrates are associated with anxiety, consumption of large quantities of soft drinks are thought to result in hallucinations, or too little protein is implicated in the appearance of obsessive rituals. In addition to accounting for observed human behavior, this hypothetical model would focus clinicians' assessment activities on the dietary sphere. Specialized measurement procedures might be developed to obtain accurate and detailed information on clients' past and present eating patterns and to monitor the nutritional components of each meal.

The model would also utilize certain clinical treatments far more than others. Carefully programmed alterations in diet would probably be seen as especially vital, while simply talking about one's problems might be regarded as

---

[1]*The Outrage* is an American adaptation of this film and may be more familiar.

a waste of time. Finally, the targets of research conducted by clinicians espousing a dietary model would be fundamentally shaped by that model. Experiments designed to clarify the functional relationships between food intake and behavior or to evaluate particular diet-assessment or diet-modification procedures would appear in large numbers and their results would have much to do with the popularity and influence of the model by which they were generated. A host of unique methodological problems might arise from such experiments and thus spawn a whole new wave of research centered on improving previous research.

The Value of Models

The model just described may or may not be an accurate one, but it does highlight the positive features of any systematic approach to clinical psychology: Even if ultimately discredited, a model can be of great value in helping the clinician to organize both thought and action and to communicate in a common "language" with colleagues.

Without a model, this is not always easy. Human behavior is extremely complex and can be examined on a variety of levels from the activity of cells and organ systems to overt motor responses to cognitive functioning and social interaction. Add to this the recognition that there is an almost endless number of ways in which behavior can be interpreted, assessed, described, researched, and altered, and it should come as no surprise that the clinical psychologist "carries on a continuing struggle against confusion" (Sundberg, Tyler, & Taplin, 1973, p. 93). One must decide which aspects of behavior deserve special attention and which can be deemphasized, which kinds of assessment data are of interest and which are less relevant, which treatment techniques merit exploration and which do not, which research targets might be fruitful and which are less promising. A model or systematic approach can help guide these decisions about phenomena which are complicated and potentially bewildering, thereby providing comfort for the clinician by bringing some order to what may have been conceptual chaos.

The appeal of a particular model as a kind of map, compass, and guide typically attracts followers whose commitment to it ranges from healthy skepticism to a zeal bordering on fanaticism. However, the personal usefulness of the models of clinical psychology to be discussed in this chapter must be distinguished from their scientific worth, which is evaluated on dimensions other than comfort, superficial attractiveness, or number of adherents. In reading what follows, therefore, it is important to keep in mind that, in scientific terms, the best clinical models are those whose implications and hypotheses can be rigorously investigated in a wide range of contexts. A good model should include a complete, efficient, and testable account of the development, maintenance, and alteration of both problematic and nonproblematic aspects of human behavior. Models which meet these requirements are open to experimental evaluation in the laboratory and systematic scrutiny in clinical application;

ideally, they will stand or fall as the data accumulate. "Only the untestable models never die. They don't even fade away, unfortunately" (Zubin, 1969, p. 6).

Some Cautions about Models

Though clinical models can help organize thinking about human behavior, guide clinical decisions and functions, and facilitate professional communication, their value is not limitless. In fact, it has been argued that the very characteristics just described as the strengths of clinical models can also be construed as their main weaknesses. If this does not confirm the pervasiveness of multiple points of view, nothing will. For example, adoption of a given model's point of view may organize one's thinking about behavior so completely that it becomes rigid, orthodox, and closed to new and potentially valuable ideas. This increases the danger of developing a fossilized rather than organized approach to clinical psychology.

Further, blind adherence to a particular model can reduce clinical function- ing to a reflexive or automatic level at which objective evaluation and subsequent modification of professional practices become increasingly unlikely. As a result, the overly model-dependent clinician may perform assessment, treatment, research, and other activities strictly in accordance with the dictates of a model because he/she has always performed them that way, regardless of experimental evidence or case results which might indicate the need for change (see Mahoney, 1976; Thorne, 1969).

Finally, a model is a bit like a geographical area in the sense that it tends to develop its own "language." This eases communication among those conversant in it, but it can obstruct discussions between "natives" and "foreigners." Often, the exchange of ideas and information between persons espousing divergent models of clinical psychology is hampered by this special kind of "language" barrier. In such cases, both parties may think they are speaking comprehensibly and understanding what they hear when, in fact, they are not getting their meaning across because their model-based terms and specialized meanings are in the way. We have heard lengthy and heated theoretical arguments of this type which ended when the participants finally realized that they agreed with one another. Fortunately, most of the problems associated with the adoption of clinical models can be significantly reduced by avoiding the overzealous commitment to them which fosters conceptual rigidity, behavioral inflexibility, and semantic narrowness. This is not to say that consistent and systematic reference to a particular model is detrimental; quite the opposite. However, understanding and appreciating other points of view can act as a kind of insurance against a narrow-mindedness which *could* be detrimental to clinicians and clients alike. We hope that the material in this chapter will be of some assistance in this regard. For those acquainted with psychodynamic, social- learning, and phenomenological personality theories, much of what follows may already be familiar, but an attempt will be made to go beyond abstract theory and outline the strategy of clinical conceptualization, assessment, and treatment which flows from each model and which can be applied in individual cases. In subsequent chapters, the specific tactics which translate these strategies into action will be considered.

One final point: None of the models to be discussed here is a single, unitary entity. Each is made up of a collection of variations on a basic theme and, thus, to adequately characterize each model, it will be necessary to describe several of these variations.

THE PSYCHODYNAMIC MODEL

The psychodynamic model is rooted in the late-nineteenth-century writings of Sigmund Freud, but it has become broad enough to include the ideas of those who revised Freud's concepts and even those who rejected them. The model is based upon the following fundamental assumptions:

1 Human behavior and its development are determined mainly by events, impulses, desires, motives, and conflicts which are within the mind (i.e., *intrapsychic*).

2 Intrapsychic factors provide the underlying causes of overtly manifested behaviors, whether or not they are problematic. Thus, just as disabling anxiety or delusions of persecution in a troubled patient would be attributed to unresolved conflicts or unmet needs, the outgoing and friendly behavior of an acquaintance might be seen as stemming from contrasting inner feelings of fear or worthlessness or from a hidden desire to be more popular than a sibling.

3 The foundations for behavior and its problems are set down in childhood through satisfaction or frustration of basic needs and impulses. Because of their potentially central role in regard to these needs, the nature and quality of early relationships with parents, siblings, grandparents, peers, and authority figures (e.g., teachers) are given special emphasis and attention. There is thus a distinct historical flavor to the psychodynamic model and a concomitant focus upon the importance of past rather than present events.

4 Clinical assessment, treatment, and research activities should emphasize the search for and the functions of subtle aspects of intrapsychic activity which, though often hidden from direct observation, must be dealt with if behavior is to be understood and behavior problems are to be alleviated.

Freudian Psychoanalysis

The Freudian approach, called *psychoanalysis,* is often thought of as a type of *medical model* (Ullmann & Krasner, 1975) because, as we saw in the last chapter, the theory focused on abnormality and came along at a time when there was strong interest in discovering organic causes for "mental illness." This atmosphere, along with Freud's own training as a physician, emphasized the parallels between his basically psychological thinking and the disease orientation to behavior which was dominant at the time. Intrapsychic conflicts and other psychological factors were seen as analogous to *disease processes* and problematic behaviors became the *symptoms* of those processes. Thus, troubled people who came to medical doctors or were confined to hospitals because of what might, according to Freud, be psychologically based problems, were still called *patients* and the standard medical and psychiatric concepts of *diagnosis, prognosis, treatment,* and *cure* were employed to deal with them. Thus, in the Freudian view, troubled people are thought to be "sick" as the result of a disorder which, though not *actually* an infectious disease, organ system malfunction, or physical injury, can nonetheless be classified or categorized like other illnesses. This medical analogy results in the handling of patients with the same compassion, respect, and concern shown by any doctor for a sick person who is not responsible for his or her disease.

The Freudian psychodynamic model was founded on a few basic principles. One of these is *psychic determinism,* the notion that behavior does not occur randomly but only in accordance with identifiable causes which are sometimes apparent and sometimes hidden from both outside observers and the behaving individual as well. From this perspective, most if not all behaviors (even "accidents") are seen as meaningful in the sense that they may provide clues to hidden conflicts and motivations (Freud, 1914). Thus, reading the word "breast" when the text says "beast," forgetting a relative's name, or losing a borrowed book may all be interpreted as expressing feelings, desires, fears, or impulses which may not appear in awareness. Freud called *unconscious* that part of mental functioning which he thought to be out of awareness and not readily accessible to it.

Another of Freud's basic postulates was mentioned in Chapter 2, namely that human behavior patterns are derived from a continuous struggle between the individual's desire to satisfy inborn sexual and aggressive instincts and the need to take into account the demands, rules, and realities of the outside world. He saw each individual faced with a lifelong search for ways of expressing socially inappropriate instinctual urges without incurring physical punishment or other negative consequences. The case of the 7-year-old boy who, after being told by his mother that he cannot go outside, proceeds to eat 46 lady fingers and throws up in the middle of her bridge party, provides a perfect example of the modification of aggressive impulse in light of the facts of reality. Indeed, Freud saw the human mind as a sort of arena where that which the person *wants* to do (instinct) must vie with the more limited dicta of what *can* or *should* be done (reason and morality) and where compromises must be hammered out.

Mental Structure   In Freud's system, unconscious primitive instincts make up the *id,* which is present at birth and contains all of the psychic energy or *libido* available to motivate behavior. Id seeks to gratify its desires without delay, and therefore it is said to operate on the *pleasure principle* (i.e., "If it feels good, do it!"). As the newborn grows and the outside world begins to impose more and more limitations on direct id gratification, the *ego* develops as a partly conscious, partly unconscious outgrowth of id and begins finding safe outlets for instinctual expression. It was our 7-year-old's ego, for example, which engineered the revenge wreaked upon his mother. Since ego adjusts to external demands, it operates on the *reality principle* (i.e., "If you are going to do it, do it quietly at least"). A third mental component, called *superego,* is another result of the socializing influence of reality. It is roughly equivalent to the "conscience," in that it contains all the teachings of family and culture regarding ethics, morals, and values. According to Freud, these teachings are internalized as superego develops, and they ultimately become the person's own ideals. One might say that superego is an intrapsychic representative of society which seeks to promote perfect, conforming, and socially acceptable behavior which is almost directly opposed to that motivated by id.

Mechanisms of Defense   Freud's three part-mental structure is constantly embroiled in internal conflicts (see Table 3-1) which result in the generation of anxiety. Ego attempts to keep these conflicts and their discomfort from reaching consciousness by employing a variety of *defense mechanisms,* usually at an unconscious level. One of the most common of these mechanisms is *repression,* where ego simply "holds" an unacceptable thought, memory, feeling, or impulse out of consciousness. An individual whose hatred is not consciously experienced may be *repressing* that hatred (when a person is aware of an impulse and *consciously* tries to deny its existence, the process is called *suppression*). However, repression takes a great deal of constant effort (somewhat like trying to hold an inflated balloon under water), and the undesirable material may threaten to "surface" at certain times.

To guard against this, ego is said to employ additional unconscious defenses. One of these is called *reaction formation,* in which the person thinks

Table 3-1   Some Examples of Intrapsychic Conflict

Conflict	Example
Id vs. ego	Choosing between a small immediate reward and a larger reward which requires some period of waiting (i.e., delay of gratification).
Id vs. superego	Deciding whether to return the difference when you are overpaid or undercharged.
Ego vs. superego	Choosing between acting in a realistic way (e.g., telling a "white lie") and adhering to a potentially costly or unrealistic standard (e.g., always telling the truth).
Id and ego vs. superego	Deciding whether to retaliate against the attack of a weak opponent or to "turn the other cheek."
Id and superego vs. ego	Deciding whether to act in a realistic way that conflicts both with your desires and your moral convictions (e.g., the decision faced by devout Roman Catholics as to the use of contraceptive devices).
Ego and superego vs. id	Choosing whether to "act on the impulse" to steal something you want and cannot afford. The ego would presumably be increasingly involved in such a conflict as the probability of being apprehended increases.

Source: Robert M. Liebert and Michael D. Spiegler, *Personality: Strategies for the Study of Man,* rev. ed. Homewood, Ill. The Dorsey Press, 1974, p. 73. © by The Dorsey Press.

and acts in a fashion diametrically opposed to the unconscious impulse. A father-hating child may thus overtly express unbounded love, affection, and doting concern for his father or, if the mechanism called *projection* is used, may attribute negative feelings to others and accuse them of mistreating their fathers. A mechanism of *displacement* actually allows some expression of id impulses, but it aims their expression at safer targets, such as coworkers or others who may be "father figures." Violent and unfair criticism of an older, somewhat senile, and totally harmless colleague, for example, might be viewed in this way. If id impulses are actually expressed by, say, behaving in a critical manner toward the father, the behavior may be *rationalized* or "explained away" by pointing out that it is "for his own good" and really expresses only loving concern. The defense mechanism which Freud saw as most socially adaptive is called *sublimation*. Here, the expression of taboo impulses is directed into productive and even creative channels such as writing, painting, acting, or dance.

While sublimation may provide a relatively permanent solution to the problem of defending against anxiety, the other mechanisms are viewed as less desirable because they are so wasteful of psychic energy. Further, they may fail under stress, forcing the troubled person to fall back, or *regress,* to levels of behavior characteristic of earlier, less mature stages of development. Partial regression may produce behaviors which are simply immature or inappropriate to one's age and social status; more profound regression is associated with the appearance of behavior which is so severely disturbed as to require hospitalization. The extent and depth of regression in a given case is partly a function of the individual's history of *psychosexual development*.

Developmental Stages   Freud postulated that, as a newborn develops, she or he passes through several psychosexual stages, each of which is named for the part of the body most closely associated with pleasure at the time. The first year or so was called the *oral* stage, because eating, sucking, and other oral activities are the predominant sources of pleasurable stimulation. If, because of premature or delayed weaning from the bottle or breast, oral needs are frustrated or overindulged, the child may fail to pass through the oral stage without clinging to, or becoming *fixated* on, behavior patterns associated with it. Adults who display and depend inordinately upon "oral" behavior patterns such as smoking, overeating, excessive talking, or "biting" sarcasm may be seen as orally fixated. Freud felt that the stronger an individual's fixation at a given psychosexual stage, the more behaviors typical of that stage would be routinely shown and the more likely it would be that regression to that level would occur under stress. Cases in which a person becomes totally dependent upon others, ceases to speak, and fails to engage in self-care and toileting behaviors are sometimes viewed by Freudians as involving a nearly complete regression to the oral stage.

Freud's second developmental period was called the *anal* stage, because he saw the anus and the stimuli associated with eliminating and withholding feces as becoming important after the oral stage. The most significant feature of this period is toilet training and anal fixation was thought to result from overly rigorous or particularly indulgent practices in this area. Adult behaviors associated with possible anal fixation include excessively "tight," controlled behavior or "loose," disorderly habits: Persons who are stingy, obstinate, highly organized, concerned with cleanliness or detail, and those who are sloppy, disorganized, and markedly generous with money might be seen as displaying anal characteristics.

The child enters Freud's *phallic* stage at about age 4 as the genitals become the primary source of pleasure. As the name of this period implies, Freud paid more attention to psychosexual development in the male than in the female. He theorized that during the phallic stage the young boy begins to have sexual desires toward his mother and wants to do away with his father's competition. This situation was labeled *Oedipal* because it recapitulates the plot of the Greek tragedy *Oedipus Rex*. Because the boy fears castration as punishment for his incestuous and murderous desires, the Oedipal complex and its attendant anxiety are normally resolved by repressing sexual desires toward the mother, emulating or *identifying* with the father, and ultimately finding an appropriate female sex partner. Freud outlined a parallel process for girls involving the Electra conflict (named for another Greek play), which ideally results in female role identity and selection of an approved male sex partner.

Freud believed that successful resolution of intrapsychic conflicts inherent in the phallic stage was difficult but crucial to healthy psychological develop-ment. Fixation at the phallic stage was seen as very common and responsible for many adult interpersonal problems, including aggression and socially discour-aged sexual practices like homosexuality, exhibitionism, and fetishism.

A dormant or *latency* period follows the phallic stage in Freud's system and extends until adolescence when the individual's physical and sexual maturity ushers in the *genital* period. In this final "stage" (which actually lasts through the adult years), pleasure is again focused in the genital area, but, if all has gone well in earlier stages, sexual interest is directed not just toward the kind of self-satisfaction characteristic of the phallic period, but toward establishment of a stable, long-term heterosexual relationship in which the needs of another are valued and considered.

Related Psychodynamic Approaches

Freud's original ideas have undergone many changes over the years since he first enunciated them. His constant alteration, editing, and supplementation of psychoanalysis make it possible to speak of many editions of Freud's theory, but he remained committed to a few cardinal principles, notably the instinctual basis of human behavior, and it was this often unpopular dogma which prompted others to create variations on the psychodynamic model. Some of these variants involved relatively minimal shifts of emphasis, while others represented a substantial break with Freud's notions. All of them share two characteristics: (1) dissatisfaction with the central role of unconscious instincts in motivation, and (2) increased recognition of the influence on human behavior of social and cultural variables.

In the less radical, "shift-of-emphasis" variations, for example, ego is characterized as a positive, creative, environmental coping mechanism in addition to being an arbiter of intrapsychic conflict. In these versions of Freud (e.g., Hartmann, 1939), ego is not seen as developing entirely out of id and its conflicts with the environment, but rather as having a certain amount of its own independent energy and growth potential which is not tied up in unconscious defensive functions. This kind of thinking is attractive to many psychoanalytical-ly oriented clinicians because it presents a more positive, less instinct-ridden portrait of human behavior.

Another important revision of psychoanalysis is embodied in the writings of Erik H. Erikson, an American psychologist who followed Freud in many respects but saw the need to emphasize the importance of social factors in human development. Erikson (1959, 1963) outlined a sequence of *psychosocial* stages which was both more elaborate than Freud's psychosexual scheme and also more oriented toward individuals' interactions with other people. At each of Erikson's eight stages (see Table 3-2), a social crisis is faced and either successfully handled or left partly unresolved. Positive outcomes at each stage facilitate the individual's ability to deal with the next crisis, while unsettled problems interfere with later development. The parallel with Freud is obvious here, as is the attention paid to the social nature of human development.

Many of those who actually rejected rather than merely revised certain aspects of psychoanalysis had originally been Freud's earliest followers. For example, Alfred Adler was one of the original members of the psychoanalytic school of thought but later disavowed the instinct theory of behavior, broke away from Freud, and developed his own approach. In Adler's *Individual*

Table 3-2   Erikson's Developmental Theory

Developmental stage	Crisis
1. Oral-sensory (birth to 1½ years)	Basic trust versus mistrust: learning to develop trust in one's parents, oneself, and the world.
2. Muscular-anal (1½ to 4 years)	Autonomy versus doubt and shame: developing a sense of self-control without loss of self-esteem.
3. Locomotor genital (4 to 6 years)	Initiative versus guilt: developing a conscience, sex role, and learning to undertake a task for the sake of being active and creative.
4. Latency (6 to 11 years)	Industry versus inferiority: receiving systematic instruction, developing determination to master whatever one is doing.
5. Adolescence	Identity versus role confusion: not "Who am I?" but "Which way can I be?"
6. Young adulthood	Intimacy versus isolation: study and work toward a specific career, selection of a partner for an extended intimate relationship.
7. Adulthood	Generativity versus stagnation: parental preparation for the next generation and support of cultural values.
8. Maturity	Ego integrity versus despair: development of wisdom and a philoso-phy of life.

Source: Bourne and Ekstrand (1976).

Analysis, the most important psychological factor in human behavior and development is considered to be not instinct but inferiority.

Noting the fact that each person begins life in a completely helpless, dependent, and inferior position, Adler suggested that behavior after birth represents a "striving for superiority" (first within the family, then in the larger social world) and that the particular ways in which each individual seeks superiority comprise a *style of life.* He considered adaptive life-styles to be characterized by cooperation, social interest, courage, and common sense, and saw maladaptive styles reflected in extreme competitiveness, lack of concern for others, and distortion of reality. Further, and perhaps most important, Adler believed that maladaptive life-styles and the behavior problems they cause are due not to unresolved unconscious conflicts but to the mistaken ideas or misconceptions the individual has about the world and other people in it. As an example, consider the little boy who discovers early that he can have a measure of control over others (and thus attain feelings of superiority) by requiring and even demanding their assistance in everything from dressing to eating. Over time, such a child might develop the misconception that he is a "special case" and that he actually cannot deal with the world and its requirements on his own. The person whose life-style evolves from such a mistaken idea might always appear frightened, hurt, sick, or handicapped in ways which demand special attention and consideration from others. (See Mosak and Dreikurs, 1973, for more details of Adlerian theory.)

Adler was not the only one of Freud's prominent adherents to strike out on his own. Otto Rank provides another example. Like Adler, Rank rejected Freud's emphasis on sex and aggression as the bases of human behavior and focused instead upon the developing child's basic dependency and inborn potential for positive growth. Rank saw the *trauma of birth* to be very significant because it involves an abrupt change from the passive, dependent world of the fetus to a chaotic outside world which requires ever-increasing measures of independence. Thus, birth provides the prototype for what Rank considered to be a basic human conflict between the desire to be dependent ("return to the womb") and the innate tendency within each person to grow physically and psychologically toward full independence. Failure to adequately resolve this fundamental conflict was, for Rank, the root of human behavior problems.

There are, of course, many other versions and revisions of Freud's ideas which are also a part of the psychodynamic model of clinical psychology. The views of dynamically oriented writers such as Carl Jung, Harry Stack Sullivan, Karen Horney, Erich Fromm, and Melanie Klein will help fill in the picture for the serious student of the model. They are summarized in standard volumes such as Munroe's *Schools of Psychoanalytic Thought* (1955) as well as in shorter papers (e.g., Mullahy, 1965). It is of interest to note that some of those who made fundamental breaks with Freud's theory actually moved so far in new directions that one might argue for their exclusion from the psychodynamic model altogether. The socially oriented ideas of men like Adler and Sullivan, for example, are quite compatible with certain versions of the social-learning and the phenomenological models, to which we now turn.

THE SOCIAL-LEARNING MODEL

Instead of emphasizing the importance or even the existence of intrapsychic conflicts, basic instincts, innate tendencies, and other unobservable constructs for the development, maintenance, and alteration of human behavior, the social-learning model focuses directly on that behavior and on its relationship to the environmental conditions which affect it. The basic assumption of all versions of this model is that behavior is primarily influenced by *learning*[2] which takes place in a *social context*.

Thus, interindividual differences in behavior are attributed in large measure to each person's unique learning history in relation to specific people and situations, not to "mental illness" or "mental health." For example, under the stressful conditions of an academic examination, a student who has heard about or had direct experience of the benefits of cheating may employ illegitimate means of achieving a high grade, while an individual who has been rewarded in the past for diligent study and total self-reliance may be far less likely to behave dishonestly. Each individual's cultural or subcultural background is seen as a part of his or her unique learning history, which plays a significant role in the appearance of both "normal" and problematic behavior (see, e.g., Ullmann & Krasner, 1975). Upon receiving a failing grade on a vitally important exam, for instance, some students' cultural values may prompt so much shame as to engender a suicide attempt while, for others, the failure may evoke a culturally traditional desire for revenge and an ensuing attack on the professor.

Interindividual similarities are accounted for within the social-learning model by pointing out the commonalities in rules, values, and learning history which are shared by most people in the same culture. Thus, students' attentiveness (or at least the absence of beer drinking and other recreational activities) during a lecture would not be seen as a collective manifestation of some intrapsychic process but, rather, as a group fulfillment of the socially learned *student role* which appears in certain academic situations for specified periods of time. The instructor's behavior would be viewed in the same way. Her or his classroom performance reflects prior social learning of appropriate *professor role* responses and may be just as situation-specific and time-limited as that of the students.

The same principles of learning which are invoked to account for behavioral differences and similarities *among* individuals are also employed to account for

---

[2]Familiarity with learning principles such as reinforcement, punishment, extinction, partial reinforcement, generalization, discrimination, and stimulus control is assumed in the discussion which follows. Those not acquainted with these terms should consult introductory texts such as Bourne and Ekstrand (1976) or Hilgard, Atkinson, and Atkinson (1971) or more clinically oriented sources like Bandura (1969).

consistencies and discrepancies *within* individuals. Behavioral consistency, which the psychodynamic model might refer to as "personality," is seen from the social-learning perspective as stemming from generalized learning and/or from the stimulus similarities which may exist among groups of related situations. For example, a person may appear calm and somewhat serious under most circumstances if that pattern of behavior has been consistently or even intermittently rewarded over a period of years and in a wide range of settings which eventually form a single class of stimuli (such as "social situations"). The social-learning model seeks to understand intraindividual *inconsistencies* and other "unpredictable" human phenomena in terms of *behavioral specificity*. Mischel (1971, p. 75) summarizes this point well:

> Consider a woman who seems hostile and fiercely independent some of the time but passive, dependent, and feminine on other occasions. What is she really like? Which one of these two patterns reflects the woman that she really is? Is one pattern in the service of the other, or might both be in the service of a third motive? Might she be a really castrating lady with a facade of passivity—or is she a warm, passive-dependent woman with a surface defense of aggressiveness? Social behavior theory suggests that it is possible for the lady to be *all* of these—a hostile, fiercely independent, passive, dependent, feminine, aggressive, warm, castrating person all in one. . . . Of course which of these she is at any particular moment would not be random and capricious; it would depend on discriminative stimuli—who she is with, when, how, and much, much more. But each of these aspects of her self may be a quite genuine and real aspect of her total being.

There are several editions of the social-learning model which, though differing substantially among themselves with respect to certain specifics, share a common core of characteristics:

1 There is an emphasis upon measurable behavior as the subject matter of clinical psychology. It is important to note here that "measurable" does not always mean "overt." The social-learning-oriented clinician may be interested in behaviors ranging from the objective and "countable" (such as number of cigarettes smoked, or time spent talking) to the subtle and covert (such as heart beats per minute, clarity of visualization, or content of thoughts). Almost any behavior can be the target of a social-learning approach; the only requirement is that an acceptable means of measuring it is available.

2 Stress is laid upon the importance of environmental as opposed to hereditary or other "given" influences on behavior. This is not to say that genetic and constitutional factors are ignored or devalued, but that they are seen as a general foundation upon which the environment shapes and builds the specifics of behavior. Genetic endowment may set certain limits on a person's behavioral or intellectual potential, but it is assumed that, within those limits, social-learning factors predominate in determining behavior. Moreover, the limits set by heredity are explored rather than assumed. The behavioral potential of a particular child with Down's syndrome (mongolism), for example, is likely to be determined by the success or failure of systematic attempts to expand it rather than by an a priori judgment of what is "possible" based on the traditional performance of such children in general (see, e.g., Thompson & Grabowski, 1972).

3 The methods and procedures of experimental science are employed as the primary means of expanding knowledge about behavior and its assessment, development, and modification. As noted earlier, clinical psychologists in general tend to be the most research-oriented of the helping professions, but, within the field, the social-learning model has led the way in operationalizing and experimentally investigating clinical subject matter in the human and animal laboratory and in applied settings such as schools and hospitals. The emphasis is upon deliberate and systematic manipulation of independent variables (e.g., treatment techniques) and careful observation of the effects of such manipulations on specifically defined and quantified dependent variables (e.g., alcohol consumption, social assertiveness, depressed behavior, or sexual arousal). When correlational research methods are employed in the social-learning model, they usually focus on overt behavior. For example, a social-learning-oriented clinician is likely to be interested in the relationship between client's estimates of, say, weekly study time and objective measures of time actually spent studying because such information might help clarify the predictive value of future self-reports. By contrast, there would be relatively little interest in conducting group research on the relationship between study time estimates and scores on a paper-and-pencil test of achievement motivation because such a relationship, whatever its nature and descriptive value, would say little or nothing about what students actually *do*.

4 Clinical assessment and treatment functions are closely tied to the results of experimental research with humans and animals. Most clinical methods of the social-learning variety are derived primarily from laboratory-based principles of learning and social behavior, and they are subjected to an immediate and continuous barrage of evaluative research conducted in laboratory and clinical settings. Further, the social-learning model encourages its practitioners to scrutinize closely the experimental evidence regarding a particular assessment or treatment procedure before deciding to adopt it and to proceed with the greatest caution in areas where there is little or no empirical guidance. Such concern for prior evaluative data is reflected in treatment contracts drawn up by some social-learning-oriented clinicians. These contracts often list the sources of experimental evidence supporting the use of a proposed technique, so that the client may be assured of its potential value (see, e.g., Stuart, 1975).

5 Clinical assessment and treatment functions are closely integrated. Overt behaviors are not viewed as symptoms of intrapsychic processes, so "diagnosis" of a client's underlying problem is not necessary. Instead, the social-learning model assumes that the same principles of learning determine both problematic and nonproblematic behaviors and therefore that clinical assessment should be designed to determine how a client's present difficulties were learned and how they are being maintained so that new, more adaptive, and individually tailored learning can be arranged. A kindergarten child's fear of school, for example, might be based upon a specific conditioned response to a particular setting, a generalized anxiety response to new situations, the intimidating presence of a particular classmate, embarrassingly poor classroom performance, or other obvious or subtle environmental factors. The social-learning-oriented clinician's treatment approach would not be based upon "standard procedures" for dealing with children diagnosed as "phobic." The specific techniques chosen might be aimed at eliminating fear of a certain room or of strange settings, development of social assertiveness, enhancement of academic skills, or other targets, depending directly upon what the assessment data have to say about the importance of various etiological and maintenance factors.

The main differences among specific versions of the social-learning model of clinical psychology usually appear in terms of the type of learning process which is emphasized (e.g., classical versus operant) and the degree to which cognitive variables play a role in assessment, treatment, and research. A brief review of the most prominent social-learning variants will illustrate this point.

Linking Learning to Clinical Problems: The Contributions of Dollard and Miller

One of the earliest social-learning approaches to behavior evolved from an attempt to translate or recast Freud's clinically derived concepts into a language consistent with experimental data on human and animal learning. This formidable task was undertaken in the 1940s by John Dollard, a sociologist, and Neal Miller, a psychologist, and culminated in the publication in 1950 of a book called *Personality and Psychotherapy.* Dollard and Miller began with the assumption that human beings do not enter the world with instincts, but with primary *needs* (such as food, water, and air) which must be satisfied. They further assumed that each person *learns* to satisfy these needs (and others which are based upon them) in somewhat different ways, thus leading to the development of individualized patterns of behavior.

For example, an infant's need for food results in strong internal stimuli (hunger pangs) which Dollard and Miller called *drives* because of their capacity to motivate or impel behavior. Early in a child's life, behavior resulting from the presence of a drive such as hunger (e.g., thrashing around and crying) may bring a person into the room with food which reduces the hunger drive and thus *rewards* or *reinforces* the behavior leading to it. In this manner, one learns to repeat behaviors which result in or are associated with drive reduction.

Of course, Dollard and Miller did not assume that all human behavior is learned through reduction of primary drives. They postulated that people acquire secondary, or *learned drives,* which function much like primary drives. Thus, a person can *learn to need* things like praise, money, or power and will learn to repeat behaviors which lead to them and abandon those which do not. In much the same way, a person can learn to be anxious in certain situations, and this anxiety can act as a drive which motivates both adaptive and maladaptive escape or avoidance behaviors. Anxiety reduction reinforces those behaviors, and it may thus establish either a useful response or a "neurotic symptom."

Dollard and Miller dealt with Freudian concepts as environmentally determined and experimentally researchable phenomena, not as intrapsychic structures. For example, they considered a person's indecision or ambivalence to be the result of incompatible approach or avoidance tendencies, rather than the product of conflict among id, ego, and superego. In their view, conflict exists when a person must choose between two or more alternative responses. The most difficult and potentially problematic of such conflicts are those of the "double approach-avoidance" variety, where each course of action has both clearly positive and clearly negative features. Much as Freud had done, Dollard and Miller stressed the importance of such conflicts and the anxiety and subsequent behavior disorders they arouse, but they employed the terminology of learning theory.

Their analysis of a typical "neurotic" conflict would be somewhat as follows: One's approach tendency toward a member of the opposite sex may be thwarted by a simultaneous avoidance tendency (e.g., based on anxiety stemming from negative social experiences and parental warnings against expressing sexual desires). The closer one gets to contact with the desired-yet-feared situation, the stronger the avoidance tendency becomes until a retreat occurs, perhaps toward a nonsocial (and thus more comfortable) alternative behavior. This withdrawal reduces anxiety but also has its negative aspects and, in addition, allows the social-approach tendency to reappear and start the whole cycle going again. Dollard and Miller saw the consequence of such conflict as a prolonged vacillation between approach and avoidance, accompanied by great psychological discomfort which may ultimately require therapeutic intervention aimed at strengthening approach tendencies, reducing avoidance tendencies, or both.

B. F. Skinner and the Functional Analysis of Behavior

Notice that, while Dollard and Miller's system eliminated some of Freud's intrapsychic notions, it retained other inferred constructs such as "drive," "motive," and "anxiety" and thus depended to some extent upon hypothesized internal processes and mechanisms to account for various aspects of human behavior. Quite a different social-learning approach has been presented by B. F. Skinner who, while also conceiving of behavior as learned, argues that nonobservable constructs such as "need" and "drive" are unnecessary for understanding it.

Instead, Skinner asserts that careful observation of and experimentation with learned, functional relationships between environmental stimuli and observable behavior will ultimately allow for a complete picture of the development, maintenance, and alteration of human behavior. Instead of introducing invisible factors (such as id or drive) into assessment, treatment, and research functions, Skinner advocates observation and description of the ways in which behavior relates to its antecedents and consequences. Since it focuses on functional relationships above all else, this approach is called *functional analysis*.

As an example of how the functional-analytic approach to clinical psychology eliminates inferred constructs, consider the notion of "need." Rather than assuming that human behavior reflects various needs (e.g., "aggressive behavior indicates a strong need for dominance"), the Skinnerian version of the social-learning model would look at the relationship between, say, aggressive behavior and its consequences. After doing so in a systematic way, it might be argued that a client's aggressive behavior has been and perhaps continues to be rewarded, at least part of the time, and that no further explanation in terms of internal need is necessary. The client has simply learned to behave aggressively.

The same thinking is applied to more severe behavior disorders. A mental hospital resident who spends the day silently staring into space, loses control over bladder and bowels, and must be fed from a spoon would not be considered "psychotic," "regressed," or "mentally ill." Instead, these behaviors (not "symptoms") would be thought of as gradually learned responses initiated by stress or other environmental factors and maintained by the tolerance and reinforcement of "crazy" behavior provided by society and especially by the hospital (see, e.g., Ayllon & Azrin, 1968; Ullmann & Krasner, 1975). Details of the Skinnerian approach to human behavior in general and to its application to the analysis of problematic behavior in particular are to be found in Skinner (1953, 1971) and Baer, Wolf, and Risley (1968).

Wolpe and Eysenck: Classical Conditioning

While Skinner's views highlight the importance of *operant* learning for clinical psychology, another aspect of the social-learning model is embodied in the writings of Joseph Wolpe (1958, 1973) and Hans Eysenck (Eysenck & Rachman, 1960). They focus upon the application of *classical* conditioning principles (Pavlov, 1927; Hull, 1943) to the understanding and elimination of human distress, particularly anxiety. This variant is an important one because it both broadens the array of working concepts available within the social-learning model and addresses a large group of anxiety-based clinical problems whose dimensions usually include client's subjectively experienced distress and which are often not specifically dealt with in functional-analytic terms.

The importance of operant reinforcement and punishment in shaping "normal" and problematic behavior is not denied in this view, but there is an accent upon the learning which takes place through the association of conditioned and unconditioned stimuli. It would be argued, for example, that a man who fearfully avoids social events may do so partly because of past negative experiences (i.e., operant conditioning: he enters a room and everyone laughs at his clothes), but also because the discomfort from those experiences has become associated with parties (i.e., classical conditioning: he gets a stomach ache upon merely receiving a party invitation). Thus, both operant and classical conditioning may be involved in the appearance of specific behavior patterns (Mowrer, 1939), but Wolpe and Eysenck provide a complement to Skinner's primarily operant position by directing attention to classical conditioning.

Albert Bandura and Observational Learning

The views of Skinner, Wolpe, Eysenck, and other social-learning theorists who focus more or less completely upon overt behaviors as the targets of clinical assessment and treatment have attracted many ardent followers, prompted the birth of specialized professional journals, and greatly enhanced the growth of the social-learning model. They have not been universally accepted, however. Some members of the social-learning "camp" feel that too little attention has been paid to the role of cognitive or symbolic (i.e., thought) processes in the development, maintenance, and modification of behavior. One of the most prominent representatives of this point of view is Albert Bandura, a Stanford University psychologist who has generated a great deal of research and writing (e.g., Bandura, 1969, 1977a; Bandura & Walters, 1963) about the ways in which cognitive activity contributes to learning.

Bandura is probably best known for his work on *observational learning,* in which he has shown that humans can acquire new behaviors without obvious reinforcement and even without the opportunity to practice. All that may be required is for the person to observe another individual, or *model,* engage in the given behavior. Later, especially if the model was visibly rewarded for his or her performance, the observer may also display the new response if given the opportunity to do so. In an illustrative experiment, Bandura, Ross, and Ross (1963) arranged for preschoolers to observe models either vigorously attacking or sitting quietly near an inflatable "Bobo" doll. In subsequent tests, the children who had observed aggression tended to match the models' behavior quite precisely, while those who had seen a passive model tended to be nonaggressive (see Figure 3-1).

Thus, a major feature of Bandura's theory is its attention to *vicarious cognitive processes.* In his view, behavior develops not only through what the

Figure 3-1 [*From Bandura, A., Ross, D., & Ross, S.A. Imitation of film-mediated aggressive models.* Journal of Abnormal and Social Psychology, **66:**3–11 (1963). *Copyright 1963 by the American Psychological Association. Reprinted by permission.*]

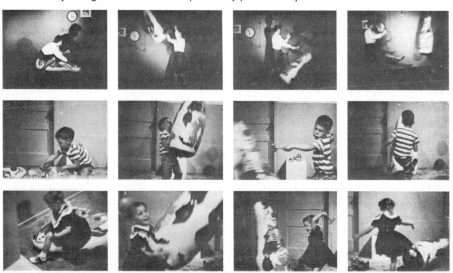

individual learns directly by operant and classical conditioning, but also through what is learned *indirectly* (vicariously) through observation and symbolic representation of other people and events. According to Bandura, the effects of vicarious processes can be as broad and significant as the effects of direct learning. They can bring about acquisition of new responses (as in the "Bobo" experiment), inhibition or disinhibition of already learned responses (as when a person violates a "don't walk" sign after watching someone else do so), and facilitation or "prompting" of behavior (as when the entire population of an airline waiting lounge forms a line at an unattended check-in counter after a single prankster stands in front of it).

In the case of the socially fearful man discussed in the last section, Bandura would point out that there are at least two sources of discomfort. One is *external* and includes the anxiety-signaling aspects of social situations themselves (e.g., other people, invitations, laughter), while the other is *internal,* or cognitive. This second source consists of thoughts generated by the fearful individual about socializing (e.g., "I will make a fool of myself," or "I will have a terrible time") which may serve to support continued avoidance.

The role of cognitive variables has perhaps an even stronger place in the social-learning theory of Julian Rotter (1954), which places broad emphasis upon the importance of *expectancies* in human activity. In Rotter's system, the probability that a given behavior will occur is dependent upon (1) what the person expects to happen after the response, and (2) the value the person places on that outcome. Thus, an individual will pay for a ticket because she or he expects that this will result in admission to a movie theater (outcome) which is showing a desirable film (value). Of course, Rotter assumes that the expectancies and values which influence, organize, and alter behavior are acquired through learning. In order to "have" an expectancy about an outcome or make a judgment regarding its value, the person must have had some direct or vicarious experience with equivalent or similar situations in the past.

To theorists like Bandura and Rotter, attention to cognitive components of behavior is an important aspect of a comprehensive social-learning model of clinical psychology and represents a "wing" of that model which emphasizes covert as well as overt behavior in the context of clinical assessment, treatment, and research (Kanfer, 1965; Meichenbaum, 1974; Mahoney, 1974; Mischel, 1973; Peterson, 1968a). This end of the social-learning spectrum, at which there is strong interest in what people "say to themselves," is of considerable importance because it helps to illustrate the breadth and diversity of the model (see Chapter 10). It also separates modern learning-oriented conceptualizations (in which all aspects of behavior are potential targets of systematic and scientific attention) from the earlier "radical behaviorism" of J. B. Watson (1913, 1924), which had placed cognitive activity "off limits" to scientific psychologists. Finally, the presence of cognitive variables in the social-learning model provides a point of contact and even of overlap with certain neo-Freudian views (recall Adler's emphasis on misconceptions) and with some versions of the phenomenological model, which is discussed in the next section.

THE PHENOMENOLOGICAL MODEL

So far we have considered models of clinical psychology in which human behavior is viewed as primarily under the influence of (1) instincts and intrapsychic conflicts or (2) the physical and social environment. A third approach, known generally as the phenomenological, or cognitive model, rejects many of the basic assumptions of the other two and asserts instead that the behavior of each human being at any given moment is determined primarily by that particular person's *perception of the world.* In other words, phenomenological theories assume that each person is unique, that each person's view of reality is just a little different from anyone else's, and that each person's behavior reflects that view as it exists from moment to moment.

As an example, consider two students who listen to the same lecture on the first day of a new term. One may be enthralled, while the other stomps out and drops the course. These divergent reactions would likely be viewed by phenomenologists as due not to differences in the listeners' ego strengths or learning histories, but to their individual perceptions of the speaker during the lecture. Most versions of the phenomenological model share the following features:

1 Human beings are seen neither as "carriers" of psychic structures and impulses nor as recipients of reinforcement, but as active, thinking people who are individually responsible for what they do and fully capable of making plans and choices about their behavior. In fairness, it should be pointed out that neither the psychodynamic nor the social-learning model fails to recognize these human attributes. Psychoanalysts who emphasize the autonomous role of ego and social-learning-oriented psychologists who focus upon individuals' capabilities for self-control (e.g., Bandura, 1969; Kanfer & Karoly, 1972) provide illustrations of this point. However, both of these models tend to look in their own way at the processes *underlying* such uniquely human characteristics as creativity, self-discipline, and decision making, rather than to focus upon those characteristics themselves.

2 Although the phenomenological model recognizes the existence of biological needs, they are deemphasized as determinants of behavior and its development. Instead, it is assumed that each person is born with a *potential for growth* which provides the impetus for behavior. This innate tendency to grow into a fully mature individual is likened to the potential of a seed to become a flower. In contrast to Freud's dark, instinct-based view and to the social-learning assumption that few behavioral characteristics are innate, the phenomenological model sees people as basically good organisms which naturally strive toward creativity, love, joy, harmony, and other positive goals.

3 Another important implication of the phenomenological view is that no one can truly understand another person's behavior unless she or he can perceive the world through that person's eyes. In line with this notion, the phenomenological model (like the social-learning model) rejects the concept of mental illness and the use of other pejorative labels for problematic behavior, and it assumes that all human activity is normal, rational, and comprehensible *when viewed from the point of view of the person being observed.* Thus, a woman who is violently hostile toward others would be seen neither as acting out id impulses nor as displaying the results of reinforcement; she is simply behaving in accordance with her perception of those around her at the time.

4 In clinical work, people cannot be dealt with as objects representing psychological processes; they are fellow human beings. There is little to be gained from accumulating historically oriented assessment data or from seeking to help a person solve a particular situational problem because (1) the past is less important than the present, and (2) helping someone to solve a problem may only create others by fostering dependence and stifling personal growth.

Phenomenological views have evolved from several sources. In part, they represent a branch of the reaction against Freud which began when Adler and Rank rejected instincts and unconscious motivation as the major bases for behavior. These and other "revisionists" emphasized the importance of individual perceptions and positive growth potential. Attention to the individual's perception of reality was also prompted by the existential philosophies of Heidegger, Kierkegaard, Sartre, and Camus which, to oversimplify, assert that the meaning and value of life and everything in it are not intrinsic, but are provided by the perceiver. Thus, for example, a person is not "actually" attractive or ugly; these qualities are "assigned" when someone else reacts to the person in question, and they reflect a different reality in the eye of each beholder.

The focus upon individual views of reality was also sharpened by the writings of a group of early twentieth-century German psychologists known as the "gestalt school" (Koffka, 1935; Kohler, 1925; Wertheimer, 1923). In contrast to the structuralism of Wundt, they asserted that the mind was more than the sum of its parts and that, with respect to perception, the individual was an active participant, not just a passive receiving station. To support their view, gestaltists pointed out that there are many cases in which a person's subjective perception goes beyond the stimuli which are "objectively" there, where the "same" object may be interpreted in different ways, and where reversible figure-ground relationships are possible (see Figure 3-2). Let us now examine a few of the phenomenological views which have grown from these roots.

Kelly's Personal Construct Theory

George Kelly developed a theory of behavior which, though not as well known as some others in the phenomenological model, provides a good place to start because it illustrates the ways in which that model relates to social-learning formulations. Kelly's (1955) theory is extremely complex, but it is based upon the single, fundamental assumption that human behavior is determined by what he called *personal constructs,* or ways of anticipating the world.

In other words, Kelly believed that individuals act in accordance with their own unique set of expectations about the consequences of behavior (note the similarity to Rotter here) and thus, that people's constructs or anticipations about life comprise their reality and guide their behavior. For example, a person may consider sharp knives to be dangerous and capable of inflicting severe harm. This construct or anticipation would lead to cautious behavior in relation to

Figure 3-2 Some perceptual phenomena which illustrate the perceiver's role in organizing "objective" stimuli: (A) "Closure" results in the appearance of a circle and a person on horseback even though many parts are omitted; (B) Reversible "figure-ground" relationship allows viewer to see a vase or a pair of silhouettes; (C) Interpretive shifts allow shaded area of a "Necker Cube" to appear as the front or back surface and enables the drawing to be seen as a young woman or an old hag. (From Introduction to Psychology, *5th ed., by Ernest R. Hilgard, Richard C. Atkinson, and Rita L. Atkinson. Copyright © 1971 by Harcourt Brace Jovanovich, Inc. Reproduced by permission of the publisher. Also from Psychology: Its Principles and Meanings,* by L.E. Bourne and B.R. Ekstrand. Copyright © 1976 by Holt, Rinehart and Winston. Reprinted by permission of Holt, Rinehart and Winston.)

sharp knives, and, since such behavior reflects an accurate anticipation of the consequences of carelessness and does in fact avoid accidents, the construct "sharp knives are dangerous" is *validated.*

Validation of personal constructs is, in Kelly's view, the major goal of every human being. He believed that human behavior does not reflect instinctual desires, the effects of external reinforcement, or the status of learned response tendencies but, rather, individuals' attempts to make sense of (correctly anticipate) the world as they see it. Kelly felt that, like the scientist who revels in the thrill of discovering why or how a phenomenon occurs and how that phenomenon can be controlled, each person is seeking to be correct about the phenomenon called life. Put more simply, there is more comfort in understanding than in confusion.

In Kelly's system, problematic behavior results when a person develops inaccurate, oversimplified, or otherwise faulty constructs. If someone has only a few broad constructs with which to anticipate and comprehend the vast number of events which occur every day, behavior based upon those constructs is almost sure to be inappropriate, ineffective, or inadequate at least part of the time. For example, a man who construes everything in life as either "good" or "bad" is going to have problems, because not all objects, events, and people can be placed on that dimension without distortion or overgeneralization. He may totally reject or unreservedly welcome the friendship of others according to some overall perception of their value and thus completely miss the positive qualities of "enemies" and the negative qualities of "allies." He may focus so completely upon his view of others that he never gives a thought to their view of him. Finally, he may tend to stereotype other people such that he sees college students, political activists, and anyone with a foreign accent as "bad" and children, grandmothers, and the clergy as "good." Such a person would probably be seen by others as selfish, unduly influenced by first impressions, strongly prejudiced, and a poor judge of character. His interpersonal relations would probably be rather stormy.

The compatibility of Kelly's views with those of cognitively oriented adherents of the social-learning model should be obvious here. It is based partly upon common interest in the role of cognitive activity in determining overt behavior and also upon the fact that Kelly saw people as capable of *learning to change* their personal constructs and, in turn, the patterns of response flowing from them. This latter notion blended cognitive, phenomenological concepts with social-learning principles and resulted in the development of new, "mixed-model" approaches to clinical treatment, first by Kelly himself and later by others (e.g., Ellis, 1962). We shall discuss the specifics of these approaches in Chapters 10 and 11.

Rogers's Self-Actualization Theory

In contrast to Kelly's relatively unheralded and mildly social-learning-flavored views, the prolific writings of Carl Rogers (1942, 1951, 1961, 1970) have more clearly differentiated the phenomenological model from all others and, in the process, made his name practically synonymous with it. Among Rogers's basic phenomenological assumptions, we find the following (1951, pp. 483–86): (1) "Every individual exists in a continually changing world of experience of which he is the center," (2) "The organism reacts to the field as it is experienced and perceived. This perceptual field is, for the individual, 'reality'," and (3) "The organism reacts as an organized whole to this phenomenal field."

Like other phenomenologists, Rogers also assumes that people have an innate motive or tendency toward growth, which he calls *self-actualization*. This motive is thought to be sufficient to account for the appearance of all human behavior, from basic food-seeking to the most sublime acts of artistic creativity. Self-actualization is defined as "the directional trend which is evident in all organic and human life—the urge to expand, extend, develop, mature—the tendency to express and activate all the capacities of the organism" (Rogers, 1961, p. 351). Rogers thus sees human behavior, whether problematic or not, as reflecting the individual's efforts at self-actualization in a uniquely perceived world. These efforts begin at birth and continue throughout life; they are sometimes unimpeded and successful, but they may also be thwarted—with problematic results.

As Rogers describes the process, a person's growth and developing interactions with the environment are accompanied by a differentiation between a "self" and the rest of the world. This results in an awareness of a part of experience which is recognized as "I" or "me." According to Rogers, all of a person's experiences, including such "self" experiences, are subject to evaluation as positive or negative, depending upon whether they are consistent or inconsistent with the self-actualizing tendency. These evaluations are made partly on the basis of direct or *organismic* feelings (as when a child evaluates the taste of candy as positive), and partly on the basis of other people's judgments. For example, a young boy may end up negatively evaluating the experience of fondling his genitals (even though the direct feelings are positive) because his parents tell him that he is a "bad boy" to do so. Thus, the "self" or "self-concept" emerges as a set of *evaluated experiences* whose positive or negative valence is often influenced by the values and opinions of others.

Sometimes, these socializing influences are of great value in the process of integrating the developing individual into society, especially when the judgments of others coincide with organismic feelings. For example, if a child practices reading skills and experiences both positive direct feelings upon gaining competence and, in addition, positive regard (evaluation) from a parent for doing so, the result will likely be a positively evaluated self-experience ("I like to read"). Here, the self-experience is in accord, or congruent, with the organismic experience and the child is able to accurately perceive his or her own behavior ("I read a lot") and the evaluation of it ("I enjoy reading").

However, according to Rogers, people value the positive regard of others so highly that they will often seek to attain it even if it means thinking and acting in ways which are inconsistent or *incongruent* with organismic experience and the self-actualizing motive. This tendency is encouraged by what Rogers calls *conditions of worth*. These are circumstances in which one can only receive positive regard from others (and, ultimately, from the self) if certain approved behaviors, values, attitudes, and beliefs are displayed. These conditions are usually set up first by parents, family, and other societal agents, but they are later maintained internally by the individual (note the similarity here to Freud's concept of superego).

The person facing conditions of worth is likely to be uncomfortable. If she or he behaves to please others, it may be at the expense of personal growth, as in the case of a woman who fulfills traditional housewife roles in spite of genuine desires to do other things.[3] On the other hand, displaying authentic feelings, values, and behaviors which are discrepant with conditions of worth risks loss of the positive regard of others and the self.

Rogers believes that to reduce, prevent, or avoid discomfort stemming from such incongruity, the individual may distort reality or the experience of it in ways that may be perceived as problematic by others. For example, a man whose parents set up conditions of worth in which displays of emotional behavior (like crying) were discouraged and unemotional "masculinity" was praised may have had to deny to himself and to others that emotional expression feels good. As an adult, his often-repeated and strongly judgmental statement that "anyone who cries is weak" actually represents a distortion of his own real feelings. Other consequences of attempts to reduce incongruity between real feelings and self-concept through distortion and misperception are legion, and, according to Rogers, the greater the discrepancy involved, the more severe the resulting problematic behavior will be. Consider a mild case: a young man with a strong interest in women claims that he is "too busy" to go out with them when, in fact, it would be too uncomfortable and discrepant with his self-concept to admit that his invitations are routinely rejected. He even goes so far as to profess manufactured disdain and disgust for members of the opposite sex. (Note the relationship here to some of Freud's ego defense mechanisms.)

In a more extreme instance, a man whose self-concept characterizes him as strongly independent, self-sufficient, and career-oriented may in fact be quite the opposite. Thus, poor grades in school, later failure to receive a desired pay raise or promotion, and less-than-adequate performance on the job (all based on lack of real interest in his field) are misinterpreted. Instead of recognizing that he may not be cut out for or very interested in his work, he asserts that others are "out to get him" or trying to make him look bad. Ideas of persecution may evolve to such proportions that he trusts no one and begins to see plots and conspiracies on every side. Ultimately, his behavior may become so troublesome as to require hospitalization.

Rogers believes that, theoretically at least, all this can be avoided. "If an individual should experience only unconditional positive regard, then no conditions of worth would develop, self-regard would never be at variance with organismic evaluation, and the individual would continue to be psychologically adjusted, and would be fully functioning" (Rogers, 1959, p. 224). Even if these optimal conditions have not been met in the past, they may be of help in the present and, accordingly, Rogers developed a therapeutic approach which employs unconditional positive regard and other factors to help troubled people reduce incongruity without having to distort reality (see Chapter 11).

Maslow and Humanistic Psychology

The writings of Abraham Maslow (1954, 1962, 1971) provide another version of the phenomenological model. Like other phenomenologists, Maslow empha-

---

[3]Incidentally, the same costs would accrue to the woman who adopts a liberated role to please feminist friends even though her genuine interests are in homemaking activities.

sized the importance of subjective experience and the unique perception of reality which each person maintains, and, in founding the movement known as humanistic psychology, he had tried to emphasize above all else that which is positive, creative, and unique about human beings. Like Rogers, Maslow sees people as capable of (and needing) self-actualization, but he suggests that failure to realize one's full, human potential is caused not so much by incongruity between self-experience and organismic experience, but by the presence of unmet needs.

These needs are viewed by Maslow as forming a hierarchy including the basic physiological requirements (like food and water) with which everyone is born as well as higher-level requisites like safety, security, love, belongingness, self-esteem, and, finally, self-actualization. In this schema, satisfaction of each need level must be preceded by the meeting of all lower-level needs. Thus, for example, one is not likely to be concerned with fulfilling the need for love and belongingness when there is uncertainty over where one's next meal is coming from. So, though each person contains the potential for full actualization, that potential cannot be sought or expressed if lower-level needs remain unfulfilled.

Maslow points out that most people are seeking to meet needs below the self-actualization level, and are thus oriented toward that which they do not have. He referred to these individuals as being "deficiency-motivated." For most people in our culture, incompletely satisfied needs usually involve security, love, belongingness, and self-esteem and, according to Maslow, often produce adult need-seeking behaviors which are "neurotic," disordered, or otherwise problematic. In relatively rare cases, however, all lower-order needs are adequately satisfied as a person develops, thus freeing the person to seek fulfillment of the highest need, self-actualization. Such people are in a position to focus upon what they can *be,* not upon what they do not *have.* This Maslow called "growth-motivation."

These fortunate few can regularly experience the full potential of humanness, and, because they are unfettered by concern over lower-level needs, they can devote themselves to the expansion of their potential in the context of a search for abstractions like truth, beauty, and goodness. Momentary experiential high points, or *peak experiences,* at which full self-actualization is reached, are common in these individuals and represent the best that is within all of us. Like other phenomenologists, Maslow underscores the importance of helping troubled people overcome the obstacles which stand in the way of the natural growth which will ultimately lead to their happiness and fulfillment.

Fritz Perls and Gestalt Psychology

Freidrich S. (Fritz) Perls was a European psychiatrist who felt the need to go beyond his original psychoanalytic training. His dissatisfaction with traditional Freudian theory and therapy first evidenced itself in his 1947 book *Ego, Hunger and Aggression: A Revision of Freud's Theory and Method.* Like others who built on Freud's views, Perls felt that there was too much emphasis placed upon sexual instincts and not enough on what he called *hunger:* an instinct or tendency toward self-preservation and self-actualization (growth). Like Freud, Perls emphasized the function of ego in facilitating growth and self-preservation by mediating between the person's internal needs and the demands of the environment. However, he thought of ego, not as a psychic structure or thing, but as a *process* whose (unattainable) goal is the reduction of tension between the person and the environment.

Ideally, as this virtually impossible balancing act continues over time, the individual grows psychologically: She or he finds new ways to meet internal needs while becoming ever-more cognizant of and able to deal with the requirements of the outside world. For this optimal growth process to take place on a continuing basis, the person must remain *aware* of his or her internal needs and feelings and of the environment. However, since each person is seen as an active participant in attending to and organizing his or her internal and external perceptions, and since the tendency to avoid conflict and keep tension as low as possible may make certain perceptions more comfortable than others, each person's awareness can become incomplete, distorted, or maladaptively distributed. When this happens, growth stops and problems start.

For example, a person with strong sexual desires who grows up in a moralistic, antisexual family atmosphere may find certain kinds of awareness-distortions temporarily comfortable but ultimately problematic. Denial or repression of sexual feelings and/or perceptions of the world as a place filled with unrelenting pressure for sexual promiscuity may occur. None of this accurately reflects either the external circumstances or the internal needs. (Note the similarity here to Rogers's concept of incongruence.)

According to Perls, when conflict avoidance prompts disturbances in awareness, classic symptoms of neurosis and neurotic defenses appear. Intense anxiety about, say, being away from home may result when a person projects her or his own hostile feelings (usually kept out of awareness) onto others, thus making everyone else seem hostile. Or, the same person may selectively attend to the ordinary risks which surround us all and, "because the world is so dangerous," refuse to go out. When disturbances in awareness become severe, there may be a loss of reality contact and consequent symptoms of psychosis.

Perls developed a treatment approach called "gestalt therapy" which is aimed mainly at restarting growth by reestablishing aware processes. We shall describe the methods involved in Chapter 11.

There are several other phenomenological approaches to behavior (e.g., May 1969), but this brief outline should suffice to convey the flavor of the model. Those interested in further, more detailed coverage of this and the other models discussed should consult the original sources already cited as well as comparative presentations provided by Hall and Lindzey (1970), Corsini (1973), Sahakian (1974), Marx and Hillix (1979), and Liebert and Spiegler (1978).

SOME IMPLICATIONS OF CLINICAL MODELS

Let us now go beyond abstract theoretical conceptualizations of the three basic models of clinical psychology and examine their implications for clinicians' assessment, treatment, and research functions. Perhaps the best way to do this is to consider the clinical strategy likely to be adopted with respect to a hypothetical case by adherents of each model. It is important to recognize, of course, that the descriptions of these strategies can provide only a general representation of their parent models, and, since there are several versions of each model, these general descriptions are bound to be less than comprehensive. Not every clinician identified with a given model will behave exactly as outlined here. Nevertheless, it is hoped that by applying the most general principles and assumptions of each model to the problems of a single troubled person, the role of model-as-guide will become clear.

Discussing the same person from three points of view can also serve to highlight an important point about clinical models: Human behavior does not have to appear in any particular form in order to be dealt with by a particular model. Behavior simply occurs and each model tries to comprehend it, whatever its content, within a specific frame of reference. Thus, people do not *actually* possess superegos or response tendencies or self-concepts; they simply *behave,* and psychologists attempt to make sense of that behavior in terms which make sense to them. Failure to recognize this important point can lead to conceptual and practical errors by clinicians who look for clients to display theoretical constructs instead of behavior.

For example, clinical students as well as full-fledged clinicians are sometimes heard to say things like "I feel pretty comfortable working with clients who have poor self-concepts, but I am really not prepared to deal with conditioned anxiety responses," or "the social-learning approach is a good one for thinking about learned problems, but it can't really handle unconscious conflicts very well." In both cases, the speaker has taken various clinical models so seriously that he or she assumes that human behavior conforms to the concepts described by theoreticians, instead of the other way around, and has failed to see that virtually *any* sample of behavior can be approached by *any* model. It is instructive, therefore to consider the behavior of a single fictitious person and to see that no model has a monopoly on describing, explaining, altering, and researching that behavior.

To help in this regard, the authors asked one representative of the psychoanalytic, social-learning, and phenomenological schools of thought to read a fictitious case report on "Mr. A" and provide (1) an initial reaction, (2) an assessment strategy, (3) some hypotheses about the etiology (cause) of the client's problems, (4) some ideas about the influence of additional assessment data, and (5) an outline of treatment. Here is the case study, followed by each clinician's responses.

A Case Example

Mr. A. is a 42-year-old Caucasian who lives in a comfortable home in the middle-class suburban area which surrounds a large city on the west coast of the United States. He has been married for 20 years, has two daughters (aged 16 and 18), and is employed as an electrical engineer at a large aircraft corporation. He identifies himself as a Protestant, but his attendance at church has always been sporadic and is now completely terminated. There are no remarkable aspects to his medical history (just the usual childhood diseases), and his general health is good. Though Mr. and Mrs. A. were on a very tight budget at the beginning of their marriage, a series of promotions and pay raises over the years has put them on comfortable financial footing.

Mr. A. is an only child. He was born in a small Midwestern city which is the home of a prestigious university. His father, now retired, was for many years head of that university's chemical engineering department and then dean of the college of engineering. His mother is also retired, but taught high school English for many years before being elevated to the post of vice principal. Mr. A. had a relatively happy and uneventful childhood. He did well in school and was a rather serious youngster who usually behaved in accordance with his parents' teachings about the importance of hard work and superior performance. His mother and father were loving but somewhat unemotional. He had never seen them display overt signs of affection for each other, and his father had become really angry only once (when Mr. A. talked about dropping out of high school).

All through his elementary and high school years, Mr. A. was part of a small group of male and female friends. Its members were a lot like him: quiet, serious, and studious. His social activities included meetings of special interest groups (i.e., the German and stamp clubs) as well as frequent movies and concerts which he attended in a group rather than on a "date." When he subsequently enrolled as an engineering student at the local university, Mr. A. continued to live with his parents and retained his well-established study and social patterns. By the middle of his junior year, he had become especially friendly with an intelligent and compatible young woman who had been in several of his required humanities courses. He had first invited her to join him and other friends for concerts, football games, and plays; later they began to socialize as a couple. Mr. A. was delighted with her company but was never physically or verbally demonstrative of his feelings. When she finally brought up the subject of marriage, he was totally surprised but thought it would be a fine idea. Mr. A.'s parents were pleased and the wedding took place right after graduation. The birth of the couple's daughters was welcome, and life settled into a pleasant and serene cycle of work, play, and child-rearing.

Problems first began to appear as Mr. and Mrs. A.'s attractive girls reached adolescence. Arguments over boyfriends, politics, effects of drug use, the existence of God, and curfews became frequent, and the family atmosphere was often that of a battleground or an armed truce. These relatively commonplace, though stressful, difficulties were later overshadowed by a set of more serious and totally unanticipated problems.

For a little over a year, Mr. A. has been experiencing attacks of dizziness, accelerated heart beat, and most recently, fainting. Though he has received extensive medical attention from his family doctor and a series of specialists, no organic basis for the problem has been detected. The rate and severity of the attacks has increased in recent months to the point that Mr. A. was forced to ask for an indefinite leave of absence from his job. Though company insurance benefits and Mrs. A's income as a substitute teacher have prevented a financial crisis, he has become increasingly depressed over his problems. After exhausting hope that the attacks would cease spontaneously, Mr. A. reluctantly accepted his physicians' conclusions that psychological factors may be involved and has called a clinical psychologist.

He reports on the phone that he never has an "attack" at home unless his older daughter is there, but that he is almost sure to become dizzy and faint shortly after leaving home for any purpose. For this reason, he cannot trust himself to drive a car, and though for awhile he tried to stay active by having his wife or a friend act as chauffeur, he is now completely housebound.

Mr. A.'s days are spent reading, watching television, or gazing out of the living room window. His appetite is poor and he is losing weight. He does not sleep well and has frequent arguments with his wife and children, during which he often accuses them of being the cause of his problems. He has become so morose about the current situation and so pessimistic about the future that the thought of suicide has entered his mind.

A Psychodynamic Approach to Mr. A.: Dr. Elliot M. Adler

I. Initial Reaction My initial impression of this case is that Mr. A. is a man whose habitual modes of adaptation and mechanisms of defense have proved inadequate to cope with the emotional turmoil and internal conflict stimulated by his elder daughter's adolescent rebellion. This defensive failure is manifested in the occurrence of intense anxiety reactions (somatically experienced as dizziness, accelerated heart beat, and fainting episodes) which were initially misinterpreted as signs of organic pathology. Subsequent defensive efforts to bind the overwhelming anxiety led to the development of phobic symptomatology and a regressive retreat to a dependent mode of adaptation. The depression, loss of appetite, and thoughts of suicide probably have a self-punitive significance, as well as representing Mr. A.'s genuine helplessness in the face of his unmanageable reactions. I suspect his symptoms are neurotically based; that is to say, they are a function of powerful (though primarily unconscious) impulses, wishes, and fantasies of an aggressive or sexual nature which are in conflict with his internalized moral standards. In short, Mr. A. is a man who is desperately afraid of being "out of control."

II. Assessment Strategy My primary tool for assessing Mr. A.'s problems would be the clinical interview. I would employ a relatively unstructured format, working under the assumption that his spontaneous verbalizations about his dilemma will prove more revealing and lead more directly to the most pertinent issues than if I imposed a predetermined sequence of questions. For example, his initial statements on the telephone direct my attention immediately to his elder daughter as a precipitating "trigger" for his anxiety reactions. Thus I would listen particularly carefully to everything he had to say about this relationship, and I would specifically explore the circumstances immediately preceding an "attack" in her presence. Since my premise is that it is not the actual events but the internal fantasies and meanings these events acquire which are the source of difficulty, I would listen for nuances of expression, slips of the tongue, or evidence of fantasy content, which might help me to assess the unconscious symbolic meanings and psychodynamics. For instance, the word "attack" suggests an act of aggression. Is he feeling attacked by someone? Or, more likely, is he afraid he might become an "attacker?" Does "attack" have a sexual connotation perhaps, as in rape, which would imply another set of unconscious impulses and fantasies. Thoughts and questions like these would play upon my mind as I listened, though I would rely on considerable substantiating material from the patient before such fleeting associations took on the weight of likely hypotheses.

In addition to evaluating the immediate precipitating events and specific internal conflicts underlying his anxiety reactions, I would want to explore the following general areas of his functioning during the course of my assessment interviews:

1 Mr. A.'s general level of ego functioning, with special emphasis on his capacity for reality testing, self-observation and insight.

2 The quality of his relationships to the most significant people in his life, past and current.

3 Contributory sources of stress affecting his premorbid functioning, such as problems at work, deaths of relatives or friends, physical health and fitness, etc.

4 I would want to hear "the story of his life" in his own words, paying particular attention to the earliest childhood memories and crucial developmental experiences.

5 I would ask for any recent or recurrent dreams Mr. A. could recall.

6 Finally, I would request that he take a diagnostic battery of psychological tests, with the specific referral request, "Assess Mr. A.'s potential for psychotic regression."

III. Etiological Hypotheses In the absence of further data I would speculate that Mr. A.'s anxiety reactions represent his fear of losing control over unacceptable impulses directed towards his elder daughter. She is, in attitude and behavior, challenging the moral foundations of his world. Presumably, this represents an age-appropriate adolescent struggle to establish an autonomous identity separate from parental influences. She must temporarily reject her parents' values as well as her previously intense emotional attachment to them: a painful and stressful process for any parent to endure. But additional hypotheses are necessary to explain Mr. A.'s inability to weather this normal life crisis. The available history suggests that Mr. A.'s intense identification with his parents' sober, conscientious though relatively passionless approach to life may have stifled his own adolescent development. Thus his daughter's rebellion strikes this man at two quite vulnerable spots in his personality at once. She is challenging the moral foundations of his overly severe conscience (superego) while arousing the stifled rebel (id) buried in his own unconscious. In this context, his anxiety reactions represent the danger signals that forbidden wishes are overwhelming his defenses while his agoraphobic symptom represents a complex compromise formation in which he attempts to escape temptation while achieving partial satisfaction and punishment for his forbidden impulses.

IV. Potential Influence of Further Assessment Data   It would not be surprising to discover that Mr. A.'s elder daughter has stirred up unconscious erotic feelings and fantasies in her father. This may be due to sexually provocative behavior on her part, or because Mr. A. has turned his erotic interests to her out of frustration in the sexual relationship with his wife. The daughter's interest in boys and her flaunting of conventional moral standards (even if only in words) would therefore represent a temptation as well as a painful rejection to this man. He would find himself simultaneously aroused by forbidden incestuous wishes as well as provoked to jealous rage by her rejection of him as an object of intense affection.

Ultimately, our assessment would have to include some hypotheses relating the current conflict and outbreak of neuroses with an aspect of his infantile past. Freud discovered that the wishes, memories, and anxieties of the infantile past remain "alive" in the repressed depths of our unconscious minds, waiting to attach themselves (by the mechanism of displacement) onto the events, experiences, and people in our current lives. If, indeed, jealous rage is at the heart of Mr. A.'s current problems, it would have to be understood as a later edition of some unresolved infantile conflict. The most obvious hypothesis in this case would be that he is reliving some aspect of his own Oedipal drama, and that the intensity of his jealousy, guilt, and anxiety is a function of this earlier and now unconscious conflict. It must be remembered that *all* of this remains highly speculative in the absence of careful and detailed confirmation in the material presented by the patient.

V. General Approach to Relief of Distress   My assessment interviews and the results of diagnostic testing would provide the necessary data to formulate my treatment strategy. The basic decision to be made is whether to institute an uncovering psychoanalytic treatment approach which would aim at exploring and making conscious the conflicting feelings, fantasies, and impulses which are resulting in Mr. A.'s symptoms, or to adopt a more supportive and active therapeutic intervention in which advice, encouragement, and possibly medication are employed to get Mr. A. back on his feet again as quickly as possible.

For the sake of this discussion, let us assume that the former approach is chosen. The analytic process would be initiated by having Mr. A. verbalize his thoughts and feelings as spontaneously as possible without regard for logical or topical consistency. As the patient began to discover that the therapist would not criticize or judge his productions, he would reveal more clearly the ideas and feelings most closely related to his pathogenic conflicts (i.e., his jealous rage and erotic feelings towards his daughter would emerge). My primary means of intervention would involve "interpretations," which consist essentially of verbal explanations of the meaning of his behavior, fantasies, or feelings. These interpretations would be intended to provide him with intellectual insight into the nature of the conflicting forces struggling within and their relation to his current and past experience. This insight will provide him with the necessary understanding with which to struggle actively to master his internal dilemma. As the analytic process deepens, the therapist will become the focus of the unconscious conflicts and drama that is beginning to emerge from repression. This provides the therapist with the opportunity to view firsthand the central pathogenic conflicts in his patient's inner life; it also presents a living theatre in which the (primarily infantile) conflicts can be resolved in a new, less destructive manner. In Mr. A.'s case, a successful psychoanalytic treatment would result in a new character structure, tolerant of a greater range of feelings and instinctual expression without recourse to unnecessary repression (or other rigid defenses), anxiety, or symptom formation.

A Social-Learning Approach to Mr. A.: Dr. Harold Leitenberg

I   Initial reaction:
   A   Based on early history, I would guess Mr. A. may want to be "perfect" in all respects, and may set unrealistic standards for himself.
   B   Inability to express feelings in a direct and nonaccusative manner.
   C   Family conflict supposedly centering on adolescent daughters. Potential marital conflict.
   D   Overly controlled and obedient to parents' value system. Afraid to rebel in a direct fashion.
   E   Agoraphobia.
   F   Depression—probably secondary to C and E.
II Probable assessment strategy
   A   Interview Mr. A. alone (probably two sessions).
      1   Depending on severity of agoraphobia, may have to do this in his home.
      2   Explore job situation. See if he wants out. See if there are any unusual pressures on job coincident with onset of agoraphobia.
      3   Explore relationship with wife. Determine if there is any reason to believe that daughters are being used as scapegoats in a marital conflict situation.
      4   Determine how interaction at home with older daughter is different from that with other members of family. Why does he continue to have "anxiety attacks" at home only in her presence?
      5   In vivo assessment of extent of agoraphobia. Set up walking "course" and instruct Mr. A. to "go as far as he can *without* any undue anxiety." Determine this when he walks alone and when he walks with me.
      6   Administer self-report questionnaires including Beck Depression Inventory, Rathus Assertiveness Schedule; Fear Survey Schedule; Rotter External-Internal Locus of Control Questionnaire.

       7 Have him record between weeks 1 and 2 anxiety level (10 point scale) on an hourly basis every day of the week; e.g., Mon. 8 A.M., 9 A.M., 10 A.M., etc.; Tues. 8 A.M., 9 A.M., 10 A.M., etc.

  B Observe spontaneous family interaction. Look for signs of positive reinforcement for agoraphobia and/or depressive verbal and motor behavior.

  C Interview all the members of the family individually *and* together. Have each member fill out a variant of Stuart's pre-family counseling inventory independently before bringing them together.

III Etiological and problem-maintenance hypotheses (if no further data were available) (letters refer to problem list)

  A Overperfectionistic and overcontrolled: probably was too frightened to go against parents' wishes and is still operating as "they expect him to."

  B Inability to directly express feelings—probably was never taught how to do this. Poor modeling from parents.

  C Family conflict. A number of hypotheses here including:

    1 Daughters are scapegoats for unstated marital conflict.

    2 His lack of control of daughters may make him feel that he is a failure as a parent (at least as *his* parents would have evaluated his performance).

    3 Potential anger at himself because his daughters are apparently more able to break loose than he was. May have released his own suppressed conflict with parents and brought into question his tendency to accept what other people have suggested for him.

  D See A.

  E Agoraphobia. Also several hypotheses:

    1 Are these symptoms being positively reinforced by other members of family? e.g., more attention and more control than he obtains otherwise?

    2 Do these behaviors enable him to escape and avoid job-related pressures? Perhaps he feels "trapped" at job and this is the only acceptable way he has for "dropping out"?

    3 Perhaps he notes somatic arousal after one of these family conflicts when he left the house. This may have terribly frightened him. Subsequent anticipation and dread of the same event can be a self-fulfilling prophecy. And of course subsequent avoidance eliminates the opportunity for extinction of anxiety.

  F Depression. I see this as secondary to agoraphobia and family conflict.

IV Potential influence of further assessment data on etiological, problem-maintenance, and other hypotheses. Depending on what I learn, I may want to explore the following somewhat more thoroughly (this is still short term for assessment purposes):

  A Unresolved conflict with parents

  B Current job situation

  C Social deficiencies, e.g., inability to express feelings directly

  D Marital conflict

  E Family interactions (reinforcement system).

V General approach to relief of distress. I would probably start on the following two areas:
   A Communication training *and* possibly behavioral contracting amongst members of immediate family.
   B Reinforced practice approach for agoraphobia (a specific form of in vivo desensitization). However, I also might eventually want to spend some time (albeit not an excessive amount of time) on unresolved conflicts with his parents and his own desires regarding job, career, life in general, etc.

A Phenomenological Approach to Mr. A.: Dr. C. H. Patterson

In contrast to (most) other therapeutic approaches, I am unconcerned about obtaining data or information prior to seeing a client or patient. If referral sources proffer such data, I will accept it, but without attempting to formulate it into a picture or conceptual model of the client, or to reach even a tentative diagnosis or formulation of the problem. Such activity could prejudice or bias the nature of the first personal contact with the client, perhaps leading to restriction of perceptions of the client and to fitting him to the preconceived formulation.

Similarly, the first contacts with the client would not be devoted to obtaining specific data or a case history. No formal psychological assessment would be attempted, and no psychological tests would be used. The interview would be structured to be unstructured; that is, to provide the client the opportunity to present himself, or project himself, in his own way, at his own rate, in his uniqueness. Whatever historical elements might be of significance in therapy would emerge at the appropriate times and places. Relationships, configurations, and cause-effect sequences would appear, leading to a perception of the client as the unique person that he is. No attempt would be made at any time to formulate diagnosis, to classify the client or his problems in any way. Concern would be with specific attitudes, feelings, emotions, and behaviors.

Diagnosis would be of concern only in recognizing possible organic (neurological or physiological) conditions. Clinical sensitivity to peculiarities, idiosyncrasies, or inconsistencies of expression, thinking, feeling, and behavior, based on clinical experience and intuition (based on a knowledge of possible organic conditions) would lead to suspicion of organic involvement and to referral for relevant medical, psychological, and neurological tests and examinations. In the present case, the history would seem to rule out such factors. Nevertheless, the possibility of organic involvement would never be irrevocably ruled out: there have been instances of clients or patients dying of a brain tumor while being treated for psychological problems.

Since no attempt at diagnosing or labeling would be made, no hypotheses regarding specific psychological etiology would be developed. In the absence of organic involvement, the general hypotheses of psychological etiology would be accepted. Furthermore, whatever the historical genesis of the problems, my concern would be with their present manifestations. The general etiology of psychological problems lies in inadequate or deleterious interpersonal relationships. Some common elements, in the past and/or the present, are lack of acceptance, understanding, respect, honesty, and love in interpersonal relationships.

Given the etiology and problem nature, the specific treatment is the provision of acceptance, understanding, respect, honesty, and love. The therapist first provides these in the therapy relationship. Under these conditions the client loses his defenses and resistance and engages in self-disclosure, openness and honesty with himself, moves to self-exploration and then understanding and acceptance of and respect for himself, and then of others. These others reciprocate, and the basis is laid for exploring his interpersonal problems with significant others and the development of mutually reinforcing and satisfying interpersonal relationships.

It is apparent that no mention has been made of the specific elements of the case of Mr. A. These are not the items of significance in treatment, and the treatment is not directed specifically at them. In a sense they are symptoms, or better, manifestations of a more general disturbance. In other words, then, treatment is essentially the same for all clients and all (nonorganic) problems. The content varies, but the nature of the process and the general outcomes are the same.

A CRITIQUE OF CLINICAL MODELS

All of the formulations just presented have a certain appeal, but they are also subject to criticisms of various kinds. To round out this chapter we should take a brief look at the kinds of problems and shortcomings which various critics have attributed to each clinical model.

Problems with Freud's Psychodynamic Model

Sigmund Freud's contribution and influence are hard to overestimate. He presented the most comprehensive and revolutionary theory of behavior ever articulated and, in the process, introduced ideas and concepts which ultimately captured the imagination of psychiatry, psychology, and other helping professions, not to mention literature, religion, sociology, and anthropology (see, e.g., Kluckhohn, 1944). In clinical psychology, Freud's influence remains, even among those practitioners who do not consider themselves to be Freudians. The intensive study of a single individual, the one-to-one assessment or treatment session, the view that overt behavior, no matter how disordered, is systematically related to identifiable psychological causes, the possibility that an individual's behavior may be influenced by factors of which he or she may be unaware, the importance of conflict, the focus on anxiety, and other features characteristic of the orientation of all "kinds" of clinicians are directly traceable to Freud. In addition, Freud's concepts have become a part of our everyday language and thus may (unconsciously?) guide the way nonpsychologists think about behavior. It is not at all uncommon to hear almost anyone refer to "Freudian slips," the Oedipus complex, unconscious motivation, defense mechanisms, or ego in the context of ordinary conversation.

In spite of its broad acceptance (for many people, clinical psychology and the psychodynamic model are one and the same), Freud's approach has been the target of continuing criticism on the grounds that:

1 Psychodynamic ideas and hypotheses such as id, ego, superego, projection, unconscious motivation, repression, and the like consist of vague abstractions which are difficult or impossible to test scientifically. The techniques which have been designed to measure various Freudian personality concepts have often shown themselves to be unreliable and invalid (see Chapter 6), and the effects of clinical treatment based on those concepts have been strongly questioned (see Chapter 9).

2 The entire basis for Freud's approach was provided by his clinical experiences with a relatively small number of upper-class patients living in Vienna around the turn of the century. This raises questions about the generalizability of his ideas to other kinds of people from other socioeconomic strata and other cultural backgrounds. Some anthropologists have suggested, for example, that psychoanalytic concepts of behavior and behavior development are not universal (e.g., Lindesmith & Strauss, 1950; Mead, 1928, 1939).

3 Psychoanalytic thinking places too much emphasis on the negative side of human character (i.e., sexual and aggressive instincts) and not nearly enough upon (1) inherent growth potential and (2) the influence of society and culture on behavior. This issue has caused many to reject Freud over the years and continues to be of concern.

4 The psychoanalytic view represents a closed system which tends to be inflexible and not easily influenced by contradictory data; any results can be interpreted as confirming Freudian principles. For example, if psychoanalytic interviews or projective tests lead to the conclusion that a person harbors strong unconscious feelings of hostility, subsequent hostile behavior would be taken as evidence for the emergence of unconscious impulses. But the appearance of calm and friendly behavior could also provide evidence for underlying hostility because it could be seen as a reaction formation. Recognition of this problem has caused some critics to call Freud's theory a "hoax" (Jurjevich, 1974).

5 The psychodynamic model makes it too easy to overinterpret behavior as indicative of unconscious motivation and related pathology, and thus may actually create problems. A man who is a successful, driving "go-getter" might become distressed to learn that he may merely be compensating for unconscious feelings of inadequacy.

6 Because it is a subtype of the medical model, Freud's approach is compatible with and serves to perpetuate an unreliable and invalid diagnostic system (American Psychiatric Association, 1968) which attaches to already troubled individuals one or more pejorative labels (e.g., "neurotic," "schizophrenic") which are not only marginally meaningful, but often socially and psychologically harmful in terms of status and eventual improvement (see Ullmann & Krasner, 1965, 1975; Szasz, 1960, 1966).

Problems with the Social-Learning Model

Since its beginnings in the late 1950s, the social-learning approach has enjoyed enthusiastic support from an ever-increasing number of adherents in clinical psychology, social work, education, psychiatry, and many other fields (see Chapter 10). For them, the model's attractiveness lies in its objective and experimentally oriented approach to human behavior: It rejects intrapsychic and subjective explanations (including notions of mental illness and the unconscious), defines its concepts operationally, relies on laboratory data rather than vague abstractions for its basic principles, ties its applied work to the results of carefully controlled research, and scrupulously evaluates the adequacy of its assessment and treatment procedures through a continuing series of critical investigations. In short, the social-learning model is seen as representing the best approach to the advancement of psychology *as a science of behavior* in the applied clinical field.

Its detractors are less convinced of all this. They suggest that:

1   The learning approach reduces human beings to a complex set of acquired responses derived from a relatively rigid and mechanistic relationship with the environment. This view is too narrow and tends to exclude genetic, physiological, constitutional, and other non-learning-based influences and, most important of all, fails to emphasize sufficiently the importance of subjective experience and each person's unique potential for positive growth. In other words, social-learning concepts deal with an individual's behavior, but ignore the individual.

2   The social-learning model is only applicable to that narrow range of human activity in which behavior is measurable. It cannot therefore adequately conceptualize or ameliorate human problems of a complex, internal nature. Thus, social-learning principles are fine for explaining and dealing with phobias and other specific and relatively simple stimulus-response relationships, "but how about grief at the loss of a loved one, shame at failures, guilt whether real or fancied over moral transgressions, a pervasive sense of impotence, and other negative affects? Likening human to animal behavior, and focusing on visible behavior rather than inner states, minimizes precisely those values, feelings, fantasies, and motives which most distinguish and trouble human life" (Korchin, 1976, p. 349).

3   The principles of learning upon which the social-learning model is based are not well established and agreed upon by learning theorists themselves. The nature and role of reinforcement in the learning process is still a matter of some debate, for example, and exemplifies the less-than-firm status of many such concepts. Further, even if all learning principles were clearly established, there is the question of whether their animal-laboratory origins allow them to be applied meaningfully to the behavior of human beings. Thus, a cat faced with an insoluble task may display "experimental neurosis," but the human behavior called "neurotic" may not be equivalent and may result from entirely different processes.

4   Social-learning approaches to clinical psychology are not as uniquely scientific or clearly validated as their practitioners would have us believe. Many

assessment and treatment procedures representing the model are based more upon clinical experience than experimental research, and, where research evidence is available, it is often not unequivocally supportive of learning-based techniques. Further, it is argued that other models can also produce research evidence for their concepts and procedures and, thus, that the social-learning view is in no sense alone in its respect for scientific method.

Problems with the Phenomenological Model

The phenomenological orientation has a strong intrinsic appeal. It gives a central role to each person's immediate experience, a kind of "given" which is easily related to by anyone who attends to such experience. Further, it emphasizes the uniqueness of humans in general and each individual in particular, thus providing comfort and reassurance that people are not just a quantitative extension of lower animals or "just like everyone else." Finally, it is an optimistic approach which focuses on the positive potential in human life and places faith and trust in the individual's capability to grow toward complete fulfillment of her or his ultimate experiential and behavioral capacities.

In spite of its refreshing and encouraging views, the phenomenological model has come in for its share of criticism. It is argued that:

1 The phenomenological approach is too narrowly concerned with immediate conscious experience and does not pay sufficient attention to the importance in determining behavior of unconscious motivation, reinforcement contingencies, situational influences, biological factors, and the like.

2 The model does not deal adequately with the *development* of human behavior. Postulation of an innate tendency toward growth or "actualization" can *account* for development but does not explain its processes. Saying that a child develops because of an actualizing tendency is like saying that one eats because of hunger; this may be true, but says little about what "hunger" is or precisely how it operates to influence behavior.

3 A related though more general criticism has been that phenomenological theories provide excellent *descriptions* of human behavior (particularly the subjective aspect of it) but are not usually focused on the scientific exploration of its functional causes. To suggest that people act as they do because of their unique perceptions of reality may be personally satisfying, but this is not very informative in terms of promoting understanding of the variables operating to develop, maintain, and alter human behaviors (including subjective perceptions).

4 Phenomenological concepts are unscientific, vague, esoteric and, in general, difficult to comprehend, let alone research. When human beings are described as "a momentary precipitation at the vortex of a transient eddy of energy in the enormous and incomprehensible sea of energy we call the universe" (Kempler, 1973, p. 255), it becomes difficult to generate testable hypotheses about their behavior. Indeed, with the exception of Rogers and his colleagues, most phenomenologists see research on human behavior as dehumanizing, needlessly fragmentary, ultimately meaningless, and thus unimportant in comparison to, say, activities designed to expand individual awareness. The

phenomenological model is therefore chided for being not only unscientific but antiscientific and therefore not likely to help advance knowledge about human behavior.

5 Phenomenological theories are not only antiscientific, they are antiintellect. In this model, reason is subordinated to feeling, and knowledge is sought through subjective experience rather than rational analysis. This goes against the grain of Western thought and antagonizes many clinicians.

6 The phenomenological model may be theoretically descriptive of the behavior of all human beings, but its clinical applicability is limited to those segments of the population whose intellectual, educational, and cultural background is compatible with the introspective nature of this approach. To those who are not in this somewhat select group, phenomenological notions may make little sense. Further, the range of problems addressed by the model is somewhat limited: To the person struggling intellectually with a crisis of identity or values, phenomenological notions may be of great subjective value, but these notions (like the tenets of most other models) may not be very useful in situations where unmet needs near the bottom of Maslow's hierarchy (e.g., food, decent housing, and a job) are the bases of human distress.

The Popularity of Clinical Models

Our coverage of the three main models of clinical psychology should make it clear that they present a kind of triple approach-avoidance conflict for the person trying to decide which one to adopt. They all present both positive and negative aspects and, even after a tentative choice is made, one still faces diversity of emphasis within each model. There seem to be no entirely objective and universally agreed upon criteria available to guide one's choice; even the advice offered at the beginning of this chapter regarding the value of scientifically testable models is based on the authors' personal bias which, though shared by many, is a bias nonetheless.

So what determines one's choice of a particular model or version of one? Freudians might suggest that unconscious motivation has something to do with it, while others would point to the role of modeling, differential reinforcement, and other learning principles. The orientation of professors and clinical supervisors often tends to be reflected by the students who come in contact with them directly or through their writings. Still others would seek the answer in congruity between a model's principles and the self-concepts of its adherents. Or, the choice may be made on the basis of "cognitive style" (Kaplan, 1964), emotional and personality characteristics (L'Abate, 1969), or just plain "personal preference" (Zubin, 1969). The truth is, we really do not know exactly *why* clinicians choose a particular model, so we are perhaps better off looking instead at *what* they tend to choose.

Here, the answers are fairly clear. Some clinicians do not make a single choice. Instead they adopt those aspects of two or more models which are personally satisfying to them. To those who value open-mindedness, flexibility, and moderation above systematic consistency, this solution to the choice-of-model problem is called *eclecticism*. To those who emphasize the value of adherence to an integrated and unitary point of view, "eclectics" are merely confused individuals destined to spin their intellectual wheels for lack of theoretical traction. In any case, the ranks of the "eclectic" or the "confused" are swelling in some groups within clinical psychology, even though (or perhaps because) a larger number of identifiable submodels are available now than ever before. Garfield and Kurtz (1976) reported that almost 55 percent of their sampling of 855 APA Clinical Division members called themselves eclectic, an increase of nearly 15 percentage points over an earlier estimate by Kelly (1961).

Other evidence presented by Garfield and Kurtz (1976) suggested that Freudian and neo-Freudian models have become considerably less popular among clinicians in the last 15 years, while phenomenological and social-learning views have gained only slightly. While these data are probably fairly accurate reflections of the *direction* of model-adoption trends within clinical psychology, they may not be entirely representative. For example, many noneclectic clinicians are not members of the Clinical Division of the APA, joining instead other model-oriented clinical groups such as the Association for the Advancement of Behavior Therapy or the Association of Humanistic Psychology. Thus, it is perhaps most accurate to say that, while there are lots of eclectics, there may be even more clinicians who identify with a particular model which is increasingly likely to be social-learning or phenomenological as opposed to psychodynamic. Garfield (1974, p. 37) put it this way: "It would appear . . . that the peak of [the psychoanalytic] orientation has already been reached."

Part Two

Learning about People

Chapter 4

Assessment in Clinical Psychology

Dictionaries commonly define "assessment" as an estimate of value or worth. A county assessor, for example, looks at a house and estimates its value. On the basis of that estimate, the homeowner's annual property tax is established. The important thing to notice here is that assessment does not take place in isolation; it is part of a process leading to a goal. The assessor (1) *collects information* (e.g., lot size, house size, number of rooms), (2) combines, integrates, or *processes* that information by reviewing from memory or notes the building's features and characteristics in relation to city standards and to other comparable structures, and then (3) *makes or guides a decision* ("This place is worth $62,000").

So while some assessments may indeed involve determination of value or worth, a more general definition of assessment would be *the process of collecting information to be used as the basis for informed decisions by the assessor or by those to whom results are communicated.* In Chapters 1 and 2, we saw that assessment was the earliest identifying function of clinical psychology and is still a mainstay of the field. However, it is important to be aware that, be it formal or informal, the process of assessment is not used only by clinicians. Almost everyone engages in some type of assessment at one time or another. Consider these examples:

1   Before choosing next term's classes and instructors, a student *collects information* by looking at a course catalog, talking to friends, reviewing uncompleted requirements, and perhaps reading a teacher-evaluation booklet. This information is then combined or *processed,* keeping many relevant factors in mind: "I need at least 12 credits to keep my scholarship, I want to be able to sleep until 10 o'clock, I want Ralph "Boom-Boom" Moscowitz (the best note taker around) in at least two of my classes, and I don't want to take more than one killer course if I can help it." Finally, a set of *decisions* is made which establishes a course list and a weekly class schedule.

2   A consumer plans to buy a car, but the particular make, model, year, and dealer are decided upon only after a considerable amount of data have been collected and processed: How much cash is available for a down payment? How large a loan payment can be managed? What new and used cars fall into the "affordable" price range and, of these, which have the features which are most desirable? What do automotive magazines, consumer publications, and knowledgeable friends say about each car? Finally, where are the best prices and most reliable service to be found?

Decisions relating to everyday social life are also guided to a certain extent by an (often unrecognized) assessment process which closely parallels that associated with clinical psychology. We hear about other people and we get to know them firsthand. The data we collect about their background, attitudes, values, behaviors, and peculiar characteristics are then processed and interpreted in light of our own standards, experience, and frame of reference. Impressions or images emerge to guide social decisions such that, when given a choice, we seek out certain individuals and avoid others. If contact is unavoidable, our social behavior may reflect prior assessments (if you have ever had to spend time with someone you dislike, you know what is meant here).

When accurate and representative social assessment data are processed efficiently and objectively, maximally beneficial decisions result. We correctly identify a "phony" or "see through" a person's tough talk to appreciate other, rarely revealed aspects of the person's behavior. Individuals who do this regularly are usually thought of as "good judges of character" and become valued sources of opinion and advice.

Unfortunately, however, social decision errors are all too likely because of problems in data collection, processing, or both. It is easy to jump to false conclusions about another person on the basis of inadequate information ("As soon as he said he hated ballet, I knew I wasn't going to like him"), an unrepresentative behavior sample (someone who is in a foul mood seldom leaves a good impression), stereotypes of various kinds ("Her accent really turned me off"), and personal biases ("I love people who wear sweaters like that!"). These and many other sources of error make the collecting of information which will guide decisions about other people an extremely hazardous process.

Yet this is precisely what the assessment function in clinical psychology is all about. And even though the clinician may have access to a wider range of more systematic assessment information than is normally available to nonprofessionals, the task of learning about and gaining a clear and accurate "working image" of other people (Sundberg, 1977) is always a challenge. That challenge is made no less awesome by the fact that the consequences of errors in clinical assessment can be far more dramatic and enduring than buying the wrong car, getting stuck in a boring course, or spending an evening with a clod.

This chapter is designed to provide an overview of how the clinical psychologist, as a human being who is not generally possessed of special or unique powers of perception and judgment and who is susceptible to at least the same number of data collection and processing errors as plague other human beings, has attempted to approach and face, if not always meet, the challenge of assessment.

COMPONENTS OF THE CLINICAL ASSESSMENT PROCESS

Four distinct though interrelated components of the clinical assessment process are illustrated in Figure 4-1. Each of them involves questions and issues with which we will have to deal in order to comprehend the process as a whole. With respect to the planning and data collection segments, for example, one might ask how much information about a person is "enough," which kinds of data are more valuable than others, how can inaccurate information be detected and eliminated, and where should information be sought. The data processing phase raises questions such as: How does the clinician go about integrating available data? Is the assessor able to remain objective and unbiased? Could a computer handle assessment data more competently than a human being? Consideration of the fourth assessment segment leads to other inquiries: What forms do assessment results take? Who uses them and for what purposes? What is the impact of assessment on the lives of those assessed? Are people protected from misuse or abuse of assessment outcome?

These and many other issues will appear as we examine the clinical assessment process more closely in subsequent sections.

Planning for Assessment

McReynolds (1975) points out that two related questions must be answered before clinical assessment can begin: (1) What do we want to know? (2) How should we go about learning it? A reply to the first of these questions is usually dictated by what one's world view says are important human variables and tends to shape the answer to the second.

FIGURE 4-1 A schematic view of the clinical assessment process.

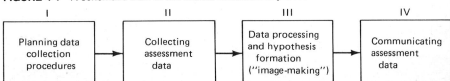

In ancient times, for example, the wishes of various gods or the positions of heavenly bodies at the moment of birth were thought to be strongly influential in the determination of human behavior and destiny. Accordingly, these variables became the focus of assessment and were measured by carefully examining the livers of sacrificed animals (hepatoscopy) or by consulting painstakingly compiled charts and tables of astronomical data (astrology). The individual being assessed was almost superfluous, since the variables addressed and the data sought were external and remote.

The world view which has shaped most clinical assessment in Western civilization is radically different. It emphasizes the importance of variables and dimensions which operate *within* or *immediately around* the individual being assessed. As we saw in Chapter 3, this general orientation toward the individual takes many forms. Personality dynamics and traits, social-learning history and current environmental factors, as well as perceptions of self and reality are each accorded varying emphasis from one clinician to the next. Regardless of specifics, however, modern clinical assessment seeks to learn things about people *by focusing on them directly*. Accordingly, the animal liver and the planetary chart have been replaced by an ever-evolving array of more useful assessment devices, mainly *interviews, tests, observations,* and *life records.*[1]

Unfortunately, the notion that clinical assessment focuses directly on individuals through reference to certain data sources provides the clinician with only the most general kinds of conceptual and procedural guidelines. The particulars of what to look for and what assessment tools to use can still vary enormously and make the planning, organization, and implementation of an efficient and useful information-gathering strategy a large part of the clinical assessment challenge.

To illustrate the problem, consider first the sheer *number* of things which can be asked about a single person. The list might begin with things like age, sex, height, and weight, and go on endlessly to include bank balance, favorite food, speed in the 100-yard dash, blood pressure, and hat size.

Potentially interesting assessment questions can also tap several interrelated *levels,* ranging from physiological functioning to relations with family and other social systems. The most commonly identified of these levels are listed in Table 4-1, along with just a few examples of data usually associated with each.

The amount and diversity of potentially available assessment data mean that we can never learn *all* that there is to know about another person. Even if total knowledge were possible, however, it would hardly be a practical goal for the clinician. An attempt to fully and intensively explore every level of assessment for a given client would doubtless turn up a lot of important information, but the process might never end and would be extremely expensive and time-consuming. It would also be likely to reveal much that is trivial,

[1]Life records (Cattell, 1965) include various kinds of "personal documents" (e.g., diaries and letters. Allport, 1942, 1965), archival and "trace" data (e.g., college transcripts. Webb, Campbell, Schwartz, and Sechrest, 1966), and other environmental and achievement measures (e.g., honors or awards. Berg and Adams, 1962).

Table 4-1   Levels of Assessment and Some Representative Data from Each

Assessment level	Type of data
1 °Somatic	Blood type, RH factor, autonomic stress response pattern, kidney and liver function, genetic characteristics, basal metabolism, visual acuity, diseases
2 Physical	Height, weight, sex, eye color, hair color, body "type," number of limbs, fingers, and toes
3 Demographic	Name, age, address, telephone number, occupation, education, income, marital status, number of children
4 Overt behavioral	Reading speed, eye-hand coordination, response to personality test items, frequency of arguments with other people, singing ability, conversational skill, interpersonal assertiveness, occupational competence, smoking habits
5 Cognitive/intellectual	Response to intelligence test items, reports of thoughts and feelings, performance on tests of information processing or cognitive complexity, response to tests of reality perception and structuring
6 Environmental	Location and characteristics of housing, number and description of cohabitants, job requirements and characteristics, physical and behavioral characteristics of family, friends, and coworkers, nature of specific cultural or subcultural standards and traditions, general economic conditions, geographical location

redundant, outdated, or irrelevant. In most instances, the value of knowing a client's driver's license number or whether she or he can juggle would be minimal.

Making Assessment Choices   So the clinician must make some choices and some compromises about (1) how much attention should be devoted to each assessment level, (2) the kinds of questions to ask at each level, and (3) what particular assessment techniques to employ.

The theoretical model adopted by each clinician plays a large role in such choices, since, as noted in Chapter 3, the dynamically oriented questions and tools favored by an orthodox Freudian will differ substantially from the functional-analytic issues and techniques emphasized by a strict Skinnerian. The clinician's familiarity with relevant research may also serve to shape the assessment strategy. Studies of the relative value of interviews, tests, observations, and life records as general data sources can be helpful guides which, along with research evidence on the *reliability* and *validity* of specific tests, observational procedures, and other tools, can make the clinician's planning task easier and more empirically oriented.

These concepts are important enough to merit a brief explanatory digression. Reliability refers to *consistency* in assessment data. It can be evaluated in several ways. If the results of repeated measurements of the same client are very similar, the assessment procedures used to generate those results are said to have high *test-retest reliability*. Another way to evaluate reliability is to examine internal consistency. If one part of an assessment method provides evidence which is similar to that coming from other parts, the method is said to be internally consistent. In the case of tests, this dimension is often called *split-half reliability*.

A third way to evaluate the reliability of an assessment is to compare results of more than one version of it. If two editions of the same test yield equivalent results, that test is said to have high *parallel-form reliability*. When several persons come up with similar data after using a particular assessment system to diagnose, rate, or observe a particular client, that system is described as having high *interrater reliability*.

The *validity* of assessment methods reflects the degree to which they actually measure what they are supposed to measure. Like reliability, validity can be evaluated in several ways (APA, 1974a). For example, if an assessment device measures all aspects of its target, it is said to have high *content validity*. An intelligence test which measures *only* memory would be low on this dimension. If a test or other measure is capable of accurately forecasting something about a client (e.g., suicide attempts, college grades), that assessment has high *predictive validity*. When two assessment devices are found to be measuring the same thing, they are said to have *concurrent validity*.

Finally, there is the concept of *construct validity* (Cronbach & Meehl, 1955). To oversimplify somewhat, an assessment has construct validity when its results are shown to be systematically related to the "thing" it is supposed to be measuring. For example, a measure of anxiety should increase under circumstances thought to increase anxiety (say, facing major surgery). If no change occurs, the measure's construct validity would be suspect. A single observation of this type is too limited to establish or dispute construct validity; a far more elaborate set of operations in a series of experiments is required (Campbell & Fiske, 1959).

To summarize the difference between reliability and validity, consider a situation in which fifty people use their eyes as an observational assessment device to determine the sex of a female impersonator. All fifty observers might agree that the person in question is a female, but they would all be wrong. Their observations would thus be *highly reliable* (consistent) but *totally invalid* because they were not accurately measuring gender.

Before leaving the subject of reliability and validity, we should mention that these concepts have recently been integrated under a broader concept called *generalizability* (Cronbach, Gleser, Nanda, & Rajaratnam, 1972). Within this framework, an assessment instrument is evaluated mainly in terms of what one can say about its results. Thus, instead of saying that a device has high test-retest reliability, one says that its data generalize over time. Generalizability theory and its accompanying data analysis procedures appear likely to play an increasingly important role in the evaluation of clinical assessment methods.

To return to the topic of assessment planning, the clinician's strategies are influenced not only by the reliability and validity of available tools, but to some degree by personal preferences and specific training experiences. A clinical psychologist may never administer a particular test simply because its use was not included in his or her graduate training program. Similarly, some clinicians use a specific set of assessment techniques almost exclusively because one or more professors at graduate school were enthusiastic about it. Those who find certain measurement tactics tedious or unrewarding are likely to seek answers to assessment questions through other procedures with which they are most comfortable.

The clinician's assessment strategy is further shaped by concern over what in electronic information theory has been called the "bandwidth-fidelity" problem (Shannon & Weaver, 1949). Just as greater bandwidth is associated with lower fidelity, the more *extensively* one explores a client's behavior, the less *intensive* each aspect of that exploration becomes (Cronbach & Gleser, 1965). In an interview, for example, the clinician could easily spend 3 hours trying to cover an extensive outline, but the result would probably be relatively superficial information about a wide range of topics. It works the other way, too. The interviewer could use the same 3 hours to explore the client's relationship with parents and friends. At the end of the interview, a lot of detailed information would be available about one part of the client's life, but there might be little or none about other parts. Cronbach and Gleser (1965) have referred to the *breadth* of an assessment device as its *bandwidth* and the *intensity* or exhaustiveness of the measure as its *fidelity*. In their terms, increasing the bandwidth of one's total assessment strategy will be accompanied by a decrease in fidelity, while increasing fidelity narrows the bandwidth.

A significant part of the clinician's assessment planning problem is to choose a package of measures that will allow both bandwidth and fidelity to be as high as possible. This choice is guided in turn by the amount of time and other resources available and also by the purpose or *goal* of the assessment enterprise. Goals have an enormous impact on assessment planning, since the questions, levels of inquiry, and techniques relevant for the problem of, say, selecting IBM executives would differ substantially from those regarding detection of brain damage in a 4-year-old child or establishing the nature of a client's anxiety prior to therapy. Accordingly, the major classes of assessment goals deserve some attention.

The Goals of Clinical Assessment   Because of the varying combinations of clients, settings, and problems with which clinicians work, the specific aims of assessment can be quite heterogeneous, but almost all of them can be placed in one of three somewhat overlapping general categories: *classification, description,* and *prediction.* Each of these goals may be sought in connection with clinical work focused on a single individual or as part of a research project in which large groups of subjects are assessed.

Classification   We saw in Chapter 2 that after clinical psychologists began working with adult clients, they came under the strong influence and supervision of medical personnel, particularly psychiatrists. This meant that clinical psychologists' assessment skills and activities were often used to reach the psychiatrically oriented goal of diagnostic classification.[2]

Assignment of each psychiatric patient to the proper category in the American Psychiatric Association's diagnostic labeling system (e.g., "neurotic," "psychotic," "mentally retarded") was seen as just as important as accurate diagnosis of physical illness because this would "ensure the proper handling and treatment of the sick and disturbed individual" (Harrower, 1965b, p. 381).

Clinicians' preoccupation with assessment for the purpose of diagnostic classification during the late 1930s and early 1940s was evident not only in their day-to-day work with individual clients but also in the kind of research they conducted. A large number of studies during this period were designed to relate specific types of responses on instruments like the Rorschach inkblot test to membership in certain diagnostic classes. Many clinical psychologists were not entirely comfortable with this search for specific indicators (called "pathognomonic signs") of diagnostic conditions, because they felt that it oversimplified the use of assessment data in ways which could result in errors (e.g., Klopfer & Kelley, 1942). Nevertheless, the goal of diagnostic classification remained prominent in clinical research and practice during the 1940s and has continued to be part of the reason why some clinicians do assessment today, especially if they work in psychiatric or other medically oriented settings. Peterson (1968a, p. 32) described the situation as follows:

> The real reason many clinicians conduct psychological examinations is that someone expects it of them. All too frequently, they administer and interpret Rorschachs, code MMPI's, and prepare reports for no clear reason beyond the scheduled expectation of a staff conference, the knowledge that they are going to be asked what "the psychologicals look like," and prescience of an embarrassed silence if they have nothing to say. The diagnosis has to be written into the record, and since someone in charge may ask for an opinion, the (psychologist) feels obliged to have one ready, with some kind of . . . data to support it.

Description   As clinical psychology began to develop a postwar professional and research identity which was increasingly independent of psychiatry, changes in clinical assessment goals began to appear. The "blind" administration, scoring, and interpretation of a few popular psychological tests for the purpose of diagnosis became increasingly distasteful to clinicians who were interested in conducting broader assessments which could result in a fuller understanding and a more elaborate *description* of the client (see, e.g., Thorne, 1948; Watson, 1951).[3]

The desire to go beyond diagnosis to seek a wider view was based partly on

[2]This is also called psychodiagnosis, differential diagnosis, or diagnostic labeling.

[3]Clinical psychologists were by no means alone in their recognition of the limited value of diagnostic labels. Adolf Meyer, one of America's most prominent psychiatrists of the early twentieth century is reported to have remarked, "We understand this case; we don't need any diagnosis" (Watson, 1951, p 22).

clinical psychology's burgeoning self-confidence, but it was also due to the conviction that people cannot really be understood simply through reference to their behavior during a short interview or a Rorschach test. It became clear that more information about people was necessary if understanding was to result. In addition, interest in the content of behavior was supplemented by a concern for its social, cultural, and physical *context*. The result was a movement by clinical psychologists toward assessment for the purpose of description of *person-environment interactions*. This movement got much of its impetus in the 1930s and 1940s from the pioneering clinical and research work of Henry Murray at the Harvard Psychological Clinic and David Rapaport at the Menninger Clinic. These men and their colleagues developed extensive batteries of interviews, tests, and observations designed to comprehensively assess "normal" people as well as those with psychological problems (Murray, 1938; Rapaport, Gill & Schafer, 1945, 1946) and to take into account the external situational context of behavior as well as its internal determinants (Wiggins, 1973).

The desirability of description as opposed to classification as an assessment goal was greatly increased by the disturbing results of research conducted in the 1950s on the reliability and validity of the standard American Psychiatric Association diagnostic classification system.[4] Many of these studies raised serious questions about the accuracy and meaning of simply attaching diagnostic labels to patients and, in addition, began to suggest that the label often had little effect on how clients were ultimately treated anyway (see,e.g., Ash, 1949; Dailey, 1953; Little & Schneidman, 1959; Schmidt & Fonda, 1956; Ullmann & Hunrichs, 1958). Further,acceptance of the medical/psychodynamic model on which diagnosis was based began to wane in the 1960s as alternative phenomeno-logical and social-learning models gained strength and as the stigma associated with being labeled was more clearly recognized (Goffman, 1961; Laing, 1967; Scheff, 1966; Szasz, 1960; Ullmann & Krasner, 1969).

All of this means that, while diagnostic labeling still takes place, broader psychological description (or "image-making") is a more popular assessment goal.[5] Interestingly, the rise of descriptive assessment has prompted many clinicians to "start over" and approach the task of classifying people and problems in new, primarily nonpsychiatric ways. The result has been proposals for classification systems which are designed to describe, not label. Instead of simply calling people "schizophrenic" or "manic-depressive" or "neurotic" on the basis of fairly narrow problem-oriented measures, clinicians may now assign individuals to more descriptive categories on the basis of extensive assessment of factors such as motivation, intrapsychic functions, openness to therapy, test

[4]This system has taken several forms over the years. Since 1968 it has been represented by the *Diagnostic and Statistical Manual of Mental Disorders* (DSM-II; American Psychiatric Association, 1968), which will soon be replaced by an updated version (DSM-III).

[5]In one study of this trend, Dollin and Reznikoff (1966) found that assessment referrals to clinical psychologists requested diagnostic labels 64 percent of the time in 1956 but only 29 percent of the time in 1966. It is of interest to note, by the way, that even though specific diagnostic labeling is not involved in descriptive assessment, it is still referred to by some traditionalists as "diagnosis" (e.g., Arbuckle, 1965; Garfield, 1974; Thorne, 1972; Tryon, 1976).

response patterns, potential for mental health, conditionability, subjective experience, relationship patterns, needs, functional relationships between behavior and the environment, behavioral excesses and deficits, and other factors. (See Adams, Doster, & Calhoun, 1977; Begelman, 1976; Borofsky, 1974; Ferster, 1965; Goldfried & Davison, 1976; Harrower, 1965b; Mahrer, 1970; and Tryon, 1976 for specific examples of psychological classification systems which represent psychodynamic, phenomenological, and social-learning points of view.)

In addition to avoiding many of the difficulties inherent in traditional psychiatric classification, description-oriented assessment makes it much easier for the clinician to pay attention to clients' strengths, assets, and adaptive functions as well as to weaknesses, liabilities, and problems. Descriptive assessment data are commonly used to provide pretreatment or "base-line" measures of clients' behavior, to guide treatment planning, to evaluate changes in problematic (and nonproblematic) behavior which result from treatment, and for many other specific clinical purposes.

Further, description-oriented assessments are of great value in the context of research in clinical psychology, personality, and behavior disorder. For example, in an extensive, large-sample investigation of the relative value of two psychological treatments for depression, assessments which *describe* clients' posttreatment behaviors (e.g., job absenteeism, time spent alone, self-reports of sadness, scores on tests of depression, and the like) would be of much greater value than those which are translated into a label (e.g., "depressive" versus "nondepressive").

Assessment aimed at description is also used in research on the development of new measurement instruments. The value of a specialized interview technique, an innovative test, or a novel observational procedure is often determined by cross-checking its findings with those of other, more established descriptive tools.

Prediction   The third major goal of clinical assessment is to make predictions about human behavior. Will client X be likely to attempt suicide? Is client Y going to harm others if released from an institution? Can client Z hold a job and live independently in the community? Questions of this kind constitute the most severe test of clinical assessment, both because accurate prediction of what any given individual will do can be extremely difficult and because the consequences of error are often socially and personally disastrous. Many angry people talk about harming their bosses, family members, or others, but only a small number of them ever carry out their threats. (Who has not said things like "I'll kill my roommate if these dishes aren't washed by tonight"?)

Obviously, it would be desirable to assess an individual and be able to determine whether she or he is simply an angry talker or a future murderer. Prediction-oriented assessment may involve (1) a search for specific aggressive or suicidal signs and response patterns on a standard psychological test, (2) more extensive assessment from a wider variety of data sources (Neuringer, 1974; Rosen, 1954), or (3) the development of special assessment instruments designed especially for prediction of relatively infrequent events such as suicide (Cohen, Motto, & Seiden, 1966; Litman & Farberow, 1961).

Assessment may also be aimed at other, less dramatic kinds of predictions which involve performance adequacy. Here, the clinician (or the industrial psychologist) is interested in selecting from a large group those individuals who will most nearly meet some future performance standard. Instruments such as the Scholastic Aptitude Test (SAT), the American College Test (ACT), and the Graduate Record Examination (GRE) provide familiar examples of predictive assessment which leads to selection. Similar approaches have been adopted by business, industry, and the military to guide selection of workers, executives, and specialists such as pilots and submarine personnel.

It is with respect to selection that the assessment goals of description and prediction show their greatest overlap. Often, descriptive assessment data constitute part of the information base from which predictions and then selections are made. A classic example of this was Henry Murray's use of his descriptive assessment approach (a combination of specialized tests, interviews, and observations) to select men for work as spies, saboteurs, and other behind-enemy-lines workers during World War II (Office of Strategic Services, 1948). Along with a staff of other psychologists, Murray set up a comprehensive assessment program which took each man from one to three days to complete and which measured everything from intelligence to stress tolerance to ability at planning murder (see Chapter 7).

This hybrid assessment goal of "description for prediction for selection" has remained visible in a variety of large-scale postwar screening programs. Some of these were focused on improving candidate selection for civilian and military jobs (e.g., Institute of Personality Assessment and Research, 1970) or for graduate training in clinical psychology and psychiatry (e.g., Holt & Luborsky, 1958; Kelly & Fiske, 1951), but perhaps the best-known descendant of the approach was the elaborate program for selecting Peace Corps volunteers (Colmen, Kaplan, & Boulger, 1964). Because these kinds of assessment programs often influence socially important decisions affecting large numbers of people, they must not only be evaluated for psychometric validity (i.e., how well assessment data predict some performance criterion), but also for their overall impact on the persons assessed and upon the business, industry, university, or other organization in which they are used. One must be concerned with (1) the actual number of correct decisions (selections) which are prompted by particular assessment procedures, (2) the cost of correct decisions in terms of money, time, and effort, and (3) the personal and other costs of selection errors (i.e., choosing inappropriate candidates or rejecting appropriate ones). Complex and elaborate decision theories, models, and procedures have evolved to deal with such issues (see Cronbach & Gleser, 1965, and Wiggins, 1973).

The goal of prediction enters into a wide variety of clinical and quasi-clinical assessment activities and, as we shall see later, has stimulated a vast body of research on the evaluation, analysis, and improvement of clinicians' prognostications about people.

The Case Study Guide   However it is arrived at, the clinician's ultimate choice of particular questions and inquiry levels gives the assessment task manageable dimensions and provides an outline of its scope. Ideally, this outline is (1) broad enough to give a general picture of the client through at least a sampling of information from each of the levels listed in Table 4-1 and (2) focused enough to allow for more intensive coverage of levels and questions especially relevant to the specific purpose of assessment.

Often, the conceptual outline which results from clinicians' assessment choices and planning is translated into written form as a *case study guide*. The idea for such an outline comes to psychology from medicine and psychiatry (Bolgar, 1965), but it has been adopted as a means of organizing assessment by most clinicians, whether or not they espouse a medical or dynamic model. A main factor behind broad acceptance of the case study approach is its flexibility. Case study outlines can be clearly tied to the assumptions of a theoretical model, or they can be open and eclectic, allowing each practitioner to use them in his or her own way. Some examples of outlines which have been suggested for use as assessment guides will illustrate this point.

Probably the most comprehensive and theoretically neutral example of a case study outline is that composed by Sundberg, Tyler, and Taplin (1973). It is designed for data collection via interview procedures with adults, but it is easy to see that much of the information could also apply to children and could be obtained through life records, tests, or observations as well. A summary of headings used in their outline is presented in Box 4-1.

Notice that, although this outline is sufficiently problem-oriented to be of use in settings where persons are seeking psychological help, it also allows the assessor to stay in touch with broader, more general, and often less problematic aspects of the client's life. Somewhat less comprehensive outlines of this type had been suggested earlier by Shaffer and Lazarus (1956) and Watson (1951).

Korchin (1976) provides another elaborate but more psychodynamically

---

Box 4-1   The Sundberg, Tyler, and Taplin Case Study Outline

A   Identifying data (name, address, occupation, marital status, and the like)
B   Reason for coming
C   Present situations
D   Family constellation (family of orientation)
E   Early recollections
F   Birth and development
G   Health
H   Education and training
 I   Work record
J   Recreation, interests
K   Sexual development
L   Marital and family data
M   Client self-description
N   Choices and turning points in client's life
O   Any additional information client wishes to add

Box 4-2 Korchin's Case Study Outline

I   Present status
    A Adaptation in life situations (major tasks in patient's life and level of functioning)
    B Symptomatic behaviors
    C Patient's motivation for clinical care and preconceptions about mental health (i.e., what are
        the patient's goals and expectations?)
    D Patient's appearance and behavior in clinic
II The manifest personality
    A Biological features (e.g., state of health, medical history, body type, physical appearance)
    B Temperament (patient's energy level, emotional appropriateness and characteristics,
        gestural characteristics)
    C Manifest personality traits (patient's self-description and description by others)
    D Interpersonal behavior (primary relationships, "stimulus value" for others, number and type
        of friends, etc.)
III Personality dynamics and structure
    A Motives and affects
    B Moral principles, social values and attitudes
    C Ego functions and identity
IV Social determinants and current life situation
    A Group memberships and roles (to what groups does client belong and what major social
        roles does client take?)
    B Family
    C Education and work
    D Social ecology
V   Major stresses and coping potential
    A Nature and source of life stresses (e.g., family, occupation)
VI Personality development
    A How did client's personality come to be?

oriented case study outline. A summary of its headings appears in Box 4-2. The psychodynamic influence is very strong here as compared with the Sundberg, Tyler, and Taplin (1973) outline. Korchin (1976) (1) refers to the person being assessed as the "patient" rather than the "client," (2) includes questions about unconscious motives, feelings, impulses, and fantasies, (3) explores ego functions, identification, and developmental "tasks," and (4) seeks to assess "personality dynamics and structure." A less elaborate but even more strongly psychodynamic outline has been presented by Saul (1957).

Representatives of the social-learning approach to clinical psychology have also adopted case study formats or outlines, the most comprehensive and influential of which is that of Kanfer and Saslow (1969). Box 4-3 contains a summary of its major topics.

Later, we shall review specific characteristics of the social-learning approach to assessment. For now, however, simply notice that the Kanfer and Saslow outline differs in two important respects from those preceding it. First, there is an intense focus on *analysis* of the relationship between the client's environment and both problematic and nonproblematic aspects of behavior. The specific antecedents, maintenance factors, and consequences of behavior are sought. Second, the outline is directly tied into future attempts at behavior

Box 4-3   Kanfer and Saslow's Case Study Outline

I   Initial analysis of the problem situation
  A   Behavioral excesses
  B   Behavioral deficits
  C   Behavioral assets

II   Clarification of the problem situation
  A   Should problematic behaviors be assigned to category IA or IB?
  B   Persons or groups who object to or support these behaviors
  C   Consequences of the problem for the patient and for significant others
  D   Conditions under which problematic behaviors occur
  E   Consequences of no change in problematic behaviors
  F   Nature of any new problems which would occur if problems were eliminated
  G   Sources of information other than patient

III   Motivational analysis
  A   Patient's ranking of various incentives or reinforcing events in terms of importance
  B   Frequency of access to various reinforcers
  C   Specific conditions under which reinforcers arouse goal-directed behaviors
  D   Do actions aimed at reaching goals correspond to verbal statements?
  E   Persons or groups exerting most effective and widespread control over current behavior
  F   Degree to which patient relates attainment of reinforcers to luck vs. his or her own behavior
  G   Major adverse stimuli
  H   Reinforcing events which can be utilized for facilitating elimination of problematic behaviors

IV   Developmental analysis
  A   Biological changes
  B   Sociological changes
  C   Behavioral changes

V   Analysis of self-control
  A   In situations in which patient can control problematic behaviors, how is control achieved?
  B   Previous aversive consequences of problematic behaviors (e.g., jail, social ostracism) and their effects on self-control
  C   Degree to which patient avoids situations conducive to problematic behaviors
  D   Correspondence between patient's verbalized degree of self-control and observations by others
  E   Conditions, persons, or reinforcers which tend to change self-control
  F   Degree to which self-controlling behavior can be used in treatment

VI   Analysis of social relationships
  A   Most significant people in patient's environment
  B   Nature of reinforcers relevant in patient's social relationships
  C   Patient's expectations of others' words and actions
  D   Others' expectations of patient (are these congruent with patient's self-expectations?)
  E   Can significant others participate in treatment? How?

VII   Analysis of the social-cultural-physical environment
  A   Norm in patient's social milieu regarding problematic behaviors
  B   Environmental limitations on access to reinforcement
  C   Aspects of patient's environment where problematic behavior is most apparent, most troublesome, or most accepted
  D   Degree to which milieu regards psychological procedures as appropriate for helping to solve problems

change. Other somewhat less comprehensive and more problem-focused social-learning outlines have been suggested by Lazarus (1973), Pomeranz and Goldfried (1970), Craighead, Kazdin, and Mahoney (1976), Peterson (1968a), and Phillips (1977).

Because phenomenologically oriented psychologists deemphasize elaborate assessment procedures, case study outlines which specifically reflect the phenomenological model of clinical psychology have not appeared.

Collecting Assessment Data

So far we have looked at some of the ways in which clinicians answer the first of the primary assessment questions noted by McReynolds (1975): "What do we want to know?" Our next step should be to examine the range of answers to his second question: "How should we go about learning it?"

Sources of Assessment Data We have seen that clinical psychologists collect assessment data from four general sources: interviews, tests, observations, and life records. In this section, we shall briefly mention some of the defining characteristics of these wellsprings of clinical information and, in addition, take note of some of the problems and limitations of the data coming from each. These short sketches are designed to serve as previews of the more detailed descriptions and evaluations of interviews, tests, and observations included in the next three chapters.

Interviews Kelly (1958, p. 330) succinctly characterized a straightforward approach to assessment as follows: "If you don't know what is going on in a person's mind, ask him; He may tell you." This simple point would be just as relevant if it were broadened to read, "If you want to know something about a person, ask," and it lies at the root of why the interview is the most basic and widely employed source of assessment data in clinical and nonclinical settings. It is popular and pervasive for other reasons as well. For one thing, inasmuch as the clinician talks with the client in a situation which is similar in many ways to ordinary social interaction, interviews provide a relatively easy and inexpensive way of collecting simultaneous samples of a person's verbal and nonverbal behavior. Second, unless the interview is to be audio or video tape-recorded, no special equipment is required and the procedure is highly "portable"; it can take place almost anywhere. Third, there is no more flexible assessment tool than the interview. Except in cases where highly structured research limitations prevail, the interviewer is free to adjust the emphasis of inquiry and conversation to those particular issues and levels which appear most relevant and important, as determined by her or his theoretical orientation or personal preference.

But what about the quality of data collected through interviews? Peterson (1968a, p. 13) comments that "the interview . . . must not be regarded as the 'truth' about the individual and his environment, but as another form of data whose reliability, validity, and decisional utility must be subjected to the same kinds of scrutiny required for other modes of data collection." Although clients' self-reports of present and future behavior are often remarkably accurate

(Hilgard, 1969; Mischel, 1968), interview data may not *always* be reliable and valid (Walsh, 1967; Yarrow, Campbell, & Burton, 1968). It may be influenced or distorted in various ways as a function of (1) characteristics of the interviewer and the questions he or she asks, (2) client characteristics such as memory and willingness to disclose accurate information, and (3) the circumstances under which the interview takes place.

The interview will be discussed and evaluated in greater detail in Chapter 5.

Tests   Like interviews, tests provide a sample of behavior. However, the stimuli to which the client is asked to respond on a test are far more standardized and consistent than is the case in most interviews. The basic idea of a test is to expose each client to exactly the same stimuli under exactly the same circumstances. Tests can be easy, economical, and convenient to administer. Often, a professional need not even be present. Further, the standardized form in which test material is presented helps eliminate bias in the content and sequence of the assessor's inquiries. Responses to most tests can be translated into scores or other quantitative form, thus making summaries of a client's behavior precise and capable of mathematical analysis.[6] In this way, test data may facilitate communication between professionals about a particular client. Finally, and perhaps most important, test data allow the clinician to objectively compare a given client's behavior with that of hundreds or perhaps thousands of other individuals who have already taken the same test. This is often helpful in the data processing stage of assessment.

Assume for instance that, on a word association test, the first thing that pops into a client's mind when the tester says "house" is "pantyhose." If the assessor had never heard this association before, it might be interpreted as being strange and perhaps indicative of some psychological problem. But if the tester has access to a book containing the associations of 12,000 subjects to the word "house," it may turn out that "pantyhose" is a fairly popular response (it is not, by the way) and thus not worthy of concern.

All these advantages, along with the fact that for many years testing was the main component of professional identity for clinical psychologists, have resulted in the widespread use of tests as clinical assessment devices. Even though the heyday of psychological testing (the 1930s through the 1950s) has clearly passed, tests are still a significant aspect of assessment (Lubin, Wallis, & Paine, 1971; Sundberg, 1961; Wade & Baker, 1977; Wellner, 1968).

However, tests are not magical devices that always reveal the "truth" about people. They must be evaluated in terms of reliability and validity, and, like other assessment techniques, they are sometimes found wanting in important respects. Anything which is not "standard" about test stimuli, including the tester, the client, or the testing situation, can threaten the value of the data obtained. These and other evaluative issues will be dealt with when we focus more directly on tests in Chapter 6.

---

[6]Certain aspects of interview data can be handled in this way as well but may involve more cumbersome procedures (e.g., Dollard & Mowrer, 1953; Matarazzo, 1965).

Observations The familiar adage that "actions speak louder than words" provides much of the basis for the clinician's desire to supplement self-report measures like interviews or tests with direct observation of a person's behavior in situations of interest. The goal here is to go beyond what a client *says* and find out what the person actually *does*.

A notable example of how observational data can alter the impression left by self-report was given by Wicker (1969, p. 42; see also Dillehay, 1973).

> In the 1930's when, according to studies of social distance, there was much anti-Chinese sentiment in the United States, LaPiere (1934) took several extensive automobile trips with a Chinese couple. Unknown to his companions, he took notes of how the travellers were treated, and he kept a list of hotels and restaurants where they were served. Only once were they denied service, and LaPiere judged their treatment to be above average in 40% of the restaurants visited. Later, LaPiere wrote to the 250 hotels and restaurants on his list, asking if they would accept Chinese guests. Over 90% of the 128 proprietors responding indicated they would not serve Chinese, in spite of the fact that all had previously accommodated LaPiere's companions.

Here, self-report and observational data provided radically different views of the anti-Chinese prejudice question, and it could be argued that the observations were more accurate than the self-reports. Indeed, observation is considered by many to be the most valid form of clinical assessment. This is because, first, it appears to be so *direct* and capable of circumventing many of the problems of memory, motivation, response style, and situational bias which so often reduce the value of interviews and tests. A smoker's self-report that five cigarettes were smoked in one day may be biased by ability to recall, a desire to appear moderate, or feelings about the assessor. An actual count of smoking frequency recorded by an observer would reflect none of these factors.

A second advantage of observational assessment is its *relevance* to behaviors of greatest interest. A child's aggressiveness, for example, can be observed and measured as it actually occurs in the schoolroom or play area where the problem has been most acute. This also illustrates a related benefit of observation: Behavior is assessed in its social and situational context rather than in the abstract. In a mental hospital, for example, careful observation of a long-term resident may reveal that the patient appears depressed only after meals or when a staff member is nearby. This information may be of greater value to a therapist than an affirmative response to the query, "Are you ever depressed?"

Finally, observations allow for description and analysis of behavior in highly specific terms and in great detail. For example, a person's sexual arousal in response to particular stimuli might be defined in terms of penile volume or vaginal blood flow, both of which can be measured with specially designed apparatus. Similarly, "psychosis" can be observed by recording the appearance and frequency over time of explicitly defined behaviors such as "strikes own body," "speaks incoherently," or "kisses water fountain."

In spite of its many advantages, observational assessment is by no means problem-free. The degree to which one can rely on information from this source may vary considerably since the reliability and validity of observational data can be threatened by observer error or bias, inadvertent observer influence on the behavior under observation, specific situational factors and the like. These problems will be discussed in Chapter 7.

Life records As people pass through life, they leave a trail of evidence of their existence and behavior in many forms, including school records, credit ratings, work records, letters, police records, photographs, awards, medical records, income tax returns, diaries, and creative products like paintings or sculpture. There is often much that can be learned about a person through perusal of such life records and, because this approach to assessment does not require the client to make any *new* responses (as do interviews, tests, and observations), there is virtually no chance that memory, motivation, response style, or situational factors can distort the data obtained. Thus, a 10-minute review of a person's grade school, high school, and college transcripts may provide far more specific, detailed, and accurate academic history information than 30 minutes of interview time spent on questions like "how did you do in school?" Similarly, reading diary entries or letters written during significant periods in a client's life can reveal "on-the-spot" feelings, ideas, behaviors, and situational details which would otherwise be either lost in the shuffle of subsequent events or distorted by imperfect recall.

Objective and subjective life records are also attractive because they provide a relatively inexpensive way of broadening one's "working image" of the client. An array of such records can often render in compact form a great deal about a person's overt and covert behavior over a long period of time and across a range of situations. In a sense, life records act like a wide-angle camera lens by bringing into view that which might otherwise be missed.

Wide-angle lenses almost always produce a certain amount of distortion, however, and records can sometimes do the same. For one thing, they tend to be superficial. Knowing that a person has a poor credit rating indicates that she or he has not fulfilled certain financial obligations, but does not in itself say why. Records may show that a person was divorced at age 18, but say nothing of how the person felt about it. Thus, records may be valuable, but not always very complete. These and other shortcomings of life records will be touched upon in Chapter 7.

The Value of Multiple Assessment Sources Clinical psychologists seldom rely on a single source of assessment data for their "working image" of a client. This is true partly because there is a multiplicity of data available within each of the four assessment sources we have described. It is virtually impossible not to observe a person's behavior in the course of an interview or a testing session and some interview data may come out of a client's responses to certain tests. Similarly, life records such as academic grades or clinic case notes usually reflect performance on tests or responses to interview questions.

Whether one multifaceted assessment source is used or data from separate sources are collected, the availability of multiple channels of assessment provides distinct advantages for the clinician. To begin with, outright lies or distortions of fact can be cross-checked. The interviewer who is told by a mental hospital resident that he or she has been there "about 6 months" may get quite a different story (e.g., 20 years) from hospital records.

It may also be the case that the whole story of a client's problems or characteristics is not clear until multiple assessment has been completed. Geer (1965) found, for example, that males who professed strong fear of dogs on a self-report were actually able to pet a dog during an observed performance test. Similarly, Nietzel and Bernstein (1976) showed that some college students who reported themselves socially unassertive were observed to be capable of strong assertive responses. In such cases, multiple assessment helps separate those individuals who *cannot* engage in certain behaviors (due to, say, lack of skill) from those who *do not* engage in them (perhaps because of the inhibitory effects of anxiety).

Another benefit of multiple assessment appears when the clinician wishes to look at the effects of a particular psychological intervention. Suppose a married couple comes to a therapist because they have been unhappy with each other and are considering divorce. If "marital happiness" based on interview data were the only measure employed, the couple's divorce following three months of clinical sessions would indicate that the marital problem was worsened by treatment. Other assessments might tell a different story, however. Observations, third-person reports, and life records (from occupational or educational settings) might show that one or both members of the former couple find their divorced status liberating as they begin to develop their interests and potentials in areas that had been previously inaccessible, such as travel, education, or job change. These satisfactions might not be reported to the therapist in an interview because the clients feel shame or guilt over divorce, because temporary depression or fear of the future seem to be more "appropriate" topics for a clinical session, or for other reasons.

Of course, multiple assessment can reveal the opposite situation as well. After being helped by a therapist to stand up for his rights, a young man may report vast improvement in self-esteem, confidence, and comfort in social situations. These positive interview data might not reveal the fact that the client has now become aggressive and somewhat obnoxious in his relations with others and that, in the long run, he is likely to suffer socially. Future social problems could be avoided, however, by detecting inappropriate behavior through observational assessment either in the client's natural environment or during role-playing sessions in the clinician's office.

Processing Assessment Data

Once assessment data have been collected, the clinician is faced with the problem of determining what those data mean. If the information gathered is to be useful in reaching the goals of classifying, describing, or predicting human behavior, it will have to be interpreted, combined, and transformed from raw form into hypotheses, images, relationships, and conclusions.

For example, knowing that a young child cries at certain measurably high intensities for precisely recorded lengths of time when placed in its crib each evening constitutes valuable assessment data. So does the observation or report that after the crying continues for varying periods, someone enters the baby's room to provide comfort. However, these carefully gathered data mean little in psychological terms until they are translated into statements like those contained in Box 4-4. This part of assessment is often referred to as data *processing,* and it is crucial. As Levy (1968, p. 8) put it (in words that owe something to existential philosophy): "Events . . . do not carry with them their own interpretation. They are innocent of any meaning except insofar as we impose it on them."

Thus, the raw data of clinical assessment—the life records, test scores, self-reports, and observations—may mean nothing until someone interprets or processes them. The processing task is a formidable one because, in most cases, some degree of *inference* is involved and inference requires a leap from known data to what is *assumed* on the basis of those data. In general, as the jump from data to assumption gets longer, inference becomes more vulnerable to error (Hoch, 1971).

Consider this simple example: A young boy is observed sitting on a lawn, playing with an earthworm which has emerged from the grass. At one point, he cuts the worm in half. It would be easy to infer from this incident that the child was cruel and aggressive and even that more serious forms of aggression, perhaps toward other people, will appear in later life. These inferences would be off the mark, however, for "what the observer could not see . . . was what the boy—who happened to have few friends—thought as he cut the worm in half: 'There! Now you will have someone to play with'" (Goldfried & Sprafkin, 1974, p. 305). In this case, a more conservative inferential statement like "the child appears to enjoy this activity" would have been more accurate.

Box 4-4   Some Statements Based on Observation of a Crying Child and Its Mother

1 Crying stops after mother enters room and begins again when she leaves.
2 Mother seems overanxious about her child's welfare.
3 Mother appears to see crying as a crisis situation.
4 Crying is rewarded by mother's attention.
5 Mother's doting attention may be a reaction formation which conceals unconscious hatred.
6 Mother's anxiety is not so much concern for the child but part of the way she feels a good mother should behave.
7 Mother displays neurotic behaviors.
8 The child is likely to become overly dependent upon mother in later life.

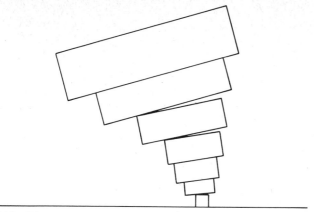

FIGURE 4-2   Can you look at this drawing without inferring anything about it?

It is easy to see that elaborate inference, especially when based upon minimal data, can be dangerous. "The untrained or careless can leap at psychological inferences and end up in an awkward position" (Hoch, 1971, p. 5). The only sure way to totally eliminate the problem of inference error is to eliminate inference altogether, but since doing so would also eliminate the meaning of most assessment data, this is not usually done. Indeed, it may be impossible for human beings to completely avoid making inferences, even in relation to the simplest stimuli. For example, the actual content ("raw data") of Figure 4-2 is a series of rectangles which gradually increase in size, angle on the page, and displacement to the left as one looks from bottom to top. However, it is difficult to avoid *inferring* more, such as that the "stack" is about to "fall over," or that the smallest "box" is about to be "crushed."

So the main questions to be dealt with in assessment data processing do not include *whether* inferences will be drawn, but center around what *kinds* of inferences to make, *how* clinicians go about making them, how *accurate* they are, and how inference error can be minimized.

Levels and Types of Clinical Inference   Clinical inferences can be characterized in terms of their *goals,* their underlying *models,* and their *levels of abstraction.* That they reflect the assessor's overall goals is illustrated in Box 4-4, where classification (statement 7), description (statement 1), and prediction (statement 8) are all represented.

Inferences also tend to be tied to the assessor's model of clinical psychology. This is because, as we saw in Chapter 3, models help the clinician take a mass of assessment data and select, organize, and summarize it in systematic, meaningful ways. This process is illustrated in Box 4-4 by statements 4, 5, and 6, which reflect the social-learning, psychodynamic, and phenomenological models respectively.

Finally, inferences vary in their level of abstraction. The clinician can make cautious, low-level inferences which do not stray very far from the original data (as in entry 1 of Box 4-4) or can attempt bolder, more generalized statements which go far beyond the "hard" data available but which are justified and supported by the assessor's experience, training, theoretical model, intuitive "hunches," and "common sense" (e.g., Box 4-4, statement 5).

At the lowest inference level, assessment data are generally taken at face value, as when a test score or composite of several scores determines whether or not a student is admitted to graduate school. Another example might be the assumption that a child enjoys television since observations reveal that he or she spends 6 hours a day in front of the set. At higher inference levels, by contrast, assessment data are expanded or generalized beyond their original limits. Thus, behavior revealed through tests, interviews, observations, and records is posited as being generally characteristic of the person and may even be used as the basis for applying summary terms like "anxious," "depressed," "hostile," "charming," and the like.

At the highest inferential level, available assessment data are processed to form an overall picture of the client in relation to her or his environment. Ideally, the "whole story" of how and why the person got to be where he or she is at the moment is reconstructed, and the client's problems and difficulties are viewed in light of this panorama. Inference at this level ventures farthest from the data originally collected, so the clinician depends upon experience and, in particular, a theoretical model to guide the statements and predictions which are made.

In actual clinical practice, assessment time and resources are too limited to allow for a complete and detailed synthesis of a single client's life, but very high-level inference does occur, usually in the form of broad statements like the following:

The patient "has revealed himself to be a passively-dependent personality entirely oriented toward pleasing various father substitutes. . . . I believe that there is a masculine identification from young childhood; that his present difficulties had their onset with the birth of a younger brother when patient was age 7. (Quoted in Harrower, 1965, p. 394)

The state of confusion and turmoil Morris was in does not approximate any standard diagnostic category, but it brings to mind . . . a *postadolescent identity crisis*. Morris was chronologically in . . . young adulthood when his peers were rapidly finding life partners with whom to share an intimacy for which he was not yet ready. . . . Morris' conflicts were typical of this condition: dependence on his mother versus rejection of her, need for the approval of others versus fear of involvement, resistance to external constraint and a deficiency in moral restraints versus a seeking for his own form of self-control and morality, and a deep confusion about himself growing out of his basic uncertainty about his sexual identity (Holt, 1971, pp. 162–163).

Three Views of Assessment Data   Whatever their type or level, the inferences drawn from assessment data depend primarily upon how those data are viewed, that is, what the data are thought to be capable of saying. For the most part, clinicians tend to conceive of assessment information in three main ways: as *samples, correlates,* or *signs* (Goodenough, 1949; Sundberg, Tyler, & Taplin, 1973). For example, consider the following bit of raw assessment data: "A person purposely took 16 sleeping pills before going to bed at a hotel last night, but was saved when discovered by a maid and rushed to the intensive care unit of a hospital."

How can this event be viewed and what kinds of inferences would follow from each perspective? The incident could be seen as a *sample* of the client's behavior and the following inferences might result:

1   The client has access to potentially lethal medication.
2   The client did not wish to be saved because no one knew about the suicide attempt before it occurred.
3   Under similar circumstances, the client may attempt suicide again.

Notice that looking at the client's behavior as a sample results in rather low-level inferences. The pill taking is seen as an *example* of what the client is capable of doing under certain circumstances. On the basis of the information provided, no attempt is made to infer *why* the individual tried suicide; more assessment would be required before specific causal statements would be justified.

However, the very same incident could be viewed as a *correlate* of other aspects of the client's life. Even though no further information is available about the client in question, knowledge gained from similar cases might guide inferences of the following type:

1   The client is likely to be a middle-aged male who is single or divorced and lives alone (this is a common set of characteristics among suicides).
2   The client is or has recently been depressed.
3   The client may have little or no emotional support from close family or friends.

Here, higher-level inferences are based upon a combination of (1) known facts about the client's behavior, and (2) the clinician's experience and knowledge of relevant statistics about what tends to correlate with that behavior. These inferences go somewhat beyond the original data with the support of empirically demonstrated relationships between and among specific variables such as suicide, age, sex, and depression. In general, the stronger the known relationships between variables, the more accurate the inferences will be.

This correlate-oriented, or *psychometric,* approach is not tied to any specific theoretical orientation. As long as they can be put into quantitative terms, assessment data of virtually any kind (e.g., ego strength scores, reinforcer preferences, personality traits, perceptions of others) can be dealt with as correlates.[7] As such, the psychometric approach to assessment data processing provides a strong link between individual-oriented clinical psychology and the more generalized field of research on human personality theories.

Finally, the pill taking may be thought of as a *sign* of other, possibly less obvious, things about the client. From such a perspective, the attempt at self-destruction could signal the presence of fairly specific and very serious problems. A sign-oriented view might result in the following kinds of inferences:

1 The client's aggressive impulses have been turned against the self.
2 The client's behavior is reflective of problematic intrapsychic conflicts.
3 The pill taking represents an unconscious cry for help.

These statements go well beyond the "hard" information in directions which are suggested by a theory of behavior. Here, assessment data provide the signs, a theory provides their meaning; the suggested relationship between a certain sign and a particular inference may stem solely from theoretical speculation.

Models, Views, and Levels   It should be fairly obvious by now that levels of inference, views of assessment data, and theoretical models are interrelated. It would be hazardous to stereotype the specific nature of these relationships, but it is safe to say in general that when assessment information is viewed primarily as a behavior *sample,* inference level is likely to be minimal and the guiding model will probably be of the social-learning type. On the other hand, conceptualizing assessment data as *signs* usually results in much higher levels of inference and often employs a psychodynamic or phenomenological model of behavior in informal, speculative fashion. In between, where assessment data are viewed as *correlates,* inferences are at low to moderate levels, and there is usually an emphasis on formal, statistical analysis of relationships among variables representing a wide range of theories.

The primary characteristics of the three views of assessment data we have described are presented in Table 4-2. The right-hand column of Table 4-2 shows that assessment data processing may be based upon formal, objective, statistical procedures, and/or informal, subjective means. The informal approach usually involves looking at assessment data as signs, while the formal approach typically sees such data as correlates.[8] Both alternatives have deep roots in the history of

---

[7]Wiggins (1973, Chapter 10) provides valuable summaries of ways in which the psychometric approach has been used to process assessment data coming from the theories of Freud, Harry Stack Sullivan, Henry Murray, George Kelly, Raymond B. Cattell, and social-learning representatives like Skinner.

[8]This is only a rule of thumb to which there are many exceptions. Prominent among them is the fact that clinicians often attempt to use *informal* procedures with data they see as correlates. As we saw in our attempted suicide case, the psychologist must somehow "mentally correlate" current information about a client with everything else she or he has heard, seen, or read about similar instances. This is a difficult task, as we shall see a bit later.

Table 4-2   Three Views of Assessment Data

Data seen as	Level of inference	Underlying theory	Source of data	Typical data processing procedures
Sign	High	Psychoanalytic or phenomenological	Interviews, tests, observations, life records	Informal; based on subjective judgments about assessment data
Sample	Low	Social-learning	Interviews, tests, observations, life records	Formal and informal; based on subjective judgments and functional analysis of client behavior
Correlate	Low to moderate	Variable	Interviews, tests, observations, life records	Formal; based on statistical analysis of assessment data

clinical psychology. The informal, subjective, strongly inferential approach is a direct reflection of Freud and his influence on clinicians' thinking. The formal, objective, data-based, statistical approach comes to the clinical field through its ties with experimental psychology and through the early work of Galton, Cattell, Binet and other psychometrically oriented pioneers. In the next part of this chapter we shall examine and evaluate the ways in which clinicians have sought to follow the subjective tradition of Freud and the objective tradition of Cattell as they make inferences about clinical assessment data.

The Process of Clinical Inference   The Hollywood image of clinical psychologists (and, of course, psychiatrists) is that of persons who are not only specially educated and trained but who are also primarily sign-oriented users of the informal approach to clinical inference. They are often portrayed as astute translators of obscure, apparently meaningless signs into clear and accurate statements about a person's past, present, or future: a kind of psychological Sherlock Holmes who can tell much from very little.

A typical example of this view appears in a 1949 film called *The Dark Past.* In it, a killer called "Mad Dog" (William Holden) and a gang of fellow prison escapees hold a psychologist, his family, and friends hostage in a remote cabin. The psychologist (Lee J. Cobb) saves the day by getting Mad Dog to talk about his life and his dreams and by noticing that one of the crook's hands is paralyzed. From these limited data, Cobb is guided by psychoanalytic theory to the correct conclusion: As a child, Mad Dog was responsible for his hated father's death, and now his crippled hand and murderous ways are symptoms of unconscious conflict about it. Mad Dog's hand immediately becomes normal after hearing Cobb's interpretation.

Clinical Intuition   To a certain extent, such fantastic inferential abilities do have their counterparts in fact. A well-known example is provided by Theodore Reik (1948) in his description of a session of psychoanalysis. The client was a young woman who was upset about the dissolution of her intimate relationship with a medical doctor:

> After a few sentences about the uneventful day, the patient fell into a long silence. She assured me that nothing was in her thoughts. Silence from me. After many minutes she complained about a toothache. She told me that she had been to the dentist yesterday. He had given her an injection and then had pulled a wisdom tooth. The spot was hurting again. New and longer silence. She pointed to my bookcase in the corner and said, "There's a book standing on its head."
>
> Without the slightest hesitation and in a reproachful voice I said, "But why did you not tell me that you had had an abortion?" The patient jumped up and looked at me as if I were a ghost. Nobody knew or could know that her lover, the physician, had performed an abortion on her. . . . (Reik, 1948, pp. 263–264)

Reik (1948) suggests that his correct inference from the data presented by the client (i.e., toothache, the injection by a dentist, the tooth extraction, the pain, the book "on its head") was based partly on an intuitive gift. It has long been supposed that clinical psychologists possess some of that same gift which, along with their special ways of thinking about people, their past experience, and their guiding theories, makes them superior at drawing high-level inferences from assessment data (Wallen, 1956).

This idealized notion stems in large degree from the reputation of Freud and his psychoanalytic followers, and it is still strongly evident today. As noted in Chapter 1, it is not unusual for a clinical psychologist to be asked if he or she is capable of reading minds, and it is even more common for the clinician to hear remarks like, "I'm not going to talk to you. You'll analyze everything I say!" It is true, of course, that certain individuals seem to be better than others at "picking up" and correctly interpreting assessment data (Sundberg, 1977), but this may not be universally descriptive of clinicians.[9]

As fact in the form of research evidence has overtaken popular fancy, the existence of special inferential capabilities among clinical psychologists has been seriously questioned. Meehl (1954, p. 28) suggests that "we have no right to assume that entering the clinic has resulted in some miraculous mutations and made us singularly free from the ordinary human errors which characterized our psychological ancestors." Peterson (1968a, p. 105) makes the point even more forcefully: "The idea that clinicians have or can develop some special kinds of antennae with which they can detect otherwise subliminal interpersonal stimuli and read from these the intrapsychic condition of another person is a myth which ought to be demolished."

---

[9]There have been attempts to establish the personal characteristics of "good judges of people" (e.g., Allport, 1961; Taft, 1955), but the attributes suggested (such as emotional adjustment, self-insight, social skill, and intelligence) have not yet been conclusively shown to be essential, nor have clinicians been shown to possess them in inordinately high proportions.

MISS PEACH   By Mell Lazarus

Cartoon 4-1 "Miss Peach" *(Miss Peach by Mell Lazarus. Courtesy of Mell Lazarus and Field Newspaper Syndicate)*

These statements reflect a large body of research which shows that when an informal approach to assessment data processing is used, clinical psychologists *as a group* (1) are not significantly better than nonclinicians at making inferences, and (2) do not make inferences which are any more accurate than could be obtained through formal, statistical procedures. To illustrate, we shall briefly review some data on the clinician versus nonclinician question and then look at some evidence related to the informal versus statistical issue.

The Clinician as Inference Expert   A classic example of research on the clinician's alleged special inference capabilities is provided by Goldberg (1959). In his study, various types of judges attempted to infer the presence or absence of organic brain damage from clients' responses to a psychological test which is widely used for such purposes. Half of the thirty clients who were judged were actually suffering organic problems; the other half were not. Test results were judged by (1) four Ph.D. clinical psychologists with 4 to 9 years' experience with the test, (2) ten M.A.-level psychology trainees who had used the test for from 1 to 4 years, and (3) eight VA hospital secretaries who had no psychology background and had never given or interpreted the test. Since the inference to be drawn from test data in this case was simply "organic" or "not organic" (of which there were fifteen cases each), the probability of being correct by chance on any given patient was .50. However, only one of the four psychologists did better than chance, and, as shown in Table 4-3, they were not any better than their students or their secretaries. In fact, the secretaries had the highest

Table 4-3   Inference Accuracy of Three Types of Judges

Group	N	% Correct	% Exceeding chance
Psychology staff	4	65	25
Psychology trainees	10	70	60
Secretaries	8	67	62
Total	22	68	54

Source: After Goldberg, 1959.

percentage of any group in terms of exceeding chance accuracy-levels. Other studies of this type conducted prior to and since the Goldberg (1959) experiment have been reviewed by Goldberg (1968a), Thorne (1972), and Wiggins (1973) and were found to present a basically similar picture. More recent data are consistent with those reviews (e.g., Garner & Smith, 1976; Levenberg, 1975).

The image of clinical psychologists as merely ordinary mortals has also been strengthened by research on their information processing ability. Studies by Kostlan (1954), Sines (1959), Golden (1964), Oskamp (1965), and Weiss (1963) suggest that having larger amounts of assessment information may increase clinicians *confidence* about inferences, but it does not necessarily improve their accuracy (see Einhorn & Hogarth, 1978 and Goldberg, 1968a for reviews). This is consistent with the notion that there simply are limits to how much data a person (clinician or nonclinician) can remember, process, and integrate, and that these limits plague the clinician who scans the vast array of assessment material which Levy (1963) calls the "psychometric matrix."

Thus, the psychologist may tend to be inordinately impressed with the first few pieces of information available and then forget or pay little attention to subsequent data (Dailey, 1952; Meehl, 1960; Sines, 1959). Or, like other people, the clinician may allow assessment information coming from certain sources (e.g., parents' report of a child's behavior) to outweigh other, contradictory information (McCoy, 1976).

Various kinds of personal bias can distort inferences. The clinician may react differently to males and females, to different age groups, or to members of certain socioeconomic, racial, or political groups (Abramovitz, Abramovitz, Jackson, & Gomes, 1973; Broverman, Broverman, Clarkson, Rosenkrantz, & Vogel, 1970; Chasen & Weinberg, 1975; DiNardo, 1975; Lee & Temerlin, 1970; Lewittes, Moselle, & Simmons, 1973; Routh & King, 1972). As suggested in Chapter 3, theoretical bias may also alter inference, since adherents of each major clinical model are likely to approach their clients with certain preconceptions about what behaviors to expect and what those behaviors mean (Pasamanick, Dinitz, & Lefton, 1959).

Further, general "folklore" and certain kinds of misremembered past experience can affect clinicians as strongly as anyone else. For example, a form of superstition called "illusory correlation" has been shown to operate in the realm of clinical inference (Chapman & Chapman, 1967; Golding & Rorer, 1972) very much the way it does in life in general. Just as your neighbor may falsely believe that it rains every time she or he washes the car, many clinical psychologists have long believed that the presence of elaborated eyes on tests that involve drawing the human figure is related to paranoid behavior in the artist, even though no firm empirical evidence for this belief exists (see, e.g., Fisher & Fisher, 1950). The fact that paranoid tendencies may still be inferred from such cues by some clinicians illustrates a type of error "to which most, or perhaps all, people are prone" (Chapman, 1971, p. 159).

The clinical psychologist may fall prey to many other influences which reduce inference accuracy. The situation in which inferences are made (e.g., school or mental hospital), the effects of fatigue, and the types of clients the clinician usually sees (and, thus, expects to see) provide additional variables (see, e.g., Beiri, Atkins, Briar, Leaman, Miller, & Tripoldi, 1966; Hunt & Jones, 1962; Thorne, 1972).

Clinical training typically received in graduate school may provide the future clinician with a lot of important and useful information and experience, but there is, unfortunately, very little evidence that it always does much to improve the ability to make accurate inferences (Hanks, 1936; Kelly & Fiske, 1951; Kremers, 1960). There are even some data available which suggest that certain aspects of clinical training may in some cases *decrease* inferential accuracy by prompting students to see problems where none exist. Soskin (1954) found, for example, that prior to taking a course on interpretation of the Thematic Apperception Test (TAT), beginning graduate students tended to see a well-adjusted person as well-adjusted. After the course, the students inaccurately saw such a client as somewhat troubled. Crow (1957) presents similarly negative evidence on the effects of certain types of clinical training.

The considerations we have reviewed so far led Wiggins (1973, p. 131) to conclude that there is "little empirical evidence that justifies the granting of 'expert' status to the clinician on the basis of his training, experience, or information processing ability."

Still, there *are* clinicians who, for whatever reasons, appear to be superior to their colleagues and intelligent lay persons in terms of inference accuracy. Is this some general, stable ability which these clinicians manifest in all cases, or is it sporadic and variable, depending upon the client, situation, and judgment task involved? The answer is not entirely clear. Some studies have shown general inferential abilities in certain persons (e.g., Cline & Richards, 1961), while other evidence suggests the opposite conclusion (e.g., Crow & Hammond, 1957). The truth may lie somewhere in between; a person's inference ability may be a joint function of some general skill as it interacts with situational variables (Bieri, Atkins, Briar, Leaman, Miller, & Tripoldi, 1966; Bruner & Taguiri, 1954; Taft, 1955). At this point, however, the correctness of this view and even the existence of general inference ability have not been clearly established (Krech, Crutchfield, & Balachey, 1962; Wiggins, 1973).

Inference by Formal versus Informal Procedures   We have seen that the Hollywood image of the clinician as a sign-oriented expert who subjectively, consistently, and often intuitively makes unerringly accurate inferences was badly tarnished in the 1950s and 1960s by research on clinical training, experience, and data processing ability. This sobering body of work was part of and largely prompted by research on a more general question about clinicians' inference ability. Many investigators wondered whether clinicians' subjective, informal efforts to interpret assessment data as signs or to mentally correlate those data with other facts are any more accurate than inferences based upon formal, statistical data processing techniques in which the clinician plays no part at all (see Gough, 1962 for a history of this question).

Because clinical psychology has roots in both the subjective and objective "camps," clinicians have traditionally been divided on the relative merits of "clinical" (subjective) and "statistical" (objective) inference procedures. Meehl (1954) notes that those who favor the informal, clinical approach see it as meaningful, organized, rich, deep, and genuine, while its critics characterize it as mystical, vague, unscientific, sloppy, and muddleheaded. Predictably, the proponents of formal, statistical inference think it is objective, reliable, precise, empirical, and sound, even though others label it artificial, trivial, superficial, rigid, and oversimplified.

More than a war of words is involved, however. The statistical versus clinical data processing issue is central to how clinicians (1) spend their time, (2) make decisions about clients, (3) shape their research, and (4) conceive of their professional identity and capabilities (Meehl, 1954). Clinicians who informally interpret psychological tests and other data, make recommendations based on their interpretations, and do research related to such activities usually do so because they believe that they (or at least their profession) are good at these things. Thus it came as a shock, to say the very least, when, in a 1954 monograph, University of Minnesota psychologist Paul Meehl reported on his review of twenty studies comparing the accuracy of predictive inferences based on informal, clinical procedures and formal, statistical procedures. He found that, in all but one case, the statistical approach equaled or surpassed the clinical approach. Later, even the sole exception to this surprising conclusion was called a tie, and, as additional research became available, the superiority of the statistical method of prediction was even more firmly established (Meehl, 1957, 1965). Table 4-4 shows the "box scores" and the kinds of variables predicted in studies covered by Meehl's reviews.

Wiggins (1973, p. 183) notes that "the impact of Meehl's review on clinical psychologists was nothing less than devastating." At least eighteen responses to it were published in the years immediately following its appearance, and most of them were critical. Detractors pointed out methodological defects in some of the reviewed studies which could have biased results in favor of statistical data processing procedures. Some felt that the variables being predicted (e.g., grades) were not like those typically dealt with by practicing psychologists (e.g., McArthur, 1956), while others suggested that the clinicians in several studies were handicapped by having inadequate or unfamiliar information about clients and about what they were supposed to predict (e.g., Holt, 1958, 1978). Thorne (1972, p. 44) put it this way: "The question must be not what naïve judges do with inappropriate tasks under questionable conditions of comparability with actual clinical situations, but what the most sophisticated judges can do with appropriate methods under ideal conditions."

The furor initiated by Meehl's conclusions and even the dark mutterings of how he had "sold the clinical approach up the river" (Holt, 1958, p. 1) could not negate the fact that inference based upon informal, subjective, "clinical" methods is not nearly as accurate as it was once assumed to be. However, this initially discouraging conclusion was not without positive aspects. Meehl's reviews, along with other reports on the clinician's limited capabilities have

Table 4-4   Summary of Outcomes of Studies Comparing Clinical Versus Statistical Predictive Inference

Source	Number of studies reviewed	Variables predicted	Outcome		
			Clinical better	Statistical better	Tie
Meehl (1954)	20	Success in school or military; recidivism or parole violation; recovery from psychosis	1*	11	8
Meehl (1957)	27	Same as above, plus personality description; therapy outcome	0	17	10
Meehl (1965)	51	Same as above, plus response to shock treatment; diagnostic label; job success and satisfaction; medical diagnosis	1†	33	17

*Later called a tie.
†Later called a tie by Goldberg (1968b).
Source: After Wiggins, 1973.

served, in the long run, to focus research attention on the problem and to advance knowledge, theory, and practice in assessment data processing. Two major lines of work have appeared in this regard.

Improving Informal Inference   The first involves investigation of how the best subjective clinical inferences are made, how they can be improved, and how they can be taught. For those engaged in this endeavor, unflattering research about clinicians' inference ability constituted a challenge, not a disaster. Thorne (1972, p. 44) suggests that "clinicians must become much more critical of the types of judgments they attempt to make, the selection of cues upon which judgments are based, and their modes of collecting and combining data." Work in these areas began in the 1960s as the clinical inference process began to undergo a kind of dissection. Researchers attempted to analyze its logic (e.g., Sarbin, Taft, & Bailey, 1960), relate it to social and physical judgment processes and errors (e.g., Bieri, Atkins, Briar, Leaman, Miller, & Tripoldi, 1966; Grossberg & Grant, 1978; Hunt & Jones, 1962), analyze the nature and influence of specific cues used by clinicians (e.g., Goldberg, 1968a; Hoffman, 1960; Oskamp, 1967), optimize the amount of assessment data to be processed (e.g., Bartlett & Green, 1966), and identify the conditions under which inference can be most reliable and valid (e.g., Watley, 1968). These efforts are continuing (e.g., Brehmer, 1976).

Using such research as a guide, it has been shown that subjective clinical inference accuracy can be improved over levels previously reported (e.g.,

Lewinsohn, Nichols, Pulos, Lomont, Nickel & Siskind, 1963), but the increment gained may not always justify the inordinate amount of extra effort and methodological sophistication required. Also, it may be that even the most superior human judges operating under optimal conditions are variable enough in their accuracy to raise questions about their suitability for the data processing task.

Consider, for example, a study by Kleinmuntz (1963) which involved distillation of the specific "rules" by which the very best clinical judges draw inferences. Knowing these "rules" could, theoretically at least, facilitate the training of less accurate, less experienced clinicians (Kagan, 1974). Kleinmuntz asked a recognized expert at drawing inferences from MMPI tests to "think aloud" while working with test results from a number of college-age subjects. The task was to decide whether each individual was "adjusted" or "maladjusted." The decision rules which emerged were transformed into a computer program which could then be used to score future subjects' MMPI scores.

The study showed that a good clinician's inference processes can be objectified (see also Nathan, 1967) and are thus potentially teachable, but it also revealed that the most appropriate "student" may be a computer; the machine used the "rules" perfectly and consistently with each new set of test data, and thus it actually did better at subsequent inference tasks than the clinician who had "taught" it! (Wiggins, 1973). Additional, related evidence for this conclusion is also presented by Goldberg (1970).

Improving Formal Inference   The performance of formal inference procedures has provided much of the impetus for the other important line of research in the "post-Meehl" era, namely the elaboration and improvement of techniques for the statistical processing of assessment data. Though it may seem that this second type of research would be likely to put clinicians out of a job, one of its by-products has been to map out the assessment tasks in which clinicians can be maximally effective.

Meehl (1954) and other reviewers and researchers in this area (e.g., Sawyer, 1966) have drawn a clear distinction between the clinical psychologist's roles in data *processing* versus data *collection*. In brief, they have highlighted the fact that, just as data processing can be formal or informal, assessment data collection can be done "mechanically" (i.e., with objective tests and life records) or subjectively (i.e., through unstructured interviews and informal observations). Thus, in a given assessment sequence, many combinations of subjective and statistical procedures are possible, and the clinician may be involved in different ways (see Table 4-5). When the studies reviewed by Meehl (1954, 1957, 1965) are reexamined in this light, as Sawyer (1966) did, it is clear that though clinicians may be generally inferior to statistical formulae at *processing* assessment data, they can make significant and often unique contributions by *collecting* and reporting their subjective judgments. The most accurate inferences found by Sawyer (1966) were based upon the formal, statistical processing of data collected by *both* mechanical and subjective techniques. "This suggests that

Table 4-5 Some Combinations of Formal and Informal Procedures for the Collection and Processing of Assessment Data.

Data collection procedure	Data processing procedure	Example
1 Formal	Formal	Psychological test scores processed by computer according to a statistical formula which predicts potential for behavior problems
2 Formal	Informal	Psychological test scores interpreted by clinician based on experience, theory, and "hunches" to establish psychiatric diagnosis
3 Informal	Formal	Clinician's subjective judgments (based on an interview) converted into quantitative ratings which are then processed by a computer or statistical formula to describe client's "personality"
4 Informal	Informal	Subjective impressions and judgments (from interviews, projective tests, etc.) interpreted subjectively to decide whether client needs to be hospitalized
5 Formal and Informal	Formal	Psychological test scores and clinician's subjective impressions and judgments all fed into computer which uses complex formula to describe client or make predictions about behavior
6 Formal and Informal	Informal	Psychological test scores and clinician's subjective impressions and judgments all scanned and interpreted by clinician to decide whether client is capable of standing trial for a crime

the clinician may be able to contribute most not by direct prediction, but rather by providing, in objective form, judgments to be combined mechanically" (Sawyer, 1966, p. 193). Thus, exploitation of the potential of formal data handling procedures has by no means shut the clinician out of the assessment process. "Sawyer's analysis reinforces Meehl's (1954) conclusion that the clinician is a highly inefficient *combiner* of data, but it also underscores the heretofore neglected contribution of the clinician as a valuable *source* of input data" (Wiggins, 1973, p. 198).

Recognition of this fact has led many practicing clinicians and researchers to focus on upgrading observational and other data *collection* skills in order to optimize the human role in clinical assessment. As an example, "clinical intuition" has been recast by many (e.g., Levy, 1963; Wallen, 1956) as skill at observing verbal and nonverbal cues coming from the client. As such, it can be developed, practiced, and improved.

At the same time, other investigators have been actively pursuing ways to expand and increase the accuracy of statistical, usually computer-oriented data processing methods. Some of these methods are thoroughly mechanical and empirical; e.g., a client's objective test scores are interpreted according to formulae which have been derived from statistical relationships between other clients' test scores and behavior (see category 1 in Table 4-5). In effect, the computer (or the diligent clinician) takes the client's test profile and "looks up" the characteristics of other people with similar profiles. Development of this type of "purely actuarial" program is difficult and expensive because it requires a large backlog of test and observational data from hundreds of previous clients. For this reason, such programs are few in number and focused only on the most popular tests, such as the MMPI (see Gilberstadt & Duker, 1965; Marks & Seeman, 1963; Sines, 1966).

To help fill in the many gaps where appropriate statistical formulae are not yet available, a kind of "hybrid" system of formal data processing has evolved. The Kleinmuntz (1963) study provides an example of this approach. In general, it involves having a computer interpret assessment data, not through use of a statistically derived formula but on the basis of clinicians' experience and theoretical beliefs which have been transformed into decision "rules." Wiggins (1973) refers to this process as "automating clinical lore." Even though this may not be an entirely empirical strategy, it may be more accurate (and certainly cheaper and more convenient) to employ a "hybrid" system than to have a human clinician interpret every test.

Indeed, the use of "hybrid" computer programs for scoring major psychological tests has become an extremely popular enterprise which can be quite lucrative for its purveyors (see Box 4-5). These programs vary considerably in their sophistication and quality, but, ideally, as more empirical data become available, automated test-interpretation systems which depend on use of "clinical lore" for decision rules will be replaced by even more adequate actuarial packages (Fowler, 1969; Wiggins, 1973).

The time and expense associated with formal, statistical approaches to assessment data processing are not their only drawbacks. Critics such as Hunt & Jones (1962) and Levy (1963) have suggested the following additional limitations and problems:

1 Actuarial techniques can be applied only where adequately developed, fully standardized assessment devices and inference formulae are available. At the moment such devices and formulae are the exception, not the rule (see Goldberg, 1974).

2 There is a certain amount of public distrust of inferences and decisions made about people on the basis of mechanical (especially computer) techniques.

Box 4-5   Sample Automated Psychological Test Report

ROCHE PSYCHIATRIC SERVICE INSTITUTE
MMPI REPORT

CASE NO: 00000   RPSI NO: 0000
AGE 37 MALE

The test items appear to have been answered truthfully with no effort to deny or exaggerate.

This patient appears to be currently depressed and anxious. He shows a pattern which is frequent among psychiatric patients. Feelings of inadequacy, sexual conflicts and rigidity are accompanied by a loss of efficiency, initiative and self confidence. Insomnia is likely, along with chronic fatigue. He is anxious, tense, and overly sensitive. Suicidal thoughts are a possibility. In the clinical picture, depression predominates. Psychiatric patients with this pattern are likely to be diagnosed as depressive reaction or anxiety reaction. The characteristics are resistant to change, although symptomatic relief may be obtained with brief treatment.

He tends to be pessimistic and complaining, and is likely to be defeatist, cynical, and unwilling to stick with treatment. He may need frequent reassurance about his medical condition. Dynamically, he is a narcissistic and self-centered person who is rigid in thought and action and easily upset in social situations.

Repression and denial are utilized as a defense against anxiety. In periods of heightened stress his anxiety is likely to be expressed in somatic symptoms. He may respond to suggestion and reassurance.

He is a self controlled, cautious person who may be somewhat feminine in his interest patterns. He is idealistic, socially perceptive, and responsive. He shows some self awareness, but he is sensitive and prone to worry. He is verbally fluent, persuasive and able to communicate ideas clearly.

This person is hesitant to become involved in social situations. He makes an effort to conscientiously carry out his responsibilities, but he is retiring and somewhat withdrawn from interpersonal relationships.

Source: Wiggins, J., *Personality and Prediction,* © 1973, Addison-Wesley, Reading, Mass. Table 5–7. Reprinted with permission.

3   New and creative discoveries about human behavior are less likely to occur if human clinicians become less involved in assessment data processing.

4   Relegation of clinicians to the data collection role decreases the chances of future improvement of human data processing skills.

5   Exclusion of the clinician from the data processing role reduces the probability that rare behavioral events and relationships will be noticed since actuarial tables and statistical formulae may not be set up to handle them.

6   Certain kinds of assessment may be more appropriately dealt with by informal means. Levy (1963) suggests that specific, "bounded" questions (e.g., will this person be likely to abuse children?) may most adequately be answered by formal data processing, while more general "unbounded" concerns (e.g., what is this person like?) are best handled through informal means.

Indeed, Levy (1963, p. 176) argues that "failure to make the bounded-unbounded distinction . . . is responsible for much of current controversy over the utility of actuarial as opposed to clinical prediction. . . . In the unbounded case, we have . . . no choice but to rely upon the clinician's deductive capacities; in the bounded case we do have this choice and can never justify not making it in favor of the statistician." Though there is still considerable disagreement over exactly what assessment questions and roles human clinicians should try to handle, Wiggins's (1973, p. 199) summary of the present situation provides a positive concluding note: "Clinicians need not view themselves as second-rate IBM machines unless they choose to engage in activities that are more appropriately performed by such machines. In the realm of clinical observation and hypothesis formation, the IBM machine will never be more than a second-rate clinician."

The Social-Learning Approach to Assessment   In the last few sections, we have seen that clinical psychologists have traditionally been concerned with formal and informal processing of assessment data which are viewed as signs or correlates. In that tradition, assessment information is interpreted in terms of psychological traits or intrapsychic dynamics, and the clinician's goal is often a prediction about the client or an abstract summary description of the client's "personality."

Clinical psychologists who adopt a social-learning model of behavior have not found these time-honored assessment concepts very appealing. Their main criticisms and alternative formulations are summarized in the following points:

1   The use of assessment data as *signs* of personality traits or psychody-namic characteristics involves too much inference and thus leaves too much room for error. In fact, social-learning advocates do not even see "personality traits," "psychological dispositions," or "personality dynamics"as useful concepts for learning about people. This is partly because, in their view, such dispositional constructs exist only in the eye and mind of the clinician who invents and uses them (Jones & Nisbett, 1971; Mischel, 1968), and partly because, "real" or not, these constructs do not seem to have much utility for accurately describing people, predicting their behavior, or planning and evaluating behavior change programs (see Bandura, 1969, Bersoff, 1973, Mischel, 1968, and Peterson, 1968a, for reviews of research supporting this view).

In fact, social-learning writers argue that part of the reason for clinicians' traditionally poor showing as data processors is that they have tended to rely upon vague trait and dynamic concepts as the bases for inferences which stray dangerously far from initial assessment information. When studies such as those of Grayson and Tolman (1950), Siskind (1967), and Auger (1974) show that clinicians do not share common definitions for important terms like "anxiety," "aggression," "ego," and "hostility," the existence of other studies reporting low reliability and validity for inferences about diagnostic labels or personality traits (e.g., Ash, 1949; Goldberg & Werts, 1966; Ullmann & Hunrichs, 1958) is easier to understand.

In view of their questionable utility, trait, state, and other dispositional concepts are seen by social-learning assessors as merely adding confusing, inference-laden, and ultimately superfluous labels to behavior samples which do not need them. For example, suppose a little girl kicks her Barbie doll across the room. Observation of that incident is seen as valuable in and of itself, and it is not improved or made more meaningful by calling it "hostility" or part of the child's "need for aggression" (Bijou & Peterson, 1971).

Accordingly, the social-learning model suggests close adherence to available data as samples of client capabilities (Wallace, 1966, 1967) rather than as bases for inference about personality traits or dynamic states. Mischel (1968, p. 10) encapsulated this idea by noting that "the emphasis is on what a person *does* in situations rather than on inferences about what attributes he *has*." Thus even the results of standard trait or dynamically oriented tests would be seen as behavior samples, not glimpses into personality or the unconscious (e.g., Goldfried, Stricker, & Weiner, 1971; Greenspoon & Gersten, 1967).

2   In spite of the early efforts of Murray (1938) and Rapaport (Rapaport, Gill, & Schafer, 1945), dispositional assessment concepts have tended to isolate people's behavior from the environment in which it occurs. Since behavior is learned in a social context, one cannot describe or predict that behavior accurately unless situational factors are systematically taken into account: A man who displays dominance on a psychological test may behave quite differently with his boss. Both the person and the environment are seen as vitally important in social-learning assessment, so the focus of data collection includes (1) client behavioral capabilities, (2) characteristics of the physical and social environment in which behavior occurs, and (3) the nature of *client-environment* interactions. This "person-situation" orientation makes the social-learning view of assessment attentive to the writings of those who emphasize the importance of environmental characteristics (e.g., Barker, 1963, 1968; Craik, 1971, 1973; Frederiksen, 1972; Moos, 1975) and compatible with broader "systems approaches" to behavior (Miller, 1971; Sundberg, 1977) in which all levels of human activity from the individual cell to international politics are seen as related, interacting components which cannot be meaningfully dealt with in isolation (Peterson, 1968a).

3   Traditional assessment practices promote an unhealthy separation between data collection and data use. Too often, assessment information is processed into descriptions or predictions which are not useful or relevant for planning or evaluating behavior-change strategies and techniques. Assessment for the sake of doing assessment is seen as a dead-end street. Social-learning writers document this point by citing research which shows that diagnostic labels often do not determine hospitalization or treatment (Bannister, Salmon, & Lieberman, 1964; Cole & Magnussen, 1966; Mendel & Rapaport, 1969) and that traditionally oriented therapists often pay little attention to the client assessment data which are available (Dailey, 1953; Meehl, 1960).

From the social-learning perspective, clinical assessment of behavior is inextricably tied to efforts at altering that behavior for the better. Toward this end, clients, situations, and client-situation interactions are described on dimensions which (1) are as precise and data-based as possible, (2) have clear and direct implications for treatment planning, and (3) can be continuously monitored during and after treatment. Thus, rather than describing a particular child's problem in vague, trait-oriented terms like "aggressiveness" or "hyperactivity," assessment would focus on the *frequencies, durations,* or *intensities* with which specific acts (e.g., striking others, running around the room) occur, the settings in which these acts appear, and the environmental factors by which they appear to be elicited and reinforced.

In general, then, the questions asked during social-learning assessment are not oriented toward *why* a person behaves in a particular way, but *what* she or he does, and *when, where,* and under what *circumstances* the activity occurs (Ullmann & Krasner, 1975). When behavior is described in this fashion, change tactics can flow directly from assessment. If assessment suggests that Sally's high-frequency whining in the classroom may be reinforced by teacher attention, a program to terminate reward of the maladaptive behavior and plan reinforcement of more appropriate alternative behaviors might be instituted. As that program begins, its effect upon the variables identified in the initial assessment would be observed and used as a guide for continuing, altering, or terminating the intervention.[10] Thus, in clinical practice, the social-learning model provides little encouragement for the clinician who engages in abstract assessment activities which are not part of an overall behavior-change effort.

The concepts and research evidence reflected in the three points just covered underlie the fundamental social-learning argument that descriptions of and predictions about behavior based upon sample-oriented assessment are more meaningful and accurate than those stemming from traditional sign-oriented assessment. In further support of their views, social-learning advocates cite other beneficial trends and empirical data:

1 Because troubled clients are not viewed by social-learning clinicians as "abnormal" or "sick," their behavior is simply described (and even classified) in objective, functional terms, thus avoiding the lasting social stigma of pejorative diagnostic or personality trait labels (Ullmann & Krasner, 1975).

2 The quality of research on the mechanisms and effects of various psychological treatments has improved greatly as a function of incorporating objective social-learning-based assessment procedures into experimental designs (Paul, 1969a).

3 The meaning of terms commonly used to describe or classify behavior problems (such as "anxiety," "incompetence," and "unassertiveness") has become clearer and more objective as a result of social-learning assessment strategies which link such general terms to specific behaviors in specific situations (e.g., Goldfried & D'Zurilla, 1969; Lang, 1968; MacDonald, 1978; Schwartz & Gottman, 1976).

4 There is a considerable body of evidence which shows that prediction of future behavior is more accurate when based on low-inference data (e.g.,

---

[10]Some psychiatrists are beginning to employ the Problem-Oriented Record (POR), an assessment approach which parallels social-learning procedures in several respects (Hersen, 1976; Wolf, 1977).

objective biographical, demographic, and behavioral characteristics) as opposed to higher-inference personality trait or test score data (e.g., Fulkerson & Barry, 1961; Goldfried & Kent, 1972; Mischel, 1973). Mischel (1968, p. 135) summarized research on this point by saying that "a person's relevant past behaviors tend to be the best predictors of . . . future behavior in similar situations."

In spite of its broad appeal and demonstrated value in clinical and research contexts, the social-learning approach to assessment is not without its critics. As might be expected, clinicians not enamored with the social-learning model tend to see objective assessment of overt behaviors in relation to specific environmental situations as too narrow and certainly inadequate for tapping the various personality traits, dynamics, and dimensions presumed to operate in their own models (e.g., Breger & McGaugh, 1965). More relevant critiques have also been advanced, however, and they have come in large measure from within (or near) the social-learning "camp" itself.

Most of the concerns stem from the fact that the social-learning approach to assessment is still in an early and rather primitive stage of development (Ciminero, 1977; Hersen & Bellack, 1976). Its specific methods are extremely diverse and often not well standardized or otherwise psychometrically sophisticated when compared to, say, psychological tests like the MMPI (Dickson, 1975; Franks, 1976; Goldfried & Linehan, 1977; Wiggins, 1973). Social learning assessments tend to be used rather inconsistently by different practitioners (Cautela & Upper, 1976; Kanfer, 1972) who, like other clinicians operating without benefit of formal actuarial formulae, often depend upon their own subjective judgment to interpret the data they collect (Wiggins, 1973). Also, though social-learning assessment provides excellent descriptions of behavior which can be used as a guide for treatment planning, it has not resolved the question of what behaviors constitute a "problem" and who sets up the definitions (Hawkins, 1975; Klein, Dittman, Parloff, & Gill, 1969; Mash & Terdal, 1976). Further, it has not yet reached a level of sophistication which allows for reliable, empirically determined choice of specific treatment techniques, especially in complex cases (Ciminero, 1977; Dickson, 1975; Goldfried & Davison, 1976; Mash & Terdal, 1976). These criticisms reveal the many unanswered questions which remain to be dealt with by social-learning oriented assessors (Goldfried & Sprafkin, 1974).

More comprehensive and detailed presentations of the theory, practice, and problems of social-learning assessment are available in several recent volumes (Ciminero, Calhoun, & Adams, 1977; Cone & Hawkins, 1977; Haynes, 1978; Hersen & Bellack, 1976; Keefe, Kopel, & Gordon, 1978; Mash & Terdal, 1976; Nay, 1979).

Phenomenology and Assessment   Many of the objections raised by social-learning theorists to traditional assessment concepts and procedures relate not only to their apparent lack of clinical, theoretical, or research utility, but also to the belief that people should not become the passive objects of study. They should not be placed in a "one-down" status, examined apart from their physical and social environment, and burdened with labels that focus on problems and weaknesses to the exclusion of potentials and strengths. In this respect the social-learning and phenomenological models are in accord. However, in line with their subjective, relationship-oriented approach, clinicians adopting a phenomenological model have suggested assessment alternatives which differ substantially from those outlined in the last section (e.g., Brown, 1972; Dana & Leech, 1974).

Some of them (e.g., Rogers, 1951) have argued against doing any assessment at all on the grounds that such procedures are inherently dehumanizing, take responsibility away from clients, and pose a threat to the quality of vital clinician-client relations. Advocates of this position are unlikely even to review assessment data which have been collected and processed by others. The assumption here is that all necessary knowledge of the client will emerge during specially conducted interviews. The characteristics of these interviews will be described in Chapters 5 and 11.

Other phenomenologists raise the possibility that assessment data *collected* through traditional sources such as personality tests can sometimes be useful clinically if they are *processed* in line with humanistic principles. For example, instead of being used to derive summary scores or abstract personality profiles, test data can be viewed as clues to how a client looks at the world (e.g., Bugental, 1963; Dana & Leech, 1974; May, 1958). In the same vein, traditional assessment data collection procedures can provide opportunities for the clinician and client to build their relationship. By discussing assessment data with the client and using these interactions as a jumping-off point for further exploration, the clinician not only shares knowledge openly, but reveals personal reactions to it, thus helping to cement a lasting partnership (Dana & Leech, 1974; Fischer, 1970; Mosak & Gushurst, 1972).

These notions are taken a step farther by phenomenologists who feel that traditional assessment devices are not ideally suited for use as relationship facilitators. They have developed and employed specialized instruments which they feel will do the job better. These include forms like the Personal Orientation Inventory (Shostrom, 1968), an "existential mental health questionnaire" (Kotchen, 1960), the Purpose-in-Life Test (Crumbaugh, 1968), and the "Who-are-you?" test (Bugental & Zelen, 1950).

Communicating Assessment Data

We have seen that raw bits of information about a client's behavior must be processed in some way before they become psychologically meaningful. However, the value of processed assessment data may still be limited unless they are organized and presented in some coherent way. This organized presentation of assessment results and the data upon which they are based are usually called a *psychological report* because, in the days when clinicians were primarily in "assessment-only" roles, the fruits of their labor were turned over to teachers, psychiatrists, and others in written form. This kind of "reporting" to other professionals is still a significant part of clinical psychology, but it is also true that many clinicians now write assessment summaries for their own use.

In either case, if the results of assessment are to have maximal value they must be presented in a way which is *clear, relevant* to the goal of assessment, and *useful* to the intended "consumer." This is often more easily said than done, and clinicians must constantly guard against a variety of problems which can make reports vague, irrelevant, and useless. To illustrate, consider the following "personality sketch." It is not as extensive as most assessment reports, but several of its characteristics are relevant to our discussion:

> You are a person of varied interests, although you pour most of your energy into a few activities that mean the most to you. In general, you show a well-balanced outlook and disposition, but when frustrated you can display temper. With those you know well you are spontaneous and expressive, but often you keep your feelings very much to yourself. You have a few defects in personality that you are aware of, particularly in connection with dealing with people. You are persistent enough, however, to achieve success in dealing with these faults. There are times when you worry too much. You will find that it suits you better to take things as they come and to show more confidence in your own future. (Wallen, 1956, p. 42)

At first glance, this sketch may appear fairly clear, relevant for describing the person in question, and reasonably useful overall. Closer examination will reveal that this is not the case. First, the terms used (such as "balanced outlook" and "defects in personality") are vague and can mean different things to different readers. Second, the statements made are so generally applicable that they are not relevant for the description of a particular individual. The combination of vagueness and generality in the sketch makes it virtually useless as a means of increasing understanding of the person described.

Careful examination of actual assessment reports often exposes the same types of problems. Let us first consider some of these problems in more specific terms and then discuss a few ideas for dealing with them.

Clarity of Reports   The first concern in preparing an assessment report must be for clarity because without this basic attribute relevance and usefulness cannot even be evaluated. This is a major problem in all human communication (Korsch & Negrete, 1972; Newman, 1974), but its impact in clinical situations is particularly strong because misinterpretation of a report can lead to misguided decisions. Hammond and Allen (1953, p. v) cite a valuable case in point:

> A young girl, mentally defective, was seen for testing by the psychologist, who reported to the social agency that the girl's test performance indicated moderate success and happiness for her in "doing things with her hands." Three months later, however, the social agency reported to the psychologist that the girl was not responding well. Although the social agency had followed the psychologist's recommendations, the girl was neither happy nor successful "doing things with her

hands." When the psychologist inquired what kinds of things, specifically, the girl had been given to do he was told "We gave her music lessons—on the saxophone."

This was not what the psychologist had had in mind for the girl, but he did not make himself clear. A related problem exists when the assessor uses jargon which the reader may not understand. Consider the following excerpt from a report on a 36-year-old man cited by Mischel (1968, p. 105):

> Test results emphasize a basically characterological problem with currently hyste-roid defenses. Impairment of his ability to make adequate use of independent and creative fantasy, associated with emotional lability and naivete, are characteristic of him. He has difficulty in repressing his unacceptable feelings and wishes, and is in the unfortunate position of being unable to make adequate use of fantasy as an alternate control. . . . Due to markedly passive-aggressive character make-up, in which the infantile dependency needs are continually warring with his hostile tendencies, it is not difficult to understand his current conflict over sexual expression.

Indeed, the writer may feel he understands the client; the question is, does the reader understand the writer? Anyone not well versed in psychoanalytic terminology would probably find such a report mystifying and, as we saw earlier, even professional colleagues may not agree on the meaning of the terms employed (see, e.g., Grayson & Tolman, 1950).[11] Readers of psychological reports also highlight factors such as excessive length (or excessive brevity), inclusion of large amounts of technical information (e.g., statistics or esoteric test scores), and lack of coherent organization as contributing to lack of communication clarity (Olive, 1972; Tallent & Reiss, 1959).

Relevance to Goals   The second basic requirement of a valuable assessment report is that it contain material which is *relevant* to the goal which prompted the assessment enterprise in the first place. If that goal was to classify the client's behavior, information relevant to a classification system would be of great importance in a report. A recommendation regarding classification could be of value as well. If description of the client's current biological, psychological, behavioral, or environmental assets and liabilities was the purpose of assessment, the report or summary should contain that description. Similarly, when a prediction about the client is desired, the assessment report should attempt to provide it, if possible. If opinions, recommendations, suggestions, or even educated guesses are requested, these should appear, unless the clinician believes that no sound basis for them exists.

These are simple, almost self-evident prescriptions, but, especially when the clinician's report is for someone else's use, assessment objectives sometimes get

---

[11]Though it may be the most frequent offender (Tallent, 1976) psychoanalytic jargon should not be singled out for criticism. Writers representing social-learning and phenomenological positions can be just as obscure in their use of language (Hallenstein, 1978).

lost. This is sometimes due to the fact that explicit goals were never stated. Although the procedure is no longer as common as it once was, clinicians may still be asked for "psychologicals" (usually a standard test battery) without being told why assessment is being done. Under such circumstances, the chances of writing a relevant report are minimal. A similar problem exists when the purpose of assessment is stated in vague terms such as, "Is this woman capable of making a good adjustment outside the hospital?" Until the assessor knows what is meant by "good," "adjustment," and exactly where "outside the hospital" is, the report may not be relevant to the assessment goal.

Unfortunately, however, there are some cases in which lack of relevance in psychological reports is due mainly to the clinician's failure to keep clearly stated objectives in mind. When this happens, the report may be a better reflection of the assessor's theoretical bias and personal style than of the client's behavior. The influence of the clinician's personal problems and perceptions on psychological reports has been documented by Filer (1952), Hammer & Piotrowski (1953), and Robinson and Cohen (1954).

Usefulness of Reports   Finally, one must ask if an assessment report or summary is useful. Does the information it contains really add anything specific and important to what we already know about the client? It is entirely possible for a report to contain very clear, highly relevant information which is already at hand through other sources. Or, a report may *sound* useful at first, but actually contain little of real value. Useless reports of either type are usually ignored, but are still written all too often (e.g., Dailey, 1953; Hartlage, Freeman, Horine, & Walton, 1968; Meehl, 1960; Mintz, 1968; Storrow, 1967; Thorne, 1972).

Reporting problems appear mainly because the assessor has either (1) not collected and processed useful information or (2) not made useful statements about the data which are available. In the former case, the clinician may have employed information-gathering techniques which are low on what Sechrest (1963) calls *incremental validity*. For example, a report may conclude on the basis of several psychological tests that a client "has strong hostile tendencies and weak control over them." If the client has already been convicted as an ax-murderer, such information provides no increment in knowledge and is functionally useless except as a confirmation of what was already strongly suspected.

In other instances, the assessor's report may have limited usefulness simply because it says nothing specific or remarkable beyond that which would be expected on the basis of general past experience, logic, and "common sense." One aspect of this issue has been called the "base-rate problem." It refers to the fact that certain kinds of things tend to be true about certain types of clients (e.g., college professors do a lot of reading) and that, if an assessment report fails to provide information which goes beyond these known base rates, it may not be useful.

A dramatic example of how knowledge of base rates in a certain population can facilitate the creation of useless though often impressive reports has been given by Sundberg, Tyler, & Taplin (1973, pp. 577–579). A clinician wrote the report which follows *without ever having seen the client*. The material contained in it is often fairly specific but is based entirely on two pieces of information: (1) that the client is a new admission to a Veterans Administration hospital and (2) that the case was to be discussed at a convention session entitled "A Case Study of Schizophrenia." In edited form, the report said:

> This veteran approached the testing situation with some reluctance. He was cooperative with the clinician, but mildly evasive on some of the material. Both the tests and the past history suggest considerable inadequacy in interpersonal relations, particularly with members of his family. It is doubtful whether he has ever had very many close relationships with anyone. . . . He has never been able to sink his roots deeply. He is immature, egocentric, and irritable, and often he misperceives the good intentions of the people around him. . . . He tends to be basically passive and dependent, though there are occasional periods of resistance and rebellion against others. . . . Vocationally, his adjustment has been very poor. Mostly he has drifted from one job to another. His interests are shallow and he tends to have poor motivation for his work. Also he has had a hard time keeping his jobs because of difficulty in getting along with fellow employees. Although he has had some relations with women, his sex life has been unsatisfactory to him. At present, he is mildly depressed. . . . His intelligence is close to average, but he is functioning below his potential. . . . Test results and case history . . . suggest the diagnosis of schizophrenic reaction, chronic undifferentiated type. Prognosis for response to treatment appears to be poor.

In writing this "report" the clinician relied heavily upon knowledge of VA hospital residents in general and upon familiarity with hospital procedures. For example, the client's relative psychological complexity was assumed because he had been referred for testing. Presumably this would not have been done in a "clear-cut" case. Also, the description given fits the "average" VA resident and thus is likely to be at least partially accurate. Further, since the case was to be discussed at a meeting on schizophrenia and since schizophrenic diagnoses are very common for VA residents, the correct classification label was fairly easy to surmise. Finally, since certain characteristics (e.g., inadequacy of interpersonal relations) are commonly thought to be typical of schizophrenics, these could be included with a high degree of confidence. In fact, the report written by a clinician who actually saw the client for assessment was very similar to the "base-rate" report (Sundberg, 1977).

This bogus document exemplifies another common feature of assessment communications which tends to reduce their usefulness: overgenerality, or the tendency to write in terms which are so broad and ambiguous that they can be true of almost anyone. One clinician of the authors' acquaintance calls this "vague-ing it up." Documents heavily laden with overly general statements have been dubbed "Barnum Reports," "Aunt Fanny Reports," or "Madison Avenue Reports" (Klopfer, 1960; Meehl, 1956; Tallent, 1958). They are similar in style to the personality sketch presented at the beginning of this section. Like the base-rate report, overly general material has the dual disadvantage of spuriously increasing a report's acceptability and impressiveness while actually decreasing its usefulness. Even though the Barnum style, all-purpose personality sketch presented earlier may not appear obviously valueless, reports not unlike it have been shown to be acceptable to and often valued by both professional and nonprofessional report consumers (e.g., Delprato, 1975; Forer, 1949; Greene, 1977; Snyder, 1974; Snyder & Larson, 1972; Snyder, Shenkel & Lowery, 1977; Stagner, 1958; Sundberg, 1955; O'Dell, 1972; Ulrich, Stachnik, & Stainton, 1963).

Presenting Assessment Data   If the foregoing material has left the impression that writing valuable assessment reports and summaries requires great care,

---

Box 4-6   An Incomplete List of Potential Topics and Issues for Use in Organizing Assessment Reports and Summaries

---

Achievement	Intellectual controls
Aggressiveness	Intellectual level
Antisocial tendencies	Interests
Anxieties	Interpersonal relations
Aptitudes	Interpersonal skills
Attitudes	Life-style
Aversions	Molar surface behavior
Awarenesses	Needs
Background factors	Outlook
Behavioral problems	Perception of environment
Biological factors	Perception of self
Cognitive functioning	Personal consequences of behavior
Cognitive skills	Placement prospects
Cognitive style	Psychopathology
Competency	Rehabilitation needs
Conative factors	Rehabilitation prospects
Conflicts	Sentiments
Content of consciousness	Sex
Defenses	Sex identity
Deficits	Sex role
Developmental factors	Significant others
Diagnostic considerations	Situational factors
Drives, dynamics	Social consequences of behavior
Emotional cathexes	Social role
Emotional controls	Social stimulus value
Emotivity	Social structure
Fixations	Special assets
Flexibility	Subjective feeling states
Frustrations	Symptoms
Goals	Treatment prospects
Hostility	Value system
Identity	Vocational topics

Source: Norman Tallent, *Psychological Report Writing,* © 1976, p. 114. Reprinted by permission of Prentice-Hall, Inc., Englewood Cliffs, New Jersey.

it has served its purpose well. Clinicians must constantly maneuver around the problems we have outlined. Often they are successful; sometimes they are not. While there is no single "right" way to present assessment data in all instances, there are some guidelines worth noting.

First, of course, is the admonition to keep the criteria of clarity, relevance, and usefulness in mind as reports and summaries are being prepared. This may be made easier by the use of some type of outline. The specific characteristics of this outline will probably be organized around the topics and issues which the clinician believes to be most important theoretically and (ideally) which are most pertinent to the goal of assessment. In fact, the report outline is often nothing more than a reorganization of the topics which originally guided the assessment process; it is designed to cover each of those topics with a degree of emphasis commensurate with its relevance and in a sequence which is logical and comprehensible to the reader. As shown in Box 4-6, the number of potential topics is large and theory-based. Any two clinicians' report outlines may be slightly or radically different depending upon their theoretical orientations and personal preferences. It would be impossible to give examples of all possible report outlines, so we shall consider just a few representatives of the three main models of clinical psychology. Illustrations of the reports or summaries which might be based upon each outline will also be presented.

A Psychodynamic Report　The following dynamically oriented outline is an edited version of the one used by Tallent (1976, pp. 121–122) for reporting on his assessment of a young man who had been in trouble with the law for "bookie" activities and assault:

    I Conflicts
        A Self-perception
        B Goals
        C Frustrations
        D Interpersonal relations
        E Perception of environment
        F Drives, dynamics
        G Emotional cathexes
        H Emotional controls
   II Social stimulus value
        A Cognitive skills
        B Conative factors
        C Goals
        D Social role
  III Cognitive functioning
        A Deficit
        B Psychopathology
  IV Defenses
        A Denial
        B Interpersonal tactics
        C Fantasy

Box 4-7   Example of an Assessment Report Based on a Psychodynamically Oriented Outline

This man is most readily understood in terms of his unusually passive, dependent approach to life and his attempts to overcome the deeply unhappy state brought about by this personality limitation.

Mr. A does not feel very adequate as a person, an attitude which is developed through experiencing a continual sense of failure in terms of his own goals, and which apparently is reinforced by others. In fact, his relations with his father very likely are the basic reason for such feeling. This person is seen by the patient as cold, rejecting, punishing, and unapproachable. He has an urge to rebel and fight against this person—an urge which has been generalized to all society, but he is afraid to give vent to his impulses. Whatever emotional support he does get (got) seems to be from the mother.

As others see him, he seems to have the essential capacity to do well if only he would try. He scores at the average level on a test of intelligence (IQ: 106), he is able to learn readily, when he wants to, and on occasion can perform unusually fast and effectively. Yet he does not typically follow through on this advantage. His willingness, sometimes even his desire, to do well fluctuates, so that in the long run he could not be regarded as a constructive or responsible person.

Other personality deficiencies also compromise his functioning. Under stress or when faced with difficult problems he becomes blocked, confused and indecisive. His thinking does not show sufficient flexibility to meet such situations so that he would be regarded as inadaptable and unspontaneous.

Mr. A's felt inadequacy causes him to feel that he is not as good as others. By way of reassuring himself on this matter he frequently during examination makes remarks that he is "like everybody else." The feeling that he is inferior includes also the sexual area where he is quite confused about his maleness. It is likely that one or more sex problems contribute to his sense of failure, although, quite understandably, he denies this and indicates a satisfactory sex life "like everybody else."

He hardly experiences the full effect of his failures, however. He protects himself by denying many events of reality, by keeping many facts about himself and others unconscious, by a general attitude of "not knowing"—an attitude of naiveness. He can hardly take corrective action about himself because he does not understand himself or his actions, or recognize the nature of his problems. Oddly enough, as already stated, this is an unhappy person, but he does not adequately recognize this fact nor does he appear to others as depressed. Yet on occasion this might be a factor in his behavior which could be personally or socially unfortunate.

This man's insecurity about himself forces him into a receptive orientation to other people. He must have friends to provide support. To achieve this he presents himself in a positive, correct light, tries to say the "right" things and even to be ingratiating and obsequious. It is important that he create the "right" effect and may resort to dramatic behavior to bring this about. "Friends" are so important to him that he sometimes must take abuse in order to hold them. He must always hold back hostile expression.

But it is perhaps in fantasy where the greatest satisfaction is derived. He dreams of being a "success" (his term)—accumulating enough money by the age of 35 so he can retire and effortlessly enjoy the comforts of the world. In his fantasy he is independent of authority, can openly express the aggression he ordinarily cannot, and flout society. He has no positive feelings about social rules (although he may profess to), but is concerned when apprehended for misconduct, possibly less for the real punishment than for how it "looks" to be known for doing what he is afraid to do. It is little wonder then that he is easy prey for an "easy money" scheme.

Source: Norman Tallent, *Psychological Report Writing,* © 1976, pp. 121–122. Reprinted by permission of Prentice-Hall, Inc., Englewood Cliffs, New Jersey.

The report based upon this outline is presented in Box 4-7.

A Social-Learning Report   Pomeranz and Goldfried (1970) describe an assessment summary outline which is fairly representative of the social-learning model. An edited version appears below:

I   Description of client's physical appearance and behavior during assessment
II Presenting problems
   A   Nature of problems
   B   Historical background of problems
   C   Current situational determinants of problems
   D   Relevant organismic variables
      1   Physiological states
      2   Effects of medication
      3   Cognitive determinants of problems
   E   Dimensions of problems
      1   Duration
      2   Pervasiveness
      3   Frequency
      4   Magnitude
   F   Consequences of problems
      1   Positive
      2   Negative
III Other problems (observed by assessor but not stated by client)
IV   Personal Assets
V   Targets for change
VI   Recommended treatments
VII Client motivation for treatment
VIII Prognosis
IX   Priority for treatment
X   Client expectancies
   A   About solving specific problems
   B   About treatment enterprise in general
XI   Other comments

The use of this outline for summarizing assessment of a male college student produced the document contained in Box 4-8. It should be noted that, although this particular example is quite brief, social-learning summaries and reports often go into considerably more detail.

A Phenomenological Report   In line with their highly flexible, subjective approach and general distrust of formal assessment, phenomenologically oriented clinicians have not suggested specific outlines for guiding the reports and summaries they may write. Thus, quite lengthy reports may be based upon a very general framework such as:

I   Client from own point of view
II   Client as reflected in tests
III Client as seen by assessor

Box 4-8   Example of an Assessment Summary Based on a Social-Learning Outline

Behavior during interview and physical description:

James is a clean-shaven, long-haired young man who appeared for the intake interview in well-coordinated college garb: jeans, wide belt, open shirt, and sandals. He came across as shy and soft-spoken, with occasional minor speech blocks. Although uneasy during most of the session, he nonetheless spoke freely and candidly.

Presenting problem:

A. *Nature of Problem:* Anxiety in public speaking situations, and other situations in which he is being evaluated by others.

B. *Historical setting events:* James was born in France, and arrived in this country seven years ago, at which time he experienced both a social and language problem. His social contacts had been minimal until the time he entered college, at which time a socially aggressive friend of his helped him to break out of his shell. James describes his father as being an overly critical and perfectionistic person who would, on occasion, rip up his homework if it fell short of the mark. The client's mother is pictured as a controlling, overly affectionate person who was always showing concern about his welfare. His younger brother, who has always been a good student, was continually thrown up to James by his parents as being far better than he.

C. *Current situational determinants:* Interaction with his parents, examinations, family gatherings, participation in classes, initial social contacts.

D. *Relevant organismic variables:* The client appears to be approaching a number of situations with certain irrational expectations, primarily unrealistic strivings for perfection and an overwhelming desire to receive approval from others. He is not taking any medication at this time.

E. *Dimensions of problem:* The client's social and evaluative anxiety are long-standing and occur in a wide variety of day-to-day situations.

F. *Consequences of problem:* His chronic level of anxiety resulted in an ulcer operation at the age of 15. In addition, he has developed a skin rash on his hands and arms, apparently from excessive perspiration. He reports that his nervousness at one time caused him to stutter, but this appears to be less a problem in more recent years. His anxiety in examination situations has typically interfered with his ability to perform well.

Other problems:

A. *Assertiveness:* Although obviously a shy and timid individual, James said that lack of assertiveness is no longer a problem with him. At one time in the past, his friends would take advantage of him, but he claims that this is no longer the case. This should be followed up further, as it is unclear what he means by assertiveness.

B. *Forgetfulness:* The client reports that he frequently misses appointments, misplaces items, locks himself out of his room, and generally is absent-minded.

Personal assets:

The client is fairly bright and comes across as a warm, friendly, and sensitive individual.

Targets for modification:

Unrealistic self-statements in social-evaluative situations; possibly behavioral deficits associated with unassertiveness; and forgetfulness.

Recommended treatment:

It appears that relaxation training would be a good way to begin, especially in light of the client's high level of anxiety. Following this, the treatment should move along the lines of rational restructuring, and possibly behavior rehearsal. It is unclear as yet what would be the best strategy for dealing with forgetfulness.

Motivation for treatment:

High.

Prognosis:

Very good.

Priority for treatment:

High.

Expectancies:

On occasion, especially when going out on a date with a female, James would take half a sleeping pill to calm himself down. He wants to get away from this, and feels what he needs is to learn to cope with his anxieties by himself. It would appear that he will be very receptive to whatever treatment plan we finally decide on, especially if the emphasis is on self-control of anxiety.

Other comments:

Considering the brief time available between now and the end of the semester, between-session homework assignments should be emphasized as playing a particularly important role in the behavior change process.

From *Clinical Behavior Therapy* by M. R. Goldfried and G. C. Davison. Copyright © 1976 by Holt, Rinehart and Winston. Reprinted by permission of Holt, Rinehart and Winston.

An example of a report organized in this phenomenological way is presented in Box 4-9. Notice that, although the clinician administered some formal psychological tests, the data from them appear in the report mainly in subjective terms.

More detailed discussions of the techniques and problems associated with writing clinical assessment reports are available in articles and books by Foster (1951), Hammond and Allen (1953), Klopfer (1960), and Tallent (1956, 1976).

Box 4-9 Example of an Assessment Summary Based on a Phenomenological Outline

Referral: Last January 24-year-old Darrell and his partner were arrested in New Jersey for collecting refunds on department store goods which they simply had picked up from the shelves. They collected $100 to $200 per day in this fashion for several months. Both young men were released on probation in March following a couple months in jail. Mr. and Mrs. Holderin are now seeking psychotherapy for their son in hopes that it will be of personal help to him and will preclude further lawbreaking.

The psychiatrist they contacted, has in turn requested a general psychological assessment prior to deciding whether to begin psychotherapy. He is particularly concerned with the possibility of schizoid functioning, especially as it might appear in the Rorshach, and with Darrell's intellectual assets.

Date of assessment: 5-6-74   *Date of report:* 5-12-74

Assessment opportunities: Extended interview, Bender-Gestalt, Wechsler Adult Intelligence Scale (partial), Rorschach, Thematic Apperception Test, human drawings, and mutual discussion of my impressions.

First appearance: Darrell showed up at my office precisely on time. He was dressed in a fashionable doublebreasted suit, wide silk tie, and silk shirt with cufflinks. He carried these well, and indeed struck me as youthfully handsome. After waiting for me to indicate where we were to go, he comfortably explained that he needed change for $10 in order to feed a parking meter. Secretaries, students, and I all scurried around looking for change as he stood by politely and nonchalantly. When he wrote a check for my services, he added the forty cents I had offered him.

Once into my office, Darrell continued to seem at ease. In a casual way he asked permission to smoke, suggested that the window be opened, and took off his jacket. Except when doing pencil work, he seemed bodily relaxed. Later, he smilingly mentioned that his idol is Alexander Mundy of the T.V. program "To Catch a Thief"—boyish in handsome appearance, a lady-killer, mod dresser with expensive entertainment tastes, sports car enthusiast, conman with class, and thief extraordinaire. Darrell remarked both that such aspirations were "unrealistic" *and* that he had thoroughly enjoyed approximating them during his recent misadventure.

Toward the end of our meeting, this suave appearance was thrown into relief as Darrell recounted his favorite horror stories, joked continuously, and drew cartoon figures complete with slapstick captions. He had also earnestly shared his educational ambitions and sought advice from me. Altogether I found him consistently easy to be with and to like—something in the manner of a teacher shaking her head but enjoying a charmingly problematic student.

Darrell as he sees himself: As mentioned, the Alexander Mundy project is a powerful and often successful one for Darrell. When he has the money, he dresses well and wines and dines well. He even owns a sports car of sorts (a Karman Ghia). And like Mundy, he has only a few male friends, but is highly successful with having his way with women. Although he would "go to pieces" if he saw a girl cry because he had hurt her, he usually lies to get what he wants and sees nothing wrong with doing so. Girls are all phony anyway, except one whom he met since being released from jail. Darrell finds he can't put on airs with her and doesn't want to. She's honest and really likes him. She even invited him to come with her and her parents to Atlantic City—"nobody ever did that for me before!" But he won't get married for at least three years, until he's sure that his criminal conviction (which she doesn't know about yet) would not hurt either of them.

Back to the Mundy style. Even in grade school Darrell was often regarded as some sort of trouble maker who wasn't properly fulfilling his potential. Darrell wouldn't tell much about these years, but he did talk about a haunting memory of a woman principal chastising him about what was going to become of him. He was quite upset when he read a few years ago about her death. But mostly Darrell focuses on his triumphs. For example, he talks his way into job after job easily, and once was able to get an extended leave of absence by making up an intricate tale about having to go to the Mayo Clinic for critical surgery. And, not caring for the "hurry up and wait" routine of military service, and missing his friends and old life, Darrell waited out the requisite six months before applying for a psychiatric discharge that would formally be an honorable discharge. He feels he really put one over on the doctor, who wrote that Darrell was prone to "impulsive outbursts." Darrell acknowledges pride in these behaviors as well as in his recent thievery—if it weren't for his partner, they would never have been caught. But he emphasizes that he doesn't want anyone else to know about his lawbreaking, and he feels it would be stupid to run the risk of again doing something that he might get caught at. He also suspects that what he did was somewhat immature—an abhorrent thought.

Darrell through the tests: Darrell plunged right into whatever I asked of him, with the effect of partially masking what I took from his frequent sidewise glances at me as discomfort and uncertainty about his ability. When asked to copy the *Bender* designs, he did so in about half the usual time. He started out carefully counting dots, asking for instructions, and so on, but wound up with the wrong number going in the wrong direction. As he noted my acceptance, he simply frowned at his mistakes and let them go. Not having planned ahead, he also ran out of space. When I mentioned these things to him and asked if they were similar to other events in his life, Darrell readily and amusedly agreed. Examples were getting arrested, not being further ahead in life at his age, and impatience with all his forms of employment (copyboy to clothes salesman).

On the *WAIS* Information section, I noticed Darrell's rapid way of speaking—sort of nonstop, in this case with all kinds of qualifiers, protestations, quick approximations, and requests for feedback. Here, he earned an average score. He acknowledged that this style is typical when a task is not intrinsically interesting and/or when it leaves no room for him to make up his own answers. "I was never any good at math, chemistry, and languages." And sure enough, when asked to repeat a series of digits, Darrell failed to score beyond average; he tried to memorize the digits, but often blurted them out, seemingly hoping that they would fall into place. We agreed that he behaves in a similar fashion while working for his father. Moreover that situation becomes exaggerated when Darrell responds to his father's chidings with even more carelessness.

For the most part, Darrell raced through the *Rorshach*, giving rapid responses and elaborations, turning the cards, and stopping abruptly with about three responses to each card. Most of the percepts involved motion, e.g., "scorpions fighting, people dancing at a costume party, men racing to dance with this girl. Keystone cops—'I'm going first; no, I'm going first,' fighting a duel, violent fight, two roadrunners colliding—'beep-beep', atomic bomb explosion, flying dinosaurs." In addition, these percepts were laced with enthusiastic rehashings of T.V. horror stories, movies, and science fiction stories. When I suggested that maybe Darrell is action-oriented, he readily agreed and gave more examples of having acted without thinking. Among these were what he called "instinctive" hitting back when physically pushed around. He denied other combativeness. When I pointed out that much of the Rorschach action seemed to be competitive, he saw no relation to his life, instead asserting that, for example, he doesn't have to compete because he's usually the first choice of the girls he wants. Nevertheless, I have a sense of his struggling in a vague way to be first in order not to be somehow put down—or squashed down.

Moving on to the *TAT* stories, I remarked to Darrell that his stories (again rapidly given) were usually straight adaptations of T.V. stories, novels, and movies. He denied that he watches these much anymore, and couldn't "go" with my observation that there were no real people, no involvements in the present, little interpersonal warmth. But he did reiterate that he has never had many friends and that girls are phony. With that, to the blank card he made up a picture of Annette (his new girl friend, 18 years old) and himself on a picnic in a beautiful meadow, just being alone together listening to music, and looking at the mountains. "Sounds childish, but I enjoy doing it."

Conclusion: In answer to the referral question, there is no evidence of autistic thinking. Although there is a general dysocial picture, it is definitely not of schizoid proportions. Moreover, Darrell has begun to let himself form closer relationships with at least Annette and his father, tentative as these may be. And under nonconfrontational circumstances, such as moments in our assessment session, he has been able to own and explore certain affects. Thus although there were certain similarities to "schizoid functioning," he can be viewed more productively as living an extended adolescence. I suspect that therapy would have to encourage him through some developmental sequences as well as current difficulties. As I see it, he could thus become more intimate with and sensitive to other persons.

For whatever it's worth, I might point out a problem *I* might have in an extended relation with Darrell, a problem which I think he's run into repeatedly. His charm and likeableness are likely to rally people to his side until he lets them down by running off or by not returning their care. Then he is either ignored or nagged, both of which demonstrate to him again that people are phony and there are no close friends. So off he goes to emulate Mundy with little concern for the consequences to others.

Source: Norman Tallent, *Psychological Report Writing,* © 1976, pp. 221–225. Reprinted by permission of Prentice-Hall, Inc., Englewood Cliffs, New Jersey.

A Note on Ethics

The collection, processing, and communication of assessment data require that the clinician have access to information which the client might not ordinarily reveal. This places a heavy responsibility upon the assessor to use, store, and report this privileged information in a fashion which safeguards the client's welfare and dignity. Currently there is growing concern over (1) how psychological assessment data are being used, (2) who may have access to confidential material, and (3) the possibility that improper or irresponsible interpretation of assessment information will have negative social, political, and economic consequences for clients.

With these concerns in mind, the clinician must first be sure that her or his inquiries do not comprise an unauthorized invasion of the client's privacy. Next, care should be taken to assure that the assessment tools employed by the clinician are not socially or culturally biased to an extent that would place certain clients (e.g., members of ethnic or racial minorities) at a disadvantage and thus give falsely negative impressions of them. Finally, the clinician must wrestle with the problem of who may have access to assessment data if he or she does not maintain sole control over them. When test scores, subjective impressions, conclusions, recommendations, predictions, and other information are communicated in report form, they may be subject to misuse by persons who see the report but are not fully qualified to interpret it as a guide to decision making. In such cases, not only is the client's privacy invaded, but the existence of assessment information may actually be a disadvantage to the client in, say, getting into graduate school or securing employment.

Minimizing and avoiding these kinds of potential problems regarding psychological assessment have been major concerns of various public officials, government agencies, citizens groups, and private individuals. Some of them advocate elimination of all psychological assessment (especially testing; see Hoch, 1971), while others are oriented toward development of safeguards designed to protect clients from assessment abuses. The latter option has been adopted by the American Psychological Association, whose *Ethical Standards for Psychologists, Standards for Providers of Psychological Service,* and *Standards for Educational and Psychological Tests and Manuals* (APA, 1968, 1974a, 1974b) contain extensive procedural guidelines for assessors to follow as they go about the sensitive task of learning about their clients.

Ethical problems and standards associated with clinical psychology will be considered in greater detail in Chapter 13.

Chapter 5

Interviewing in Clinical Psychology

The interview is by far the most widely employed tool in clinical psychology. It plays a prominent role in many forms of psychological treatment and, as we have seen, is a major component of the clinical assessment which precedes, accompanies, and follows treatment. The use of interviews to provide help to troubled persons will be considered more specifically in later chapters, but it should be kept in mind that much of what will be said in this chapter about assessment interview procedures and problems applies to treatment interviews as well.

This is not a "how-to-interview" chapter. Even the many books and articles available on the subject (e.g., Bernstein, Bernstein, & Dana, 1974; Bingham, Moore, & Gustad, 1959; Deutsch & Murphy, 1955; Fenlason, 1952; Fensterheim, 1972; Garrett, 1942; Gill, Newman, Redlich, & Sommers, 1954; Gorden, 1969; Kahn & Cannell, 1957; Menninger, 1952; Morgan & Cogger, 1972; Oldfield, 1941; Sullivan, 1954; Whitehorn, 1944) do not provide wholly adequate substitutes for the supervised practice of interview skills. Thus, the material covered here should be viewed only as a preliminary orientation to and evaluation of the interview as an assessment data source.

What Is an Interview?

An interview is not an extraordinary thing. In simplest terms, it is a conversation which has a purpose or goal (Bingham & Moore, 1924; Matarazzo, 1965). Consider the following interchange between A and B:

A: How did you spend the weekend?

B: Well, it was pretty quiet. I slept in on Saturday and then watched a football game in the afternoon. That night, my wife's brother came over with their 8-year-old boy. He's a real pain. Anyway, we sat around and talked most of the night. Drank a lot of beer and smoked some dope.

A: Were you home on Sunday, too?

B: Most of it. I didn't feel too great in the morning so I just sat around a lot. Later I watched the Packers game on TV. I really just wanted to have a quick supper and go to bed early, but my wife kept griping about how we never go anywhere. Finally, I had to take her out to eat. I wasn't all that hungry, but she didn't care. The worst part was that we had a flat on the way home, and I ruined a perfectly good shirt while I was changing the damn thing.

If A were B's friend and coworker and the interaction took place while passing the time on the way to the office on Monday morning, it would simply be part of a conversation like billions of others which occur every day. But this same exchange could just as easily have been part of an interview in which A (a clinician) is gathering information about B and his life-style. The distinction between social conversations and an interview, then, is based not upon their content but upon whether or not they serve a particular purpose.

Interviews have been a part of everyday life for centuries. They occur in the form of interactions between employers and prospective employees, lawyers and witnesses, pollsters and citizens, parents and teachers, doctors and patients, and, of course, clinicians and clients. It is important to recognize, therefore, that clinicians have merely adopted and refined the interview; they did not invent it.

Clinical Interview Situations

The fact that interviews so closely resemble other forms of conversation makes them a natural source of clinical information about people, an easy means of communicating information to them, and a convenient context for attempting to help them. As noted in Chapter 4, interviews are flexible, relatively inexpensive, highly portable and, perhaps most important, capable of providing the clinician with simultaneous samples of clients' verbal and nonverbal behavior. These advantages make the interview useful in a variety of clinical situations, including the following:

1 Intake This is perhaps the most common type of clinical interview situation. The client voluntarily or, in the case of some juveniles, criminals, and others, involuntarily contacts the clinician because of some problem in living. The psychologist may have little or no information about the client, so the intake interview or interviews are designed mainly to establish the nature and context of the problem. Information gathered in this situation may be used by the interviewer to decide whether or not she or he (or the agency she or he represents) is an appropriate source of help, further assessment services, or whatever. The interviewer must ask, "Can I/we work with this person?" "Is this problem within my/our area of expertise?" "Can I/we do any good?" If, on the basis of one or more intake interviews, the answer to such questions is "no," the clinician usually refers the client to another psychological, psychiatric, medical, or social agency for appropriate alternative services. If further contact is seen as desirable, assessment or treatment is scheduled for future sessions. Most individual clinicians conduct their own intake interviews, but, in many agencies (e.g., county mental health clinics) and group practices, social workers or other personnel may perform this function.

2 Problem identification The decision to accept or refer a client on the basis of intake information rests, in part, on the nature of the client's problems. For this reason, many intake interviews are aimed, partly at least, at problem identification. There are other clinical situations, however, in which a decision to work with or refer the client has already been made or is not at issue. In such situations, interviews may be focused *entirely* upon identification or elaboration of the client's problems.

When the interviewer is oriented toward or is asked for a *classification* of the problem, "diagnosis" of some sort usually occurs. This can take the form of a label (e.g., "manic-depression," "paranoid schizophrenia," "anxiety neurosis") from the American Psychiatric Association diagnostic system, but it may also involve a "personality-type" characterization (e.g., "passive-dependent," "anal-compulsive"). Other, less psychiatrically oriented clinicians and those not required by their work setting to classify people commonly use problem-identification interviews to develop broader descriptions of the client and the environmental context in which his or her behavior occurs.

Interviews designed to *classify* client problems are most commonly associated with admissions procedures in mental hospitals and other inpatient or outpatient facilities where a "diagnosis" is required for statistical or other purposes. Similar interviews may also occur when psychologists serve as diagnostic consultants to psychiatrists, courts, schools, or others who are interested in such questions as "Is Mr. P. competent to stand trial?" "Is Mrs. L. psychotic?" "Is Jimmy G. mentally retarded?"

Interviews focused upon *describing* a client and his or her problems in broader, more comprehensive terms usually occur in the context of the full-scale clinical exploration which often precedes treatment by the assessor or other professional. Here, the interviewer elicits a detailed account of the client's strengths and weaknesses, current life situation, and history, often following outlines such as those presented in Boxes 4-1, 4-2, or 4-3. In agencies employing a "team" approach, part of the problem-identification task is undertaken by social workers who use interviews to collect *social history* information from the client and those well acquainted with her or him.

3 Orientation Often, people participating in psychological assessment or treatment in clinical or laboratory settings do not know exactly what to expect, let alone what is expected of them. This is especially true if they have had no previous contact with clinical psychologists or other "helping professionals." To make these new experiences less mysterious and more comfortable, many clinicians conduct special interviews (or reserve segments of interviews) for the purpose of acquainting the client with the assessment, treatment, or research procedures to come.

Orientation interviews can be beneficial in at least two ways. First, because the client is encouraged to ask questions and make comments, misconceptions or misinformation which might obstruct subsequent sessions can be dealt with and corrected. As an example, some clients may assume that whatever they say to a clinician will be repeated to other members of the family. Fears of this kind (which could alter the client's cooperativeness) can be allayed during an orientation interview or segment, thus avoiding future problems.

In addition to eliminating inaccurate expectations, orientation interviews can communicate new, adaptive expectations designed to facilitate later interactions. Often, this is done by clearly describing or illustrating (through films, video tapes, or audio recordings) the kinds of things that "good" clients are expected to do in assessment or treatment. Thus, the prospective client learns what is coming and what will be expected in the way of cooperation, effort, self-disclosure, honesty, and the like. In most cases, clients are free to choose not to participate in the activities described. This freedom, along with accurate expectations on the part of those who do participate, tends to make clinic or laboratory assessment and treatment sessions more efficient and effective (Bednar, Melnick, & Kaul, 1974; Bednar & Kaul, 1978; Frank, 1973; Goldstein, 1971; Heitler, 1976; Orne & Wender, 1968).

4 Termination Closely related to the problem of orienting clients to forthcoming clinical experiences is that of satisfactorily terminating those experiences. For example, persons who have just completed a series of assessment sessions involving extensive interviews, tests, and observations are often understandably anxious to know "what the doctor found," how the information will be used, and who will have access to it. Such concerns can be particularly acute when the assessor has acted as consultant to a school, court, or psychiatrist. An interview (or segment) designed to explain or reiterate the procedures and protections involved in transmission of privileged information, and to provide, where possible, a brief summary and careful interpretation of assessment results can go a long way toward alleviating any uncertainty or distress that clients and their families may feel in relation to assessment.

In research settings, a termination interview is usually referred to as "debriefing." This usually includes a full explanation of the project in which the volunteer client has participated and revelation of any deceptions employed in it. Debriefings can be more complete and detailed than the research orientation interviews which precede them. Further, they permit and even encourage the volunteer client to ask questions and make comments about procedures, hypotheses under study, data analysis, and results. Talking with volunteers in this way is aimed at assuring that no element of the research experience has left a harmful or disturbing residue. This is in keeping with standards of general and research ethics laid down by the American Psychological Association (APA, 1977; see Chapter 13). Candid debriefings may also benefit the clinician, since it is often under such after-the-fact circumstances that she or he finds clues to what may actually be determining volunteers' behavior in the laboratory (Orne, 1962).

Completion of clinical treatment which may have been quite intensive and/or extended also requires some form of termination interview. Many "loose ends" need to be tied up: There is gratitude and affection to be expressed and accepted, reminders to be given about the handling of future problems, plans to be made for follow-up contacts, and reassurance given to the client about his or her ability to "go it alone." Treatment termination interviews can be emotional or businesslike events. In either case, they serve the important purpose of making the transition from treatment to posttreatment as smooth and productive as possible.

5 Crises When a person's problems in living are of a highly immediate, stressful, and pressing nature and normal problem-solving skills prove inadequate to deal with the situation, the person is said to be in a crisis (Caplan, 1961). Often, people in crises appear for help at clinical facilities or call a "hot line," suicide prevention center, or other 24-hour crisis service (see Chapter 12). In such cases, the interviewer does not have the luxury of scheduling a series of assessment sessions to be followed, perhaps, by some form of treatment. The crisis must be dealt with on the spot, often in only a few minutes, and several interview goals which would otherwise be distributed over sessions must be combined. The interviewer attempts to provide support, collect assessment data, and take some action to help. This usually means dealing with the client in a calm, concerned, and accepting fashion, asking relevant informational questions (e.g., "Have you ever tried to kill yourself?" "What kinds of pills do you have in the house?"), and working on the immediate problem directly or through referral to relevant medical, social, or psychological services.

One or two well-handled interviews during a crisis may be the beginning and the end of contact with clients whose need for assistance was temporary and situation-specific. For others, the crisis interview leads to establishment of a contract for subsequent (and more relaxed) assessment and treatment sessions.

6 Observation As already noted, interviews (and tests) provide an opportunity to observe various aspects of client behavior. On rare occasions, clinicians conduct special interviews designed to see how a person deals with certain circumstances. Here, the interview merely provides a context for observation of the interviewee's reaction to stressful, ambiguous, conflict-laden, or other situations. This sort of "interview" will be more thoroughly described when we consider observational assessments in Chapter 7. It should be noted, however, that these are special-purpose techniques which are not commonly used in clinical settings. They are far more applicable in research or personnel selection activities.

Interview Structure

Probably the most basic variable in clinical interviews conducted for any purpose is *structure:* the degree to which the interviewer determines the content and course of the conversation (Peterson, 1968a; Rotter, 1971). At one end of the structure continuum are totally *nondirective* interviews where the clinician does as little as possible to interfere with the natural flow of the client's speech and choice of topics. At the other end are highly *structured* interviews which, because of their rigid, question-and-answer format, resemble a kind of interrogation. Interviews of the first type are aimed primarily at client comfort, while those of the second are designed primarily to gather a maximum amount of specific information. In between are many blends which are usually referred to as *guided* or *directed* interviews.

Some excerpts from a few clinical interactions may make the structure dimension clearer. Consider first this segment from a nondirective intake interview.

Clinician: [Your relative] didn't go into much detail about what you wanted to talk about, so I wonder if you'd just start in at wherever you want to start in with, and tell me what kind of nervousness you have.

Client: Well, it's, uh, I think if I were to put it in, in a few words, it seems to be a, a, a complete lack of self-confidence in, and an extreme degree of self-consciousness. Now, I have always been a very self-conscious person. I mean every, just about, since I was probably fourteen years old the first I remember of it. But for a long time I've realized that I was sort of using people as crutches. I mean I, a lot of things I felt I couldn't do myself I did all right if someone was along.

Clinician: Um-hm.

Client: And it's just progressed to the point where I'm actually using the four walls of the house as an escape from reality. I mean I don't, I don't care to go out. I, I certainly can't go out alone. . . . It's sort of a vicious circle. I find out I can't do it, and then I'm sure the next time I can't do it.

Clinician: Um-hm.

Client: And it just gets progressively worse. I think the first that I ever noticed it. . . . (Wallen, 1956, p. 146)

The client continued a narrative which included information about the problem's onset and duration, her occupation and marriage, her father's death, and other topics. Notice that the clinician hardly says a word although, as we shall see, there are things he could have done nondirectively to encourage client speech if she had not been so talkative.

Let us now go to the other extreme and listen to a highly structured conversation. The example chosen is from a type of problem-identification session called a *mental status interview*. It covers a planned set of topics in a roughly programmed order. Outlines for this type of interview are provided by

Sands (1972), Stevenson and Sheppe (1959), Spitzer, Fleiss, Burdock, and Hardesty (1964), Wells and Ruesch (1945), and Wing, Cooper, and Sartorius (1974). Many mental status interviews occur after a person has been admitted to a psychiatric hospital.

 Clinician: Good morning. What is your name?

 Client: Randolph S———.

 Clinician: Well, Mr. S———, I would like to ask you some questions this morning. Is that all right?

 Client: Fine.

 Clinician: How long have you been here?

 Client: Since yesterday morning.

 Clinician: Why are you here?

 Client: I don't know. I think my wife called the police and here I am.

 Clinician: Well what did you do to make her call the police?

 Client: I don't know.

 Clinician: What day is today?

 Client: Tuesday, the 12th.

 Clinician: What year is it?

 Client: 1977.

 Clinician: What city are we in?

 Client: Chicago.

 Clinician: Who is the mayor of Chicago?

Similar questioning would deal with many other topics and capacities including family and friends, occupation, physical and psychological problems, recent and long-term memory, retention and recall of information, general knowledge, and the like. Notice how the interview structure clearly determines the material covered and establishes a fairly rapid pace.

 In the following guided interview, both nondirective and structured features appear.

 Clinician: You say that you are very jealous a lot of the time and this upsets you a great deal.

 Client: Well, I know it's stupid for me to feel that way, but I am hurt when I even *think* of Mike with another woman.

 Clinician: You don't want to feel jealous but you do.

 Client: I know that's not the way a "liberated" woman should be.

 Clinician: What is your idea of how a liberated woman should feel?

 Client: I don't know. In many ways I feel I have changed so much in the last year. I really don't believe you have the right to own another person—and yet, when it happens to me, I feel really hurt. I'm such a hypocrite.

 Clinician: You're unhappy because you are not responding the way you really would like to?

 Client: I'm not the person I want to be.

 Clinician: So there's really "double jeopardy." When Mike is with someone else, it really hurts you. And, then when you feel jealous, you get down on yourself for being that way.

Client: Yes, I guess I lose both ways. (Morganstern,1976, p. 64)

Here, the interviewer encourages the client to express herself freely, but also places some limits on the topic by asking a specific question.

The structure of a given interview is heavily dependent upon its purpose. While some clinicians adopt a highly nondirective or rather structured interview approach under virtually all circumstances, the majority tend to adjust structure to accommodate the situation. For example, by their very nature, orientation interviews may require more interviewer guidance than do conversations aimed at problem identification. Similarly, crises often demand more structure than might be needed during a routine intake interview. Structure may change during the course of an interview. As we shall see later, many intake and problem-identification interviews begin in a very nondirective way and become increasingly structured as conversation continues.

Structure also depends, in part, upon the theoretical orientation, training, and personal preferences of the interviewer. There is far too much variability among individual clinicians to justify stereotypes for each clinical model, but it is safe to say in general that followers of Rogers's version of the phenomenological approach tend to provide the least interview structure. Freudians usually provide somewhat more. Other phenomenologists, neo-Freudians, and social-learning types are likely to be the most verbally active and/or directive.

These differences are very general, however. As noted in Chapter 3, models help organize and orient the clinician, but they do not always provide guidance for handling every client and circumstance. Thus, it should come as no surprise that there is often a great deal of similarity among experienced clinicians of varying theoretical persuasions in the way specific interview situations are handled (see, e.g., Fiedler, 1950; Klein, Dittman, Parloff, & Gill, 1969). One suspects that this is due, in part, to the fact that, though no one has developed the one "right" way to interview, certain very broad strategies and tactics have proven valuable in practice and have thus been adopted and taught by skilled clinicians representing every model.

These general strategies and tactics are most easily examined in the context of the *guided* interview because it usually contains them all. In the sections to follow, we shall consider the anatomy and execution of guided interviews as a means of reviewing the full range of conversational procedures commonly employed by clinical psychologists. Characteristic emphasis or deemphasis on each of these procedures by proponents of various clinical models will be noted where appropriate.

STAGES IN THE INTERVIEW

Like many other events which take place over time, interviews are commonly thought of as having a beginning, a middle, and an end. This is a considerable oversimplification, however, since such neat stages may not be present or discernible in all instances.

Intake or problem-identification interviews are most likely to pass through three fairly clear segments. They usually begin with efforts at making the client comfortable and ready to speak freely (stage 1), continue into a central information-gathering phase (stage 2), and end with summary statements, client questions and, if appropriate, plans for subsequent meetings (stage 3). In later assessment interviews, the length and clarity of these stages vary. As the client gets to know the clinician and the clinical situation, stage 1 will probably grow shorter while stage 2 gets longer. Similarly, stage 3 may be very brief until the final assessment interview, when it may take up most of the time available.

Treatment interviews sometimes follow a different three-stage format. A session may begin with the client's report of thoughts and events since the last meeting, continue with whatever treatment procedures are being employed, then conclude with a summary of current progress, plans for the next meeting, and/or "homework" assignments.

Other interview situations, such as those relating to crises, orientation, and termination, may not be organized around a beginning-middle-end framework at all. Nevertheless, the three-stage model does offer a convenient guide for organizing our review of the course and tactics of "typical" clinical interviews.

Stage 1: Beginning the Interview

Especially during initial interviews, the clinician must give careful attention to the first minutes of contact. The client is likely to be at least a little uncomfortable about talking to a stranger (especially a "shrink") about personal matters, and this apprehension may be intensified by uncertainty or misunderstanding about what the psychologist will be doing. As a result, many clients enter the interview with a kind of wait-and-see attitude which prompts them to be a bit "cagey" and careful about what they say. If this were to continue throughout the conversation, little valuable assessment information would be generated.

Most clinicians see the establishment of *rapport*—a harmonious and comfortable working relationship—as their main task during the first part of initial interviews. This can be done in many ways, most of which are related to common sense and courtesy. Since a client's anxiety and uncertainty can be greatly eased by demystification of the interview, a warm smile, friendly greeting, and a handshake are excellent and very human opening features. Offering a chair and assisting with the disposal of overcoats, umbrellas, or packages are similarly humanizing rituals. For clients who smoke, an invitation to do so and a conveniently placed ashtray can be comforting. "Small talk" about the weather, difficulty in finding the office, features of the building, or other topics also ease the client's transition into the interview situation and make it less strange and foreboding.

As noted earlier, interviews can occur almost anywhere, but certain circumstances seem especially conducive to rapport-building for most clients. Except for those individuals whose cultural background might cause such surroundings to be threatening, interviews are best conducted in a comfortable private office. This is because, first, most people seem to find it easier to relax when they can get comfortable physically. Second, it is far easier to assure the client of the interview's confidential nature when no one else is present or within earshot.

Several other office characteristics can aid rapport. The height, relative comfort and placement of chairs provide good examples. A reassuring equality is established when two people sit a few feet apart on similar chairs of equal height. If the clinician sits in a high backed, massive chair behind a huge desk which is six feet from the client's smaller, lower seat, rapport may be impaired.[1] The appearance of the office and the frequency of interruptions are also relevant. A clear (or at least neatly organized) desk, along with instructions to secretarial staff to hold phone calls and prevent other intrusions, lets the client know that she or he has the clinician's full attention. This, in turn, helps convey sincere interest in what the client may have to say, and it tends to evoke reciprocal cooperation. These simple steps are particularly important for clients who are reticent about taking up a busy professional's time, since they show that the clinician is not champing at the bit to get on to other things.

Objects in the office can influence rapport. Though some clinicians purposely display bizarre paintings or other art objects as projective test stimuli (see Chapter 6), most interviewers choose less dramatic pieces which are noticeable enough to serve as topics for initial "small talk," but are not upsetting. Care should also be taken about things which are left lying about. The clinician's academic interest in homosexuality, for example, could threaten some clients if a pile of books on the subject were placed close by.

This list of rapport-building techniques could be extended almost indefinitely; the point is that, from the beginning, the clinician tries in every way possible to create a warm, comfortable environment and a relationship which will encourage the client to speak freely and honestly about whatever topics are relevant to the interview (see Goldstein, 1976).

Skilled clinicians can set up remarkable rapport during the first stage of an initial interview but, even for them, the process continues into the second and third stages, and into subsequent contacts as well. Like other social relationships, the one between client and clinician takes time to grow. Once that relationship has taken root, however, the initial interview can move into its second, or formal information-gathering stage.

Stage 2: The Middle of the Interview

Transition to the "middle" of an initial interview should be as smooth and easy for the client as possible. The way in which this is accomplished and the ways in which the clinician conducts the second stage will illustrate many of the major interview tactics in use today.

Nondirective Techniques   In most cases, clinical interviewers begin the second stage with nondirective techniques, usually an *open-ended* question or request. Common examples are: "What brings you here today?" "What would

---

[1]This and other statements about rapport-building are not meant to be absolute; some clients may prefer talking to clinicians who are in a throne-like position.

you like to talk about?" "Perhaps you would like to tell me about the problems you referred to on the telephone." A major advantage of the open-ended approach is that it frees the client to begin in his or her own way. This is especially important when the matters of greatest concern are difficult to bring up directly and immediately; an open-ended invitation to talk allows the client to ease into painful or embarrassing topics gradually and without feeling pressed.[2] Relatively nonstressful beginnings of this type are generally believed to aid rapport because they communicate the clinician's willingness to listen to whatever the client has to say.

, Contrast the open-ended initiations suggested above with "binding" statements like: "You said you thought there was a sex problem. Is it yours or your wife's?" "What kind of work do you do?" "Are you here to talk about your own problems or someone else's?" Notice how openings of this type tend to prematurely focus the conversation upon topics which may be inordinately threatening or even irrelevant. An interview whose second stage begins with and continues to employ "binding" tactics often degenerates into a superficial question-and-answer session in which the client may feel put-upon, misunderstood, and frustrated. Accordingly, such "interrogation" procedures are usually reserved for situations in which the client's behavior indicates that spontaneous speech will not be forthcoming.[3]

Use of open-ended questions or comments is not restricted to the beginning of an interview's second stage. Such devices are called upon whenever the clinician wishes to *prompt* the client's verbal behavior while influencing its content as little as possible. Classic remarks like "Please go on," "Tell me a bit more about that," and "How did you feel about that?" exemplify continued implementation of a nondirective strategy.

That strategy is normally supplemented by a variety of tactics designed both to help the client express herself or himself freely and fully and to enhance rapport by communicating the clinician's understanding, interest, and acceptance. The most general of these tactics, called *active listening,* includes both verbal and nonverbal elements. We will discuss the latter in a subsequent section. Verbally, active listening involves responding to the client's speech in ways which, without interrupting it, indicate understanding and encouragement to go on. The clinician's "mm-hms" in the nondirective interview excerpt presented earlier represent one type of verbal active listening. Others include comments such as "I see," "I understand," "I'm with you," or "Right."

A related strategy is called *paraphrasing.* Here, the clinician restates what the client has said in order to (1) show that she or he has been listening closely, and (2) give the client a chance to hear and possibly correct the remark if it was

---

[2]Often, clients begin with a "ticket of admission" problem which may not be the one of greatest concern to them. The functional reason for the client's visit may appear only after varying amounts of diversionary conversation.

[3]Again, this is not always the case. Rogers (1967) provides an example of continued, and ultimately fruitful, use of nondirective interviewing with a withdrawn institutionalized client (see Chapter 11).

misinterpreted. Rogers calls this *reflection* and emphasizes not only restating content, but also highlighting client feelings. Let us consider some illustrations:

A.   *Client:* Sometimes I get so mad at my husband, I could kill him.
     Clinician: You would just like to get rid of him altogether.

B.   *Client:* Sometimes I get so mad at my husband, I could kill him.
     Clinician: He really upsets you sometimes.

Notice that in example A, the clinician merely reworded the client's remark. In example B, he or she reflected the *feeling* contained in the remark. Both versions could have been combined as "sometimes he upsets you so much you would just like to get rid of him."

Most clients respond to paraphrasing by continuing to talk, usually along the same lines as before and, often, in greater detail. When this is what the clinician wishes to happen, some form of paraphrasing is preferable to a direct question, since the latter might change or restrict the conversation. This is illustrated in the following interactions:

A.   *Client:* What it comes down to is that life just doesn't seem worth living sometimes.
     Clinician: Sometimes it all just seems to be too much.
     Client: Yeah, and I don't know what to do when I feel that way. I don't really think I want to die, not really. But I also dread the thought of another day starting. For example . . .

B.   *Client:* What it comes down to is that life just doesn't seem worth living sometimes.
     Clinician: How often do you feel that way?
     Client: Oh, off and on.

Later we shall see that there is a definite place for questions such as that asked by the interviewer in example B, but unless one feels that one knows enough to start pinpointing specifics, interrupting with several such questions early in the interview will probably limit the initial picture of the problem and may cause the client to feel harassed. Further, immediate use of direct queries can suggest to the client that she or he should "shut up" and wait for the next question. In general, this is not a great boost to rapport.

Paraphrasing can be profitably used as a clarification device in situations where the clinician is confused about what a client has said. Consider the following:

Client: I told my husband that I didn't want to live with him any more so he said "fine" and left. Well, when I got back, I found out that the son-of-a-bitch kept all our furniture!

If, as is probably the case, the interviewer does not fully comprehend the sequence of events described, he or she could simply say "what?", but that might be interpreted by the client as an insult (or as an indication that the clinician is a dunce). Instead, a combination of paraphrase and request for clarification serves nicely:

Clinician: OK, let's see if I've got this straight. You told your husband you didn't want to live with him, so *he* left. You later came back to your house from somewhere else and found he had taken the furniture?

Ideally, the client will either confirm this interpretation or fill in the missing pieces. If not, the clinician may wish to use more direct questioning procedures, which we shall now discuss.

Directive Techniques   As already stated, most interviewers supplement nondirective tactics with those of a more directive nature. These typically take the form of *questions* which, on first hearing, may sound casual and similar to those which are part of everyday conversation. In fact, their form, length, wording, and content are often the result of careful (though usually on-the-spot) planning.

For example, the clinician usually wants to avoid asking "binding" questions which may (1) damage rapport and (2) bias assessment data by forcing the client to choose a possibly artificial or inaccurate response supplied by the interviewer.

Look at the following illustrative questions:

A. "Do you feel better or worse when your husband is out of town?"

B. "How do you feel when your husband is out of town?"

Example A offers a clear, but possibly irrelevant two-choice situation. This is a "do you walk to work or carry your lunch?" question, for which the most valid answer may be "neither." Unfortunately, some clients are not assertive enough in the interview situation to ignore the choice, so they settle for one unsatisfactory response or the other. Unless there is a special reason for offering the client only a few response alternatives (e.g., to test assertiveness), skilled interviewers usually prefer to ask direct questions in a form which gets at specific information, but which also leaves the client free to choose his or her own words (see example B above).

Experienced clinicians also seek to avoid asking questions which suggest their own answers. Notice the implications contained in these queries:

A. "You don't actually vomit when you get upset at parties, do you?"

B. "You've suffered with this problem a long time?"

Perhaps the client always throws up at parties or just noticed the problem last week. However, questions such as these communicate fairly clearly what the interviewer expects to hear, and some clients will oblige by biasing their response. Questions like "How do you feel at parties?" or "How long have you had this problem?" provide far better alternatives.

Along similar lines, inquiries which are based upon unwarranted assumptions are generally avoided in clinical interviews. These are "Do you still whip your old father?" questions. No matter what response is given, it is likely to be misunderstood and muddy the assessment waters. There should be little trouble detecting the hidden assumptions in the examples below:

    A. "How bad is your insomnia when you are depressed?"

    B. "How much weight would you like to lose?"

If the client sleeps especially soundly when feeling low or had not recognized a weight problem, such questions cannot be answered without contradicting the clinician, feeling insulted, or both. A careful interviewer would be more likely to explore these same issues with questions more like these:

    A. "You said you are often depressed. How do you feel during those times?"

    B. "If you could make any changes in your life or in yourself, what would they be?"

Combining Interview Tactics   Because the interview is so flexible, clinicians are free to combine some or all of the conversational tactics we have described. It is very common to initiate and facilitate the client's speech with open-ended requests, paraphrasing, prompts, and other active listening techniques, then to use more directive questions and comments to "zero in" on topics or specific points of special interest and importance.

However, directive procedures do not always take over completely as the interview progresses. They continue to be mixed and blended with less directive tactics. A prime example of this is provided by the concept of *repeated scanning and focusing*. Here, the interviewer first scans a particular topic nondirectively, then focuses upon it in more directive fashion. An example is presented below:

Clinician: You mentioned that your family is back East. Could you tell me something about them?

Client: There's not much to tell. There's Dad, Mom, and the twins. They all seem to like it back there so I guess they'll stay forever.

Clinician: What else can you say about them?

Client: Well, Dad is a retired high school principal. Mom used to be strictly a housewife but, since us kids have grown, she's been working part time at a supermarket. The twins are both college seniors now.

Clinician: How did you get along with your folks when you lived at home?

Client: Really fine. I've always thought they were great people and that's probably why they had so little trouble with me. Of course, now and then, there would be a problem, but not often.

Clinician: What kinds of problems were there?

The interviewer might go on to explore several very specific issues about the client's relationship with both parents, then move on to another topic, again beginning with scanning procedures and progressing to more focused questions.

As noted earlier, clinicians who most strongly emphasize rapport and other relationship factors tend to use a combination of interview tactics which is heavily weighted toward the nondirective side (Porter, 1943). Social-learning interviewers also see a good client-clinician relationship as vital, but mainly as the context for assessment of specific information (not as the only item of importance). Their mixture of tactics thus tends to be more directively weighted (Linehan, 1977; Meyer, Liddell, & Lyons, 1977; Morganstern, 1976; Peterson, 1968a; Phillips, 1977). The potential for other mixes and blends of the interview tactics we have described is virtually endless, making it possible for proponents of every model and submodel to settle on a characteristic style.

Stage 3: Closing the Interview

The last stage of an interview can provide valuable assessment data as well as an opportunity to further enhance rapport. As available time grows short, the interviewer may initiate the third stage with a statement like this:

> We have been covering some very valuable information here and I appreciate your willingness to tell me about it. I know our session hasn't been easy for you. Since we're running out of time for today, I thought we could look back over what we've covered and then give you a chance to ask *me* some questions.

Notice that the clinician gets several things across here. First, the impending conclusion of the interview is signaled. Second, the client is praised for cooperativeness and, at the same time, reassured that the clinician understands that the interview has been stressful. Third, a plan for the final minutes is suggested; it includes an opportunity for the client to pose questions or make comments which may have been formed before and during the interview, but which were not verbalized for various reasons.

The clinician's recap of the session serves both to summarize interview content and to check again that she or he has not misheard or misunderstood anything of obvious importance. Questions and comments from the client during this stage can be quite enlightening, especially when they disclose unsuspected misconceptions or information gaps. It may be surprising for the client to ask for the interviewer's name (if it had already been given) or for a drug prescription (when the clinician is not an M.D.), but such things help alert the psychologist to special communication problems or inappropriate client expectations. Thus, this part of the conversation (especially when it ends a first contact) becomes a miniature version of the termination interview described earlier. It usually concludes with leave-taking rituals (e.g., "It was good of you to come," "Have a nice weekend") and, when appropriate, confirmation of plans for some sort of future contact with the interviewer or other professional.

The last segment of interviews may sometimes evoke unexpected, unusual, and important client behaviors. It is not unheard of for a client to "drop bombshells" during this period: "By the way, did I tell you that I am terminally ill?" or "Oh gosh, look at the time. I have to hurry to a meeting with my parole officer. He is especially picky with murderers." Remarks like these are a bit extreme, but illustrate the fact that some clients do not want the interview to end and attempt to prolong it by revealing obviously relevant data. Other individuals disclose such information more or less inadvertently. They may assume the interview is "over" and thus drop whatever pretense or other protective cover may have been in use earlier. For all these reasons, the clinician devotes as much care to the final stage of the interview as to those which precede it.

COMMUNICATION IN THE INTERVIEW

So far, we have been talking mainly about the general and specific *procedures* employed by skilled clinicians to set up and conduct conversations with their clients. Use of a judicious combination of these procedures is generally regarded as a vital component of effective rapport-building and fruitful information-gathering. However, there are other factors which contribute significantly to interview quality. Chief among these is the clarity of *communication* between interviewer and interviewee. All the clinician's skill at posing good questions, encouraging the client to talk, or making smooth transitions from topic to topic may be of little value if he or she does not understand what the client is saying and *vice versa*.

The basic problem in interview communication (and most other human interactions for that matter) is that of message transmission. The speaker must put the message she or he means to convey in transmittable form (e.g., words, gestures, and the like) and then send it. The listener must receive the message and interpret it within his or her own frame of reference. Unfortunately, communication lapses can occur at many points along the line in both verbal and nonverbal channels.

Because skilled clinicians are anxious to avoid communication problems, they take great pains to maximize the clarity of the messages they send, and to be sensitive to and sure about the messages they receive. Let us consider an example of poor clinical communication and then look at some of the ways verbal and nonverbal "breakdowns" of this type can be made less likely. In the following hypothetical exchange, the speakers' thoughts are in parentheses:

Clinician: (I wonder what his teen-age social life was like.) Tell me a little about the friends you had in high school.

Client: (I had dozens of social acquaintances, but only one person who was a really close friend.) There was just one, a guy named Mike.

Clinician: (So he was pretty much of a loner.) How did you feel about that?

Client: (It was fine. I had a great time, went to lots of parties, had lots of dates, but knew I could always depend on Mike to talk with about really personal things.) I enjoyed it. Mike and I got along really well.

Clinician: (Not only was he a social isolate, he claims to have liked it that way. I wonder if he is being honest with himself about that.) Did you ever wish you had more friends?

Client: (For crying out loud, he makes it sound like it's a crime to have one really close friend. I think we've talked enough about this.) No.

Verbal Communication In the illustration just presented, the clinician used "friend" to refer to casual as well as intimate acquaintances. This word was accurately received but, because it had a different meaning for the client, led to misunderstanding. The conversation could have gone on in this fruitless way for quite a while before the interviewer and the client straightened out their problem.

The most extreme version of verbal miscommunication is exemplified by cases in which the interviewer and client literally do not speak the same language,[4] but less drastic gaps can be more subtle and far more difficult to recognize. Although the client and clinician may technically be speaking the same language (and thus assume they understand one another), the interviewer must be aware that educational, social, racial, cultural, economic, religious, or other differences between them can seriously reduce or even wipe out communication. Unless the clinician is familiar with the client's background and frame of reference, takes it into account, and asks for clarification when verbal referents are unclear, the interview will probably suffer. Consider this example:

Client: When I'm in such heavy situations, I just get real uptight.

Clinician: What makes you uptight?

Client: Well, the whole thing. Everybody kind of hanging out and running around. I can't seem to get it together with anybody, so I guess I freak out.

Clinician: And then what happens?

Client: I usually go home and go to sleep. But I'm usually pretty bummed out.

Clinician: Are you saying that you don't fit in with these people and that's what makes you feel bummed out?

Client: Well, I don't know. These are my friends, I guess—but it never seems to work out. (Morganstern, 1976, pp. 67–68)

Do these two people understand each other? We do not know for sure, and, as long as the interview goes on this way, neither do they. Accordingly, the clinician will at some point need to request clarification of the client's words. She or he might have done so right away, as follows:

Client: When I'm in such heavy situations I just get real uptight. . . .

Clinician: I think I have some idea of what you are saying, but everyone has slightly different interpretations. So I wonder if you can help me get a better understanding of what you mean. For example, when you say that you're uptight in these situations, what does that mean for you?

Client: Well, uptight, you know. Tense.

Clinician: You mean your muscles get tense?

Client: My neck gets very sore—and I get a headache lots of times.

Clinician: Anything else happen that you notice?

Client: Well, either because of my neck or my headache, I start sweating a lot.

---

[4]This is not as farfetched as one might suppose. The authors have heard many "interviews" between foreign-born M.D.'s and residents of state mental hospitals which resulted in utter confusion for all concerned.

Clinician: So when you say you're uptight you are really experiencing it physically. What kinds of things do you say to yourself when this happens?

Client: I'm thinking, man you are really paranoid. You just can't relax in any situation. You are really a loser. And then I want to get out of there fast. . . . (Morganstern, 1976, p. 68) Here, the amount and clarity of information transmitted are increased manyfold.

Clients can become just as confused as clinicians, but those reluctant to appear "stupid" or to question a person "in authority" may not reveal their dilemma. They may simply go away mad. Some evidence on this point comes from a study conducted in a medical setting by Korsch and Negrete (1972). Their data showed, among other things, that communication from doctors to patients' mothers in a pediatric clinic was obstructed by the use of medical terms and that client confusion and dissatisfaction often resulted. For example, a "lumbar puncture" (spinal tap) was sometimes assumed to be an operation for draining the child's lungs and "incubation period" was interpreted by one mother as the time during which her child had to be kept in bed.

Circumventing similar problems in clinical psychology is often difficult, but it can be facilitated by attention to certain guidelines. Skilled interviewers try to avoid (or at least explain) jargon, ask questions in a direct and straightforward way (i.e., "What experiences have you had with masturbation?", not "Do you ever touch yourself?"), and request frequent feedback from their client (e.g., "Is all this making sense to you?").

In addition, clinicians try to assure that their verbal behavior conveys interest, patience, concern, and acceptance. Expressions by the interviewer of hostility, belligerence, impatience, ridicule, belittlement, or prejudgment are not generally desirable. Goldstein (1976) has summarized some conversational dos and don'ts from Wolberg (1967) which illustrate the kinds of verbal communications which clinicians prefer (and avoid). Two examples are presented in edited form below:

1. *Client:* I feel helpless and I think I ought to end it all.
   Unsuitable responses:
   A. You better snap out of it soon.
   B. Well, that's a nice attitude, I must say.
   Suitable responses:
   A. I wonder what is behind this feeling.
   B. You sound as if you think you're at the end of your rope.
2. *Client:* I am considered very intelligent.
   Unsuitable responses:
   A. An opinion with which you undoubtedly concur.
   B. The troubles you've gotten into don't sound intelligent to me.
   C. Even a moron sometimes thinks he is intelligent.
   Suitable responses:
   A. How do you feel about that?
   B. That sounds as if you aren't sure of your intelligence.

Nonverbal Communication   As with all human beings, a constant stream of nonverbal behavior accompanies virtually all of the client's (and the interviewer's) verbal behavior. Indeed, the nonverbal communication channel usually remains open even when the verbal channel is shut down. This has been understood by perceptive individuals for centuries (see McReynolds, 1975), and, in 1905, Freud summarized the point well: "He that has eyes to see and ears to hear may convince himself that no mortal can keep a secret. If his lips are silent, he chatters with his finger-tips; betrayal oozes out of him at every pore" (pp. 77–78). Since both members of an interview dyad are sending and receiving nonverbal messages, the clinician must not only be sensitive to incoming signals but also to those that she or he may be transmitting as well.

A representative sample of nonverbal interview dimensions is presented below.

1   Physical appearance—e.g., height, weight, grooming, style and condition of clothing, unusual characteristics (e.g., partial paralysis, missing limb), muscular development, hairstyle

2   Movements—e.g., gestures, repetitive arm, hand, head, leg, or foot motions, tics or other apparently involuntary movements, pacing, handling of cigarettes, matches, or other objects

3   Posture—e.g., slouching, rigidity, crossed or uncrossed arms or legs, head in hands

4   Eye contact—e.g., constant, fleeting, none

5   Facial expressions—e.g., smiles, frowns, grimaces, raised eyebrows

6   Emotional arousal—e.g., tears, "wet" eyes, sweating, dryness of lips, frequent swallowing, blushing or paling, voice or hand tremor, rapid respiration, frequent shifts in body position, "startle" reactions, inappropriate laughter

7   Speech variables—e.g., tone of voice, speed, slurring, lisp, stuttering, blocking, accent, clarity, "style," sudden shifts in topic, omission of relevant content

In addition to "picking up" the nature of nonverbal client behaviors, clinicians also look for consistencies and inconsistencies between the verbal and nonverbal channels. The statement "I feel pretty good today" will thus be given less credence if the speaker is on the verge of tears than if a happy smile is evident.

Similarly, the interviewer attempts to coordinate his or her own verbal and nonverbal behavior so as to give the client unambiguous messages. Telling a client to "take your time" will carry more weight as a statement of relaxed, patient interest if it is said slowly and quietly than if it is blurted out while rapidly tapping a foot. Friendly eye contact, some head nodding, an occasional smile or laugh (when appropriate), and an attentive posture helps let the client know that the interviewer is listening closely. Overdoing it may backfire, however. A constant smile, a continuously knitted brow, sidelong glances (accompanied by dramatically slow "mm-hmms"), and other theatrics may only convey interviewer anxiety (Wallen, 1956).

Most clinicians agree that observation of nonverbal dimensions begins at the moment that client and clinician meet and continues until they part. They often differ, however, as to what nonverbal behavior means. Interviewers committed to a sign-oriented approach are likely to draw higher-level inferences from nonverbal behaviors than those adopting a more sample-oriented stance.

For example, a social-learning interpretation of an increase in respiration, perspiration, and "fidgeting" while a client talks about sex would probably be that some emotional arousal is associated with that topic. Other clinicians would go further. Phenomenologists might look at the form of specific "fidgeting" gestures (such as brushing lint off a shirt) and see a denial of sexual feelings or a request that the interviewer "keep away." Psychodynamic interviewers may go another step to postulate that nonverbal behaviors (e.g., twirling a ring on a finger) are symbolic representations of sexual activity or other unconscious impulses (e.g., Feldman, 1959; Garner, 1970).[5] Whatever level of inference stems from it, however, nonverbal behavior serves as a powerful communication channel and a valuable source of supplementary interview data.

A General Note   There are many aspects of clinical interviewing which we have not covered due to limitations on our space and our goals. Dealing with silences, how to address the client, the pros and cons of note-taking, handling personal questions, and the advisability and timing of confronting a client's inconsistencies are just a few of the additional issues with which clinicians are faced in interview situations. The reader interested in further, more detailed exploration of interviewing techniques is referred to the general references listed at the beginning of this chapter.

RESEARCH ON THE INTERVIEW

It is now time to look at some research on the interview as a social event and as a source of assessment data.

Social Interaction and Influence in the Interview

Until 1942, when Carl Rogers published the first transcripts from phonographic recordings of therapy interviews, the exact nature of clinical interactions had been unknown.[6] Afterward, interview research began to grow rapidly. At first, it focused on basic issues like the effects of recording and the relative accuracy and completeness of clinicians' summaries versus electrical recordings of the same

---

[5]Moderate to high-level inferences about nonverbal behavior in nonclinical contexts are also common, as exemplified by popular books such as *Body Language* (Fast, 1970) and *Man Watching: A Field Guide to Human Behavior* (Morris, 1977) as well as more scholarly works (e.g., Harper, Wiens, & Matarazzo, 1978).

[6]Rogers's recordings were considered scandalous at the time since tradition ruled out all but narrative case reports. The fact that he was a *psychologist* (not a psychiatrist) doing therapy with an adult made Rogers's revelations even more distasteful to those not yet accustomed to the expanding roles of postwar clinicians.

interview (Covner, 1942, 1944; Snyder, 1945). However, once it was established that recording devices were not significantly disruptive and provided the most complete picture of the interview, researchers struck out in many new directions.

Descriptive Research   One of these new directions involved descriptive research aimed at relating interview variables to rapport-building, therapy effectiveness, and other interpersonal dimensions. Some studies focused on differences in specific interview tactics used by Rogerians and non-Rogerians (e.g., Porter, 1943; Seeman, 1949; Snyder, 1954; Strupp, 1960), while others were aimed at defining interview variables like client "resistance" (Snyder, 1953), interviewer "ambiguity" (Bordin, 1955), and relationship "warmth" (Rausch & Bordin, 1957). Still other investigators engaged in detailed analyses of the audible content of conversations as a means of better understanding the interview process (e.g., Auld & Murray, 1955; Leary & Gill, 1959, Mahl, 1959). One team of researchers devoted years to the content analysis of just the first five minutes of a single interview (Pittenger, Hockett, & Danehy, 1960).

Researchers also sought to describe interviews (and the people and relationships in them) in terms of *noncontent* variables. Specialized equipment was used to collect information about things like the physiological arousal (e.g., heart rate) of interviewer and client (e.g., Dimascio, Boyd, Greenblatt, & Solomon, 1955; Greenblatt, 1959), and the stability, idiosyncrasies, and "equilibrium" of their speech and silence durations (e.g., Lennard & Bernstein, 1960; Saslow & Matarazzo, 1959). It has been suggested that data of this type can be used operationally to define various types of clients (e.g., "schizophrenics" versus "normals") and such interview concepts as "empathy," "transference," and "insight" (Matarazzo, 1965).

Experimental Research   Descriptive clinical and laboratory research of the 1940s and 1950s generated large amounts of data about the interview which highlighted its complexity as a social event. An additional dimension of this complexity was revealed by experiments which confirmed that interviews are not only data gathering contexts, but *social influence* situations as well. Research of this type was stimulated in large measure by Skinner's (1948, 1957) conceptualization of verbal behavior as a set of response classes which can be modified by its consequences.

Dozens of *verbal conditioning* studies soon began to appear. They showed in general that not only can fairly simple response classes (like the use of plural nouns) be affected by reinforcement, but that more clinically relevant interviewee verbalizations (such as positive or negative opinions, reports of family memories, expression of feelings, self-evaluations, and delusional speech) are alterable through contingent interviewer feedback (see reviews by Greenspoon, 1962; Kanfer, 1968; Krasner, 1958, 1965; and Salzinger, 1959).

Other research indicated that noncontent variables in the interview (e.g., duration and frequency of client speech and silence) can also be systematically influenced by the clinician. In several studies, for example, duration of interviewee speech was increased when the interviewer nodded his head or said "mm-hmm" while listening (Kanfer & McBrearty, 1962; Matarazzo, 1965). Work by Matarazzo and his colleagues (e.g., Matarazzo, Weitman, Saslow, & Weins, 1963) showed other ways in which interviewer and interviewee speech duration may be related. When an interviewer increased and then decreased the duration of his own utterances over three parts of a conversation, interviewees did the same. When he decreased then increased his speech length, interviewees again followed suit. This is called *synchrony* (see Figure 5-1).

A quick glance at verbal conditioning and other interviewer-influence data might give the impression that interview assessment would be routinely facilitated by social reinforcement of client speech and/or by increasing the clinician's speech duration. Unfortunately, the problem is not that simple. For one thing, during assessment, interviewers are anxious to avoid direct reinforcement of specific types of statements since this may bias the data generated. And in any case, all the relationships described in published research do not seem to hold universally. As an example, synchrony was observed originally during experimentally controlled interviews. Though it has also appeared in other settings (i.e., conversations between astronauts and their ground control stations; Matarazzo, Weins, Saslow, Dunham, & Voas, 1964), it was not found in a therapy situation (Matarazzo, Weins, Matarazzo, & Saslow, 1968). Further,

Figure 5-1 Interviewer influence on duration of interviewee speech. *(From the* Handbook of Clinical Psychology, *edited by Benjamin B. Wolman. Copyright © 1965 by McGraw-Hill Book Company. Used with permission of McGraw-Hill Book Company.)*

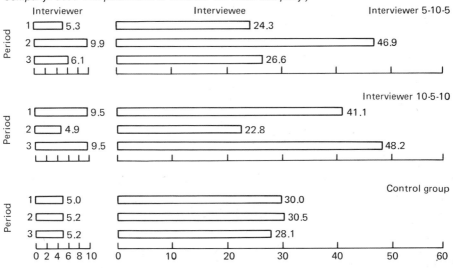

Mean duration of single units of speech, seconds

the use of "mm-hmm's," especially when they are not contingent on specific responses, does not always produce increased interviewee verbal behavior (e.g., Siegman, 1976) and may even decrease it (Siegman, 1972, 1975). Davis (1971) presented data which suggest that social competition may operate instead of or along with social reinforcement in some interviews.

Findings such as these suggest that the *situation* in which the interview takes place and the *social roles* of the participants may significantly alter the nature of the interaction. In therapy, for example, the synchrony-producing influence of clinician upon client may be moderated, obscured, or even reversed by the client's influence upon the clinician. In other words, unless the clinician experimentally controls utterance durations (as in Figure 5-1), they may increase with quiet clients and decrease with those who are more talkative (e.g., Heller, Meyers, & Kline, 1963; Lennard & Bernstein, 1960). Pope, Nudler, VonKorff, and McGee (1974) showed that the relative status of interviewer and interviewee can influence their interactive behavior. When novice student interviewers talked to other students in an experimental setting, synchrony in verbal productivity occurred, but it disappeared when higher-status professionals did the interviews.

There have been many other laboratory experiments on social influence in the interview and the literature continues to grow (see reviews by Heller, 1971; Jourard, 1969; Matarazzo, 1962, 1965; Matarazzo & Weins, 1972; Weins, 1976). Some of the data are surprising. For example, it appears that "warm" interviewers do not always enhance interviewee speech (Heller, 1972; Heller, Davis, & Meyers, 1966) and that self-disclosure may actually be facilitated by interviewers who are reserved (even hostile) and who transmit messages that are somewhat ambiguous (Ganzer & Sarason, 1964; Heller, 1972). This may be because, under moderately stressful experimental circumstances, certain subjects feel they should try to please the interviewer by "telling all." It appears doubtful however, that stress-producing interviewer behaviors aid client verbalization and disclosure in actual clinical assessment interviews (Heller, 1972).

In summary, research on interview interaction and influence has shown these areas to be extremely complicated aspects of social behavior which are under the influence of a wide array of interviewer, client, relationship, and situational factors. The data published so far show encouraging progress in researchers' technical and conceptual sophistication, but they do not tell the individual clinician the "right" way to conduct interviews (Richardson, Dohrenwend, & Klein, 1965). Indeed, because there probably is not a single "right" way for all interviewers to talk to all clients under all circumstances, the greatest value of past and future interview research is in providing scientific information about what is likely to happen when various combinations of people, tactics, and situations occur in the context of clinical assessment.

Reliability and Validity of Interview Data

It is virtually impossible to speak of interview reliability and validity as if they were fixed characteristics of all clinical conversations. In light of research described in the last section, it should be obvious that the degree to which an interviewee gives the same information on different occasions or to different interviewers (reliability) and the degree to which that information is accurate (validity) may depend upon the clinician, the client, and the circumstances under which the interview takes place. Exactly how strongly these factors affect interview reliability and validity is still unknown (Morganstern, 1976), so it is possible to give only a general idea of the value of the interview as a data source.

Reliability   Some writers have estimated interview reliability by looking at the degree to which different judges agree on the *inferences* (e.g., ratings, diagnoses, or personality trait descriptions) drawn from conversations with the same client (Berg, 1966; Matarazzo, 1965). Unfortunately, this confounds the reliability of what the client *said* with the quality of the interviewer's inference system (e.g., the diagnostic categories). For example, if a client tells two clinicians the same thing and they each draw different conclusions from it, it seems fair to say that the interview was reliable, but that the interviewers' inferences were not.

It seems more relevant to ask about the reliability of interview data themselves. Theoretically, one would expect clients' responses to be very similar from one interview to the next or from one interviewer to the next, but there is surprisingly little clinical information on this point. The data which are available come mainly from survey research and indicate that when innocuous information (such as age) is requested, or when interinterview intervals are short, reliability can be quite high (e.g., Sobell & Sobell, 1975; Vaughn & Reynolds, 1951).

Other interview data may be less reliable, especially when reports are widely separated in time. Wenar & Coulter (1962), for example, found that only 43 percent of the parents they talked to gave consistent information about their children's history (e.g., age at toilet training) when interviews were separated by 3 to 6 years. Other research on parents' reports about their children's behavioral history reveals that reliability tends to be particularly low on questions about vague issues such as "overactivity" and quite high on more easily defined questions such as stuttering (Lapouse & Monk, 1958). Further, reports on child-rearing practices such as toilet training and weaning tend to change from interview to interview, usually in the direction of making the parents appear more up-to-date and in line with the latest trends (Robbins, 1963). Perhaps because clinical interview reliability is presumed or because, in typical clinical situations, there is little interest in obtaining the same information more than once, most evaluative research on the interview has focused upon its *validity*.

Validity   Interview data can be extremely accurate in absolute terms and, in comparison to other assessment tools, may be the best source of clinical information. In a study cited by Thorne (1972), for example, answers to the question, "Are you homosexual?" were more valid indicators of sexual orientation than any combination of psychological tests. Similarly, Mischel

(1968) cites evidence that what people say they will do is a better predictor of future behavior than test scores. This is hardly surprising, but one should also keep in mind that the validity of interview responses can be reduced under certain circumstances.

A client's response to "Tell me something about your marital problems" might be very different from his answer to the question, "Why can't you get along with your spouse?" (Ganzer & Sarason, 1964; Heller, 1972; Pope & Siegman, 1968; Thomas, 1973). Further, salient interviewer characteristics such as age, sex, or race may alter interviewee candor (e.g., Benney, Reisman, & Star, 1956; Cantril, 1944; Grantham, 1973; Erlich & Riesman, 1961; Hyman, Cobb, Feldman, Hart, & Stember, 1954; Katz, 1942; Ledvinka, 1971).

Clients may also misremember or for some reason purposely distort various types of information. Even simple, easily verified factual data such as use of cream in coffee, possession of a driver's license, grade point average, and children's height, weight, and date of birth are occasionally reported inaccurately (Cannell & Kahn, 1968; Doering & Raymond, 1935; Pinneau & Milton, 1958; Walsh, 1967; Yarrow, Campbell & Burton, 1970). The probability of some distortion may be even higher when the information sought is of a more emotionally charged, sensitive, or less specific nature, such as drug use, annual income, religious beliefs, criminal record, sexual behavior, child-rearing practices, behavior disorders, or occasions and length of mental hospitalization (Ball, 1967; Chess, Thomas, & Birch, 1966; Dirks & Kuldau, 1974; Fidler & Kleinknecht, 1977; Mednick & Shaffer, 1963; Schwitzgebel & Kolb, 1974; Sobell, Sobell, & Samuels, 1974). Clients are often understandably wary about what they will tell about themselves and to whom; a friend may laugh at tales of your vegetable imitations, but a psychiatrist or psychologist might treat them more seriously. The desire to present oneself in a particular light to a "mental health professional" has been called "impression-management" (Braginsky, Braginsky, & Ring, 1969; Goffman, 1959), and it can lead to invalid interview data (Sherman, Trief, & Sprafkin, 1975).

Situational factors of various kinds may also affect the validity of interview data. It is not hard to understand that the things a person would say to an interviewer on national television might differ from information given in a private consulting room. And even in private, self-disclosure may vary as a function of the topics discussed and whether or not candor and frankness are expected in the situation (Heller, 1971; Wilson & Rappaport, 1974).

Interviewer Error and Bias   Even reliable and valid interview data are of little clinical value if they are twisted in some way by the interviewer. Thus, it is impossible to conclude an evaluation of the interview as a data source without some mention of its susceptibility to distortion. Unfortunately, this susceptibility is rather strong.

Distortion may be accidental, as when the client's words are not recorded accurately by the interviewer. Unless the interaction is captured on audio or video tape, potentially important information may be lost or misrepresented

MISS PEACH   By Mell Lazarus

Cartoon 5-1   Miss Peach by Mell Lazarus. *(Courtesy of Mell Lazarus and Field Newspaper Syndicate.)*

simply because the volume of incoming data was so large. Sometimes, "errors" are deliberate. Schwitzgebel & Kolb (1974) quoted an interviewer hired to conduct structured inquiries as saying: "One of the questions asked for five reasons why parents had put their child in an institution. I found most people can't think of five reasons. I didn't want [the boss] to think I was goofing off, so I always filled in all five."

Personal biases, preferences, and various kinds of prejudice may strongly affect the conclusions reached by clinical (and nonclinical) interviewers. In an early, but still relevant study by Rice (1929), social workers' judgments of why skid-row bums had become destitute were found to be related to personal views, not just interview data. Thus, a prohibitionist interviewer saw drinking as the cause of poverty in 62 percent of the cases, while a socialist said the interviewees were poor mainly because of general economic conditions. More recent research clearly indicates that interview-based diagnoses are strongly influenced by nonrelevant factors. To cite two examples, Mehlman (1952) and Raines and Rohrer (1955, 1960) showed that interviewers tend to have "favorite" diagnoses which they apply more often than any others. Similarly, Temerlin (1968) found that psychologists' and psychiatrists' diagnoses of a client may be determined by prejudicial information given to them before they ever hear the client speak.

One possible way around such problems would be to employ a mechanical interviewer and, indeed, computer interviewing is now a part of some medical and psychological assessment procedures (Angle, Hay, Hay, & Ellinwood, 1977). Clients communicate with the computer through a television screen and a typewriter and appear to accept this human-nonhuman interaction quite well (Greist, Klein, & Van Cura, 1973; Slack & Van Cura, 1968). This approach virtually eliminates error and bias in both inquiry and response recording. Even so, computers are not likely to replace humans or entirely eliminate human judgment (and error) in interview-based assessment because the flexibility of a live clinician is an indispensable part of interviewing. However, computers *are* likely to produce great time and energy savings in the gathering of routine information. They can also reduce distortion in the clinical assessment process by providing yet another mechanical means of data collection to supplement more subjective procedures.

A Final Note   Research on the interview as an assessment data source does not justify a single, all-encompassing conclusion. As Garfield (1974, p. 90) put it, "The interview has been used in so many different ways for various purposes, by individuals with varying skills, that it is a difficult matter to make a final judgment concerning its values." A lot depends upon the skill of the interviewer, but the exact nature of what "skill" means is still not entirely clear. Although the interview will undoubtedly continue to occupy a primary assessment role in clinical psychology, it must also remain the object of research. Peterson's (1968a) concluding statement is still timely: "We are not justified in extolling the virtues of the interview as a clinical procedure at the present time. It is widely used. It makes sense. But its merit as a clinical procedure needs far better documentation than is available to date, and its improvement as a procedure awaits appropriate experimental investigation" (p. 129).

Chapter 6

Testing in Clinical Psychology

As we saw in Chapter 2, the history of clinical psychology as a science and as a profession is intimately related to the development, administration, and interpretation of psychological tests. And even though clinicians now perform many functions in addition to or instead of testing (Garfield & Kurtz, 1976; Kelly, 1961), various kinds of tests remain a part of clinical research and practice (Buros, 1974, 1975; Lubin, Wallis, & Paine, 1971; Wade & Baker, 1977). It is therefore essential that we consider the nature and characteristics of psychological tests, the means through which they are constructed, and the results of research on their value as assessment tools.

What Is a Test?

In simplest terms, a test is nothing more than a particular way of observing and describing a person's behavior in a standard situation (Cronbach, 1970; Peterson, 1968a; Sundberg, 1977). Tests present certain planned stimuli (inkblots or true-false questions, for example) and ask the client to respond to them in some way. The client's reactions are recorded as the test's *results,* to be used as sample, sign, or correlate in the clinician's overall assessment strategy. Accordingly, the data generated by tests may lead to very conservative, situation-specific statements (e.g., "The client appeared confused and disoriented during testing and was correct on 15 out of 60 items") or, at the opposite pole, to sweeping, high-level inferences (e.g., "The client's ego boundaries are so ill-defined as to make adequate functioning outside an institution very unlike-ly"). Most commonly, test results are used to guide inferences which are between these extremes.

Tests have been likened to highly structured interviews because they ask the testee to respond to specifically programmed assessment stimuli presented in a predetermined sequence. They also share certain characteristics with observa-tional assessments by providing an opportunity for the clinician to watch and listen as the client deals with the test and the test situation. In some ways, however, tests are distinct from other assessment techniques. For example:

1 A test can be administered in a nonsocial context. The items are often presented in writing to a client who sits alone and records his or her responses on an answer sheet. Here, no observational assessment supplements test data.

2 A given client's test results can often be compared mathematically to the responses of hundreds or even thousands of other persons who have taken the same test. When a large amount of previous test data (called *norms*) are available for comparison with each new client's responses, the test is said to be *standardized*[1].

3 Tests may be administered to clients in groups as well as individually. College entrance examinations, which are usually given in an auditorium or other large room, provide a good example of how masses of people can be assessed at the same time through tests.

What Do Tests Test?

There are thousands of psychological tests in existence today. They are designed to be administered to infants, children, adolescents, adults, senior citizens, students, soldiers, mental patients, office workers, prisoners, and every other imaginable group (see Anastasi, 1976 and Cronbach, 1970, for book-length summaries). Further, tests appear in many *modes* or *styles*. Some pose direct, specific questions ("Do you ever feel discouraged?"), while others ask for more general reactions to less distinct stimuli ("Tell me what you see in this drawing"). Some are presented in paper-and-pencil form, while others are given orally. Some require use of verbal skills ("What is a chicken?"), and others ask the client to perform various tasks ("Please trace the correct path through this puzzle maze").

Recognition of the pervasiveness and variety of tests in our society can lead to the mistaken assumption that each test instrument is in a class by itself and that testers are seeking to measure thousands of different things about human behavior. Actually, many tests have very similar purposes and can be grouped into a surprisingly small number of categories. The vast majority of tests seek to measure (1) *intellectual functioning*, (2) *personality characteristics*, (3) *attitudes, interests, preferences,* and *values,* or (4) *ability*. We shall consider some examples

---

[1]Cronbach (1970) reserves the term "standardized" for tests which are administered in precisely equivalent fashion by each tester. This is an important point because we shall see that differences in testing procedure can influence test results.

in each of these categories a bit later. For now, it is worth noting that the tests most commonly used by clinical psychologists are those of intellectual functioning and personality (Lubin, Wallis, & Paine, 1971; Wade & Baker, 1977). This is partly because clinicians tend to be oriented toward such things in their own treatment and research work, and partly because other people expect them to provide data and advice on these variables.

Once it is understood that tests focus on only a few basic goals, it may seem reasonable to ask why there are so many in each category. One reason is that testers are constantly seeking to improve the reliability and/or validity of existing instruments. This results in new editions of older tests.

Another reason for the proliferation of tests is that there is constant interest among testers in measuring things in new and more sophisticated ways. For example, psychologist A may feel that the anxiety test developed by psychologist B does not really "get at" anxiety very well, and so she or he constructs a new instrument. Psychologist C, who espouses a different clinical model, may argue that A and B are both "off base" with their tests and so comes up with yet another "more meaningful" device. This sequence has been especially noticeable in personality testing, but it is evident in varying degrees in other test categories as well.

A third factor responsible for the sometimes bewildering array of tests is that testers' interests keep getting more specific, thus prompting the development of special-purpose tests. In intelligence testing, for example, instruments are available for use with infants, the physically handicapped, and persons not fluent in English or from specific cultural backgrounds. Similarly, surveys of general preferences or interests have been followed by special-purpose tests aimed at assessing, say, the way adolescents spend leisure time or the things children find rewarding. A quick glance at the latest *Mental Measurements Yearbook* (Buros, 1978) or other test compendia (e.g., Chun, Cobb, & French, 1975; Comrey, Backer, & Glaser, 1973; Goldman & Saunders, 1974; Goldman & Busch, 1978) will reveal dozens of additional specialized instruments such as the Abortion Questionnaire, the College Drinking Questionnaire, the Ego Strength Scale, the Fear-of-Death Scale, the Post-Suicidal Attempt Scale, and the VD Questionnaire. Fascinating historical accounts of many now-forgotten tests are contained in Reisman (1966) and DuBois (1970).

Test Construction Procedures

Curious (or angry) members of the public often raise a basic question about psychological tests: "How do shrinks come up with these things?" The answer can get rather complex, but it is fair to say that tests are constructed in two basic ways: *rationally* and *empirically*.

The rational technique begins by asking, "What kind of test and test items would make sense for assessing the topic of interest?," and it then proceeds to build a test which answers that question. It is thus a kind of "common sense" approach to test construction.

The procedure can be illustrated through an absurd example. Suppose one

wished to have a test which could reliably and accurately identify adult humans
as male or female. Since the rational approach would involve sitting down and
thinking about the kinds of things that might differentiate the sexes, the
clinician's own view of what makes males and females different would shape the
content of the test.

If physical characteristics are seen as crucial, and a true-false format is
preferred, the test might contain items such as:

1   I have a penis.
2   I have a vagina.
3   I once had a penis.
4   I once had a vagina.
5   I shave my face.
6   I have a beard.

Another clinician might feel that a performance test would provide more
accurate assessment and would list *tasks* which he or she feels males and females
will deal with in different ways. Such a test might include the following requests
which are thought to be approached differently by men and women:

1   Please look at your fingernails.
2   Please look at the heel of your shoe.
3   Please look at the ceiling.
4   Please take off your shoes.
5   Please cross your legs.
6   Please pick up these books and carry them across the room.

A third individual might believe that physical characteristics and performances
are only surface indicators of sex and that "real" maleness or femaleness can be
measured only by tapping the unconscious. The resulting test might try to look at
unconscious themes by asking the client to fill in incomplete sentences such as:

1   A dependent person is_____.
2   Strength is_____.
3   The trouble with most men is_____.
4   Most women are_____.
5   I like to_____.
6   There is nothing worse than_____.

In any case, the form and content of a rationally constructed test will reflect in
large measure the *tester's* perception of what should be tested and how.

The main alternative to rational construction procedures is the empirical
approach. Here, instead of trying to decide ahead of time what test content
should be used to measure a particular construct, the tester lets the content
"choose itself." Thus, in building a sex test, the clinician might amass a large
number of self-report test items, performance tasks, inkblots, or whatever, and

then administer all of them to a large group of people who have *already been identified* (through self-report, observation, chromosome tests, or the like) as males or females. Responses to all the test material would then be examined to see if any items, tasks, or other stimuli were consistently handled differently by men and women.

When such stimuli are identified, they form the initial content of the test, *whether or not they make any sense intuitively.* It might be, for example, that the things which reliably discriminated males from females included "true" responses to items like "my nose runs a lot," "coffee makes me sleepy," or "my shoes are too tight." Similarly, success at a task like lifting a chair off the floor while bending at the waist may also have separated the two sex groups. The reasons *why* such items or tasks separate males from females may become the subject of additional theoretical research, but, for practical purposes, testers are usually willing to employ a good empirically constructed test in spite of the fact that its power cannot be clearly explained.

How does the would-be test builder decide whether to start with rational or empirical procedures? Several factors may be decisive. For one thing, the rational approach is generally faster, easier, and less expensive; it does not necessitate initial administration of many items to many people in order to settle on those which will actually comprise the test. These features may make rational procedures particularly attractive to the clinician who does not have easy access to a large pool of test material and willing subjects or who is forced by circumstances to come up with a test on relatively short notice.

Rational procedures may also be favored by clinicians who are engaged in research aimed at testing a particular theory. That theory may hypothesize, for example, that people differ mainly in terms of "nebbishness." Assuming no nebbish test is available, the researcher who wishes to explore this hypothesis through testing will need an instrument which corresponds to what the theory says nebbishness is and how it should be measured. Development of a Neb Test would thus likely proceed on rational grounds.

On the other hand, clinicians who are not as concerned with theoretical notions and who have time and other resources available to them may find the empirical approach far more desirable, especially when attempting to make specific predictions about people. If the tester's task is to identify individuals who are likely to graduate from law school, for example, it makes good sense to find out if successful lawyers respond to certain test stimuli in a way which is reliably different from law school dropouts.

Sometimes, rational and empirical techniques are combined, as exemplified by the *internal consistency* approach to personality test construction. Here, data from rationally chosen items or from existing tests of particular interest are analyzed through complex mathematical procedures to determine which are correlated and which are not. Groups of correlated items are identified as *scales* which are thought to be relatively pure measures of personality dimensions such as needs or traits (Maloney & Ward, 1976).

Rational-empirical test construction combinations appear in other contexts as well. For example, the person who wishes to construct a true-false test using empirical procedures is immediately faced with a problem: Of the millions of true-false items which could be included in the initial piloting of a test, the tester must somehow decide which ones to try. This is usually done on rational grounds; items will be selected from older, valued tests or might just be those the clinician feels ought to be tried out. Similarly, empirical procedures often appear in the development of rationally constructed tests. If administration of a new "rational" instrument reveals that certain of its items are better at discriminating various target groups (e.g., good versus poor typists), those items are more likely to be retained in subsequent editions of the test than are items with little or no "power."

This last point should serve as a reminder that regardless of how a test is constructed *initially,* its value as an assessment instrument must ultimately be established on empirical grounds through research on its reliability and validity (see Chapter 4). That requirement is emphasized and elaborated in an official American Psychological Association document called *Standards for Educational and Psychological Tests and Manuals* (APA, 1974a). Later in this chapter we shall look at how various tests have fared when scrutinized by reliability/validity research. For now, let us consider the nature and content of some prominent representatives of each of the four psychological test categories identified earlier.

MAJOR TYPES OF TESTS

Intellectual Functioning

It is fitting that we begin our exploration of psychological tests with measures of intelligence, since, as noted in Chapter 2, the early history of clinical psychology is basically the early history of intelligence tests.

Almost everyone would agree that intelligence is a good thing to have, but there is little consensus about what intelligence actually *is*. After reviewing a large number of definitions of this elusive construct, Frank (1976) concluded that "the situation is characterized much more by confusion than by agreement" (p. 126). This state of affairs has generated the half-joking suggestion among clinicians that "intelligence is whatever intelligence tests measure." Indeed, the history of intelligence test development reveals that each tester proceeded initially on rational grounds and that each of the instruments which resulted (218 of them in Buros's 1974 *Tests in Print*) reflects its creator's view of how best to measure intellectual functioning.

Intelligence test builders have been influenced to a certain extent in their rational approach by models or theories about the essential nature of intelligence. This is not the place to describe these theories (for reviews, see Reisman, 1966 or Maloney & Ward, 1976) but, to cite one major dimension, some writers describe intelligence primarily as a general characteristic (called *g*) while others see it as made up of several (as many as 120) specific intellectual functions (called *s*) such as word fluency, reasoning, and memory. The practical relevance of *g, s,* or other intelligence theories for our purposes is actually rather limited, however, mainly because test authors have not followed theory all that closely. Though one can find a certain theoretical flavoring in the major intelligence tests described below, none of them really reflects, say, the *g* or *s* approach clearly enough to provide any definitive validation of one theory or another (Maloney & Ward, 1976).

The Binet Scales   We saw in Chapter 2 that Alfred Binet was certainly not the first person to develop a measure of intelligence, but that his original test and the revisions based upon it have been among the most popular and influential means of assessing the mental ability of children. In its earliest form (1905), Binet's test consisted of thirty questions and tasks, including things like unwrapping a piece of candy, following a moving object with the eyes, comparing objects of differing weights, repeating numbers or sentences from memory, recognizing familiar objects, and the like (Frank, 1976). The child's test score was simply the number of items passed.

Beginning with a 1908 revision (and in every version since then) the tasks in Binet's test were *age-graded.* This means the items are arranged so that younger children would normally be expected to pass the earlier ones while progressively older children would normally be expected to pass progressively later ones. Binet and his collaborator, Theodore Simon, observed the test behavior of about 200 children and suggested, for example, that 3-year-olds ought to be able to identify their eyes, nose, and mouth, name simple objects in a picture, repeat a two-digit number and a six-syllable sentence, and give their last name. At 7 years, success at tasks such as finding missing parts of drawings, copying a written sentence and simple geometric figures, and identifying denominations of coins was expected. Items to be passed at the eleventh-year level included criticism of absurd sentences, definition of abstract concepts, and rearranging words to form a sentence. A child's *mental age* was seen as the highest age level at which *all* test items are passed (plus credit for any correct responses at higher levels).

The 1908 scale covered ages 3 to 13 and was brought to America by Goddard (see Chapter 2). Though immensely popular, the Binet-Simon test was seen as having several shortcomings. Some users were dissatisfied because the test tended to place more emphasis on verbal skills and knowledge than on the child's capacity for judgment. Others noted that the test was too easy at lower age levels and too difficult at the upper end (Reisman, 1966). Binet attempted to correct some of these problems in a 1911 revision of his test, but a far more influential version was to be written on the other side of the Atlantic in 1916 by Lewis Terman, a Stanford University psychologist.

Terman and other users of Binet's test had been aware for some time that expressing a child's intelligence mainly in terms of "mental age" was less than satisfactory, mainly because it was imprecise and left too much room for misinterpretation: "If a child's mental age equalled his chronological age, he was considered 'regular' (average) in intelligence; if his mental age was higher, he was 'advanced'; if his mental age was lower, he was 'retarded'" (Reisman, 1966, pp. 105–106). Terman's edition of the Binet-Simon was called the Stanford Revision or the Stanford-Binet and soon became *the* intelligence test in American clinical psychology. The Stanford-Binet was standardized on a larger sample (1400 white subjects) than had been used for Binet's 1911 revision and across a wider age range (Terman's test was usable for persons from age 3 to 16).

More important, however, was the fact that Terman adopted an idea suggested in 1912 by German psychologist William Stern for numerically representing the relationship between mental and chronological age. Stanford-Binet results were expressed as the *intelligence quotient* (or IQ) which results when mental age (MA) is divided by chronological age (CA) and multiplied by 100. Thus, a 6-year-old whose mental age comes out as 8 on the Stanford-Binet would have an IQ of $[(8 \div 6) \times 100]$, or 133.

Terman suggested at one point that various IQ ranges be given labels such as "average," "feebleminded," and "genius," but he later expanded the list to range from "very superior" and "superior" through "high average," "average," "low average," "borderline defective," and "mentally defective." Similar systems are also in use to help classify persons at the lower end of the IQ scale as "mildly," "moderately," "severely," or "profoundly" retarded (Ullmann & Krasner, 1975). Although the original intent of such labels may have been to provide a shorthand summary of a particular person's score relative to others of his or her age (Merrill, 1938), IQ figures and the labels based upon them are often overemphasized, misused, and misinterpreted, especially by those unfamiliar with their meaning. For this reason, among others, the collection and use of IQ data have become the center of considerable controversy, as we shall see later.

Terman and Merrill revised and improved the Stanford-Binet in 1937 and again in 1960 using larger, more diverse (but still all-white) standardization samples. In 1972, the 1960 test was restandardized using a stratified sample of 2100 children representing diverse socioeconomic, geographical, racial, and cultural subgroups.

The 1960 edition is appropriate for clients from 3 to 18 and is the one most popular with clinicians today. Its items begin at the 2-year-old level and proceed upward in half-year steps until age 5, after which there are 1-year steps to age 14. The rest of the test items are at higher levels labeled "average adult," "superior adult I," "superior adult II," and "superior adult III." At each level, there are six items or tasks (with the exception of "average adult," which contains eight) arranged in order of increasing difficulty. The subject's *basal age* is the highest age level at which she or he passes all items, while the *ceiling age* is the level at which all items are failed.

The items themselves vary widely in order to tap memory, vocabulary, motor skills, comprehension, logic, problem solving, reasoning ability, abstract thinking, and the like. Box 6-1 contains examples of the types of tasks which appear at various age levels.

Box 6-1   Items of the Type Included in the 1960 Edition of the Stanford-Binet

Age 2:	Place geometric shapes into corresponding openings; identify body parts; stack blocks; identify common objects.
Age 4:	Name objects from memory; complete analogies (e.g., fire is hot; ice is _____); identify objects of similar shape; answer simple questions (e.g., "Why do we have schools?").
Age 6:	Define simple words; explain differences (e.g., between a fish and a horse); identify missing parts of a picture; count out objects.
Age 8:	Answer questions about a simple story; identify absurdities (e.g., in statements like "John had to walk on crutches because he hurt his arm"); explain similarities and differences among objects; tell how to handle certain situations (e.g., finding a stray puppy).
Age 10:	Define more difficult words; give explanations (e.g., about why people should be quiet in a library); list as many words as possible; repeat 6-digit numbers.
Age 12:	Identify more difficult verbal and pictured absurdities; repeat 5-digit numbers in reverse order; define abstract words (e.g., "sorrow"); fill in missing word in a sentence.
Age 14:	Solve reasoning problems; identify relationships among points of the compass; find similarities in apparently opposite concepts (e.g., "high" and "low"); predict the number of holes which will appear when folded paper is cut and then opened.
Superior Adult I:	Supply several missing words for incomplete sentences; repeat 6-digit numbers in reverse order; create a sentence using several unrelated words (e.g., "forest," "businesslike," and "dismayed"); describe similarities between concepts (e.g., "teaching" and "business").

Determination of IQ via the Stanford-Binet no longer involves merely dividing mental age by chronological age. That simple procedure from the 1916 version of the test has been replaced by use of IQ tables which correct the simple MA/CA $\times$ 100 formula by taking into account the mean and variance in IQs at each age level in the standardization sample. Thus, if a 6-year-old scores a mental age of 9 (which is not only high relative to his or her chronological age, but also higher than most 6-year-olds in the population on which the test was standardized), he or she would receive an IQ of 156 rather than the 150 which would have resulted simply from calculating MA/CA $\times$ 100. Such "corrected" scores were arrived at by setting up Stanford-Binet IQ tables in which the mean IQ at each age level is 100 with a standard deviation of 16. Thus, the modern IQ score for a given client represents degree of deviation from the average of her or his age level. An IQ of 100 is "average" for the age, 116 would be 1 standard deviation above average, and 84 would be 1 standard deviation below average.

In spite of its near universal acceptance and use with children, the 1937 Stanford-Binet continued to be criticized for its strong emphasis upon verbal aspects of intelligence and for its relative inappropriateness with clients over age 18. This second criticism became especially important as clinicians began to work more and more with adults during the 1930s.

The Wechsler Scales   One of the most prominent of these clinicians was David Wechsler, chief psychologist at New York's Bellevue Psychiatric Hospital. In the early 1930s, he began developing an intelligence test designed specifically for adults, and the result of his efforts, the Wechsler-Bellevue (W-B) Scale was published in 1939. This new test differed in several important ways from the Stanford-Binet, even though some W-B tasks were borrowed or adapted from it. First, of course, it was aimed at adults, 17 and older. Second, it did not attempt to measure mental age, which Wechsler felt was not a useful concept. Instead, the W-B was a *point scale* in which the client receives credit for each correct answer and in which IQ does not reflect the relationship between mental age and chronological age, but a comparison of points earned by the client to those earned by persons of equal age in the standardization sample.

A third distinguishing feature of the Wechsler-Bellevue was that its items were arranged in groups or *subtests* based on similarity. Each subtest contained increasingly difficult items. For example, on the "digit span" subtest, the client is asked to repeat various numbers, starting with three digits and progressing to nine digits. The score on this subtest is determined by the maximum number of digits the client is able to repeat without error. Similar tasks are included in the Stanford-Binet, but they are scattered throughout the test (i.e., a two-digit task at the 2.5-year level; a six-digit task at age 10) rather than occurring in one place. The W-B contains six *verbal* subtests (information, comprehension, arithmetic, similarities, digit span, and vocabulary) and five *performance* subtests (digit symbol, picture completion, block design, picture arrangement, and object assembly).

In its original form, the W-B had some deficiencies, the most serious of which was an inadequate standardization sample (1700 white New Yorkers aged 7 to 70). Nevertheless, its use for adult testing was common during and after World War II. In 1955, Wechsler revised and restandardized his test on a more representative sample of over 2000 white and nonwhite individuals (aged 16 to 74) living in all parts of the United States. This revision was called the Wechsler Adult Intelligence Scale, or WAIS, and has become the most popular adult intelligence test in use today (Lubin, Wallis, & Paine, 1971). Like the W-B, the WAIS has six verbal and five performance subtests and the client is given a Verbal IQ, a Performance IQ, and a Full Scale IQ (which combines the other two). Some examples of the types of items included on the WAIS are presented in Box 6-2.

The structure of the WAIS allows not only for IQ scores, but for the drawing of inferences from *patterns* of subtest scores. Some clinicians use WAIS subtest patterns or variability ("scatter") to help them arrive at a diagnostic label for the client, to assess the possibility of brain damage, or to describe certain personality dynamics.

Some time after publication of the W-B, Wechsler became interested in extending the point-scale test format for use with children. In 1949, the Wechsler Intelligence Scale for Children (WISC) appeared. The WISC was made up of twelve subtests (six verbal, six performance) of which only ten were usually administered. The subtests were similar to those listed for the W-B, but easier. The WISC was standardized on 2200 white children from all parts of the United

Box 6-2 Items of the Type Included in the Wechsler Adult Intelligence Scale (WAIS)

Information:	What is the shape of an orange?
	What does bread come from?
	What did Shakespeare do?
	What is the capital of France?
	What is the Malleus Malleficarum?
Comprehension:	Why do we eat food?
	What should you do with a wallet found in the street?
	Why do foreign cars cost more than domestic cars?
	What does "the squeaky wheel gets the grease" mean?
Arithmetic:	If you have four apples and give two away, how many do you have left?
	How long will it take a person to walk 20 miles at 3 miles per hour?
	If four people can finish a job in 6 days, how many people would it take to do the job in 2 days?
Similarities:	Identify similar aspects of pairs like: hammer-screwdriver, portrait-short story, dog-flower.
Digit span:	Repeat in forward and reverse order: 2- to 9-digit numbers.
Vocabulary:	Define: chair, dime, lunch, paragraph, valley, asylum, modal, cutaneous.
Picture completion:	Find missing objects in increasingly complex pictures.
Block design:	Arrange blocks to match increasingly complex standard patterns.
Picture arrangement:	Place increasing number of pictures together to make increasingly complex stories.
Object assembly:	Arrange parts of puzzles to form recognizable objects (e.g., dog, flower, person).

States, but because they ranged in age only from 5 to 15, the WISC was not generally useful for the very young. The Wechsler Preschool and Primary Scale of Intelligence (WPPSI) was developed later, but still only reached the 4-year-old level.

In 1974, a new version of the WISC called the WISC-R was published. It also includes six verbal and six performance subtests although, again, only five of each are actually administered. The content of the WISC-R items was changed to make it more meaningful to children, and the entire test was standardized on a new sample of 2200 white and nonwhite children from varying socioeconomic levels and geographical locations.

Other Intelligence Tests A variety of other intelligence instruments is also in use today. The most prominent of these are designed to assess intelligence without emphasis on verbal skills. It is important that such tests be available, since, as noted earlier, some clients may be too young or, for other reasons, unable to do well at verbal tasks. Tests such as the Cattell Infant Intelligence Scale, the Peabody Picture Vocabulary Test, and the Porteus Maze Test allow

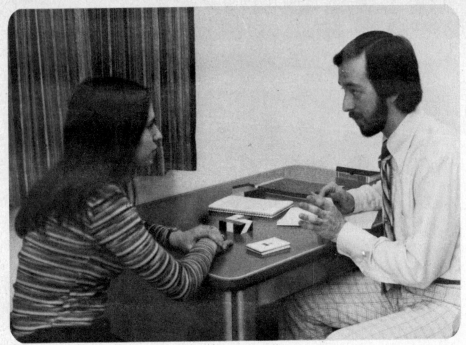

Figure 6-1 Administration of the WAIS.

the clinician to collect data on intellectual functioning in clients of this type (see Anastasi, 1976 or Yang & Bell, 1975 for details on such tests). They also provide a "backup" in cases where the clinician suspects that a client's performance on a standard IQ test may have been hampered by anxiety, specific verbal deficits (caused, say, by differences in cultural background), or other situational factors. If the client does better on special purpose or performance-oriented intelligence tests, the initial low IQ score can be better understood and will be less subject to misinterpretation.

Ability Tests

Many clinicians think of intelligence as mental ability and often refer to most of the tests described in the last section as general mental ability instruments. However, there is a significant number of other tests which are designed to tap more specific abilities. These include *aptitude* and *achievement* tests. Aptitude tests are designed to predict success in an occupation or an educational program. The Scholastic Aptitude Test (SAT), which is widely used to establish high school students' potential for college-level work, provides an example familiar to most undergraduates.

Achievement tests measure proficiency at certain tasks; that is, how much does the person know or how well can he or she do? The Wide Range Achievement Tests and the Graduate Record Examination (GRE) are two well-known instruments of this kind. Still other familiar tests combine features of aptitude, ability, and general intelligence instruments. The American College Test (ACT) is of this type.

The more specific the ability or aptitude tested, the less familiar the test is likely to be. If you have never heard of the Seashore Méasures of Musical Talents, the Crawford Small Parts Dexterity Test, the Meier Art Judgment Test, or the Minnesota Clerical Test, it is probably because they are administered in situations where very specialized abilities are of interest. It is also important to note that, in general, ability testing is more often done by personnel officers and educational, vocational, and guidance counselors than by clinical psychologists. The reader interested in further detailed information about specific ability testing of this type should consult Anastasi (1976) or Buros (1974).

Clinicians' interest in ability testing is usually related to assessment of specific cognitive capabilities or deficits. Sometimes this involves using general ability (intelligence) tests in special ways. As noted earlier, clinicians may seek to draw inferences about specific cognitive abilities, deficits, or even brain damage from the *pattern* of scores on instruments such as the WAIS or the WISC. However, the clinician may also choose from a variety of special-purpose tests which are designed to detect deterioriation in mental function caused by brain damage or other factors (Haynes & Sells, 1963).

Some of these tests emphasize perception and memory. For example, the Benton Visual Retention Test (Benton, 1968), the Bender Visual Motor Gestalt (or Bender-Gestalt; Bender, 1938) and the Memory-for-Designs Test (Graham & Kendall, 1960) ask the client to copy or draw from memory geometric figures or other designs. Other tests in this category are aimed at assessing the client's ability to form concepts and engage in other types of abstract thinking. The most popular instruments of this type are the Goldstein-Scheerer Tests of Abstract and Concrete Thinking (Goldstein & Sheerer, 1941). The five tests in this package include a block design copying task (similar to that included on the WAIS), a geometric figure copying task using sticks of varying length, and several sorting tasks in which the client is asked to sort out and arrange various kinds of objects according to concepts such as color, shape, or function. Again, the reader interested in detailed coverage on tests of this type, including the Lowenfeld Mosaic Test (Lowenfeld, 1949) and the Vigotsky Test (Vigotsky, 1934), should consult Anastasi (1976), Frank (1976), and Buros's *Yearbooks*.

Attitudes, Interests, Preferences, and Values

Information about a person's attitudes, interests, preferences, and values is most often collected in our society by pollsters, vocational and educational counselors, and social psychologists, but clinical psychologists often find such data useful as well. For example, before beginning to work with a distressed couple, the clinician may wish to get some idea about each spouse's attitudes and values relating to marriage and to his or her role in it. Similarly, if one wishes to use reward procedures to help a client alter her or his behavior, it is important to know what kinds of things she or he prefers: Dispensing chocolate-chip cookies to a child who is nauseated by them would hardly provide a desirable reward. Finally, it may be instructive for the clinician to know that the interests of a client who is severely conflicted about entering the medical profession are totally unlike those of successful physicians.

The many tests available to assess attitudes, interests, preferences, and values tend to overlap a lot (it is difficult to measure, say, interests without also measuring preferences), so there is little to be gained from trying to attach specific labels to each instrument in this category. It is important, however, to be aware of some of the more commonly used tests, such as the Strong Vocational Interest Blank (SVIB) and the Kuder Preference Record. These are paper-and-pencil instruments designed to assess clients' preferences for various pursuits, occupations, academic subjects, recreational activities, and types of people. Each results in an interest profile which can be compared with composite profiles gathered from members of occupational groups such as biologists, engineers, army officers, carpenters, police, ministers, accountants, salespeople, lawyers, and the like.

Generalized life orientations are often assessed via the Allport-Vernon-Lindzey Study of Values (Allport & Vernon, 1931; Allport, Vernon, & Lindzey, 1970), a paper-and-pencil instrument which asks the client to choose from among two or four alternatives about things like use of leisure time, interest in various news items, and the importance of various activities. The resulting profile of values shows the relative strength of six basic interests: theoretical ("intellectual"), economic, aesthetic, social, political, and religious. Other, more phenomenologically oriented, general value assessments include the Purpose-in-Life Test (Crumbaugh, 1968) and the Paths of Life Test (Morris, 1948).

There are also a large number of tests designed to assess more specific attitudes, interests, preferences, and values. None is as widely used as the SVIB, but each has a certain theoretical or practical appeal for some clinicians. For example, the social-learning model of clinical psychology has generated several tests aimed at illuminating client preferences and attitudes as a prelude to treatment planning and implementation. Among the most prominent of these is the Reinforcement Survey Schedule (Cautela & Kastenbaum, 1967), a list of situations and activities whose items are to be rated in terms of their desirability for the client. Special versions of this test for use with children and psychiatric inpatients have also been developed (Cautela, 1977). Other tests, such as the Pleasant Events Schedule (MacPhillamy & Lewinsohn, 1972), the Mediator-Reinforcer Incomplete Blank (Tharp & Wetzel, 1969), and the Children's Reinforcement Survey (Clement & Richard, 1976) provide additional examples of social-learning preference assessments.

Assessment of specific values and attitudes also make up part of Stuart and Stuart's (1975) Pre-marital Counseling Inventory. Each member of a couple contemplating marriage is asked to indicate their agreement or disagreement with fourteen statements which reflect values in and expectations about a permanent relationship (e.g., "the husband is breadwinner and his needs should come first" and "it weakens sexual attraction when men and women often see each other nude"). Major discrepancies in responses to items such as these are seen as highlighting areas of potential conflict which require compromise or, in some cases, careful rethinking of matrimonial plans.

The reader may have noticed that many of the things assessed by tests described in this section are related to the client's personality. Indeed, some would suggest that one's attitudes, interests, values, and preferences make up a large part of what is commonly thought of as personality. The overlap between these areas is well recognized, but there are also a vast number of psychological tests whose goal is the measurement of many other aspects of that elusive construct called personality, and it is to these instruments that we now turn our attention.

Personality Tests

"Personality" is the most commonly used term to describe and account for the individual differences and behavioral consistencies in human beings, and even though it is used on an everyday basis by almost everyone, there is not much agreement as to what exactly is meant. Some theorists see personality as an organized collection of traits, others hypothesize dynamic relationships among intrapsychic forces, while still others point to recurring patterns of behavior. As was the case with intelligence, the breadth and vagueness of the notion of personality mean that clinicians and personality researchers are free to assess it in a multitude of ways, usually in accordance with their own theoretical model of human behavior and clinical psychology (see Chapters 3 and 4). This is probably why there are more tests in the personality category than in any other (Buros, 1974, lists 440 of them). We cannot even begin to cover the vast array here, and so this section will be restricted to a brief look at several of the most prominent personality tests now in clinical use. Readers interested in more detailed treatment of personality and personality assessment strategies should consult specialized texts such as Hall and Lindzey (1970), Lanyon and Goodstein (1971), Liebert and Spiegler (1978), Mischel (1971), or Wiggins (1973).

There are two major types of personality tests: *objective* and *projective*. Objective tests present relatively clear, specific stimuli such as questions ("Have you ever wanted to run away from home?") or statements ("I am never depressed") or concepts ("Myself" or "Large dogs") to which the client is asked to respond with direct answers, choices, or ratings. Most often, objective personality tests are of the paper-and-pencil variety and can be scored mathematically (sometimes by machine), much like the multiple-choice or true-false exams used in large college classes. Some objective tests focus on only one aspect of personality such as anxiety, dependency, or ego strength, while others are designed to provide a more comprehensive overview of many personality dimensions.

Projective tests are mainly associated with the psychodynamic model of clinical psychology. Beginning with Freud's notion that people tend to defend themselves psychologically by attributing to other people and things those aspects of their own personality which are unacceptable, Frank (1939) broadened the concept of projection. Frank's "projective hypothesis" suggested that there is a general "tendency of people to be influenced in the cognitive mediation of perceptual inputs by their needs, interests, and overall psychological organization" (Exner, 1976, p. 61). In other words, each individual's personality will determine, in part at least, the way she or he sees and interprets things. Frank (1939) labeled tests which specifically encourage clients to display this tendency as "projective methods." In general, these methods or tests elicit reactions to ambiguous or unstructured stimuli (such as inkblots or incomplete sentences) which are interpreted as a reflection of (primarily unconscious) personality structure and dynamics. Some projective tests involve a paper-and-pencil format, but more often the client gives an oral response to each item. These responses are transcribed or tape recorded by the tester for later scoring.

Though projective test responses can often be converted to numerical form, the scoring process is far more subjective and inferential than is the case with objective tests. This is primarily because projective tests collect "raw" verbal responses which must somehow be transformed into numbers. Objective tests structure things so that the client does the transformation for the tester by choosing "true" or "false" or some other specific, quantified response. Both approaches can be hazardous since either the client or the clinician is forced to make inferences about the test. George Kelly (1958, p. 332) summarized the problem beautifully: "When the subject is asked to guess what the examiner is thinking, we call it an objective test; when the examiner tries to guess what the subject is thinking, we call it a projective device."

Objective Personality Tests The first objective personality test developed by a psychologist was Woodworth's (1919) Personal Data Sheet which was used during World War I to help screen soldiers for psychological problems. It was a short, simple form asking for "yes" or "no" answers to questions such as: "Have you ever been afraid of going insane?" "Did you have a happy childhood?" "Does it make you uneasy to cross a bridge?" These items were selected because they reflected problems and symptoms reported at least twice as often by previously diagnosed neurotics as by "normals." Additionally, no item was retained in the test if more than 25 percent of a normal sample answered it in an unfavorable manner; it was assumed that a behavior reported by more than a quarter of the normal population could not indicate pathology (Anastasi, 1976). Item selection and retention procedures such as these were a prelude to later, more sophisticated empirical test construction procedures.

The MMPI Among the hundreds of objective personality measures which have appeared since Woodworth's early effort, none has been more influential or more widely used than the Minnesota Multiphasic Personality Inventory (MMPI). This test was developed during the late 1930s at the University of Minnesota by Starke Hathaway (a psychologist) and J. C. McKinley (a psychiatrist) as an aid to psychiatric diagnosis of clinical patients. The MMPI was one of the first personality tests to be constructed empirically. Hathaway and

McKinley took a large pool of items from older personality tests and other sources and converted them into statements to which a client can respond "true" "false," or "cannot say." These were administered to thousands of normal persons as well as others who had already been labeled as displaying some psychiatric disorder.

Certain response patterns tended to show up. When compared to normals, members of various diagnostic groups showed statistically different reactions to certain items. For example, a particular group of items tended to be answered in the same general way mainly by depressed persons, while another group of items was answered in a particular way by persons diagnosed as schizophrenic. Eight such item groups were identified as discriminating normals from nonnormals and as being associated with a certain diagnostic category. These item groups were called *scales*. Later, two additional groupings were identified as being responded to differently by males and females and by shy, introverted college students. Thus, there are ten *clinical scales* on the MMPI; their names and examples[2] of the kinds of items included in each are presented in Box 6-3.

Also included in that box are four *validity scales*. These are groups of items designed to assist the tester in detecting various kinds of bias or distortion in MMPI responses. The *L* (or *lie*) scale consists of fifteen statements which, if answered honestly, would reveal mildly negative things about the client (such as the fact that he or she does not stay informed about world events every day). The assumption here is that if the client denies trivial negative behaviors or thoughts, he or she will probably not be honest about more serious problems covered on other items. The *F* (or *frequency*) scale contains items which are rarely endorsed by normals, but which were not associated with any particular diagnosed group either. A high *F* scale score is thus interpreted as indicating carelessness in responding, a purposeful attempt to appear deviant, or some related factor. The *K* (or *correction*) scale is designed to detect a client's tendency to be overly defensive or overly disclosing about problems. A high score on the *K* scale is taken as evidence that the severity of problems revealed in other parts of the test was played down by the client. A low *K* score suggests that certain problems may have been overstated. In either case, the *K* scale is used as a guide for "correcting" scores on scales 6 through 10 in Box 6-3. This is in contrast to the other validity scales which are used mainly to check on the degree to which extraneous factors may have reduced the test's overall value as a personality assessment device.

There are 550 items on the MMPI. When a client takes the test, her or his responses to 400 of these items are converted into clinical and validity scale scores. Originally, the MMPI clinical scales were taken literally; a person showing a high depression or schizophrenia score was likely to be given

---

[2]In order to avoid biasing the responses of readers (or their friends) who might take the MMPI, its actual items are not presented. Incidentally, the MMPI item format has been widely parodied: A "Maryland Malpractice and Pandering Inventory" has circulated as a joke among clinicians for years. It contains items such as: "I used to tease vegetables." "The sight of blood no longer excites me." "I use shoe polish to excess." (See also Walker & Walsh, 1969.)

Box 6-3 MMPI Scales and Simulated Items

Validity (or test-taking attitude) scales

? (Cannot Say) Number of items left unanswered.

L (Lie) Fifteen items of overly good self report, such as "I smile at everyone I meet." (Answered True.)

F (Frequency or Infrequency) Sixty-four items answered in the scored direction by 10 percent or less of normals, such as "There is an international plot against me." (True)

K (Correction) Thirty items reflecting defensiveness in admitting to problems, such as "I feel bad when others criticize me." (False)

Clinical scales:

1 or **Hs** (Hypochondriasis). Thirty-three items derived from patients showing abnormal concern with bodily functions, such as "I have chest pains several times a week." (True)

2 or **D** (Depression) Sixty items derived from patients showing extreme pessimism, feelings of hopelessness, and slowing of thought and action, such as "I usually feel that life is interesting and worthwhile." (False)

3 or **Hy** (Conversion Hysteria) Sixty items from neurotic patients using physical or mental symptoms as a way of unconsciously avoiding difficult conflicts and responsibilities, such as "My heart frequently pounds so hard I can feel it." (True)

4 or **Pd** (Psychopathic Deviate) Fifty items from patients who show a repeated and flagrant disregard for social customs, an emotional shallowness and an inability to learn from punishing experiences, such as "My activities and interests are often criticized by others." (True)

5 or **Mf** (Masculinity-Femininity) Sixty items from patients showing homoeroticism and items differentiating between men and women, such as "I like to arrange flowers." (True, scored for femininity.)

6 or **Pa** (Paranoia) Forty items from patients showing abnormal suspiciousness and delusions of grandeur or persecution, such as "There are evil people trying to influence my mind." (True)

7 or **Pt** (Psychasthenia) Forty-eight items based on neurotic patients showing obsessions, compulsions, abnormal fears, and guilt and indecisiveness, such as "I save nearly everything I buy, even after I have no use for it." (True)

8 or **Sc** (Schizophrenia) Seventy-eight items from patients showing bizarre or unusual thoughts or behavior, who are often withdrawn and experiencing delusions and hallucinations, such as "Things around me do not seem real" (True) and "It makes me uncomfortable to have people close to me." (True)

9 or **Ma** (Hypomania) Forty-six items from patients characterized by emotional excitement, overactivity, and flight of ideas, such as "At times I feel very 'high' or very 'low' for no apparent reason." (True)

0 or **Si** (Social Introversion) Seventy items from persons showing shyness, little interest in people, and insecurity, such as "I have the time of my life at parties." (False)

Source: Norman Sundberg, *Assessment of Persons,* © 1977, p. 183. (Reprinted by permission of Prentice-Hall Inc., Englewood Cliffs, New Jersey.)

corresponding diagnostic labels. It soon became obvious, however, that elevation of a particular scale does not always mean that the client in question belongs in the associated diagnostic category (Anastasi, 1976).

Recognition of this problem prompted (1) a trend toward calling the clinical scales by number (1-10) rather than by name, and (2) plotting all scale scores on a graph and analyzing both the resulting profile (not just the highest score) and the relationships among its points (a sample profile is presented in Figure 6-2).

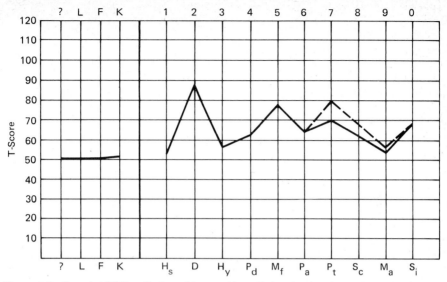

Figure 6-2 Sample MMPI profile for a 34-year-old married professional man. The solid line is the uncorrected profile; the dashed line represents K-scale corrections. *(From Dahlstrom, W. G., Welsh, G. S., & Dahlstrom, L. E. An MMPI Handbook, vol. 1, rev. ed., © by University of Minnesota Press. Reprinted by permission).*

Maloney and Ward (1976, p. 335) contrast the old single-scale-oriented approach to MMPI interpretation with current profile analysis procedures:

> Consider the diagnosis of "psychopathic deviate" (now called anti-social personality disorder). Under the old formulation, elevation on scale 4 (psychopathic deviate) was considered sufficient to make this diagnosis. However, it has been found that elevations on this scale occur with considerable frequency in both the normal population and other diagnostic groups. As a result, the differential diagnostic usefulness of scale 4 by itself is quite limited and suspect. However, with the profile approach, there are considerable data to suggest that a coded profile of 4-9 (. . . scale 9 is "hypomania"), with the relative absence of elevations on other clinical scales, and especially in the presence of a "supernormal" neurotic triad (scales 1, 2, and 3), is much more indicative of a psychopathic condition (Meehl, 1972).

The clinician conducts the profile analysis by comparing the client's chart with those of other clients. As we saw in Chapter 4, this can be done purely "clinically" by recalling previous clients, or "statistically" by reference to books containing sample profiles and the characteristics of the people who produced them (Carkhuff, Barnett, & McCall, 1965; Dahlstrom & Welsh, 1960; Dahlstom, Welsh, & Dahlstrom, 1972; Drake & Oetting, 1959; Gilberstadt & Duker, 1965; Hathaway & Meehl, 1951; Hathaway & Monaches, 1961). We also noted in Chapter 4 that there are several companies which offer machine scoring of the MMPI along with computer interpretation based upon actuarial formulae or *automated clinical lore.* The popularity of such services among clinicians is indicated by a report that one scoring and interpretation service alone processes 1600 MMPIs per week (Butcher, 1972).

In addition to being the most popular objective personality test in clinical use today, the MMPI has spawned over 6000 research reports and literally hundreds of other related tests and scales, many of which go far beyond the test's original purpose of assessing "those traits that are commonly characteristic of disabling psychological abnormality" (Hathaway & McKinley, 1967, p. 1). For example, there are now over 300 new groupings of MMPI items, each of which is purported to measure some aspect of personality such as ego strength, anxiety, dependency, dominance, social status, and prejudice (Anastasi, 1976; Butcher, 1972). These new groupings or scales can be used in conjunction with the MMPI as a whole or as a separate test (such as the Taylor Manifest Anxiety Scale; Taylor, 1973). Shorter, less cumbersome versions of the MMPI have also been developed. Called the "Mini-Mult" or "Midi-Mult," these truncated editions are by definition less comprehensive and designed mainly for quick classification and screening purposes.

The CPI   The California Psychological Inventory (CPI; Gough, 1957) is another prominent example of a broad-range, empirically constructed, objective personality test. In contrast to the MMPI, the CPI was developed specifically for assessing personality in the "normal" population. Though about half of its 480 items come from the MMPI, the CPI items are grouped into different, more diverse, and positively oriented scales including sociability, self-acceptance, responsibility, dominance, self-control, and ten others. There are also three validity scales which serve basically the same purpose as those on the MMPI. The CPI was standardized on 13,000 males and females from all parts of the country and in all socioeconomic categories. Some observers see the CPI as one of the best personality tests available today because of the representativeness of its standardization sample and its relatively high reliability. The test has been used to predict delinquency, parole outcome, academic grades, and the likelihood of dropping out of high school (Anastasi, 1968). There is some evidence as well that certain CPI scales can be effectively used in other cultures (e.g., Gough & Sandhu, 1964).

Other objective personality inventories in rather wide clinical use include the Personality Research Form (Jackson, 1967), the Edwards Personal Preference Schedule (EPPS; Edwards, 1959), the Sixteen Personality Factors Questionnaire (16PF; Cattell & Eber, 1962), and the Guilford-Zimmerman Temperament Survey (Guilford & Zimmerman, 1949).

Social-Learning Tests   Most traditional objective tests generate data which are used as signs or correlates. They are associated with moderate to high levels of inference about personality traits and dynamics or about the future behavior which those traits or dynamics will determine. However, proponents of the social-learning model of clinical psychology see personality as nearly synonymous with behavior and have therefore constructed a number of objective tests which, unlike those described so far, are designed to gather behavior samples upon which only a minimal amount of inference is to be based. These tests tend to be short, simple, and rationally constructed.

Probably the most frequently employed "personality test" that is oriented toward the social-learning approach is the Fear Survey Schedule (FSS). It is simply a list of objects, persons, and situations which the client is asked to rate in terms of fearsomeness. The several editions of this test (e.g., Akatagawa, 1956; Geer, 1965; Lawlis, 1961; Wolpe, 1964; Wolpe & Lang, 1964, 1969) contain from 50 to 122 items and use either 1 to 5 or 1 to 7 scales for the fear ratings. The FSS is often used to assess the "popularity" of various fears, to identify persons with specific fears, and even to help assess changes in response over the course of fear-reduction treatment. A few items from the FSS are presented in Box 6-4.

Although the FSS is used primarily in clinical and research settings to sample an individual client's self-reported reactions to various stimuli and situations, some users of the test (e.g., Tasto, Hickson, & Rubin, 1971) have collected the responses of large numbers of college students and used them as a standardization sample against which to compare new clients' scores. In fact, these same researchers have set up a standard-score fear profile sheet (very much like the MMPI profile in Figure 6-2) which provides a graphic display of the relative strength of client fears in five areas: small animals, hostility, isolation and loneliness, physical destruction and pain, and morals and sex.

Among other social-learning objective tests focused upon anxiety, one finds the State-Trait Anxiety Inventory (Spielberger, Gorsuch, & Lushene, 1970), the Social Avoidance and Distress Scale (Watson & Friend, 1969), the Social Anxiety Inventory (Richardson & Tasto, 1976), the S-R Inventory of Anxiousness (Endler, Hunt, & Rosenstein, 1962), the Rathus Assertiveness Schedule (Rathus, 1973), the Conflict Resolution Inventory (another assertiveness test; McFall & Lillisand, 1971), and the Social Anxiety Survey Schedule (Cautela, 1977). Social-learning researchers and therapists have also developed a variety

Box 6-4 Sample Items from the FSS-II

1 Snakes
2 Death of a loved one
3 Seeing a fight
4 Being a passenger in a car
5 Failing a test
6 Arguing with parents
7 Hypodermic needles
8 Swimming alone
9 Making mistakes
10 Strange dogs
11 Being alone
12 Heights
13 Closed places
14 Cemeteries
15 Roller coasters

Source: Geer, 1965.

of nonfear-related tests which reflect the straightforward, self-report features of the FSS. A sampling of these tests would include the Depression Adjective Checklist (Lubin, 1965), the Beck Depression Inventory (Beck, 1972), the Multiple Affect Adjective Checklist (Zuckerman & Lubin, 1965), the Marital Precounseling Inventory (Stuart & Stuart, 1972), the Marital Conflict Form (Weiss & Margolin, 1977), the Couple Interaction Survey Schedule (Cautela, 1977), and the Smoking Behavior Inventory (McFall & Hammen, 1971): The reader interested in detailed material on the content, development and use of social-learning test instruments should consult Cautela (1977), Tasto (1977), Hersen and Bellack (1976), or Mash and Terdal (1976).

Projective Personality Tests   In spite of the fact that projective tests were not formally named until 1939, the use of projective assessment methods goes back at least to the 1400s, when Leonardo da Vinci is said to have selected his pupils partly on the basis of the creativity and talent they displayed while attempting to find shapes and patterns in ambiguous, unstructured forms (Piotrowski, 1972). In the late 1800s Binet adapted a parlor game called "Blotto" to the assessment of "passive imagination" by asking children to tell what they saw in inkblots (Exner, 1976). Galton constructed a word association test in 1879, and Carl Jung was using a similar test for clinical assessment by 1910 (see Zubin, Eron, & Schumer, 1965). These relatively informal projective "methods" or "techniques" later evolved into projective *tests* when their content was standardized such that each client was exposed to the same stimuli in the same way (English & English, 1958). It should be noted, however, that not all clinicians are equally willing to apply the term "test" to projectives. Some feel that such instruments are best thought of as "response elicitation techniques" because they depend so heavily upon the individual psychologist's interpretive skills (Levy, 1963).

Technically, any test or stimulus can be used projectively if the clinician is willing to interpret client responses as indicative of personality structure or dynamics,[3] and thus there has been considerable discussion and disagreement among interested parties about just what it is that defines a test or test procedure as "projective" (Lindzey, 1961, Shneidman, 1965, and Zubin, Eron, & Schumer, 1965 present descriptions of the controversy). Lindzey (1961) suggested a set of criteria which, though not universally accepted as strictly defining projective assessments, has been widely influential in outlining their general nature. According to these criteria, projectives:

1   Are sensitive to unconscious personality dimensions.
2   Permit the client a broad range of responses.
3   Are capable of measuring many different aspects of personality.

---

[3]Exner (1976, pp. 66–67) notes that answers to certain intelligence test items may provide projective clues about personality: "The best answer to the question, 'why does the state require people to get a license in order to get married?' is that it is for purposes of record keeping. However, if a subject says, 'To prevent the scourge of VD from being inflicted on unsuspecting women,' then the answer . . . conveys something about the peculiar interests of the respondent."

4 Leave the client unaware or at least unsure of the specific meaning of his or her responses.

5 Generate a large amount of complex assessment data.

6 Employ relatively ambiguous stimuli.

7 Can be interpreted so as to provide an integrated picture of the client's personality as a whole.

8 Are capable of evoking fantasy material from the client.

9 Have no right or wrong answers.

Projective methods defined roughly in this way have been classified by various writers according to the nature of the stimuli they use, the way in which the tests are constructed, interpreted, or administered, their designated purpose, and the kind of client response they elicit (Lindzey, 1959). Classification by client response is probably the clearest strategy for our purposes, so the following sections will correspond to Lindzey's (1961) labeling of projective tests as evoking *associations, constructions, completions, choices* or *orderings,* and *expressions* from the respondent. We shall have space to consider only a few examples in each group, but a vast quantity of more detailed information about these and other projectives is available in such references as Exner (1976), Harrison (1965), Lindzey (1961), Murstein (1963), Rabin and Haworth (1960), Shneidman (1965), Sundberg (1977), and Zubin, Eron, and Schumer (1965).

Association Tests In this category are projective tests that ask clients to look at an ambiguous stimulus and tell what they see in or associate with it. Without question, the most widely known and frequently employed projective of this type is the Rorschach Inkblot Test. It is a set of ten colored and black-and-white inkblots created by Hermann Rorschach, a Swiss psychiatrist, between 1911 and 1921. Although many researchers in Europe and America had previously employed inkblots in the assessment of fantasy, imagination, and perception (Zubin, Eron, & Schumer, 1965), it was Rorschach who first attempted to use such stimuli for diagnosis and personality assessment.

Actually, he began with geometric figures cut from colored paper and only later switched to inkblots, partly as a result of having read about an inkblot test of fantasy developed by Hens, a Polish medical student (Reisman, 1966). By 1918, Rorschach had put together a set of fifteen blots and was hard at work on a personality classification and diagnostic system with which to use them. When the inkblot test finally appeared in 1921 (after having been reduced to ten blots by the publisher to cut costs), it was not well received, to say the least. European test experts such as Stern "denounced it as faulty, arbitrary, artificial, and incapable . . . of understanding human personality . . ." (Reisman, 1966, p. 163). Rorschach's book, *Psychodiagnostik,* which described his test and its interpretation, sold few copies.

This probably would have been the end of the Rorschach test[4] if David Levy, an American psychiatrist studying in Switzerland in 1920–21, had not learned about it from one of Rorschach's colleagues. Levy brought a copy of the

---

[4]It certainly was the end of Rorschach who died a year after his book was published.

test back to the United States and, in 1927, instructed a psychology trainee named Samuel Beck in its use. Beck stimulated interest in the Rorschach by publishing the first American report involving its use and, in 1937, providing a much-needed standardized procedure for administering and scoring the test. Another scoring manual appeared that same year (Klopfer & Kelly, 1937, 1942) and the Rorschach was on its way to wide popularity among American psychologists who, until then, had no global test of personality available to them (Reisman, 1966). The growing clinical use of the test was paralleled by a virtual explosion of research on its characteristics, reliability, validity, scoring, and interpretation. Today, there are over 3000 books and articles about the Rorschach (Maloney & Ward, 1976).

The test itself is quite simple. The client is shown a series of ten cards, one at a time. An inkblot (similar to that pictured in Figure 6-3) appears on each card and the client is asked to tell what she or he sees or what the blot could be. The tester records all responses verbatim and makes additional notes about response times, how the card was being held (e.g., upside down, sideways) while a response occurred, noticeable emotional reactions, and the like. Next, the tester conducts an *inquiry* or systematic questioning of the client about the parts or characteristics of each blot that prompted the responses given.

The initial reactions to the blots and the comments made during the inquiry are then transformed or coded into more manageable form through the use of a scoring system. The coded responses are then interpreted as signs of personality and personality disorder. This usually involves attention to the *location, determinants, content,* and *popularity* of the client's responses. Anastasi (1968, p. 496) describes these dimensions as follows:

Figure 6-3   Inkblot similar to those used in the Rorschach *(Norman D. Sundberg,* Assessment of Persons, *© 1977, p. 207. Reprinted by permission of Prentice-Hall, Inc., Englewood Cliffs, New Jersey).*

Location refers to the part of the blot with which the examinee associates each response. Does he use the whole blot, a common detail, an unusual detail, white space, or some combination of these areas? The *determinants* of the response include form, color, shading and "movement." Although there is of course no movement in the blot itself, the respondent's perception of the blot as a representation of a moving object is scored in this category. Further differentiations are made within these categories. For example, human movement, animal movement, and abstract or inanimate movement are separately scored. . . .

The treatment of *content* varies from one scoring system to another, although certain major categories are regularly employed. Chief among these are human figures, human details (or parts of human figures), animal figures, animal details, and anatomical diagrams. Other broad scoring categories include inanimate objects, plants, maps, clouds, blood, x-rays, sexual objects, and symbols. A *popularity* score is often found on the basis of the relative frequency of different responses among people in general. For each of the 10 cards, certain responses are scored as popular because of their common occurrence.

Assume, for example, that a client responded to Figure 6-3 by saying, "It looks like a bat" and during subsequent inquiry noted that "I saw the whole blot as a bat because it is black and is just sort of bat-shaped." If one of the popular scoring systems (e.g., that of Beck or Klopfer) were used, these responses would probably be coded as "WFC' + AP," where W indicates that the whole blot was used *(location),* F means that the blot's form (F) was the main *determinant* of the response and C' means that achromatic color was also involved. The + shows that the form described seemed to correspond well to the actual form of the blot, A means that there was animal *content* in the response, and P indicates that "bat" is a *popular* response to this particular card.[5]

The clinician may draw inferences from several aspects of Rorschach test responses. Some normative data exists (e.g., Ames, Leonard, Metraux, & Walker, 1959; Beck, 1937) to help establish particular responses as common or unusual and there has even been an attempt to computerize the interpretive task (Piotrowski, 1964). For the most part, however, inference is based upon experience with the test and the use of general interpretive guidelines. Sundberg (1977, p. 208) provides a summary of such guidelines which, though oversimplified and incomplete, nevertheless conveys the flavor of the inferences which often stem from coded responses:

Using the whole blot suggests integration and organization; many small details indicate compulsiveness and over-control, and the use of white space suggests oppositional and negativistic tendencies. The presence of much poor form, uncommon responses, and confused thinking suggests a psychotic condition. Responsiveness to color is supposed to represent emotionality, and in the absence of good form, it suggests uncontrolled emotions and impulsivity. Responses mention-

[5]There are at least five reasonably distinct systems for scoring the Rorschach (see Exner, 1976), so a given response may be coded in various ways; further, each scoring system is probably used somewhat differently by each individual clinician.

ing human movement indicate imagination, intelligence, and a vivid inner life. . . . Content also has much potential for interpretation. . . . Knives, guns, mutilated bodies, and angry interactions suggest strong hostility.

Some users of the Rorschach think response content is particularly valuable and have developed specialized content scoring systems which purportedly detect anxiety, hostility, aggression, homosexuality, and other personality dimensions (e.g., Elizur, 1949; Walker, 1951; Wheeler, 1949).

In addition to interpreting responses to individual cards, the clinician may look for recurring sequences or patterns of responses within and across cards. Further, certain test statistics contained in a "structural summary" are interpreted. The overall number of responses (called productivity), the frequency of responses coded in certain categories, and various ratios and relationships between and among category frequencies are seen as significant. For example, because most people tend to use blot form more often than color in determining their responses, the appearance of a high proportion of color-dominated determinants may be taken as evidence for weak emotional control. In one interpretive system, there are twenty-two response percentages and ratios available for interpretation (Exner, 1974).

The client's overt behavior in response to the Rorschach testing situation itself is also attended to by the clinician. Evidence of tension, enjoyment, or confusion, attempts to impress or abuse the examiner, and other behavioral cues are becoming an increasingly important part of Rorschach interpretation (e.g., Friedman, 1953; Goldfried, Stricker, & Weiner, 1971). A sample of inferences which might be drawn from the structural summary, response content, and test-taking behavior of a client given the Rorschach is contained in Box 6-5.

A number of variants on the Rorschach have appeared since its 1921 publication. The most notable examples include techniques for administering the test to pairs or groups of subjects (Cutler & Farberow, 1970; Harrower & Steiner, 1945) and the development of new sets of blots (e.g., Harrower, 1945; Holtzman, 1961; Wheeler, 1938). With the possible exception of the Holtzman (1961) Inkblot Test, none of these procedures has gained anywhere near the following associated with the Rorschach itself (Lubin, Wallis, & Paine, 1971).

Another association-type projective test worthy of note here involves the word association format. This format was pioneered by Galton (1879) and Jung (1910) for use in the laboratory and clinic, respectively: The most widely used version is the Kent-Rosanoff Free Association Test (Kent & Rosanoff, 1910), a list of 100 common words. The clinician says each word and the client is to give his or her association to it (e.g., "up"—"down," "table"—"chair"). Inference from the test is based upon the degree to which the client deviates from the associations given by a standardization sample. A 60-word association test containing stimuli thought to be especially relevant to psychosexual conflicts is also available (Rapaport, Gill, & Schafer, 1945, 1946), but is not prominent.

Construction Tests This type of projective asks the client to create or construct a story or other product on the basis of test stimuli. Among such tests,

Box 6-5   Example of Inferences Based on the Rorschach

In a context of severe intellectual and emotional confusion, we see a conflict centering primarily about a life-death struggle within the self, and about bodily integrity, personality integrity, and self-identity. Things somehow do not seem "right" to him as he turns away from the outside world and focuses on himself, especially on his body and its functions. He feels mutilated, dismembered rather than whole, worthless, and as if he is a lower form of life. Specifically, there is attention directed to alimentation, elimination, the rectum, and other bodily features associated with elimination. There is also concern about sex, but its specific relation to this disordered economy is not certain. All of these difficulties, particularly as they relate to body processes are seen as the result of external assault upon him, as if others have unjustifiably done something to him and damaged him. In fact, in his current state of despair, he tends to see others as at fault and he is critical. In this manner, oppositional tendencies which are now quite strong are pushing for expression and he feels they are justifiable.

This inner state of dysphoric turbulence is seen in a loss of spontaneity, in a marked sense of insecurity, helplessness, and uncertainty, and in social relations which are characterized by tentativeness. He is overcautious. Thus, he is remarkably ineffectual and unadaptable, and unable to come to grips with problems. In novel situations or under pressure, his judgment would not be at all reliable. In a personality not comfortably defended against psychosis, the term "paranoid" intrudes itself. The possibility of further regression with depersonalization, depression, and bodily delusions has to be considered.

Source: Orbach, C.E. and Tallent, N., "Modification of Perceived Body and Body Concepts Following the Construction of a Colostomy." *Archives of General Psychiatry,* 1965, 12, 126-135, copyright 1965, American Medical Association.

the Thematic Apperception Test (TAT) is the most popular by far. Unlike the Rorschach, the TAT presents relatively recognizable stimuli consisting of thirty drawings of people, objects, and landscapes (see Figure 6-4). In most cases, only about ten of these cards (one of them blank) are administered; the subset chosen is determined mainly by the client's age and sex. A separate set of cards depicting black people is also available. The examiner shows each picture and asks the client to make up a story about it, including what led up to the scene, what is now happening, and what is going to happen. The client is also encouraged to say what the people in the drawings are thinking and feeling. For the blank card, the respondent is asked to imagine a drawing, describe it, and then construct a story about it.

The TAT was designed in 1935 by psychologists Christiana D. Morgan and Henry Murray at the Harvard Psychological Clinic (Murray, 1938, 1943). It was based not only upon a general projective hypothesis, but also upon the assumption that, in telling a *story,* the client's needs, wishes, and conflicts will be reflected in a character (usually the heroine or hero with whom the client identifies (Lindzey, 1952). Like the Rorschach, the TAT was not an original idea. Drawings and pictures had been used much earlier by Binet and others to assess the development of children's intelligence and imagination (Binet & Simon, 1905; Brittain, 1907; Libby, 1908) and a few tentative efforts at using picture-based fantasy as an aid to diagnosis had been made (e.g., Schwartz, 1932; Van Lennep, 1951). However, the TAT broke new ground by attempting to use respondents' stories as clues to personality.

Figure 6-4   Drawing of the type included in the TAT. *(Reprinted by permission of the publishers from Henry A. Murray,* Thematic Apperception Test, *Cambridge, Mass.: Harvard University Press, copyright © 1943 by the president and fellow of Harvard College, © 1971 by Henry A. Murray.)*

Originally, the TAT was part of a battery of assessment devices being used in Murray's research project on the broad description of "normal" personality (see Chapter 4). "The implications of this technique for investigating the personality of patients were immediately obvious, however, and the clinical use of the test soon outstripped its research application" (Zubin, Eron, & Schumer,

1965, p. 394). Today, the TAT is second only to the Rorschach among projective tests in terms of clinical use. The body of published research and other material related to it is massive (over 1500 references in the 1972 *Mental Measurements Yearbook*).

As with the Rorschach, there is not one "right" way to analyze the meaning of clients' responses to TAT cards. As early as 1951, Shneidman identified at least twenty systems for scoring and interpretation and new methods have continued to appear (Harrison, 1965; Zubin, Eron, & Schumer, 1965). Analysis can focus upon both the *content* and the *structure* of the TAT stories. Content refers to *what* is described: the people, the feelings, the events, the outcomes. Structure involves *how* the story is told: the logic and organization, the use of language, the appearance of speech disfluencies, misunderstanding of instructions or stimuli in the drawings, obvious emotional arousal, and the like. Though many interpretive approaches (especially some of the early ones) emphasize story content, the potential importance of structure (including the client's overt behavior while working on the test) has received increasing recognition (e.g., Holt, 1958; Kagan, 1956; Murstein, 1963).

The original interpretive scheme suggested by Morgan and Murray (1935) takes a "hero-oriented" approach in which responses are read for the *needs* (e.g., achievement, aggression, affiliation) and *presses* (perceived environmental influences such as criticism, affection, or physical danger) which are associated with the main character and which Murray viewed as fundamental aspects of personality. The frequency and intensity of each need and press are scored on a 1 to 5 scale, and the themes and outcomes of each story are noted as well. This system was oriented toward an exploration and description of personality, not toward clinical diagnosis.

Other scoring approaches, particularly those which are also associated with personality research as opposed to clinical application, have used even more formal quantitative procedures to describe TAT stories (e.g., Dana, 1959; McClelland, Atkinson, Clark, & Lowell, 1953). Efforts along these lines have resulted in the appearance of some normative TAT response data (e.g., Eron, 1950; Lindzey, Bradford, Tejessy, & Davids, 1959; Murstein, 1972; Rosenzweig & Fleming, 1949) which clinicians can compare to stories told by their own clients. However, some interpretive systems make little or no use of formal scoring procedures (e.g., Henry, 1956), while others combine preliminary quantitative analysis with subjective interpretation of the resulting numbers (e.g., Bellak, 1947).

Scoring may focus primarily on the "hero" of each story, or on more general themes and interpersonal relations. The range of possibilities is clearly shown in Shneidman's (1951) *Thematic Test Analysis,* which contains specific examples of how fifteen prominent users of the TAT went about scoring and/or interpreting the stories told by a single hospitalized client.

Of the many approaches available, most users of the TAT in clinical situations seem to prefer those which are less structured, more intuitive, and which use response norms, formal scoring criteria, and personality theories only as general guides (Harrison, 1965; Sundberg, 1977). They may utilize Murray's need and press concepts and some psychoanalytic thinking, but perhaps most commonly they develop an idiosyncratic combination of principles derived partly from theory and largely from logic and clinical experience. An example of a TAT story and a clinician's interpretation of it are presented in Box 6-6.

Among the many construction tests inspired by or similar to the TAT are:

1　The Children's Apperception Test (CAT; Bellak, 1954), whose cards depict animal characters rather than human beings. It is used with 3- to 10-year-olds.

2　The Blacky Pictures (Blum, 1949), another children's test showing a small dog ("Blacky") and his family in a series of psychodynamically symbolic situations, including one in which a knife falls toward Blacky's tail.

Box 6-6　Example of Inferences Based on the TAT

The following responses were given by a 25-year-old, unmarried male to a TAT card which shows a young boy looking at a violin which rests on a table in front of him:

> This child is sick in bed. He has been given sheet music to study, but instead of the music, he has come across a novel that interests him more than the music. It is probably an adventure story. He evidently does not fear the chance that his parents will find him thusly occupied as he seems quite at ease. He seems to be quite a studious type and perhaps regrets missing school, but he seems quite occupied with the adventure in the story. Adventure has something to do with ocean or water. He is not too happy, though not too sad. His eyes are somewhat blank—coincidence of reading a book without any eyes or knowing what is in the book without reading it. He disregards the music and falls asleep reading the book.

A segment of a skilled TAT user's working notes on this story is presented below (Holt, 1978, pp. 166–167). After listing several indicators of psychosis (perceptual distortion, arbitrariness, peculiarities, delusional ideation, blandness, interpersonal isolation), he concludes:

> On the basis of this story alone, I feel certain that there is a schizophrenic process present, even though not necessarily a pure schizophrenia. Slightly pretentious, facade tone, helped along with basic fact of perverse refusal to acknowledge presence of violin, strongly suggests that he *does* see violin but consciously thinks that he's being "clever" or "original," or is out-tricking the examiner (whom he might see as trying to trick him) by ignoring it or seeing it as a book. That he is aware of it on some level is suggested by the fact that the basic theme, p Parental Imposed Task→ n Auto Resis, passive Aggression, comes through. Consistent also is statement at the end: he *disregards* the music. Not a psychopath trying to act smart—too schizzy.
>
> 　*Sick in bed as a child* may be an autobiographical theme. He's almost certainly "sick" (that is, psychotic) now, and so that may be enough explanation for it. But most psychotics don't [see the card this way]; therefore it becomes plausible that he may have had long illnesses as a child, cutting him off from other kids, and→ to fantasy escape—dreams of travel and adventure.
>
> 　Sentence 3 may also describe his overt behavior: nonchalant, seemingly "at ease," really frightened underneath.
>
> 　Above are almost all hypotheses, to be confirmed or excluded by later stories.
>
> 　*Strong passivity* throughout—especially in outcome. Also suggestion of *flight* and *avoidance* of very passive sort—drastic enough to include denial of threatening aspects of reality.
>
> 　*Nothing holds his interest long*—not even adventure novel. Hero soon withdraws into *own* fantasy, to conviction of knowing what's in book without reading it even though "took a chance" to read it, and finally withdraws into sleep.

3 The Make-a-Picture-Story (MAPS; Shneidman, 1949) which has been called a "do-it-yourself TAT" because the client first constructs pictures by placing cutout human and animal forms on a printed background, and then tells stories about them.

4 The Auditory Apperceptive Test (Stone, 1950), consisting of recorded sounds (e.g., typewriter, windstorm) about which the subject is asked to create a story.

5 The Rosenzweig Picture-Frustration Study (Rosenzweig, 1949), which presents twenty-four cartoons showing one person frustrating another in some way (e.g., "I'm not going to invite you to my party"). The client's task is to say what the frustrated person's response would be.

There is even evidence that some social-learning-oriented clinicians have experimented with TAT-like pictures to assess cognitions occurring in particular situations (see Meichenbaum, 1976). For a more comprehensive list and description of construction-type projective tests see Zubin, Eron, and Schumer (1965).

Completion Tests These involve presenting the subject with part of a stimulus (usually a sentence) and asking the subject to complete it in his or her own way. The underlying assumption here is that the way in which the client chooses to finish the sentence will be a reflection of motives, conflicts, or other personality dimensions. Like the other types of projective techniques discussed so far, the incomplete sentence format had previously been used as a measure of intellect (Ebbinghaus, 1897, cited in Reisman, 1966). Its use as a projective personality assessment technique is usually dated from tests described by Payne (1928) and Tendler (1930), but more widely used versions did not appear until the 1940s.

Today, the most popular completion test is the Rotter Incomplete Sentences Blank (Rotter & Rafferty, 1950). It contains forty sentence "stems" such as: "I like. . . ." "My father. . . ." "I secretly. . . .". Client responses are compared to extensive data provided in the test manual and are given a 7-point rating of adjustment or maladjustment depending upon the degree of deviation from established norms. Item ratings are then totaled to provide an overall adjustment score.

These relatively objective scoring procedures are primarily associated with Rotter's test and a few other fairly short research-oriented sentence-completion instruments aimed at assessing fairly specific aspects of personality (e.g., Exner, 1973). Most other completion tests attempt to provide more general personality descriptions, tend to be longer (up to 240 items), more diverse in content, and rather heavily dependent upon the clinician's experience and skill to guide inferences. Included in this category are sentence-completion tests by Sacks (1950), Stein (1947), Forer (1950), and Holsopple and Miale (1954). P. Goldberg (1965) presents a comprehensive review of these and many others.

Choice or Ordering Tests In this category are projective instruments which ask the client to arrange test stimuli in some order or to make choices from an array of stimuli according to preference, attractiveness, or some other dimension. Tests of this type are relatively few in number and not particularly popular with clinicians, but this was not always the case.

In the 1940s and 1950s, for example, the now-obscure Szondi Test (pronounced "zon-dee"; Szondi, Moser, & Webb, 1959) was used by many clinical psychologists (Sundberg, 1969). This instrument was developed around 1947 by Lipot Szondi, a Hungarian psychiatrist who believed that liking or disliking a particular type of person was due in part to certain genetically determined traits or drives which are shared with that person. The test was designed to illuminate these drives by asking the client to choose the two most liked and the two most disliked persons from each of six groups of photographs. These groups each contained eight pictures of European mental patients diagnosed as sadistic murderers, hysterics, catatonic or paranoid schizophrenics, manic-depressives, or the like.

Each diagnostic category was represented once in each set of photographs. The pictures were less than flattering, to say the least (see Figure 6-5), which probably made choosing one's "most liked" characters more difficult than picking those at the other end of the spectrum. According to Szondi, a client's consistent choice of a certain diagnostic type as most liked or disliked revealed the presence of unconscious or overt drives shared with that particular type. An equal distribution of both "like" and "dislike" in a particular diagnostic group was thought to indicate ambivalence in that area of behavior, while ignoring a category altogether meant that the client did not share the drives of its members.

Accounts differ as to how the Szondi Test found its way to America. Reisman (1966) credits David Rapaport with its importation, but Harrison (1965) suggests that one of Szondi's students introduced it. Whatever the case, after a brief period of popularity (over 300 published references were compiled by Rapaport in 1954, and for a while there was even a *Szondi Newsletter*), the test faded from the scene as a result of its limited usefulness in diagnosis and the questionable nature of the theory upon which it was based.

The Kahn Test of Symbol Arrangement (Kahn, 1955) exemplifies a contemporary choice/ordering projective. Here, the client is shown sixteen plastic objects of various shapes (stars, animals, crosses, circles, hearts) and asked to place them into categories such as "love," "hate," "bad," "good," "living," "dead," "large," and "small" (Harrison, 1965). The client's choices about which objects go in which categories are recorded, and, in addition, the client is asked to free associate to each object in order to illuminate its symbolic meaning for her or him. The arrangements of objects are then interpreted in light of the meaning of each symbol and used to support inferences about the client's unconscious personality processes.

The Tomkins-Horn Picture Arrangement Test (Tomkins, 1957) combines aspects of ordering procedures with those of construction techniques such as the TAT. It presents the client with twenty-five trios of drawings depicting a person engaged in various activities. The client is to arrange each trio in the sequence of his or her choice and then tell a story about the action depicted. Interpretation is

Figure 6-5 Photos from the Szondi Test *(Szondi, L., Moser, U., & Webb, M. W. The Szondi Test in Diagnosis, Prognosis and Treatment. © 1959 by J. P. Lippincott, Philadelphia. Reprinted by permission).*

based upon sequence arrangement norms and upon subjective judgments about the meaning of the stories told. This test has much in common with the Make-a-Picture-Story (MAPS) described earlier and also shares features with Van Lennep's (1951) Four Picture Test.

Expressive Tests   These procedures ask the client to directly express herself or himself in some way, most commonly by drawing a picture. Several tests of this type enjoy great popularity today. Most notable is the Draw-a-Person Test (DAP; Machover, 1949) which, as its name implies, merely asks the client to draw a person. A similar test (called Draw-a-Man) had been developed earlier by Goodenough (1926) who used the quality, detail, and complexity of drawings to estimate children's intelligence. In the DAP, however, various aspects of personality are inferred from the drawings produced by adults or children. Each client may be asked to make several drawings; the initial instructions to draw a person may be followed by requests to draw a person of the opposite sex, a family, self, mother, and so on. Some users of the test ask the client to answer questions or tell a story about their drawings, but the primary rationale for the procedure is that the drawings themselves can reveal significant personality data.

Using psychoanalytic theory as her guide, Machover (1949) suggested that the inclusion, exclusion, and characteristics of each body part, along with the placement, symmetry, organization, size, and other features of the drawing as a whole were indicative of the client's self-image, conflicts, wishes, fears, and perceptions of the world. For example, the appearance of large eyes may be related to paranoid thinking ("keeping my eyes open" or "people watching me"), problems in drawing the nose (a phallic symbol) could reflect castration anxiety, while the stability of the figure's stance might represent feelings of security. A sample drawing and the inferences based upon it are presented in Figure 6-6.

Two other projective drawing tests are also widely used. Buck's (1948) House-Tree-Person Test asks the client to draw each of those objects and then discuss them in an extended interview. The Bender-Gestalt Test, described earlier as a measure of intellectual deterioration, is also interpreted as a projective indicator of personality and personality disorder when the nature and symbolic meaning of errors and distortions in the copied figures are focused upon. Additional drawing tests are available (e.g., Caligor, 1952) but do not appear to be in general use.

Among the many nondrawing projectives of the expressive type, one finds methods involving finger painting (e.g., Napoli, 1947), psychodrama (Moreno, 1946), and puppet play (e.g., Woltmann, 1951).

The Status of Testing in Clinical Psychology

Though the actual number of psychological tests available has continued to expand year after year, the enthusiasm which once surrounded them has not (e.g., Bersoff, 1973; Lewandowski & Sarcuzzo, 1976; Lubin & Lubin, 1972). Especially during the 1930s through the 1950s, tests were touted as being almost like x-rays or semimagical pathways to measuring intelligence, personality, ability, or whatever (Reisman, 1966), and every clinical psychology student was

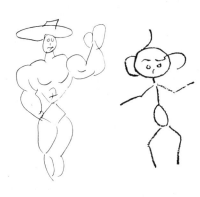

Beneath the obvious attempts at an impressive figure of masculine prowess, there are more subtle trends of the opposite: of inadequacy and inconsequentiality. The muscles of the drawn figure have been inflated beyond the hard and sinewy, into a puffy softness as if it is a figure made of balloons; the legs taper down to insubstantiality and, finally, absent feet, and an incongruous hat is placed on the boxer making comical his lifting of one gloved hand in victory. . . On the one hand, emblematic of his defenses, his drawn achromatic person is the "twenty-year-old" boxer with muscles flexed and a weight-lifter's build. Beneath this inflated image, however, on the crayon drawing of a person—which, due to the impact of color, tends to tap the relatively deeper levels of personality (Hammer, 1958)—he offers now only a "six-year-old boy" who then looks even more like an infant than a child: with one curlicue hair sticking up and the suggestion of diapers on (. . . shown here in black and white). The ears are rather ludicrous in their standing away from the head and, all in all, the total projection in this drawing is that of an infantile, laughable entity, rather than the impressive he-man he overstated on the achromatic version of a person. Beneath his attempts to demonstrate rugged masculinity (which may have culminated into the offense with which he is charged), the patient experiences himself as actually a little child, dependent and needing care, protection, and affection.

Figure 6-6 DAP drawings (done by an 18 year-old male who was caught stealing a television set) and interpretations *(Reprinted from Emanuel Hammer, "Projective Drawings," in A. I. Rabin, ed., Projective Techniques in Personality Assessment, pp. 375–376. Copyright © 1968 by Springer Publishing Company, Inc. New York. Used by permission).*

required to take intensive testing courses. Writing as late as 1965, one distinguished clinician remarked that "It is hard to conceive . . . of anyone in the field of clinical psychology reaching the postdoctoral level without being thoroughly well-versed in the Rorschach" (Harrower, 1965b, p. 398). Yet such a thing is now not only conceivable, but happens quite often (Shemberg & Keeley, 1970), as your authors can personally testify.

The decline of psychological testing from the heights it once occupied (when virtually every client was routinely given some combination of the WAIS, the Rorschach, and the TAT) has been brought about by several factors. For one thing, as noted in Chapter 4, there has been a general shift away from traditional classification-oriented diagnostic assessment in clinical psychology, so the use of tests for that purpose has decreased. Second, many clinicians simply do not like the "tester" role, which they see as not only subservient to psychiatry, but artificial and potentially damaging to relationships with clients (Breger, 1968; Rosenwald, 1963). More general concerns have also emerged in recent years as clinical psychologists, the public, the government, and individual clients have placed tests and the testing process under far more intense scrutiny than ever before. This increased caution and conservatism regarding psychological tests stem from (1) research on the reliability, validity, and other psychometric characteristics of many instruments, (2) growing awareness of the susceptibility of tests to bias of various kinds, (3) recognition that certain tests, particularly those assessing intelligence, may place members of certain minority groups at a disadvantage, (4) concern that collection and storage of test information may constitute an invasion of the respondents' privacy, and (5) worry that tests and test data are too easily misused or misinterpreted. In this section, we shall consider some of the arguments related to each of these issues.

Psychometric Properties of Tests   One of the most fundamental criticisms leveled at psychological tests is that they do not do their job very well, i.e., that they tend to be unreliable, invalid, or both (e.g., Mischel, 1968). While it is probably unfair to say that this is true about all tests under all circumstances, research on their psychometric properties has not generally been favorable. This research is far too voluminous to be described on a test-by-test basis here (see Anastasi, 1976, for a comprehensive review), but can be summarized as follows.

First, *in general, the reliability of psychological tests tends to be fairly high but not uniformly so.* Reliability coefficients for certain MMPI scales are as low as .00, for example, but parallel form, test-retest, and split-half reliabilities are commonly .80 to .96 for major intelligence tests, and in the .80s for prominent objective personality tests. Similarly, aptitude and ability tests such as the GRE, the Miller Analogies Test (MAT), the Medical College Admission Test (MCAT), and the Law School Admission Test (LSAT) display reliability coefficients ranging from .71 to .97. Tests of interests and values, such as the Kuder Preference Record, the Strong Vocational Interest Blank, and the Allport-Vernon-Lindzey Study of Values have produced reliabilities from the .70s to the low .90s.

Reliability is somewhat difficult to compute in the case of projective tests because split-half, parallel form, and test-retest approaches often do not make sense with such instruments. Attempts to determine reliability in the traditional sense for the Rorschach, the TAT, and other major projectives have produced variable and mostly unimpressive results (Garfield, 1974; Korchin, 1976). Projective test advocates often point instead to the relatively high levels of agreement shown by different clinicians using similar scoring systems. Whether such data say more about the tests or their users is a matter of some debate, however.

Second, *the validity of psychological tests has in general been less impressive than their reliability.* To a certain extent, this must be the case since, mathematically, a test can never be more valid than it is reliable, but the discrepancy between reliability and validity is sometimes very great. Indeed, there are few tests in existence today whose validity is spectacularly high in absolute terms. In relative terms, it is probably fair to say that the closer test content or tasks are to the content or tasks being predicted or assessed (i.e., the criterion), the higher the validity will be (Mischel, 1968; Thorndike et al., 1921).

For example, aptitude and ability tests which ask testees to provide information or perform tasks directly related to academic, occupational, or other skills are consistently among the most valid tests available. Tests such as the GRE, MCAT, and LSAT are often equal or superior to undergraduate grades at predicting graduate school performance, and a combination of test scores and undergraduate grades provides an even better prediction (i.e., student selection) than would occur if only tests *or* grades were used (Anastasi, 1976). Examples of other relatively high-validity aptitude-ability tests include the MAT and the Differential Aptitude Test whose correlation with subsequent academic performance is in the .40 to .80 range.

The major intelligence tests appear to be next in terms of relative validity. These tests, and especially their verbal sections, correlate with academic performance, specific skills (such as reading, arithmetic, and language use), and teacher ratings in the .17 to .75 range. It is apparently the case, however, that teacher ratings are significantly better than IQ scores at predicting academic performance (see Frank, 1976).

When intelligence tests are used to draw inferences about a client's psychiatric disorder or personality characteristics, validity data have for the most part been disappointing (Cronbach, 1970). Frank (1976, p. 158) suggests a reason for this: It is naïve "to assume that even if personality factors, normal or abnormal, do influence performance on tests of intelligence, that these factors will be the only ones that influence the test results. . . . A subject's age, sex, education, socioeconomic status, and level of intelligence affect performance as does a subject's attitude toward being tested and the examiner's attitude toward the subject."[6]

Probably because their content is so far from the criteria they aim to describe or predict, traditional tests of personality have been found to be among the least valid psychological assessment instruments. Even widely used objective tests have failed to clearly establish their validity relative to, say, simple self-reports or bibliographic information (e.g., Fulkerson & Barry, 1961; Mischel, 1968). The MMPI, for example, has been described as a "mess" (Norman, 1972) and a "psychometric nightmare" (Rodgers, 1972). It was based upon a seriously deficient diagnostic system, its scales have been shown to have limited reliability, and the sample on which the test was standardized was too small and unrepresentative of diverse geographical, racial, and cultural variables. The ability of the test to make all but the roughest distinctions between diagnostic categories (e.g., normal versus abnormal; neurotic versus psychotic) has been strongly questioned, and, because many of the scales are highly correlated, its potential for truly individualized profiles is limited. Research on projective instruments is even less encouraging. Correlations between projective test data and various criteria have tended to range from only .20 to .40 (Sundberg, 1977). Peterson (1968a, p. 3) summarized evaluative research on personality tests by saying that "the cumulative negative evidence is quite compelling and strong positive evidence for validity and utility is nowhere to be seen."

There are many theoretical and practical reasons for such conclusions. Loevinger (1965) points out that the absence of good tests of this type "results not from lack of interest or of willingness to make a good test but from the

[6]In spite of data to the contrary, clinicians still use IQ test "scatter" and other indicants to draw inferences about client personality or behavior disorders (Garfield, 1974). Possible reasons for this and other empirically unjustified test uses will be considered later.

intrinsic difficulties of personality measurement" (p. 91). For example, the personality criteria these tests try to describe or predict are themselves often vague, multidimensional, and surprisingly variable, depending upon situational and other factors. In addition, the meaning of personality test items (e.g., "I enjoy people") or response alternatives (e.g., "often" or "rarely") may vary considerably among clients. Galton recognized this problem when he invented the questionnaire: "There is hardly any more difficult task than that of framing questions which are not likely to be misunderstood, which admit of easy reply, and which cover the ground of inquiry" (Galton, 1883, p. 279). Finally, the basic question of whether to use test responses as samples or signs is still not resolved. No wonder validity suffers!

Distortion of Test Scores   As noted at the beginning of this chapter, tests are designed to collect assessment data under standard conditions. When such conditions are not standard, test scores may be distorted or biased in ways which can mislead the clinician who tries to draw inferences from them. A multitude of factors other than those the tester wishes to measure has been shown to significantly alter the outcome of almost all types of tests. For example, Mussen and Scodel (1955) demonstrated that after having been sexually aroused by photographs of nude females, college men gave more sex-related responses to the TAT when it was administered by a young, informally dressed male graduate student than when given by a man who was older and more formal.

Test administration procedures such as instructions can also influence client responses. As part of their investigations of impression-management tactics used by mental hospital residents, Braginsky, Grosse, and Ring (1966) gave a true-false psychological test accompanied by varying sets of instructions. In one condition, the test was described as an index of mental illness on which "true" responses indicated pathology. Other patients were told that the test measured self-insight and that "true" responses were associated with readiness to leave the hospital. Instructions clearly altered test results. The "mental-illness" test prompted high scores from those who wished to stay in the hospital and lower scores from those who wanted to leave. The "self-insight" instructions prompted the opposite pattern: patients wishing to leave scored higher than those wanting to stay. Instructional effects also appear on IQ tests (e.g., Engleman, 1974), personality tests such as the Rotter Locus of Control Scale (Deysach, Hiers, & Ross, 1976), and even simple Fear Survey Schedules (e.g., Lick, 1977), while selective verbal reinforcement has been shown to alter projective test results (e.g., Greenspoon, 1962; Stewart & Patterson, 1973).

On some tests, the structure of the items and response alternatives may influence results. Suppose a tester wants to know how parents feel about allowing their children to display aggression toward them. The tester may write an item which says "no child should be permitted to strike a parent" and ask the client to "agree" or "disagree." In this case, the client must mentally construct an alternative such as "a child should be encouraged to strike a parent" in order to guide the decision to agree or disagree. Each person may construct different mental alternatives, however, thus making the psychological content of the items variable among clients (Loevinger, 1965).

On tests where the client's responses must be recorded verbatim by the tester, the problem of information loss (already noted for the interview) appears again. To the extent that *all* of what a client says and does is important to the quality of test data, limitations on the ability of any human being to capture an entire testing session accurately can clearly lower that quality.

The circumstances under which a test is given can be important. Bernstein (1956) found that TAT responses contained less emotion and were more optimistic when a tester was in the room than when the client took the test alone. This is perfectly understandable, since, as is the case in many interviews, clients often do not wish to appear "sick" or strange when in the presence of a psychologist. Sometimes, the examiner can produce emotional arousal which actually reduces the client's test score. Handler (1974) reports a case in which a child's IQ rose from 68 to 120 simply by eliminating the disruptive presence of the psychologist. When later IQ tests were administered with the examiner present, the child's score never surpassed 79.

Handler (1974, pp. 54–55) tells another story which highlights the importance of physical surroundings during testing:

> I did a study on the Draw-A-Person Test at Michigan State University. It concerned the relationship between GSR [galvanic skin response] and figure drawing anxiety indices. I attached a polygraph to each subject and asked him to draw human figures. In the study, most of the drawings looked like they were done by back ward patients in a mental hospital. At that time, the Psychology Department was housed in a large, double quonset hut, and I had a tiny, windowless, dimly lit room to use for my research. It was filled with a great deal of apparatus, including a rather imposing looking polygraph console. The walls were covered with sound-deadening materials, which gave the room the eerie quality of a padded cell, or at least of an isolation booth. The subject entered the room reluctantly through two double doors, which I immediately proceeded to slam shut. He was asked to sit in a chair with double armrests, and I attached recording electrodes to the fingers of the nonpreferred hand. Then I turned on the polygraph. . . . I was so involved in collecting data that I did not realize the fantastic stress situation created for all the subjects, who probably thought that, at the very least, they would receive a shock sometime during the experimental period. No wonder the drawings looked so bad.

More general environmental factors may influence test scores as well. Webb (1971) found, for example, that MMPI scale scores tended to be higher for urban clients than for those living in rural areas.

Another source of test data distortion is suggested by the argument that some clients tend to respond in particular ways to all items, regardless of content. This tendency has been called response *set* (e.g., Cronbach, 1946), response *style* (e.g., Jackson & Messick, 1958), and response *bias* (e.g., Berg, 1955). Some clients are thought to exhibit *social desirability* responses, whereby they tend to endorse statements or self-descriptions which are socially acceptable and approved (e.g., honesty and fairness) and reject those which are less valued (Edwards, 1957). Clients have also been suspected of *acquiescent* response styles (e.g., Jackson & Messick, 1961), in which they tend to agree with or endorse virtually any self-descriptive test item. Defensive, deviant, and overly disclosing styles have also been postulated.

The strength and significance of response styles as influencers of test data have been hotly debated matters (see Rorer, 1965; Wiggins, 1973), and it is also not clear whether response tendencies represent stable client characteristics (e.g., Edwards, 1970) or temporary behavior patterns dictated and reinforced by the circumstances under which the test is taken (Mischel, 1968). In any case, the client and her or his point of view while taking the test should not be ignored when evaluating test data.

Other client variables may also be important determinants of test data quality. The value of an adult test containing items like "What is the current gross national product?" or "Describe your self-concept" would be lowered considerably if given to a 2-year-old child. Similarly, clients whose cultural and environmental background leaves them unfamiliar with the concepts and vocabulary of middle-class, white America often look bad on psychological tests reflecting those ideas and terms (e.g., Eells, Davis, Havighurst, Herrick, & Tyler, 1951). While this does not appear to be a source of bias in some cases (e.g., the SAT; Anastasi, 1976), the influence of one's background on intelligence test scores has become a matter of great concern, especially to culturally distinct and/or disadvantaged minority groups within our society.

One approach to the problem has been to use culture-specific instruments such as the Black Intelligence Test of Cultural Homogeneity (BITCH; Williams, 1972) with persons thought to be discriminated against on standard tests, but this merely shifts cultural bias elsewhere. Another approach involves construction of intelligence tests which are not strongly influenced by culture-specific experiences or the presence of particular verbal skills. Examples of some of these tests were given earlier. Additional instruments designed for cross-cultural use include the Leiter International Performance Scale (Leiter, 1936), the Culture Fair Intelligence Test (Cattell, 1940), and the Raven Progressive Matrices (Penrose & Raven, 1936). As already noted, certain early drawing tests (e.g., Goodenough's Draw-a-Man) were also originally designed as nonverbal, culturally neutral measures of intelligence. Unfortunately, hopes for "culture fair" tests have been dampened by research which shows that cultural and other environmental factors influence such tests as much or, in some cases, more than standard instruments (see Anastasi, 1976 for a review and Bernardoni, 1964 for a parody of cross-cultural measures).

Expert psychometricians do not find this surprising and argue that, instead of ignoring IQ tests or attempting to *remove* their cultural and subcultural bias, testers should *examine* the differential performance of certain groups in order to identify specific deficits and motivate corrective programs. Anastasi (1968, pp. 558–559) summarizes this view succinctly:

Tests cannot compensate for cultural deprivation by eliminating its effects from their scores. On the contrary, tests should reveal such effects, so that appropriate remedial steps can be taken. To conceal the effects of cultural disadvantages by rejecting tests or by trying to devise tests that are insensitive to such effects can only retard progress toward a genuine solution of social problems. Such reactions toward tests are equivalent to breaking a thermometer because it registers a body temperature of 101.

Social-learning and other assessors make a related suggestion for reducing irrelevant cultural effects: When specific predictions (e.g., about academic or occupational performance) are desired, use instruments which sample as directly as possible the particular behaviors and skills of interest. When this is done, the opportunity for extraneous characteristics to distort performance is greatly reduced.

The examples of potential sources of test score bias discussed here barely scratch the surface of the problem. Readers interested in more intensive study of this issue should consult sources such as Anastasi (1976), Handler (1974), Hoch (1971), Masling (1960, 1966), Murstein (1965), Palmer (1970), Peterson (1968a), Sarason (1954), Sattler and Theye (1967), and Sundberg (1977).

Abuse of Tests   Like all assessment procedures, tests involve entry by the clinician into the privacy of clients' thoughts and overt behaviors. The extent to which such entry is appropriate, desirable, or even legal is currently a matter of intense debate and litigation. Many observers contend that there are too many tests, too much testing, and too much accumulation of test information in data banks and elsewhere. They also argue that much of this testing and test data are irrelevant, inaccurate, and too easily misused or misinterpreted (often to the client's detriment) by those who gain legitimate or illegitimate access to them. Overdependence upon summary IQ scores by ill-informed test data consumers (and the general public) provides an excellent case in point.

During the mid-1960s, both houses of Congress conducted hearings on psychological testing, particularly as used in educational and vocational selection. These inquiries were prompted in part by serious, knowledgeable test critics and also by the appearance of nonexpert books with sensational titles like *The Brain Watchers* (Gross, 1962), *The Tyranny of Testing* (Hoffman, 1962), and *They've Got Your Number* (Wernick, 1956). Senator Sam Ervin (of Watergate fame) noted: "We have received numerous complaints that some of the questions contained in . . . personality inventories relating to sex, religion, family relationships, and many personal aspects of . . . life constitute an unjustified invasion of privacy" (Ervin, 1965, p. 880).

Many subcommittee members were incensed by some of the things that they learned about test content and quality. In particular, the inclusion of useful but apparently silly or overly intimate items from empirically constructed tests like the MMPI acted as lightning rods for Congressional wrath. Representative Rosenthal of the House Special Subcommittee on Invasion of Privacy fumed: "I will tell you what. I am impressed to the point where if the House were still in session today, and I don't think they are in session, I am prepared to offer a bill on Monday to prohibit the giving of psychological tests by any Federal agency, under any circumstances, at any place, and to make it a Federal crime for any Federal official to do it" (quoted in the *American Psychologist,* November 1965, p. 982).

The rising concern over invasion of privacy and other issues has been called an "anti-test revolt" (Anastasi, 1968) and has resulted in or reaffirmed restrictions on certain types of testing in certain settings. For example, personality tests have been eliminated from routine selection procedures for federal employees, and IQ tests are banned or restricted in New York City and San Francisco schools (Bersoff, 1973). In one extreme case in Texas, a school district governing board ordered test results burned (Nettler, 1959).

As noted earlier, the APA is sensitive to these issues and has officially urged its members to reduce the possibility of abuse in the testing field by adhering to its *Standards for Educational and Psychological Tests and Manuals.* The existence of these standards embodies the pro-test argument that when developed, evaluated, administered, interpreted, communicated, and publicized with due regard for scientific principles and the rights and welfare of clients, psychological tests can make a positive contribution to society. For additional material on this highly sensitive set of issues, see Cronbach (1975), Berdie (1965), and "Testing and Public Policy," a special issue of *The American Psychologist* (1965).

Testing Today   One might anticipate that awareness of the many problems associated with testing would have had a devastating impact on clinicians' use of tests, especially for personality assessment. In fact, as noted earlier, testing is

Cartoon 6-1   *(© by Jules Feiffer. Reproduced by permission).*

still an active enterprise in this country, and clinical psychologists in direct service settings show no signs of abandoning even their most poorly validated instruments (Lubin, Wallis, & Paine, 1971; Reynolds, 1979; Wade & Baker, 1977). Why is this the case?

For one thing, as ordinary mortals, clinical psychologists form habits and find them hard to break. Graduate training often tends to set career-long patterns of assessment practices which may take on strong emotional overtones. In other words, clinicians may do what they were taught to do and then continue doing so because it is what they have always done.

Of course, such habit patterns are not based entirely upon blind adherence. Many clinicians read and attend to data about their tests in somewhat selective ways. With respect to evaluative data on the Rorschach, for example, Korchin (1976, p. 240) points out that "with no effort at all, anyone can draw subsets which either prove or disprove [its] claims." Further, negative *research* findings about a test may simply be seen as irrelevant or at least not central to that test's use in *clinical* settings: "Published indexes of validity . . . are but rough guides, for the psychologist must reach his own judgments of clinical validity and meaningfulness in each particular case" (Tallent, 1976, p. 14). Sometimes, negative evidence is even recast as providing support for a test. After acknowledging the effects of situational factors on TAT responses, for example, Korchin (1976, p. 247) argues that "the fact that the TAT changed sensibly when subjects were aroused shows that it can capture state changes *as well as* durable personality dispositions."

It must also be recognized that certain clinicians, for reasons which are not clearly understood, are able to draw remarkably accurate inferences from test data. Almost every practitioner knows of at least one MMPI, TAT, or Rorschach "ace" whose reputation shores up general confidence in particular tests. Finally, most clinical psychologists are themselves reinforced for using even the least scientifically supported tests by the fact that, now and then (and sometimes more than that), they make their own extraordinarily precise or insightful inferences on the basis of test data.

When these factors are added to the traditional view of clinical psychologists as test experts, the societal demand for testing services, and the relative lack of alternative assessment devices which are as quick and easy to use, the continued popularity of psychological testing is not at all mysterious. Amrine (1965, p. 859) put it this way: "Tests and testers are . . . attacked by the right and left, from outside of psychology and from inside. Meanwhile, the sale and use of tests increases steadily because to thousands of users psychological tests even as presently designed appear to be better than the alternative of no tests." Thus, though more stringent standards and limitations regarding the use of tests in many spheres appear likely, testing in clinical psychology will be with us for a long time (see Petzelt & Craddick, 1978).

Chapter 7

Observation in Clinical Psychology

Observation of the behavior of other people is the most fundamental aspect of interpersonal assessment for clinicians and nonclinicians alike. As was noted in Chapter 4, we all base innumerable social judgments on informal assessment, much of which depends on the appearance and actions of others. Indeed, the notion that "seeing is believing" frequently prompts us to place extra emphasis upon observation of what people *do* as opposed to what they (or others) *say* they do. A single class with a monotonously droning professor may cause some students to drop the course, no matter how good it is said to be, and the sight of a harmless "town drunk" careening down the sidewalk often results in precautionary street-crossing behavior by less intoxicated pedestrians. It is even rumored that persons seeking companionship through computer dating services do not entirely trust the interview or test data upon which match-ups are usually made and insist upon observing their potential date on videotape or in some other way before committing themselves to a meeting.

Clinical psychologists also collect and analyze observational data in the context of their assessment activities. This has been described formally as "the selection, provocation, recording, and encoding of that set of behaviors and settings concerning organisms 'in situ' which is consistent with empirical aims" (Weick, 1968, p. 360). Sundberg and Tyler (1962) put it more simply: "Watch 'em.'' The appeal of the "watch 'em" approach is clear. It provides a direct, firsthand look at behaviors of clinical interest and, in the process, provides a rich source of clues about the causes of those behaviors (Goldfried, 1976). The particular reason for choosing observational assessment will vary somewhat from case to case and across research projects, but, in general, the goal is either to (1) collect information which is not available in any other way, and/or (2) supplement other kinds of data as part of a multiple assessment approach.

For example, consider the situation in which a teacher and a "problem" pupil give quite different but equally sincere reports of why they fail to get along: "He's a brat"; "She's mean." A clearer, less biased picture may emerge from observations of relevant classroom interactions by neutral parties. In other instances, knowing what a person can or will do in a given situation is so important that only observation can suffice. As we saw in Chapter 6, selection of persons best able to perform in certain vocational or military capacities must depend on demonstrated ability at a job-related task, because what a person *says* he or she can or would like to do may not be relevant. Similarly, knowing that a mental patient "feels better" and wishes to leave the hospital is less valuable than observing that person's ability to hold a job, use the bus system, do grocery shopping, and meet the other demands and responsibilities of everyday life.

As a supplement to other methods of data collection, observation can broaden and elaborate the total assessment picture and, in turn, lead to a more comprehensive understanding of the client. This is particularly true when intermethod discrepancies or similarities are revealed. Observations may show, for example, that a "religious fanatic" arrested for disturbing people on the street by "talking crazy" gives excellent sermons in the hospital chapel. Recognition that this individual is capable of appropriate behavior under certain circumstances could do much to enhance the hospital staff's conception of her or his problems. In the same way, observers' reports that a person claiming to have quit smoking is or is not lighting cigarettes in their presence can provide valuable information to the clinician or researcher interested in evaluating an antitobacco program.

We have seen that, even when administering tests or conducting interviews, the astute clinician is also gathering observational data about how the client handles the assessment situation. However, the emphasis placed upon observational information and the way in which it is used in an overall assessment strategy vary considerably among clinicians. Some see the client's overt behavior as providing only supplementary clues to personality traits and dynamics which will be revealed more fully through tests or interviews. For others, observable behavior plays a larger role in guiding inferences about underlying personality or pathology and may even be given a weight equivalent to self-reports or test scores. In both cases, observations are used as *signs* of more fundamental, unobservable constructs. As Shaffer and Lazarus (1952) put it, "In the clinical situation, the easily observed superficial behavior is usually less important than unrecognized behavior patterns and motive systems which must be inferred by the clinician to make the behavior meaningful" (p. 70).

On the other hand, many clinicians and researchers regard observational data as behavior *samples* which represent the most direct, important, and scientific assessment channel available. These individuals usually subscribe to a social-learning model and use observation to describe person-situation interactions rather than to draw inferences about hypothesized underlying characteristics of clients.

In general, the more importance clinicians attribute to observational data, the more systematic they are likely to be in gathering and analyzing such data. At one end of the spectrum are the relatively informal, usually retrospective anecdotal accounts of client behavior. These "free-ranging" observations (Wallen, 1956) are a kind of by-product of other assessment efforts. The following excerpt from a report which followed administration of the Stanford-Binet to a 12-year-old boy provides a clear example:

> John's principal difficulties were on tests requiring precise operations, as in the use of numbers. With such tests he became insecure and often seemed confused with slips of memory and errors in simple calculations. He asked to have instructions repeated, was dependent on the examiner, and easily discouraged. Although cooperative and anxious to do well, it was extremely hard for him to master a task (such as "memory span") in which he was required to be exact by fixed standards. (Jones, 1943, p. 91)

Interviews provide similar but less-structured observational opportunities. Since Freud's day, interviews have played a role in the evolution of monumental psychological theories as well as in day-to-day decisions about individual clients.

Clinicians who place even greater emphasis on overt actions have improved upon casual observation in at least two ways. First, they have developed numerous methods for more accurately and systematically watching and quantifying behavior. Second, they have demonstrated the feasibility of and refined the procedures for collecting observational data in situations other than interviews or tests. Together, these developments have made it possible for modern clinicians and researchers to observe scientifically a wide range of human behavior in a multitude of settings. In this chapter, we shall describe and evaluate some of the observational systems and techniques now available and in use.

Some Historical Notes

Overt behavior existed long before language, so it is probably safe to say that observation preceded the interview as a source of human assessment data. A prehistoric person probably learned fairly quickly how to judge the intentions or tendencies of other prehistoric persons on the basis of their actions (e.g., an offer of food; a raised club), and the importance of observation did not diminish as language developed. In ancient Greek and Chinese civilizations it was suggested that conclusions about an individual could sometimes be drawn on the basis of physical and behavioral characteristics. In the Western world, the practice of interpreting physical features and behaviors came to be called *physiognomy* or *physiognomics* (McReynolds, 1975) and, as we saw in Chapter 2, ultimately led to the appearance of the personality classification systems of Gall, Lombroso, Kretschmer, and Sheldon. It is important to remember, however, that physiognomy also involved behavioral observation. Homer provides an early literary illustration in his *Iliad:*

> There is nothing like an ambush for bringing a man's worth to light and picking out the cowards from the brave. A coward changes color all the time; he cannot sit still for nervousness, but squats down, first on one heel, then on the other; his heart thumps in his breast as he thinks of death in all its forms, and one can hear the chattering of his teeth. But the brave man never changes color at all and is not unduly perturbed from the moment when he takes his seat in ambush with the rest. (Translation by Rieu, 1950; quoted in McReynolds, 1975, p. 488.)

Later, the writings of Pythagoras, Hippocrates, Plato, Aristotle, and Galen elaborated on the relationship between overt behavior and personality characteristics. In a ninth-century B.C. treatise attributed to Aristotle, for example, it is suggested that "sluggish movements denote a soft disposition, quick ones a fervent one . . . the deep and full voice denotes courage, when high and slack it means cowardice" (quoted by McReynolds, 1975, p. 492).

Even the Bible contains references to assessment via behavioral observation. In order to help Gideon defeat the Midianites with the smallest possible force, God tells how to identify the most able soldiers:

> Now therefore go to, proclaim in the ears of the people, saying, whosoever is fearful and afraid, let him return and depart early from Mount Gilead. And there returned of the people twenty and two thousand; and there remained ten thousand. And the Lord said unto Gideon, The people are yet too many; bring them down unto the water, and I will try them for thee there. . . . So he brought down the people into the water; and the Lord said unto Gideon, Everyone that lappeth of the water with his tongue . . . him shalt thou set by himself; likewise everyone that boweth down upon his knees to drink. And the number of them that lapped, putting their hand to their mouth, were three hundred men; but all the rest of the people bowed down upon their knees to drink water. And the Lord said unto Gideon, By the three hundred men that lapped will I save you, and deliver the Midianites into thine hand. . . . (Judges 7:2–7)

Obviously, the best warriors will be those who remain alert to danger, even when drinking.

McReynolds (1975) describes the way in which assessment by observation was kept alive in classical works and in the writing of authors such as Francis Bacon (1605), Thomas Wright (1601), John Bulwer (1644), Marin de la Chambre (1650), and Christian Thomasius (1691), each of whom saw psychological significance in speech patterns, body movements, facial expressions, hand gestures, or other overt signs. Thus the foundations of what we now call observational assessment, content analysis of speech, gesture and movement analysis, and research on the relationship between facial expressions and emotion were laid down centuries ago. Like the test and the interview, clinical observation is the modern form of an old tradition, a part of what McReynolds (1975) calls the "living past."

APPROACHES TO CLINICAL OBSERVATION

At the beginning of this chapter, we quoted Weick's (1968) definition of observational methods as "the *selection, provocation, recording,* and *encoding* of . . . behaviors" (italics added). This definition is a particularly good one because it highlights the elements which are fundamental to nearly every type of observational system. The clinical observer must first *select* those persons, classes of behavior, events, situations, or time periods which are to be the focus of attention. Second, a decision must be made about whether to *provoke* (i.e., artificially bring about) behaviors and situations of interest or to merely wait for them to happen naturally. Third, plans must be made for the way in which observations are to be *recorded:* Observer memory, audio or video recording devices, physiological monitoring systems, timers, and counters are all possible choices. Finally, a system for *encoding* raw observations into usable form must be developed. A large sheet of paper filled with marks representing a client's body movements or a tape recording of a married couple's argument are of little value unless the information contained in them can be translated into manageable and interpretable dimensions such as "frequency of specific movements per minute" or "percent time spent making negative statements." This is probably the most difficult and technically demanding aspect of any observational procedure.

Although each observational enterprise must solve the same set of problems regarding target selection, mode of operation, recording technique, and encoding system, the decisions reached by individual clinicians or researchers are seldom the same. Differing assessment goals, unique client populations, specific environmental limitations, and other factors all act to produce a wide array of approaches to clinical observation.

The clearest way to organize this array is in terms of the *settings* employed. At one extreme, there is *naturalistic* observation, where the assessor looks at behavior as it occurs in its most natural context (e.g., in a home, school, factory, or playground). *Controlled,* or *experimental,* observation (Peterson, 1968a; Wiggins, 1973) lies at the other extreme. Here, the clinician or researcher sets up some sort of special situation in which to observe behavior. Often certain aspects of each of these classic approaches are blended to handle specific assessment needs, and there are many versions or subtypes of both naturalistic and controlled observation (see Table 7-1). One of the most important ways in which these variants differ from one another is in terms of the observers' role (Wiggins, 1973). *Participant* observers are visible to the clients being watched and may even interact with them in some cases. *Nonparticipant* observers are not visible, although, in most cases, the clients are aware that observation is taking place. As

Table 7-1 Overview of Observation Systems

Setting: **Naturalistic**

Observer role:	Participant						Nonparticipant					
Recording system:	Human		Mechanical		Both		Human		Mechanical		Both	
Encoding system:	sign	sample	sign	**sample**	sign	sample	sign	sample	sign	sample	sign	sample

Setting: **Controlled**

Observer role:	Participant						Nonparticipant					
Recording system:	Human		Mechanical		Both		Human		Mechanical		Both	
Encoding system:	sign	sample	sign	sample	sign	sample	sign	sample	sign	sample	sign	sample

noted earlier, other significant observational dimensions include the characteristics of the recording system (human, mechanical, or both) and a decision about whether data are used as signs or samples.

In order to present a reasonably complete (though certainly not exhaustive) picture of the technical smorgasbord called clinical observation, we shall describe naturalistic and controlled observational systems which focus upon several kinds of behavior. The examples chosen will illustrate the use of (1) participant and nonparticipant observers, (2) human, mechanical, and combined recording procedures, and (3) informal and formalized encoding systems which deal with behavior as samples and signs. More comprehensive and detailed coverage of this material is available in Ciminero, Calhoun, and Adams (1976), Cone and Hawkins (1977), Goldfried (1976), Haynes (1978), Hersen and Bellack (1976), Keefe, Kopel, and Gordon (1978), Mash and Terdal (1976), Nay (1979), Sundberg (1977), and Wiggins (1973).

Naturalistic Observation

Watching a client behave spontaneously in a natural setting such as his or her home, school, or job has some obvious advantages. For one thing, it is realistic. The people, situations, and events involved provide a background for observation which is obviously relevant for understanding the nature of the client's behavior and the factors which appear to prompt, maintain, or alter that behavior. Additionally, naturalistic observation may be done in subtle ways which provide a very accurate view of behavior, uncluttered by the client's self-consciousness or attempts to convey a particular impression. Since the natural environment is present all the time, there is great potential for long-term, even continuous, observation, which would be difficult or impossible in a laboratory or other controlled setting.

The classic case of naturalistic observation is the anthropological field study in which a scientist literally joins a tribe, subculture, or other social unit of interest in order to observe its characteristics and the behavior of the individuals within it (e.g., Mead, 1928; Williams, 1967). Here the observer is a participant in every sense of the term, and observations are usually recorded informally in anecdotal notes which later appear as a detailed and organized account called an *ethnography* (e.g., Barnett, 1960).

In psychology, one of the closest approximations to this kind of naturalistic observation was accomplished by Festinger, Riecken, and Schachter (1956) when, without identifying their profession, they joined a group of people who firmly believed that the world was about to come to an end. Their report, *When Prophesy Fails,* provides an insider's look at the social processes which take place when important beliefs are discomfirmed.

The work of Roger G. Barker provides another example of firsthand, naturalistic observation whose intensity approaches anthropological proportions. In an effort to understand the ecology of human behavior, Barker and his colleagues sought to observe as much of it as possible and to capture the richness, variety, and details of its interactions with the environment. This involved participant (but noninteractive) observation of children on a continuous basis from morning until night as they went about a normal day's activities in their home town (Barker, Schoggen, & Barker, 1955; Barker & Wright, 1951, 1955). No attempt was made to select particular behaviors, situations, or events for special attention. Observations were recorded in notebooks as narrative "day records" (see Box 7-1) and later encoded as "behavioral episodes" (see Figure 7-1). When episodes involved other people, they were coded in sign-oriented fashion as representing "nurturance," "resistance," "appeal," "submission," "aggression," "avoidance," and the like. When looking at Box 7-1, notice the amount of observer inference involved in the narratives (e.g., "He looked briefly at me *as if wondering what I thought*").

The amount of data generated by these procedures is staggering. One 8-year-old girl, for example, had 969 behavioral episodes involving 571 objects in the course of a single day. The Barker group was aware that this full-scale ecological approach results in far too much information (even after encoding) to be presented in anything short of a book-length report and suggested more practical alternatives, including periodic rather than continuous observation. Recognition that "voluminous amounts of reliable data that cannot be summa-

Box 7-1 Excerpt from a Day Record

5:39: Raymond tilted the crate from side to side in a calm, rhythmical way.
Clifford's feet were endangered again. Stewart came over and very protectively led Clifford out of the way. [Observer's opinion.]
Raymond slowly descended to the ground inside the crate.
When Stewart came back around the crate, Raymond reached out at him, and growled very gutturally, and said, "I'm a big gorilla." Growling very ferociously, he stamped around the "cage" with his arms hanging loosely. He reached out with slow, gross movements.
Raymond reached toward Clifford but didn't really try to catch him.
Then he grabbed Stewart by the shirt.
Imitating a very fierce gorilla, he pulled Stewart toward the crate.
Stewart was passive and allowed himself to be pulled in. He said "Why don't you let go of me?" He spoke disgustedly and yet not disparagingly.
Raymond released his grasp and ceased imitating a gorilla.
He tilted the crate so that he could crawl out of the open end. As he crawled out, he lost control of the crate and it fell over on its side with the open end perpendicular to the ground.
Stewart said, "Well, how did you get out?"
Raymond said self-consciously, "I fell out," and forced a laugh.
He looked briefly at me as if wondering what I thought.
5:40: He slowly and carefully crawled inside and went directly through the crate and out the open end.
Stewart and Clifford got in front of Raymond and tried to get him to chase them and continue imitating a gorilla.
Raymond stood immobile and didn't cooperate.
Finally Stewart said to Clifford, "Maybe if he'll follow us through, then we can crawl out this end. Then we can tip it up and have him caught again."

Source: Barker & Wright, 1951.

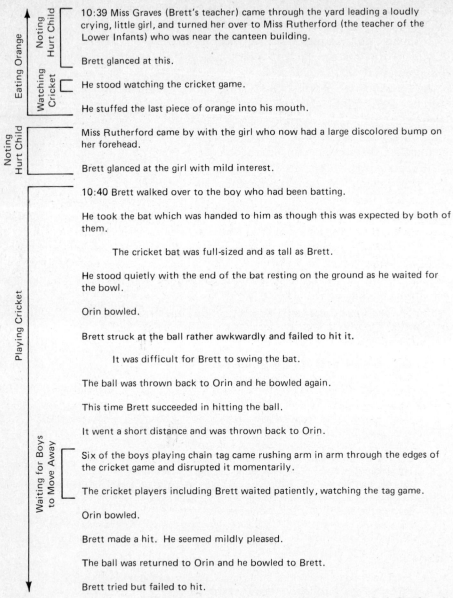

10:39 Miss Graves (Brett's teacher) came through the yard leading a loudly crying, little girl, and turned her over to Miss Rutherford (the teacher of the Lower Infants) who was near the canteen building.

Brett glanced at this.

He stood watching the cricket game.

He stuffed the last piece of orange into his mouth.

Miss Rutherford came by with the girl who now had a large discolored bump on her forehead.

Brett glanced at the girl with mild interest.

10:40 Brett walked over to the boy who had been batting.

He took the bat which was handed to him as though this was expected by both of them.

The cricket bat was full-sized and as tall as Brett.

He stood quietly with the end of the bat resting on the ground as he waited for the bowl.

Orin bowled.

Brett struck at the ball rather awkwardly and failed to hit it.

It was difficult for Brett to swing the bat.

The ball was thrown back to Orin and he bowled again.

This time Brett succeeded in hitting the ball.

It went a short distance and was thrown back to Orin.

Six of the boys playing chain tag came rushing arm in arm through the edges of the cricket game and disrupted it momentarily.

The cricket players including Brett waited patiently, watching the tag game.

Orin bowled.

Brett made a hit. He seemed mildly pleased.

The ball was returned to Orin and he bowled to Brett.

Brett tried but failed to hit.

Figure 7-1   Excerpt from playground observation of a boy named Brett. *(Baker, R. G. The Stream of Behavior. © 1963 by Irvington Publishers, Inc. Reprinted by permission of the publisher.)*

rized may be as useless as unreliable data" (Mash & Terdal, 1976, p. 269) continues to prompt assessors to collect their observational data intermittently and/or to focus mainly on those aspects of behavior and behavior-environment interaction which are of special theoretical or practical importance.

Psychologists interested in child development, for example, have devised observation systems aimed at specific categories of behavior which are thought to be indicative of particular stages or levels of physical, cognitive, and social functioning (e.g., Arrington, 1932; Bayley, 1965; Gesell & Amatruda, 1947; Piaget, 1947; Wright, 1960). Similarly, social psychologists have developed observational tools which help them to record and encode the complex interplay of behaviors occurring in groups. Bales's (1950) interaction coding system classifies the responses of each member of small groups as representing things like "disagreement," "solidarity," "tension release," and "request for orientation." In business and industry, psychologists have devised methods such as the "Critical Incident Technique" (Flanagan, 1954) to observe and record those particular behaviors which characterize good versus poor workers.

The targets of naturalistic observation in clinical psychology have sometimes been behaviors used to infer personality characteristics (e.g., Santostefano, 1962) or intelligence (e.g., Lambert, Cox, & Hartsough, 1970), but the primary focus has been upon assessing the nature of and/or changes in problems which brought the client to the clinician. These include everything from nail-biting and cigarette smoking to troublesome thoughts, from problematic self-expression to maladaptive social interactions and psychotic behavior.

Like their nonclinical counterparts (e.g., the Barker and Bales systems), early clinical observation usually involved the drawing of various kinds of inferences from behavior. The observer not only inferred the meaning of behavior, but also decided which behaviors to report and which to omit. Consider the following anecdotal observation:

> Joan spent the entire science period wandering from group to group instead of helping Rose as she was expected to. She interrupted many of the others, telling them they were doing the work wrong. She asked a lot of (foolish) questions ("Does filter paper make certain things go through or just keep certain things out?") and was teased a good deal by the boys. By the time Rose was finished she returned; Rose was quite angry, but they made up and Joan helped put things away. (Cronbach, 1960, p. 537)

This excerpt paints a rather negative portrait of Joan, but tells only part of the story of her behavior and *only from the observer's point of view.* Was her question about filter paper "foolish"? Was she right in telling her classmates that they were making errors? Was she also displaying positive behaviors that were not described? These questions are not answered by the anecdote.

Further, another observer's view might have rendered a somewhat different picture. Box 7-2 contains the notes of four observers who watched the same ten-minute film, *This Is Robert,* which showed a boy in classroom and playground situations. Notice the different images generated by each viewer. Cronbach (1960, p. 535) summarizes the problem well: "Observers interpret what they see. When they make an interpretation, they tend to overlook facts which do not fit the interpretation, and they may even invent facts needed to complete the event as interpreted."

Box 7-2   Excerpts from Four Observers' Notes on the Same Film[*]

Observer A: (2) Robert reads word by word, using finger to follow place. (4) Observes girl in box with much preoccupation. (5) During singing, he in general doesn't participate too actively. Interest is part of time centered elsewhere. Appears to respond most actively to sections of song involving action. Has tendency for seemingly meaningless movement. Twitching of fingers, aimless thrusts with arms.

Observer B: (2) Looked at camera upon entering (seemed perplexed and interested) Smiled at camera. (2) Reads (with apparent interest and with a fair degree of facility). (3) Active in roughhouse play with girls. (4) Upon being kicked (unintentionally) by one girl he responded (angrily). (5) Talked with girl sitting next to him between singing periods. Participated in singing. (At times appeared enthusiastic.) Didn't always sing with others. (6) Participated in a dispute in a game with others (appeared to stand up for his own rights). Aggressive behavior toward another boy. Turned pockets inside out while talking to teacher and other students. (7) Put on overshoes without assistance. Climbed to top of ladder rungs. Tried to get rung which was occupied by a girl but since she didn't give in, contented himself with another place.

Observer C: (1) Smiles into camera (curious). When group breaks up, he makes nervous gestures, throws arm out into air. (2) Attention to reading lesson. Reads with serious look on his face, has to use line marker. (3) Chases girls, teases. (4) Girl kicks when he puts hand on her leg. Robert makes face at her. (5) Singing. Sits with mouth open, knocks knees together, scratches leg, puts fingers in mouth (seems to have several nervous habits, though not emotionally overwrought or self-conscious). (6) In a dispute over parchesi, he stands up for his rights. (7) Short dispute because he wants rung on jungle gym.

Observer D: (2) Uses guide to follow words, reads slowly, fairly forced and with careful formation of sounds (perhaps unsure of self and fearful of mistakes). (3) Perhaps slightly aggressive as evidenced by pushing younger child to side when moving from a position to another. Plays with other children with obvious enjoyment, smiles, runs, seems especially associated with girls. This is noticeable in games and in seating in singing. (5) Takes little interest in singing, fidgets, moves hands and legs (perhaps shy and nervous). Seems in song to be unfamiliar with words of main part, and shows disinterest by fidgeting and twisting around. Not until chorus is reached does he pick up interest. His especial friend seems to be a particular girl, as he is always seated by her.

[*]The observers were told to use parentheses to indicate inferences or interpretations. The numbers used refer to scenes in the film and were inserted to aid comparison.
Source: Cronbach, L. J., *Essentials of Psychological Testing*, © 1959 by Harper & Row, Pub., Inc. © 1960, Lee J. Cronbach. (Reprinted by permission of Harper & Row, Publishers, Inc.)

Attempts to improve on anecdotal accounts in naturalistic clinical observation have taken many forms. To reduce unsystematic selection and reporting of client behaviors, most modern clinical observation schemes purposely focus the observer's attention on behaviors of particular interest. Some versions of this approach employ *retrospective* procedures (Wiggins, 1973) in which certain of the client's past behaviors are revealed or recalled.

For example, life records may be scanned to gather information about particular behaviors in a client's past. School, police, court, and juvenile authority records have been used as a means of evaluating preventive and remedial treatment of delinquent and predelinquent children (e.g., Alexander & Parson, 1973; Cohen, 1972; Cohen & Filipczak, 1971; Slack, 1960; Schwitzgebel & Kolb, 1964; Tenber & Powers, 1951), while changes in academic grades have provided indices of reduction of test anxiety (e.g., Allen, 1971). Similarly, records of parole violations, return to combat duty, or visits to the dentist have helped assess the impact of interventions with prisoners, soldiers, and fearful dental patients (e.g., Fox, 1954; Ludwig & Ranson, 1947; Patuxent, 1973; Wroblewski, Jacob, & Rehm, 1977).

In clinical research, life records may be of value in testing theories related to the causes of behavior problems. Barthell and Holmes (1968) were interested in the hypothesis that social isolation early in life and particularly during adolescence is related to the subsequent diagnosis of schizophrenia. As a partial test of this hypothesis, they looked up the high school yearbooks of people labeled "schizophrenic" or "neurotic" and compared the activities listed for these individuals with nonlabeled students from the same schools. A similar use of life records is illustrated by research which relates factors such as age, marital status, employment history, and education to the development of schizophrenia and to chances for improvement (e.g., Phillips, 1968; Zigler & Phillips, 1960).[1]

More commonly, retrospective observation involves asking persons familiar with the client to report on the presence, frequency, intensity, duration, or form of specific categories of behavior as displayed in the recent past.

Hospital Observations   The Wittenborn Psychiatric Rating Scales (Wittenborn, 1955) provide an excellent example. This system contains fifty-two scales, each of which is made up of three or four descriptive statements (see Table 7-2). Psychiatric ward staff observe a hospitalized client several times per day or week and then choose the statement in each scale which best describes the client's behavior. The pattern of statement choices is then translated into scores which, on the basis of previous factor-analytic research, are thought to be indicative of certain diagnostic categories. For instance, high scores on scales 3 and 13 (and others like them) are interpreted as indicative of paranoid schizophrenia, while acute anxiety is inferred from high ratings on such scales as 4. Other score patterns are related to conversion hysteria, manic state, depressed state, schizophrenic excitement, paranoid conditions, hebephrenic schizophrenia, and phobic compulsiveness.

A similar system called the Inpatient Multidimensional Psychiatric Scales, or IMPS (Lorr, Klett, McNair, & Lasky, 1962), has been widely used in hospital settings by ward personnel who observe and interview their clients. The IMPS contains seventy-five items, each of which is either rated by the observer/ interviewer on 5 or 9 point scales or responded to with a "yes" or a "no" (see Box 7-3). These data are translated into scores on ten dimensions including excitement, hostile belligerence, paranoid projection, grandiose expansiveness, disorientation, and conceptual disorganization. The scores can then be plotted as a profile (a little like an MMPI) which provides a broad description of the client.

---

[1]These illustrations of retrospective or *archival* observation represent only part of a broader observational approach called *nonreactive* or *unobtrusive* measurement, which has been used in clinical psychology and other behavioral sciences to learn about people's behavior without altering it in the process. A comprehensive description and discussion of these techniques is contained in a fascinating, often humorous book by Webb, Campbell, Schwartz, and Sechrest (1966).

Table 7-2   Sample Scales from the Wittenborn Psychiatric Rating Scales

Scale	Score	Descriptive statement
1	0	Gives no evidence of difficulty in sleeping.
	1	Without sedation may have difficulty in falling asleep, or sleep is readily or spontaneously interrupted.
	2	Without sedation long periods of wakefulness at night.
	3	Acute insomnia; without sedatives gets less than 4 hours sleep in 24.
3	0	No evidence that he imagines people (who probably are wholly indifferent to him) have an amorous interest in him.
	1	Believes (without justification) that certain persons have an amorous interest in him.
	2	Believes (without justification) that a sexual union has occurred or has been formally arranged for him.
4	0	No evidence for obsessional (repetitive, stereotyped) thinking.
	1	Obsessive thoughts occur but can be banished without difficulty.
	2	Patient is able to banish obsessive thoughts but only with difficulty.
	3	Cannot banish or control obsessive thoughts.
10	0	Eats adequate serving.
	1	Eats indifferently and may leave food unless urged to finish.
	2	Voluntarily eats very little and may require coaxing or spoon-feeding.
	3	Refuses to eat.
13	0	No evidence of social withdrawal.
	1	Does not appear to seek out the company of other people.
	2	Definitely avoids people.
21	0	No apparent intrapsychic difficulty in carrying out plans.
	1	Fluctuating attitude toward his plans.
	2	Unable to stick to or carry out any plan.

(Reprinted by permission of the author.)

Some other well-known systems of this type include the "NOSIE-30" (Honigfeld, Gillis, & Klett, 1966), the Fergus Falls Behavior Rating Sheet (Lucero & Meyer, 1951), the Minimal Social Behavior Scale (Farina, Arenberg, & Guskin, 1957), the Psychiatric Status Schedule (Spitzer, Endicott, Fleiss, & Cohen, 1970), the Patient Observational Record Form (Flanagan & Schmid, 1959), and the Hospital Adjustment Scale (McReynolds, Ballachey, & Ferguson, 1952). See Walls, Werner, Bacon and Zane (1977) for a more comprehensive list.

Because observations which contain surplus meaning "are not the simple data that are basic to scientific research and measurement" (Loevinger, 1965, p. 82), many of the newer clinical observation systems used in natural settings not only select and specify the targets to be observed, but also seek to greatly reduce

Box 7-3   Samples from the Inpatient Multidimensional Psychiatric Scales (IMPS)

Compared to the normal person to what degree does/is the client:
1   Exhibit an attitude of superiority
2   Ramble off the topic discussed
3   Assume bizarre positions
4   Unrestrained in showing feelings
5   Blame others for difficulty
6   Believe he has unusual abilities or talents
7   Believe people are against him
8   Make unusual facial grimaces

observer/coder inferences which are very much a part of the Wittenborn, IMPS, and other early techniques. These new systems involve *immediate,* not retrospective, observation. They require the observer to look at a client's behavior and to record or encode that behavior as it occurs without drawing inferences. When such observations are made at regular intervals (e.g., once per hour), the process is called *time sampling.* When only certain activities are observed (e.g., mealtime interactions, cigarette smoking), it is usually called *event sampling.* Often both techniques are involved, as when observations are made once per minute during particular events such as mother-child interactions.

One of the first immediate observation systems used with inpatients was the Behavioral Study Form (BSF) developed by Schaefer and Martin (1966, 1975) at Patton State Hospital in California. The BSF requires ward personnel (usually nurses) to observe clients approximately every 30 minutes and to record the presence of specific behaviors. A list of these behaviors and a sample record sheet are presented in Figure 7-2. At each observation point, the nurse records a "mutually exclusive" behavior (which defines the client's general activity) and any "concomitant" behavior which may accompany that activity. The client's location and other relevant facts are also noted. Data collected over a period of days, weeks, or months can easily be summarized in tables containing, for example, average time spent sleeping, rocking, pacing, watching TV, or whatever. This information can also be presented in a graph such as the one in Figure 7-3. Because the observation targets are clearly spelled out and easily defined as present or absent, the Schaefer and Martin system leaves little room for target selection or inference by the observers. As we shall see later on, these features increase the likelihood that different observers will use the system reliably.

The Behavioral Study Form has served as the basis for some of the more elaborate observation systems now used in psychiatric hospitals. The most prominent examples of these are the Behavior Observation Instrument (BOI; Liberman, DeRisi, King, Eckman, & Wood, 1974) and the Time Sample Behavior Checklist (TSBC; Paul & Lentz, 1977). The latter is probably the most sophisticated and fully researched instrument of its kind. Other, independently

Watch Especially for:

19- head in hands HH
18- Working- assigned
16- Talking to others
GENERAL CODE

Mutually Exclusive Behaviors
1. Walking   4. Sitting
2. Running   5. Lying down
3. Standing

Concomitant Behaviors
6   Drinking
7   Eating — meals
7a   Eating — other than meals
8   Grooming (describe)
9   Group meeting
10   Medication
11   Reading
12   Receiving pay
13   Rocking
14   Pacing
15   Smoking
16   Talking to others
17   TV
18   Working — assigned
19   Other

Location
A   Dining room
B   Hall or lounge
C   Sleeping quarters
D   Lavatory
E   Outside

Patient _____ *Susan R.* _____

Admission _____

Followup:

(1)   2   3   4   5   6   7   8   9

Date: ____ *August 24, 1967* ____

Time	Code	Location
0630	3-8	D
0700	3-6	B
0730	4-15	B
0800	3-10	A
0830	4-18	A
0900	3-18	A
0930		
1000	4-19 HH	B
1030	4-19 HH	B
1100	3-19 Buying item	B
1130	3-18	A
1200	4-7	A
1230	3-16 (Employee)	B
1300	4-11	A
1330	4-9	A
1400	4-9	A
1430	4-9	A
1500	Unavailable	
1530	1	E
1600	3-11	A
1630	3-18	A
1700	3-18	A
1730	4	D
1800	4-16	E
1830	3	C
1900	3-16	C
1930	3-17	B
2000	3-11	A
2030	2-19 (screaming)	B
2100	5	C

Figure 7-2 Coding system and sample record from an early hospital observation system (*Schaefer, H. H. & Martin P. L. Behavioral Therapy, 2nd ed. © 1975 by McGraw-Hill Book Company, New York, Reprinted by permission.*)

developed, schemes for observing the status of and the changes in the behavior of hospital patients include a Barker-like coding system constructed by Ittleson, Rivlin, and Proshansky (1970), the Behavior Observation System of Harmatz, Mendelsohn, and Glassman (1973), and the Resident Activity Manifest (Cataldo & Risley, 1974). Walls, Werner, Bacon, and Zane (1977) list dozens more.

Barker-style ethological observations have also been used in hospital settings by clinicians interested in getting a detailed view of children's behavior

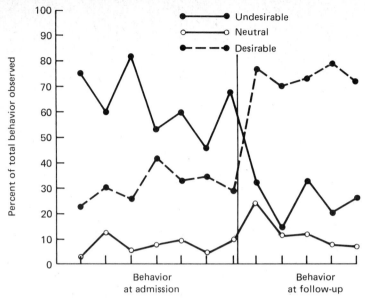

Figure 7-3 Graphic record of three behavior categories under observation. *(Schaefer, H. H. & Martin, P. L.* Behavioral Therapy, *2nd ed. © 1975 by McGraw-Hill Book Company, New York. Reprinted by permission.)*

problems. Rather than attempting to observe and record *all* aspects of the client's behavior, however, certain general subcategories (e.g., social behavior) become the focus of a *long-term* functional analysis which reveals the relationships between these behaviors and the environmental stimuli which precede and follow them. Using this approach, Hutt and Hutt (1968) found that autistic children are more likely to engage in such bizarre motor behavior as hand flapping when new people or objects are introduced into their environment. Other clinically important information about the nature and environmental determinants of children's problematic and nonproblematic behavior can also be gathered in this way (e.g., Currie & Brannigan, 1970; Evans, 1971; Hutt & Ounsted, 1966).

The amount of time and effort involved makes ethologically-oriented observation the exception rather than the rule in functional analysis (Wiggins, 1973), but the approach has clear relevance for clinical work (Hutt & Hutt, 1970). A variant has been used, for example, to gather information on everyday behaviors such as eating and drinking as a prelude to helping clients who overindulge in those activities (e.g., Gaul, Craighead, & Mahoney, 1975; Kessler & Gomberg, 1974; LeBow, Goldberg, & Collins, 1976, 1977).

School Observations The desire to observe children's behavior for clinical purposes has spawned a large number of systems specially designed for use in schools, playgrounds, and other relevant settings. In the tradition of early experimental sociologists (e.g., Dawes, 1934; Thomas, 1929), recording and coding systems designed by Bijou (Bijou, Peterson, & Ault, 1968) and O'Leary (O'Leary & Becker, 1967; O'Leary & O'Leary, 1972) use symbols to represent the behavior of children and the adults around them during time-sample observations collected several times each minute. The symbols (and their definitions) described by Bijou, Peterson, and Ault (1968) in a study done in a nursery school are presented in Figure 7-4. Notice that, like other observation systems of this type, the data gathered can easily be summarized in quantitative form. In this case, percentages could be calculated to summarize how much time a child spent verbalizing to or touching adults or other children.

Classroom observation may focus on a single child and those with whom the child interacts or, by rotating observer attention, the behavior of several target children or even of a whole class can be assessed (e.g., Bushell, Wrobell, & Michaelis, 1968; O'Leary, Becker, Evans, & Saudargas, 1969; Thomas, Becker, & Armstrong, 1968). Similar coding schemes are available for observing children's indoor and outdoor play (Walls, Werner, Bacon, & Zane, 1977).

Home Observations   Naturalistic observational assessment procedures are also available to measure clinically relevant behaviors which occur mainly in the client's home. As has been the case in other areas, early clinical observations in homes tended to contain a lot of inference and unsystematic target selection (e.g., Ackerman, 1958). More recently, however, lower-inference home observation systems have evolved.

In many ways, these are really just extensions of the procedures already described for use in schools. One of the first practical, scientific home observation packages was designed by Gerald Patterson (Patterson, Ray, Shaw, & Cobb, 1969) for use in the homes of young predelinquent boys. This system places trained observers in the client's living area for an hour or two, usually just before dinner.[2] The observers avoid interacting with the family and concentrate on recording the behavior of one member at a time during successive 5-minute periods. Each type of behavior observed (e.g., talking, crying, hitting, laughing, ignoring) is summarized by one of twenty-nine symbols similar in nature to those used by Bijou and O'Leary. Patterson, Cobb, and Ray (1973) provide details of this system. Other systems are available as well (e.g., Lavigueur, Peterson, Sheese, & Peterson, 1973; Mash, Terdal, & Anderson, 1973), some of which have been used not only to assess individual clients but to gather normative data on the behavior of both disruptive and nondisruptive children (e.g., Delfini, Bernal, & Rosen, 1976).

When adult social interaction at home is the target of observational assessment, more complex recording and encoding systems are usually needed. To measure the at-home social skills of depressed clients, for example, Lewinsohn and Shaffer (1971) had observers record family interactions at mealtimes on a time-sampling basis. The encoding system categorized verbal

---

[2]This and most other observation procedures described in this chapter are set up only after the client or a person responsible for the client gives consent.

Symbol	Definition	Symbol	Definition
	First Row **(Social Contacts)**		**Second Row** **(Sustained Activity)**
(box with diagonal, upper-left triangle filled)	*S* verbalizes to himself. Any verbalization during which he does not look at an adult or child or does not use an adult's or child's name. Does not apply to a group situation.	*(box with dot)*	*Sustained activity in art. S* must be sitting in the chair, facing the material and responding to the material or teacher within the 10-sec interval. Responding to the material includes using pencil, paint brush, chalk, crayons, string, scissors or paste or any implement on paper, or working with clay with hands on clay or hands on implement which is used with clay, or folding or tearing paper. Responding to the teacher includes following a command made by an adult to make a specific response. The behavior must be completed (child sitting in his chair again) within two minutes.
(box with circle)	*S* verbalizes to adult. *S* must look at adult while verbalizing or use adult's name.		
(box with diagonal, lower-left triangle filled)	*S* verbalizes to child. *S* must look at child while verbalizing or use child's name. If in a group situation, any verbalization is recorded as verbalization to a child.	*(box with dot)*	*Sustained activity in storytime. S* must be sitting, facing the material, or following a command given by the teacher or assistant. If the *S* initiates a verbalization to a peer, do not record sustained activity in the 10-sec interval.
S	Child verbalizes to *S*. Child must look at *S* while verbalizing or use *S*'s name.		
△	Adult verbalizes to *S*. Adult must look at *S* while verbalizing or use *S*'s name.	*(box with dot)*	*Sustained activity in show-and-tell. S* must be sitting, facing the material, or following a command given by the teacher. If the *S* initiates a verbalization to a peer, do not record sustained activity in that 10-sec interval.
s	Adult gives general instruction to class or asks question of class, or makes general statement. Includes storytelling.	*(box with dot)*	*Sustained activity in reading. S* must be sitting in the chair, facing the material and responding to the material or the teacher within the 10-sec interval.
(box with two vertical lines)	*S* touches adult. Physical contact with adult.	*(box with dot)*	*Sustained activity in writing. S* must be sitting in the chair, facing the material and responding to the material or the teacher within the 10-sec interval. Responding to the material includes using the pencil (making a mark), or holding the paper or folder. Responding to the teacher includes responding verbally to a cue given by the teacher.
(box with horizontal line)	*S* touches child with part of body or object. Physical contact with child.		
V	Adult touches *S*. Physical contact with adult.	*(box with dot)*	*Sustained activity in arithmetic. S* must be sitting in the chair, facing the material and responding to the material or the teacher within the 10-sec interval. Responding to the material or teacher includes using the pencil or eraser or holding the paper or folder or responding verbally to cue.
T	Child touches *S* with part of body or object. Physical contact with child.	*(box with diagonal)*	Sustained activity did not occur in interval.

Figure 7-4 Part of a symbol-coding system for observation of children *(Bijou, S. W., Peterson, R. F., & Ault, M. H.* Journal of Applied Behavior Analysis, *1968, 1, 175-191. © 1968 by the Society for the Experimental Analysis of Behavior, Inc. Reprinted by permission.)*

behavior as self-initiated *actions* (e.g., questions, comments, requests for information, complaints) or positive and negative *reactions* to the behavior of others (e.g., approval, laughter, criticism, disagreement). These and other dimensions (such as speed of reaction to others) were then used to examine differences between depressed and nondepressed persons (e.g., Libet & Lewinsohn, 1973) as well as changes in depressed behavior as a function of treatment (Lewinsohn & Shaffer, 1971).

Gottman (1974) has used a similarly complex coding system for the assessment of couple interactions. Each verbal statement is categorized in terms of its (1) *content* (e.g., question, opinion, command, feedback), (2) *affect* (positive, negative, or neutral), and (3) *impact,* or *intent* (e.g., puts spouse down, puts self up). Two aspects of Gottman's work merit special mention. The first involves the use of sequential or *time-series* analysis of the observational data (Gottman, Markman, & Notarius, 1977). This complex mathematical technique allows the assessor to look not only at the influence of one person on the other at a given point (as when a wife insults her husband) but also at the influence of previous interactions upon later ones. This means that negative "spirals" (where one bad interaction leads to more of the same), positive "spirals," and other long-term social sequences can be more easily discovered than is the case with analytic procedures which merely present "percent of time spent" summaries. The second interesting feature of Gottman's home observation procedure is the use of tape recorders rather than human observers to collect the raw data. Transcripts of the tapes were scored by trained coders.

Observation by "Insiders"   So far, the naturalistic observation systems we have described employ trained undergraduates or other special personnel as participant or nonparticipant observers of client behavior. As we shall see later, there is some question about whether these "outsiders" can do their job without inadvertently influencing the behavior they are to watch, so some clinicians and researchers have arranged to have observational data collected by persons who are part of the client's day-to-day world. We have already seen examples of this: The IMPS and Wittenborn scales are completed by nurses or other ward personnel.

Similarly, observation of children in classrooms and at home has been accomplished by training teachers, parents, and even other children to collect and record data regarding specific behaviors (e.g., Christopherson, Arnold, Hill, & Quilitch, 1972; Eyberg & Johnson, 1974; Hall, Fox, Willard, Goldsmith, Emerson, Owen, Davis, & Porcia, 1971; Hall, Axelrod, Tyler, Grief, Jones, & Robertson, 1972; Kubany & Sloggett, 1973; Osborne, 1969; Surratt, Ulrich, & Hawkins, 1969).

The use of "insiders" as observers of adult behavior for clinical purposes is less common, but not unknown. For example, in the context of efforts to help clients quit smoking, a clinician or researcher may ask for corroborative reports of success (or failure) from family members, employers, coworkers, or friends (e.g., Best, 1975). Such reports may also be solicited as part of the assessment of problems with and change in drug use (e.g., O'Brien, Raynes, & Patch, 1972), sexual activity (e.g., Rosen & Kopel, 1977), social interaction (e.g., Wills, Weiss, & Patterson, 1974) and other adult behaviors.

Self-Observation   Though "insiders" usually have a less obstructed view of a client's behavior over a broader range of locations and time than would be available to an outside observer, no one spends as much time with the client as the client does. It should not be too surprising, therefore, that in many clinical and research settings, clients may be asked to observe and record their own behavior. This is called self-recording or *self-monitoring*. It is usually done by adults or young adults, though children can sometimes be successful at it as well (e.g., Broden, Hall, & Mitts, 1971; Clement, 1974; Thoresen & Mahoney, 1974).

Self-monitoring often requires the client to keep a written record of the frequency or duration or intensity of certain aspects of his or her behavior. A simple chart may be used to record the occurrence of events such as exercise, headaches, pleasant thoughts, hair pulling, giving or receiving praise, and the like. Table 7-3 contains two examples of self-monitoring charts which can be carried around on index cards.

Frequency or duration records can be of great value in assessment, but they leave some important questions unanswered. In looking at Table 7-3, for example, one might want to know what happened to interrupt studying, which subjects were hardest to understand, the circumstances under which sex took place, and the level of sexual enjoyment experienced by the client. To gather information of this type, more elaborate self-monitoring charts called "behavioral diaries" are used.

Figure 7-5 contains an illustration of a diary used for recording smoking behavior. Notice that space is provided for notation of the time at which each cigarette is lit as well as for information about the physical and social setting and the mood which preceded smoking. Similar diaries detailing specific behaviors,

Table 7-3. Part of Completed Self-Monitoring Charts for Study Habits and Sexual Encounters

Part I: Study habits record form			Part II: Sexual encounter record form			
Date	Start study	Stop study	Date	Time of Day	Date	Time of Day
2/13/79	6:30 P.M.	7:15 P.M.	2/13/79	7:00 P.M.	3/14/79	7:15 P.M.
2/13/79	8:15 P.M.	9:30 P.M.	2/15/79	8:30 A.M.	3/14/79	8:00 P.M.
2/14/79	6:00 A.M.	7:30 A.M.	2/15/79	9:00 P.M.	3/14/79	9:30 P.M.
2/14/79	9:00 P.M.	9:15 P.M.	2/21/79	5:30 P.M.	3/14/79	11:30 P.M.
2/15/79	7:00 P.M.	8:15 P.M.	2/21/79	6:45 P.M.	3/16/79	2:00 A.M.
2/15/79	9:00 P.M.	11:00 P.M.	2/21/79	9:00 P.M.	3/16/79	6:00 A.M.
2/16/79	2:00 P.M.	3:30 P.M.	2/25/79	6:30 A.M.		

DAILY RECORD

Name _____ Date _____

Time	Intensity of craving*	Was cigarette smoked? (✓)	Place	With whom	Mood
1.					
2.					
3.					
4.					
5.					
6.					
7.					
8.					
9.					
10.					
11.					
12.					
13.					
14.					
15.					
16.					
17.					
18.					
19.					
20.					

*indicate the intensity of your craving on a scale of 1 to 5: 1 = no perceptible craving; 2 = slight craving; 3 = moderate craving; 4 = fairly strong craving; 5 = intense craving.

Total number of cigarettes smoked _____

Figure 7-5 Behavioral diary for recording smoking behavior. *(From Pomerleau, O. F. & Pomerleau, C. S.* Break the Smoking Habit, © *Research Press, Champaign, Illinois. Reprinted by permission.)*

their antecedents, and their consequences are commonly used in clinical practice and in research to structure self-monitoring of eating habits (e.g., Stuart & Davis, 1972), social-interaction styles (e.g., Wills, Weiss & Patterson, 1974), thoughts (Mahoney, 1971; Meichenbaum, 1976), and other targets. Sometimes, clients are asked to summarize the data they collect on a graph in order to get a visual image of the target behavior and the progress they make once treatment begins. For recent reviews of self-monitoring procedures and applications see Bellack and Schwartz (1976), Evans and Nelson (1977), and Nelson (1977).

Observation Aids Human sensory systems such as sight and hearing are restricted in their ability to detect and discriminate what happens in the environment, making the human observer a "limited instrument for recording physical events" (Rugh & Schwitzgebel, 1976, p. 79). To assist imperfect humans in their observation tasks, mechanical and/or electronic devices are often brought into play. For example, various kinds of mechanical devices are sometimes used to assist self-monitoring, especially when frequency or duration measures are of primary concern. The client may carry some sort of counter which is pressed each time a target behavior occurs. Daily totals can then be read off the counter and recorded on a record sheet or graph. Commercially available golf-stroke or knitting counters may be used, though specially designed single or multiple response counters are sometimes provided by the clinician. A miniature abacus disguised as a leather-and-bead bracelet has been used to allow subtle yet accurate self-monitoring (Mahoney, 1974), while moving pennies or toothpicks from one pocket or purse area to another can provide an even simpler alternative (Watson & Tharp, 1972).

Precise monitoring of the duration of target responses may be aided by various kinds of clocks, watches, and timers. The study-time record presented in Table 7-3, for example, was obviously calculated through the routine use of a wall clock or wristwatch, but, in other cases, a common electric clock or stopwatch can be turned into a cumulative timer. For example, the client may be asked to set a clock to "noon," plug it in each time she or he begins some activity (e.g., studying, exercising, sleeping), and unplug it each time the activity stops. The time on the clock face at the end of the day would thus display the duration of the target behavior for that day (Mahoney & Thoreson, 1974). A stopwatch carried in the client's pocket or purse can be used in the same way.

The use of mechanical aids in naturalistic observation is by no means restricted to self-monitoring. A wide variety of devices has been employed to help or even replace human observers in many clinical and research settings. Some of these tools are rather simple. Observers often use stopwatches to keep track of intervals during time-sampling sessions, and hand-held counters may be employed to record each instance of a particular target behavior (see Cooper, 1974). More complex mechanical aids may be used to record and store larger amounts of information in usable form. These often take the form of "event recorders," which allow an observer to record the occurrence of one or more target behaviors on a strip of paper which moves along at a constant speed. A different button or key on the recorder is pressed when a particular behavior (e.g., hitting another person, laughing, blinking) occurs, so a review of the paper tape reveals the pattern or sequence of all the behaviors observed as well as how often and at what rate each one occurred.

A running record of behavior can also be provided by mechanical devices (usually switches and counters) which are directly connected to the client in some way. This is typified by systems aimed at measuring physical activity, which is a variable of both clinical and research interest with depressed, hyperactive, and certain other clients. Schulmann and Reisman (1959) objectively assessed hyperactivity by having clients wear self-winding watches on their wrists and ankles. Similar movement-sensitive counters, switches, or strain gauges worn on the body or placed under chairs or beds have been used to assess activity level (Epstein & LaPorte, 1978), stability while standing (Terekhon, 1974), motion during sleep (Siegel & Sameroff, 1971; Vietze, Foster, & Friedman, 1974), tics and other movements while seated (Barrett, 1962), and even the forcefulness of toothbrushing (Heath & Wilson, 1974). In one study, the activity of retarded sheltered workshop employees was monitored by switches attached to the tools they used (Schroeder, 1972).

Electronic data collection devices have also played a role in naturalistic observation procedures. Audio and video tape recorders have been employed to help gather larger amounts of continuous data than would be possible using human observers. Families and other social groups have been tape-recorded in their natural environment (e.g., Johnson & Bolstad, 1974), and, as part of a study designed to assess fear of dentistry, Kleinknecht and Bernstein (1978) placed television cameras in the waiting rooms and treatment operatories of practicing dentists. The cameras were connected to a video tape deck which recorded the overt behavior of patients in both settings. Later, the tapes were viewed by trained observers who used time-sampling procedures and a special coding system to quantify the patients' behaviors.

The advent of tiny, solid-state transmitters has allowed audio recordings of a client's verbal behavior to be made even when that client is nowhere near the tape recorder. This involves having the client wear a tiny microphone attached to a pocket-size wireless transmitter which sends a signal to a remote receiving point where it is stored in a standard tape recorder. Equipment of this kind has been used to record the verbal interactions of adolescents (e.g., Purcell & Brady, 1966), psychiatric inpatients (e.g., Moos, 1968), and married couples (e.g., Soskin & John, 1963). Information about nonverbal behavior such as heart activity (e.g., Weiss & Engel, 1971), brain waves (e.g., Jacobson, Kales, Lehmann, & Zweizig, 1965), or galvanic skin response (e.g., Thackray & Orne, 1968) can also be gathered through radiotelemetry.

Combinations of mechanical and electronic observational aids appear in devices which sense movement or other aspects of behavior and transmit this information by radio waves to a monitoring station nearby. Kupfer, Detre, Foster, Tucker, and Delgado (1972) employed such a device (worn as a wristband) to measure the physical activity of depressed inpatients, and Herron and Ramsden (1967) placed a pressure sensor and a miniature transmitter in the heel of clients' shoes to record locomotion. Information about pressure, movement, and other variables relevant to dealing with clients who suffer from tension-produced dysfunctions of the face and jaw has been communicated by radio from sensor-transmitters placed in eyeglasses (Rugh, 1971) or on teeth (Kavanaugh & Zandler, 1965).

Additional examples of the application of mechanical and electronic technology to the development of instrumentation for use in naturalistic observation abound in the clinical literature. Excellent reviews of these applications and the equipment and principles associated with them have been provided by Miklich (1975) and Rugh and Schwitzgebel (1977).

Controlled Observation

The major appeal of naturalistic observation is, as we have seen, that it can result in large samples of free, spontaneous, and "real" client behavior occurring under circumstances of relevance and interest to the clinician. Some of the assets of observation in natural settings can sometimes become liabilities, however, especially when observation targets are low in frequency. Suppose, for example, that the clinician wishes to observe a client's response to stress. To accomplish this goal using naturalistic procedures, human or nonhuman observers would have to continuously monitor the client's behavior in settings where stressful events might occur. Because there is no guarantee that the client would actually encounter clinically relevant stress on a given day or in a given situation, much of the time and effort expended in this enterprise is likely to be wasted.

Further, because naturalistic observation usually takes place in an uncontrolled environment, even if a stressor or other relevant situation appears, many things can happen to foul up the assessment. The client may temporarily move out of the observer's earshot or line of vision, or his or her verbal behavior may be drowned out by someone else's conversation, a television set, a radio, or even a passing airplane. Worse yet, the client may get assistance in dealing with the situation of interest simply because a family member, friend, or coworker happened to be around. How would the client have reacted without help? The assessor cannot know unless the same situation recurs when the client is alone and under observation.

The fact that the situation of interest may not soon occur again points to another limitation of naturalistic observation: Repeated assessment of a client's reaction to certain low-probability events is often nearly impossible. Thus, precise measurement of client improvement or deterioration during treatment or over time may be seriously hampered. For the clinical researcher, this problem is very important, because comparison of the behavior of many people under identical conditions is a cornerstone of most experimental designs.

One way of dealing with some of the difficulties associated with naturalistic observation is to set up special circumstances under which to observe a client's behavior as she or he reacts to planned, standardized events. This is usually called *controlled observation* because the clinician maintains control over the nature and timing of the assessment stimuli in much the same way as do users of the tests described in Chapter 6. Controlled observations are also referred to as situation tests, miniature situations, analogue assessments, and contrived observations.

As was true in the case of early naturalistic observations, the first controlled observation systems and procedures tended to involve a great deal of inference. For example, Barker, Dembo, Tamara, and Lewin (1941) set up a frustration situation by first allowing nursery school children to play with highly desirable toys in a fenced area, then locking the youngsters out. The varying reactions and strategies displayed by each child (see Figure 7-6) were interpreted as evidence of maturity, constructiveness, regression, and other inferred characteristics. Earlier, Hartshorne and May (1926) studied personality traits such as honesty by

Figure 7-6 Sketch of varying reactions to controlled frustration situations. *(From* Child Psychology, *4th ed., by J. J. B. Morgan. © 1942 by Holt, Rinehart and Winston. Reproduced by permission of Holt, Rinehart and Winston.)*

placing children in situations where they could steal money without fear of being detected. In social psychology, special interactions called Leaderless Group Discussions (Bion, 1946) were set up and individuals were rated on variables such as "showed initiative," "motivated others to participate," or "offered good solutions" (Bass, 1954). Personality traits such as prominence and sociability were inferred from the ratings.

During World War II, military psychologists devised controlled observations which were aimed at assessing personality traits as well as objective behavioral capabilities. In the Operational Stress Test, for example, would-be pilots were placed in a flight simulator and asked to manipulate various controls. The candidates did not know that the tester was purposely trying to confuse and frustrate them and cause them stress by giving increasingly complicated instructions accompanied by lots of negative feedback (e.g., "You're making too many errors"; Melton, 1947). During the test, the assessor made ratings of the candidate's reaction to criticism and stress, and these ratings supplemented objective data on skill with the simulator.

Traits of initiative, dominance, cooperation, and group leadership were inferred from another series of wartime observational assessments developed by the staff of the Office of Strategic Services (OSS) to help select espionage agents and other special personnel. The assessments were based on earlier work by

German and British military psychologists and included group tasks such as transporting a log across a stream (without going in the water) and moving a heavy object over an imaginary chasm between two 10-foot-high walls.

These were difficult tasks, but the "highpoint of fiendish ingenuity" (Cronbach, 1960, p. 568) was represented by the "construction test" in which a single candidate was assigned to build a 5-foot cube-shaped frame out of large wooden poles and blocks resembling a giant "tinker toy" set. Because the test was supposed to measure the candidate's organizational and leadership ability, he was given two "assistants" (actually, psychologists) who called themselves "Buster" and "Kippy."

> Kippy acted in a passive, sluggish manner. He did nothing at all unless specifically ordered to, but stood around, often getting in the way. . . . Buster, on the other hand, . . . was aggressive, forward in offering impractical suggestions, ready to express dissatisfaction, and quick to criticize what he suspected were the candidate's weakest points. . . . It was their function to present the candidate with as many obstructions and annoyances as possible in ten minutes. As it turned out, they succeeded in frustrating the candidates so thoroughly that the construction was never . . . completed in the allotted time. (OSS, 1948, p. 103)[3]

Box 7-4 contains an excerpt from a typical test session.

Since World War II, milder versions of the OSS "situational tests" have been used as part of the process for selection of police officers (Mills, McDevitt, & Tonkin, 1966) and other personnel (Bray, Campbell, & Grant, 1974; Lopez, 1966). In current clinical and research settings controlled observations take many forms, almost all of which are much less sneaky than those used by the OSS under the pressures of wartime. In some cases, the "control" involved consists merely of asking clients (usually couples, families, or parent-child pairs) to come to a clinic or laboratory and have a discussion, attempt to solve a problem, or just talk while under observation by TV cameras, tape recorders, or human coders (e.g., Alexander, 1973; Bugenthal, Love, & Kaswan, 1972; Toepfer, Reuter, & Maurer, 1972). In other instances, the client or clients are presented with a structured task or situation designed to elicit behaviors of relevance to clinical assessment.

Role-Playing Tests The clinician and/or several other persons may create a make-believe situation in which the client is asked to *role-play* his or her typical behavior. Role-playing has been advocated by various clinicians for many years (e.g., Borgatta, 1955; Rotter & Wickens, 1948; Stanton & Litwak, 1955) and serves as the cornerstone of *psychodrama* (Moreno, 1946) and other psychodynamic and phenomenological treatment approaches (e.g., Kelly, 1955; Perls, 1969), but it was not until the late 1960s that it became a part of systematic, low-inference programs of clinical assessment (McFall, 1977). The most

---

[3]The fact that "Kippy" and "Buster" were Army privates and often got to torment high-ranking officers "set an untouchable record for job satisfaction among psychologists" (Cronbach, 1960, p. 568).

Box 7-4   Excerpt from OSS Construction Task Session

Staff member (calling toward the barn): Can you come out here and help this man for a few minutes?

Buster and Kippy: Sure, we'll be right out.

Staff member: O.K., Slim, these are your men. They will be your helpers. You have ten minutes.

Slim: Do you men know anything about building this thing?

Buster: Well, I dunno, I've seen people working here. What is it you want done?

Slim: Well, we have got to build a cube like this and we only have a short time in which to do it, so I'll ask you men to pay attention to what I have to say. I'll tell you what to do and you will do it. O.K.?

Buster: Sure, sure, anything you say, Boss.

Slim: Fine. Now we are going to build a cube like this with 5-foot poles for the uprights and 7-foot poles for the diagonals, and use the blocks for the corners. So first we must build the corners by putting a half block and a whole block together like this and cinching them with a peg. Do you see how it is done?

Buster: Sure, sure.

Slim: Well, let's get going.

Buster: Well, what is it you want done, exactly? What do I do first?

Slim: Well, first put some corners together—let's see, we need four on the bottom and four topside—yes, we need eight corners. You make eight of these corners and be sure that you pin them like this one.

Buster: You mean we both make eight corners or just one of us?

Slim: You each make four of them.

Buster: Well, if we do that, we will have more than eight because you already have one made there. Do you want eight altogether or nine altogether?

Slim: Well, it doesn't matter. You each make four of these, and hurry.

Buster: O.K., O.K.

Kippy: What cha in, the Navy? You look like one of them curly-headed Navy boys all the girls are after. What cha in, the Navy?

Slim: Er—no. I am not in the Navy. I'm not in anything.

Kippy: Well, you were just talking about "topside" so I thought maybe you were in the Navy. What's the matter with you—you look healthy enough. Are you a draft dodger?

Buster: What kind of work did you do before you came here? Never did any building, I bet. Jeez, I've seen a lot of guys, but no one as dumb as you.

Slim: Well, that may be, but you don't seem to be doing much to help me.

Buster: What—what's that? Who are you talking to, me? Me not being helpful—why, I've done everything you have asked me, haven't I? Now, haven't I? Everything you asked me. Why, I've been about as helpful as anyone could be around here.

Slim: Well, you haven't killed yourself working and we haven't much time, so let's get going.

Buster: Well, I like that. I come out here and do everything you ask me to do. You don't give very good directions. I don't think you know what you are doing anyway. No one else ever complained about me not working. Now I want an apology for what you said about me.

Slim: O.K., O.K., let's forget it. I'll apologize. Let's get going. We haven't much time. You build a square here and you build one over there.

Buster: Who you talking to—him or me?

Kippy: That's right—how do you expect us to know which one you mean? Why don't you give us a number or something—call one of us "number one" and the other "number two"?

Slim: O.K. You are "one" and he is "two."

Buster: Now, wait a minute—just a minute. How do you expect to get along with people if you treat them like that? First we come out here and you don't ask us our names—you call us "you." Then we tell you about it, you give us numbers. How would you like that? How would you like to be called a number? You treat us just like another 5-foot pole and then you expect us to break our necks working for you. I can see you never worked much with people.

Slim: I'm sorry, but we do not have much time and I thought—

Kippy: Yes, you thought. Jeez, it doesn't seem to me that you ever did much thinking about anything. First you don't ask our names as any stupid guy would who was courteous. Then you don't know what you did before you came here or whether you are in the Army, Navy, or not, and it's darn sure you don't know anything about building this thing or directing workers. Cripes, man, you stand around here like a ninny arguing when we should be working. What the hell is the matter with you, anyway?

Slim: I'm sorry—what are your names?

Buster: I'm Buster.

Kippy: Mine's Kippy. What is yours?

Slim: You can call me Slim.

Buster: Well, is that your name or isn't it?

Slim: Yes, that is my name.

Kippy: It's not a very good name—Dumbhead would be better.

Source: OSS, 1948.

common use of role-playing in controlled observation has been in the assessment of social competency, self-expression, or assertiveness.

Sometimes, the procedures are simple and structured, as in the Situation Test (ST) developed by Rehm and Marston (1968) to explore college males' social skills. In the ST, the client sits with a person of the opposite sex and listens to a tape recorded description of the scene to be role-played. The woman (an assistant to the clinician) then reads a question or statement such as "What would you like to do now?" or "I thought that was a lousy movie," and the client is asked to respond as if the situation were real. In the Social Behavior Situations Test (SBT; Twentyman & McFall, 1975), social situations are also created via tape recording, but the client listens alone. The tape may contain material such as: "You are on a break at your job. You see a girl who is about your age at the canteen. She works in another part of the store and consequently you don't know her very well. You would like to talk to her. What would you say?" (Twentyman & McFall, 1975, p. 386). After hearing the tape, the client is asked to act as if he were actually in the situation and to carry on an interaction over an intercom with a female assistant in the next room. In both the ST and the SBT, clients' behaviors are coded and judged for anxiety, response latency, speech disfluencies, overall adequacy, and other variables.

For added realism, some social situations have been presented on videotape (Goldsmith & McFall, 1975; Melnick, 1973), but most controlled social skill assessments employ live human beings in the role-play. Another example is provided by the Forced Interaction Test (Twentyman & McFall, 1975) in which a female assistant enters a room and sits down next to the male client. The client's task is to imagine himself in a classroom and to initiate and maintain a 5-minute conversation with the assistant. Similar, though somewhat more elaborate "live" observational procedures for assessing social skills have also been used by many other investigators (e.g., Arkowitz, Lichtenstein, McGovern, & Hines, 1975; Borkovec, Stone, O'Brien, & Kaloupek, 1974; Glasgow & Arkowitz, 1975; MacDonald, Linquist, Kramer, McGrath & Rhyne, 1975). Response dimensions of importance on these tests include talk time, length of silences, nodding, eye contact, and self-disclosure.

Role playing has also been used to assess client assertiveness. In the Behavioral Assertiveness Test (Eisler, Miller, & Hersen, 1973; Eisler, Hersen, Miller, & Blanchard, 1975), for example, hospitalized males were prompted to respond to a female assistant in various make-believe social situations (e.g., a person steps in front of the client in a supermarket check-out line; a steak ordered rare arrives well done). Their behavior was videotaped and then analyzed using a coding system which covered variables such as response latency and compliance. In other studies (e.g., Bloomfield, 1973; Serber, 1972) no assistants were employed; the clinician role-played directly with the client. This is also commonly done in clinical work where the use of assistants is not feasible or may be inappropriate.

Tape recordings are sometimes used to help standardize the stimuli in role-played assessment. The client listens to a tape recording which simulates various social situations and then responds to each of them as she or he normally would in everyday life. Tapes allow for the easy creation of a variety of social settings and events which would be difficult to reproduce in the clinic or laboratory and which are not easy to observe elsewhere.

Taped stimuli have commonly been used to assess the social competency and assertiveness of college students (e.g., Arkowitz, Lichtenstein, McGovern,

Box 7-5   Sample Situations from the BRAT

Narrator: In this scene, picture yourself standing in a ticket line outside of a theatre. You've been in line now for at least ten minutes, and it's getting pretty close to show time. You're still pretty far from the beginning of the line, and you're starting to wonder if there will be enough tickets left. There you are, waiting patiently, when two people walk up to the person in front of you and they begin talking. They're obviously all friends, and they're going to the same movie. You look quickly at your watch and notice that the show starts in just two minutes. Just then, one of the newcomers says to his friend in line:
Newcomer: "Hey, the line's a mile long. How 'bout if we cut in here with you?"
Person in Line: "Sure, come on. A couple more won't make any difference."
Narrator: And as the two people squeeze in line between you and their friend, one of them looks at you and says:
Newcomer: "Excuse me. You don't mind if we cut in, do you?"
(Bell sounds as cue for *S* to respond.)

Narrator: Imagine that this morning you took your car to a local Standard station, and you explicitly told the mechanic to give you a simple tune-up. The bill should have been about $20. It's now later in the afternoon and you're at the station to pick up your car. The mechanic is walking over to you.
Mechanic: "Okay, let me make out a ticket for you. The tune-up was $12 for parts and $8 for labor. Uh, grease and oil job was $6. Antifreeze was $5. Uh, $4 for a new oil filter. And, uh, $5 for rotating the tires. That's $40 in all. Will this be cash or charge?"

Source: McFall & Marston, 1970.

& Hines, 1975; MacDonald, 1978; McFall & Marston, 1970). A few examples of the taped situations presented in an early version of the Behavioral Role-playing Assertion Test (BRAT; McFall & Marston, 1970; McFall & Lillesand, 1971) are reproduced in Box 7-5. Clients' responses to these situations are usually recorded and then rated for overall assertiveness, response latency, disfluency, response duration and other related factors. Situations of a similar type have also been included on tapes developed for use with psychiatric inpatients (e.g., Goldsmith & McFall, 1975; Goldstein, Martens, Hubben, VanBelle, Schaaf, Wiersma, & Goedhart, 1973).

There is even a tape that "talks back." In order to assess the firmness and generality of clients' assertion skills (especially involving refusal of unreasonable requests), McFall and Lillesand (1971) used an Extended Interaction Test in which the client's refusal to submit to a demand was met with gradually escalating insistence on the part of a taped antagonist (see Box 7-6). Presumably, a person who can withstand repeated requests is more assertive than one who caves in after an initial attempt at refusal.

The Extended Interaction Test provides an example of one approach to assessing the generality of client behavior through controlled observation, but there are others as well. Some involve administration of new, different items from tests like the BRAT to measure the range of situations in which a client is skilled or assertive (e.g., Edelstein & Eisler, 1976), while others attempt to

---

Box 7-6   Excerpt from the Extended Interaction Test

Narrator: You are feeling really pressed for study time because you have an exam on Friday afternoon. Now, you are studying at your desk, when a close friend comes in and says, "Hi. Guess what. My parents just called and offered to pay for a plane ticket so I can fly home this weekend. Great, huh!? The only problem is, I'll have to skip my Friday morning class, and I hate to miss out on those notes; I'm barely making it in there as it is. Look, I know you aren't in that class, but it'd really be a big help if you'd go to the class Friday and take notes for me so I could go home. Would you do that for me?"

(*S* responds. If refusal . . .)

"I guess it is kinda crazy to expect you to do it, but, gee, I've got so many things to do if I'm gonna get ready to leave, and I don't want to waste the time asking around. Come on, will you do it for me this once?"

(*S* responds. If refusal . . .)

"Look, what're friends for if they don't help each other out of a bind? I'd do it for you if you asked. What do you say, will you?"

(*S* responds. If refusal . . .)

"But I was *counting* on *you* to do it. I'd hate to have to call my folks back and tell them I'm not coming. Can't you spare just *one* hour to help me out?"

(*S* responds. If refusal . . .)

(Sarcastically.) "Now look, I don't want to *impose* on your *precious* time. Just tell me. Will you do it or do I have to call my folks back?"

(*S* responds.)

Source: McFall & Lillesand, 1971.

observe the client in naturalistic settings (e.g., Frederiksen, Jenkins, Foy, & Eisler, 1976). Because the first strategy may not be realistic and because the second strategy is usually difficult to carry out, a third, somewhat controversial approach has appeared in recent years. It involves creating a *staged naturalistic event* (Gottman & Markman, 1978) consisting of controlled observational circumstances of which the client is either unaware or about which he or she has been misinformed. The idea is to take a systematic look at behavior in a *controlled* setting that appears *naturalistic* to the client or, in short, to have the best of both observational worlds.

For example, McFall (e.g., McFall & Twentyman, 1973) has reported some creative procedures for assessing the generality of college students' assertiveness outside the laboratory setting. Clients volunteering for an assertion training study were telephoned by a research assistant who posed as a fellow student and who made a series of seven increasingly unreasonable requests (see Box 7-7). Scores on this test corresponded to the point at which the client switched from "yes" to "no" in response to the caller's pleas. After each call, the client was contacted again and informed about the real nature and purpose of the interaction.

An unobtrusive test has also been used to measure generalized social skills in male psychiatric inpatients (Goldsmith & McFall, 1975). Here, the client is asked to meet and carry on a conversation with a total stranger (who is, as usual, the clinician's confederate). The client thinks he is being evaluated on how well he completes three tasks: (1) initiating the conversation, (2) asking the other person to lunch, and (3) terminating the conversation. What the client does not know is that "the confederate had been programmed to confront him with three

---

Box 7-7   Excerpt from Unobtrusive Telephone Assessment of Assertion

"Hi, may I speak to (subject)? (Subject)? You're taking intro psych, aren't you? Well, I'm Tom Blake. I don't think you know me, but I'm in (professor)'s lecture, too. I don't know anyone in the class, so I got your name off the registration list they have in the psych office."

Request 1: "I really hate to bother you, but I have some questions on some of the lecture material. Do you think you could help me for a few minutes?" (*S* responds. If no refusal . . .)

Request 2: "I think all I really need is to look at your notes. Do you think we could arrange that?" (*S* responds. If no refusal . . .)

Request 3: "Actually, I haven't made it to all the lectures, so I'll need to borrow your notes for awhile to fill in what I've missed. Okay?" (*S* responds. If no refusal . . .)

Request 4: "Well, (subject), to tell you the truth, I haven't been to class since the last exam, so I'll probably need your notes for two days. Would that be all right?" (*S* responds. If no refusal . . .)

Request 5: "Let's see now. I have a paper due on Wednesday (five days before exam), so I won't be able to get them before that. Could I get them sometime on Thursday?" (*S* responds. If no refusal . . .)

Request 6: "Oh, wait a minute! I've got a chemistry exam on Friday. Could I get them after that? That would be three days before the psych exam." (*S* responds. If no refusal . . .)

Request 7: "Now that I think about it, I'll probably need a night to recover from the chem exam, so is it all right if I get them Saturday instead, for the two days before the exam? (*S* responds.)

Source: McFall & Twentyman, 1973.

'critical moments': not catching the subject's name, responding to the lunch invitation with an excuse that left open the possibility of lunch at an alternative time, and saying 'Tell me about yourself' at the first convenient pause in the conversation" (McFall, 1977, p. 168). Similar contrived situations which involve some deception have also been used in psychiatric settings by Gutride, Goldstein, and Hunter (1973), Hersen, Eisler, and Miller (1974), and Weinman, Gelbart, Wallace, and Post (1972). Behavior observed through these unobtrusive techniques is usually scored on dimensions such as assertiveness, eye contact, comfort, skill, and pleasantness.

This type of observation involves deception and possible invasion of privacy, so it must be set up with great care and with due regard for client welfare and dignity. The proponents of unobtrusive controlled observation have recognized and sought to avoid its potential dangers (e.g., Hersen & Bellack, 1977) and are quick to point out that its value may be limited to measuring certain specific behaviors (such as refusal) rather than more complex interactive social skills (e.g., McFall, 1977).

Performance Measures   In most of the controlled observations described in the previous section, the client is asked to act "as if" a situation or event were taking place. There are other procedures, however, in which the client is actually faced with some version of a clinically relevant situation so that her or his behavior can be observed. Some of these observations are focused upon social interaction. A client may be asked to carry on a real conversation with a person who is not programmed to respond in any particular way (e.g., Argyle, Bryant, & Trower, 1974) or a couple may be given an issue to discuss (e.g., Gottman, Markman, & Notarius, 1977). A mother's style of interaction with her child may be observed during play (e.g., Wahler, Winkel, Peterson, & Morris, 1965), cooperative work on a structured task (e.g., Santostefano, 1968), or other activities (e.g., Smith, 1958; White & Watts, 1973).

Controlled observations of performance have also focused upon consummatory behaviors such as eating, drinking, or smoking. For example, the eating style (e.g., amount, speed, preferences) of normal and/or obese individuals has been recorded during a meal or snack offered in a laboratory or other controlled setting (e.g., Abramson & Wunderlich, 1972; Nisbett, 1968; Schachter & Gross, 1968). Alcoholic and nonalcoholic drinkers have been observed in specially constructed cocktail lounges (see Figure 7-7) or living rooms located in hospitals (e.g., Miller, Hersen, Eisler, & Hilsman. 1974; Miller, Becker, Foy, & Wooten, 1976; Sobell, Schaefer & Mills, 1972; Williams & Brown, 1974), and the details of cigarette use (puff rate, depth of inhalation, number of puffs) have been scrutinized in volunteers smoking under observation in simulated social settings (e.g., Frederiksen, Miller, & Peterson, 1977).

Another important and increasingly popular type of performance measure in controlled settings is the physiological activity (e.g., heart rate, respiration, blood pressure, galvanic skin response, muscle tension, and brain waves) which appears in relation to various stimuli and situations. This type of observational

Figure 7-7   Simulated bar located in a hospital setting. *(Courtesy of G. Alan Marlatt. Reprinted by permission.)*

assessment appears almost everywhere in the clinical literature (see reviews by Epstein, 1976; Kallmann & Feuerstein, 1977; Kopell & Rosenbloom, 1975; Lang, 1971). An early example is provided by Malmo, Shagass, and David (1950) who showed a film about headache to a client with a severe headache problem and measured an increase in her forehead muscle tension while she watched. R. S. Lazarus (1967) studied stress reactions by recording a variety of physiological responses in volunteer subjects while they watched a graphic film about primitive circumcision rituals.

More recently, clinicians have begun to study the effects of common and unusual erotic stimuli (presented via film, videotape, slides, or audiotape) on various indexes of sexual arousal, including penile volume and vaginal blood flow (e.g., Barlow, Becker, Leitenberg, & Agras, 1970; Geer, 1977; Sintchak & Geer, 1975; Zuckerman, 1971). These measures have been used extensively in the assessment of problematic sexual behavior (e.g., Abel, 1976; Barlow, 1977). Figure 7-8 shows a graph of a client's penile erection in response to audiotapes describing three types of foot and sandal fetish material.

Assessment of the physiology of fear in controlled settings has also occupied many clinical researchers. In a classic study, Paul (1966) used measures of heart rate and sweating taken just before giving a talk to help identify speech-anxious clients. These measures were repeated following various anxiety-reduction treatments to aid in the evaluation of their effects. The wide range of physiological assessments of anxiety is covered in reviews by Borkovec, Weerts, and Bernstein (1977) and Lang (1977).

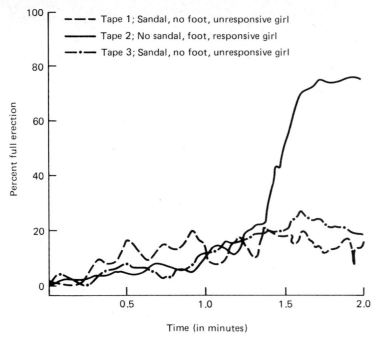

Figure 7-8 Erectile responses to various foot-related stimuli. *(Abel, G. G., Blanchard, E. B., Barlow, D. H., & Mavissakalian, M.* Journal of Applied Behavior Analysis, *1975, 8, 247–260. © 1975 by the Society for the Experimental Analysis of Behavior, Inc. Reprinted by permission.)*

Probably the most popular performance measure in controlled observation is designed to assess overt anxiety in relation to specific objects and situations. These are usually called *Behavioral Avoidance Tests* (BATs) because they confront the client with the very thing which he or she fears and then record the type and degree of avoidance displayed. Relatively informal BATs had been conducted with children as early as the 1920s (e.g., Jones, 1924), but it was not until the early 1960s that systematic avoidance-testing procedures became a common form of controlled observational assessment. A. A. Lazarus (1961) was among the first clinicians to carefully observe clients' reactions to controlled fear stimuli (such as heights and closed places) in a BAT, but the research prototype of the procedure was developed by Peter Lang.

In a study of the effects of systematic desensitization (see Chapter 10) on snake phobia, Lang and Lazovik (1963) asked each of their clients to enter a room which contained a harmless caged snake and to approach, touch, and pick up the animal. The clients were given a score based on whether they were able to look at, touch, or hold the snake. In subsequent versions of the BAT, many other fear stimuli (e.g., rats, spiders, cockroaches, dogs) have been used and the "look-touch-hold" coding system for scoring clients' responses has been replaced by more elaborate and sophisticated measures. These include recording how close (in meters) the client is able to come to the fear target, maximum amount of interaction achieved (see Box 7-8), length of time between entering the test room and making physical contact with the target, overt behaviors during the test (see Table 7-4), and changes in physiological arousal (e.g., heart rate, respiration, galvanic skin response). Usually, the client is asked to approach the feared target but, occasionally, BATs are set up to measure how long the client can look at a frightening stimulus (e.g., Rutner & Pear, 1972) or how close the client will allow that stimulus to approach her or him (e.g., Levis, 1969).

Controlled performance tests have also been developed to assess fear of certain *situations* rather than small animals. Paul's (1966) use of contrived test speeches to assess clients' discomfort about public speaking was an early example of this type of assessment. Others include asking persons who fear heights or closed places to climb fire escapes or sit in a small, dark test chamber (e.g., Miller & Bernstein, 1972; Ritter, 1970).

EVALUATION OF OBSERVATIONAL ASSESSMENT

Observational methods have become increasingly popular clinical assessment tools in recent years. This is due in part to the fact that, as noted in Chapter 4, direct and objective observation of behavior can help avoid many of the inference problems which reduce the reliability and validity of some traditional interview and test procedures. Social-learning-oriented theorists, researchers, and clinicians have been among the more enthusiastic proponents of observational assessment, arguing forcefully that this approach provides the most realistic view of exactly those client behaviors which are of greatest clinical relevance for understanding and alleviating distressing human problems (e.g., Bandura, 1977; Bersoff, 1973; Bijou & Peterson, 1971; Mischel, 1973).

Indeed, observations are sometimes thought of as being like photographs

---

Box 7-8   Approach Scale for Use in Observing Snake BAT

 0   Refuses to enter.
 1   Walks halfway to cage.
 2   Stands in front of cage.
 3   Reaches toward cage but does not touch it.
 4   Touches cage with one hand.
 5   Touches cage with both hands.
 6   Puts any part of one hand inside cage.
 7   Puts any part of both hands inside cage.
 8   Touches snake with one hand.
 9   Touches snake with both hands.
10   Grasps snake with one hand.
11   Grasps snake with both hands.
12   Lifts animal with one hand.
13   Lifts animal with both hands.
14   Removes any part of animal from cage with one hand.
15   Removes any part of animal from cage with both hands.
16   Removes entire animal from cage with one hand.
17   Removes entire animal from cage with both hands.

Table 7-4 Timed Behavioral Checklist for Observing Snake BAT

Behavior observed	Observation period					
	1	2	3	4	5	6
1 Halting, indirect approach						
2 Extraneous hand and arm movements						
3 Arms rigid						
4 Hands restrained (in pockets, behind back, clasped)						
5 Hand tremors						
6 Face muscles tense (tics, grimaces) or "deadpan"						
7 Face pale or flushed						
8 Moistens or bites lips						
9 Breathes heavily						
10 Swallows "hard"						
11 Perspires						
12 "Negative" verbalizations (moans, etc.)						

Based on Paul (1966).

which provide an accurate picture of human behavior. But just as a photograph of a particular scene is a product of the scene itself, the equipment used, the photographer's techniques, and the developing process, data from observational procedures are determined by many factors other than the behavior of the clients (Kent & Foster, 1977). As we shall see, some of these factors can actually distort the assessment picture. It should be clearly understood, therefore, that the mere act of observing human behavior does not automatically establish the resulting data as reliable and valid (Cone, 1977).

To illustrate, let us consider a hypothetical situation in which a clinician or researcher is working with a distressed married couple and decides to include observational procedures as part of an overall problem-assessment enterprise. A controlled situation is set up in which the couple is asked to talk about one of their problems and attempt to resolve it while being observed and videotaped through one-way glass. Later the videotape is scored by trained observers using some type of coding or rating system. A summary of the couple's behavior would result (e.g., "couple spent 63 percent of the session in negative interaction"; "couple scores 9 on a 10-point level-of-distress scale") and might be accompanied by the explicit or implicit suggestion that this is a sample of how the husband and wife relate to one another. Such an observational procedure is certainly direct and obviously objective, but is it necessarily reliable and valid?

Reliability in Observational Assessment

The first question that must be asked about observational data is, "Are they reliable?" Usually, this refers to the issue of *interrater agreement*.[4] To what extent do two or more observers arrive at the same scores or ratings or conclusions with respect to the behavior they watched? If interobserver agreement is low, such that our hypothetical couple's interaction was characterized in very different ways by different individuals, one cannot place much confidence in the observation. The assessor would have to either "believe" one particular observer or average all observers' data in some way. Neither alternative is very attractive because (1) there is usually little basis for trusting one observer above others, and (2) averages of widely discrepant scores represent a mathematical but not a behavioral reality (the couple's *average* scores from unreliable observers may not reflect their actual behavior at all).

The reliability of modern clinical observation systems which use trained observers is usually very high; coefficients of .80 to 1.00 are not at all uncommon (e.g., Paul & Lentz, 1977). Even when clients observe their own behavior through self-monitoring, agreement between their data and those of external observers is sometimes in the .90s (Kazdin, 1974). Such gratifying figures do not always appear, however (especially in self-monitoring studies), and when they do, it is usually because the clinical assessor has been aware of and successfully avoided many pitfalls which can threaten the reliability of observational data.

Task Complexity   For example, the complexity of the observers' task can affect the degree to which they agree with one another. If observers must make many difficult discriminations in recording, coding, or rating their own or other people's behavior, reliability will probably be lower than if fewer, easier judgments are required (e.g., Arrington, 1932, Cavior & Marabotto, 1976; Epstein, Miller, & Webster, 1976; Johnson & Bolstad, 1973; Jones, Reid, & Patterson, 1975; Mash & McElwee, 1974; Thomas, Loomis, & Arrington, 1933). In the case of our imaginary married couple, this means that the clinician would be more likely to get reliable observational data using, say, a 15-category rather than 100-category coding system; observation will also be more reliable if clients do not engage in a large number of short duration responses in quick succession.

Knowledge of Reliability Checks   Another factor which can affect reliability is the observers' knowledge that their agreement is being monitored. When people are first trained to use a particular observation system, they tend to work very hard during practice sessions and pay close attention to the task, partly because they are clearly being evaluated. Later, when "real" data are being collected, the observers may get sloppy, especially if they think no one is checking up on reliability (e.g., Reid, 1970; Romanczyk, Kent, Diament, &

---

[4]Obviously, split-half or parallel-form questions are less relevant, and test-retest reliability would be of importance only in observing behaviors which are not expected to change very much over time.

O'Leary, 1973; Taplin & Reid, 1973). The same can be said for clients who self-monitor their behavior (e.g., Lipinski, Black, Nelson, Ciminero, 1975). The best protection against lowered reliability stemming from this problem appears to be random checking of performance. Thus, our clinician should tell the observers that their agreement about the observed couple's behavior will be checked from time to time but that they will not be told when (Taplin & Reid, 1973).

Observer Training   The training given to observers can also alter reliability. Suppose, for instance, that the observers of our married couple are told to record laughter as a category in their coding system but no definition of laughter is given. One observer might count belly laughs but not giggles, while another would include everything from a quiet titter to violent guffaws. Obviously, reliability will suffer. The authors have found that, in training observers to use the coding schemes presented in Box 7-8, satisfactory reliability was achieved only after each item received careful discussion and a clear definition. When observers are left to define for themselves what is meant by specific coding categories or, worse, global constructs (like "hostile" or "happy"), the reliability of observational data drops dramatically (e.g., Hawkins & Dobes, 1977).

Even high reliability coefficients do not always mean that an observation system is being used consistently by all observers. To put it bluntly, observers sometimes cheat, especially when they want to please their employer and when they are unsupervised. This usually takes the form of altering scores in order to enhance agreement (e.g., O'Leary & Kent, 1973). Obviously, our clinician would be wise to supervise the coding of the couple's behavior and to see to it that reliability coefficients are calculated by someone other than the observers.

Another situation in which high reliabilities may be misleading is when there is "observer drift" (Johnson & Bolstad, 1973; O'Leary & Kent, 1973). When observers work together in unchanging pairs or groups, they tend to form their own particular well-agreed-upon version of the coding or rating system so that, over time, each pair or group "drifts" away from the others. Within each pair or group, reliability may be very high, but if new pairings are made or if between-pair reliabilities are calculated, interobserver agreement would be much lower (e.g., Kent, O'Leary, Diament, & Dietz, 1974). The clinician can combat this problem by constant rotation of observer pairs and/or periodic retraining of all observers (Johnson & Bolstad, 1973; Kent & Foster, 1977).

Interpreting Reliability Figures   Yet another subtle question arises when high reliability figures are encountered: How were they calculated? There are many complex mathematical issues involved here which would take us far afield (see Hartmann, 1977 and Kent & Foster, 1977 for detailed discussions), but they basically involve questions of what a reliability coefficient means.

For example, suppose that our clinician reported interobserver agreement 95 percent of the time. Depending upon how this figure was calculated, it could either mean that there was strong agreement about what the observers *saw* or about what they did *not* see. If "agreement" is registered only when two observers record the occurrence of the same behavior at the same time, the 95 percent would be impressive indeed. However, if agreement also means that each of two observers did *not* record the occurrence of a particular behavior, the agreement percentage could be inflated by chance or other factors. In an extreme case, both observers could be asleep and still be in perfect agreement.

Several mathematical procedures are currently available to control or correct problems of this type, but they are still not used uniformly enough to warrant unequivocal faith in the reliability figures cited in observational assessment literature (Kent & Foster, 1977). To summarize, interobserver agreement in clinical observation can be extremely high, but effort and care must be used to reach and maintain satisfactory and meaningful levels.

Validity of Observational Assessment

The next set of questions one must ask about observational procedures has to do with validity: Are these procedures measuring what they are supposed to measure, and how well are they doing it? At first glance, direct observation of client behavior would appear to rank highest in validity among all clinical assessment approaches. Instead of hearing about behavior in interviews or speculating about behavior through tests, the clinician using observation can actually watch the "real thing." Indeed, there is considerable evidence that some types of immediate or retrospective observation provide a more useful image of clients' current and future behavior than some interviews or tests (e.g., Fiske, 1978; Lanyon & Goodstein, 1971; Mischel, 1968). At the very least, observation can provide assessment data which are just not available through other sources.

To a certain extent, however, enthusiasm for the obvious *directness* of clinical observation has tended to cause a deemphasis on proving its *validity* in traditional terms (Johnson & Bolstad, 1973). After all, if we *observe* aggression in our married couple, are we not *measuring* aggression, and is not that enough to establish the validity of our technique? The answer is an unqualified "yes" only if we can show (1) that the behaviors coded (e.g., raised voices or hands) constitute a satisfactory and functional definition of aggression, (2) that the data faithfully reflect the nature and degree of aggression which occurred during observation, and (3) that the clients' behaviors while under observation accurately represent their reactions in similar, clinically important but unobserved situations.

Often, these criteria are clearly satisfied. When a number of nonparticipant observers repeatedly see a child engaging in violent, dangerous, and unprovoked attacks on siblings and peers at home and in school, and when these data agree in detail with the verbal reports of parents and teachers, the validity of observational data would be difficult to question. In other instances, however, the requirements for establishing validity of observation are far less easily met. Many questions and issues must be dealt with before we can be confident that we are getting a valid picture of clinically relevant aspects of client behavior.

Defining Observation Targets   Probably the most basic issue relating to the validity of observational assessment involves clarification of what is being measured. Typically, when a clinician sets out to develop an observation system for, say, assertion or depression, she or he uses what we referred to in Chapter 6 as a rational approach. The assessor tells the observers what to look for and code, and the behaviors named are quite often based mainly upon how that assessor happens to think assertion or depression can be detected in behavior. Thus, basic measurement decisions, such as what behaviors or aspects of behaviors (e.g., frequency, intensity, duration) to code or rate and how these are defined, often "reflect the whim and habits of the individual investigator" (Kent & Foster, 1977, p. 319). The result is that each clinician or researcher may say that she or he is observing assertion or depression or whatever when, in fact, each may be measuring very different things.

For example, one clinician might assess assertiveness by observing clients' ability to refuse unreasonable requests, while another focuses more on skill at direct expression of positive affect. To a certain extent, this reflects a problem of definition which may never be resolved to everyone's satisfaction, but it is important to ask what the observation system actually tells us about the client. If that system focuses on frequency of blinking as a definition of depressed behavior, it may give us a very reliable view of the client's blinking, but it will probably be a totally inadequate index of what most people think of as depression.

One way to assess the validity of an observation is to ask, "What is it related to?" Does blinking decrease when the client reports feeling better? Do people receiving bad news show higher blinking rates? If one is actually observing part of a phenomenon of interest, sensible relationships of this type should emerge (Cronbach & Meehl, 1955). If, on the other hand, it is merely *assumed* that an observation system automatically captures a meaningful picture of depression, assertion, or whatever, the clinician runs the risk of collecting samples of behavior which have little or no importance outside the measurement situation. This serious problem has been given surprisingly little attention by developers and users of observational assessment, partly because, as already noted, the validity of observation seems so obvious.

Even so, some efforts have been made to formally validate observational assessment. Jones, Reid, and Patterson (1975) summarize a series of studies designed to explore the relationship between certain categories in their Behavioral Coding System (BCS) and other variables. For example, in order to assure that child behaviors coded as "noxious" or "deviant" by the BCS were also perceived that way by those normally around the child, mothers were asked to rate all BCS categories (noxious or not) for "deviancy." As it turned out, the mothers' ratings confirmed the noxiousness of the "noxious" categories. In other studies, BCS "deviant behavior" data were compared to mothers' ratings of their children's noxiousness and changes in BCS data were related to the administration of various treatment procedures. Jones, Reid, and Patterson (1975) also describe research which shows that children who had been previously identified by others (e.g., school officials) as aggressive were, in fact, aggressive when observed through the BCS.

Some researchers have approached the validity question by attempting to design their observations empirically rather than rationally. For example, instead of deciding ahead of time (and perhaps incorrectly) what particular behaviors reflect assertion or depression or anxiety, an assessor may code virtually all client behavior occurring during observation. Patterns of behavior which emerge are then correlated with other data (e.g., self-reports, physiological arousal, life records, third-party accounts) about the client's reaction to the observed situation and to other relevant situations. If a particular pattern of observed behavior (e.g., shaking and whimpering) is strongly associated with high scores on other measures also designed to assess anxiety, that behavior pattern can then be referred to as "anxious" with greater confidence than if the assessor had simply decreed that shaking and whimpering indicate anxiety. If, in addition, the "anxious" behavior increases and decreases under circumstances which are more or less stressful or it changes for the better following some form of treatment, evidence for the anxiety-related meaning of the behavior becomes even stronger. This approach was used by Kleinknecht and Bernstein (1978) in developing an observation system for measuring patients' fear while in a dental office.

An even more elaborate and sophisticated strategy for building validity into an observation system is embodied in Goldfried and D'Zurilla's (1969) *behavior-analytic* model. Here, the assessor first does a careful exploration of the construct to be measured and then custom-tailors the observation to that construct. The best example of an observation system based on this strategy is MacDonald's (1978) College Women's Assertion Sample. In order to observe assertiveness or lack of it under controlled circumstances, MacDonald (1978) first asked college women to describe situations in which assertion could occur. This resulted in over 800 examples. The fifty-two clearest and most frequently mentioned situations were retained and a new group of college women was asked to rate the assertiveness of dozens of possible responses in each. Responses receiving consistent ratings became examples of submission, assertion, and aggression. With all these data in hand, MacDonald (1978) then made a tape recording of her fifty-two situations and could ask college-age clients to role-play responses to them, knowing that this controlled observation contained both highly relevant stimuli and a coding system which reflects what many people do think of as assertion.

Because behavior-analytic procedures are so elaborate and time-consuming, there are only a few other examples of their use in the development of observation systems (e.g., Goldsmith, 1973). As the use of clinical observation grows, however, these and other techniques aimed at clarifying and systematizing just what *is* measured in observational assessment are likely to become more common.

Observer Effects   No matter how reliable observers are, they must also be as objective and accurate as possible about what they see if their data are to be valid (see Waller & Leske, 1973). No one is perfect, however, so the clinician or researcher has several things to worry about with respect to his or her observers. First, there is the problem of observer *error*. Just as an interviewer or tester may for some reason record or remember certain client responses more accurately than others, an observer can also make mistakes. Kennedy and Uphoff (1939) found, for example, that even on a simple task like recording subjects' guesses in an ESP experiment, error occurred 1.13 percent of the time. Rosenthal (1966) describes additional data of this kind.

Second, the quality of observational data may be compromised by observer *bias*. Human beings are not perfect recording devices. They may see things which are not objectively there to see, partly because, as the gestalt school of psychology emphasized, there is a perceptual tendency in human beings to "complete" or "close" incomplete stimulus patterns (see Figure 3-2). Thus, an observer may *see* a child raise a hand toward another child, but *record* the behavior as "striking" rather than hand raising. The act of striking may never have occurred, except in the observer's brain.

In a paper called "Seeing's believing," Johnson (1953) tells about a radiologist who concluded that a button revealed in an x-ray was on the patient's vest when, in fact, it had lodged in the patient's throat. The error probably occurred because, as Rosenthal (1966, p. 6) put it "buttons occur more frequently on vests than in throats." Johnson (1953, p. 79) concluded: "Our assumptions define and limit what we see, i.e., we tend to see things in such a way that they will fit in with our assumptions even if this involves distortion or omission." In the Kennedy and Uphoff (1939) study cited earlier, observer errors were not random. Those who were "believers" in telepathy made 71.5 percent more errors which artificially *increased* subjects' telepathy scores than those who were "nonbelievers." Similarly, the "nonbeliever" observers made twice as many errors which *decreased* telepathy scores than did the "believers." Additional evidence on this point is reviewed by Carpenter (1977), Rosenthal (1966), and White (1977).

Even life records, which are clear and apparently objective, can be subject to distortion by observer bias. For example, if a grade school teacher dislikes a particular student for some irrelevant reason, that child may become a "discipline problem" because the teacher is overly attentive to the child's minor rule violations and often asks a counselor, vice principal, or other school authority to help "straighten this kid out." All the special attention may appear on school records, while the original teacher bias does not. This distortion of the situation becomes "fossilized" in the records, where it may repeatedly and cumulatively influence the impressions of upper grade teachers, school counselors, and clinical psychologists (see Rosenthal & Jacobson, 1968).

Even assuming the absence of significant errors or bias in existing records, there is still no guarantee that they will be read with total objectivity since the clinician may not always be dispassionate. She or he may be particularly impressed by certain records (e.g., from a prison) while glossing over others (e.g., athletic awards, letters). An important source of observer bias lies in information available prior to seeing clients. Suppose that, just before their first observation session, a clinician told his or her observers that the clients to be assessed "fight like cats and dogs." Under certain circumstances, this statement could lead the observers to "see" hostility whether or not it was actually there.

The effects of such biasing information can be especially strong if observers are asked to make broad, general ratings of or statements about behavior. In a well-known example of the phenomenon, psychiatrists, psychologists, and graduate students were asked to listen to a taped interview in which an actor portrayed a perfectly well-adjusted man (Temerlin, 1968). When they listened under neutral conditions, 57 percent of the observers rated the "client" as "healthy," while 43 percent called him "neurotic." No one thought he was psychotic. However, responses were strongly biased if the tape was described as either that of a "perfectly healthy man" or a person who "looks neurotic but actually is quite psychotic." In the former case, 100 percent of the listeners rated the "client" as "healthy." In the latter, an average of nearly 30 percent diagnosed the man "psychotic," and over 60 percent called him "neurotic."

In a study involving visual observation and global descriptions (Rapp, 1965, cited by Johnson & Bolstad, 1973), eight pairs of observers watched a child in a nursery school. One member of each pair was told that the client was feeling "under par," while the other was told the child was feeling "above par." In seven of the eight pairs, the observers' descriptions differed significantly and corresponded with their implanted expectations.

More recent research has shown that rewarding conformity to prior expectations and discouraging nonconformity can enhance bias in observers (O'Leary, Kent, & Kanowitz, 1975), but it is important to note that, when highly specific and well defined behavioral coding systems rather than global ratings are used, observers are relatively immune to the effects of externally imposed bias (Kent, O'Leary, Diament, & Dietz, 1974; Schuller & McNamara, 1975 cited by Kent & Foster, 1977; Walter & Gilmore, 1973).

Reactivity of Observation   In addition to worrying about observer bias, the clinician utilizing observational assessment must also be concerned about "client bias," or more properly, *reactivity:* Clients may react to being observed by intentionally or unintentionally altering the very behaviors which are of greatest clinical interest. This parallels the issues of response bias and impression management in tests and interviews. The problem of reactivity in observation can easily be illustrated at any social gathering by turning on a tape recorder. Noticeable changes in everyone's behavior usually occur immediately, and they last either until the machine is switched off or the novelty disappears. Awareness of the possible reactivity of clinical observation has a long history (e.g., Covner, 1942; Polansky, Freeman, Horowitz, Irwin, Papanis, Rappaport, & Whaley, 1949), but the magnitude and dimensions of the problem are still unclear.

Some social and clinical psychologists have advanced arguments and presented data which suggest that even obvious observational procedures have only a minimal and short-term influence on subjects or clients, after which their behavior regains its natural spontaneity (e.g., Bijou, Peterson, Harris, Allen, & Johnson, 1969; Heyns & Lippit, 1954; Purcell & Brady, 1966; Werry & Quay,

1969; Wright, 1967). For example, Mercatoris and Craighead (1974) found that the amount of appropriate behavior shown by retarded adult women did not change when they were watched by a visible observer as opposed to a hidden television camera. Similarly, Hagen, Craighead, and Paul (1975) found no differences in mental hospital staff behavior when an observer was present as opposed to when observation was done through hidden microphones.

Other data suggest, however, that there can be reactive effects associated with observation. Zegiob, Arnold, and Forehand (1975), for example, reported increases in mothers' play, positive verbal statements, and other behaviors when mother-child interactions were overtly as opposed to covertly observed. Samph (1969, cited in Wildman & Erikson, 1977) found that teachers "used more praise, accepted student ideas more, and criticized students less when observers were present in the classroom than when data were collected unobtrusively with a tape recorder" (Wildman & Erikson, 1977, p. 269).

There is also strong evidence that self-monitoring can be reactive. For example, smoking behavior usually decreases when smokers record each cigarette they light (e.g., McFall & Hammen, 1971), and other behaviors such as eating, nail-biting, hallucinating, alcohol intake, tics, child management skills, and studying often change when self-observed (see Ciminero, Nelson & Lipinski, 1977 for a review). In fact, because self-monitoring usually produces *beneficial* changes in recorded behavior (e.g., reduced eating or hallucinating or increased studying or social interaction) the procedure has been used as a form of therapy as well as a clinical assessment device.

Fortunately or unfortunately, self-monitoring does not *always* alter the behaviors it is meant to record. Little or no change in depression, obsessive ruminations, hair pulling, nail-biting, overeating, and other targets has been reported in some clients who observed their own responses (Bayer, 1972; Jackson, 1972; Kazdin, 1974; Mahoney, 1971, 1974; McNamara, 1972). In light of all this conflicting research, it is not easy for the clinician to reach firm conclusions about whether awareness of observations will actually alter clients' behavior. Kent and Foster (1977, p. 289) put it this way: "There seems little reason to doubt that the presence of an observer may, in fact, affect the behavior of those he observes. But the number of factors determining the magnitude and direction of behavior change may be so great that manifest reactivity is scattered and almost completely unpredictable."

The determining factors to which Kent and Foster (1977) refer include observers' age, sex, visibility, and eye contact, as well as the duration of observation, the physical setting, client anxiety and prior experience with observers, the use of mechanical versus human observers, and the like (Kent & Foster, 1977; Wildman & Erikson, 1977). Similarly, the reactivity of self-monitoring may depend upon (1) the client's expectation or wish to change the observed behavior in a particular direction, (2) the number and nature of the behaviors recorded, (3) whether observations are continuous or intermittent, and (4) whether data are recorded before or after each target behavior occurs (see Ciminero, Nelson, & Lipinski, 1977).

Thus, not all clinical observation is always going to be strongly reactive, but the possibility of reactivity can almost never be ignored. To be on the safe side, the clinician would probably want to make observation of clients as unobtrusive as possible (perhaps using two-way mirrors or mechanical or electronic devices to keep coders out of sight) and would schedule assessment sessions which are long enough to give clients plenty of time to get used to being observed.

Representativeness of Observed Behavior Even after obvious reactive effects have dropped out (e.g., the client no longer looks at or refers to the observer or TV camera), observed behavior may not provide a truly *representative,* or *ecologically valid* (Brunswick, 1947), picture of the client. This may be true for many reasons. The client may have a headache or a hangover on the day of an observation. A death or birth in the family may have just occurred. A child may be observed immediately after a scolding or just before participating in some eagerly awaited activity. These and any number of other factors can result in temporary patterns of depressed, euphoric, hyperactive, or "spaced-out" behavior which may be quite atypical of the client.

Further, the situation in which the person is observed may alter or place limits on behavior. Mother-child and other family interactions, for example, may differ when observed at home rather than in a laboratory (e.g., Moustakas, Sigel, & Schalock, 1956; O'Rourke, 1963) and a child's social-interaction style with a hated or feared peer will probably be quite different from that shown toward a valued friend. Factors of this type must always be kept in mind by the careful user of observational techniques.

There are other worries as well. It is sometimes the case that features of the situation in which observation takes place exert an influence all their own by directly or subtly suggesting to the client what behaviors are appropriate or expected. When this happens, the observation is not only reactive in terms of general client-awareness problems; it is also likely to *produce* certain specific behaviors through the influence of guiding social cues that Orne (1962) called *demand characteristics.* If a clinician observes a married couple in a setting which contains strong social cues regarding how the clients should behave (e.g., "We would like to measure just how much fighting you two actually do"), she or he runs the risk of learning more about the effects of the situation than about the behavior of the people being assessed.

This problem of situational bias reducing the representativeness of observed behavior tends to occur most often in controlled settings, though it can appear in naturalistic observation as well. The reason for this mainly appears to be that, in most controlled observations, the client must go to some specially identified place to be observed and is thus acutely aware of what is going on. Further, specific instructions about the observation are usually given to enlighten and orient the client and to help him or her recognize when assessment begins and ends.

There is abundant evidence that the social and situational cues provided by these and other features of observation can alter client behavior radically. For example, Orne and Schiebe (1964) monitored male college students undergoing a period of isolation in a small, well-lighted room. Half the subjects were told that the room was a sensory deprivation chamber. In this condition, the experimenter wore a white coat, conducted a medical history interview, asked the subject to sign a medical release form, and displayed an "emergency tray" of drugs and equipment which were part of the "precautionary measures" in the laboratory. He also mentioned that release from the chamber was possible by pressing an emergency alarm if "the situation becomes difficult" and that a physician was available if "you should feel upset." The other subjects were told they were in a control group. There was no white coat, no interview, no "emergency tray," and no "emergency alarm." Once in the isolation room, the two groups differed markedly in behavior. Control subjects appeared relaxed and comfortable. They rested or slept, worked on various time-filling tasks, and said little. "Sensory deprivation" subjects, on the other hand, were restless, slept very little, expressed discomfort or feelings of disorientation, and "gave an impression of almost being tortured" (Orne & Schiebe, 1964, p. 11).

Similar situational effects involving instructions have also been shown to operate in the assessment of social skills, fears, and other clinical targets. For example, in a study designed to measure assertiveness, Nietzel and Bernstein (1976) asked college students to respond to a series of tape recorded social situations similar to those described earlier in this chapter (McFall & Marston, 1970). Each subject heard the tape twice, once in a "low demand" situation, where she or he was asked to give "your natural reaction" and once under "high demand," in which responses were to be "as assertive as you think the most assertive and forceful person could be." Other subjects heard low or high demand instructions twice. The assertiveness of the subjects' responses in each condition was scored on a 5-point scale. The results are summarized in Figure 7-9. Obviously, instructions in the assessment situation not only had an initial

Figure 7-9 Instructions significantly increased or decreased subject's rated assertiveness in this study of situational influence in observation. Subjects given consistent instructions did not change over time. *(Nietzel & Bernstein, 1976.)*

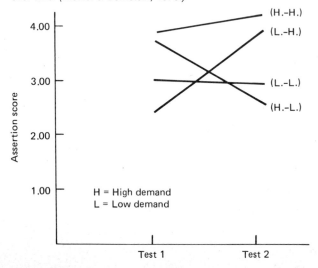

effect, but were capable of significantly altering subjects' behavior from test to test. Other situational factors, such as the identity of the person to whom a response is given, can also alter clients' level of assertion (Eisler, Hersen, Miller, & Blanchard, 1975).

In anxiety assessment, the instructions given, the presence or absence of an experimenter, the characteristics of the physical setting, and other situational variables have been found to strongly influence the amount of fear clients display during BATs (e.g., Bernstein, 1973; Bernstein & Nietzel, 1973; Miller & Bernstein, 1972; Smith, Diener, & Beaman, 1974). The behavior of children under observation in their own homes can be made to look "good" or "bad" depending upon what their parents think the assessor wants to see (Johnson & Lobitz, 1974).

A variety of research strategies have been suggested to minimize the effects of situational bias in observational assessment (Bernstein & Nietzel, 1977; Borkovec & O'Brien, 1976), but the problem cannot be entirely eliminated. As long as the stimuli present when the client's behavior is being observed are "different from the stimulus complex when [the client] is unobserved, we cannot assume that behavior during observation, even after it has stabilized, represents 'typical' behavior" (Wildman & Erikson, 1977, p. 271). The best a clinician can do is minimize or eliminate as many cues as possible which might obviously bias or guide client behavior. At the same time, it would probably help if a naturalistic setting can be created. Comfortable living-room furniture is usually preferable to a sterile lab table and rickety folding chairs. Home or school observations may be even better, if feasible.

The ultimate means of assuring the representativeness of observational data is, of course, the continuous use of totally unobtrusive measures such as those mentioned earlier (Webb, Campbell, Schwartz, and Sechrest, 1966). An example of this strategy is contained in McFall and Twentyman's (1973) programmed telephone calls to subjects in their assertion study, but practical and/or ethical considerations will usually place limits on the utility of extensive nonreactive measurement in many clinical and research settings.

A final word   By now it should be obvious that, like interviews and tests, observation is a far from perfect clinical assessment tool. Nevertheless, it has many advantages which make it one of the most valuable devices available. The challenge for the clinician or researcher is to use observation in a way which minimizes the influence of the various distorting factors we have discussed, so that the data generated can have maximum value in an overall assessment plan.

Part Three

Helping People Change

Chapter 8

Clinical Intervention: Overview

All kinds of people try to change your behavior. Politicians work for your vote. Advertisers persuade you to buy their product. Your parents encourage you to abide by their wishes. Friends transform you through their affection. Enemies arouse you by their antipathy. Some people even change your behavior without trying. You may go to embarrassing lengths to imitate your heroes or to catch the eye of someone whom you secretly admire.

Almost every form of human interaction involves some attempt by one party to influence the other to behave in a certain fashion. Social contact involves a chain of influences, some of which are benign and uncalculated while others are coercive and deliberate. Some people are very strong influencers and can move us to behave in entirely novel ways. Others are ineffective influencers who have an insignificant impact on us.

Behavior influence is not always interpersonal. As Krasner and Ullmann (1973) have pointed out, our behavior is altered and maintained by the physical as well as the social environment. As one simple example, consider the effect the weather has on your conduct; when was the last time you went swimming in a sleet storm?

Behavior influence can also be very much a private matter. Our memories of the past affect the way we live in the present. And our fantasies about the future can either be an inspiration or a detriment to our current activities.

While it is possible to speak of behavior influence in general terms by merging all its different forms into a common concept, our task in this chapter is to concentrate on one specific type of behavior influence: that exerted by the clinical psychologist. When a psychologist, in a professional capacity, seeks to influence someone's behavior, we often describe the psychologist's activity as an *intervention*. Intervention is a broad concept. Depending on the qualities of the intervention, we could describe it more specifically as consultation, education, psychotherapy, group therapy, family therapy, or play therapy. If we knew more about the orientation of the clinician and his or her training and theoretical leanings, we could qualify the nature of the intervention even further, using such terms as case consultation, administrative consultation, gestalt therapy, client-centered therapy, rational-emotive therapy, or social-learning therapy. In this chapter, clinical intervention is the umbrella term we will use to describe the explicit, professional attempts by the psychologist to change clients' behavior in a desirable direction.

Intervention is one of the six professional functions of the clinical psychologist. "To intervene" literally means "to come between in action; to intercede or interfere." When we speak of a psychologist's intervention, we could be referring to many types of "coming between": *consultation and education,* where the psychologist comes between some audience and its needs for specific knowledge; *program development,* where the psychologist comes between some social problem and the need for an innovative solution; or *psychotherapy,* where the psychologist comes between an individual and the individual's personal problems in living. It is this latter type of "coming between," psychotherapy, which we typically think of as the clinical psychologist's most traditional form of intervention. In Chapter 12, we will discuss alternative forms of intervention like consultation and program development, but our focus here will be on psychotherapy and its variations, such as group therapy, marital therapy, and family therapy. In Chapters 9, 10, and 11, we will present the three dominant perspectives on psychotherapy: psychodynamic, social-learning, and phenomenological, but in this chapter, our attention will be directed at learning about the common features of all psychotherapeutic approaches and about the shared core of assumptions and practices of all psychotherapists.

WHAT IS PSYCHOTHERAPY?

The literal translation of psychotherapy would be "treatment of the psyche." While this is not a really sufficient definition of the activity, it does suggest a number of implications that will help us understand the fundamental substance of psychotherapy.

The Participants

To speak of "treating psyches" suggests that there are psyches or personalities in a state of distress and dissatisfaction. The extent to which an individual's thoughts or feelings or emotions are disturbed can vary a great deal. In some the disturbance is great, resulting in an inability to meet the minimal demands of living. Employment may be terminated, suicide may be attempted, hospitalization may occur. In others the disturbance may be less extreme, but still very upsetting. An unhappy marriage, a lack of self-confidence, a nagging fear, a general sense of unworthiness, an identity crisis, depression, sexual problems, and insomnia are a few of the problems that often motivate people to enter psychotherapy. The essential feature is that some aspect of a person's functioning has become disturbed enough that she or he decides to seek the help of a professional. Quite simply, the individual is suffering. His or her own resources, the help of friends, the long-awaited vacation, and the understanding of the family no longer seem to be sufficient antidotes for the suffering that the person is experiencing. When the point is reached where the problem is defined as requiring the intervention of a professional, we have the first participant in psychotherapy: the *client.*

The second participant in psychotherapy is the *therapist.* The therapist is someone who by special training and experience is prepared to help the client overcome the disturbance that has motivated the desire for treatment. The therapist should possess skills that will enable her or him to understand the client's disturbance and then interact with the client in such a way that the client learns to cope with the presenting problems more effectively.

In addition to some form of advanced training, the psychotherapist is expected to possess certain personal characteristics that will contribute to the effect of therapy. The ability to listen to clients and convey to them a sense of understanding and sensitivity without being judgmental is one very important quality of the therapist. The capacity to combine warmth and support for troubled clients with a resolve to confront them with their own responsibility for change is another vital attribute. The therapist should also convey a sense of confidence to the client. Another way of saying this is that the therapist must believe that psychotherapy will be effective. Many clinicians cite the need for the therapist to project *genuineness, empathy,* and *unconditional positive regard.* These are called Rogerian qualities because Carl Rogers claimed that they are the necessary and sufficient conditions to bring about therapeutic change.

This emphasis on personal characteristics has sometimes led to the suggestion that "everyday experiences" or "natural ability" are more important than professional training for making a good therapist. Some therapists rely on their charisma or "healing personality" to accomplish their goals and eschew any consistent, well-developed theory of therapy. Even among schools of psychology as a whole, certain psychotherapeutic approaches (e.g., some forms of phenomenological therapy) tend to emphasize extensive professional training far less than others (e.g., psychoanalysis).

While there is a vast literature on the importance of the "good" therapist's qualities (e.g., Gurman and Razin, 1977; Meltzoff and Kornreich, 1970), there is also great emphasis placed upon the characteristics of the "good" psychotherapy client. The type of person who is likely to benefit most from psychotherapy is thought to be verbal, intelligent, motivated to change, perhaps even moderately anxious about the need to change, able to communicate with the therapist, and "psychologically minded," a characteristic which simply means that the person appreciates the importance of psychological factors in determining behavior. As some cynics like to point out, the ideal psychotherapy client is someone who would probably continue to be successful whether he or she received therapy or not. This criticism is largely unfair because it ignores the fact that psychotherapy is seldom practiced under conditions involving either the ideal client or the ideal therapist.

Interest in therapist and client characteristics has progressed past focusing on the personal attributes of the therapist or client in isolation. There is now a concern for their interactive quality. This perspective has given rise to the concept of therapist-client *matching*, which Berzins (1977) has defined as "the idea that certain therapist-patient pairings are more desirable than others. The empirical delineation of this problem requires an understanding of the conditions under which, regardless of the characteristics of therapists and patients considered separately, the *interaction* of these characteristics proves decisive for the processes or outcomes of psychotherapy" (p. 222).

Today, most clinicians are not aware of the admittedly skimpy research available on various matching strategies, and they rely instead on such stereotypes as "opposites attract" or "like cures like." Furthermore, in many clinical settings, the assignment of clients to therapists is a haphazard affair accomplished through a quick glance at the calendar and the intuitions of a receptionist (Berzins, 1977). On purely pragmatic grounds, however, we should not neglect the question of maximizing therapeutic effects by searching for optimal therapist-client matches. "Even a reasonable probability that *some* therapist-patient pairings are ineffectual . . . suggests that psychotherapy research must move beyond the separate assessment of therapist and patient characteristics to serious investigation of the interaction of these characteristics" (Berzins, 1977; p. 223).

The Therapeutic Relationship

The uniqueness of psychotherapy stems not from its cast of characters, but from the very special relationship that develops between therapist and client. What are the characteristics that make the therapeutic relationship unique?

First of all, the relationship is one in which both parties should clearly be aware of why they are there and what the rules and goals of their interaction should be. The relationship is not accidental. It is not one in which the parties should be confused about the roles they are to play. The relationship should be a voluntary one initiated by the client and accepted by the therapist.[1]

Psychotherapy often begins with a therapeutic contract (e.g., Karoly, 1975) which specifies the goals of treatment, the procedures to be employed, any potential risks, and the individual responsibilities of client and therapist. In many instances, the contract is negotiated informally, with both parties simply

---

[1]In many cases the client is not a voluntary participant. A client sometimes enters therapy when someone (e.g., a parent, judge, or spouse) becomes distressed by the client's behavior and compels the individual to seek help. Of course, therapy proceeds very differently when the client is not a voluntary participant.

exchanging information about what they expect therapy to accomplish. In other instances, the contract may take the form of a signed document which states quite precisely the obligations of each participant. In either case, one effect of "contract making" is to help the therapeutic relationship become one in which the client is an active, cooperative agent, a planner of and decision maker about his or her own changes.

The major purpose of the therapeutic relationship is to induce the client to behave in a manner which both the therapist and the client consider to be more desirable. Therapists are also changed by their clients on occasion, but that sort of change is incidental to what most clinicians regard as the primary objective of the relationship: beneficial change for the client.

Psychotherapy is more than just purchased friendship. Although the therapist may be friendly and sympathetic, the therapeutic relationship must involve more than compassion. Therapy sometimes requires the clinician to be a cool, objective assessor of clients and, at other times, an active detective who locates client resistances and pushes through them. The therapist must be willing to combine support and fondness for clients with a willingness to challenge them to give up old ways of behaving in exchange for new, frightening, but more adaptive behaviors.

The intensity of the therapeutic relationship gives rise to all too many temptations for the therapist to discard a professional orientation toward clients in favor of more spontaneous, "natural" reactions such as sexual attraction, pity, frustration, hostility, and boredom. Most therapists try to be very alert to the way in which their personal needs intrude upon the therapy process. Learning to detect these needs and deal with them is one of the major reasons why some therapists undergo a period of therapy themselves. The therapist attempts to form a meaningful, attentive relationship with the client without losing sight of the fact that the relationship must advance the client's attempt to change. As Korchin (1976) observes, the therapeutic relationship requires a "balance of attachment and detachment."

The relationship between client and therapist is also characterized by several moral and ethical commitments on the therapist's part that function to insulate the relationship from the heat of outside forces. Confidentiality is probably the most essential of these commitments. The therapist does not reveal information which the client shares in therapy. The client's privacy must be protected. In addition, therapists have a clear obligation to regard the welfare of their clients as their main priority.[2] With very few exceptions, the therapist's actions must be directed by a singular concern: "What is best for my client?"

The Techniques of Psychotherapy

There are literally dozens of specific psychotherapeutic techniques. Every system of psychotherapy has its preferred procedures, and every therapist has a unique style of employing those procedures. The therapist's methods are usually

---

[2]There are, of course, some exceptions. See Chapter 13 for a fuller discussion of situations which compel the psychologist to break confidentiality.

Box 8-1 Three Views of the Therapeutic Relationship

The major systems of psychotherapy take varying positions on the meaning of the psychotherapy relationship. Therapists of all theoretical persuasions attribute a considerable amount of importance to the therapeutic relationship and will work very carefully to establish a good one. However, beyond the broad generalization that psychotherapists prefer a strong therapeutic relationship to a weak one, there are several views on the ideal nature of the client-therapist relationship and the role it should play in therapy, depending upon the perspective: phenomenological, psychoanalytic, or social-learning.

Many phenomenologically oriented therapists regard the therapeutic relationship as the single most essential element in therapy. Carl Rogers, the founder of client-centered therapy (Rogers, 1942, 1951, 1954), takes the position that the client-therapist relationship is the crucible in which all the necessary and sufficient ingredients for therapeutic change are generated. According to Rogers (1951):

> Stress is upon a direct experiencing in the relationship. The process is not seen as primarily having to do with the client's memory of his past, nor with his exploration of the problems he is facing, nor with the perceptions he has of himself, nor the experiences he has been fearful of admitting into awareness. The process of therapy is, by these hypotheses, seen as being synonymous with the experiential relationship between client and therapist. Therapy consists in experiencing the self in a wide range of ways in an emotionally meaningful relationship with the therapist. The words—of either client or counselor—are seen as having minimal importance compared with the present emotional relationship which exists between the two. (pp. 172–173)

In psychoanalysis, the relationship between client and therapist is seen as a means to the goal of insight. The psychoanalyst strives for a different type of relationship from the Rogerian therapist. In psychoanalysis, the therapist-client relationship is an instrument for achieving a specific purpose, which is to show the client how his or her present behavior is determined by experiences in earlier developmental periods of life. Psychoanalysts usually speak of the *transference relationship* or simply *transference* to refer to the fact that after a period of therapy the client begins to carry over and attach to the therapist the friendly, hostile, and ambivalent attitudes and feelings which the client formerly felt in relation to parents or other significant persons. As a consequence, the original pathogenic conflicts of early familial relationships are repeated in relation to the therapist. In order to encourage transference, the analyst will remain a rather passive and somewhat detached figure. In psychoanalysis, the relationship is not as spontaneous or genuine in the sense of being typically "human" as it is for the Rogerian therapist. The analyst's detachment or aloofness is practiced; it is a strategic calm, a studied technique for encouraging transference. The following bits of advice from Freud clearly reveal his highly instrumental view of the therapeutic relationship:

> I cannot recommend my colleagues emphatically enough to take as a model in psychoanalytic treatment the surgeon who puts aside all his own feelings, including that of human sympathy, and concentrates his mind on one single purpose, that of performing the operation as skillfully as possible. (Freud, 1912; p. 121)

> The analytic technique requires the physician to deny the patient who is longing for love the satisfaction she craves. The treatment must be carried through in a state of abstinence; I do not mean merely corporal abstinence, nor yet deprivation of everything desired, for this could perhaps not be tolerated by any sick person. But I would state as a fundamental principle that the patient's desire and longing are to be allowed to remain, to serve as driving forces for the work and for the changes to be wrought. (Freud, 1915; p. 173)

Social-learning therapists tend to view the therapy relationship as an important but not sufficient condition of therapy. It is seen more as a useful *context* in which more specific behavior-change techniques are introduced. Alan Goldstein (1973), in his brief overview of social-learning therapy, reveals the typical social-learning view that a good relationship is an important preface to subsequent and more vital techniques.

> In most cases, it is required that an atmosphere of trust be established if any therapeutic intervention is to be effective. This usually is accomplished quickly by the therapist through his establishing that (1) he understands and accepts the patient, (2) that the two of them are working *together*, (3) and that the therapist has at his disposal the means to be of help in the direction desired by the patient. (Goldstein, 1973; p. 221)

based on some formal theory of behavior, personality, and behavior disorder in general and of the client's problem in particular (see Chapter 3). In other words, although therapists usually remain flexible, their behavior is guided by some general principles of treatment; it is not random.

Various psychotherapeutic approaches differ in the extent to which their theories of personality and behavior disorder are related to specific techniques. For example, psychoanalysts have developed a very complex theory of personality but do not specify exactly what procedures are to be used in applying this theory to a given case. Many social-learning theorists, on the other hand, attempt to provide in great detail the exact procedures to be employed in treatment.

Treatment approaches also vary in terms of the kinds of changes they are designed to produce. Thus, social-learning therapists are likely to deal directly with the problem as the client initially presents it (along with other difficulties that might contribute to the primary complaint). For example, a mother who reports depression and fears that she will kill her children would be encouraged to reexamine her marital role and other day-to-day problems. She might be assigned a variety of "homework assignments" involving her relationship with her husband, disciplinary methods for her children, or the development of new, out-of-the-house activities for herself. By contrast, the psychoanalyst would be more inclined to work on possible underlying causes of the mother's depression. Therapy might be aimed at helping the client understand how her current symptoms are due, say, to feelings of inadequacy as a mother because of failure to meet her own mother's rigid and unrealistic standards. Finally, a phenomenological therapist might deal with the problem by helping the mother experience it and herself more clearly. The goal might be for the client to discover her potential for creating alternatives in her life that would free her from the one-sided or distorted way of life in which she now feels trapped.

Notwithstanding all these differences, there are several techniques which are common to almost all psychotherapeutic strategies. The basic methods of psychotherapy are mainly psychological in nature rather than physical or medical. Psychiatrists may prescribe psychoactive drugs on occasion, and some phenomenologically oriented therapists may employ physical stimulation (usually in the form of sensory awareness exercises), but these are usually viewed not as the real foundation of therapy but as helpful supplements to the main psychological ingredients of treatment. Let us now consider a few major psychological methods of clinical intervention.

1 Fostering Insight Achieving insight into psychological problems was, of course, a chief objective of Freud who described it as "re-education in overcoming internal resistances" (Freud, 1904; p. 73). While Freud was most interested in a particular type of insight (the recognition and analysis of unconscious influences), most therapists aim for insight in the more general sense of greater self-knowledge. Clients are expected to benefit from learning about the reasons why they behave in certain ways because such knowledge is

Box 8-2   Eclectic Psychotherapy

The list of psychotherapy "brand names" continues to grow. In addition to the old standbys like client-centered, gestalt, psychoanalytic, and social-learning therapy, we are now witness to such phenomena as est (Erhard Seminars Training), whose followers pay hefty fees to grapple with the meaning of phrases like "what is, is." In "prosperity training," students learn that "money is spiritual."

One of the great paradoxes of this proliferation of psychotherapeutic approaches is that the majority of therapists pledge allegiance to no single system, preferring instead to select from several theoretical models the one approach that best fits a given client. This orientation is known as *eclecticism* or *eclectic psychotherapy*. Eclectics do not consider themselves to be anti- or atheroetical clinicians who simply reach into a grab bag and randomly yank out a technique. The choice of technique is still a principled one, but it is based on the exigencies of each individual case rather than on the dictates of a general theoretical system.

In one recent survey (Garfield & Kurtz, 1976), the majority of clinicians contacted identified themselves as eclectics. As a result, Garfield and Kurtz (1977) conclude that any investigation of psychotherapy which concentrates on specific theoretical orientations is "studying only a minority of those engaged in psychotherapeutic practice" (p. 83).

Because it is not a "school" of psychotherapy, eclecticism has not attracted a large number of vocal adherents, nor has it been popularized by any famous founders. Frederick Thorne (1950, 1967, 1973) is probably the best-known advocate of an eclectic approach, and even he appears to be a somewhat reluctant spokesman: "Eclecticism carries with it none of the special advantages of uniqueness, newness or proprietorship of special knowledge implicit in the special schools whose adherents often turn such attributes to personal advantage" (Thorne, 1973; p. 449).

Thorne is careful to distinguish his version of eclectic therapy from any approach that is simply a hodgepodge of technique. Eclecticism requires a valid formulation of each clinical case. In Thorne's words,

> Probably the most important consideration in using the eclectic approach is the condition of the client, his mental and existential status, his momentary needs, his symptomatic status, and the underlying dynamics of the condition. The eclectic therapist gives attention to all these factors, balancing short-term needs versus long-term therapeutic goals. As case handling unfolds, the client reveals more and more of his problems, and gets deeper and deeper into underlying causes. The eclectic tends to reject stereotyped formulas for dealing with problems and instead tends to react extemporaneously to new developments. The selection of methods proceeds continuously and responsively as the developments of case handling transpire. (p. 470)

presumed to contribute to the development of new behaviors. The psychotherapist's rationale for fostering a client's insight is a little like the well-known justification for studying history: to know the errors of the past in order to avoid repeating them in the future.

Therapists of all theoretical persuasions seek to promote self-examination, self-knowledge and self-analysis in their clients. There are numerous approaches to this goal. Some procedures are quite structured and deal with a specific type of content; dream analysis would be an example. Other therapists might try to promote insight by directly asking their clients to examine the reasons for, motives behind, and implications of certain behaviors (e.g., "What does that tell you about yourself?," or, "What relationship do you see between your troubles with your boss and the dislike you express for your father?"). Social-learning therapists emphasize a special kind of insight. They stress the importance of helping the client to fully understand how behavior is functionally related to past learning and current environmental factors.

A common technique for developing insight is for the therapist to offer an *interpretation* of the client's behavior. The purpose of interpretation is not to convince the client that the therapist is necessarily right about the significance of some event, but to motivate the client to examine more carefully his or her own behavior and perhaps draw some new conclusions about its meaning. Interpretations can come in many forms, as Jerome Frank (1973) has noted in his very influential book, *Persuasion and Healing:*

> The simplest form of interpretation consists of repeating something the patient has said, perhaps with some change in emphasis, so that he becomes more clearly aware of it. In a roughly ascending scale of degree of inference and amount of complexity, other forms of interpretation are summarizing, in order to coordinate and emphasize certain aspects, verbalizing the feelings that seem to lie behind the patient's utterances, and confronting him sharply with attitudes implied by his statements that he had not recognized. Complex interpretations may indicate similarities between a patient's feelings toward important contemporaries, including the therapist. They may also suggest symbolic meanings of his statements or link them to a theoretical scheme. (p. 222–223)

2   Reducing Emotional Discomfort   Clients sometimes come to a therapist in such a state of emotional upheaval and anguish that it is quite difficult for them to participate very actively in therapy. In such instances, the therapist will try to reduce the client's level of distress enough to allow the person to begin working on the problem. Therapists usually do not strive to entirely eliminate a client's discomfort because, in so doing, they might also eliminate any motivation for working toward more lasting change. The challenge is to diminish extreme distress without sapping the client's desire to deal with enduring problems.

There are many approaches to achieving reduction in client discomfort. Probably the most common method is to use the therapeutic relationship as a booster to the client's emotional strength. Clients typically gain some emotional stability and renewed confidence simply by knowing that the therapist is now a personal ally, a buffer against the onslaughts of a hostile, seemingly merciless world. Other therapists offer direct reassurances. This may take the form of some statement like "I know that things seem almost hopeless right now, but I think you will be able to make some important changes in your life."

3   Encouraging Catharsis   One special strategy for reducing intense emotions is simply to encourage their free expression in the protective presence of the therapist. This technique is known as *catharsis,* i.e., the release of pent-up emotions that the client has been afraid to acknowledge for a long period of time. The therapist may encourage the client to give voice to those emotions, believing that through their release they will be dispelled or eased. At the very least, catharsis may result in the client becoming less frightened of certain emotions. In some therapies, catharsis is a goal in itself, while in others (e.g., social-learning), it is seen only as a minor event.

4 Providing New Information Psychotherapy is almost always educational. The therapist will provide new information intended to correct gaps or distortions in clients' knowledge. Certain areas of adjustment are plagued quite regularly by misinformation, sexual functioning being the most notable example. There are several available methods for correcting misinformation. Some therapists offer direct advice to their clients, adopting for a limited period of time a role more like a teacher than a therapist. Others may suggest reading material relevant to the topic, a process sometimes known as *bibliotherapy*. Still others rely on more indirect maneuvers—a shrug of the shoulders, a skeptical facial expression, an exaggerated interpretation—to suggest to clients that there are other, more functional or accurate ways of perceiving the world around them.

5 Assigning Extratherapy Tasks Therapists often ask clients to perform certain tasks outside of the therapy session for the purpose of encouraging the transfer of positive changes to the "real world." This is known as therapy "homework." Harper (1959) describes homework as follows:

> The therapist and the patient agree on certain actions (based on the patient's changed conceptions of himself and his environment) with which he is to experiment between one psychotherapeutic session and the next. The patient reports on his successes and failures regarding these attempted changes in his behavior, and then he and the therapist make plans for additional changes. As the patient experiences gratification from successful accomplishments in new modes of behavior, his self-esteem grows. This, in turn, enables him to execute still more improvements in his behavior. (p. 6)

Social-learning therapists are the most enthusiastic advocates of homework assignments, believing them to be the most effective way to promote the generalization and maintenance of new reactions and skills learned in the therapist's office or in other formal settings.

6 Developing Faith, Hope, and Expectancy for Change Of all the procedures common to all systems of therapy, raising clients' faith and expectancy for change is the ingredient most frequently mentioned as a crucial contributor to therapeutic improvement. In fact, many scholars attribute the success of psychotherapy to its ability to arouse the clients' belief that they can be helped, rather than to any specific techniques. The curative power of faith is, of course, not restricted to psychotherapy. The effects are well known in medicine: in fact, the "history of medical treatment can be characterized largely as the history of the placebo effect" (Shapiro, 1971; p. 442). A placebo is

> . . . any therapy, or that component of any therapy, that is deliberately used for its nonspecific, psychologic, or psychophysiologic effect, or that is used for its presumed specific effect on a patient, symptom, or illness, but which, unknown to patient and therapist, is without specific activity for the condition being treated. (Shapiro, 1971; p. 440)

All methods of treatment whether they be medical, psychological, religious, or mystical involve potent placebo effects. Clinicians are so accustomed to thinking about the role of placebo effects in psychotherapy that they have even coined additional terms to designate their influence. The most popular of these have been *expectancy effects* (Wilkins, 1971, 1973), *nonspecific effects* (Shapiro, 1971), and *demand characteristics* (Orne, 1962). These designations refer to various aspects of the same general idea: that psychotherapy achieves its successes, in part, because of its capacity to generate clients' expectancy for improvement.

In the psychotherapy literature, client expectancies have been defined as the prediction of an "outcome that is looked for with the belief, faith, confidence, and conviction of being found" (Meltzoff & Kornreich, 1970; p. 256). Frank equated expectancy for improvement with such concepts as optimism, hope, and faith, all of which involve "the perceived probability of achieving a goal" (Frank, 1973; p. 136).

An emphasis on expectancy-placebo effects in psychotherapy does not mean that the theory-directed techniques, which serve to distinguish one therapeutic approach from another, are unimportant. It does mean, however, that one important element (some might say the *most* important element) of any effective therapy is that it causes the client to believe that positive changes in life are attainable (Bandura 1977b).

Psychotherapy enjoys a special reputation among the general public. It is viewed as a somewhat mysterious treatment that is powerful enough to correct even the most aberrant behavior. Part art and part science, psychotherapy profits from the mystique that surrounds both fields. Clients who begin psychotherapy often do so with the belief that they are about to engage in a unique, almost irresistibly powerful experience conducted by an expert with skills and training sufficient to work miracles. The perceived potency of psychotherapy is further enhanced by the fact that clients usually come to therapy after having fretted for a long time about whether they really "need" treatment. By the time this internal debate is resolved in favor of seeking help, the client already has a large emotional investment in making the most of a treatment which is regarded with a mixture of fear, hope, and relief.

For their part, therapists attempt to maximize the client's faith in the power of psychotherapy. The therapist attempts to assure the client that the therapist understands the problem and is confident that, by working together, they will be able to achieve some desired changes. The perception by a client that "I have been heard and understood and can be helped" is an extremely important one in therapy. Among the procedures which encourage this perception are some of the general techniques already described—the formation of a nurturant but professional relationship, interpretations, catharsis, and the alleviation of emotional panic.

In addition, most therapists offer the client a *rationale* for why psycho-therapy will be effective. In place of the client's uncertainty about what therapy will involve, the therapist will attempt to structure the experience in such a way that the client understands how and why beneficial change should occur. Jefferson Fish, a self-described "placebo therapist" observes:

One of the strong points in the therapist's role as a socially sanctioned healer is his status as an expert on psychotherapy. Because of this status, patients frequently give their therapists considerable freedom in structuring their expectations about their own therapy. Thus, most patients want to know what psychotherapy will be like; and they tend to be quite accepting when their therapists provide them with such "information." (Fish, 1973; p. 46–47)

Having initially structured therapy in such a way as to increase the client's motivation and expectancies for treatment, the therapist will attempt to insure that the client experiences some success in therapy as soon as possible. The success might be a small one whose nature depends on the specific therapeutic approach involved—a minor insight arrived at after a simple interpretation by the therapist, the successful completion of a not-too-difficult "homework" assignment, the "feeling better" that clients experience after an initial cathartic experience. Whatever the means, the objective is for therapy to bring about the kind of change that the client expects it should. The therapist will encourage the client to view it as progress, as a sign that therapy can help. The task for the therapist is to build the client's confidence that he or she is not a hopeless case.

There is a cumulative impact to the trickle of small changes that clients observe in the initial stages of therapy. They begin to be persuaded that they can change, that they can control their lives, that their problems are understandable. A sense of despair and hopelessness starts to give way to a fragile but uplifting feeling of capability and even self-mastery. There is a sparkle of self-confidence, a hopeful glimpse of a new self-image.

Thus, at their fullest strength, therapeutic expectancies can exert a circular effect. At the beginning of therapy, the client's faith in the therapist and treatment are strengthened to the point that the client believes in the possibility of making desired improvements. When some changes, regardless of their magnitude or their content, are actually experienced, the client's expectancies are confirmed and they grow. As a result, the client believes that larger, more meaningful changes can be attained, and she or he pursues them with reinforced expectations. Meanwhile, the therapist enhances the client's blooming self-esteem by pointing out that all changes are the result of the client's own effort.

In short, when successful, all forms of psychotherapy relieve dysphoric feelings, rekindle the patient's hopes, increase his sense of mastery over himself and his environment, and in general restore his morale. As a result, he becomes able to tackle the problems he had been avoiding and to experiment with new, better ways of handling them. These new capabilities decrease the chance that he will become demoralized again and, with good fortune, enable him to continue to make gains after psychotherapy has ended. (Frank, 1973; p. 330)

We can now return to the question, "What is psychotherapy?" Our answer (for others, see Frank, 1973, and Harper, 1959) emphasizes the following qualities:

1 Psychotherapy consists of an interpersonal relationship between at least two participants, one of whom (the therapist) has special training and expertise in handling psychological problems.

2 The other participant is a client who is experiencing some problem in emotional, behavioral, and/or interpersonal adjustment and who has entered the relationship in order to alleviate this problem.

3 The psychotherapeutic relationship is a nurturant but purposeful alliance in which several methods, largely psychological in nature, are employed to bring about the changes desired by the client and approved by the therapist.

4 These methods are based upon some formal theory regarding psychological problems in general and the specific complaint of the client in particular.

5 Regardless of theoretical preferences, most therapists will employ several of the following intervention techniques: fostering insight, reducing emotional discomfort, encouraging catharsis, providing new information, assigning extratherapy tasks, and raising clients' faith in and expectancy for change.

MODES OF PSYCHOTHERAPY

So far, we have been discussing psychotherapy almost entirely in its most popular mode: that of individual, or one-to-one, treatment. This classic arrangement still forms the backbone of most clinical treatment work. In Chapters 9, 10, and 11, when we describe the goals, procedures, and effects of psychodynamic, social-learning, and phenomenological approaches to psychotherapy, the emphasis will be upon individual interventions. However, it is important to recognize that clinical intervention can also be undertaken with *groups* of clients. These groups may consist of unrelated individuals or they may be composed of family members. In the former case, the treatment enterprise is usually called *group therapy;* in the latter, it is called *marital* or *family therapy.*

Group Therapy

Group therapy amounts to more than just simultaneous therapy for several individuals. Although primarily inspired by the economic need to ease the shortage of professional personnel around World War II, group therapy has progressed to the point that it is now regarded as a unique and valuable form of intervention in its own right. Group therapy is seldom recommended today solely because of its economy, but rather because it is seen, on clinical grounds, to be the intervention of choice for many types of clients.

Group therapy is practiced with a wide variety of styles and techniques. Indeed, every major model of clinical psychology has treatment groups based on its principles. There are analytic groups, client-centered groups, transactional analysis groups, encounter groups, gestalt groups, and social-learning groups. Groups are also a popular form of intervention within many nonprofessional self-help organizations. Weight-control groups, assertiveness groups, consciousness-raising groups, and Alcoholics Anonymous are common examples. Certain groups assume a special identity because of one idiosyncratic quality. Marathon groups which run for long, uninterrupted periods of time provide a good illustration.

This wide range of theory and practice makes it very difficult to talk meaningfully about any uniform process of group therapy. Nonetheless, Yalom (1975) argues that behind all the stylistic differences there are some essential similarities in effective therapy groups. Most group therapists emphasize the importance of interpersonal relationships and assume that pathology or unhappiness or maladjustment can be reduced to difficulties in the development or maintenance of interpersonal relations. Group therapists also assume that during the course of a group, clients will sooner or later "be themselves" and manifest their maladaptive interpersonal behaviors. Once these behaviors have been exhibited, other group members can provide corrective feedback about them, thus prompting the learning of new, more effective interpersonal syles. Finally, opportunities to correct problem behaviors are accompanied by the chance for group members to exhibit their areas of strength, sensitivity, and empathy. As a result, group therapy not only challenges harmful habits and beliefs but may strengthen and support positive behavior as well.

Like various systems of individual psychotherapy, many approaches to group therapy appear to share common "curative factors." Though some of these factors are very similar to those found in one-to-one treatment, most of them are thought to be unique to groups, thereby accounting for the special usefulness often attributed to this form of treatment. A full discussion of the curative factors in group therapy is contained in Yalom's (1975) authoritative text, *The Theory and Practice of Group Psychotherapy*. In summary, these factors include:

1 Sharing New Information As you will remember, this was also an important characteristic of individual psychotherapy. In groups new information is likely to be imparted from two different sources. First, the group leader or therapist may offer advice or instructions from time to time. However, direct advice also comes from the other members of the group who share with one another their own experiences and lessons of the past. The multiple perspectives of the group as a whole will probably constitute a richer store of new information than would usually be the case with a single therapist.

A major feature of group-generated information and feedback is its *consensuality*. The impact of new information is magnified by the agreement on which it is based. While it may be tempting to discount feedback from one friend or even one therapist, it becomes progressively more difficult to dismiss the similar opinions of eight or ten observers as biased or inaccurate. In numbers there is strength, especially when the numbers all agree.

2 Instilling Hope This is almost identical with the concept of expectancy for change discussed previously. As with individual psychotherapy, there should be confidence in the competence of the therapist and a belief that the treatment can be helpful. As in individual work, group therapy can be introduced with a rationale that buoys the hope of new members, but there are also special features of groups that increase the positive expectancies of their members. Probably the most important of these features is the opportunity for group members to observe positive changes taking place in others. An individual client might search for changes in her or his behavior only to become impatient and discouraged at what is felt to be an exasperatingly slow pace of improvement. However, detecting slow but positive changes in others may lead to the recognition that everyone grows at about the same pace and may thereby sustain faith in the effectiveness of the group.

3 Universality Groups dramatize the fact that everyone struggles with problems in living. One of the most valuable lessons that group members learn is that they are not alone in their misery or their fear or their disappointment. This discovery is important because many persons are very secretive about their problems, which restricts their ability to find out that they are not unique. A group allows its members to share their problems and, in the process, to derive some comfort from the knowledge that "there are others just like me." Learning about the universality of one's problems can soothe anxiety about "going crazy" or "losing control." Further, knowing that others have overcome similar problems may make it easier to believe in one's own capacity for change.

4 Altruism Not only do groups allow the sharing of problems, they also encourage the mutual display of personal resources. Groups give clients a chance to shine, to find out that they can be helpful to other people. Just as group therapy produces new insights into interpersonal weaknesses, it also confirms the presence of interpersonal strengths. In addition to being clients, group therapy members also serve as one another's therapists. The "helpee" role intertwines with the "helper" role. Clinicians often refer to the positive emotions that follow altruistic behavior as "feelings of self-worth." Whatever the name, group members are usually exhilarated by the experience of being able to help and care for another person.

5 Interpersonal Learning By their very nature, therapy groups require interpersonal behavior. At the beginning of a group, the contacts between members are likely to be formal, hesitant, and guarded. As the group progresses and members come to know one another, these contacts become progressively more spontaneous, intimate, and direct. A properly conducted therapy group is an ideal setting in which to learn new interpersonal and social skills. It is a small, nurturant community whose members are motivated to help their colleagues. It presents repeated opportunities to practice fundamental social skills with different types of people and with the advantage of almost immediate feedback on performance. Groups also contain numerous models for imitative learning— one of the most efficient ways to learn novel behaviors. Yalom (1975, p. 22) comments on the broad interpersonal quality of group therapy in the following terms:

Group therapy patients, somewhere between the third and sixth month of therapy, often undergo a shift in their therapeutic goals. Their initial goal, relief of suffering, is modified and eventually replaced by new goals, usually interpersonal in nature. Thus goals change from wanting relief from anxiety or depression to wanting to learn to communicate with others, to be more trusting and honest with others, to learn to love. One of the early tasks of the therapist is to facilitate this translation of symptoms into interpersonal constructs.

6 Recapitulation of the Primary Family Many group therapists regard the therapy group as a "reincarnation" of clients' primary families. This quality is sometimes described as *family reenactment,* and it is thought to be a curative factor because it allows clients to deal with those early family experiences that still color, confuse, and corrupt their current functioning.

Yalom (1975) suggests that there is value in exploring the past family "spirits" that still may haunt the group as long as the primary focus of the group remains in the here-and-now.

Group events, member sibling rivalry, therapist-parents, and regressive group fantasies all pitch the patient back to his early life in the family. He reenacts early family scripts in the group and, if therapy is successful, is able to experiment with new behavior, to break free from the locked family role he once occupied. He recaptures the past and, again if therapy is successful, does so, much less arbitrarily; in fact, the patient changes the past by reconstituting it. (p. 98)

Recapitulation of the family is group therapy's counterpart to the transference relationship in individual psychodynamic therapy. Group members will often react to group leaders or other members as if they were parents. The major distinction between these two phenomena is that transference is usually considered a much more crucial factor for success in psychoanalysis than family reenactment is for effective group therapy.

7 Group Cohesiveness Cohesiveness can be thought of as the "attractiveness of a group for its members" (Frank, 1957). Yalom (1975) suggests such synonyms as "groupness" and "we-ness" to describe the experience of group cohesion. While the concept is somewhat difficult to define, its manifestations are quite clear when experienced by a group. Members of cohesive groups are accepting of one another and they are likely to form close, supportive group relationships. They are willing to listen to and be influenced by the group. They participate in the group readily, feel secure in it, and are relatively immune to outside disruption of the group's progress. Cohesive groups also permit the expression of hostility, provided such conflicts do not violate the norms of the group. Attendance is reliable in cohesive groups, and premature termination of treatment is not usually a problem (Yalom, 1975).

Group cohesiveness is often regarded as the most important of the curative factors. Its value in group therapy is approximately that of the therapeutic relationship in individual psychotherapy. Yalom (1975) considers cohesiveness to be a "necessary precondition" for effective group treatment and one which enhances the development of the other curative factors. Cohesiveness exerts its beneficial influence in many ways. The *acceptance* that members receive from the group may counteract their own feelings of worthlessness. The *public esteem* of the group comes to be a reference point which influences members' own *self-esteem*. The effect of this influence is usually an increase in personal self-esteem, because it is common for groups to evaluate individual members more favorably than the individuals evaluate themselves. The greater the group cohesion, the more probable it is that each member will agree with the group judgment. Group members, in turn, will strive to change in order to confirm the group's impression. The effect is something like a *group fulfilling prophecy* where members are motivated to "not let the group down." Behaviors once thought by the individual to be "impossible" may be performed largely because of the group's supportive demand that they at least be attempted.

Kaul and Bednar (1978) have attempted to summarize the qualities that make group therapy a clearly distinct intervention. As already noted, the presence of several clients is not a sufficient discriminator. Kaul and Bednar suggest that groups offer four types of learning that are not present and cannot be duplicated by individual psychotherapy. These four learning influences are closely related to Yalom's curative factors, and they serve the useful purpose of summarizing and integrating Yalom's longer list of concepts. You might think of these four factors as higher-order constructs under which the previous curative factors can be subsumed. According to Kaul and Bednar (1978, p. 179), the four types of learning unique to group therapy are:

> **1** Members may profit as a consequence of learnings based upon their participation in, and evaluation of, a developing social microcosm;
> **2** Group members may benefit as a consequence of giving and receiving feedback in the group;
> **3** Individuals may improve as a result of consensual validation derived from the group; and
> **4** Individuals may profit from the relatively unique opportunity to be reciprocally involved with other group members as both helpers and helpees.

The Practice of Group Therapy

Group Composition   Therapy groups usually consist of between six and twelve members. The number needs to be large enough for the special qualities of a group to emerge without being so large that interactions become difficult or trivial. If a group is too small, the full advantages of universality and cohesiveness may be jeopardized. Greater risks are more common, however, when groups become too large. With larger groups there is a tendency for feedback to become more mechanical and superficial. There may also be less sensitive exploration of others' viewpoints. Another major problem with larger groups is that "isolates" (members who make infrequent contributions) are more likely.

An important question facing the group leader relates to the type of client that should be accepted into a group. Initial assessment of group candidates is often not as structured as one might encounter in individual psychotherapy. Most group therapists rely on an interview to screen prospective members. They try to exclude brain damaged individuals or those who are paranoid, hypochondriacal, suicidal, extremely narcissistic, sociopathic, drug or alcohol addicted, or psychotic (Yalom, 1975). According to Yalom, "these patients seem destined to fail because of their inability to participate in the primary task of the group; they soon construct an interpersonal role which proves to be detrimental to themselves as well as to the group" (1975, p. 221).

Group leaders disagree on whether groups should be *homogenous,* where members are similar on dimensions such as age, sex, and type of problem, or *heterogenous,* in which there is a mix of different types of clients. From a purely pragmatic perspective, heterogenous groups are much easier to form. They also have the clinical advantage of exposing members to a wider range of people and perspectives. To the extent that a therapist wants her or his group to be representative of the "real world," a heterogenous group would be preferred. The major advantage of homogenous groups is that they facilitate a more direct focus on symptom improvement. This emphasis is understandable since the group's identity is often defined in terms of a common problem which initially motivated treatment.

Group Duration   How long does group therapy last? What is the length of the usual group session? Questions about time are very important in group therapy because practitioners believe that the quality of group interactions is influenced by the amount and the nature of time which members spend together. Questions of timing remain open and frequently debated, however.

Some groups, like old soldiers, never die. These groups become virtually organic, continuing to function over long time periods, adding new members as old ones depart. Other groups are time-limited, lasting only for a specific number of sessions. These groups may be open to new members, but more often they are closed and continue only with the initial participants.

Group sessions are typically longer than sessions of individual psychotherapy. Two hours is probably the most common length. Group sessions need to be longer for the obvious reason that it takes more time for eight clients to talk than only one. It also tends to take more time for a group to reach a meaningful level of dialogue.

Lengthy sessions are a defining characteristic of marathon approaches to group treatment. Bednar and Kaul (1978) suggest that while there is no clear demarcation between marathon and other group approaches, it is generally assumed that a marathon session would last from 6 to 48 hours or more. According to Bednar and Kaul:

The rationale for the value of the marathon approach seems rather straightforward; people pretend and defend less as they become increasingly fatigued. Advocates of the marathon approach argue that the typical one to three hours of group meetings do not provide sufficient time for the erosion of social facades. Additionally, they assert that as a member's store of available energy is depleted, that member becomes more apt to show his or her true feelings, act more transparently, and attempt novel modes of behavior. Finally, it is held that merely removing an individual from the typical environment may make learning occur more readily.

The critics of marathon techniques have remained unpersuaded by these arguments. They have wondered why if someone is too tired to pretend, they aren't also too tired to practice new behaviors or engage themselves constructively with other members. They have asked why one might assume that new learnings would transfer from the specific marathon setting to the more typical world of the member. Finally, the critics have asked whether changes elicited under such conditions would persist. (p. 782)

The Group Therapist The group therapist must walk a narrow line between exerting too much control over the group and allowing it to "run free" without a focus, anchor, or goal. The effective group therapist is probably best thought of as a "first among equals" who, while not being the sole mediator of change, remains responsible for keeping the group on course and maximizing the opportunities for group members to help themselves. Korchin (1976) describes the effective therapist in the following terms:

> The role of the therapist, particularly initially, focuses on creating, building, and maintaining the group culture. As strangers to each other, the members look to the leader for defining the basic rules of therapy. He, in turn, lays down by example as well as precept the basic principles by which the group is to function, though these may change over time as a group culture and norms emerge. The therapist must be alert to potentially disruptive factors and be prepared to intervene as necessary. A group process can be threatened by continued absences or lateness, by clique formations or scapegoating, and it is the therapist's task to minimize them. (p. 395)

Marital and Family Therapy

Marital and family discord have become two of the most common problems encountered by the clinical psychologist. Indications of the magnitude of these problems cannot be missed. More than one of every three marriages ends in divorce. The tragedy of family breakdowns is revealed by frightening increases in the rates of child abuse, adolescent suicide, runaways, substance abuse within families, and parental desertion. A burgeoning professional literature on the theory and treatment of disturbed families and marriages has appeared (Ables and Brandsma, 1977; Ackerman, 1958; Bell, 1961; Haley, 1971; Lederer and Jackson, 1968; Liberman, 1970; Patterson, 1971; Satir, 1967).

Marital Therapy In marital therapy the "client" is the marriage, or more accurately, the married couple. (Because of the changing nature of living

Box 8-3 An Example of Group Therapy

This brief transcript will give you a better idea of what goes on in a group. It is taken from a book by Thomas Verny (1974) who reports it to be a verbatim account of about a half hour of group interaction (minus irrelevant remarks, repetitions, and hesitations).

Beth: After last week's session, I was very very angry. I even thought I shouldn't be in this group any longer. I just feel like the claws are at me all the time.

Dora: I was feeling very worked up too.

Fred: I just want to say one thing. That is, last week I felt the strangest tension and I couldn't decide whether it was me and I wanted to leave. Then I thought: This is ridiculous.

Beth: I almost . . . that is why I almost didn't want to come this week. I have got work to do and it is hard, and I don't need any extra tension in my life, specially this hounding that I have been getting for the past weeks.

Dora: Do you have any idea . . . do you realize, why you have been getting all this? I give it to you because I am so irritated with you for not doing anything about your situation.

Beth: I get out and I do as much as I can. [pause] Besides, I don't think that's the real reason for you and everyone else attacking me.

Dora: Well, if you don't believe me you can tell me what you think.

Beth: You're jealous of me.

Dora: Okay that's true, but don't put this into that category, because the reason I've been on you has got nothing to do with jealousy.

Beth: Sometimes I would just like to tell you to go and screw off.

Dora: Well then, why don't you? How about your apartment, have you been able to do anything about that?

Beth: No.

Dora: Are you angry with me for asking that question?

Beth: No.

Dora: Would you like to have a nice apartment?

Beth: Yes, and I would also like to have a permanent relationship with a man and lots of other things.

Therapist: My question is, "When are you finally going to get better?"

Beth: When I stop letting the world control me. When I stop getting scared. When I start trusting myself a little bit more.

Therapist: What will you do in order to be that kind of a person?

Beth: Well, last week I deliberately put my movie script down and I rested when I felt like it. I walked outside and decided I was not going to punch myself out for this thing.

Dora: You are scared of losing Tom.

Beth: Not only Tom. I am scared of him [pointing to therapist] thinking that I am a bitchy person. I am not happy. I am not particularly happy with my circumstances but I have to learn how to accept it.

Therapist: You are always shifting; it is like going through shifting sands; we can never really get through to the core of Beth, which has kept her going to psychiatrists for the last four or five years.

Beth: To me, the core is a void. I don't know what's in there. [pause] Unless you see someone opening up their guts, you think nothing is happening. [turning to the therapist] I don't know what to say to you.

Dora: I don't think that's what he means at all.

Beth: I wasn't supposed to grow up. I wouldn't be loved if I grew up. I certainly wouldn't be loved if I would be any smarter or better in my work than my brother or my father or my mother. That's why when I get punched up, I just fall apart.

Fred: I'm not punching you up. Not at all.

Beth: I have the feeling that I'm doing a lot of rehashing.

Therapist: Yes, you are.

Beth: Well, I'm just answering questions.

Therapist: Yes, just being the nice girl and answering questions.

Beth: That's right. I am being a nice girl.

Therapist: When are you going to stop being just a nice girl and be yourself?

Beth: I'm afraid people will say, "There goes number-one bitch."

Therapist: I would much prefer you being the number-one bitch than the number-one qvetch.

Dora: Is that a Jewish word?

Beth: Yes, it is. It means a person who complains chronically.

Annette: Groups are filled with them.

[general laughter]

Bill: How can we help you now?

Beth: By letting me know that I wouldn't be disliked if I got angry.

Several people: Why don't you try us?

Jim: There is one quality that I like in Beth and she seems to have this more than any other woman in this group, and that is the fact that she often laughs at herself. Isn't that right? Like, when you said qvetch, and suddenly [sic], you know, there was a smile on her face. She kind of lit up.

Therapist: That is why I say [turning to Beth] you are just playing at being neurotic.

Beth: That's something else that's upsetting me. Why do I think that I am so neurotic. I feel very funny now. I am embarrassed. [silence] I am wondering how everybody feels.

Therapist: Why is there always a need for talking?

Beth: Because I never get anything back. The only time I get anything back is when things are going poorly with me.

Therapist: Why don't you rely on your own resources? You have talked; you have thought about yourself; you have looked inward; why can't that be helpful in itself? Why do you need to hear from Henry and Joe and Jean and everybody else?

Dora: You know what Beth? I think you want more and more and more and nothing is quite enough.

Jim: I am really getting hostile with you Beth, because Tom made a statement that you were playing at being neurotic, and whether it's right or wrong, it is a significant phrase and you don't even hear it.

Therapist: I think one of the reasons that you were embarrassed a few minutes ago was because you were not playing neurotic. It was a new role and an unfamiliar one.

Beth: Because I was talking all about myself. I think I was embarrassed because I was taught that it's wrong to be alone, to be by yourself, to be on your own.

Boris: I think you were embarrassed when you were being yourself, because most of the time I don't get Beth. I get a very good actress, but I don't get Beth.

Beth: That terrifies me.

Therapist: Well then get terrified. You don't look terrified.

Dora: I think that it's terribly hard for you to know when you are yourself and when you are not, but it is certainly something that you need to discover.

Therapist: One of the things that I know you do is that you play to audiences all the time and I don't mean you as an actress, but you as Beth who is acting.

Dora: And here is an audience.

Therapist: Constantly you think "How is this going to please them, displease them, what is their reaction going to be?"

Jim: You know, now that you mention about Beth's acting, I took her home after last week's session. I was the only one present and I was just astounded because she behaved as if the room were full of people. I had the feeling that, on some occasions, she was talking to people who were not even in the room. She would go to the door, and she was saying lines through the door and to various parts of the room, probably playing for me, or something. It was like watching a weird performance. She opens the door but she doesn't really open it, she flings it open.

Rosemary: Beth, this is not criticism, this is feedback. Not one of us can see ourselves the way we really are. When you are ready to hear him or anybody else who gives you feedback, then perhaps you'll be ready to stop doing things that you yourself don't like doing.

Jim: Even in the group you do a lot of acting, and half of the time I can't hear what you are saying, and often it isn't connected with anything.

Beth: I don't recall making all these scenes and acting like a mad woman.

Therapist: If you could only stop, Beth, arguing and just concentrate and understand, just observe your pattern, I think it would really be helpful to you.

Beth: How often do I repeat this with other people? Dora said that I do this. Joe says this. And Jim is saying it.

Therapist: And Dan said it when he was in the group. Everybody who has known you has said it at one time or another. You tune out or you get involved with yourself.

Dora: And nobody can break it.

Beth: Yes, and I am wondering why. I am hearing it now, I am recognizing it.

Source: Verny, 1974; pp. 78–83.

arrangements in our culture, marital therapy is increasingly referred to as "couples therapy" in order to reflect the fact that it is intended for persons involved in a long-term, intimate relationship, not just those who are legally married.) This treatment is also described as being "conjoint" therapy, which simply means that both members of the couple see the same therapist(s) within the same sessions.

Marital therapy can be preceded, followed, or accompanied by individual psychotherapy for either or both of the spouses. Individual psychotherapy in addition to marital therapy is recommended when one of the members of the couple is suffering from some problem which is largely unrelated to the relationship.

Marital therapy is not the same as two psychotherapies for the price of one (or even for the price of two). In marital therapy the focus is on a *disturbed relationship*. This emphasis is different from working with a *disturbed individual in a relationship* which would be a proper goal for individual psychotherapy. The need for marital therapy usually arises out of the conflicting expectations and needs of the couple. A wife who was initially attracted to her husband because of his dashing charm and "playboy" image now finds these same qualities to be obstacles to the emotional security and fidelity which she currently expects from their relationship. A husband may come to feel that what he once admired as "spunkiness" in his wife is now a threat to his dominance of the marriage. Intimate relationships are most frequently beset by problems in the areas of sexual satisfaction, personal autonomy, dominance-submission, responsibility for child-rearing, money management, fidelity, and the expression of disagreements and hostility. The goals and techniques of the marital therapist will depend on which of these conflicts is the most pressing for any given couple. Although the theoretical orientation (psychoanalytic, phenomenological, or social-learning) of marital therapists will influence their choice of particular procedures, the range of differences between practitioners of marital therapy is probably smaller than that which would exist between the same people practicing their version of individual psychotherapy.

If there is a common theme among marital therapists it is their emphasis on *problem solving*. Problem solving involves teaching the couple how to solve their own problems more constructively. It does not mean that the therapist intervenes and solves the couple's problems for them or even that the therapist directly advises the couple how to solve their problems. The therapist's task is to facilitate the couple's working together in order that they can learn new ways to handle the inevitable problems of a close relationship.

The touchstone of problem solving is teaching the couple how to communicate more effectively with each other. "Improving communications" is such a basic ingredient in all couple therapy that it runs the risk of becoming a cliché; yet its actual role in therapy is central.

Working with communication involves efforts at changing not only the way spouses talk to each other but also how they think about their relationship. Therapists often discover that when there is some problem in a relationship, the members of the couple become preoccupied with deciding whose fault the problem is. They devote their energies to blaming each other, to thinking about the past, to stating demands in a way that ensures they will not be met, and, finally, to withdrawing and avoiding one another. Among the multiple tasks of improved communications are: teaching the couple to accept mutual responsibility for working on their problems, maintaining a focus on the here-and-now of their relationship, fostering expression of preferences rather than demands for obedience, and negotiating compromises and solutions to specific problems which the couple had long ago decided to be insoluble.

A brief excerpt from one type of couple therapy drawn from Ables and Brandsma (1977) illustrates several of these themes. In this example the therapist (T) is trying to help the wife (W) learn to give up her tendency to blame her husband for certain of his behaviors that she finds irritating:

T: I do think that what Pete is saying is an important point. There are things that are going to be different about you and each of you is going to think the things you do maybe make more sense than the other person's, and that's probably going to be pretty much of a reality. You're not going to be able to change all those. You may not be able to change very many of them. And everybody is different. They have their own predilections to do things a certain way and again what's coming through from you is sort of like damning those and saying those are wrong; they're silly, they don't make sense, I don't understand them or whatever. You may not understand them but they are a reality of each of you. That's something you have to learn how to deal with in some way. Otherwise, you . . . the reason I'm stressing this is I think it plays a large part in your criticalness.

W: Well, I do find it difficult to cater to, I guess that's the word, cater to some idiosyncrasies that I find or think are totally foolish. I am intolerant. I am, and I find it very difficult. I find it almost impossible to do it agreeably and without coming on as "Oh, you're ridiculous."

T: I guess what would be helpful would be if you could come on honestly enough to say "I don't like them" or "It doesn't sit well with me" without having to add the additional value judgment of whether they're foolish or ridiculous or whatever. That's the part that hurts. It's when you damn him because of these things—that's gonna hurt. I'm sure from Pete's point of view they make sense for his total economy of functioning. There's some sense to why he does things the way he does, just as there is for why you do things the way you do. It's not that they're foolish. They make sense in terms of where you are, what you're struggling with, and what's the best way you can deal with right now. I'm not trying to say that means you have to like them, but when you come across and say "It's ridiculous or foolish"—that's the part that makes it hurt.

W: Well, tell me again how to say it, because I find it hard to say anything except "That's really stupid—that's silly." I know you said it a minute ago but I lost it.

T: Well, anytime you can say it in terms of how it affects you and say with it, like "It's hard—I find it hard to take," that doesn't say "I find you're an ass for wanting to do that such and such a way." It's just that, "I find it hard to take—I get upset in this circumstance" or whatever. Stay with what your feelings are rather than trying to evaluate Pete. You know if you say "Good Lord, nobody in his right mind has to have that done that way."

W: That's about the way. [Husband laughs]

T: Those are the things that are going to get to him.

W: Well, there are many, many things like this and I'm sure I don't handle them well, but I find it very difficult to be tolerant of things that are so different from my nature.

T: I understand that.

[The therapist goes on to note an incident in which the husband was displeased but withstood his irritation the best he could without attacking his wife.] (pp. 92–94)

Family Therapy   Although they are similar in many respects, marital therapy and family therapy evolved for different reasons. Marital therapy was the natural outgrowth of the fact that many clients frequently complained of marital problems. The roots of family therapy are more indirect, stemming from the fact that individuals who made large improvements during individual therapy or institutional treatment often had a relapse when they returned to their families. This observation, along with other clinical insights and research, led to several theories of psychopathology which emphasized the family environment and parent-child interactions as causes of maladaptive behavior (Bateson, Jackson, Haley, and Weakland, 1956; Lidz and Lidz, 1949; Sullivan, 1953).

Family therapy also differs from marital therapy in that it usually begins with a focus on the problems of one member of the family rather than the entire family system. Therapists often speak of the "identified client" as the person in the family who has been singled out as the one with the problem. Typically, the identified client is a male child (often of adolescent age) whom the parents come to label as a "behavior problem" or as "unmanageable." While family therapy may begin with a focus on the symptomatic member, the therapist will soon try to reframe the problem in terms of disturbed family processes or faulty family communication. While keeping the well-being of the identified client as a crucial concern, the therapist will encourage all family members to see (1) their own contribution to the problem, and (2) the positive changes that each member can make.

As with marital therapy, the most common goal of family therapy is improved communications. For example, disturbed families seem to rely on coercion as their major means of communication. The message from both parents and children is often of the form, "Do what I want or you'll be sorry." The therapist must try to teach all family members alternative, noncoercive ways of communicating their needs. Other areas of family communication which the therapist might work on include teaching parents the importance of consistency in rule setting and discipline, encouraging each member of the family to communicate clearly and directly with one another, minimizing scapegoating of

the identified client, and helping the family members examine the appropriateness of what they expect from the rest of the family.

Virginia Satir (1967), one of the best-known practitioners of family therapy,
offers the following example of how the family therapist tries to help parents and
children communicate more directly with one another:

> The therapist helps parents to understand their children and receive "feedback"
> from them.
>
> He asks the parents to explain the child's behavior, thus making covert
> explanations overt so they can be dealt with. He challenges any solely negative
> interpretations and answers covert questions parents are asking about their children.

Mother: His pleasure is doing things he knows will get me up in the air.
Every minute he's in the house ... . constantly.
Therapist: There's no pleasure to that, my dear.
Mother: Well, there is to him.
Therapist: No. You can't see his thoughts. You can't get inside his skin.
All you can talk about is what you see and hear. You can say it *looks* as though
it's for pleasure.
Mother: All right. Well, it looks as though, and that's just what it looks
like constantly.
Therapist: He could be trying to keep your attention, you know. It is very
important to Johnny what Mother thinks.

> He asks the child to explain his own behavior:

Father: I mean, he never wanted me to stay and watch him play baseball.
Therapist: Tell me, how did you explain this to yourself? Why did you
think he didn't want you to watch?
Father: Well, that's the trouble, I never have been able to figure it out.
Therapist: Well, one way to find out is to *ask*. Let's ask Johnny. He can
tell you. Maybe he is uneasy when Dad is around.
Son: I'd just get embarrassed, sometimes.
Therapist: You'd get embarrassed.
Son: Uh huh. Cause he had Patty with him and Patty is always making a
fuss. The other guys would laugh . . .

> He helps the child to express frustration and anger and delineate situations
> which precipitate anger:

Therapist: Do you kind of get mad at Daddy when he gets mad at you?
Son: Yeah, and sometimes he gets real mad and pinches my ear.
Therapist: He pinches your ear. Do you feel like hitting him back?
Son: Yeah. I get real mad sometimes.
Therapist: So what keeps you from hitting him?
Son: Well he's, uh, he's bigger than me." (pp. 151–152)
Among the problems for which family therapy might be preferred are

family crises, marital or sexual problems, and conflicts about values, beliefs, life-styles, or goals (Korchin, 1976).

EVALUATION OF THERAPEUTIC INTERVENTION

The evaluation of psychological treatment is a major concern of at least three different audiences, and each audience has its own values that influence its definition of mental health as well as criteria that are used in assessing mental health (Strupp and Hadley, 1977; see Table 8-1). First, there is the client, the consumer of the service, who understandably has a more than casual interest in the success of an activity in which he or she has invested much personal effort, time, and money. The client usually asks two very simple questions of therapy: "Did it help me?" and "Was it worth the expense?"

The second source of evaluation is the therapist, who also has a considerable investment in delivering psychotherapy to clients and who needs to know if her or his efforts are worthwhile or if they need to be modified in some way.

The final evaluative audience for psychotherapy is society, which in this case

Table 8-1   Three Perspectives of Mental Health

Source	Standards/values	"Measures"
I. Society	Orderly world in which individuals assume responsibility for their assigned social roles (e.g., breadwinner, parent), conform to prevailing mores, and meet situational requirements.	Observations of behavior, extent to which individual fulfills society's expectations and measures up to prevailing standards.
II. Individual	Happiness, gratification of needs.	Subjective perceptions of self-esteem, acceptance, and well-being.
III. Mental health professional	Sound personality structure characterized by growth, development, self-actualization, integration, autonomy, environmental mastery, ability to cope with stress, reality orientation, adaptation.	Clinical judgment, aided by behavioral observations and psychological tests of such variables as self-concept, sense of identity, balance of psychic forces, unified outlook on life, resistance to stress, self-regulation, ability to cope with reality, absence of mental and behavioral symptoms, adequacy in love, work, and play, adequacy in interpersonal relations.

Source: Strupp, H. H. & Hadley, S. *American Psychologist,* 1977, *32,* 187–196. Copyright 1977 by the American Psychological Association. (Reprinted by permission.)

refs to any third party having an interest. A third party can be a spouse, parent, friend, lover, teacher, judge—anyone who is concerned about the changes that psychotherapy can produce in one or more clients. Third parties also can take on a cumulative quality; that is, if we add together all the individual third parties with an interest in psychotherapy, we can speak of society in the traditional sense of an organized, cooperative social group which is concerned that the practice of psychotherapy produce desirable effects for the community at large.

Evaluating therapy is a dominant research activity within clinical psychology. This activity takes two forms. The empirical assessment of the ultimate *effects* of treatment is known as *outcome research* and will be discussed in some detail in the next several pages.

The other major form of psychotherapy research is known as *process research*. Typically, process studies focus on the ongoing interaction between therapist and client as therapy unfolds. It examines changes that occur within therapy sessions. Many psychologists have argued that there is no useful or necessary distinction between process and outcome research. For example, Kiesler (1971) argues that the dichotomy is an unfortunate one which obscures the fact that all psychotherapy research intends to measure change of some kind. Process research assesses *in-session* changes at several points in time, while outcome research assesses *extratherapy* changes taking place between the beginning and end of treatment (and during follow-up). Kiesler advocates that the process-outcome distinction be discarded and that we refer to "in-therapy (interview) studies and extra-therapy (in-situ) investigations" (p. 46).

Psychotherapy outcome research is a topic which now occupies one of the largest literatures in clinical psychology (Garfield and Bergin, 1978; Meltzoff and Kornreich, 1970; Smith and Glass, 1977). Our purpose in this section is not to summarize the results of this unwieldy literature, but to describe briefly the basic methodology, the "how-to" involved in the evaluation of psychotherapy effects.

For a long time the basic question posed by the clinical researcher was: "Is psychotherapy effective?" Researchers gradually came to discover that this question was too broad to be answered meaningfully, and they abandoned it in favor of Paul's (1969a) now famous reformulation: "What treatment, by whom, is most effective for this individual with that specific problem, under which set of circumstances, and how does it come about?" (p. 44).

Kazdin (1978) has organized Paul's "ultimate question" into three goals of outcome research: (1) determine the efficacy of a specific treatment; (2) compare the relative effectiveness of different treatments; and (3) assess the individual components of treatment that are responsible for change in a particular problem or client.

In order to accomplish any of these goals, the psychotherapy researcher, like all researchers, is faced with one task: to design and conduct the evaluation in such a way that the results may be interpreted unambiguously (Underwood, 1957). This obligation is deceptively easy to describe, but exasperatingly difficult to execute. In fact, it is quite reasonable to argue that it is impossible to execute an evaluation which yields completely unambiguous results (Mahoney, 1978) for the simple reason that any human activity is a fallible effort.

Despite this recognition of fallibility, researchers strive to conduct the best evaluations they can. Most of them prefer to evaluate psychotherapy through the use of a scientific experiment. Now a scientific experiment is a very complex enterprise, the true meaning of which continues to evoke heated debate among philosophers as well as scientists. For our purposes, we shall describe an experiment as *an attempt to discover the causes of certain events by making systematic changes in certain factors and then observing changes that occur in other factors.* Researchers call the factors *they* change (or manipulate) the *independent variables,* while the factors in which resulting changes may be *observed* are termed the *dependent variables.*

Within-Subject Research

In psychotherapy research there are two basic experimental strategies. One is called *within-subject* research; the other is known as *between-subject* research. Both approaches share the common essence of an experiment; i.e., they both examine the comparative effects of varying conditions (independent variables) on the performance of a participant or group of participants. However, each approach uses different methods.

In within-subject designs, the comparisons of interest are made on the same subjects at different points in time. The within-subject experiment requires that the dependent variables be measured on several occasions in a certain sequence. The experiment is usually begun by observing the dependent measures before any manipulation of independent variables has taken place. This period is referred to as the *baseline,* and it provides an estimate of the preintervention, or existing, level of the dependent measure. Following the baseline, the *intervention* phase of the experiment is introduced. In this phase the independent variable is manipulated by the experimenter and the dependent measures are observed to detect any deviations from their baseline levels.

In evaluating the effectiveness of psychotherapy, the baseline period would involve observing the client's behavior for several days before any treatment was initiated. The intervention phase would correspond to the period of active treatment during which regular assessments of the client's progress would be made.

Although there are several types of within-subject experiment designs, two are used in the great majority of cases and therefore deserve special comment. The best-known of this pair is the *ABAB, or reversal,* design, which evaluates the effects of a treatment by alternating the baseline when there is no treatment (A) with the intervention when treatment is in effect (B). The length of each phase is determined by many factors, but usually each phase is continued until the client's behavior (the dependent measures) becomes relatively stable. If behavior fluctuates reliably and substantially in conjunction with the sequential experimental phases, the experimenter gains confidence that his or her

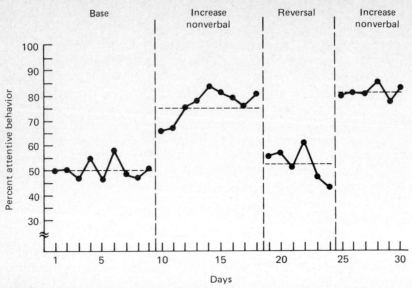

Figure 8-1 Example of a reversal design. This study showed the effects of presenting, withdrawing, and re-presenting teacher approval (smiles and physical contact) for attentiveness in retarded students. *(Kazdin, A. E. & Klock, J. Journal of Applied Behavior Analysis, 1973, 6, 643–654. © 1973 by the Society for the Experimental Analysis of Behavior. Reprinted by permission.)*

treatment is, in fact, responsible for the changes observed. An example of an ABAB evaluation of a clinical intervention is provided in Figure 8-1.

The other important within-subject design is the *multiple-baseline* design which evaluates an intervention without withdrawing treatment, as is required in the reversal design. Although this is a major advantage in psychotherapy research (where there are both clinical and ethical objections to interrupting treatment at arbitrary times), the multiple-baseline design is used less frequently than its ABAB counterpart. Multiple-baseline designs allow the researcher to observe simultaneously several dependent measures while applying the intervention of interest to only one of them. In other words, baseline conditions are in effect for all dependent variables except the one to which the treatment is applied. This procedure can be continued so that the treatment is applied to different variables, one at a time, while all other measures continue under baseline conditions. The experimenter gains confidence in the effects of a given treatment if a dependent measure changes only when the intervention is being applied to it. A cause-effect relationship is strengthened even more if this finding is repeated, or *replicated,* on each of the measures.

The need for several different baselines can be filled in a number of ways (Kazdin & Kopel, 1975), but usually the experimenter focuses on several behaviors in the same individual, applying treatment to a given behavior while the others remain at baseline. Imagine a study which evaluated the effects of social praise by hospital staff on the behavior of psychotic patients. In this

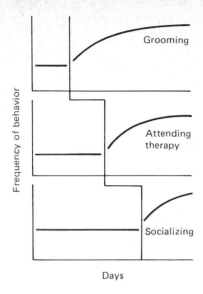

Frequency of behavior

Grooming

Attending
therapy

Socializing

Days

Figure 8-2 Data from a multiple-baseline
design. *(Kazdin, A. E. & Kopel, S. A. Behavior Therapy, 1975, 6, 601–608. © 1975 by
Academic Press, New York. Reprinted by
permission.)*

hypothetical experiment, three behaviors were examined—grooming, attending
occupational therapy, and socializing on the ward. The intervention (social
praise) is introduced at different points in time for the three behaviors; each
"new" intervention begins on the day following the termination of the baseline
phase for each behavior.

As Figure 8-2 shows, each behavior improved when, *and only when,* "its"
intervention was introduced. For example, attending therapy did not increase
during the time that social praise was being given for grooming. The fact that
each behavior changed only when social praise was being given for it makes it
very unlikely that some other factor (e.g., weather, the influence of other
patients) could account for such a specific pattern of results.

Within-subject research has the advantage of requiring only a small number
of subjects. In fact, the logic of within-subject designs permits the use of only
one subject, in which case the term "single subject" or "$N = 1$" research is used.
Of course, within-subject comparisons can also employ a group of participants,
all of whom are treated the same throughout the experiment.

Between-Subject Research

In research of the between-subject variety, the comparisons of interest are
drawn between groups of subjects that are exposed to different intervention
conditions. The simplest example of this approach is an experiment where there
are only two groups of subjects—an *experimental* group and a *control* group.
Subjects randomly assigned to the experimental condition are given some special
experience (in the case of psychotherapy research this would be some sort of
treatment) while the control group subjects are "left alone." Dependent
measures are collected for both groups prior to the experiment (this is called the
pretest) and shortly after it is over (the *posttest*). These same measures may also

be repeated at longer posttreatment intervals; this is usually described as *follow-up*. Once the pretest equivalence of the experimental and control groups is established, any differences between the groups, at either the posttest or follow-up, are assumed to be due to the treatment which only the experimental group received.

One traditional difference between the within-subject and between-subject strategies is that in the latter case statistical analyses are usually used to assess the magnitude or *significance* of the difference between treated and untreated subjects. A mean score and a measure of variability are computed for each group and a statistical test is applied to determine whether the between-group differences are likely to have occurred by chance. In within-subject research, such inferential statistics are usually not used because the researcher is more interested in demonstrating that the performance of a subject is reliably related to the sequential manipulations of the independent variable. The within-subject researcher feels that statistics are not necessary to demonstrate such control; a person can look at a graph of the subjects' performance and simply "see" the differences. (For a discussion of the pros and cons of performing statistical analyses on within-subject data see Gentile, Roden, and Klein, 1972; Glass, Wilson, and Gottman, 1973; and Hartmann, 1974.)

Psychotherapy outcome research has progressed to the point where the simple two-group (experimental versus control) design is no longer adequate for dealing with the questions which researchers now seek to answer. Even if large differences appear between the treatment and the no-treatment group, little is learned about the effects of psychotherapy except, perhaps, that it is more effective than doing nothing at all. This type of design cannot reveal whether the treated subjects' improvement was due to the specific techniques of the therapeutic approach, the characteristics of the therapist, or the pervasive capacity of therapy to generate faith and expectancy for improvement (i.e., nonspecifics, or placebo effects). This simple design is also unable to answer the question of whether the particular treatment tested would be more effective than some alternative approach.

A traditional way of answering such questions is to build all the factors of interest, along with the appropriate controls, into the experimental design. The major advantage of such *factorial designs* is that they compare several factors that might be responsible for therapeutic change. Thus, one group of subjects might receive a complete treatment "package" while another gets only that part of treatment thought to be most important to its effectiveness. Yet another group might be exposed to procedures which are impressive enough to generate faith in or hope for improvement but which are not actually very helpful. A fourth group might get no treatment at all.

By comparing the results in each of these groups, the experimenter can begin to determine whether the complete treatment package is (1) better than no treatment, (2) better than what could be gained from expectancy or placebo effects, and (3) better than a "streamlined" version. If another group of subjects had been given a completely different form of treatment, the experimenter could have also compared her or his own approach with an alternative approach. Paul (1966) provides an excellent description of a classic factorial design in his *Insight vs. Desensitization in Psychotherapy*. It is often said that well-designed experiments possess a high degree of *internal validity* (Campbell & Stanley, 1963). Internal validity refers to the degree to which the design of an experiment allows one to be confident that the results are due to the specific factor or factors being manipulated rather than some other, unintended factor.

Between-subject research is popular among psychotherapy researchers because it allows them to manipulate several different variables simultaneously rather than sequentially, as is required by within-subject designs. Between-subject designs are expensive, however; it takes many subjects and a large research staff to compose and treat the groups necessary for the statistical analyses used.

As noted throughout this section, there are many types of within-subject and between-subject designs. To give some idea of the complexity of methods which can be used to evaluate the effects of psychotherapy, we have listed twelve of the most common experimental designs in Table 8-2 (Mahoney, 1978). In this table an O refers to an observation or an assessment. An $X, Y,$ or Z refers to some form of treatment. The table describes twelve of the most common designs used to evaluate the effects of some intervention. Designs 1 to 7 are within-subject designs, while designs 8 to 12 are between-subject. For definitive discussions of these and other research designs, see Campbell and Stanley (1963) and Cook and Campbell (1979).

Analogue Research

Whether researchers advocate within- or between-subject designs, most agree that the best way to assess the outcome of psychotherapy is to conduct research on actual therapy offered by trained clinicians to bona fide clients in real treatment settings. The ideal experimental study would be to select clients seeking treatment for a certain problem and assign them randomly to different treatment and control conditions using trained therapists and measuring outcome on several different indexes of therapeutic change collected by persons "blind" to the conditions under which the clients had been treated. Unfortunately, this ideal is achieved so seldom as to be almost nonexistent in the psychology outcome literature.

The obstacles to the ideal psychotherapy experiment are numerous. In most cases, the essential requirements of an adequate experimental design cannot (or should not) be met in a "real-life" clinical context. For example, both clinical and ethical considerations prevent the random assignment of clients to different treatment and control conditions. Few clients are willing to tolerate being put into a no-treatment condition simply for the sake of good science. And for their part, therapists are reluctant to stand by and allow clients to be assigned to control conditions that appear to have little probability of bringing about constructive changes.

These problems usually are accompanied by an even more basic impedi-

Table 8-2 The 12 Most Common Experimental Designs Used to Evaluate the Effects of Some Intervention

Design	Symbol	Within-subject design	Comments
1 Posttest only	X0	A person or group experiences a manipulation (X) (e.g., therapy), and the dependent variable is then measured (0).	Extremely weak and uninformative design; no strong conclusions can be drawn.
2 Pretest-posttest	0X0	The dependent variable is measured (0) before and after the experimental manipulation (X).	Weak design; it may be concluded that there was (or was not) a change in the dependent variable, but one cannot determine whether this change would have occurred anyway (without the experimental manipulation).
3 Reversal	0X0X0	Two separate manipulations of the independent variable are each preceded and followed by measurement of the dependent variable.	More adequate design in that it can replicate the observed effect of an experimental manipulation; conclusions are limited to the subject or group in question, however, and this design does not rule out the possible influence of factors other than the independent variable; reversal may pose practical and ethical problems in some situations.
4 Equivalent time samples	0X0X0X0X0X	An extension of the reversal design in which an independent variable is sequentially presented and removed (or otherwise manipulated) with alternating measurements of the dependent variable.	Moderately adequate design in the sense of multiple replication and possible control of some time-related factors; limitations include the possibility that the effects of a manipulation may change due to its repeated presentation and withdrawal.

Table 8-2   (cont.)

Design	Symbol	Within-subject design	Comments
5 Multiple baseline	0X000 00X00 000X0	The timing of an experimental manipulation is systematically varied across different behaviors or situations.	Moderately adequate design in that it includes replication and partial control of time-related factors; limitations vary with the specific procedures.
6 Time series	000X000	The stability of a dependent variable is measured; deviations from that stability after an experimental manipulation are used to infer causal relationship.	Somewhat controversial in terms of adequacy; limitations include failure to rule out factors that changed simultaneously with the experimental manipulation and failure to replicate.
7 Changing criterion	$0X_10X_20X_3$	Similar in some respects to equivalent time samples design, except that the value of the independent variable is systematically altered; if changes in the dependent variable reliably covary with these manipulations, a causal relationship is inferred.	Moderately adequate design that shares many of the strengths and weaknesses of the equivalent time samples design; in addition, this may be problematic with some patterns of criterion change.

Design	Symbol	Between-subject design	Comments
8 Multiple baseline	0X000 00X00 000X0	The timing of an experimental manipulation is systematically varied across persons or groups.	See multiple baseline design within subjects (5).
9 Control group	0X0 0 0	Subjects are randomly assigned to an experimental or control condition (usually groups); the independent variable is manipulated only in the experimental condition, but the dependent variable is measured (pre and post) in both.	Generally adequate design whose limitations include failure to evaluate the effects of being observed or participation in *any* experiment.

Table 8-2   (cont.)

Design	Symbol	Between-subject design	Comments
10 Solomon four group	0X0 0 0 X0 0	Subjects are randomly assigned to four conditions (usually groups), two of which will receive the experimental manipulation—one of these is tested (i.e., the dependent variable is measured) before and after the manipulation; the other is tested only after; in the two control conditions, one is tested pre and post, the other only post.	Very adequate design in that it controls for the effects of testing; limitations include failure to evaluate the contribution of participating in *any* experiment.
11 Attention and control group	0X0 0 0 X0 0 0Y0 Y0	Subjects are randomly assigned to six conditions (usually groups), four of which are identical to those in the Solomon design; the two remaining receive some form of contact or attention designed to control for simple participation in an experiment.	Very adequate design; major limitation is failure to control for subject expectancies.
12 Placebo and control group	0X0 0 0 X0 0 0Z0 Z0	Identical to Design 11, except that the two added conditions receive an experimental manipulation that has an equal degree of credibility or probable effects as the true experimental manipulation; the placebo's probable effects are evaluated by subjects.	Very adequate design; the placebo condition simultaneously controls for participation and expectancy.

Treatment of various kinds is designated as "X," "Y," or "Z." Assessments are designated as "0."

Source: Mahoney, M. *Journal of Consulting and Clinical Psychology*, 1978, *46*, 660-672. © 1975 by the American Psychological Association. (Reprinted by permission.)

ment to research on psychotherapy: There are few clinical situations in which the researcher can obtain a sufficient number of clients who meet the criteria for inclusion. Another problem is that it is almost impossible to control for external factors that may influence clients' behavior. Commenting on this problem, Kazdin (1978, p. 674) has observed, "in outpatient psychotherapy, clients may receive additional experiences (e.g., encounter group or marathon sessions) or counsel (e.g., from a physician) while participating in a given treatment. In inpatient treatment with psychiatric patients, it may be difficult to control ongoing treatments (e.g., drugs) and other factors (e.g., release from the hospital) that can influence treatment or its evaluation."

Add to these obstacles the practical problems of enlisting experienced therapists to participate in a study, convincing agency administrators to invest time and finances in the research, and collecting meaningful outcome measures from clients who invariably seem either to have moved or obtained unlisted phone numbers, and you can sympathize with the psychotherapy researcher's sense of futility in conducting a "real-life" evaluation of treatment outcome.

There are really two approaches to these problems of psychotherapy outcome research. One is for researchers to summon all their creativity and tenacity and conduct the best clinical research they possibly can while at the same time recognizing that certain questions cannot be answered with certainty in a nonlaboratory study. The other approach is to try to bring psychotherapy research questions into the laboratory. In doing so, the researcher "buys" the control afforded by the laboratory by sacrificing some of the realism inherent in actual clinical settings.

In recent years, the second strategy has become an increasingly popular one. This approach, in which the variables and conditions of clinical situations are approximated in a more controlled experimental setting, is called *analogue research* (Cowen, 1961; Kazdin, 1978; Paul, 1969a). The advantages of psychotherapy analogue research are that it: (1) allows control of many extraneous variables that could not be controlled in the clinic, (2) makes possible an increased number of participants, (3) permits replication of results, (4) allows selection of subjects and research personnel on any of several dimensions (e.g., demographic characteristics, experience, type of problem, personality features), and (5) allows variables such as the number, length, and conduct of treatment sessions to be held constant across all subjects.

Analogue research tries to resemble actual clinical conditions as much as possible. To the extent that the analogy is a close one, with considerable similarity between laboratory variables and their clinical counterparts, the experiment is thought to possess *external validity*. External validity refers to the degree to which the design of an experimental study allows one to be confident that the results are generalizable to settings other than the one in which the experiment took place (Campbell & Stanley, 1963).

There are four basic dimensions upon which the similarity between clinical and analogue settings are assessed (Bernstein and Paul, 1971). The first is *subject characteristics* and *recruitment*. In analogue research, subjects are often college undergraduates who volunteer for the experiment for a variety of reasons (e.g. course credit or requirement, monetary incentives, curiosity) which may have very little to do with a desire to overcome a distressing problem. In general, the degree to which an analogue experiment's results can be generalized to a clinical population will depend on the extent to which the reasons for subjects' volunteering are similar to those that compel clients to seek treatment.

The second dimension to be considered in evaluating the adequacy of analogue research is the nature of the *target problem*. Within the social-learning literature, subjects reporting a fear of small animals (e.g., rats) have commonly been used in experiments on the effects of several anxiety-reduction techniques. Critics (Cooper, Furst, and Bridger, 1969; Bernstein and Paul, 1971) have contended that, as a target problem, the fear of small animals such as snakes, mice, dogs, and moles may have little relevance to clinical anxiety unless the intensity of clients' fear or amount of behavioral disruption is very high. In many studies, both may be rather low.

The third dimension of interest is *therapist characteristics*. In most analogues the "therapists" are graduate students in clinical psychology who have some limited clinical experience but who have seldom been independently responsible for the conduct of psychotherapy. It is doubtful that they possess the general clinical skills, specific techniques, and commitment to client improvement which ideally characterize the competent, practicing clinician.

The final dimension on which to compare clinical and analogue activities involves the *treatment techniques* themselves. In most instances analogue treatments are *standardized* on several dimensions, which simply means that these dimensions are specified and held constant across all participants. "Research applications may hold constant the number of treatment sessions across groups; the duration of treatment sessions; the material, tasks, or topics discussed within sessions; and so on" (Kazdin, 1978; pp. 680–681). This degree of standardization is seldom encountered in psychotherapy where the intervention is usually tailored to the unique needs and personality of each individual client. Bernstein and Paul (1971) suggest that, in many analogues, treatment techniques are frequently attenuated, simplified, grossly altered, or even omitted in order to meet the demands of the academic calendar, administrative red tape, cost, and convenience. Such modifications may so distort the nature of a technique that it bears very little resemblance to the clinical procedure it was intended to represent.

Thus, the use of analogue designs introduces a dilemma for the psychotherapy researcher because it almost always involves a trade-off in research priorities. The gains in internal validity that analogues can provide must be balanced against the sacrifices in external validity that they often require. Researchers' enthusiasm for analogue research is often tempered by their recognition of this problem. The objection is not to analogy per se. It can always provide data on general behavior-change processes, whether they accurately represent clinical variables or not (Kiesler, 1971). The objection is to *rigorless* analogy which is accomplished merely by substituting the language of one domain for the terminology of another, rather than by the thoughtful "fine tuning" of experimental variables and the empirical assessment of only those dimensions that are likely to increase an experiment's generality.

Because of the potential usefulness of the analogue research approach, many researchers have attempted to modify and improve it. The suggested remedies for rigorless analogy have been numerous. One proposal is that, in small animal phobia studies, research subjects should include only those individuals whose fear is severe enough to disrupt their daily activities (Rosen, 1975). Another alternative involves selection of target problems that are more relevant to the overall functioning of the research participants (Borkovec, Stone, O'Brien, and Kaloupek, 1974). This recommendation has led to increased clinical analogue research with participants who suffer from interpersonal anxieties, sleep disturbances, and social unassertiveness.

As Paul (1969a) has pointed out, the "ultimate" outcome question ("What treatment, by whom, is most effective for this individual, with that specific problem, under which set of circumstances, and how does it come about?") cannot be answered in any single investigation. Therefore, the maximum benefit from any type of outcome evaluation, whether it be an uncontrolled case study, a factorial experiment in a clinical setting, or an experimental analogue, will be achieved by integrating individual investigations into a sequence or program of related studies. Paul (1969a) has noted that, as "the field of behavior modification enters the experimental era, all levels and approaches to the ultimate question may be expected to continue. It is to be hoped, however, that each approach will be seen in perspective, in its relationships both to other approaches and to the actual level of product obtained, so that future generations may view the field as a composition of 'artisans' or 'scientists,' rather than as cultists bound by historical inheritance" (p. 61).

Chapter 9

Clinical Intervention: Psychodynamic Models

During most of the twentieth century, efforts at relieving human suffering through psychological interventions have been based primarily upon the psychodynamic theories of Sigmund Freud. His *psychoanalysis,* which developed simultaneously as a method of treatment, a theory of personality, and a means of conducting observational research on human behavior, revolutionized the psychiatry of his time and altered forever the ways in which people think about themselves and their actions. Freud's voluminous writings also served to stimulate many of his followers (and their followers) to explore, extend, and revise his ideas. Today there is a broad spectrum of psychodynamically oriented theories which range from classical or "orthodox" psychoanalysis (which closely follows Freud's tenets) to systems which not only reject many of Freud's basic beliefs, but actually overlap with phenomenological or social-learning models (see Chapter 3). There is a corresponding array of psychodynamic clinical treatment approaches, and our aim in this chapter is to describe the background, techniques, and effectiveness of a few prominent examples. The logical point to begin our discussion is with Freud's own treatment methods.

PSYCHOANALYTIC TREATMENT

Most observers agree that Sigmund Freud was the founder of psychotherapy as we know it today. His one-to-one method of studying and helping people, his systematic search for relationships between a person's history and current problems, his emphasis on thoughts and emotions, and his focus on the therapist-patient relationship pervade nearly all modern clinical treatment modalities, regardless of their underlying theoretical models. But where did Freud's ideas come from?

It will not be possible here to provide anything resembling a complete account of Freud's life or the evolution of his thought, so a brief sketch will have to suffice. More complete coverage can be found in a highly readable presentation by Fancher (1973) as well as in many other sources (e.g., Ford & Urban, 1963; Munroe, 1955). Those seeking even more detailed material should consult Ernest Jones's monumental three-volume biography, *The Life and Work of Sigmund Freud* (1953, 1955, 1957), or translations of Freud's own works (e.g., Brill, 1938; Freud, 1953–64).

The Beginnings of Psychoanalytic Treatment

Freud was born in Freiberg, a town now in Czechoslovakia, on May 6, 1856, the son of a Jewish wool merchant. His family moved to Vienna, Austria, where, at the remarkably early age of 9, Freud entered Gymnasium, a sort of advanced high school. He was originally interested in a career in law or politics, but, just prior to graduation, an essay on nature by the poet Goethe prompted him to concentrate on natural science instead. Fancher (1973, p. 13) quotes a letter in which Freud describes the essay's effect: "The urge to understand something about the mysteries of the world and maybe contribute somewhat to their solution became overwhelming." Thus, in 1873, at the age of 17, Freud entered the University of Vienna medical school. He soon found that research interested him far more than routine coursework, and he spent most of his time working on several research projects in the university's Institute of Physiology. As a result, Freud did not complete his medical degree for 8 years.

His efforts during this period resulted in the discovery of the location of the sex organs in the male eel and in the accumulation of a great deal of new information about neurology. One of his projects showed that supposedly separate parts of a fish's nervous system were actually connected, a fact which would later be confirmed by the discovery of the neuron as the basic unit of nervous activity. More important than these studies themselves was Freud's introduction by several distinguished teachers to the then new concept of neurological *mechanism*. This view held that the activity of the nervous system in animals and humans was based on electrochemical factors which obeyed newly discovered laws of physics and chemistry. An implication of mechanistic theory was that, ideally, human behavior could be explained in *physical* terms and that lawful relationships existed both within people and between people and their environment. As we shall see, these notions had a profound effect upon Freud's later work.

While Freud possessed a brilliant scientific mind, a medical degree, and the most advanced orientation to neurology possible in his day, he had little else. He was unmarried and continued to live with his parents, who supported him

Figure 9-1 Sigmund Freud (1856–1939) *(Courtesy of Historical Pictures Service, Inc., Chicago, Illinois. Reprinted by permission.)*

financially because, in the 1880s, it was virtually impossible to make a living as a research scientist. This fact, coupled with the desire to marry his sweetheart, Martha Bernays, caused Freud to alter the course of his career in the direction of the more lucrative field of medical practice.

In 1882, Freud began 3 years of clinical training at Vienna General Hospital. You will recall that this was an era when the medical model of behavior disorder was resurgent and that there was diligent searching for the presumed organic causes underlying all mental illness. The director of the Vienna Hospital psychiatric clinic was Theodor Meynert, an eminent authority on brain anatomy and pathology whose work and theories greatly impressed Freud. Meynert believed, for example, that certain patterns of neural activity in the brain correspond to certain thoughts or memories or feelings, and thus that complex psychological phenomena are ultimately due to nerve cell activity which, in turn, is based on electrochemical factors.

Here, then, was a psychological extension of the mechanistic views Freud had absorbed while in medical school, and he realized that the best way to blend his research interests in neurology with his clinical work was to study and treat diseases of the nervous system in humans. By 1886, Freud had enough background (and money) to begin the independent private practice of medicine. He also got married in that year. One of the people who helped Freud begin his private practice was Joseph Breuer, a senior medical colleague and close friend. We shall soon see that Breuer's early attempts to work with and cure certain unusual symptoms in his patients helped lead Freud to the development of psychoanalysis.

Like other physicians of his time, Freud was often confronted with patients who showed symptoms of neurological damage or disease for which no organic cause could be found. Many of these cases displayed what Freud considered to be "neurological nonsense." For example, patients sometimes complained of impossible conditions, such as insensitivity or paralysis which affected their entire hand, but not their arm. Others suffered paralysis of the legs during the day, but walked in their sleep. Patients of this type were called *neurotics* and since the cause, let alone the cure, for their problems was so obscure, most well-heeled physicians ignored and even disparaged them, often assuming that neurotic symptoms were either phony or the result of basic character defects.

Freud could not afford to be so picky, and he often found himself dealing with the most common type of neurotic: those displaying *hysterical* (i.e., nonorganic) paralyses, amnesia, anesthesia, blindness, speech loss, and the like (see Ullmann & Krasner, 1975, for detailed coverage of hysterical behaviors). Standard treatment for hysteria at the time mainly involved the use of "wet packs" and baths (hydrotherapy) or electrically generated heat (electrotherapy), neither of which was particularly effective. In fact, Freud became convinced that whatever benefits patients received from these procedures were due to the effects of *suggestion*. Accordingly, he began to experiment with techniques which could maximize the benefits of suggestion, foremost among which was *hypnosis*.

It is important to realize that while, today, the study and use of hypnosis is quite respectable, in Freud's time it was generally regarded as a cheap magician's trick and far beneath the dignity of serious physicians and scientists. This view was prompted in part by the novelty and strangeness of hypnotic phenomena, but mainly by the obvious theatrics and bizarre theories of Anton Mesmer, the chief early promoter of hypnosis (see Ullmann & Krasner, 1975). Nevertheless, hypnosis was being studied seriously by a few courageous individuals, several of whom had attempted to use it to cure hysterical disorders.

Freud's familiarity with hypnosis began when, at the conclusion of his training at Vienna Hospital, he spent 6 months studying in Paris with Jean Charcot, director of the neurology clinic at the Salpêtrière asylum. Charcot showed that hysterical symptoms could be created and temporarily removed through induction of a hypnotic trance and thus that hysteria and hypnosis were related phenomena. In fact, Charcot believed that only hysterics could be hypnotized. Later, in the French city of Nancy, Freud visited a clinic organized by Ambrose-August Liebault and Hippolyte Bernheim. These two physicians believed that the ability to be hypnotized was not a symptom of nervous disorder, but a routine phenomenon attainable with normal individuals. Liebault and Bernheim used direct hypnotic suggestions to remove hysterical symptoms (e.g., "you will now be able to walk"), but with limited, often temporary success. Freud's use of hypnotic suggestion produced equally mediocre results, but around 1890 he began to combine hypnosis with a new technique he had learned from his colleague, Joseph Breuer.

This technique, called the *cathartic method,* had been stumbled upon by Breuer while attempting to relieve a wealthy young patient, "Anna O.," of an array of hysterical symptoms, including headaches, a severe cough, neck and arm paralyses, involuntary squinting, anesthesia in both elbows, and other problems. These difficulties began during her father's terminal illness and intensified following his death. She began to display extremes of mood which went from wild agitation, excitement, and even hallucinations during the day to calm, trancelike states in the evenings. Breuer was struck by the fact that these "trances" strongly resembled hypnosis. Fancher (1973, p. 48) describes what happened next:

> Breuer discovered that if Anna were permitted while in the hypnotic state to recite the contents of all her hallucinations from the day, then she invariably would leave the trance state and enjoy a period of almost normal tranquility and lucidity during the following late night hours. . . . Anna came to refer to the exercise of reciting her hallucinations as the "talking cure," or . . . "chimney sweeping."

This "talking cure" did not eliminate Anna's daytime disorders, however, and, to Breuer's dismay, new symptoms began to appear. It was in attempting to cure one of these, a sudden inability to drink liquids, that Breuer made the discovery which would later start Freud on the road to psychoanalysis:

> During one of Anna's hypnotic states . . . she began describing to Breuer an Englishwoman whom she knew but did not especially like. The woman had a dog that Anna particularly despised. Anna described how on one occasion she entered the woman's room and observed the dog drinking water from a glass. When the event occurred, Anna was filled with strong feelings of disgust and loathing, but out of politeness she was unable to express them. As she recited this account to Breuer, she for the first time permitted herself the luxury of expressing fully and animatedly her negative feelings about the dog's drinking. When she emerged from the trance she immediately asked for a glass of water, which she . . . drank without the slightest difficulty. (Fancher, 1973; p. 49)

Removal of Anna's fear of drinking was permanent and was apparently brought about by her vivid recollection of a forgotten event while in a trance. It occurred to Breuer that other hysterical symptoms might be caused by other forgotten memories and that their recall might be the key to curing them. He began hypnotizing Anna and asking her to remember everything she could about each of her symptoms. "To his immense gratification, he discovered that every symptom could be traced back to a traumatic or unpleasant situation for which all memory was completely absent in the waking state. Breuer found that whenever he could induce Anna to recall those unpleasant scenes and, more importantly, to *express the emotions* they had caused her to feel, the symptoms would disappear" (Fancher, 1973; pp. 49–50; italics added). For more details on the case of Anna O., see Breuer and Freud (1896, 1966).

Freud began using the cathartic method and had good success with it, but he found that there were serious drawbacks as well. For one thing, not all of his patients could be hypnotized. In addition, Freud found that recall of memories and expression of the emotions associated with them are most beneficial when the patient is able to remember what happened after hypnosis is removed. To make the treatment more widely applicable and to facilitate *conscious* recognition of early memories, Freud began to look for new, nonhypnotic means of helping patients locate the lost memories so important to the cure.

He first tried a "pressure technique" which he had seen Bernheim use at the Nancy clinic to help patients recall memories which had been artificially blotted out by hypnotic suggestion. As used by Bernheim, this technique simply involved pressing a hand against the patient's forehead and suggesting that she or he could remember. Freud's adaptation of this method consisted of having the patient relax with eyes closed and recite the memories which came to mind when he placed a hand on the patient's forehead. The recall process was often helped by having the patient lie on a couch, but Freud found that significant memories did not always appear immediately, no matter how strongly he suggested that they would. Often, however, the patient recalled an insignificant memory which brought others to mind in a sequence which ultimately led to the one apparently responsible for a symptom. Thus, Freud ultimately abandoned the laying on of hands and simply instructed his patients to continuously report whatever thoughts, feelings, or memories came to mind. This later became known as *free association,* a mainstay among the psychoanalytic techniques to be described later.[1]

Throughout most of the 1890s Freud's treatment of "neurotic" patients focused mainly upon helping them to consciously remember important, usually unpleasant, memories and emotions which they had repressed and which had been protected from recall by various *defense mechanisms* (see Chapter 3). He also spent a great deal of time on the construction of a model of nervous system functioning which could not only explain the development, maintenance, and cure of neurotic symptoms, but of normal, everyday behavior as well.

Freud called his work in this area the "Project for a Scientific Psychology." Its specific features are too numerous and complex to be described here, but they included postulation of nerve energy or excitation called "Q" which could "fill up" or *cathect* a given nerve cell and which could be discharged by that cell. Freud also suggested that there was a neural force he called "ego" which inhibited the discharge of various neurons. Where ego energy was strong, nervous activity was controlled and adjusted to the requirements of the external environment. Where ego energy was weak, neural discharge was less inhibited. Thus, controlled or impulsive behavior was determined by natural forces and factors in the person's nervous system.

The "project" clearly reflected Freud's neurological sophistication and objective, scientific outlook. He was a person who wanted to understand human behavior as a phenomenon which followed natural laws. Unfortunately, he was never able to construct his neurological model so that it could account for all aspects of neurosis. In particular, he was unable to find an adequate *neurological* reason why painful or traumatic events and memories should be automatically repressed by the nervous system. In 1896, Freud abandoned his efforts at explaining neurotic behavior on strictly neurological grounds and began to concentrate instead on *psychological* explanations.

This was brought about, in part, by logical and theoretical difficulties with his neuronal model, but also by a growing conviction that the causes of neurotic problems were more complex than he had initially supposed. He had originally found, for example, that many of his patients recalled early memories of sexual trauma, usually molestation by a parent or other close relative, and he assumed that such events were the basis for most hysterical symptoms. By the turn of the century, however, Freud was convinced that this "seduction theory" was too simpleminded and that there were other, more important causal factors to be considered. For one thing, he simply could not believe that the seduction and sexual abuse of children was as widespread as would be indicated by the high frequency of hysterics. Second, and more important, Freud had begun to pay attention to *dreams* (his patients' and his own) and had deduced on the basis of

---

[1]Incidentally, Freud may have hit upon this technique through a lost memory of his own. Fancher (1973) reports that, when Freud was a teen-ager, he read an essay by Ludwig Borne called "The Art of Becoming an Original Writer in Three Days." In that essay Borne suggested that the would-be writer should spend 3 days writing down everything that comes to mind "without any falsification or hypocrisy" and that amazingly new and surprising thoughts would appear.

his neurological model that they represent the fulfillment of *wishes*. He found that many of these wishes or fantasies are socially unacceptable and thus appear only when defenses are somewhat relaxed during sleep, and even then only in disguised form.

In an intellectual leap which in many ways changed the world, Freud then suggested that, like dreams, hysterical symptoms can be based upon unconscious wishes and fantasies, not just on memories of actual events. Thus, a patient's "memory" of childhood seduction by a parent might actually be a *fantasy* or *wish* about such an encounter.

The implications of this new theory were staggering and ultimately led Freud to develop his most controversial concepts: infantile sexuality, the Oedipus/Electra conflict, and the instinctual basis of human behavior. It altered his approach to therapy as well. Psychoanalytic treatment of neurosis shifted from the recovery of memories to the illumination of unconscious wishes.

The Goals of Psychoanalytic Treatment

Generally speaking, the goal of classical psychoanalytic therapy is to help the patient learn to think and behave in more adaptive ways by understanding himself or herself better. In theory, when a patient understands the real, often unconscious reasons *why* she or he feels and acts in maladaptive ways and sees that those reasons are no longer valid, she or he will not have to continue behaving in those ways. The analogy comes to mind of the Japanese soldier left on a remote Pacific Island during World War II with orders never to surrender. Decades after the war ends, the soldier is still in hiding, holding out against an enemy which no longer exists, except in his own mind. When someone finally finds him and he understands that things have changed and his original orders no longer apply, he can stop acting like a hunted animal and start living productively in the larger world.

In psychoanalytic treatment, it is not enough for the therapist to say "the war is over" by simply describing the unconscious material that he or she thinks may be at the root of the patient's problems. The patient must make these discoveries for herself or himself with help and guidance from the therapist. This process of self-understanding ideally includes *intellectual* recognition of one's innermost wishes and conflicts, *emotional* involvement in discoveries about oneself, and the *systematic tracing* of the manner in which unconscious factors have determined past and present behaviors and affected relations with other people.

Thus, the main goals of psychoanalytic treatment are (1) intellectual and emotional *insight* into the underlying causes of the patient's behavior and behavior problems and (2) *working through* or fully exploring the implications of those insights.

One of the more popular myths about psychoanalysis is that insight about one's entire life comes in a single, sudden flash, accompanied by the explosive release (or "abreaction") of all pent-up emotional energy from the past and followed by the total and permanent disappearance of the patient's problems.

There is not much truth in this image. Although Freud's patients were often relieved of a symptom following recovery of specific repressed memories, he came to believe that the removal of a symptom (no matter how dramatically it occurs) was usually only a part of therapy and that if more important unconscious material were not unearthed, new symptoms would appear.[2] Thus, "making the unconscious conscious" (Freud, 1914) is a gradual process which takes place over many analytic sessions, some of which are more emotional than others. This continuous effort at self-exploration is often slowed by dead ends, false leads, and a variety of psychological defenses thrown up by the patient to prevent conscious awareness of long-hidden truths.

Even after these truths are revealed, the therapist still has to promote the *working through* of insights and the defenses which kept them from consciousness for so long. The idea here is for the patient to recognize how pervasive the unconscious problems, conflicts, and defenses are so that he or she can learn to recognize the signs of their presence and prevent their full return. It would do little good, for example, for a patient to recognize that she has had unconscious feelings of anger toward her mother in the past if she does not also see that she deals with women in the present *as if* they were her mother and that her problems in relation to these women are actually based on unconscious hostility and/or attempts to defend against it. In simpler terms, insight provides the outline of a patient's story; working through fills in the details.

Reaching the rather ambitious goals set by classical psychoanalysis, which often involve no less than the minute "dissection" and gradual reconstruction of the patient's personality, requires a lot of time (three to five sessions each week for 2 to 15 years), a lot of money (fees can run as high as $100 per hour), and a great deal of therapist skill in creating the circumstances for progress and in nurturing that progress as it occurs. The ways in which the therapist works at this formidable task are described in the next section.

PSYCHOANALYTIC TREATMENT TECHNIQUES

One of the fundamental assumptions of psychoanalytic theory is that the patient's most important fantasies, feelings, and conflicts are unconscious and protected by psychological defenses. No matter how hard the patient tries, therefore, it is unlikely that the patient alone can penetrate the depths which he or she has avoided for so long. This is where the therapist comes in. She or he must create an atmosphere in which the patient can engage in real self-exploration; she or he must show the patient how and where to look for important material and must help the patient integrate and make sense out of the things which emerge.

The specific ways in which all this is done will be somewhat different for each analyst and for each patient, but there are a few techniques and strategies

[2]This "symptom substitution" theory has been repeatedly cited by dynamically oriented therapists in their critiques of "symptom treatment" through social-learning approaches (e.g., Breger & McGaugh, 1965).

which usually occur. We shall be discussing each of these separately, but it is important to keep in mind that, in practice, they are interwoven in a multitude of combinations rather than "done" in a certain order.

Free Association

This is one of the most basic techniques developed by Freud to help unearth unconscious material. As noted earlier, free association evolved as part of the search for a nonhypnotic way to recover past memories, and it involves asking the patient to follow a single "fundamental rule": to say everything which comes to mind without editing or censorship.

> The patient is requested to report everything that occurs to him in the analytic session. He is asked to verbalize everything that occurs to him in the original sequence and form without any modification or omission. He is asked to assume a passive attitude toward his train of thought; in other words, to eliminate all conscious control over his mental processes to which he gives free rein. . . . (Alexander, 1937; pp. 40–41)

The rationale for free association is that, by removing the constraints of logic, social amenities, and other rules, unconscious material will begin to surface.

The most common, though not universal, approach is to have the patient free associate while lying on a couch. The analyst sits out of the patient's view in order to avoid interfering in any way with the associative process. In early analytic sessions the therapist may have to give some instructions (e.g., "just say whatever occurs to you regardless of how important or unimportant it may seem"), but later the patient becomes familiar enough with the role to begin free associating without a prompt. Sometimes relevant material appears fairly directly:

Patient: God, It's been a long day. I haven't had to work this hard since I was in high school. Back then I used to work part-time on my uncle's farm and part-time in a drugstore. The farm work was really hard. Sometimes when it was hot, I thought I was going to die out in those fields. It was a lot nicer when I visited the farm as a small child. Dad and Mom used to take me and my sister to the farm on weekends and us kids would play all day. We used to go in the barn a lot and it seems like we played some secret game or something (pause). Now I remember! We played doctor and my sister and my two cousins and I would take turns being the doctor and examining each other's genitals. We knew we weren't supposed to do it though and I remember being scared to death that we'd get caught. . . .

Recall of this sort is often accompanied by emotions appropriate to the original event. The patient quoted above may have blushed or experienced anxiety while recounting the incident.

Because of the operation of defenses, the unconscious bases for the patient's current problems are seldom automatically and clearly revealed in memories, feelings, and wishes. Much more often, free association merely gives glimpses of and clues to the underlying causes of distress. It is the therapist's task to try to make sense of the bits and pieces which emerge. *Patterns of association* are often important. Consider the following excerpt from the free association of a middle-aged male:

Patient: My dad called long-distance last night. It was nice to hear from him, but I can never quite feel comfortable when we talk. Once we get through the usual "hello and how are you" part, there just doesn't seem to be anything to say. (long silence) I almost fell asleep there for a minute. I used to do that a lot in college. I must have slept through half my classes. Once I woke up and saw the professor standing over me, shaking me, and the whole class was laughing.

The fact that thoughts about father led to memories about a threatening authority figure could have significance, especially if this pattern is repeated in other sessions. It could mean that the patient still has unresolved feelings of fear and hatred in relation to his father, feelings which will need to be clarified, recognized, and dealt with.

Much of what the patient says during free association is defensive in nature. The patient whose mind "goes blank" or who comes up with only trivial details of the day or who obviously edits what is said is seen as throwing up barriers to self-exploration. The following excerpt from an analytic-style session with "S" (Murray, 1938, quoted in White & Watt, 1973; pp. 257–258) provides an excellent example of patient defenses (the analyst is denoted as "E"):

S: The thing uppermost in my mind at present is the hour exam I just had. Rather easy exam. I wasn't feeling particularly brilliant this morning. I don't know whether I made any mistakes or not. Quite a bit hinges on this exam

Figure 9-2 The classical psychoanalytic therapy situation *(From* Psychology and Life, *7th Edition by Floyd L. Ruch. Copyright © 1963, 1967 by Scott, Foresman and Company. Reprinted by permission.)*

because I want to get a scholarship for the second semester. If I get it, I will be able to carry through my work to my Master's degree. If I don't, I don't believe I'll be able to make it. It's hard to borrow money these days. I would like to keep on at college though because with the kind of work I get here I will get the kind of job I want. I am particularly interested in research work and this course that I am taking fits me for that.

E: I am afraid you are telling me a story rather than telling me what is coming into your mind. (After the first few sentences S has been giving a reasoned statement of his financial position. This is contrary to instruction and hence constitutes the first manifestation of resistance.)

S: I have an experiment this afternoon and I'm darned if I know what it is about. (This remark may contain a double meaning: S is wondering what the present session is about, as well as the afternoon's experiment. But he has abandoned his first form of resistance, the next topic being a good example of free associations.)

S: I wonder how my Dad is getting along. He is on his last legs, so to speak. Dad and I never got along very well. I remember one time when I was a youngster I was supposed to be watching some cows that were grazing near an orchard. I got so interested in reading that I forgot about the cows and they entered the orchard and ate some of the fruit off the trees. Dad was angry as the devil. He came around the corner and made a bee-line for me and I ran and he, being the old backwoods type, took a healthy swing at me with his foot as I went by and he slipped and nearly broke his arm on the wet grass. (At this point S turned around on the couch to look at E.)

E: What did you think when you turned around?

S: The reason I turned around was to look directly at you.

E: Why did you want to look directly at me?

S: If you are trying to put over a point and look directly at the person it is generally better. In sales work, for instance . . . (Again S has departed completely from free association to the idea of making a point and selling an argument. This is another form of resistance, similar to the first. At the same time he has dramatized his feeling toward E. Doubtless annoyed because E corrected him on account of his first lapse from the fundamental rule, he thinks of an earlier incident in which he lapsed from duty but eluded his father's wrath, and indeed turned the tables by being the cause of his father's hurting himself. This line of thought, however, awakens so much anxiety that he has to turn around to make sure that E is not getting angry. At this point E agains reminds S of the fundamental rule.)

S: (Long pause.) I am to report what comes into my mind and nothing seems to come in. I don't care much for your paintings that you have, or whatever they are.

E: What don't you like about them?

S: I have disagreeable memories of paintings of that type. The framed diploma is a plain-looking thing to have on the wall. Is that yours, by the way?

E: Tell me what comes into your mind about it.

S: I thought it might be yours, but when I look at the inscription, it says "M.D.," so I guess that can't be yours. (For a moment S appears to free associate, but he has chosen another method of resistance, that of describing objects in the room. Almost at once his feelings betray themselves: he criticizes the objects, and leads up to a very neat indirect way of saying to E, "You are no doctor.")

It is important to remember that, according to analytic theory, the therapist will initially be faced with resistance and many other forms of defense in free associative material. These defenses must be recognized by the analyst and made clear to the patient in the process of continued analytic probing (we shall return to this point later).

The Use of Dreams

Because they are viewed as the expression of wishes and fantasies usually kept from consciousness, dreams play an important role in psychoanalysis. At one time, Freud went so far as to call them "the royal road to the unconscious." However, there is a difficulty faced by the analyst in using dream material: While the patient's defenses are *relatively* relaxed during sleep, they are not totally absent, and a certain amount of distortion and defense is still operative. Therefore, dreams are usually thought to express unconscious wishes in versions that are sufficiently well disguised to avoid traumatizing (and waking) the sleeper. Nevertheless, because the unconscious material is believed to be closer to the surface in dreams than during waking hours, great importance is attached to them in psychoanalysis. An entire session or series of sessions may be consumed in recounting and discussing a single dream.

The patient's description of a dream reveals its *manifest content* or obvious features. If a person dreams that he or she is running through the woods and suddenly falls into a pool of cold macaroni salad, this story is the manifest content. Manifest content often contains relatively unimportant features and events associated with the dreamer's activities that day (this is called "day residue") or may merely supply convenient ways of satisfying temporary wishes without the dreamer having to waken. A hungry person may dream of food, for example.

For psychoanalytic purposes, however, the most interesting aspect of dreams is their *latent content:* the unconscious ideas, wishes, and impulses which appear in the form of a safe *compromise* between total repression and full expression. The process of transforming unacceptable material into more acceptable manifest content is called *dream work*. The many forms which dream work may take have been the subject of extensive psychoanalytic writing, beginning with Freud's own *Interpretation of Dreams* (1900). By way of summary, analytic theory and clinical experience suggest that dream work involves *displacement, condensation, alogic, dramatization, substitution, devaluation,* and *symbolization* (Fancher, 1973; Munroe, 1955).

Most aspects of manifest dream content are viewed as *symbols*, or representatives of something else. In spite of the popular belief that certain dream content (e.g., a snake) *always* "means" something specific (e.g., a penis), Freud did not believe that dreams could be understood in this inflexible fashion (he is said to have pointed out that "sometimes a cigar is just a cigar"). Most analysts do assume, however, that manifest content has *some* symbolic significance, the specifics of which may differ for each person or even from dream to dream.

For example, a very meaningful unconscious impulse (such as the desire to have extramarital sex) might be *displaced* to a position of minor importance in the dream (a massage parlor or body-building advertisement glimpsed from a moving car). In some cases, an apparently innocuous dream event (such as one's brother leaving for a vacation) may be seen as a *substitute* for taboo wishes (e.g., the brother's death). Dream work may also *devalue* significant material. Munroe (1955) tells of a prudish woman who often dreamed of being only partly clothed or even naked in public without feeling at all embarrassed. Presumably, she defended against unconscious sexual wishes by making them seem unimportant.

A great deal of potentially valuable unconscious material may be expressed by dreams in greatly *condensed* form. Again, Munroe (1955) provides an excellent example in a dream in which the patient reports: "I am afraid of the dog." To the analyst, this may mean (1) the patient is afraid of God (which is "dog" spelled backwards), (2) the patient seeks to hide his fear, even from himself, and (3) by equating God with a dog, the patient expresses contempt for a Supreme Being. Similar "shortcuts" also appear in dreams as *alogical* sequences (e.g., when there is a sudden shift of time or place) or as *dramatizations:* Two people fighting may represent conflicting tendencies within the dreamer.

In addition to dream work, *waking* defense mechanisms may operate to hamper the analyst's attempts to get at latent content. Usually, the patient is asked to describe the dream as accurately and completely as possible, but the report may be unconsciously edited and organized more logically than was the case in the dream itself. This Freud called *secondary revision.*

To help identify those aspects of a dream which have the greatest unconscious significance (and thus the greatest need for defense), some analysts ask their patients to repeat a dream two or more times. Later versions will almost always differ from the initial story, and it is assumed that the changes, omissions, and additions which occur reflect unconscious efforts to better disguise or defend highly charged material.

A more common procedure is to ask the patient to free associate to certain features of manifest content. In the process, unconscious material may be revealed. Consider this dream reported to Dr. Robert Lindner by a female patient whose father and mother (who was confined to a wheelchair by paralysis) had a violently unhappy marriage:

> I was in what appeared to be a ballroom or dance hall, but I knew it was really a hospital. A man came up to me and told me to undress, take all my clothes off. He was going to give me a gynecological examination. I did as I was told but I was very

frightened. While I was undressing, I noticed that he was doing something to a woman at the other end of the room. She was sitting or lying in a funny kind of contraption with all kinds of levers and gears and pulleys attached to it. I knew that I was supposed to be next, that I would have to sit in that thing while he examined me. Suddenly he called my name and I found myself running to him. The chair or table—whatever it was—was now empty, and he told me to get on it. I refused and began to cry. It started to rain—great big drops of rain. He pushed me to the floor and spread my legs for examination. I turned over on my stomach and began to scream. I woke myself up screaming. (Lindner, 1954; pp. 134–135)

Lindner describes how this manifest content is used as raw material for free association:

"Well," she said after a brief, expectant silence, "what does it mean?"

"Laura," I admonished, "you know better than that. Associate and we'll find out."

"The first thing I think of is Ben," she began. "He's an intern at University, you know. I guess that's the doctor in the dream—or maybe it was you. Anyhow, whoever it was, I wouldn't let him examine me."

"Why not?"

"I've always been afraid of doctors . . . afraid they might hurt me."

"How will they hurt you?"

"I don't know. By jabbing me with a needle, I guess. That's funny, never thought of it before. When I go to the dentist I don't mind getting a needle; but with a doctor it's different. . . . I shudder when I think of having my veins punctured. I'm always afraid that's what the doctor will do to me."

"Has it ever been done?"

She nodded. "Once, in college, for a blood test. I passed out cold."

"What about gynecological examinations?"

"I've never had one. I can't bear to think of someone poking around inside me." Again silence; then, "Oh," she said, "I see it now. It's sex. I'm afraid the doctor in the dream *is* Ben. He wants me to have intercourse, but it scares me and I turn away from him." (Lindner, 1954; p. 135)

This "insight" seems to have come too easily and was too obvious. The analyst feels sure there is more to it.

". . . Other men have made love to you."

"Yes," she said, sobbing now, "but I only let them as a last resort, as a way of holding on to them a little longer. . . . I'd do anything to keep them from getting inside me—poking into me . . . like the needle, I guess."

"But why, Laura?"

"I don't know," she cried, "I don't know. Tell me."

"I think the dream tells you," I said.

"The dream I just told you?"

"Yes. . . . There's a part of it you haven't considered. What comes to your mind when you think of the other woman in your dream, the woman the doctor was examining before you?"

"The contraption she was sitting in," Laura exclaimed. "It was like a—like a wheel chair—my mother's wheel chair—my mother's wheel chair! Is that right?"

"Very likely," I said.

"But why would he be examining *her?* What would that mean?"

"Well, think of what that kind of examination signifies for you."

"Sex," she said. "Intercourse—that's what it means. So that's what it is—that's what it means! Intercourse put my mother in the wheel chair. It paralyzed her. And I'm afraid that's what it will do to me. So I avoid it—because I'm scared it will do the same thing to me. . . . Where did I ever get such a crazy idea?" (Lindner, 1954; p. 136–137)

Notice how free association to dream content led the patient to an insight which will provoke further exploration of her past and of unconscious material not yet revealed.

Certain dreams are thought to have particularly important latent content. It has even been suggested that the *first* dream reported to the analyst may contain a capsule summary of all major problems (Blanck, 1976). More frequently, however, a *series* of dreams is used in the process of analysis. Attention to multiple dreams often reveals established *patterns* of latent content and helps to avoid errors which can occur when too much emphasis is placed upon a single dream. Hall (1953) provides an excellent example of this process in his analysis of several dreams reported by an 18-year-old male patient.

Another point to keep in mind about the use of dreams in psychoanalysis is that they provide ideas, clues, and hypotheses for further probing far more often than they provide "final answers." The caution with which one must approach analysis of even "obvious" dream content, symbols, and associations is clearly spelled out by Bonime (1962):

> If a woman were dreaming of a snake which associatively became established as a penis, it would still be necessary, if one is to achieve insight into her personality through her dream symbol, to establish the quality of experience with a penis which was symbolized by that snake. If she were a professional dancer largely preoccupied by a desire to be seductive, and if she had performed the dance of a snake charmer, then the penile snake could symbolize her desire to charm men or control them by her sexual allure. . . .
>
> If a woman had been made pregnant before a promised marriage by a man who later deserted her, the penile snake in her dream might represent the quality of deceit or poisonousness, or both, not only in men but also in any human being who offered intimacy. If she had had a puritanical upbringing and yet indulged in a sexual affair, the penile snake might represent hidden "sinful" desires or actual secret activities of a sexual nature. . . . By still further extension, the snake could refer . . . to yearnings for other types of self-indulgence [or] self-gratification. . . . (p. 36)

Attention to "Everyday Behavior"

One of Freud's primary concepts was that of *psychic determinism* (see Chapter 3), the notion that most, if not all, human behavior is related to or caused by conscious *and* unconscious mental processes. An obvious consequence of this view, spelled out in his *Psychopathology of Everyday Life* (1901, 1914), is that, like neurotic symptoms, much of our day-to-day behavior is in some way reflective of unconscious wishes, fantasies, impulses, and defenses.

Accordingly, the psychoanalyst strives to be consistently sensitive to all of a patient's verbal and nonverbal behavior appearing in treatment sessions or in accounts of intersession activities. This means maintaining an "evenly divided" or "free-floating" attention to trivial as well as momentous events, to purposeful acts and accidental happenings, to body language as well as spoken language. Any or all of these may help expose habitual psychological defense tactics and the secrets they are assumed to protect. Psychoanalytic theory has generated numerous examples of potentially meaningful everyday behaviors. Two of the better-known categories, *mistakes* and *humor,* are discussed below.

Mistakes   In the midst of the Watergate cover-up, former President Nixon made the following statement in a speech to Congress: ". . . join me in mounting a new effort to replace the discredited president. . . ." He actually meant to say ". . . to replace the discredited present welfare system. . . ," but other possibilities on his mind may have been revealed in this slip of the tongue. Such "Freudian slips," or *parapraxes,* are thought to be quite obvious indicators of the speaker's actual, often unconscious feelings (former Texas Governor John Connally once said that he hoped then Vice-President Agnew ". . . would be exonerated and found guilty . . ."). Equally blatant "slips of the pen" may also reflect indirectly expressed feelings: "Dear Madeline: Your party was just divine. Thanks so much for inviting us. We can wait to see you again. . . ."

Such "easy to interpret" parapraxes are common in everyday life and, while the analyst may use them to help the patient's self-exploration, he or she also focuses upon errors which are more subtle, often apparently meaningless, and thus presumably reflective of carefully protected unconscious material which has temporarily slipped out. Brenner (1974) mentions a case in which a young male patient who was interested in body building referred to "physical culture" as "physible culture." This "accidental" mistake had no immediate meaning for either patient or therapist, but, following psychoanalytic method, the patient was asked to free associate to the word "physible." His first association was the word "visible" and from there he continued until an unconscious wish to exhibit his nude body (and to see others naked) was revealed.

Many other simple, everyday mistakes may also take on psychoanalytic importance. The failure of a writer to detect an embarrassing or unkind slip of the pen during proofreading could be seen as a further expression of unconscious wishes. Other "accidental" events, especially those in which the patient has at least partial responsibility, may also be seen as wishful. The waiter who spills hot soup on an elderly male customer or the woman who inadvertently incinerates some of her husband's important paperwork might be asked in analysis to free associate to various elements in these "accidents." The result might be an inference that the waiter was actually attempting to execute a father substitute

Box 9-1 Freud's Analysis of a Slip of the Tongue

In his *Psychopathology of Everyday Life*, Freud (1901) describes his analysis of a slip of the tongue made by a young male acquaintance. It reveals how, according to psychoanalytic theory, significant material emerges in extremely subtle ways.

In the course of his conversation with Freud, the young man quotes in Latin Virgil's *Aeneid:* "Exoriare aliquis nostris ex ossibus ultor" ("Let someone arise from my bones as an avenger"). In doing so, he left out "aliquis" ("someone"). To help the man find the meaning of this error, Freud asked him to free associate to "aliquis."

The associations included dividing the word into "a" and "liquous" as well as other words like "reliquien" (meaning "relics"), "liquefying," "fluidity," and "fluid." He then thought of the relics of Simon of Trent which he had seen two years earlier, then of blood sacrifices, then of a newspaper article called "What St. Augustine Says about Women." Later, he thought of St. Januaris and the miracle of his blood (which is supposed to liquefy on a certain holy day each year) and the fact that the miracle was once delayed.

The young man then became disturbed and he stopped associating. Freud asked what was wrong and was told that the new association was too intimate to reveal and involved a young lady from whom he was expecting some news. At this point, Freud said that the news involved the possibility that the woman was pregnant.

The man's astonishment at having his secret (which was far more shocking in 1900 than it is now) uncovered was relieved somewhat as Freud explained his method. The references in free association to liquid, blood, calendar saints, regularly occurring miracles of flowing blood, concern over a delay in the miracle, and the like all led Freud to see the man's conscious and unconscious preoccupation with menstruation and possible pregnancy.

and that the wife was expressing strong feelings of competitiveness toward her husband.

Forgetfulness is another prime example of presumably motivated error. Here, we are not talking about cases in which a person purposely "forgets" something (e.g., a dental appointment), but about instances in which a memory lapse occurs without obvious cause. If a patient forgets the manifest content of the dream she or he had planned to describe, the analyst may suspect that the dream contained material too threatening to remember under the scrutiny of analysis. Sometimes a patient achieves an important insight into an unconscious wish and suddenly forgets what it was, apparently as a defense against acknowledging unflattering personal characteristics.

Often, a loss of memory outside the treatment session is discussed in subsequent analysis. Brenner (1974) tells of a patient who inexplicably forgot the name of a familiar friend at a party. As the patient free associated to this event, it was construed to have important unconscious meaning:

As he talked about it, it developed that the name of the acquaintance was the same as that of another man whom he knew and toward whom he had strong feelings of hatred which made him feel very guilty. . . . In addition he mentioned that the acquaintance was crippled, which reminded him of some of his wishes to hurt and injure the namesake whom he hated. . . . In order to avoid becoming conscious of his destructive fantasies . . . he repressed the name which would have made the connection between the two. (p. 130)

The complexity of unconscious processes that may be extracted from apparently routine mistakes is revealed in the following example:

> A patient, while driving her husband's car, stopped so suddenly in traffic that the car behind her crumpled one of the rear fenders. . . . The analysis of this mishap revealed a complicated set of unconscious motives. . . . For one thing, the patient was unconsciously very angry at her husband. . . . Smashing up his car was an unconscious expression of this anger, which she was unable to display openly and directly against him. For another thing, she felt very guilty as a result of what she unconsciously wanted to do to her husband . . . and damaging his car was an excellent way to get him to punish her. . . . For a third thing, the patient had strong sexual desires which her husband was unable to satisfy and which she herself had strongly repressed. These unconscious sexual wishes were symbolically gratified by having a man "bang into my tail," as she put it. (Brenner, 1974; p. 139)

It is often pointed out that psychoanalytic theory seems to leave no room for real accidents or innocent mistakes. This is not strictly true. Events over which a person has no control (e.g., being injured when a plane crashes through one's roof) are seen as genuine accidents, but if the victim can be seen as in any way responsible for the mishap, there is a potential for unconscious significance. The authors know of a woman who returned from the grocery store on a snowy winter day and, in the process of carrying several heavy bags of groceries into the house, fell on the ice and broke her leg. Upon hearing the commotion, her psychiatrist husband ran outside, saw her writhing in pain on the ground and shouted, "Why did you do this to me?" Using analytic logic, the husband presumed that, though the fall was probably due to snow and ice, his wife's failure to ask for help or to carry only one bag at a time had expressed an unconscious desire to get more loving care and attention from him or to punish him by adding the nursing of an invalid to his daily responsibilities.

Thus, the suggestion that accidents and errors in speech, writing, or memory may be due simply to fatigue, impatience, the pressure of time, or other mundane factors is countered by the analytic view that such external factors merely *facilitate* an accident or error; its particular form is determined by unconscious processes.

Humor   Jokes and witticisms are everywhere, and though at first glance they hardly seem the stuff of which psychoanalytic hay is made, Freud noted that humor usually contains either overt or covert expressions of *hostility* or *aggression*. The transformation of angry feelings into humor is called *wit work* and is closely analogous to the *dream work* discussed earlier. Thus, displacement, condensation, and other processes can easily be seen in certain jokes. Puns are particularly good examples of *condensation* in which at least two meanings are conveyed by a single word: "The elephant circumcisor told me his job had good and bad points. The pay is lousy but the tips are big." Here, in addition to condensation in the word "tips," there may be some *displacement* of aggression toward whoever or whatever might be symbolized by the elephant.

Indeed, when one considers how many jokes and stories (not to mention Don Rickles' entire repertoire) present situations in which a person or group is made to look foolish, is injured or killed, or in some other way gets the short end of the stick, it is easy to see how Freud reached his conclusions. More interesting perhaps is the fact that, although in theory there are jokes which are "harmless," Freud was hard put to give a single good example.

According to psychoanalytic theory, jokes provide a safe outlet for anger and hostility which, if expressed directly, might bring angry retaliation or at least unacceptable feelings of guilt. Because the joke disguises at least part of the aggressive impulse, a certain amount of psychic energy which would have otherwise been used in continued repression of that impulse becomes unnecessary and is released in the form of laughter. Thus, the jokes a person makes or those she or he finds funny may be examined by the analyst in helping that person toward self-understanding. The details of Freud's theory of humor are covered in his *Jokes and Their Relation to the Unconscious* (1905) and in Grotjahn (1957).

Analysis of Resistance

As noted earlier, the psychoanalyst assumes that the patient will display various forms of *resistance* in the course of any attempt to expose threatening unconscious material. We have already seen some examples of resistance in the context of free association and dream analysis, but there are many other forms as well. All of them are considered important because (1) they help highlight the topics, areas, events, and time periods about which the patient is most defensive (and thus which require the most intense exploration), and (2) they provide current examples of habitual defenses which, with the analyst's help, the patient can gradually learn to recognize and ultimately abandon. Because real progress can only be made in the absence of resistance, psychoanalysis is fundamentally involved with removing it.

The ways in which resistance can appear to the psychoanalyst are too numerous to catalog here. We shall give just a few examples in order to illustrate the range of possibilities (see Fine, 1971, especially Chapters 8, 9, and 10 for more detailed coverage).

Fairly obvious resistance to the whole psychoanalytic enterprise (or particular phases of it) is often inferred from a patient's repeated absence from or lateness for treatment sessions. Unwillingness to speak about certain topics,[3] refusal to lie on the traditional couch, regularly falling asleep, or failure to pay the therapist's bill are often interpreted in the same way.

Other manifestations of resistance may be more subtle. The appearance of depression or the expression of hopelessness when a major breakthrough is about to occur is sometimes viewed as the patient's way of delaying painful insights. "At the point where feelings of hopelessness arise, many therapists are

---

[3]Or refusal to speak at all. There is a case on record of a patient who said nothing in therapy for two years! (Fine, 1971).

tempted to switch to some other technique, convinced that the standard analytic approach has failed. This is precisely what the patient is trying to get them to do. . . . His hopelessness has a manipulative purpose, to drive other people away, and allow him to wallow in his misery" (Fine, 1971; pp. 123–124). Thus, when, to an outside observer, the patient appears to be expressing despair over inadequate progress after months or years of analysis, he or she may be seen by the therapist as actually fighting *against* progress and change.

A similar interpretation may be made in the face of other patient behaviors. A common example is a pattern called *intellectualization*. Here, important emotions are seen as repressed, but the patient does not appear overtly uncooperative. Instead, she or he simply substitutes logic and reason for the feelings which are so valued in analysis. Thus, in discussing a parent's death, the patient might very calmly say something like "well yes, I was sad, but actually we had all been expecting this to happen so there was no shock. Besides, I was responsible for making all the arrangements and that really took up all my energy." Other patients avoid dealing directly with their own problems by insisting on an estimate of how long treatment will take or by attempting to engage the analyst in conversations or debates about the effectiveness of various therapeutic techniques, the relative merits of differing theories of behavior disorder, or other esoteric topics.

Less cerebral resistance tactics have also been identified by psychoanalysts. For example, when threatened by analytic probing, some patients may develop various physical symptoms for which there is no organic cause. A chronic cough, blurred vision, a lingering cold, a sudden speech impediment or other hysteria-like problems may make conversation and other work during analytic sessions impossible or may even prevent sessions from taking place. On occasion, these symptoms (such as failure to eat) can even be life-threatening. Resistance is also suspected by analysts when other, related behavior patterns appear. *Regression,* in which the patient "goes backward" in development by, say, remaining in bed, abandoning grooming and toileting habits, crying, and requiring constant care, may be viewed as a severe and potentially permanent obstacle to analysis.

Other behaviors (often called "acting out") are also seen as resistant. The initiation of or return to alcohol or drug abuse, participation in particularly dangerous recreational activities, or some other fairly dramatic life change may be construed as the patient's way of escaping the anxiety brought about by the possible uncovering of repressed material. Dangerous as these last few tactics are for the patient, acting out can sometimes be hazardous to the therapist as well. Analytic patients have, on rare occasions, attempted to injure or kill their therapists, presumably as part of a desperate attempt to avoid recognizing the truth about themselves. In a few tragic cases, these extreme measures have proven disastrous or fatal to the analyst.

The final form of resistance to be discussed here is probably the most difficult for nonanalytically oriented observers to recognize or accept. We refer here to cases in which the patient feels (1) that external rather than intrapsychic factors are primarily responsible for problems, (2) that problems are getting worse, or (3) that he or she has a right as a consumer to be given evidence of the value of the psychoanalytic approach. In each instance, the patient makes a reasonable statement or request, but, to the therapist, it is seen as diverting attention from the intrapsychic dynamics presumed to underlie all behavior problems. It should be understood, therefore, that if the analyst focuses attention on *why* the patient wants to know about the value of analysis or the reason for slow progress instead of giving a straightforward answer, the goal is not necessarily to evade the issue, but to follow psychoanalytic principles. Those principles dictate that any patient behavior that interferes with the analytic process should be dealt with as a defense so that, ultimately, the unconscious material which is believed to *truly* underlie the patient's problems can be made conscious.

Analysis of the Transference

It was noted in Chapter 8 that, in all forms of therapy, a *relationship* of some kind develops between therapist and client. In psychoanalysis, this relationship is not only an essential working context but also an important source of raw material for probing the unconscious and its defenses. The patient's feelings toward and relationship with the therapist are called the *transference*.[4] It is thought to develop on at least two levels. The first involves fairly obvious, realistic, mostly conscious feelings, as when the patient expresses gratitude for the therapist's help or respect for her or his erudition. At this level, there is a *therapeutic alliance* (Zetzel, 1956) which facilitates the treatment process.

At another, mostly unconscious level, however, the transference relationship is thought to contain attitudes and reactions which are directly related to the patient's unconscious intrapsychic conflicts, many of which go back to early childhood and lie at the root of current symptoms. Thus, the patient may have reactions to or feelings for (and against) the analyst which are determined not by the therapist's actual characteristics or behavior, but by the ways in which the patient related to significant people in the past.

This assumption is based upon Freud's belief that time does not exist in the unconscious. The earliest unconscious conflicts will always be active (unless made conscious and worked through) no matter how much time goes by and will make their presence known in many problematic ways, including disrupted interpersonal relationships.

Theoretically, at least, unconscious factors may color the patient's interactions with anyone who evokes childhood conflicts, but the therapist appears to be an especially likely candidate. There are several reasons for this. For one thing, the analyst is in a position of high status and power in relation to the patient who comes for help in time of trouble. This identifies the therapist as an *authority* and immediately brings to mind images of a parental figure. These images are intensified by the fact that the therapist usually conveys a *caring*

[4]The therapist's feelings about the patient are referred to as *countertransference*.

attitude. The analyst is there to help, no matter what the patient's problems may be. It is easy for the patient to associate this attitude with the actual or wished-for attributes of her or his parents. In addition to all this, the therapist tries to be nonjudgmental and to accept with equanimity whatever the patient reveals about himself or herself. This tends to foster feelings of trust and confidence which are, again, reminiscent of real or fantasized attitudes toward parents or other valued persons from the past. Finally, because the analyst traditionally maintains an "analytic incognito" by revealing little or nothing about herself or himself, the analyst becomes a sort of blank screen (not unlike the blank card on the TAT) on to which the patient is free to project all sorts of attributes, characteristics, and motives.

This means that, while the patient may sometimes unconsciously see the therapist as a loving parent, he or she may also react as though the therapist were a vengeful father, a seductive mother, a hated rival, a jealous lover, or any one of a hundred other figures. The specifics depend, in large measure, upon the particular nature of the patient's unconscious difficulties. When the patient-therapist relationship creates a "new edition" or miniature version of the patient's overall problems, it is referred to as the *transference neurosis* and may become a central focus of analytic work.

The appearance of the transference and transference neurosis was noted by Freud quite early in his work. It often took the form of female patients' erotic love for or fantasies about Freud. He concluded that these women were actually expressing childhood wishes about their fathers, for whom he had been symbolically substituted.

The apparent reproduction of early unconscious conflicts is not only theoretically fascinating; it is remarkably convenient. The analyst can work with important problems from the past as they occur in the present through the transference. It is for this reason that most of the therapist's attention is centered on events occurring during treatment sessions rather than between them.

As was the case with resistance, there are endless ways in which transference and transference neurosis can be displayed by the patient. Again, we shall only describe a few examples. Among the more obvious of these is the appearance of *dependence* on the therapist. The patient may show up early for every session,[5] express reluctance to leave at the end of the hour, telephone for advice or comfort at all hours of the day or night, make demands upon the analyst, or bend over backwards to please the analyst. As Freud found, the development of intense feelings of love for the analyst is not uncommon and may sometimes reach dramatic proportions. Some patients become so caught up in fantasizing about a hoped-for love affair with the analyst that nothing else seems important to them. When the therapist fails to reciprocate, strong feelings of disappointment and/or anger often appear. The patient might become depressed and may even make a suicidal gesture.

[5]It has jokingly been pointed out that you cannot win in analysis because you are dependent if you show up early, resistant if you show up late, and compulsive if you are right on time.

Intense *negative* feelings about the therapist also reflect transference. The patient may, at some point in therapy, decide that the analyst is incompetent (and stupid, to boot). Although these sentiments are expressed in no uncertain terms and on repeated occasions, the patient may not terminate therapy. To the therapist, this means that the patient is not simply an unhappy customer, but one who is using the therapeutic relationship to express feelings which are actually aimed at a parent or other significant person. Negative transference may also appear in less direct and far more childish ways. Fine (1971) tells of a 16-year-old patient who attempted (successfully) to annoy the analyst by calling him on the telephone fifteen or twenty times an hour, sometimes identifying himself as Christopher Columbus.

Transference and transference neuroses must be handled with care. Rather than merely reacting to them, the analyst tries hard to *understand the meaning* of the patient's positive and/or negative feelings. If the analyst responded "normally" to a confession of love or a verbal attack, the patient would probably not learn very much and a premature termination of therapy could occur. The trick is to keep the transference active and visible without forcing the patient out of therapy. If this can be done, the unconscious material involved can be dealt with, made conscious, and worked through. When all these goals are accomplished, the patient's analysis is usually seen as complete.

It is worth pointing out, by the way, that analysis and working through of the transference tend to take much longer than the analysis and working through of a specific symptom. Thus, while psychoanalysis may begin because of a particular complaint (e.g., anxiety attacks), it is very likely to continue long after that problem disappears because the patient's real difficulties are believed to be revealed in the transference.

Making Analytic Interpretations

So far, we have outlined the major *sources* of unconscious material and the psychoanalytic techniques used to help tap them. We have also seen that because of the operation of defense mechanisms, the "real" meanings of dreams, free associations, jokes, everyday behavior patterns, treatment obstacles, and transference are usually not clear to the patient. Indeed, the patient is seen as being least likely to understand these things simply because, unconsciously, he or she does not want to.

The analyst, on the other hand, is much better able to hypothesize about the unconscious determinants of patient behavior. The analyst is trained to look for hidden meanings and, because she or he is ideally a somewhat detached and objective observer, the possible significance of the patient's verbal and nonverbal behavior is thought to be easier for the analyst to detect. The problem, of course, is how to help the patient see and accept uncomfortable things while, at the same time, not overwhelming him or her with too much insight before he or she is ready to handle it. This is where the *analytic interpretation* comes in. Through questions and comments about verbal and nonverbal behaviors, free associations, dreams, and the like, the analyst seeks to provide guidance and direction to the patient's self-exploration. When the patient is resistant and defensive or when she or he is unable (unwilling?) to see the potential meaning of some event, the therapist attempts to point this out and sometimes offers suggestions for new ways to look at things.

Ideally, the analyst's interpretations are not simply statements of how he or she construes the patient's behavior or problems. After all, the analyst could easily be wrong. The interpretive process is somewhat more tentative and continuous, a kind of constant prodding of the patient to consider alternative views, to reject easy, obvious explanations and to search instead for deeper meanings. As Munroe (1955, p. 307) puts it, "the *interpretive comment* of the analyst provides the major integration of the therapeutic procedure." In other words, interpretations move analysis along by promoting insight and the working through of those insights. Without interpretations, the patient might never make progress.

It is all too easy to assume from movies and other carriers of cultural stereotypes that anything of potential unconscious significance is interpreted to the patient as soon as its meaning seems clear to the analyst. In the Lee J. Cobb film mentioned in Chapter 4, the captive analyst immediately understands his criminal patient's symptoms through a dream, gives his interpretation, and solves the problem. This unrealistic portrayal ignores at least three things: (1) the material emerging in an analytic session is not usually easy to interpret, (2) it is not all of equal importance, and (3) the patient may not be ready to accept a simple, straightforward explanation even if the analyst has a correct one to offer. Thus, the therapist faces three important questions as she or he works at the delicate and difficult task of giving valid and usable interpretations: What could this dream (or association or response) mean? Is it related to important new unconscious content? Is now the time to say something to the patient about it?

A correctly timed comment or question can result in a step forward; it ". . . stirs up the patient in one way or another. It brings his whole personality into the office of the analyst and provides a kind of emotional re-education on the spot" (Munroe, 1955; p. 307). The word "emotional" is important here because it is assumed that when an interpretation is on target, important, and well-timed, it will evoke positive (or negative) *feelings* in the patient which may help promote insight. On the other hand, most analysts feel that a correct interpretation of important material may arouse *too much* emotion (or other strong defenses) if it is given before the patient is ready to make constructive use of it.

It is of little consolation to the therapist if a brilliant explanation of, say, an obscure dream feature ("I think the garbage disposal represents your unconscious desire to destroy your mother") causes the patient to stomp out of the room or to calmly suggest that the analyst needs a vacation. As a kind of rule of thumb, an interpretation is best delivered at the point where the patient is nearly aware of something important, but has not yet verbalized it. Ideally, ". . . one 'tells' a patient what the patient *almost* sees for himself and one tells him in such a way that the patient—not the analyst—takes 'credit' for the discovery"

(Menninger, 1958; p. 134). In simplest terms, the therapist tries to say just the right things at just the right times. When he or she succeeds, the analytic interpretation becomes a tool which has been likened to the surgeon's scalpel (Munroe, 1955).

The analyst's interpretations can reflect rather narrow hypotheses about fairly specific relationships (like the low-level inferences discussed in Chapter 4), or they can deal with much broader conceptualizations (like those associated with high-level inferences). Some interpretations are made clearly and directly, especially when the patient is thought to be ready for a straightforward presentation, while in other instances, the analyst will merely hint at her or his hypotheses so that the patient can deal with the new idea gradually. Several illustrations of analytic interpretation are presented below.

Interpreting Resistance   We have said that the analyst's first job (besides establishing a good working relationship) usually involves identifying and overcoming resistance to the analytic process. The patient can be made aware of his or her resistant strategies and tactics in many ways.

Patient: I've been thinking; we've spent five sessions together now and have gotten exactly nowhere. How long does it take for me to start seeing some changes?

(If the analyst were sure that this is a resistant tactic and that the patient ought to be confronted, a rather direct and specific interpretation might be offered):

Therapist: I don't know the answer to that question, but it seems to me that by bringing it up, you could be attempting to avoid talking about other things.

A less direct interpretation could also be used:

Therapist: I don't know the answer to that question, but I wonder why you asked it.

In this case, it will probably take longer for the patient to recognize the defensive aspect of the question, but the insight will be less abrupt.

After an analyst has had time to observe continuing patterns of resistance, she or he may venture a more elaborate interpretation:

Patient: I'm sorry to be late, doctor, but I got a long distance call from my brother-in-law just as I was leaving the house to come here. He told me that my sister has gotten sick again and wanted to know if I had some cash to spare to help tide them over with the medical bills. I told him 'yes' but I really don't know how I can afford to do it and still keep coming to see you. Sometimes everything falls on me at once.

Therapist: You know, last session we began to see that your feelings toward your parents were not all positive. I think we are on to something important in that area. Today you start off by saying that, through no fault of your own, you may not be able to continue in therapy. This seems to be a recurring thing, both here and in your childhood. Whenever you are threatened by what you are learning about yourself, a disaster always seems to occur which diverts our attention. You used to get out of trouble this way as a child, too. Whenever your parents became angry with you for avoiding responsibility, you always found a way to show that someone else had prevented you from doing what you should have done. Has this ever occurred to you?

In cases where the patient already has insight into her or his defensive tactics, an interpretive comment may aid in the working through or elaboration of that insight:

Therapist: I think your failure to recall your dreams lately is really just another manifestation of your "playing dumb" technique. You discovered that you do this with your husband when he wants you to do things for him that you don't want to do, and you do it in here, too.

Interpreting Other Analytic Productions   We saw earlier that dreams produce one type of raw material for analytic interpretations. The use of the "wheelchair" dream illustrated how an analyst might very gently lead a patient to an understanding of latent content. In other circumstances, the interpretation might have been more direct (e.g., "I think your anger toward your father comes out very strongly in this dream").

Here are two other examples of interpretation based upon various analytic products:

You know, it's very interesting that whenever you say something that is a little bit nasty to anyone you smile. After you've been a little bit aggressive, you become *very* agreeable and nice, and I notice it here. I wonder if when you were with your father you discovered that the only way to keep him from attacking you was to become more sociable, amiable, in this kind of smiling, passive way. . . . (Barton, 1974; p. 33)

It is quite interesting that most of the jokes you tell are at the expense of people who are deformed or crippled or handicapped in some way. I wonder what this means. I wonder if by attacking the weakness in others you are trying to deny the weakness in yourself.

Interpreting the Transference   Because it is thought to be so intimately related to the patient's early intrapsychic conflicts, the characteristics of the transference are prime targets for analytic interpretation. After observing the development of a patient's dependence, the analyst might remark: "I notice that you often seem to deal with me in the same way you dealt with your parents as a child. You seem to want me to protect you and help you through the difficulties you are facing." The same interpretation could also be couched in less obvious terms: "I get the feeling that you would like me to somehow magically solve all your problems, and I wonder if you have ever felt that way about anyone else."

Often, accurate interpretation of transference leads to a negative reaction from the client. This reaction must itself be interpreted. For example:

Patient: I have a confession to make. I know I never could have come through these last two months without you to help me. I love you.

Therapist: If we examine why you feel that way about me we might discover who I represent to you when I provide psychological support.

Patient: Oh God! Can't you even take a compliment like a human being? What kind of person are you? I was trying to tell you how I feel about *you;* I wasn't saying anything about me! Can't you come off your analytic throne for even one minute?

Therapist: You have expressed love for me. That has been very hard for you to do. It is important to understand why you are able to do it in relation to me now when you couldn't before. It is also important for us to understand why you got so angry just now when I did not respond as you wanted me to.

An exchange like this is likely to lead to an exploration of the patient's ability and inability to express tender feelings toward others, particularly toward parents, and may uncover a strong need to be reassured about self-worth. In the process, the patient may find that unreturned love does not mean one is worthless. It may also finally become clear that his or her parents were simply not able to be loving and that nothing he or she could have done as a child would have changed that fact. Insight about this matter may be worked through in later sessions as the analyst and patient repeatedly consider interpretations of the transference.

With the aid of interpretations, the patient is led to understand and work through all aspects of the transference. As the months and years of treatment go by, this process ultimately leads to a change in the therapist-patient relationship. The patient not only sees how her or his defenses and unconscious conflicts caused problems; she or he learns to deal differently with the world, beginning with the therapist. The patient learns that the forces of the past no longer need dictate the behavior of the present. The analyst is *not* the patient's parent, and neither is his or her boss or spouse. Ideally, this knowledge and emotional understanding will liberate the patient to deal with life in a more rational, realistic, and satisfying manner.

Unfortunately, our outline of psychoanalytic techniques is just that, a sketchy outline. It has left out many details and oversimplified others. Much more complete coverage of the approach is contained in Munroe (1955), Greenson (1967), Menninger (1958), Kernberg (1976), Fenichel (1941), and, of course, Freud (e.g., 1949). Extended case examples are also available in Barton (1974), Fine (1973), and Greenwald (1959).

Applications

In its classic form, psychoanalysis is used in a one-to-one relationship with "neurotic" adults over a period of several years. We shall see later that the classical approach has been varied in several ways to make it shorter and more applicable to group and family settings and younger patients, but the typical recipient of psychoanalytic treatment is a relatively intelligent and sophisticated adult who has the time and financial resources to embark upon an extended intellectual and emotional adventure.

Thus, a "good" analytic patient should be motivated to seek help and to work at solving problems. She or he must be capable of following the "fundamental rule" of free association and must be able to form an interpersonal relationship with the therapist. Further, the patient should be able to think logically about the world, including her or his own behavior, and to maintain contact with reality. Finally, the patient must have enough courage to focus on and accept the fact of his or her mental problems (Ford & Urban, 1963). These requirements rule out, for the most part, the use of orthodox psychoanalysis with persons who are labeled as "psychotic." The intensity and severity of their behavior problems often result in their confinement to mental hospitals or other institutions, and they often do not display the responses and effort required for analytic work.

The kinds of problems most often dealt with in psychoanalytic treatment are those involving anxiety, guilt, depression, and maladaptive interpersonal relationships. A brief sampling of these problems would include hysterical disorders, sexual orientation disturbances, phobias, general anxiety, sexual dysfunctions (e.g., impotence, frigidity), inappropriate aggressiveness or timidity, unsatisfying social relations, inability to work productively, insomnia, and marital conflicts.

VARIATIONS ON PSYCHOANALYSIS

Like all great thinkers, Sigmund Freud attracted many followers, both in his own lifetime and after his death. Some of these people sought to preserve his ideas and techniques in their original form, while others advocated changes ranging from minor alterations to wholesale rejection of fundamental principles. These changes not only provided alternatives to psychoanalytic theory (as noted in Chapter 3); they also suggested a broader range of therapeutic techniques than had been "legal" under orthodox Freudian tenets. In this section, we shall describe a few of these treatment innovations, beginning with those which are least distinct from the original model and progressing to those incorporating more radical changes.

Psychoanalytically Oriented Psychotherapy

Many therapists employ psychoanalytic treatment procedures in ways which depart somewhat from the guidelines originally set down by Freud. Although some of these individuals still see themselves as engaging in psychoanalysis, traditional Freudians prefer the phrase *psychoanalytically oriented psychotherapy*. That phrase encompasses a number of nonorthodox analytic procedures, but is probably most closely associated with the approach developed by Franz Alexander and some of his colleagues at the Chicago Psychoanalytic Institute during the 1930s and 1940s.

The treatment philosophy of the "Chicago group" has been spelled out in several well-known books (e.g., Alexander & French, 1946; Alexander, 1956, 1963). We shall focus on the more notable features of the approach, most of which grew out of doubts about the importance of traditional therapeutic practices. For example, Alexander and his coworkers questioned the belief that treatment must be intense, extended, and fundamentally similar in all cases. They also sought ways to expand the applicability of psychoanalysis to two previously excluded patient groups: the young and the more severely disturbed.

Alexander (1963, p. 273) summarized his views this way: "Psychoanalytic principles lend themselves to different therapeutic procedures which vary according to the nature of the case and may be variably applied during the treatment of the same patient." This flexibility appears in many aspects of psychoanalytically oriented psychotherapy. For one thing, not every patient is seen for the traditional five sessions each week. It is thought that while some persons may benefit from such intense effort, others may not. Daily sessions may foster too much dependence on the analyst or may become so routine that the patient begins to pay too little attention to them.

On the other hand, by reducing the frequency of sessions, the patient has more time to reflect upon what happens in each one and to test in the real world what is being learned about himself or herself. Further, the emotional involvement of the patient in each session may be higher if the sessions occur less often. And since the total cost of treatment is lowered, a less intense edition of psychoanalysis can be more attractive to those with limited means. In a given case, the frequency of sessions may vary as circumstances dictate. Early in treatment the patient may need to be seen every day. Later on, the sessions may take place less often; other patterns might appear as well. Alexander even suggested that temporary interruptions in treatment could be beneficial by testing the patient's ability to live without therapy and to reduce reliance on the therapist. Alexander and French (1946) reported that their form of psychoanalysis can be completed in sixty-five sessions over about a year and a half; in many cases, even less time is needed.

Another way in which psychoanalytically oriented psychotherapy displays flexibility is in its plan for treatment. Traditional psychoanalysis is usually rather lengthy due to the perceived need for fully exploring and working through resistance, insights, and the transference. Alexander suggested that not all patients need such extensive attention and that many can benefit from shorter treatment. Persons whose problems are relatively mild, who are fairly well-adjusted except for a particular difficulty, or who are more seriously disturbed than the usual analytic patient are seen as candidates for less extensive treatment aimed at *support* rather than at the uncovering and reconstruction associated with full-blown analysis.

Alexander also placed heavy emphasis upon producing *corrective emotional experiences* in therapy, not just insight. The idea here is to help the patient not only to see that old conflicts need no longer run her or his life, but to use the transference to let the patient *resolve* those old conflicts in a better way.

"Re-experiencing the old, unsettled conflict *but with a new ending* is the secret of every penetrating therapeutic result . . ." (Alexander & French, 1946; p. 338).

To aid in the promotion of corrective emotional experiences, the analyst may attempt to *control* the character of the transference. A transference neurosis may be allowed to develop or, if its appearance is not seen as beneficial in a certain case, might be avoided. This control is exerted in several ways, such as by making or avoiding interpretations that are likely to foster transference of infantile reactions. The therapist may also attempt to purposely alter the *countertransference*. If feelings toward the patient help promote a corrective emotional experience, they may be directly expressed. If not, the therapist may ". . . replace his spontaneous countertransference reactions with attitudes which are consciously planned . . . according to the dynamic exigencies of the therapeutic situation" (Alexander, 1956; p. 93). In other words, in this version of psychoanalysis, transference is not only analyzed, it may be manipulated; countertransference is not only a spontaneous reaction which the analyst comes to understand through his or her own personal analysis; it is a potential treatment tool.

A general rule in Freudian analysis is that the patient should not make major life decisions while treatment is underway. This is designed to prevent bad decisions caused by maladaptive impulses, false or partial insights, neurotic defenses, or other factors. In contrast, the analytically oriented therapist may encourage those life changes which the patient and analyst agree make sense. This procedure is based upon the assumption that the therapeutic relationship is not only a context for self-exploration; it is also a place in which to rehearse ideas for progress which must then be tested in real life. The changes made sometimes involve manipulation of the patient's external environment and are often initiated by the therapist. A patient whose despair is due in part to the fact that she or he is in an unsatisfying job might be encouraged to look for a better position. Here, the therapist clearly performs a guidance function which is more active and direct than that found in orthodox analysis.[6]

At various points in treatment, psychoanalytically oriented psychotherapists make use of a number of other unorthodox techniques including the following:

1   The patient may sit up and face the analyst rather than lie on a couch.
2   Normal conversation may be substituted for free association.
3   Various drugs or hypnosis may be used to promote self-exploration.
4   The nature of present problems and their solution is emphasized. Childhood conflicts are explored mainly to show that they no longer need to exist.
5   The patient's family may be consulted (or even offered treatment) as part of a total effort at helping the client. A family therapy group might thus result.
6   Nonverbal communications including play (for children), artistic crea-

---

[6]It should be noted that, in spite of their theoretical restrictions, orthodox analysts sometimes actually do give advice (Munroe, 1955; Strupp, 1972).

tions, or leisure activities may become an additional source of material for analysis.

The Ego Analysts

Psychoanalytically oriented psychotherapists accept most of Freud's basic tenets but revise his procedures. Another, more independent group of therapists, usually referred to as *ego analysts,* stray even further from the strict Freudian path by arguing that the psychoanalytic preoccupation with sexual and aggressive instincts as the bases of behavior and behavior disorder is too narrow. Wolberg's (1967) summary of the ego-analytic position is presented in edited form below:

    1 Behavior is determined by forces other than instinct. These include responses encompassed under the concept of ego.

    2 The ego has an autonomy separate from both instinct (id) and reality.

    3 The ego prompts drives for environmental mastery and adaptive learning which are separate from sexual and aggressive instincts.

    4 Female sexuality is on a par with rather than inferior to male sexuality.

    5 The classical topography (id, ego, superego) does not explain the structure of the psychic apparatus.

    6 Therapy is more than a means of exploring and working through early childhood experiences. It is a relationship experience which contains positive-growth potentials that can lead to self-actualization.

    7 Activity and flexibility are essential to therapy.

    8 An optimistic rather than a pessimistic viewpoint is justified with regard to the human potential for creativity and love.

These views led the ego analysts "to explore the complexity in behavior that each person develops and with which he *directs his own activity and deals constructively with his environment"* (Ford & Urban, 1963; p. 181; italics added). Notice here that people are presumed to be capable of using ego functions to control their behavior and organize that behavior in positive as well as negative ways. This more optimistic view of human beings has much in common with the phenomenological approach (see Chapters 3 and 11). It led analysts such as Heinz Hartmann (1958), David Rapaport (1951), Melanie Klein (1960), Freud's daughter Anna (1946), and Erik Erikson (1946) to use psychoanalytic treatment techniques for the exploration of patient's adaptive ego functions as well as their basic id instincts. For more on the theory and practice of ego analysis, see Munroe (1955), Ford and Urban (1963), Kohut (1971), or Guntrip (1973).

Psychoanalytically oriented psychotherapy and ego analysis are characterized primarily by *revision* of Freudian concepts and techniques, not by outright revolt against them. However, there have been many other therapists who have moved much further away from Freud. These individuals retained a psychodynamic orientation, but deemphasized in varying degrees the importance of Freud's theory of instincts, infantile sexuality, and the unconscious determination of behavior. The treatment techniques developed by such "rebels" are our next topic.

Alfred Adler's Individual Psychology

Alfred Adler was one of Freud's earliest followers and was also the first to formally defect from the ranks of orthodox psychoanalysis. The reasons for his departure and the alternative theory he formulated are outlined in Chapter 3.

Since Adler believed that people's problematic life-styles were based largely upon *misconceptions* which they hold, his approach to treatment was primarily focused upon exploring and altering those misconceptions. Where a strict Freudian might see a student's vomiting before school each day as a defense of some kind, the Adlerian analyst would probably suggest that the problem was a manifestation of general tension brought about by some misconception (e.g., "I must do better than anyone else" or "the teachers are out to make me look bad") upon which the student bases part of his or her life-style (Munroe, 1955). In Freudian analytic therapy, this person's vomiting might be explored through free association or other means in order to understand its defensive function and to probe the impulses it may be designed to repress. In Adler's individual psychology, the symptom would be discussed as one illustration of the patient's mistaken attitudes and maladaptive life-style. The patient would then be helped to form new, more appropriate attitudes and given encouragement to go out and consciously change his or her style in the direction of what Adler called *social interest, courage, and common sense* (e.g., Adler, 1963).

Mosak and Dreikurs (1973) have succinctly outlined the goals of Adlerian psychotherapy:

> **1** To establish and maintain a good therapeutic relationship (i.e., a therapeutic alliance, in Freudian terms).
> **2** To uncover the patient's lifestyle and goals, as well as to explore how they affect him/her in daily life.
> **3** To give interpretations which lead the patient to gain insight into his/her lifestyle and its consequences.
> **4** To reorient the patient's attitudes so that they support a more adaptive lifestyle; to translate the patient's insight into constructive action.

Adlerian Treatment Techniques

Patient-Therapist Relationship Adlerians do not usually use a couch. Their goal is to create a cooperative relationship between equals in a working environment. Accordingly, the patient and therapist normally sit face to face in similar chairs. The feelings and reactions expressed toward the therapist (transference) are seen not as reflecting unconscious childhood conflicts but are interpreted as the patient's habitual style of dealing with people *like* the therapist. "The patient . . . expects from the therapist the kind of response he has trained himself from childhood to believe that people or certain people will give him" (Mosak & Dreikurs, 1973; p. 55).

The therapist also watches for life-style clues in the *scripts,* or standard interpersonal ploys and games, that the patient creates in treatment. Usually, the therapist is expected to play a particular part. For example, the patient may repeatedly enact the "poor soul" role which she or he consciously or unconsciously hopes will bring out a nurturant response from the therapist. This may be typical of the patient's maladaptive way of getting love and attention.

Handling Resistance   As with transference, resistance is seen by Adlerians as a sample of the patient's usual way of operating, in this case, a way of avoiding material which may be unpleasant. In addition, however, resistance may reflect the fact that the patient and therapist have different *goals*. The therapist's goal is to explore the patient's basic life-style and misconceptions, but, because clinging to one's misconceptions is thought to maintain feelings of security, the patient may use a maladaptive life-style to protect those misconceptions from exposure. When the patient's goal is to maintain the status quo in this way, he or she will appear resistant (e.g., "I can't understand what you are talking about," "I'm too upset to talk about this now"). The therapist may handle such resistance not only by interpreting its meaning, but also by pointing out the goal discrepancy. A discussion of goals may then result which, for the moment at least, reestablishes therapist-patient cooperation.

Dreams   Like Freud, Adler believed dreams were an important source of information to be utilized in treatment, but he saw them not as the compromised fulfillment of wishes from the past, but as a *rehearsal* of how the patient might deal with the problems in the future. The moods created in a dream are seen as setting the stage for the next day's activities. "If we wish to postpone action, we forget the dream. If we wish to dissuade ourselves from some action, we frighten ourselves with a nightmare" (Mosak & Dreikurs, 1973; p. 58).

Adler also used dreams as an indication of therapeutic progress. If, for example, a new patient reports short dreams in which there is little action, this might reflect a passive approach to dealing with problems. As treatment proceeds and the patient begins to experiment with a more active life-style, her or his dreams should become more active as well (Dreikurs, 1944). Some Adlerians use the nature of the patient's dreams to guide them in deciding when to terminate therapy (Rosenthal, 1959).

The Life-style Investigation   In addition to attending to dreams, resistance, transference characteristics, nonverbal behavior, and other informal material, some Adlerians (e.g., Dreikurs, 1954) explore the patient's life-style in a more systematic way. The focus here is on the patient's family and his or her position in it, the earliest memories which can be recalled (these are thought to reflect the life-style), basic mistakes or misconceptions, and the assets and strengths the patient possesses. The summary of a life-style investigation is presented in Box 9-2.

The Use of Interpretation   We mentioned earlier that in Adlerian therapy resistance and transference are usually handled by *interpreting* them as examples

Box 9-2   A Sample Life-style Summary

Summary of family constellation

John is the younger of two children, the only boy, who grew up fatherless after age 9. His sister was so accomplished at almost everything that, early in life, John became discouraged. Since he felt he would never become famous, he decided perhaps he could at least be notorious, and through negative traits brought himself forcefully to the attention of others. He acquired the reputation that he was pretty obnoxious and a "holy terror." He was going to do everything his way, and nobody was going to stop him. He followed the guiding lines of a strong, masculine father from whom he learned that the toughest man wins. Since notoriety came with doing the disapproved thing, John early became interested in and engaged in sex. This also reinforced his feelings of masculinity. Since both parents were handicapped and still "made it," John apparently decided that without any physical handicaps, the sky would be the limit for him.

Summary of early recollections

"I run scared in life, and even when people tell me there's nothing to be scared of, I'm still scared. Women give men a hard time. They betray men, they punish them, and they interfere with what men want to do. A real man takes no crap from anybody. But victory is hard to come by because somebody always interferes. I am not going to do what others want me to do. Others call that 'bad' and want to punish me for it but I don't see it that way. Doing what I want is merely part of being a man, and why should anyone want to interfere with my being a man?"

"Basic mistakes"

1 He exaggerates the significance of real masculinity and equates it with doing what he pleases.
2 He is not on the same wavelength as women. They see his behavior as "bad"; he sees it as only "natural" for a man.
3 He is too ready to fight, many times just to preserve his sense of masculinity, and not because of the issue he is allegedly fighting over.
4 He perceives women as the enemy, even though he looks to them for comfort.
5 Like Moses, victory is snatched from him at the last moment.

Assets

1 He is a driver. When he puts his mind to things, he makes them work.
2 He engages in creative problem solving.
3 He knows how to get what he wants.
4 He knows how to keep the world busy with him.
5 He knows how to ask a woman "nicely."

Source: Mosak, H. H. & Dreikurs, R. "Adlerian Psychotherapy," in R. J. Corsini (ed.), *Current Psychotherapies.* © 1973 by Peacock Publishers, Inc., Itasca, Illinois, p. 57. (Reprinted by permission.)

of the patient's maladaptive life-style. Interpretation is used in the same general way to promote insight about the life-style–meaning of the patient's dreams, problems, interpersonal relationships, and other behavior. Where Freud interpreted in order to promote insight into *past causes* of current problems, Adler interpreted in order to promote insight into the nature and purpose of the patient's *present* life-style.

Instead of using it as a scalpel, the Adlerian employs interpretation as a mirror in which the patient can see how she or he copes with life (Mosak & Dreikurs, 1973). When this is done and the patient sees what it is that he or she is doing, it becomes much harder to maintain maladaptive ideas and behaviors. In comparison to the strict Freudian approach, there is relatively little worry among Adlerians about the details of phrasing and timing interpretations because they do not see the patient as particularly delicate.

Advice and Encouragement   While Freud pointed out that patients must sometimes be encouraged to do things they may have been afraid of in the past, in general the strict psychoanalyst is supposed to remain objective and rather detached most of the time. This restriction was relaxed somewhat by psychoanalytically oriented therapists, but Adler broke the rules altogether. The Adlerian therapist is much more openly involved in the business of advising and encouraging the patient. As long as the patient does not become dependent upon the therapist for advice and encouragement, it is seen as an essential part of translating insight into action.

For example, once a patient realizes that her exaggerated dependence on her husband is part of her overall style of seeking protection (and controlling others), the therapist might point out several alternative ways in which she might start to change. In other cases, the therapist might offer more direct advice (e.g., "get a part-time job"), especially when the patient needs some help to get started toward a more adaptive life-style.

Other Treatment Procedures   Adlerians often make use of a variety of other techniques to help make patients aware of the problematic aspects of their life-style and to prompt them to change for the better. Many of these are very similar to some of the tactics employed by certain proponents of social-learning and phenomenological treatment (see Chapters 10 and 11). Included among these procedures are:

1   Modeling   Ideally, the therapist exemplifies certain values and attitudes and behaviors that the patient might wish to emulate. "The Adlerian therapist presents himself as 'being for real,' fallible, unconcerned with prestige considerations, able to laugh at himself, possessing courage, caring—a model for social interest" (Mosak & Dreikurs, 1973; p. 60).

2   Task setting   Adler advocated getting patients to go out and do new things which would help the treatment process. "Acting as if" was one favorite method. When patients express a longing to be different than they are, the therapist may assign them to act (for, say, a week) *as if* they really were the way they want to be. This helps patients see that change is possible and, with time, could become permanent.

The patient may be asked to focus on and actually *try* to perform the very behaviors he or she wishes to stop. An insomniac might try to stay up all night and a person who always seems to be crying might try to cry constantly. By not using a style in which the patient fights against these behaviors, the patient often finds that they disappear.

There may be other tasks as well. "A 50-year-old man who professed 'genuine' intention to get married but simultaneously avoided women was instructed to seek one meaningful contact with a woman (how to do so was up to him) every day" (Mosak & Dreikurs, 1973; p. 61; see also Box 9-3).

3 Creating images   The patient is sometimes given a kind of summary image of his or her life-style. This image can then be used on a day-to-day basis as a reminder of the style she or he is trying to alter. "Superman," "The Beggar King," and "Miss Perfection" are just a few examples.

4 The push button technique   When patients believe themselves to be at the mercy of their emotions, the therapist might help them learn that this is a misconception. The patient is asked to imagine with eyes closed some past unpleasant experience and notice the negative emotional feelings which result. The patient is then told to "push a button" and switch the attention to some past pleasant event. The appearance of accompanying positive emotions and the possibility of switching back and forth between affective states help to illustrate the degree of control over emotion that the patient actually has.

Applications   The Adlerian approach is obviously appropriate for use in one-to-one treatment with the kinds of patients who might be seen in Freudian psychoanalysis, but much of its appeal lies in the fact that it can also be applied with other types of patients in individual, group, and family contexts as well. Because reality contact and the ability to form a transference relationship were deemphasized by Adler, he was able to work with persons labeled "psychotic" and with criminals as well.

Adler also worked with "normal" individuals because he believed that one can have problems in living due to misconceptions and a maladaptive life-style without being an officially diagnosed patient. This view resulted in the establishment of community education centers which were designed to *prevent*

Box 9-3   An Example of Adler's Task Setting

Adler often employed task setting as a means of helping depressed people. In the example below, note the charming combination of good humor and practical advice.

> To return to the indirect method of treatment: I recommend it especially in melancholia. After establishing a sympathetic relation I give suggestions for a change of conduct in two stages. In the first stage my suggestion is "Only do what is agreeable to you." The patient usually answers, "Nothing is agreeable." "Then at least," I respond, "do not exert yourself to do what is disagreeable." The patient, who has usually been exhorted to do various uncongenial things to remedy this condition, finds a rather flattering novelty in my advice, and may improve in behavior. Later I insinuate the second rule of conduct, saying that "it is much more difficult and I do not know if you can follow it." After saying this I am silent, and look doubtfully at the patient. In this way I excite his curiosity and ensure his attention, and then proceed, "If you could follow this second rule you would be cured in fourteen days. It is—to consider from time to time how you can give another person pleasure. It would very soon enable you to sleep and would chase away all your sad thoughts. You would feel yourself to be useful and worthwhile."
>
> I receive various replies to my suggestion, but every patient thinks it is too difficult to act upon. If the answer is, "How can I give pleasure to others when I have none myself?" I relieve the prospect by saying, "Then you will need four weeks." The more transparent response, "Who gives *me* pleasure?" I encounter with what is probably the strongest move in the game, by saying, "Perhaps you had better train yourself a little thus: do not actually *do* anything to please anyone else, but just think out how you *could* do it!"

Source: Adler, 1964; pp. 25–26.

the development of behavior disorder by providing parents and teachers with information and advice about child-rearing and family relations. These centers have continued to grow in number in various parts of the world and, in many ways, anticipated the community psychology movement of the 1960s and 1970s (see Chapter 12).

Other Psychodynamic Therapies

In discussing psychoanalytically oriented psychotherapy, the ego analysts, and Adler's approach, we have merely scratched the surface of all the variants on and rebellions against Freud's model of treatment. Box 9-4 gives some idea of the many additional systems available today. The work of many of the therapists and theorists included in that table (e.g., Stekel, Ferenczi, Reich, Federn) paralleled the effort of the "Chicago group" and the ego analysts to expand the range of techniques, patients, treatment settings, and presenting problems which could be associated with psychoanalysis. Others (e.g., Horney, Sullivan, Fromm) sought to use basic psychoanalytic concepts in the context of treatment which places heavy emphasis upon the cultural and interpersonal environment of

---

Box 9-4 Modifications in Psychoanalytic Therapy

I Alternate systems of analytic psychotherapy based on theoretical or ideological differences from Freudian classical analysis.
   1 The non-Freudian systems.
      a The *individual psychology* of Alfred Adler.
      b The *analytical psychology* of Carl Jung.
      c The *will therapy* of Otto Rank.
   2 Neo-Freudian systems based on the cultural emphasis.
      a The *holistic* approach of Karen Horney.
      b The *interpersonal relations* school of Harry Stack Sullivan.
      c The *cultural* approach of Erich Fromm.
II Attempts to streamline, abbreviate and speed up the process of psychoanalytic therapy.
   1 Stekel's *active analytic* psychotherapy.
   2 Ferenczi's experiments with *active* techniques.
   3 The Chicago school of *brief* psychoanalytic therapy.
III Expansions of Freudian classical analysis in various directions.
   1 The "object-relations approach" of Guntrip, Winnicott, Fairbairn, and the British school.
   2 The "eight stages of man" and Erikson's extension of Freud's theory of character development.
   3 Character analysis of Wilhelm Reich.
   4 Kohut's approach to the treatment of narcissistic character disorders.
IV Modifications based on the shift in emphasis to ego psychology.
   1 Federn's ego psychology and the psychotherapy of the ego boundaries.
   2 Wolman's interactional psychoanalytic therapy.

Source: Kutash, 1976; pp. 89–90.

the patient. Still others (e.g., Jung and Rank) followed in Adler's footsteps by breaking sharply with Freudian principles and founding relatively distinct alternative treatments.

Together, these psychodynamic systems have helped keep psychoanalytic and related therapy procedures in step with modern clinical problems and societal needs. Without them, the psychodynamic approach to human distress might not have remained one of the "big three" in clinical psychology.

Another important point about some of the variants on psychoanalysis is that, as noted earlier in this chapter, many of them have actually helped lay the groundwork for certain procedures associated with social-learning and phenomenological models. For example, when Otto Rank broke with Freud, he developed a therapeutic approach which deemphasized the unconscious and the importance of detailed exploration of the past. Instead, Rank sought to employ the patient's own innate *will to health* as a vehicle for promoting mature independence. In therapy, Rank treated his patients like responsible individuals (not sick people) and emphasized the importance of the therapy relationship itself as a major growth experience. He saw the therapist as a *facilitator* of the client's inherent potential for growth, not as a relentless prober of the unconscious. These concepts provided a part of the base upon which Carl Rogers would later build his phenomenologically oriented client centered therapy (see Chapter 11).

Similarly, Harry Stack Sullivan (like Adler) did therapy in ways which are compatible with today's social-learning approach (see Wachtel, 1977). Ford and Urban's (1963) outline of the usual sequence of events in Sullivanian therapy (Box 9-5) shows the systematic approach and attention to overt behavior patterns which is a hallmark of learning-based clinical interventions.

Box 9-5 Summary of the Therapeutic Sequence in Sullivanian Therapy

a   Initial review of the problem.
b   Reconnaissance of the behaviors relevant to the problem.
c   Decision as to general outlines of the difficulty and the course therapy shall pursue.
d   Careful and detailed study of the subject's response repertoire.
e   Identification of the anxieties, avoidance patterns, and the interpersonal situations in which they occur.
f   Rendering these patterns explicit to the subject.
g   Making explicit the fact of intervening anxiety.
h   Drawing out the effects of these anxiety patterns on the remainder of the subject's behavior.
i   All of the foregoing reduces the intensity of anxiety and permits the operation of other responses in its stead.

Source: Ford, D. H. and Urban, H. B. *Systems of Psychotherapy.* © 1963 by John Wiley & Sons, New York. (Reprinted by permission.)

EFFECTIVENESS AND OTHER RESEARCH ISSUES IN PSYCHODYNAMIC THERAPY

It is probably safe to say that when most people think of "psychotherapy," they imagine a pipe-smoking therapist and a patient on a couch. This was once a reasonably accurate stereotype, since, as we have seen, psychodynamic treatment was the first systematic approach to the exploration and solution of human psychological problems. For many years it dominated clinical interventions and was immensely influential in shaping professional ideas about what therapy is and how it should be conducted.

Today, its popularity and dominance are somewhat reduced. This is partly because its underlying theoretical model has been challenged by phenomenological and social-learning alternatives (see Chapter 3) and partly because, in spite of modern revisions, it is still seen as too expensive, lengthy, and intellectual to be useful in dealing with non-middle-class people and problems (see Chapter 12). Beyond these issues, critics have also focused upon the question of the effectiveness or benefits of psychodynamic therapy.

One of the most frequent arguments is that the psychodynamic approach has seldom been evaluated by quantitative, empirical research. Analysts are frequently depicted as being suspicious of or even downright hostile to controlled, quantitative studies of therapy outcome. Indeed, some advocates of the psychodynamic model have argued that their treatment methods are too complex, too multifaceted, and too subjective to be evaluated fairly by quantitative methods.

Nevertheless, there *has* been a considerable amount of quantitative research on psychodynamic treatment, especially psychoanalysis, which many psychologists appear either to ignore or remain uninformed about. A large amount of this research has been summarized by Wallerstein and Sampson (1971) and Fisher and Greenberg (1977). The most thorough and recent review of research on psychoanalysis is provided by Luborsky and Spence (1978). The journal *Psychoanalysis and Contemporary Society* is a good source for additional examples of this research.

The types of research questions asked about psychodynamic treatment are quite similar to the questions posed about other forms of therapy. Luborsky and Spence (1978) discuss four main areas of research in psychoanalytic treatment: (1) What kinds of clients are best suited for psychoanalysis? (2) What kinds of therapists are best suited to perform it? (3) What changes or outcomes are produced by psychoanalysis? and (4) What is the nature of change throughout the process or course of treatment?

Questions concerning outcome have received the least attention in the psychoanalytic literature. Most studies have focused only on a group of treated clients who, at the end of treatment, are rated by their therapists on some sort of improvement scale. Control groups are usually not included. Psychoanalysis has only rarely been directly compared to other forms of psychotherapy. Cartwright's (1966) study is probably the best known, but its importance is diminished by an obvious problem with its sample size: There were only four patients.

Research on the *process* of psychoanalysis has been both more frequent and of generally higher quality. For example, a considerable amount of research has been performed on the effects of therapists' interpretations. Accuracy of interpretation and level of empathy have been shown in some studies to be positively related to the final outcome of treatment.

Despite the gradually increasing sophistication of research on psychoanalysis, most analysts would probably still agree with Luborsky and Spence's (1978) judgment: "Quantitative research on psychoanalytic therapy presents itself, so far, as an unreliable support to clinical practice. Far more is known now through clinical wisdom than is known through quantitative, objective studies" (p. 358). Later, they add that "few, if any, quantitative research findings have changed the style or outcome of psychoanalytic practice (Luborsky & Spence, 1978; p. 360). Without disparaging the value of clinical wisdom, we would argue that no form of psychotherapy should remain too long aloof from the findings of well-controlled research. The ultimate scientific status of psychoanalysis, or any other therapy, depends on empirical investigation of its methods rather than on the consensual approval of its practitioners.

Chapter 10

Clinical Intervention: Social-Learning Models

Social-learning approaches to clinical problems are often referred to as *behavior modification,* or *behavior therapy.*[1] Whatever the label, the model has become famous. In recent years, behavior modification has regularly been described, misunderstood, praised, and condemned in the press, television, and movies (e.g., *A Clockwork Orange*) and has become a part of our popular vocabulary. While at one time the public's stereotype of psychologists and psychiatrists was that of professionals who primarily understood and practiced Freud's brand of therapy, social-learning techniques are rapidly augmenting or replacing psychodynamic images in the popular conception of psychology. This new stereotype misses the target only by a little: Most clinicians, regardless of their own theoretical background, *are* familiar with the basic principles of behavior therapy and employ its techniques on many occasions.

The term "behavior therapy" first appeared in a 1953 paper by Lindsley,

[1]Throughout this chapter we will use the terms *behavior modification* and *behavior therapy* interchangeably, even though some writers insist that the two are not synonymous. Among those psychologists who emphasize the difference between the two concepts, those with an operant or Skinnerian orientation prefer the name *behavior modification,* leaving *behavior therapy* to clinicians who operate from a Hullian and/or cognitive framework. These theoretical differences will become more meaningful as we progress through this chapter.

Skinner, and Solomon which described operant conditioning with psychotics. Though these authors did not continue to use the term, Eysenck (1959) did, and he is often given credit for introducing it. In point of fact, Arnold Lazarus, a South African psychologist, was the second person to use the term in print, publishing a 1958 article on behavior therapy in the *South African Medical Journal.*

While we may quibble about "who was first," there is no argument that the recent growth of social-learning-oriented interventions has been astounding. Behavior modification has also become one of the most popular research areas in clinical psychology. Twenty years ago there was not a single professional journal devoted exclusively to research on social-learning approaches in clinical psychology and psychiatry. Now there are eleven. The major behavioral journals in order of their appearance are: *Behaviour Research and Therapy* (1963), *Journal of Applied Behavior Analysis* (1968), *Behavior Therapy* (1970), *Journal of Behavior Therapy and Experimental Psychiatry* (1970), *European Journal of Behavioral Analysis and Modification* (1975), *Behavior Modification* (1977), *Cognitive Therapy and Research* (1977), *Child Behavior Therapy* (1978), *Advances in Behavior Research and Therapy* (1978), *Behavioral Assessment* (1979), and the *Journal of Behavioral Assessment* (1979).

A similar rate of growth has occurred in the publication of textbooks and handbooks dealing with behavior modification. The first book with "behavior therapy" in the title was Eysenck's *Behavior Therapy and the Neuroses* published in 1960 (Kazdin, 1978). Today, there are hundreds of books about many aspects of behavior modification, and many of them are updated each year. Several social-learning-oriented interest groups and societies have been formed, the most influential of which is the Association for the Advancement of Behavior Therapy (AABT). There are at least a score of behavioral newsletters, catalogs of equipment for behavior modifiers, and special bibliographies of behavioral publications. There is even a special code of ethics for behavior modifiers (AABT, 1977).

Perhaps the best indicator of the increasing complexity of the area is the proliferation of concepts that represent various "splinter" groups. Thus, we have *broad spectrum behavior therapy, narrow band behavior therapy, cognitive behavior therapy, cognitive behavior modification, language behavior therapy, rational behavior therapy, psychobehavioral therapy* and *psychodynamic behavior therapy* (Wilson, 1978). We doubt that there is much to be gained by inventing new brand names or by trying to acquaint you with the subtle differences they may represent. More valuable lessons can be learned from studying the historical origins of behavior modification and paying special attention to those developments that shaped the unique qualities of modern social-learning interventions.

In a very comprehensive book published in 1978, Alan Kazdin discusses several scientific and professional foundations of behavior modification. In this chapter, we will focus on six of these areas: early Russian research on conditioning, comparative psychology, Watsonian behaviorism, learning theory,

B. F. Skinner and operant conditioning, and applications of learning therapy to human behavior and psychotherapy. For more elaborate coverage of these topics and several others, consult Kazdin (1978, especially pp. 49–185).

FOUNDATIONS OF BEHAVIOR MODIFICATION

Conditioning Research in Russia

The impact of Russian conditioning research on behavior modification was transmitted through the early twentieth century work of three men: Ivan Sechenov, Ivan Pavlov, and Vladimir Bekhterev. Each of these scientists was trained in medicine, each was more a physiologist than a psychologist in orientation, and each advocated objective, mechanistic explanations of behavior, including those human behaviors that had always been considered to be highly subjective. Of greatest importance, each insisted that behavior be studied through scientific, empirical methods.

Sechenov's work came first. Aside from championing the empirical method, Sechenov made two important contributions to a behavioristic psychology. First he claimed that all behavior, mental and physical, voluntary and involuntary, was composed of reflexes that ultimately were elicited by the environment. Thus, he saw the ultimate cause of behavior as external. Second, Sechenov believed that the reflexes that formed complex human behavior were acquired through learning. Sechenov's theory of learning was based on Aristotle's concept of associationism, the idea that responses are learned when they are associated repeatedly with certain stimuli.

Pavlov's work on conditioning salivation in dogs is well known, at least by anyone who has taken introductory psychology. Pavlov discovered that if you repeatedly pair an *unconditioned stimulus* that elicits a reflex *(or unconditioned response)* with a neutral stimulus, the previously neutral stimulus becomes a *conditioned stimulus* which will now elicit a response *(the conditioned response)* which resembles the original reflex. A diagram of this process is presented in Figure 10-1.

In his famous experiments, Pavlov demonstrated that food would elicit salivation and that after pairing a tone with the food several times, the tone itself would be able to elicit salivation. Pavlov also discovered *higher-order conditioning* when he noticed that his own presence, after many associations with the tone and food, also elicited the dog's salivation. Thus, Pavlov's greatest contributions were his study of the precise conditions under which one form of learning (often called *Pavlovian, classical,* or *respondent conditioning*) took place and his demonstration of the specific effects that changes in those conditions would have on the conditioning process.

Bekhterev also studied conditioning, although he was more interested in overt motoric responses than was Pavlov. Bekhterev studied simple motor reflexes in humans using mild electric shock to the hands and feet as the unconditioned stimulus. Bekhterev was very enthusiastic about the implications of conditioning. He argued that psychology would be replaced by a more

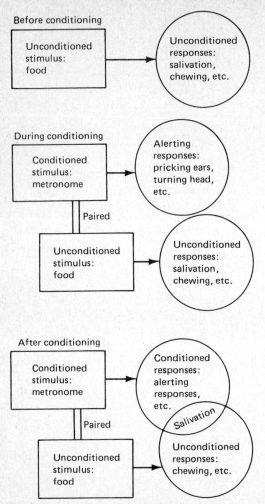

Figure 10-1 The course of Pavlovian conditioning. Before conditioning, food, an unconditioned stimulus, elicits unconditioned responses like salivation and chewing. During conditioning, a metronome, the potential conditioned stimulus, comes on a few moments before the food is given. The food still elicits various responses, while the metronome elicits only the usual alterness to a new sound. After a number of conditioning trials, the metronome elicits a new set of responses that includes some overlap (for example, salivation) with the original unconditioned response. *(Brown, R., and Herrnstein, R. J. Psychology.* © 1975 *by Little, Brown and Company. (Reprinted by permission.)*

objective discipline which he termed *reflexology*. Bekhterev's greatest historical contribution was his attempt to apply the principles of reflexology to behavioral disturbances. For example, Kazdin (1978) notes that at the beginning of the twentieth century Bekhterev was using conditioning to treat several types of disorder including hysterical deafness and sexual deviations. Pavlov also was aware of the clinical value of conditioning, particularly in understanding the causes of various behavior disorders.

Comparative Psychology

Comparative psychology involves the study of animal behavior. It is important to the development of behavior modification for several reasons, but chiefly because it gave support to Darwin's claim that there was a continuity in the behavior of humans and animals. Because of this continuity, the laws of animal learning that were being discovered in the late nineteenth and early twentieth centuries were thought to apply to humans as well.

Watsonian Behaviorism

John B. Watson "was responsible for crystallizing an existing trend toward objectivism" in psychology (Kazdin, 1978, p. 63). Watson received his Ph.D. in 1903 from the University of Chicago where the orientation to psychology was "functional." This meant that psychologists studied how human consciousness operated. The method of study was introspection, or the careful, trained observation of one's own mental processes. However, Watson was also exposed to the methods of physiology and biology at Chicago, and he became dissatisfied with functionalist psychology which, by comparison to the "hard" sciences, was too subjective in content and method for his tastes.

Watson's view of a more objective, behaviorist psychology was first published in 1913 in a paper called "Psychology As the Behaviorist Views It." In this article Watson described two essential qualities of behaviorism. First, introspection as a methodology was to be rejected and replaced with external observation, the method used by the animal psychologists. Second, psychologists must abandon the study of consciousness and focus instead on overt behavior and its relation to environmental stimuli. Watson's system came to be known as *S-R psychology* because of his emphasis on stimulus-response bonds through which all behavior could be explained. For example, thinking was seen as actually involving small movements of the vocal cords, and emotions were the product of physiological changes in certain organs. According to Watson:

> In each adjustment there is always both a *response or act* and a *stimulus or situation* which call out that response. Without going too far beyond our facts, it seems possible to say that the stimulus is always provided by the environment, external to the body, or by the movements of man's own muscles and the secretions of his glands; finally, that the responses always follow relatively immediately upon the presentation or incidence of the stimulus. These are really assumptions, but they seem to be basal ones for psychology. Before we finally accept or reject them we shall have to examine into both the nature of the stimulus or situation, and of the response. If we provisionally accept them we may say that the goal of psychological study is the *ascertaining of such data and laws that, given the stimulus, psychology can predict what the response will be; or, on the other hand, given the response, it can specify the nature of the effective stimulus.* (Watson, 1919, pp. 9-10)

Watson was very active in popularizing behaviorism and claiming that it could be used to solve human problems. His most extravagant allegation was that if he were given one dozen healthy infants, "well-formed, and my own specified world to bring them up in . . . I'll guarantee to take any one at random and train him to become any type of specialist I might select—doctor, lawyer, artist, merchant, chief, and yes, even beggarman and thief, regardless of his talents, penchants, tendencies, abilities, vocations and race of his ancestors" (Watson, 1930, p. 104). Partly as a result of this kind of enthusiasm, the literature of the 1920s contained many articles describing how behaviorism could be used to solve the problems of education, abnormal behavior, and society in general (Willis & Giles, 1978).

Learning Theory

By the 1930s the major topic of research in American psychology had become the psychology of learning and the construction of theoretical systems which explained learning processes. These learning theories were similar to the principles of conditioning set forth by the Russian physiologists in that both learning and conditioning are explanations for the acquisition and maintenance of new responses. But learning theories attempted to explain a much wider range of behavior (including speech and voluntary motor behavior) than the conditioning theories which were concerned with discrete responses of a narrow kind (knee jerks, eye blinks, startle responses).

Edward L. Thorndike was one of America's first learning theorists. He was interested in the voluntary, or *instrumental,* behavior of animals. For example, how does a cat learn to escape from a cage in which it is confined? Thorndike found that the most important factor in the development of a new response was the consequence of that response. Responses are strengthened or weakened according to the *law of effect,* which held that

> of several responses made to the same situation, those which are accompanied or closely followed by satisfaction to the animal will, other things being equal, be more firmly connected with the situation, so that, when it recurs, they will be more likely to recur; those which are accompanied or closely followed by discomfort to the animal will, other things being equal, have their connections with that situation weakened, so that, when it recurs, they will be less likely to occur. (Thorndike, 1911, p. 244)

This law of effect was the theoretical forerunner of B. F. Skinner's concepts of reinforcement and operant conditioning, of which more will be said later.

Another early learning theorist was Edwin Guthrie, whose major statement on learning was contained in his 1935 book, *The Psychology of Learning.* Guthrie's theory was quite similar to Watson's: Learning occurs as a result of contiguity or close association between stimuli and responses. Unlike Thorndike, Guthrie did not believe that reinforcement played a major role in learning. According to Guthrie, reinforcement simply prevents the organism from performing some new behavior which could break up the previously formed associations between a stimulus and response.

Other important names in the history of social-learning models are Clark

Hull, America's most influential learning theorist throughout the 1930s and 1940s and Edward Tolman, the founder of *purposive behaviorism.* Hull attempted to synthesize the classical conditioning of Pavlov and the instrumental conditioning of Thorndike under a single theoretical system. His work has had a great influence on the later learning theories of such eminent psychologists as Kenneth Spence (1956), O. Hobart Mowrer (1960), and Neal Miller (1951). Hull's theory has also been cited as a theoretical foundation for several modern behavior therapy techniques, most notably Wolpe's systematic desensitization.

Tolman emphasized the role of such intervening variables as *expectancy, cognition,* and *meaning* in his learning theory. He made an explicit distinction between learning and performance: An organism may learn or could know what the correct behavior in some situation would be without necessarily performing that behavior. Tolman suggested that reinforcement acts to *regulate* overt performance but does not "teach" us which responses are correct. As you shall see, Tolman's ideas were very similar to those expressed by modern social-learning theorists. Many of the social-learning model's more cognitive therapy methods described later are quite compatible with Tolman's "purposive behaviorism."

Each of the learning theorists mentioned above was aware of the possible implications of his work for understanding and modifying human behavior. This was especially the case for Guthrie, who offered several procedures (to be discussed later) for altering undesirable behaviors and for Hull, whose work was the basis for Dollard and Miller's classic book, *Personality and Psychotherapy* (1950), which attempted to translate psychoanalytic theory into learning terms. A similar effort at recasting conventional therapeutic concepts into the language of learning theory was made in Julian Rotter's *Social Learning and Clinical Psychology* (1954).

Skinner and Operant Conditioning

According to strict behaviorists, operant conditioning is the process by which most "voluntary" forms of behavior are developed. Of course, the most important figure in the application of operant conditioning to an understanding of human social conduct is B. F. Skinner, whose *Science and Human Behavior* (1953) is regarded as one of the foundations of modern behavior therapy (Rimm and Masters, 1979). The basic premise of operant conditioning is deceptively simple: Behavior is learned and strengthened as a result of its consequences. The term "operant" suggests a person whose behavior operates or acts upon the environment to produce consequences. In turn, these consequences influence the probability that the behaviors which preceded them will recur in the future. Learning not to touch a hot stove by getting burned provides a simple example of this process.

The main effect of operant conditioning is that randomly emitted, trial-and-error behaviors are progressively "shaped" into meaningful patterns of activity as a result of their outcomes. Positive or rewarding consequences (reinforcers) strengthen the likelihood of previous operants, while aversive consequences weaken the probability of similar future responses. Skinner's own research concentrated on the role of reinforcement as the major determinant of behavior.

There are five principles which define the core of operant conditioning. Four of these are represented in Figure 10-2, which depicts the possible combinations of presenting or withdrawing either positive or negative events following some behavior. Presenting a positive reinforcer following some behavior is called *positive reinforcement,* a process which, as the arrow in Cell I indicates, strengthens the behavior. Having a beer after a study session is a common form of positive reinforcement. Cell II describes one type of *punishment* in which a negative consequence is presented after some behavior and results in a decrease in that behavior's future probability (see "hot stove" example above).

Cell III represents a second form of *punishment* which occurs when a previously available positive event or state is removed following emission of some behavior. For example, having one's car stolen while unlocked would probably decrease the future probability of such careless behavior. *Negative reinforcement* (Cell IV) results in an *increase* in the probability of a behavior's future occurrence by removing something unpleasant following that behavior. Thus, headache relief after taking aspirin tends to strengthen future aspirin taking. Both positive and negative reinforcement always strengthen behavior, while both kinds of punishment decrease the future probability of the behaviors preceding them.

Figure 10-2 Techniques and effects of operant conditioning. The arrows in each cell indicate that behavior preceding various consequences will be strengthened (↑) or weakened (↓).

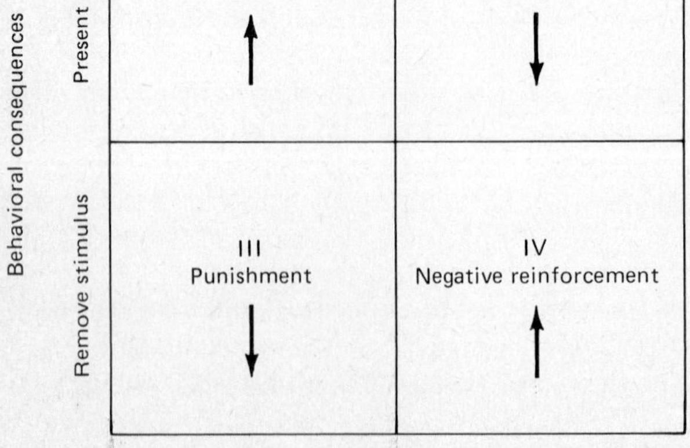

Nature of behavioral consequences

		Positive	Negative
Behavioral consequences	Present stimulus	I Positive reinforcement ↑	II Punishment ↓
	Remove stimulus	III Punishment ↓	IV Negative reinforcement ↑

The fifth operant principle (not presented in Figure 10-2) is *extinction*. Extinction refers to the weakening or elimination of behavior as a result of the absence of both positive *and* negative consequences. A simple example of this process would be giving up on telephoning someone after repeatedly failing to get an answer. There are, of course, many other concepts and principles associated with operant conditioning. For more extensive coverage of this material, see Ferster and Perrott (1968), Holland and Skinner (1961), and Reynolds (1968).

Applications of Learning Theory to Human Behavior and Psychotherapy

We have seen that within the first 25 years of the twentieth century, eminent Russian physiologists had published important work on conditioning, Watson had articulated the principles of behaviorism, psychologists were increasingly applying the findings of experimental research on animals to explain human behavior, and theorists such as Thorndike were beginning to propose increasingly complex models of the manner in which new behavior was learned. One effect of all these developments was that psychologists were more and more interested in applying the laws of conditioning and learning to the investigation and treatment of behavior disorders.

An early illustration of this trend was the discovery that emotional responses resembling human neuroses could be experimentally induced in laboratory animals. Pavlov observed examples of *experimental neuroses* in his dogs after exposing them to electric shock as an unconditioned stimulus or requiring them to make very difficult sensory discriminations. The dogs' symptoms included agitation, barking, biting the equipment, and forgetting things they had previously learned. While these findings were incidental to Pavlov's major interest in conditioned reflexes, in the 1940s Jules Masserman of Northwestern University deliberately studied the conditioning and deconditioning of experimental neuroses in cats as an analogy to psychopathology and psychoanalytic treatment. Investigation of experimental neuroses in a variety of animal species quickly became a popular research topic. Kazdin (1978) reports that W. Horsely Gantt, another early researcher of experimental neuroses, had a dog named Nick whom Gantt claimed remained neurotic for more than 12 years.

The discovery of experimental neuroses in animals soon led to research on apparently similar problems in humans. The most famous of these studies is a classic experiment reported in 1920 by John B. Watson and his graduate student, Rosalie Rayner (with whom Watson was presumably conditioned to fall in love and later marry). A 9-month-old infant, Albert B., was first presented with several stimuli such as a white rat, a dog, a rabbit, a monkey, masks, and a burning newspaper. He showed no fear toward any of these objects, but he did become very upset when a loud noise was sounded by striking a steel bar with a hammer. He was startled by the noise, his breathing was affected, and he trembled and cried during later presentations of the noise.

Nick, in happier days, on his farm. Nick's hard life was not entirely relieved by his retreat to the farm, for it was here that Gantt tried to teach him how to swim only to run into problems on three separate occasions—once when he threw Nick into the water, a second time when Nick got tangled up in his own chain, and finally when Nick got his foot caught in Gantt's bicycle and was dragged for some distance. Gantt (1944) observed, "After each of these he appeared less friendly toward me for several days . . ." (p. 84). *(From W. H. Gantt, Experimental Basis for Neurotic Behavior. Published with the sponsorship of the American Society for Research in Psychomatic Problems. New York, 1944. Reprinted by permission.)*

In order to see whether Albert's fear could be conditioned (à la Pavlov) to formerly nonfrightening objects, Watson and Rayner associated the loud noise with a white rat. The rat was brought to Albert and, as soon as he began to reach for it, the noise was presented. After several such pairings over a 1-week period, the rat alone elicited a strong emotional reaction in Albert. According to the authors, "the instant the rat was shown the baby began to cry. Almost instantly he turned sharply to the left, fell over on his left side, raised himself on all fours and began to crawl away so rapidly that he was caught with difficulty before reaching the edge of the table" (Watson & Rayner, 1920; p. 5). The investigators were also interested in whether this conditioned fear had generalized to other objects so they presented several stimuli which only two months earlier had not upset Albert. This time the effects were different. Albert was quite squeamish when confronted with a rabbit, a fur coat, Watson's own hair, and even a Santa Claus mask. Albert's fear persisted in less extreme form during assessments conducted over a 1-month period.

The child was removed from the research setting before anything could be done to completely remove his fears, but, a few years later, Mary Cover Jones, another of Watson's students, investigated several techniques for reducing fear reactions in a group of institutionalized children. Two methods were found to be most successful: *direct conditioning,* in which a fear stimulus was associated with some pleasant activity like eating, and *social imitation,* where the fearful child watched other children who were not afraid of the object in question (Jones, 1924a).

These two methods were investigated more carefully in Jones's (1924b) case history of Peter, a report which is as well known among psychologists as the Watson and Rayner report on Albert. Peter was a 3-year-old boy who was afraid of many things, particularly rabbits. Social imitation was used first. According to Jones, "each day Peter and three other children were brought to the laboratory for a play period. The other children were selected carefully because of their entirely fearless attitude toward the rabbit . . .". (Jones, 1924b, p. 310). The rabbit was present during these play periods, and, with the fearless examples of the other children, Peter was able to become more comfortable as he gradually came closer to the animal in a sequence of "toleration" steps (e.g., tolerates rabbit 12 feet away in a cage, tolerates rabbit 3 feet away in a cage, can touch rabbit when free in room, squats defenseless by rabbit, holds rabbit in lap, lets rabbit nibble his fingers).

Peter's progress was jeopardized by a couple of unfortunate events over which Jones had little control. He contracted scarlet fever which interrupted treatment for 2 months, and he had a nasty encounter with a big dog that badly frightened him while he and his nurse were getting into a taxicab. At this point direct conditioning was introduced. Peter was placed in a high chair and fed his favorite food while a caged rabbit was placed gradually closer to him at each session. Sometimes other children were present during the sessions.

Direct conditioning eliminated Peter's fear of rabbits. There was also some evidence that the deconditioning generalized to Peter's fear of other stimuli. For example, he showed no fear toward a mass of angleworms or a box of frogs. Peter himself best summed up the happy results of this case by announcing one fateful day, "I like the rabbit."

The experiments by Watson and Rayner (1920) and M. C. Jones (1924a, b) had a tremendous impact on the history of behavior modification because they suggested that conditioning could account for both the acquisition and treatment of fear reactions. The range of problems to which conditioning was applied during the 1920s and 1930s was very wide, covering children's fears, sexual disorders, substance abuse, and several neurotic conditions (Yates, 1970). Interest in the clinical use of conditioning persisted despite the failure of some investigators to replicate initial results (Kazdin, 1978). O'Leary and Wilson (1975) review a case reported by English (1929) who attempted to condition a 14-month-old girl to be afraid of a large wooden duck by banging a metal bar with a hammer each time the girl reached for the duck. After fifty such pairings the infant's enthusiasm for the duck was unabated, so English used a larger and noisier hammer. Still the child remained unafraid, although several professionals in the building complained about all the racket. Amazed and probably somewhat disappointed by the little tyke's nerves of steel, English theorized that the usual rambunctiousness and uproariousness of the girl's three older brothers had made her immune to the aversive properties of noise.

The Recent History of Behavior Therapy

Official recognition of "behavior therapy" occurred in the late 1950s and early 1960s, a time when there were several reasons why clinical psychology was receptive to social-learning approaches to treatment. Eysenck's challenges to the effectiveness of psychotherapy, widespread dissatisfaction with the usefulness of clinical assessment, and discontent with the implications of the medical model of behavior disorder were particularly influential. Each of these forces was mentioned in Chapter 4 and is discussed more fully in Chapter 12. For present purposes, it is important to recognize that these factors caused clinicians to view social-learning approaches to behavior change as very attractive alternatives to traditional forms of psychotherapy.

Behavior therapy was formally initiated in three countries: South Africa, England, and the United States. To a certain degree, developments in each country were independent of the others, but there was also an interesting pattern of mutual dependency and collaboration. In South Africa, psychiatrist Joseph Wolpe was conducting animal and human research which culminated in the publication of his book, *Psychotherapy by Reciprocal Inhibition* (1958). The work of two of his psychologist students, Stanley Rachman and Arnold Lazarus, was to receive worldwide attention as well. Lazarus, you will remember, was one of the first to use the term "behavior therapy," and Rachman has been very influential in the progress of behavior therapy and research in England since 1960. The South Africans were a very mobile group: Wolpe visited Eysenck in England and then moved permanently to the United States in 1962; Lazarus has resided in this country since 1966 (Kazdin, 1978).

In England, the two most important influences on behavior therapy have been Hans Eysenck and M. B. Shapiro, both of whom are affiliated with the Institute of Psychiatry at the University of London and Maudsley Hospital. Eysenck introduced the term "behavior therapy" to England in 1959 and published the first systematic text on behavior therapy in 1960 (Kazdin, 1978). England's "Maudsley group" (which also included Rachman, Issac Marks, and Michael Gelder) included prolific researchers who investigated the effectiveness of many behavioral techniques including flooding, aversion therapy, and several varieties of desensitization (all to be discussed later).

Kazdin (1978) lists several professionals in the United States who pioneered the clinical use of social-learning treatment techniques. During the 1920s, William Burnham practiced several procedures that were very similar to modern behavioral methods. In the early 1930s, Knight Dunlap used the method of *negative practice* to eliminate bad habits. Voegtlin and Lemere used chemical aversion (their term was "conditioned reflex treatment") to treat alcoholics at the Shadel Sanitarium in Seattle, Washington (Shadel, 1944). Andrew Salter employed a therapeutic strategy he called "conditioned reflex therapy" which was based on classical conditioning and involved exercises to increase emotional expressiveness as well as other techniques that resembled many current behavioral methods (Salter, 1949). Throughout the 1950s and 1960s operant conditioning methods were increasingly used in the treatment of psychotic patients and troubled children (see Ullmann & Krasner, 1965).

The situation in the United States was different from that in either South Africa or England because, despite the use of frequent examples of learning-based techniques, there was no integrated, systematic movement toward behavior therapy. Another way of saying this is that in the United States there were behavior therapists long before there was behavior therapy. The crystallization of behavior therapy in America was the result of two factors: (1) a recognition of the behavior-therapy movement in England, particularly the work of Eysenck, and (2) the publication of several books in this country that provided an overall, unified framework for behavior modification. Most notable in this latter category are Skinner's (1953) *Science and Human Behavior*, *Conditioning Techniques in Clinical Practice and Research* (Franks, 1964), *Case Studies in Behavior Modification* (Ullmann & Krasner, 1965), *Research in Behavior Modification* (Krasner & Ullmann, 1965), Wolpe's 1958 book, and *Behavior Therapy Techniques: A Guide to the Treatment of Neuroses* (Wolpe & Lazarus, 1966).

As you can see from Table 10-1, the definition of behavior therapy has undergone considerable revision over the years, but, according to three recent

Table 10-1   A Brief History of Definitions of Behavior Therapy

Source	Definition of Behavior Therapy
Eysenck (1964)	The attempt to alter human behavior and emotion in a beneficial manner according to the laws of modern learning theory.
Ullmann and Krasner (1965)	A field including many different techniques, all broadly related to the field of learning—but learning with a particular intent, namely, clinical treatment and change.
Wolpe and Lazarus (1966)	The application of experimentally established principles of learning to overcome maladaptive habits.
Yates (1970)	The attempt to use the empirical and theoretical knowledge resulting from experimental research in psychology and related disciplines in order to explain the genesis and maintenance of abnormal behavior and to apply that knowledge to the treatment or prevention of abnormalities by means of controlled experimental studies of the single case, both descriptive and remedial.
Krasner (1971)	The application of behavioral principles derived from the experimental laboratory by modifying human behavior labeled as deviant.
Kazdin (1978)	The application of experimental findings from psychological research for the purpose of altering behavior.
Wilson (1978)	Treatment techniques that involve a commitment to measurement, methodology, concepts, and procedures derivable from experimental psychology.
Rimm and Masters (1979)	Any of a large number of specific techniques that employ psychological (especially learning) principles to constructively change human behavior.

reviews of the field (Kazdin, 1978; O'Leary & Wilson, 1975; Rimm & Masters, 1979), the common, essential principles of behavior therapy are the following:

1 There is a presumed continuity between normal and abnormal behavior which implies that the basic laws of learning apply to all types of behavior. Maladaptive behaviors are acquired through the same psychological processes as any other behaviors (see Chapter 3).

2 Therapeutic techniques should be based on the empirical findings and theoretical foundations of experimental psychology. In its early years, behavior therapy relied primarily on the findings of S-R learning theory, but today its empirical foundations are much broader.

3 Therapy is aimed at the modification of specific, overt, maladaptive behaviors. The cognitions and emotions which accompany overt behavior are also dealt with, but in a more concrete, direct manner than in many other therapeutic approaches. Treatment is carefully tailored to the unique needs of each client.

4 There is a focus on the client's present problems. This here-and-now emphasis results in much less preoccupation with early childhood experiences or historical material than is usually the case in, say, psychoanalysis.

5 There is a strong commitment to the experimental evaluation of treatment. The behavior therapist attempts to employ techniques which have been scientifically validated through experimental group designs or single-subject methodology.

6 There is a recognition that emphasis on problem-focused techniques and empirical validation of treatment does not reduce the need for behavior therapists to be sensitive persons who are concerned for the welfare of their clients. Like clinicians of any other theoretical persuasion, behavior therapists strive to exercise good clinical judgment and sound ethical practices when providing their services and conducting their research.

CONTEMPORARY BEHAVIOR-THERAPY TECHNIQUES

In the remainder of this chapter, we will describe some of the techniques that compose the core of behavior therapy. We will trace the historical development of each procedure, describe its current applications, and discuss empirical evidence for its effectiveness.

Systematic Desensitization

Systematic desensitization (SD) is one of the best-known, most frequently employed, and thoroughly researched techniques in behavior therapy. It is used most often to reduce maladaptive, learned anxiety (such as phobias) but has also been applied to a host of other clinical problems, some of which appear at first glance to have little to do with anxiety.

Historical Background   As noted earlier, interest in applying learning principles to the problem of eliminating strong fears has been lively for decades.

The demonstrations by Watson and Rayner that fear could be learned through conditioning (i.e., in Albert's case) and by Mary Cover Jones that it could be unlearned through the same mechanism (i.e., in Peter's case) were prime examples. In addition, learning theorist Edwin Guthrie proposed several learning-based techniques during the 1930s for breaking maladaptive habits. For instance, Guthrie suggested that one way to overcome fear was to begin with an example of the frightening stimulus that was so weak that anxiety did not occur and then gradually increase the strength of the stimulus until it could be presented at full strength without eliciting discomfort (Guthrie, 1935). During the 1920s, Johannes Schultz, a German psychologist, developed a technique called "autogenic training." It involved a combination of hypnosis, relaxation, and autosuggestion with which clients themselves induced states that were incompatible with distressing emotions such as anxiety.

However, the first clearly defined package of social-learning-oriented treatments for clinical use in anxiety reduction was Joseph Wolpe's *systematic desensitization*. Wolpe described this treatment package in his 1958 *Psychotherapy by Reciprocal Inhibition*. Wolpe had been doing research in South Africa on the conditions under which cats would develop "experimental neuroses." Like Masserman (1943) before him, Wolpe found several "neurotic" manifestations. For example, after animals had been shocked on repeated occasions while eating, they resisted being put in the cages where the shocks had taken place, and they acted emotionally and refused to eat when finally placed in those cages.

Wolpe reasoned that if conditioned anxiety could inhibit eating, the reverse might also be true; eating might inhibit conditioned anxiety (as it had done in the case of Peter). Luckily for the cats, Wolpe was right. Relying on a principle called *reciprocal inhibition,* he hand-fed fearful cats in the cages where their anxiety had been learned. According to Wolpe (1958): "If a response antagonistic to anxiety can be made to occur in the presence of anxiety-evoking stimuli so that it is accompanied by a complete or partial suppression of the anxiety responses, the bond between these stimuli and the anxiety responses will be weakened" (p. 71).

Many of the animals benefited from this procedure and their emotional behaviors were reduced. However, some cats remained "neurotic." Wolpe moved these cats into rooms that were less and less like the conditioning room until they were willing to eat. After an animal was able to eat in one of these rooms without showing anxiety, Wolpe moved it to a setting which was a bit more like the feared environment. He continued this process of feeding the cats in places that were more and more like the original conditioning setting until they were able to eat in the feared cage itself.

Desensitization Procedures   After having cured his cats, Wolpe (1958) began to extend his methods to humans who suffered with maladaptive anxiety. His first task was to find a response which was sufficiently incompatible with anxiety to inhibit its unwanted occurrence. He selected three types of inhibiting responses: deep muscle relaxation, interpersonal assertion, and sexual arousal.[2] In each instance the principle was presumed to be the same: People cannot be anxious while they are relaxed or assertive or sexually aroused. Deep muscle relaxation has become the most popular anxiety inhibitor in clinical treatment involving systematic desensitization. However, assertion or sexual arousal may also be employed, especially when the anxiety to be inhibited relates to interpersonal or sexual problems.

The most common relaxation technique is called *progressive relaxation training* (e.g., Bernstein & Borkovec, 1973), a shorter version of a method pioneered by Jacobson in 1938. The client is taught to become physically and mentally relaxed by going through a series of exercises in which sixteen different groups of muscles are tensed for a few seconds and then released while the client focuses on the sensations of relaxation that follow. You can get some idea of what these exercises feel like by tightly clenching your fist for about 5 seconds and then abruptly releasing the tension. The flow of relaxation you will feel is a mild version of what can be experienced by tensing and relaxing muscles throughout the body.

Relaxation training initially takes approximately 40 minutes per session. After four to six sessions and some practice at combining the exercises for several muscle groups, the client may be able to achieve deep relaxation in less than 10 minutes. Relaxation may be attained through other methods if for some reason the client is unable to perform the exercises or the therapist has a preference for another technique. Hypnosis is used on occasion, as are drugs such as methohexitol sodium.

The next step in desensitization is to introduce anxiety-arousing situations in a gradual fashion. Wolpe used two types of graded *hierarchies*. There were *in vivo* hierarchies, where clients were actually exposed to gradually more threatening versions of what they feared, and *imaginal* hierarchies, in which clients imagined or visualized a series of increasingly frightening scenes. In each case, the specific order of real or imagined scenes is determined by the client. Hierarchy construction is often more difficult than it might appear. The main problem is wording and arranging items so that each one elicits just a bit more anxiety than the one before it. Too large an increase in arousal between items will make progress up the hierarchy difficult, while too small an increase may make for a needlessly long and boring course of treatment. An illustrative imaginal desensitization hierarchy is presented in Box 10-1.

Clinicians today usually use imaginal hierarchies, often for the sake of convenience. It is obviously much easier and cheaper to have a submarine phobic imagine a submerged cruise than to actually arrange a trip to the bottom

---

[2]Eating has not been completely abandoned as an anxiety inhibitor. In a recent case report (Tarler-Benlolo & Love, 1977), a woman who feared sexual encounters with her husband was instructed to munch her favorite food, macadamia nuts, while becoming gradually more sexually intimate. The technique worked, a new form of oral sex was discovered, and a cascade of bad jokes about nuts soon followed.

Box 10-1   An Example of a Desensitization Hierarchy

Below is an example of a desensitization hierarchy used by James Geer (1964) in his treatment of a 17-year-old high school girl who had a "morbid fear of contracting a case of nits in her hair." The numbers in parentheses indicate the session(s) of desensitization during which that item was presented.

1   Writing the words "bug" and "lice." (1)
2   While reading in school you notice a small bug on your book. (1)
3   While walking down the sidewalk you notice a comb in the gutter. (1)
4   You are at home watching television when an ad concerning a dandruff removing shampoo comes on. (2)
5   You are reading a *Reader's Digest* article that goes into detail concerning the catching and curing of a case of lice. (2)
6   You look at your desk top and notice several bobby pins and clips upon it. (3)
7   You are in a department store, and the saleslady is fitting a hat on you. (3)
8   At a store you are asked to try on a wig and you comply. (3)
9   You are watching a movie and they show a scene where people are being deloused. (4, 5, and 6)
10 At school, in hygiene class, the teacher lectures on lice and bugs in people's hair. (4 and 5)
11 A girl puts her scarf on your lap. (5)
12 In a public washroom you touch the seat of a commode. (6)
13 You are in a beauty shop having your hair set. (6)
14 A girl sitting in front of you in school leans her head back on your books. (6 and 7)
15 While sitting at home with your sister, she tells you that she used someone else's comb today. (7 and 8)
16 While sitting in the local snack bar a friend tells you of her experiences when she had a case of lice. (8 and 9)
17 You are combing your hair in the washroom when someone asks to borrow your comb. (9)
18 A stranger asks to use your comb and continues to ask why not when you say no. (9)
19 While standing looking at an ad in a store window, someone comes up beside you and puts their head near yours to see too. (10)
20 A stranger in the washroom at school hands you her comb and asks you to hold it for her. (10)
21 Your sister is fixing your hair when she drops the curlers on the floor, picks them up, and uses them in your hair. (11)
22 A stranger notices a tangle in your hair and tries to help you by combing it out with her comb. (11)

of the sea. In vivo hierarchies are often desirable, however, and have been employed with success alone, or in combination with imaginal stimuli (e.g., Bernstein & Beaty, 1971; MacDonald & Bernstein, 1974).

After training in relaxation and the construction of the hierarchy, desensitization proper is begun. In imaginal procedures, the client is relaxed and asked to visualize as vividly as possible the easiest item on the hierarchy. If the client can imagine the scene without any anxiety for 10 seconds, the next scene will be presented. If any anxiety is felt, however, the client indicates this to the therapist by some prearranged signal (e.g., raising the index finger), and she or he is instructed to stop visualizing the scene. After regaining complete relaxation, the client will again be asked to picture the item for a shorter duration (e.g., 3 to 5 seconds). Visualization times for that scene are gradually increased until the client imagines it twice for the full duration without anxiety. This general sequence is continued until the client comfortably handles all the items.

It is thought that the inhibition of anxiety in relation to imaginal scenes will gradually transfer to their real-life equivalents, but the client is also urged to seek out real-world counterparts of the visualized scenes in order to consolidate and reinforce progress and to assess the generality of the treatment effects. Completion of a hierarchy typically takes between three and five sessions, though it is possible to finish a short hierarchy in a single meeting.

Applications   Systematic desensitization has been applied to fears of almost everything, including high places and low places, closed spaces and open spaces; an ark's worth of mammals, reptiles, birds, insects, and fish; encounters with women, with men, with strangers and with noise, dirt, and death. Desensitization has even been used to relieve less common fears that sound as if Woody Allen invented them. These include fear of balloons, wind, the year 1952, feathers, violins, dirty shirts, and short people.

Desensitization is also used in cases where anxiety is not immediately obvious. For example, when anxiety causes complex, coordinated patterns of behavior to break down, clients may focus on the disruption itself, not the anxiety causing it. Complaints about inability to concentrate, poor memory, confusion, speech disfluency, sexual dysfunction, or impairment of motor skills (e.g., typing) can quite often be dealt with through desensitization of the situations which are stimulating the initial anxiety. Similarly, the appearance of certain kinds of maladaptive, bizarre, or seemingly irrational behaviors such as amnesia, obsessions, compulsions, delusions, hysterical paralysis, drug abuse, alcoholism, or unusual sexual practices are sometimes found to be motivated by efforts to avoid certain anxiety-provoking stimuli or situations.

Finally, prolonged anxiety may cause real *physical damage* to various organ systems and result in "psychosomatic" or psychophysiological disorders (e.g., ulcers). In other cases anxiety may produce physical symptoms such as headaches, high blood pressure, or chronic fatigue. Where actual damage has occurred, medical treatment is of course required but in either case, anxiety reduction through desensitization may help eliminate one of the factors causing these problems.

Variations on Desensitization   The popularity and effectiveness of SD have led to a proliferation of methods based upon it. *Group desensitization* has been used for some time in situations where several clients share a common fear. In group desensitization, a single hierarchy is used with all the clients and progress up the hierarchy is geared to the pace of the slowest individual.

In vivo desensitization is probably the most popular variant on SD. As noted earlier, the client is exposed to actual anxiety-arousing objects or situations, presented in a gradual fashion, often in real-life settings. Standard relaxation procedures are frequently eliminated from in vivo desensitization because of the obvious impracticality of having a client walk around, say, an airport or a zoo while keeping his or her muscles completely relaxed. As an alternative, therapists may act as anxiety inhibitors by accompanying their clients on in vivo "field trips." Sometimes the client is asked to engage in some behavior that is incompatible with strong anxiety. An interesting application of this latter approach was treating severe elevator phobia by having clients eat a multicourse, gourmet meal while seated in an elevator as it moved up and down (Bryntwick & Solyom, 1973).

Cue-controlled relaxation is another means of inhibiting anxiety in real-life settings, either as part of in vivo desensitization or some type of stress management procedures. The technique involves first training the client in standard progressive relaxation. After becoming totally relaxed, the client is instructed to subvocalize a *cue word* like "calm" or "relax" with each exhalation. The therapist pronounces the cue word along with the client for several trials and the client continues alone for several more pairings. After a few weeks of practicing this procedure, the client is presented with some frightening (real or imagined) stimulus in the office and told to take a deep breath and subvocalize the cue word upon exhalation. If relaxation is achieved, the client is encouraged to use the cue to prevent or deal with maladaptive anxiety in real-life encounters.

Effectiveness and Other Research Issues   Regarding the effectiveness of SD, Gordon Paul concluded that "for the first time in the history of psychological treatments, a specific therapeutic package reliably produced measurable benefits for clients across a broad range of distressing problems in which anxiety was of fundamental importance" (Paul, 1969b, p. 159). Paul's conclusion has been reevaluated over the years (e.g., Davison & Wilson, 1973) with the result that social-learning-oriented clinicians are generally confident about the efficacy of desensitization, especially when it is applied to its most appropriate target: clear-cut, conditioned, maladaptive anxiety.

The major research question surrounding desensitization today is not so much *whether* it is effective, but *why*. Wolpe's original counterconditioning explanation has been challenged by a vast amount of research and many behavior therapists no longer subscribe to it (Kazdin & Wilcoxon, 1976; Wilkins, 1971). Several mechanisms have been proposed as alternative explanations for desensitization's success. Among the most popular are the following:

1   That desensitization depends on *cognitive factors* that modify the way the client thinks about a feared object. For example the technique may produce a strong belief or *expectancy* that a fear can be overcome. The credibility of desensitization therefore ensures its success as a treatment (e.g., Marcia, Rubin, & Efran, 1969).

2   That the therapist acts as *social reinforcer* for the client's nonfearful responses (e.g., Leitenberg, Agras, Barlow, & Oliveau, 1969).

3 That as the client recognizes progress up the hierarchy, future non-phobic behavior is supported through *self-reinforcement* (e.g., Meichenbaum, 1972).

4 That clients learn to *shift their attention* from threatening to nonthreatening properties of phobic situations (e.g., Wilkins, 1971).

5 That anxiety is *extinguished* via the presentation of conditioned emotional stimuli (hierarchy scenes) without any aversive consequences (e.g., D'Zurilla, Wilson, & Nelson, 1973; Lader & Mathews, 1968).

Hundreds of research investigations have yet to resolve the question of the mechanism by which desensitization produces its effects (see reviews by Davison & Wilson, 1973; Kazdin & Wilcoxon, 1976; Wilson & Davison, 1971). Whether future research will be any more conclusive is uncertain. In any event, systematic desensitization now stands as one of the best validated treatment techniques available to the clinical psychologist.

Flooding and Implosion

Like desensitization, *flooding* is a technique used for anxiety reduction but, unlike desensitization, it involves *extended* exposure of a *nonrelaxed* client to anxiety-eliciting stimuli of *high* intensity. Flooding is based on the principle of extinction, i.e., that conditioned fear stimuli gradually lose their aversive quality when the client is repeatedly or continuously exposed to them without any actual harmful consequences. In flooding, persons are prevented from avoiding or escaping a situation they fear in order to help them learn that the situation is not actually threatening. Flooding is a little like the common-sense "sink-or-swim" technique whereby a child who fears water is thrown into the deep end of the pool (one hopes for extinction of fear, not the child).

Implosion or implosive therapy is very similar in procedure to flooding. The main difference is that implosion often presents fear stimuli that are more intense than those actually found in life and sometimes includes material which psychoanalytic theory suggests would be important in causing a certain fear (Stampfl & Levis, 1973). For example, in treating someone with a fear of toads, the implosive therapist might use imagined scenes of toads along with others depicting castration, Oedipal conflicts, parental rejection, and bodily injury.

Historical Background Kazdin (1978) points out that flooding had its modern origin in two types of laboratory experiments. The first was Masserman's work on experimental neurosis in which it was demonstrated that an animal's experimentally induced anxiety could be eliminated by forcing the animal back into the feared setting. Experiments on avoidance learning also suggested the therapeutic value of forced exposure (e.g., Solomon, Kamin, & Wynne, 1953).

Although there are few references to techniques resembling flooding in early clinical literature, there is no doubt that similar methods have been employed nonsystematically for many years. Aphorisms such as "face your fears," "the only thing to fear is fear itself," and "look fear in its face" are all supported by the same rationale as flooding.

Flooding Procedures   Flooding is usually conducted imaginally, though it can be done in vivo. In either instance, exposure times must be long enough for anxiety to begin to dissipate. Exposure should never be terminated while the client is still anxious because this would reinforce avoidance behavior. Flooding sessions usually last 45 minutes to an hour, although it is sometimes necessary for them to last 2 or more hours before a decrease in anxiety is noted. An excerpt from a session of implosion is provided in Box 10-2.

Applications   Flooding is often used for problems where desensitization has previously proven to be unsuccessful. One problem for which flooding appears to be especially popular is agoraphobia. Literally translated, agoraphobia is "fear of the marketplace," but in current parlance it means a fear of public places, especially those that are too crowded or too empty. Clinical agoraphobics are usually women who present a cluster of symptoms including panic attacks, depression, fear of being away from any place that represents safety, depersonalization, and "fear of fear" (Goldstein & Chambless, 1978). Flooding is also frequently employed for obsessive-compulsive disorders.

Effectiveness and Other Research Issues   Although empirical research has not yet isolated the exact mechanism responsible for flooding's effectiveness, the major research effort has been to compare desensitization with flooding in an attempt to discover which technique is more effective (Barrett, 1969; DeMoor, 1970). This question has not been resolved and may never be. While neither technique has been shown to be uniformly superior, it is probably fair to say that

---

Box 10-2   An Example of Implosive Therapy

Below are some excerpts from a transcripted session of implosive therapy with a snake phobic. These quotes should give you an idea of how implosive techniques are practiced and why most clinicians rarely use them.

> Close your eyes again. Picture the snake out in front of you, now make yourself pick it up. Reach down, pick it up, put it in your lap, feel it wiggling around in your lap, leave your hand on it, put your hand out and feel it wiggling around. Kind of explore its body with your fingers and hand. You don't like to do it, make yourself do it . . .
> Let it, let it bite at your finger. Put your finger out, let it bite, let it bite at your finger, feel its fangs go right down into your finger. Oooh, feel the pain going right up your arm and into your shoulder. You want to pull your hand away, but leave it there.
> Okay, feel him coiling around your hand again, touching you, slimy now, he is going up on your shoulder and he crawls there and he [is] sitting on your chest and he is looking you right in the eye. He is big and he is black and he is ugly and he's coiled up and he is ready to strike and he is looking at you.
> Feel him bite, put your head down towards him, put your head down, let him bite at your face, let him bite as much as he wants. Feel him bite, he is putting his head, his little head up by your ear and he is snapping at your ear. Feel him snap at your ear.

Source: Hogan, 1968, pp. 427–428.

most behavior therapists prefer desensitization. This preference may be based on several factors, not the least of which is the conventional belief that desensitization is the less intrusive and discomfiting of the two methods.

Assertion Training

The 1970s have become known as the decade of individual independence, an era committed to the pursuit of selfhood (or selfishness) and often criticized for what some would call its narcissistic preoccupations. Partial testimony to the character of the period is the spate of self-help books urging people to do their own thing, explore their (and others') erogenous zones, be creatively aggressive, and say no and not feel guilty. Though *assertion training* has sometimes been identified as behavior therapy's contribution to this phenomenon of self-promotion, it is more than just another manifestation of the "me generation"; it is also an important clinical tool whose beneficial effects for many clients extend far beyond the boundaries of current social trends.

Contrary to popular belief, assertiveness is not merely aggressiveness or the ability to stand up for one's rights. It is best defined as *the appropriate expression of feeling in ways which do not infringe upon the rights of others* (Alberti & Emmons, 1974; Wolpe & Lazarus, 1966). Thus, telling your boss that you will not agree to some unreasonable request requires assertion, but so does telling your friends that you were moved by their recent expression of sympathy. Assertion is not the same as aggression. Responding to the person who pushes ahead of you in a supermarket check-out line by saying "pardon me, there is a line here; please wait your turn" is assertive. Saying "get your ass out of here before I hit you with this pot roast" is aggressive and not a goal of assertion training. Finally, assertiveness does not preclude politeness or altruism. An assertive individual will make sacrifices to help others ("why don't you check-out first; I'm not in a hurry"), but *only* because he or she wishes to do so, not because of fear of expressing objections.

All too often, people know exactly what to say and do in a difficult social situation (and chide themselves later for not having said or done it) but, because of thoughts like "I have no right to make a fuss" or "he won't like me if I object," they suffer in silence. Increasing social awkwardness, continuous self-blame and, sometimes, varying degrees of depression are common results. Assertion training is designed to (1) teach clients how to appropriately express themselves (if they do not already have the skills), and/or (2) eliminate cognitive obstacles to clear self-expression. The benefits usually include a general sense of well-being and the establishment of patterns of thought and overt behavior which help the client achieve social and material rewards, including greater satisfaction from life (Rimm & Masters, 1979).

Historical Background   Assertion training was anticipated by several earlier therapeutic procedures. For example, Moreno's (1946) psychodrama used role-playing techniques which encouraged participants to act spontaneously and express feelings more freely. In George Kelly's (1955) *fixed-role therapy,* clients were asked to assume the role of some model whose outlook on the world and actual behavior were less inhibited and constricted than their own (see Chapter 11). Through this type of identification, the client was expected to learn the benefits of behavior which today would be described as assertive.

The first systematic description of assertion training was offered by Andrew Salter in his *Conditioned Reflex Therapy* (1949). Salter prescribed a number of *excitatory* techniques for "inhibited" clients. Among these methods were use of "feeling talk" (e.g., "I absolutely despise crows"), expression of contradictory opinion, "facial talk" (making facial expressions consistent with emotions), improvisation, acknowledging and accepting compliments, and using the word "I" in conversation.[3]

The most influential figure in the evolution of assertion training, however, was Joseph Wolpe, who advocated using assertive behavior as an anxiety inhibitor as early as 1949. Wolpe found assertive responses to be particularly effective in inhibiting interpersonal anxiety and began training his clients in specific assertion skills. The development of assertion training has been explosive in recent years, as evidenced by the multitude of books, articles, workshops, and courses devoted to it. Popularization of assertion training has not detracted from its usefulness in clinical settings, however, and it remains today a solid component of social-learning treatment.

Assertion Training Procedures   Unlike other techniques discussed in this chapter, assertion training has not been clearly standardized into a specific set of procedures. Rather, a wide assortment of methods is employed. Though it can be done on a one-to-one basis, assertion training often takes place in small groups and usually includes four general components: (1) defining assertion and distinguishing assertion from aggression and submissiveness, (2) discussion and identification of clients' rights and the rights of others in a variety of social situations, (3) identification and elimination of cognitive obstacles to assertion, and (4) development and/or practice of assertive behavior (Lange & Jakubowski, 1976).

This last component usually begins with role-playing or rehearsal of various social interactions, often with the therapist taking the client's role and modeling appropriate assertiveness. Next, the client tries the same behavior. This effort is reinforced and suggestions are made for even further improvement. After additional, more refined rehearsals, the client is asked to try out the new thoughts and actions in real-life settings. Successes and failures are then discussed and analyzed at future sessions, where new or slightly adjusted skills are developed and practiced. This sequence continues until the need for further training disappears.

---

[3]These techniques are also part of gestalt therapy and other phenomenologically oriented treatment approaches discussed in Chapter 11.

Applications Many types of clients can benefit from assertion training, although few enter a therapist's office and request it specifically. Couples suffering marital discord, college students who have interpersonal problems, shy and introverted adults, alcoholics, drug abusers, withdrawn psychotics, and people who rely on aggression to coerce others are often helped by assertion training as part of an overall clinical intervention.

Effectiveness and Other Research Issues Since the late 1960s, research on the effects of assertion training has been popular among social-learning-oriented clinicians. Most of this work has been done with college students or psychiatric inpatients and has attempted to ascertain the relative effectiveness of the modeling, behavioral rehearsal and feedback components of assertion training. While the results are complex and difficult to summarize, it would seem that with college students, almost any training technique is sufficient to produce behavioral changes. Psychiatric patients seem to require a more elaborate treatment package in which modeling may be especially important (see Bellack & Hersen, 1977).

Although most research demonstrates that subjects receiving some form of training do significantly better than those who receive either a placebo or no treatment, it has been difficult to show that new assertive behavior transfers to in vivo contexts. Few studies have examined the issue of generalization of treatment effects. Those that have (Hersen, Eisler, & Miller, 1974; Kazdin, 1974; McFall & Marston, 1970; Nietzel, Martorano, & Melnick, 1977) often discover a disappointingly small amount of transfer of recently developed assertiveness.

Assertion research has received considerable criticism. A major concern is that most of it has been limited only to negative or "refusal" assertion which involves expression of dissatisfaction and saying "no" to unreasonable requests (see Box 10-3). Assertion in which the client communicates positive affect, gives and receives compliments, or expresses tender feelings has for the most part been ignored by researchers or is added to a study only as an afterthought.

Modeling

A very important mechanism in social-learning theory is *modeling,* or observational learning. Bandura (1969) claims that "virtually all learning phenomena resulting from direct experiences can occur on a vicarious basis through observation of other persons' behavior and its consequences for them" (p. 118). In many instances, learning through modeling is far more efficient and effective than learning through direct reinforcement. Observation of competent models can eliminate the hazards and negative consequences of unguided trial-and-error behavior (imagine the problems if everyone had to be hit by a car before knowing how to cross streets safely!). Highly sophisticated behaviors such as speech require appropriate models, as do complex chains of motor behavior such as driving. Of course, many behaviors *can* be developed through direct

---

Box 10-3 Exercises in Assertion Training

The training situations used in most recent assertion research concentrate on what is often termed "denial" or "refusal" assertion and are similar to those used in assessing assertion (see Chapter 7). Below are three examples taken from some of our own research.

1 You have just moved into a new apartment with two other friends. They have been looking for a fourth person with whom to share the apartment. The two friends come to you and inform you that they have found a fourth person. The proposed roommate happens to be someone whom you secretly dislike.
2 You are eating in a very nice restaurant with some friends. The waiter comes and you order a steak, telling him you want it "rare." A little later, the waiter brings you your steak, and you discover that it is well-done. The waiter asks, "Will there be anything else?"
3 You are leaving your job late on a Friday afternoon. You are hurrying home because you have made dinner plans for that evening with some friends. At the door of the office, you are stopped by your boss who says, "I'd like you to work tonight for a couple of hours because we have a job that must be completed by tomorrow."

Source: Nietzel, Martorano, and Melnick, 1977.

---

experience and reinforcement, but the process of learning is often shortened by the opportunity to observe the performance of models.

In addition to developing new behaviors, modeling has two other effects (Bandura, 1969). Observation of the consequences of a model's behavior may either *inhibit* or *disinhibit* imitative behavior in an observer (would you pet a dog that just bit your friend?). Observing the behavior of others can also *facilitate* the performance of similar responses already present in the repertoire of the observer (taking one's place in line is a common example).

Historical Background Modeling long has been recognized as an important influence on behavior. Psychological theories of imitation were proposed by Lloyd Morgan (1896) and Gabriel Tarde (1903), the French judge and sociologist. Tarde developed a theory of criminality based on the idea that crime is acquired almost exclusively through imitation. These early theorists viewed imitation as an innate characteristic of humans. Later, psychologists began to explain modeling in terms of conditioning (Allport, 1924) and reinforcement (Miller & Dollard, 1941) principles.

The replacement of instinct theories with those that emphasized learning variables was, as noted earlier, a dominant feature of American psychology in general throughout the first half of the twentieth century. In the laboratory, Wolfgang Kohler, one of the founders of gestalt psychology, demonstrated that chimpanzees would imitate other chimps and men, particularly in situations with which they were familiar. L. W. Cole claimed some evidence for imitation among raccoons (Boring, 1950).

You have already encountered one of the earliest therapeutic examples of modeling in Jones's (1924a, b) use of *social imitation* to overcome conditioned fear in children. Bandura (1969) also credits Masserman (1943) with the early use of modeling to remediate experimental neuroses produced in laboratory animals. According to Bandura, the opportunity for Masserman's inhibited animals to observe a fearless cagemate was sufficient to reduce avoidance behavior in some of them.

Modeling Procedures   Modeling has been used to treat many different types of clinical problems including social withdrawal among adults and children, obsessive-compulsive behaviors, unassertiveness, antisocial conduct (including physical aggressiveness), and early infantile autism (see Nay, 1976). Probably its most common use, however, is in the reduction of fears.

In simplest form, a modeling approach to the elimination of fearful avoidance would involve having a client observe a live or symbolic (filmed or videotaped) display in which one or more models fearlessly perform the behavior which the client avoids. The observable consequences for the models are always positive, or at least not negative.

A wide range of variations on the basic modeling package has been developed. The most common of these is called *participant modeling*. In this procedure, live modeling is supplemented by giving the client an opportunity to

These frames are from a modeling film used to treat snake phobics. The film depicts children and adults in progressively more threatening interactions with a king snake. *(From A. Bandura, E. B. Blanchard, and B. Ritter,* Journal of Personality and Social Psychology, *1969, 13, 173–199. Copyright by the American Psychological Association. Reprinted by permission.)*

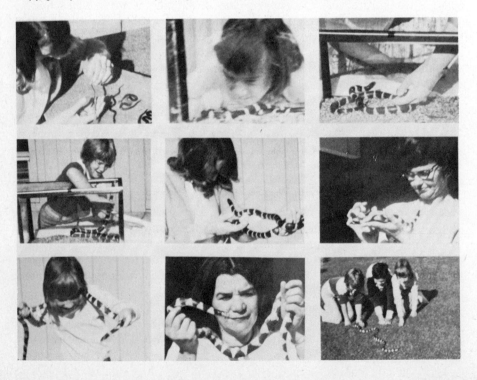

make guided, gradual contact with the feared object under controlled or protected circumstances. This guided contact may be further supported by the use of *response induction aids,* which are special props or procedures that make feared responses a little easier or less threatening. For example, Bandura, Jeffery, and Wright (1974) reported that induction aids such as gloves and physical assistance enhanced the effectiveness of modeling in reducing clients' fear of snakes.

Another recent innovation in modeling techniques is *covert modeling* (Kazdin, 1974). Here, clients observe the activities of *imagined* therapeutic models rather than watching live or videotaped displays. The basic covert modeling package involves three components: imagination of situations where fear is expected to occur; imagination of one or more persons comfortably dealing with these situations, and imagination of favorable consequences for the model.

Effectiveness and Other Research Issues   For the most part, outcome research on modeling for fear reduction and other goals has shown it to be effective in producing beneficial changes (e.g., Bandura, 1971; Rosenthal, 1976). Many questions remain unanswered, of course, but it would still be fair to conclude that modeling techniques have shown great promise in dealing with the problems to which they have been applied.

A primary concern of much present-day modeling research is the investigation of several procedural variations that are intended to bolster the effectiveness of the modeling paradigm. Participant and covert modeling are two important examples. Other research has shown that observers are especially influenced by models with whom they share characteristics, by models that are prestigious, by models that are rewarded for their acts, and by multiple models (Bandura, 1969).

In a very interesting variation in the customary modeling procedure, Meichenbaum (1971) proposed that the display of some fearful behavior by models could actually enhance modeling effects if presented as the initial part of a more complete demonstration in which the model ultimately copes with and overcomes the fear. He termed this technique *coping modeling* and suggested that it would strengthen treatment because it enhances observer-model similarity and provides useful information on how to deal successfully with a fear. While not universally supported, some studies have replicated Meichenbaum's (1971) finding that coping models produce stronger effects than "mastery models," who display total fearlessness and competence (e.g., Kazdin, 1973).

Aversion Therapy

Aversion therapy is a set of techniques which use painful or unpleasant stimuli to decrease the probability of some unwanted behavior. Drug abuse, alcoholism, overeating, smoking, and disturbing sexual practices are typical targets of aversion therapy. Most aversion methods are based on classical conditioning. Stimuli which elicit problem behavior are paired, Pavlov-style, with a noxious stimulus (e.g., a person is shocked as he sits at a simulated bar and begins to reach for a bottle of Scotch). Continuation of this sequence should result in a decrease in the positive value of the eliciting stimuli until the unwanted behavior is reduced if not eliminated.

Aversion therapy may also employ punishment. In such cases, the aversive stimulus is delivered just after the client performs the problematic behavior (e.g., shock would occur immediately after taking a drink of alcohol).

Historical Background Aversion techniques have been used on an unsystematic basis for centuries. Ullmann and Krasner (1969) report that the Romans encouraged sobriety among their citizens by placing an eel in the wine cups of intemperate drinkers. Throughout the first half of the twentieth century, aversion techniques were frequently used to treat certain behavioral problems. The conditioning work of Bekhterev and Pavlov suggested the possible clinical utility of conditioning aversions to previously positive stimuli. Thus, it is not surprising that it was another Russian, Nikolai Kantorovich, who, in 1930, was the first to use aversion conditioning (electric shock to the hands) for the treatment of alcohol abuse. As noted earlier, one of the first major applications of aversion therapy in the United States was reported by Voetglin and his associates at the Shadel Sanitorium in Seattle.

Aversion Therapy Procedures The noxious stimuli used in aversion therapy usually take one of two forms: electric shock (to the hands, feet, or legs) or drugs which either induce nausea or temporarily suppress breathing. Substances with a foul taste or smell have also been used, but only rarely (e.g., Busch & Evans, 1977; Colson, 1972).

In one example of electrical aversion, Blake (1965) used shocks along with relaxation training and instructions about the negative consequences of drinking to treat a group of alcoholics. Participants were shocked on half of the occasions on which they sipped alcohol. Termination of the shock occurred only when subjects spat out the alcohol, a procedure known as *aversion relief*. Follow-up interviews indicated a 54 percent rate of abstinence after 6 months and 52 percent abstinence after one year.

Hsu (1965) investigated a more extreme electric shock procedure. With electrodes attached to the subject's head, levels of shock just less than those that would have rendered the subject unconscious were administered when alcoholic beverages were selected and sipped. Daily treatments took place for 5 days, followed by 1- and 6-month "booster sessions." Of forty male volunteers, only sixteen completed the full treatment sequence.

Reimringer, Morgan, and Bramwell (1970) reported a chemically based aversion technique for the elimination of "persistent physical or verbal violence, deviant sexual behavior, and lack of cooperation and involvement" among inmates at a state mental hospital. The technique was procedurally simple. Following a preset schedule, the patient received an intravenous, 20-mg dose of succinylcholine, a neuromuscular blocking agent that produces brief paralysis of the diaphragm and suppression of breathing 34 to 40 seconds after administration. Inmates were conscious during the paralysis, and the experience was described as intensely terrifying. Upon suppression of breathing, the "talking phase" of the technique began. This involved verbal admonishments to discontinue unacceptable behaviors along with suggestions to increase positive "constructive socialization." Suggestions were repeated until the inmate was able to respond verbally to the attending staff.

Another illustration of chemical aversion is supplied by Raymond (1956). He reported successful use of apomorphine-based conditioning with a hospitalized, 33-year-old male fetishist against whom numerous charges had been lodged involving malicious attacks on and damage to "prams" (baby carriages) and handbags. According to the police, he was responsible for twelve diverse incidents which had occurred over several years, e.g., setting prams on fire, driving a motorcycle into them, smearing mucus on a handbag. One prosecutor was moved to label the patient "a menace to any woman with a pram." Treatment involved repeatedly pairing the fetish objects with drug-induced nausea. After several sessions over a period of days, the patient claimed to be repulsed by the objects of his former affections and even relinquished some pram photos he had kept surreptitiously for years. At a 6-month booster session, a film of the fetish objects was paired with nausea.

A continuing controversy in aversion therapy is whether there is a basis for preferring chemical or electrical events as the noxious stimuli. From an aesthetic viewpoint it is probably a toss-up. For a time, the prevailing sentiment appeared to favor electrical methods, although this preference was justified more on the basis of procedural efficiency and control than on outcome comparisons. Davidson (1974) has described seven advantages usually associated with electrical methods: (1) greater temporal precision, (2) greater suitability for frequent repetitions, (3) fewer medical complications, (4) fewer apparatus requirements, (5) fewer staff needed, (6) less traumatic implementations for staff, and (7) wider applicability. However, recent opinion (Elkins, 1975) suggests that the positive effects of chemical aversion may have been underestimated in early investigations because the procedures were often carelessly or incorrectly applied.

It has been suggested that certain types of aversion are more appropriate for behaviors that involve a particular sensorimotor system. For example, associations between nausea and overeating or overdrinking might be biologically and psychologically easier to establish than connections between, say, overeating and pain. On the other hand, shock may be more easily associated with sexual or aggressive misbehaviors than would chemically induced sickness (e.g., Wilson & Davison, 1969).

A newer form of aversion therapy called *covert sensitization* requires the client to simply visualize or imagine aversive consequences that could accompany unwanted behavior. According to Little and Curran (1978), covert sensitization usually proceeds as follows:

The covert sensitization client, after receiving several sessions of relaxation training, is asked to relax and imagine a sequence of events leading up to a hypothetical problematic performance. The client is then asked to imagine a series of aversive events (typically, nausea and vomiting) just as the point in the imaginal sequence is reached when initial reinforcement is about to be received. The aversion trial is concluded with a suggestion to the client that relief is experienced coincident with an imaginal turning away from the target stimulus. Escape trials are alternated with aversion trials. In the escape trials, the client successively imagines that he or she has an urge to commit the target behavior, begins to experience aversive consequences (typically, nausea), resists the undesired urge, and consequently feels fit and self-satisfied. The therapist attempts to facilitate the client's visualization by describing both types of scenes and by providing an especially detailed and exaggerated description of the aversive consequence. (p. 513)

Joseph Cautela, the originator of covert sensitization, describes the following scene to be visualized by an alcoholic client:

You are walking into a bar. You decide to have a glass of beer. You are now walking toward the bar. As you are approaching the bar you have a funny feeling in the pit of your stomach. Your stomach feels all queasy and nauseous. Some liquid comes up your throat and it is very sour. You try to swallow it back down, but as you do this, food particles start coming up your throat to your mouth. You are now reaching the bar and you order a beer. As the bartender is pouring the beer, puke comes up into your mouth. You try to keep your mouth closed and swallow it down. You reach for the glass of beer to wash it down. As soon as your hand touches the glass, you can't hold it down any longer. You have to open your mouth and you puke. It goes all over your hand, all over the glass and the beer. You can see it floating around in the beer. Snots and mucus come out of your nose. Your shirt and pants are full of vomit. The bartender has some on his shirt. You notice people looking at you. You get sick again and you vomit some more and more. You turn away from the beer and immediately you start to feel better and better. When you get out into the clean fresh air you feel wonderful. You go home and clean yourself up. (Cautela, 1966, p. 37)

Covert sensitization offers several advantages over the actual use of shock or chemically induced aversion (Cautela & Rosenstiel, 1975). Few side effects have been noted, although some investigators have reported a tendency for aversive associations to generalize to nontargeted stimuli (Ashem & Donner, 1968). Special equipment or medical personnel are not required, and the procedure can be applied repeatedly in many different kinds of settings. In addition, because the client's own experiences are used, a wider variety of stimuli are available which, when presented in imagery, may better approximate those encountered in the natural environment. These advantages are reduced somewhat by the fact that some patients report difficulty in maintaining clear visualizations, which necessitates extensive imagery training.

Effectiveness and Other Research Issues   Our judgment about the effects of aversion therapy is that, in most cases, it has a rather limited impact on the problem to which it is applied. While few behavior therapists doubt that they can temporarily discourage a client from uncontrolled drinking or aberrant sexual acts by applying some powerfully repugnant agent, most remain skeptical about how permanent these changes will be (e.g., Redd, Porterfield, & Andersen, 1979).

The goal of any treatment should be change that is *durable* and that will *generalize* to the environment in which a client lives. On both these grounds, aversion therapy is often found lacking. One major reason is that aversion therapy, by itself, does not teach clients new, alternative behaviors that can replace their maladaptive ones. This is particularly important in the treatment of problematic consummatory behaviors such as overeating, smoking, drug abuse, or sexual deviations. In the sexual area, for example, problems usually reappear if clients do not develop other sexual outlets that are satisfying to them and acceptable to society (Serber, 1972).

The data on covert sensitization are mixed. Its practical advantages (e.g., flexibility, ease of administration) are numerous, but the existing literature is based primarily on studies which lack necessary controls. Little and Curran (1978) conclude that covert sensitization may be effective in producing desired changes in sexual preferences, but that the data do not support its effectiveness for alcoholism, smoking, or obesity.

Finally, we should add that many clinicians do not use aversion techniques simply because they personally find them unpleasant, unethical, or both. Others feel that shocking clients or making them vomit can harm the therapeutic relationship. As a result, most therapists use aversion methods only as a last resort after nonaversive procedures have failed to produce beneficial changes.

Contingency Management

Contingency management is a generic term describing any operant (Skinnerian) technique which attempts to modify a behavior by controlling its consequences. *Shaping, time-out, contingency contracting,* and *token economies* are some specific names for various types of contingency management. We shall describe each of these later. In practice, contingency management refers to the contingent presentation and/or withdrawal of reinforcers and aversive stimuli following certain behaviors. "Contingent" simply means that the manipulation of consequences occurs *if and only if* the behavior to be strengthened or weakened has occurred.

Historical Background   The use of rewards and punishments as a means of controlling behavior has, of course, existed for a long time. The idea that psychologists discovered that rewarding a behavior results in its increase while punishing it produces a decrease would reflect the grandest arrogance. The Old Testament depicts God as an effective contingency manager who practiced extinction (responding to the provocation of his sons and daughters, "I will hide my face from them" — Deuteronomy 32:19–20) as well as time-out and punishment (when the Israelites disobeyed God, He sent them to the wilderness for 40 years).

The same principles were used by correctional workers during the 1800s. For example, Alexander Maconochie, governor of a British penal colony, was convinced that the prison's deplorable conditions needed reform. Maconochie developed a plan by which a prisoner could gain early release by earning a sufficient number of "marks" through industry and good conduct. Another important feature of the system was its organization into graduated phases which resemble those of many contemporary token economies. The five phases were: (1) rigid discipline and absolute confinement; (2) labor on a chain gang; (3) limited freedom within certain areas; (4) "ticket-of-leave" or conditional freedom; and (5) total freedom.

Fuller (1949) reported one of the first uses of contingency management with a mental patient. The case involved a retarded 18-year-old boy whom Fuller described as a "vegetative idiot." He was completely immobile, mute, and able to take only liquid or semisolid nourishment. Despite this history, the client was taught to move his right arm through operant conditioning. The reinforcer for this behavior consisted of a brief squirt of warm sugar-milk into the boy's mouth.

Applications Contingency management has been applied to a broader range of problems than any other social-learning method. Autism, temper tantrums, learning difficulties, hyperactivity, retardation, juvenile delinquency, aggression, hallucinations, delusions, depression, phobias, sexual disorders, and psychosomatic complaints are only a few of the targets that have been dealt with through contingency management.

A special advantage of contingency management is its flexibility. It is suitable for the very young and the very old. It can be tailored to the unique complaints of an individual or applied to the common needs of a group or even a community. Its principles are relatively easy to learn, thus making it possible to train friends, relatives, teachers, and peers to employ contingency management in real-life settings.

Contingency management can also be used by an individual to modify his or her own behavior. This process is known as *self-control* (Goldiamond, 1965) and can be thought of as the ability to regulate personal behaviors by arranging appropriate reinforcement contingencies. The overweight person who permits herself or himself to eat only at narrowly specified times, only in the kitchen, and only in the presence of family is practicing a form of self-control. Specific components of self-control include self-instructions, self-monitoring, self-reinforcement, and self-evaluation, each of which has been shown to have some clinical utility (e.g., Kanfer, 1975).

Contingency Management Procedures Complete accounts of the wide range of contingency management techniques are available in many texts (e.g.,

Leitenberg, 1976; Nay, 1976; O'Leary & Wilson, 1975; Redd, Porterfield, & Andersen, 1979). Some idea of this range can be gathered from the following four examples:

1 Shaping   Also called *successive approximation,* shaping is a procedure for developing new behaviors by initially reinforcing any act that remotely resembles the ultimately desired behavior. Gradually the criterion for reinforcement is made more stringent until only those responses matching the final standard are rewarded. Shaping is very useful for instigating behaviors that appear to exceed the present capacities of a person. Therefore, it is often used to teach speech to children who are mute, toilet habits to those who are incontinent, and self-help and occupational skills to the retarded.

2 Time-out   Time-out is a special example of extinction which reduces the frequency of some unwanted behavior by temporarily removing the person from a setting where reinforcers for that behavior are available. The most common example is sending a child to a quiet, boring room for a short time following some act of mischief. Time-out is advocated as a method of controlling tantrums and is based on the principle that ignoring a child's "bad" behavior will decrease it, especially if alternative "good" behavior is also reinforced. It may be the case that enthusiasm for time-out is strongest among those clinicians who have no children of their own and have therefore not had the opportunity to learn, in the words of Odgen Nash, that

> Children aren't happy with nothing to ignore
>
> And that's what parents were created for.

3 Contingency contracting   Contracting is a recently popular form of contingency management where a formal agreement, often in written form, between therapist and client spells out the consequences of certain behaviors on the part of both parties. It thus systematizes and organizes the use of many behavior change methods.

Boudin (1972) employed contingency contracting to control amphetamine and barbiturate use by a female graduate student. Behavior of both the client and therapist during the 3-month treatment was specified in a detailed treatment contract. The client was required to (1) prepare a weekly schedule of her activities, (2) contact the therapist three times each day so that he could monitor her activities, (3) solicit the therapist's advice regarding her handling of any "potentially dangerous situations" (ones in which the probability of using drugs was increased), (4) formally and publicly commit herself to total drug abstinence, (5) self-administer shock from a portable dispenser contingent upon drug-procurement behaviors, (6) establish a joint bank account with the therapist in which all of her money was deposited, (7) forfeit $50 for each instance of actual or suspected drug use (checks were to be made payable to the Ku Klux Klan, a group particularly disliked by the client). For his part, the therapist agreed to arrange his schedule so that he was accessible to the client at all times and to countersign checks necessary to meet her living expenses.

The success of contractual arrangements depends, in part, on the therapist's willingness to enforce the agreements with the specified contingencies. In this case, the therapist exercised decisive control at three points: He refused to permit the client to discontinue therapy upon her request on the fourth day of treatment, he promptly paid the Ku Klux Klan $50 when the client reported the use of amphetamines, and he established firm contingencies and stimulus control that allowed the client to complete an important research report. Follow-up 2 years later revealed the client to be drug-free.

4   Token economies   A token economy is a procedure for implementing the principles of contingency management to alter a wide variety of behaviors in a person or group of people. You might think of it as a scaled-down monetary system in which people are paid in a special currency (tokens) for performing designated behaviors. A token economy is not much different from the ordinary principle of being compensated for one's labors, except that token economies are often established in institutional settings where residents had previously become accustomed to receiving rewards on a noncontingent basis.

As used in institutions, the token economy usually consists of four basic components. First, *target behaviors* must be specified. This means that the staff and, often, the clients designate what behaviors they hope to increase or improve through the program. Social interaction, self-help skills, and physical exercise are common target behaviors for chronically institutionalized mental patients. Second, there must be some medium of exchange or *token* which participants earn when and only when they perform the target behaviors. Gold stars and colored slips of paper are popular among children. Adults' tastes run toward poker chips, green stamps, or metal "coins." Third, there must be *back-up reinforcers:* the goods or services for which tokens may be exchanged. Food, recreational privileges, "vacations" from the hospital, and more luxurious living conditions are common back-ups. Finally, the *rules of exchange* must be established by all participants. Rules include the number of tokens to be earned by performing given target behaviors as well as the number of tokens necessary to purchase any back-up. Exchange rules are often altered over the course of a token economy in order to avoid "inflation" or "deflation" of the currency.

The first report of a token economy in a psychiatric institution was published by Ayllon and Azrin (1965), who increased the rate of self-care behaviors and completed work assignments in a group of chronic female patients. Following Ayllon and Azrin's study, the use of token economies in psychiatric hospitals increased at a rapid rate (Kazdin & Bootzin, 1972). There was also a dramatic increase in the application of token economy procedures to other populations. Several investigators used token systems to control delinquent and antisocial behavior (e.g., Burchard, 1967; Cohen, 1968), and token programs were soon introduced to elementary school classrooms for the purposes of reducing disruptions and promoting learning (e.g., O'Leary & Becker, 1967). Special programs for Head Start participants, retardates, alcoholics, drug addicts, and autistic children were developed according to token economy principles (Kazdin & Bootzin, 1972).

More recently, token economies have been extended beyond institutions and introduced directly into the community. For example, Miller and Miller (1970) increased the rate of community organization activities among poor people through a token economy. A variety of conservation and environmental protection efforts have also been promoted through token programs that are applied either to large geographical areas or relatively dense populations (Nietzel, Winett, MacDonald, & Davidson, 1977).

Effectiveness and Other Research Issues In terms of sheer frequency, research on contingency management is unmatched by any other social-learning intervention technique. Perhaps the most remarkable feature of all this research is the consistency with which it finds operant methods to be effective in modifying specific behaviors in desired directions. There are exceptions to this pattern, of course, but they are strikingly few in number.

The most troublesome aspect of contingency management is the perplexing problem of generalization. The nagging question is not about whether the techniques produce change, but whether the changes are durable as well as generalizable (Keely, Shemberg, & Carbonell, 1976; Nietzel & Moore, 1978). Thus, among the principal research goals in the field at this time are (1) development and evaluation of procedures deliberately designed to promote the transfer of new behaviors to natural settings, and (2) demonstration of the continuation of improved behaviors over time.

Another major trend in contemporary research on applied operant methods is the investigation of their success in dealing with problems that go beyond "mental health." Several broad social problems such as energy conservation, racial discrimination, unemployment, and mass transportation have all been approached from an operant perspective (Nietzel, Winett, MacDonald, & Davidson, 1977). At the other extreme, behavioral and psychological events that underlie various physical illnesses have also been modified by contingent reinforcement (Katz & Zlutnick, 1975; Pomerleau & Brady, 1979; Williams & Gentry, 1977).[4] The use of operant technology to control internal, autonomic responses is known as *biofeedback,* which is our next topic.

Biofeedback

Biofeedback is really just a specialized use of contingency management, but it is unique for two reasons. First, the behaviors to be controlled or changed are internal, autonomic responses which for many years were thought to be entirely involuntary and therefore not subject to deliberate modification; heart rate,

---

[4]This is part of a more general movement toward applying behavioral sciences to the understanding, prevention, and cure of health-related problems. This movement is now called *behavioral medicine.*

blood pressure, brain waves, galvanic skin responses, and distribution of blood flow are primary examples. Second, biofeedback requires special equipment which monitors the activity of interest and then communicates or provides "feedback" on this activity to the client. Feedback is transmitted either through a visual display (e.g., a meter or graph) or an auditory stimulus (e.g., a varying tone).

Historical Background   The most important figure in the development of biofeedback is Neal Miller (1969), who demonstrated that rats could learn to increase and decrease autonomic functions on the basis of contingent reinforcement (direct brain stimulation). The fact that the rats were immobilized with the drug curare ruled out the possibility that the autonomic changes were merely artifacts of muscular movement.

Miller was not the first to investigate the conditioning of autonomic behavior. Kazdin (1978) reports that K. M. Bykov had demonstrated in the mid-1950s that physiological responses could be *classically* conditioned to previously neutral stimuli, but Miller showed that visceral activity was also subject to the principles of *operant* conditioning.

Despite the troubling fact that Miller and several other researchers had difficulty replicating the results of the early studies with animals, many investigators throughout the 1960s began to show that humans could control such activity as brain waves and heart rate.

Applications and Procedures   Biofeedback has been used to treat several kinds of disorders. Probably the most common targets are essential hypertension (high blood pressure), migraine headaches, Raynaud's disease (a problem of reduced blood flow that can lead to gangrene in the hands or feet), and cardiac arrhythmias (irregular heart beats). EEG (electroencephalogram) conditioning, popularly known as "electric zen," can increase the percentage of alpha wave production and is often used as a special form of relaxation or meditation training.

In each of these applications, the procedure is fundamentally the same. A painless apparatus which monitors and feeds back information about physiological activity is attached to the client who then uses some preferred mental or physical strategy to change the internal response in a clinically desired direction. In most cases, the reinforcer for change is simply the knowledge of results provided by the feedback; however, feedback may be supplemented on occasion by praise from the therapist or by monetary rewards (Blanchard & Epstein, 1978).

Effectiveness and Other Research Issues   At this point there is not enough evidence to conclude that biofeedback is a clinically useful technique. It is important that this fact be kept in mind because, of all the techniques described in this chapter, biofeedback tends to generate the most endorsements and claims of success. Most of those claims have very little scientific support (e.g.,

Birnbaumer, 1977). O'Leary and Wilson (1975, p. 282) made several important points about the current status of biofeedback methods:

> First, most of the research with humans has involved "normal," volunteer subjects, and with few exceptions, the results have been statistically significant but too small to have much substantive or clinical significance. . . . Second, it has not been adequately demonstrated that the results obtained in the highly artificial laboratory situation will generalize to the natural environment or that the gains which have been achieved will be maintained over a long term follow-up. Systematic studies controlling for subject expectancies and placebo effect have yet to be carried out. . . . Finally, comparative outcome studies are necessary to show that alternative treatment methods, which might require less in the way of expensive and highly sophisticated physiological apparatus, are not equally effective.

Cognitive Behavior Therapy

Introducing a section called "cognitive behavior therapy" may suggest that the techniques already described in this chapter do not involve any cognitive factors. This is not the case. One can no more expect a client to participate in a psychotherapeutic technique without thinking about the experience than one can expect a sprinter to run a race without moving his or her legs. Any therapy technique, behavioral or otherwise, stimulates a multitude of cognitions: Will this treatment work? Why will it work? What if it doesn't work? Why didn't I think of trying this? When will I start to notice some improvement? In addition to thinking about these questions, clients must depend on cognitive processes to understand a therapist's communications, to visualize material in procedures like desensitization or covert modeling, and to reflect on the changes they make or fail to **make in** therapy.

Thus, **all** **therap**eutic interventions involve some cognitive processes, but some procedures are particularly oriented toward changing distinct, maladaptive cognitions. These techniques compose what is known as *cognitive behavior therapy* or simply *cognitive therapy*. Cognitive therapy can be defined as a treatment approach that attempts to modify overt behavior by influencing a client's thinking processes (Rimm & Masters, 1979). Ledwidge (1978) lists the following techniques as examples of cognitive behavior therapy: coping skills training, anxiety management, stress innoculation, emotion-response routine, idealized self-image technique, misattribution therapy, problem-solving training and self-instruction training. Time projection, thought stopping, and Aaron Beck's (1970) cognitive therapy for depression and other targets are frequently used procedures that should be added to this roster. Detailed descriptions of these techniques can be found in Mahoney (1974) and Meichenbaum (1974).

Cognitive behavior therapy is primarily a phenomenon of the 1970s. Ledwidge (1978) reports that no research articles on cognitive therapy appeared in a behavioral journal prior to 1970. There are now more than fifty reports in the behavioral journals and a journal devoted entirely to cognitive therapy, *Cognitive Therapy and Research,* has been founded.

   While clinical research interest in cognitively oriented therapy has expanded rapidly and fruitfully among social-learning advocates in the 1970s, the
alteration of clients' maladaptive thoughts has been of central interest to other
therapists for decades. Probably the best-known pre-1970 champion of cognitive
therapy (other than Adler) is Albert Ellis, founder of rational-emotive therapy,
or RET.[5]

   Ellis (1973) stated the core principles of RET as follows: "[W]hen a highly
charged emotional Consequence (C) follows a significant Activating Event (A),
A may seem to but actually does not cause C. Instead emotional Consequences
are largely created by B—the individual's Belief System. When, therefore, an
undesirable Consequence occurs, such as severe anxiety, this can usually be
quickly traced to the person's irrational Beliefs, and when these Beliefs are
effectively Disputed (at point D), by challenging them rationally, the disturbed
Consequences disappear and eventually cease to reoccur" (p. 167).

   To illustrate these principles, Ellis (1973) provides the following example.
Suppose we have a man who has a very bad day at work. He arrives late, forgets
his office keys, spills coffee on his desk and misses two important appointments.
He may think to himself, "I did lousy at my job today." He is correct, he did do
a bad job. This is what Ellis calls the Activating Event (A), a happening that is
undesirable, unwanted, or obnoxious. Next the man may think, "This is
horrible, what a schmuck I am; if I don't get with it I'll get fired which will serve
me right for being so worthless." These ideas are a reflection of the person's
Belief System (B), and according to Ellis, they account for or produce the
emotional consequences (C) of anxiety, depression, and worthlessness which
this man may experience.

   To summarize the ABCs of RET: Psychological problems result not from
external stress but from the irrational ideas that people hold which lead them to
command, insist, and dictate that their wishes and desires must be met in order
for them to be happy. Thus the task in RET is to attack these irrational,
unrealistic, self-damaging beliefs and to instruct clients in more rational or
logical thinking patterns that will not upset them.

   Historical Background   Ellis (1973) acknowledges numerous precursors to
his RET system. Among early philosophers, the stoics, and particularly
Epictetus, believed that "men are disturbed not by things, but by the view they
take of them." Literature provides other examples. Shakespeare, for instance,
has Hamlet observe: "there is nothing either good or bad but thinking makes it
so."

   Ellis also notes that modern psychotherapists influenced the development of
RET. Chief among these was Alfred Adler, whose motto "everything depends
on opinion" is a keystone of RET philosophy. Several therapists who employed

---

[5]Rational-emotive therapy has also been called rational behavior training (Goodman &
Maultsby, 1974), systematic rational restructuring (Goldfried, Decenteceo, & Weinberg, 1974), and
cognitive restructuring (Ledwidge, 1978).

"Why doesn't she call? I don't understand. She said she'd call at 5:00. It's 5:15 already. maybe she's been in accident. Maybe she's lying in a ditch somewhere. I'd better call her and make sure she's ok. No, what if she's not hurt. What if she's with a MAN. I can't call her. She'll think I'm too pushy. They never like pushy men. But it's 5:20 already and she SAID she'd call— I didn't make her say that. She might really be hurt and bleeding somewhere. But what if I call her and she doesn't want to talk to me? God-damned women."

Cartoon 10-1 Courtesy of the Western Psychological Association.

a forceful, directive, highly active therapeutic style (e.g., Hippolyte Bernheim, Andrew Salter, Frederick Thorne, Alexander Herzberg, and Wilhelm Stekel) also anticipated RET.

Ellis's first formal presentation of RET was in a paper he presented to the American Psychological Association in 1956, but the most complete and informative formulations are contained in his *Reason and Emotion in Psychotherapy* (1962) and the *Handbook of Rational-Emotive Therapy* (Ellis & Grieger, 1977). In his more recent descriptions of RET, Ellis has emphasized its similarity with the more cognitively oriented forms of behavior therapy: "In fact, in many ways broad spectrum behavior therapy and RET are almost synonymous" (Ellis, 1973, p. 175).

RET Procedures Ellis (1973) claims that RET is an appropriate treatment for almost all emotional problems with the exception of severe schizophrenia, extreme mania, organic brain damage, and mental retardation.

The style of the RET therapist is active, challenging, demonstrative, and often abrasive. Ellis advocates the use of a strong, direct form of communication in order to persuade clients to let loose the irrational ideas with which they indoctrinate themselves into misery. Here is a brief excerpt from an initial RET session between a therapist (T) and a young woman (C) who presented several problems, among them the abuse of alcohol.

C: . . . my tendency is to say *everything.* I want to change everything; I'm depressed about everything; *et cetera.*

T: Give me a couple of things, for example.

C: What I'm depressed about? I, uh, don't know that I have any purpose in life. I don't know what I—what I am. And I don't know in what direction I'm going.

T: Yeah. But that's—so you're saying, "I'm ignorant!" (client nods) Well, what's so awful about being ignorant? It's too bad you're ignorant. It would be nicer if you weren't—if you *had* a purpose and *knew* where you were going. But just let's suppose the worst: for the rest of your life you didn't have a purpose, and you stayed this way. Let's suppose that. Now why would you be so bad?

C: Because everyone *should* have a purpose!

T: Where did you get the *should?*

C: 'Cause it's what I believe in. (silence for a while)

T: I know. But think about it for a minute. You're obviously a bright woman; now, where did that *should* come from?

C: I, I don't know! I'm not thinking clearly at the moment. I'm too nervous! I'm sorry.

T: Well, but you *can* think clearly. Are you now saying, "Oh, it's hopeless! I can't think clearly. What a shit I am for not thinking clearly!" You see: you're blaming yourself for *that.*

C: (visibly upset; can't seem to say anything; then nods)

T: Now you're perfectly *able* to think.

C: Not at the moment!

T: Yes you are! Want to bet?

C: (begins to sob)

T: What are you crying about now?

C: Because I feel so stupid! And I'm afraid!

T: Yeah. But "stupid" means "I'm putting myself down for acting stupidly."

C: All right! I didn't expect to be put on so *fast.* I expected a moment to catch my breath and see who you *were;* and to establish some different kind of rapport.

T: Yeah. And that would be nice and easier; but we would really waste our time.

C: Yes, I guess we would.

T: But you're really upset because you're not giving the right answers—and isn't that *awful!*

C: Yes. And I don't think that anybody likes to be made a, a fool, a fool of!

T: You *can't* be made a fool of!

C: (chokes a little)

T: You see, that's the *point:* that's impossible. Now, why *can't* you be made a fool of?

C: (angry outburst) Why don't you stop asking me!

T: (interrupting) No! You'll never get better unless you *think*. And you're saying, "Can't we do something *magical* to get me better? And the answer is: "No!"

The therapist's frontal assault on the client's irrational beliefs is not restricted to cognitive interventions. Role-playing, sensory awareness exercises, desensitization, assertion training, and specific homework assignments also will be employed by the RET therapist in an attempt to provide a behavioral complement to cognitive change.

Effectiveness and Other Research Issues Ellis (1973) lists more than twenty-five experimental studies of RET and an even greater number of independent case reports which indicate a record of significant improvement associated with RET. The basic principles of RET have also been investigated in research studies which generally support the idea that emotional distress is associated with specific irrational beliefs (see reviews by Ellis, 1977, and DiGiuseppe & Miller, 1977). Several studies have compared RET with some other techniques like systematic desensitization. An interesting result of some of the best-controlled of these studies (e.g., Meichenbaum, Gilmore, and Fedoravicius, 1971) is that while desensitization appears more effective for clients with a specific phobia, RET may be more appropriate for clients who are anxious in several different kinds of situations.

A Final Note

In describing contemporary behavior therapy we have concentrated on specific techniques such as desensitization, flooding, contingency management, and biofeedback. This emphasis should not be taken to imply that behavior therapists are simply technicians who match problems with specific treatment methods in an automatic way. Behavior therapists, like clinicians of other theoretical persuasions, are committed to the welfare of the people they treat and attempt to convey a sense of support and caring during the therapy process. Technical proficiency is not a substitute for the special therapeutic relationship that a client and clinician can and do share.

Chapter 11

Clinical Intervention: Phenomenological Models

In Chapters 9 and 10 we described approaches to clinical intervention which operate largely on the assumption that human behavior is primarily a product of either intrapsychic conflicts or environmental influences; the most fundamental concept in classical psychodynamic therapy is *instinct,* while in most social-learning treatments, various kinds of *reinforcement* are central. As noted in Chapter 3, however, there is another alternative, a "third force" in clinical psychology which deemphasizes both instinct and reinforcement and focuses instead on *conscious experience* as the basis for the development, maintenance, and modification of human behavior. This *phenomenological* approach offers a very optimistic portrait of humans as creative, growing beings who, if all goes well, consciously guide their own behavior in directions which will ultimately realize their fullest potential as unique individuals. When problems arise in the form of various behavior disorders, they are usually seen as stemming mainly from disturbances or gaps in *awareness* which can be eliminated through various kinds of therapeutic experiences.

Obviously, the notion of working on behavior problems by increasing clients' conscious awareness reflects some of the psychodynamic principles upon which phenomenological treatments are partly based (see Chapter 9). Just as obviously, approaching each client as a unique individual who is guided by her or his own thoughts bears a close relationship to the more cognitively oriented versions of social-learning treatments (see Chapter 10). In fact, the interrelationships and commonalities in the theory and practice of all three models of clinical intervention are becoming increasingly obvious to some observers (e.g., Krasner, 1978; Wachtel, 1977; Wandersman, Poppen, & Ricks, 1976). Nevertheless, some of the goals and many of the techniques of phenomenologically oriented treatments are quite distinct. In this chapter we shall describe the background, procedures, and effectiveness of a few of the most prominent phenomenological intervention modes.

It will soon become clear that, just as was the case with psychodynamic and social-learning methods, a few common themes unify the many different terms and techniques associated with the phenomenological approach to clinical treatment. To set the stage for our discussion, let us briefly review some of these commonalities:

1 There is a clear emphasis upon promoting the client's *growth* as a person rather than upon the facilitation of skill at "playing the game of life." In other words, phenomenological therapists are fundamentally concerned with helping clients try to become aware of and reach their own unique potential as individuals. They deemphasize the client's interpersonal or behavioral "skills," coping "strategies," or "adjustment" to the environment. The underlying assumption here is that, when the client more nearly approaches his or her full potential, he or she will be capable of finding solutions to the external problems of living without help from anyone else. In fact, actively helping a client to solve particular problems is viewed as counterproductive: If the client makes use of the *therapist's* solution, the opportunity will be missed to let her or his own feelings and ideas be a guide. In addition, the client may become dependent upon the therapist and less inclined to take responsibility for seeking independent resolutions of future difficulties.

2 Because clients are viewed by phenomenological therapists as fully responsible individuals who are potentially capable of handling their own lives, the roles of the client and therapist are considered to be comparable in status. If in psychodynamic therapy there is an "expert doctor–naive patient" relationship and in social-learning interventions there is a "teaching assistant–student" relationship, in phenomenological treatment the clinician and client are more like "gardener and flower." The therapist facilitates growth which is inherent in the client, but both may grow and benefit from the relationship.

3 The relationship between the client and the therapist is seen as the primary vehicle through which growth takes place. This means that the immediate, moment-to-moment experience of the therapy situation is what helps the client. Thus, for an insecure client, discussion of and insight into the past or making plans for handling future problematic situations would be viewed as far less helpful than actually being in a relationship where another person nonjudgmentally *accepts* and *values* the client despite his or her own lack of self-assurance. This experience is thought to be helpful because it may prompt the client to begin perceiving himself or herself in more positive terms. The point is that, in phenomenologically oriented treatment, the client-therapist relationship is not a special, isolated context for talking *about* early conflicts, how those conflicts appear in the present, or possible new responses to the environment. It is seen as a *real interpersonal relationship* which, quite apart from the topics discussed or the "techniques" used, gives the client human *experiences* which themselves promote growth.

4 Because the immediate experience of the therapy relationship is so important, the focus of phenomenological treatment seldom if ever strays far from what is going on between client and therapist in the session. As noted in Chapters 3 and 4, this usually means that there is relatively little formal assessment of the client's past. The assumption is that the past is gone, cannot be changed, and in any case is not as important for the client's future as what happens in the present.

5 Like social-learning therapists, phenomenologically oriented clinicians assume that most of their clients are not "sick," "disordered," or in any other way basically different from "normal" people, no matter how bizarre or unusual those clients appear to be. However, rather than emphasizing unique learning experiences as the foundation of most behavior problems, phenomenologists typically see their clients as behaving in line with their own unique perceptions of the world. Therefore, the therapist seeks to understand the client's problems by trying to look at the world through the client's eyes. It is hoped that, in the process of revealing her or his perceptions to the therapist, the client will become much more clearly aware of those perceptions and how they guide behavior.

With these general themes in mind, let us now begin to examine some specific examples of phenomenological treatment.

THE CLIENT-CENTERED THERAPY OF CARL ROGERS

Probably the best-known and most influential of the phenomenological approaches to clinical intervention is the *client-centered therapy* of Carl Rogers (1942, 1951, 1959, 1961, 1970). Though Rogers' initial training as a psychologist was in a psychodynamic tradition, he ultimately rejected the principles of that tradition and founded instead an approach to treatment which, by the 1940s, had provided clinical psychology with its first systematic alternative to Freud. As we shall see, Rogers also established a tradition of doing research on the process and outcome of psychotherapy.

Some Background on Client-Centered Therapy

Carl Rogers was born on January 8, 1902, the fourth of six children in a close knit, conservative Protestant family. Religion and the concepts of individualism, self-reliance, and hard work were important early influences. "There was no drinking, dancing, card playing, theatre going, and little social life . . ." (Sollod, 1978, p. 95) in Rogers' youth; in fact, he reportedly had only two dates all during high school (Reisman, 1966). His family moved to a farm when Rogers was 12, and he became interested in agriculture, particularly the scientific, experimental aspects of it. By the age of 14, Rogers had become a student of scientific agriculture and learned "how experiments were conducted, how control groups

Figure 11-1   Carl Rogers (1902–) by John T. Wood, courtesy of Carl Rogers.

were matched with experimental groups, how conditions were held constant by randomizing procedures . . ." (Rogers, 1961, p. 6).

Rogers became an agriculture major at the University of Wisconsin but, because of his family background, was leaning toward becoming a minister. In his junior year, he spent 6 months at a World Student Christian Federation conference in China, during which time he began to question the very conservative religious views of his parents and to become inclined toward more liberal forms of Christianity. As a result, after graduation he enrolled in New York City's Union Theological Seminary, an institution whose liberal orientation fit Rogers' newly developing religious views.

While at the seminary, Rogers and some of his fellow students formed an independent seminar group whose aim was to search for truth through thought and discussion about personal ideas, concepts, and doubts. There was no instructor. "The majority of the members of that group, in thinking their way through the questions they raised, thought themselves right out of religious work. I was one" (Rogers, 1961, p. 8). In 1925, after 2 years at Union, Rogers enrolled in Teachers College at Columbia University to study psychology.

At least as early as his China trip, Rogers had been wrestling with the concept of authority. In religion, in education, in family life, he had learned that those "in authority" want to tell people what to do, how to think, and what values to adopt. Yet he had begun to question the wisdom and ultimate correctness of this approach, not only as a force in his own life, but in the lives of others. While at Teachers College, Rogers found that he was not alone in his concern. Through William Kilpatrick, a faculty member, he learned about *progressive education,* among whose concepts was the notion that education should enhance the personal growth of students by pacing lessons to the student's level of reading and by tailoring material to student needs. Progressive education advocates such as Kilpatrick and John Dewey also advocated use of *guided discussion* to help students find things out for themselves rather than merely using lectures or readings to *tell* students the right answers or conclusions.

Rogers' training in child therapy at Columbia began under the guidance of Leta Hollingsworth and continued during a year-long internship at the Institute for Child Guidance in New York. You will remember from Chapter 2 that child guidance clinics at this time were run primarily by psychiatrists, so Rogers was exposed to a strongly Freudian treatment model. Though he "gained much" (Rogers, 1959, p. 186) from this experience, Rogers became as uncomfortable with the concept of therapist-as-authority as he had been with the notion of teacher-as-authority. Thus, after he took his first job as a psychologist in the child study department of the Rochester (New York) Society for the Prevention of Cruelty to Children (a child guidance agency), Rogers became increasingly unhappy with the prevalent dynamic psychiatric approach to clients and their problems. At this point (the early 1930s) Rogers was not really sure what alternative to pursue, but he felt that there had to be a better way to go about clinical work.

The beginning of an alternative appeared when Rogers became aware of Otto Rank's approach to therapy, mainly through the influence of Rankian social workers at Rochester and through the writings of Jessie Taft, a Philadelphia psychologist/social worker. Taft had developed an approach she called *relationship therapy.* It was a form of treatment "which can take place only when divorced from all hint of control" (Taft, 1951, p. 94). Taft's procedures reflected the basic tenets advanced by Rank: "The individual client . . . is a moving cause, containing constructive forces within, which constitute a will to health. The therapist guides the individual to self-understanding, self-acceptance. It is the therapist *as a human being* who is the remedy, not his technical skill. . . . The spontaneity and uniqueness of therapy lived in the present carry the patient toward health" (Meador & Rogers, 1973, p. 121; italics added).

These ideas sat well with Rogers. They fit nicely with the principles of progressive education which had impressed him so much in graduate school, they reflected his own growing distrust of authoritarian treatment in which the therapist was in an "expert" role superior to the client, and they evoked ideals stemming from his childhood: ". . . the individualism of the American frontier, the belief in self-reliance, the conviction that the individual could learn to do what was necessary for him to learn and do" (Meador & Rogers, 1973, p. 120).

As the 1930s passed, Rogers became increasingly aware of the shortcomings of traditional assessment and treatment concepts. For example, after using the psychoanalytic approach espoused by Healy (see Chapter 2) to help a fire-setting youngster see that his maladaptive behavior was based upon unconscious conflicts over masturbation, Rogers was jolted to discover that the client's behavior did not improve. It came as a shock to realize that "Healy might be wrong" (Rogers, 1961, p. 10). At another point, Rogers reread the transcript of an interview with a mother that, years earlier, he had thought was excellent: "I was appalled. Now it seemed to me to be a clever legalistic type of questioning by the interviewer which convicted this parent of her unconscious motives, and wrung from her an admission of her guilt. I now knew from my experience that such an interview would not be of any lasting help to the parent or the child. It made me realize that I was moving away from any approach which was coercive or pushing in clinical relationships . . ." (Rogers, 1961, p. 11).

As a result of experiences like these, Rogers began to incorporate into his clinical work some alternative ideas about nonauthoritarianism and the therapeutic value of a good human relationship. Contrary to then popular belief, Rogers began to think that "it is the *client* who knows what hurts, what directions to go, what problems are crucial, what experiences have been deeply buried. It began to occur to me that unless I had a need to demonstrate my own cleverness and learning, I would do better to rely upon the client for the direction of movement . . ." (Rogers, 1961, pp. 11–12).

In 1937, Rogers, began to put some of these ideas in writing. His first book, *The Clinical Treatment of the Problem Child,* was published in 1939, and though it was mainly a practical handbook which described the full range of child-therapy techniques then available, it contained two noteworthy features. First, of course, was Rogers' bias toward relationship therapy. Second, his orientation toward experimental research, which came from his early experiences in agriculture and from the influence of experimental psychologists at Teachers College, became evident. He was among the first to recognize the need for careful, scientific research to substantiate the alleged value of any treatment technique, including his own favorite. Rogers pointed out, for example, that, although many therapists extol the value of relationship therapy, "since their criteria are largely intangible measures such as the freedom from minor tensions and the greater degree of personal comfort achieved, any measurement of success is difficult indeed. From those who are most interested in relationship therapy, we find no mention of the degree or proportion of success . . ." (Rogers, 1939, p. 200). The same year that his book was published, Rogers left his job at the child study department and became director of the brand new Rochester Child Guidance Center.

By 1940, Rogers was beginning to move more rapidly toward the development of a systematic approach to treatment which incorporated his own ideas and those of the people and movements which had influenced him. Three important things happened in that year. First, Rogers participated in a symposium on therapy organized by Goodwin Watson, a Columbia University psychology professor. At that meeting, Rogers described the virtues of relationship therapy, but also heard Watson endorse some very similar ideas in ways which may have helped shape Rogers' thinking (Sollod, 1978). Second, Rogers moved from his clinical service job in Rochester to his first academic position (as a full professor!) at Ohio State University. This new job meant that he would be teaching graduate students, a task which almost invariably makes a professor keenly aware of what she or he does and does not know. The academic world provided a setting which helped prompt Rogers to elaborate his views. "It was in trying to teach what I had learned about treatment and counseling to graduate students . . . that I first began to realize that I had perhaps developed a distinctive point of view of my own . . ." (Rogers, 1961, p. 13).

He became sure of this as a function of the third major event of 1940. On December 11, Rogers gave an invited talk to the Psi Chi[1] chapter at the University of Minnesota. In that talk, entitled "Some Newer Concepts in Psychotherapy," he systematically presented for the first time his notions about doing therapy, including use of a *nondirective* approach which allows clients to solve their own problems without influence or judgments from the clinician. This involved (1) relying heavily upon the client's individual drive toward growth, health, and adjustment rather than upon treatment "techniques" to produce benefits, (2) emphasizing the *present moment* in therapy rather than the past as a key to change, and (4) focusing upon the therapeutic relationship and the experience of it as a promoter of client growth (Rogers, 1974). The reaction to what Rogers subsequently called the "birth" of nondirective therapy was intense. "I was totally unprepared for the furor the talk aroused. I was criticized, I was praised, I was attacked, I was looked on with puzzlement" (Rogers, 1974, p. 8). Then, as now, Rogers' ideas appealed to some people as just what was needed as an alternative to the "all-knowing expert" approach of psychoanalysis and some of its variants. Freudians and other traditionalists were strongly critical, for obvious reasons.

Being at the center of controversy prompted Rogers to state his position even more clearly, and, in 1942, he published a full-length account of nondirective therapy in a book called *Counseling and Psychotherapy*. In this book, Rogers advocated "a counseling relationship whose characteristics were the warmth and responsiveness of the therapist, a permissive climate in which the feelings of the client could be freely expressed, and a freedom for the client from all coercion or pressure. A client in such a relationship would gain understanding of himself . . ." which then allows him or her to take positive steps toward self-help (Meador & Rogers, 1973, p. 122). Rogers' scientific research orientation continued to be strongly evident in this book. He reported

---

[1]A national psychology honorary organization which is still very active today.

on the careful content analyses of clinical interviews which, for the first time, had been phonographically recorded.

In 1945, Rogers organized and became executive secretary of the University of Chicago Counseling Center. During the 12 years that followed, Rogers continued to develop and evaluate his treatment approach which, by 1946, he was calling *client-centered* rather than "nondirective" therapy. This change was designed to emphasize the primary role of the client's inherent potential for growth, and was formalized in Rogers' 1951 book, *Client-Centered Therapy.*

Over the years, Carl Rogers continued to practice and do research on psychotherapy and to apply his expanding views in an ever-broadening range of contexts. After leaving Chicago, he spent 4 years at the University of Wisconsin and then moved to the Western Behavioral Sciences Institute in La Jolla, California. He is now located at his own Center for Studies of the Person, also in La Jolla. A distinguished series of books has resulted from his clinical experience. These include *On Becoming a Person* (1961), *Freedom to Learn* (an application of his concepts to education, 1969), *Carl Rogers on Encounter Groups* (1970), and *On Becoming Partners: Marriage and Its Alternatives* (1972).

Let us now examine the process of Rogerian therapy.

The Client-Centered Approach

It was tempting to call this section "Techniques of Client-Centered Therapy," but such a title would not capture the spirit of Rogers' approach. He argues that therapy is a *process,* not a set of techniques. He is a strong advocate of the notion that a therapist cannot solve a client's problems by *telling* or by *teaching* her or him anything: "No approach which relies upon knowledge, upon training, upon the acceptance of something that is *taught,* is of any use. . . . It is possible to explain a person to himself, to prescribe steps which should lead him forward, to train him in knowledge about a more satisfying mode of life. But such methods are, in my experience, futile and inconsequential. The most they can accomplish is some temporary change, which soon disappears, leaving the individual more than ever convinced of his inadequacy" (Rogers, 1961, pp. 32–33).[2] The *real* process of therapy in Rogers' view is an "if . . . then" proposition: If the *correct circumstances* are created by the therapist, the client will spontaneously begin to change and grow. In other words, the therapeutic process will take place on its own, driven by the client's growth potential, only when the proper atmosphere is present and regardless of specific "technique" or session content.

All this is related to Rogers' self theory, which we sketched in Chapter 3. The argument is, basically, that people are thwarted in their growth by the influence of evaluations and judgments imposed upon them by others. This creates *conditions of worth* and may force the person to distort or force out of awareness some of their own real feelings. When this happens, various kinds of

---

[2]Rogers thus writes off both psychodynamic and social-learning treatment approaches.

symptoms appear. Thus, if an accountant really wanted to be an artist but had to
ignore those feelings due to family pressure, depression might be the ultimate
result. The growth process would stop as the person's behavior (e.g., professing
satisfaction with accountancy) became increasingly out-of-line, or *incongruent,*
with real feelings.

Therapy, in general terms, is aimed at providing the client with *new
experiences* that will restart the growth process. These new experiences mainly
involve relating to a person (the therapist) who will deal with the client in ways
which do not sustain conditions of worth, which accept the client as he or she is,
and which value the client as a person. Ideally, if such characteristics had been
present in the client's past relationships, they would have prevented psychological problems; their appearance in the present can still be helpful, however. For
this reason, the Rogerian therapist tries to provide *an interpersonal relationship
which the client can use to further personal growth.*

According to Rogers, this type of relationship cannot be manufactured or
role-played: phoniness would be detected by the client and would not be
beneficial. For Rogers, the only way to generate a growth-enhancing relationship is for the therapist to really adopt and express three interrelated *attitudes.*
These are: *unconditional positive regard, empathy,* and *congruence.*

Unconditional Positive Regard   The most basic and pervasive therapeutic
attitude in Rogers' system is that of unconditional positive regard. It conveys
three main messages: that the therapist (1) *cares about* the client as a person, (2)
accepts her or him, and (3) *trusts* the client's ability to change and grow. This
may seem to be a simple and easily adopted stance (after all, any good therapist
cares about clients), but, in practice, it is not accomplished without some
difficulty.

For example, there are many ways to "care" about someone. One can be
quite superficial about it, as when ending a conversation or business transaction
with words like "take care, now" or "have a nice day." The recipient of
messages like these probably does not attach much importance or meaning to
them, and the person who uttered the words will probably not be automatically
counted as a close, caring friend. Rogerians wish to go well beyond this kind of
routine caring.

At the other extreme, a caring attitude can be so strong and possessive as to
be incapacitating to the person who is cared for. A child who is constantly *told*
how much his or her parents care and how that caring resulted in painful
self-sacrifice ("your mother and I went without so you could go to college") may
end up feeling burdened with guilt. Similarly, a young man who dotes on his
fiancée and tries never to let her be away from him may actually cause her to feel
stifled and overwhelmed by the intensity of his caring. In these situations, one
suspects that the caring expressed is partly for the child or fiancée and partly
selfish. Rogerians try to avoid crippling their clients with caring.

The ideal of "regard" in Rogers' concept of unconditional positive regard
is that of *nonpossessive caring* in which genuine positive feelings are expressed

toward the client in a way which is liberating, not limiting. There are many ways in which this can be done. The simplest involves merely *telling* the client "I care about you." This straightforward statement often has an important place in therapy but can be interpreted as superficial, especially if overused. Therefore, in most instances, Rogerians also try to *show* the client that they care.[3]

The therapist's *willingness to listen* is a very important manifestation of this attitude. Patient, warm, and interested in what the client has to say, the therapist does not interrupt the client or try to change the subject or give any other verbal or nonverbal signs that she or he would rather be doing something else. In addition to merely listening, the therapist seeks to *understand* the client's feelings and perceptions from the client's point of view (this is discussed in more detail in the section on empathy, below). For many clients, talking to someone who is really willing to listen and who really wants to understand is a new and exhilarating experience which provides the impetus for an unprecedented degree of self-expression.

The "unconditional" aspect of the therapist's unconditional positive regard is manifested in a willingness to *accept* the client as he or she is, without judgment or evaluation. Rogers believes that the experience of being prized as a human being, regardless of the nature of one's feelings or behaviors, can be a valuable and growth-producing experience, especially for clients whose development has been hampered by the presence of conditions of worth and other evaluative pressures. Acceptance of the client means that the therapist must refrain from many activities sometimes associated with the therapist role.

For one thing, she or he *avoids interpretations*. When the client expresses a feeling (e.g., "I love my children very much"), the Rogerian ideal is to view that feeling as reflecting the client's perception at that moment. To interpret the statement as part of a defense against unconscious hostile feelings would not be seen as consistent with an accepting attitude. If the client's stated feelings are indeed inaccurate, the assumption is that he or she will eventually discover the more genuine emotion as the self-expression process goes on.

Rogerians also try very hard to *avoid evaluative judgments* about their clients. This means, for example, that the therapist will not "summarize" the client with a diagnostic label or in any other way define for the client what her or his problems involve. It also means accepting the client's reported feelings and behaviors as those of a valued person, no matter what those feelings and behaviors may involve. Often this is not an easily attained goal. Consider your own reaction to a person who says "I wish my mother were dead" or "it doesn't really bother me to cheat on my husband; he's so dumb he'll never find out anyway" or "I never wanted any of my children, and I plan to kick them out of the house as soon as they are of legal age."

Fortunately, Rogers' concept of unconditional positive regard does not require the therapist to *approve* of feelings like these. In fact, the goal is neither

---

[3]If the therapist really does *not* care about the client, Rogers would suggest that a different therapist be brought in rather than attempting to fake a positive attitude.

to approve nor disapprove but, as noted above, to *accept* these feelings as a real part of a person whom the therapist cares about. In other words, while the therapist may have an evaluative reaction to the client's *thoughts* or *actions,* ideally he or she can be nonjudgmental *about the fact that they occurred.* Further, the therapist can still prize the client as an individual. This ideal is illustrated in the following interaction:

Client: That was the semester that my brother died and everything seemed to be going down the tubes. I knew how important it was to my parents that I get into medical school, but I also knew that my grades would be lousy that year unless I did something. To make a long story short, I bought a term paper and cheated on almost every exam that semester.

Therapist: It was a really rough time for you.

Note that the therapist focuses upon the client's *feelings* in the situation, not upon the ethical status of the behavior. Obviously, a major aspect of unconditional positive regard involves the separation of a client's worth *as a person* from the worth of the client's *behavior.* Rogers believes that family life would be greatly improved and psychological problems would be less prevalent if a similar distinction were more common outside of therapy (see Rogers, 1961, Chapter 16).

The "positive" component of unconditional positive regard is the therapist's implicit *trust* in the client's potential for growth and problem solving. Rogers believes that if clients perceive a therapist's lack of trust in their growth potential, they are unlikely to grow and may become dependent. On the other hand, "the more sincerely the therapist relies on the client to discover himself and to follow his own processes of change, the more freely the client will do just that" (Meador & Rogers, 1973, p. 138). Here again, the therapist must abandon some traditional notions about his or her role in treatment. She or he must try not to be the "expert" who overtly or covertly tells the client what is "wrong" or guides the client toward "better" ways of thinking and behaving. In particular, Rogerians try not to (1) give advice, (2) take responsibility for clients, or (3) make decisions for clients.

These are often very difficult rules to follow, especially in cases where the therapist feels sure that he or she knows what is "best" for the client or when it appears that without "good advice" the client will make a mistake. Yet trust in the client's resources must be more than rhetoric if it is to promote growth. This means that the client must be allowed to make bad decisions or experience problems even if they could have been averted through action or advice by the therapist. The assumption here is that while advice or intervention might have solved or prevented some problems, others would be created: the therapist would take the role of a superior, the client would become more dependent and, most important, both client and therapist would have a little less faith in the client's ability to deal with problems requiring independent decision making.

Rogers believes so strongly in the importance of trusting the client that he holds to his view even in the face of possibly tragic actions. This is illustrated in the following excerpt from the treatment of a depressed young woman:

Client: . . . I cannot be the kind of person I want to be. I guess maybe I haven't the guts—or the strength—to kill myself—and if someone else would relieve me of the responsibility—or I would be in an accident—I—I—just don't want to live.

Therapist: At the present time things look so black to you that you can't see much point in living.

Client: Yes—I wish I'd never started this therapy. I was happy when I was living in my dream world. There I could be the kind of person I wanted to be—But now there is such a wide, wide gap—between my ideal—and what I am . . .

Therapist: It's really a tough struggle—digging into this like you are—and at times the shelter of your dream world looks more attractive and comfortable.

Client: My dream world or suicide. . . . So I don't see why I should waste your time—coming in twice a week—I'm not worth it—What do you think?

Therapist: It's up to you. . . . It isn't wasting my time—I'd be glad to see you whenever you come—but it's how you feel about it—if you don't want to come twice a week—or if you do want to come twice a week?—once a week?—It's up to you.

Client: You're not going to suggest that I come in oftener? You're not alarmed and think I ought to come in—everyday—until I get out of this?

Therapist: I believe you are able to make your own decision. I'll see you whenever you want to come.

Client: (note of awe in her voice) I don't believe you are alarmed about—I see—I may be afraid of myself—but you aren't afraid for me.

Therapist: You say you may be afraid of yourself—and are wondering why I don't seem to be afraid for you?

Client: You have more confidence in me than I have. I'll see you next week—maybe. (Rogers, 1951, pp. 46–47)

The client's concluding statement appears accurate. The therapist *does* have more confidence in the client than she has in herself. Ideally, this will only be a temporary situation for, presumably, she will begin to share that confidence from within. Rogers points out, however, that the therapist cannot halfheartedly adopt a trusting attitude and expect the client to grow: "To me it appears that only as the therapist is completely willing that *any* outcome, *any* direction, may be chosen—only then does he realize the vital strength of the capacity and potentiality of the individual for constructive action" (Rogers, 1951, p. 48). This does not mean that Rogers expects the worst from clients who are given real trust and freedom by their therapists. Quite the contrary. "It is as [the therapist] is willing for death to be the choice, that life is chosen; for neuroticism to be the choice, that a healthy normality is chosen" (Rogers, 1951, p. 49).

Empathy Rogers' approach is, as we have said, phenomenological: human behavior is seen as a product of each person's unique perceptions. Thus, in order to understand a client's behavior, and help the client understand it as well, the therapist must come as close as possible to seeing the world as the client sees it.

According to Rogers, when the therapist lets the client know that she or he really understands (or at least wants to understand) what the client sees and feels, the chances for a useful therapeutic relationship are enhanced. In Rogerian terms, this involves a striving for *accurate empathy* or *empathic understanding*.

Empathy requires that the therapist be immersed in an effort to *perceive* the client's feelings, but it does not dictate that the therapist actually *experience* those feelings (Rogers, 1951). This is an important point because, if a therapist actually felt the client's fear or anger, the therapy session could become nothing but a place for two people to be frightened or angry together! It is also vital to recognize that empathy is not achieved by *sympathizing* with the client. A comment like "I'm really sorry that you feel so depressed" reflects kindness and sympathy, but not empathy.

Similarly, a therapist who merely *tells* the client that he or she empathizes will not convey an empathic attitude. It is all too common, in therapy and in everyday life, to hear people say "I really know how you feel" or "I understand what you are going through" or "I've felt that way myself." If, as phenomenologists believe, each person's perceptions are unique, it takes far more work on the therapist's part to approximate a genuine understanding of what it feels like to be any particular client. In fact, it can be argued that when someone uses an easy phrase such as "I know how you feel," they are actually conveying a *lack* of interest in really trying to understand. Imagine your own reaction if, after giving someone a lengthy account of your complex feelings about, say, a grandparent's death, you hear them say "right, I've felt the very same way." It would probably be easy to question the degree to which they (1) know how you feel or (2) want to know how you feel.

Conveying a Rogerian-style empathic attitude is not easy, especially for therapists brought up and trained to focus upon intellectual analysis. In order to illustrate the problem and the empathic ideal, we present below an excerpt from the beginning of a therapy session with a young male client. As you read the excerpt and after you are finished, try to be aware of your reactions to it.

Client: I don't feel very normal, but I want to feel that way. . . . I thought I'd have something to talk about—then it all goes around in circles. I was trying to think what I was going to say. Then coming here it doesn't work out. . . . I tell you, it seemed that it would be much easier before I came. I tell you, I just can't make a decision; I don't know what I want. I've tried to reason this thing out logically—tried to figure out which things are important to me. I thought that there are maybe two things a man might do; he might get married and raise a family. But if he was just a bachelor, just making a living—that isn't very good. I find myself and my thoughts getting back to the days when I was a kid and I cry very easily. The dam would break through. I've been in the Army four and a half years. I had no problems then, no hopes, no wishes. My only thought was to get out when peace would come. My problems, now that I'm out, are as ever. I tell you, they go back to a long time before I was in the Army. . . . I love children. When I was in the Philippines—I tell you, when I was young I swore I'd never forget my unhappy childhood—so when I saw these children in the Philippines, I treated them very nicely. I used to give them ice cream cones and movies. It was just a period—I'd reverted back—and that awakened some emotions in me I thought I had long buried. (A pause. He seems very near tears.) (Rogers, 1951, pp. 32–33)

Many therapists would react to such material with sympathy and with a wish to intellectually understand (i.e., "figure out") the client. In doing so, they use what Rogers has called an *external frame of reference.* That is, they attempt to understand by being an outside observer and applying their own values, ideas, and theoretical principles to what the client says and does. Examples of therapist thoughts based upon an external frame of reference are presented on the left side of Table 11-1. On the other hand, the therapist could adopt an *internal* frame of reference which reflects a desire to understand what it must be like to be this client. The right side of Table 11-1 contains some of the therapist's thoughts which might result. Notice the difference in content and tone.

Of course, the Rogerian therapist must not only *adopt* an empathic attitude; she or he must *communicate* it to the client. This is done both verbally and nonverbally, through some of the active listening modes we described in Chapter 5. Of particular value in conveying empathy is the use of *reflection,* an interview method that serves the dual purpose of (1) communicating the therapist's desire for or attainment of emotional understanding and (2) making the client more clearly aware of his or her own feelings.

The use of reflection is probably one of the most misunderstood aspects of

Table 11-1   Some Therapist Thoughts Which Reflect Internal Versus External Frames of Reference

External	Internal
I wonder if I should get him started talking.	You're wanting to struggle toward normality, aren't you?
Is this inability to get under way a type of dependence?	It's really hard for you to get started.
Why this indecisiveness? What could be its cause?	Decision making just seems impossible for you.
What is meant by this focus on marriage and family?	You want marriage, but it doesn't seem to you to be much of a possibility.
The crying, the "dam" sound as though there must be a great deal of regression.	You feel yourself brimming over with childish feelings.
He's a veteran. Could he have been a psychiatric case? I feel sorry for anybody who spent four and one-half years in the service.	To you the Army represented stagnation.
What is this interest in children? Identification? Vague homosexuality?	Being very nice to children some-how has meaning for you. but it was—and is—a disturbing experience for you

Source: Rogers, 1951, pp. 33–34.

client-centered therapy because, to an outside observer, the therapist may appear to be stating the obvious or merely repeating what the client has said. In a famous joke about this approach, Rogers is supposed to have responded in the following way to a livid fellow duck hunter who threatens to shoot Rogers if he doesn't relinquish a disputed kill: "You feel this is your duck."

In actuality, much more is going on in a Rogerian therapy session than repetition of the client's statements. In the first place, reflection itself is not just repetition or even pure paraphrasing. It involves the *distillation* and "playback" of the client's feelings. The person who does this well is, according to Rogers, more likely to be helpful. Let us look at some examples.

Client: This has been such a bad day. I've had to keep myself from crying three or four times. The worst part is, I'm not even sure what's wrong!

The therapist's response could be externally oriented (e.g., "Well what exactly happened?"), but a reaction which attempts to communicate empathy would probably be along these lines:

Therapist: You really do feel so bad. The tears just well up inside. And it must be a little scary to not even know why you feel this way.

At first glance, the clinician may seem to be a parrot, but look more closely. The client never *said* she felt bad; the therapist inferred it by taking the client's point of view. Similarly, the client never said her sadness frightened her—the clinician *felt* that this might be the case if she or he were in the client's shoes. If the therapist is wrong about either or both of these points, the client has the opportunity to correct the reflection. Right or wrong, the clinician has let the client know that he or she really wants to understand.

Another point about communicating empathy through reflection: the therapist's nonverbal message may be as important as what is said (see Chapter 5). Tone of voice, facial expression, body posture, and other cues can all add to (or detract from) an empathic attitude. This is somewhat difficult to illustrate on the printed page, but Rogers (1951), p. 28) provides a useful example:

Here is a client statement: "I feel as though my mother is always watching me and criticizing what I do. It gets me all stirred up inside. I try not to let that happen, but you know, there are times when I feel her eagle eye on me that I just boil inwardly."

A response on the counselor's part might be: "You resent her criticism."

This response may be given empathically, with the tone of voice such as would be used if it were worded, "If I understand you correctly, you feel pretty resentful toward her criticism. Is that right?" If this is the attitude and tone which is used, it would probably be experienced by the client as aiding him in self-expression. Yet we have learned, from the fumblings of counselors-in-training, that "You resent her criticism" may be given with the same attitude and tone with which one might announce "You have the measles," or . . . "You are sitting on my hat."

The best way to get a feel for this nonverbal dimension of empathy is to watch and listen to Rogers or a skilled Rogerian in action.[4] One of the better

---

[4]Rogerians are certainly not the only therapists who convey empathy to their clients, but they are more likely to emphasize it in therapeutic sessions.

opportunities to accomplish this is provided by a well-known film in which Rogers interviews "Gloria" as a demonstration of his approach (Rogers, 1965). Similar material is contained in other films (e.g., Rogers, 1978) and on tape recordings distributed by the American Academy of Psychotherapists (see footnote 5).

A third point which should be understood about communicating empathy is that the process is rather slow. The therapist's use of reflection may or may not appear to get anywhere in a single session, but Rogers believes that, over time, the empathic attitude gives even the most aloof or withdrawn client a sense that the therapist understands her or him. The *continuous experiencing* of this understanding attitude will, according to Rogers, ultimately lead to client growth.

Congruence   Throughout the last two sections, we have repeatedly emphasized the importance of real rather than manufactured empathy and unconditional positive regard. This emphasis is only part of Rogers' general belief that the more *genuine* the therapist is in all aspects of his or her relations with the client, the more helpful the therapist will be. The idea is that the therapist's feelings and actions should be *congruent,* or consistent, with one another. "This means that I need to be aware of my own feelings . . . [and willing] to express, in my words and my behavior, the various feelings and attitudes which exist in me" (Rogers, 1961, p. 33). According to Rogers, when the therapist is genuine or congruent, she or he sets up a *real* human relationship. In strong contrast to the Freudian view, Rogers argues: "It does not help to act calm and pleasant when actually I am angry and critical. It does not help to act as though I know the answers when I do not. . . . Put in another way, . . . I have not found it to be helpful or effective in my relationships with other people to try to maintain a facade; to act in one way on the surface when I am experiencing something quite different underneath" (Rogers, 1961, pp. 16–17). Rogers believes in the value of congruence ". . . even when the attitudes I feel are not attitudes with which I am pleased, or attitudes which seem conducive to a good relationship" (Rogers, 1961, p. 33).

Congruence represents a rather extraordinary requirement and one which is often difficult for a clinician (or anyone else) to satisfy. The therapist must abandon any parentlike notion that expressing a particular reaction or feeling would "not be good for the client" and just go ahead and be genuine. In so doing, the therapist abdicates responsibility for the client's life, expresses confidence in the client's ability to handle the therapist's feelings, and, if those feelings are at all negative, shows a willingness to risk a temporary setback in the relationship. The hope is that, in the long run, the client's awareness that the therapist is for real (not just someone who is paid to be nice) will aid in the self-actualization process.

In order to get an idea of how congruence might promote trust, think of a close and valued friend. Chances are that, sometime in the past, that friend told you things you might not have wanted to hear. Maybe it was that you were overdressed or that you had been hard to get along with or that you were wrong about something. Once you know that your friend will say what he or she really feels (i.e., is congruent in dealing with you), even if it does not always make you happy, it may be easier for you to trust the validity of what that person may say today or next week. However, if you know that your friend sometimes tells you only what she or he thinks you want to hear, your faith in that person's reactions ("you really look great," "I agree with you completely," "you are one of my favorite people") might be considerably reduced.

In a way, then, a good Rogerian therapist will treat a client like a friend. He or she will not try to be something that he or she is not, partly because this would be seen as detrimental to the *therapist's* personal growth and partly because it would be poor modeling.

Let us consider a sample of therapist-client interaction which illustrates one of the ways in which congruence can be displayed:

Client: I really have been feeling better about a lot of things since we started seeing each other. If my father had been warm as you are, I think my childhood would have been a lot easier. (pause) It sounds silly to say it, but I wish you could be my father.

Therapist: I think it would be nice to have you for a son.

This client's statement could have prompted a Freudian to analyze the evident transference, or in some other way remain emotionally distant; the Rogerian's response was a reflection of how he *felt*.

Consider another example:

Client: You really look tired doctor. Don't you feel well today?

Therapist: (who really feels rotten) Oh no, I'm fine. Anyway, how you feel is more important.

Here is an obvious case of therapist incongruence. The client is not only likely to see right through the therapist's facade; she or he will probably end up feeling guilty for making a sick person work when that person would rather be at home. The clinician could just as easily have said "I do feel pretty sick, but I very much wanted to have our session today." If this actually reflects the therapist's feelings, it will help strengthen the therapeutic relationship.

Finally, imagine this interchange:

Client: I just feel so hopeless. Tell me what I'm doing wrong in my life.

Therapist: I guess when you are feeling this bad it would be nice if someone could come along and tell you just what is going wrong and maybe how you can put everything right again. I really wish I could do all that, but I can't. I don't think anyone else can either.

Notice the therapist's reflection of client feeling plus the direct expression of: (1) her genuine wish to be able to understand and solve the client's problems and, (2) her admission that she is simply not capable of such a feat. A therapist who does not have all the answers but who says "Don't you think it would be better if you figured that out for yourself?" would, according to Rogers, be incongruent. He or she would be conveying the subtle suggestion that he or she *knows* what is wrong but won't tell. Such a message might actually promote client inferiority, not growth.

The Nature of Change in Client-Centered Therapy

We said earlier that client-centered therapy represented an "if . . . then" assumption: If the right conditions were created by the therapist, then the client will change and grow. It is now time to describe the dimensions along which, according to Rogers, the change and growth takes place.

Increased Awareness   The experience of therapy is believed to bring clients in closer contact with the true nature of their own feelings, many of which may have been previously denied or otherwise kept out of awareness. Further, the focus of awareness tends to shift from the past or the future to the immediate present: how the client is feeling here and now. These shifts and increases in awareness usually carry with them an increasing focus upon the *self* rather than upon specific symptoms as the target of exploration.

Increased Self-Acceptance   Over time, the client becomes less self-critical and more self-accepting. She or he is more likely to take responsibility for her or his feelings and behavior and less likely to blame external circumstances or other people for those feelings and behaviors. The client spends less time trying to deny those things about the self which are not ideal. The client may later decide to try to change some of these things, but they are no longer disowned. Some of the increase in self-acceptance is thought to be based upon the gradual discovery that, in spite of things which may be less than admirable, the client is, at bottom, a basically good person.

Increased Interpersonal Comfort   As therapy progresses, the client becomes more comfortable in human relationships. Defensive interpersonal games and similar strategies designed to keep other people at a distance are abandoned and the client begins to experience the pleasure of letting others know him or her as he or she really is.

Increased Cognitive Flexibility   As has been noted by Kelly (1955) and others, people tend to have problems when they see the world in rigid, black-and-white terms (e.g., "all men are despicable," "all teachers are uncaring"). Successful client-centered therapy is seen to result in a "loosening up" of limited (and limiting) views of the world such that the client is able to perceive the endless variability which exists. The cognitions which result (e.g., "the behavior of some men is indeed despicable, but this is not always true") are likely to promote less problematic behavior.

Increased Self-Reliance   The client is likely to end up feeling less dependent upon others and more confident about personal resources and abilities. This includes greater self-reliance about decision making, problem solving, and stress management, but it also includes a greater focus on the self as a source of *evaluation*. A growing client is seen as one who becomes less dependent upon the views and reactions of other people as a barometer of self-worth and more oriented toward internal evaluations. In behavioral terms, the client may become less fearful in social-evaluative situations (e.g., speeches, tests, parties) because she or he comes to feel that what she or he thinks of herself or himself is at least as important as what others think of her or him. Rogers sees these changes as resulting from a shift in the client's *valuing process*. The client becomes less concerned with "shoulds" and "oughts" (e.g., "I should love being a student") and more concerned with how he or she actually feels (see Box 11-1). Thus, the growing client is likely to separate (as the therapist did) her or his worth as a *person* from the quality or adequacy of her or his *behavior*.

Rogers believes that the changes which take place along these dimensions over the course of successful therapy are relatively consistent from one client to the next. He has summarized these changes in a *therapy process scale* which is presented in edited form in Box 11-2.

Improved Functioning   In addition to the internal, psychological changes just described, Rogers notes that overt benefits also follow successful client-centered therapy.

The client's behavior changes in these ways: he considers, and reports putting into effect, behavior which is more mature, self-directing, and responsible than the behavior he has shown heretofore; his behavior becomes less defensive, more firmly based on an objective view of self and reality; his behavior shows a decreasing

---

Box 11-1   Self-evaluation versus Evaluation by Others

Here are some examples of thoughts based upon concern over evaluation by others (left column) and those based upon a greater focus on self-evaluation (right column).

1 I should never be angry at anyone.	1 I should be angry at a person when I deeply feel angry because this leaves less residual effect than bottling up the feeling, and actually makes for a better and more realistic relationship.
2 I should always be a loving mother.	2 I should be a loving mother when I feel that way, but I need not be fearful of other attitudes when they exist.
3 I should be successful in my courses.	3 I should be successful in my courses only if they have long-range meaning to me.
4 I have homosexual impulses, which is very bad.	4 I have homosexual impulses, and these are capable of expressions which enhance self and others, and expressions which achieve the reverse.

Source: Rogers, 1951, p. 149 and p. 151.

Box 11-2 Seven Stages in the Process of Therapeutic Change

Stage 1: Communication is about externals. There is an unwillingness to communicate self. Feelings and personal meanings are neither recognized as such nor owned. Constructs are extremely rigid. Close relationships are construed as dangerous.

Stage 2: Feelings are sometimes *described* but as unowned past *objects* external to self.

Stage 3: There is much description of feelings and personal meanings which are not now present. These distant feelings are often pictured as unacceptable or bad. . . . There is a beginning recognition that any problems that exist are inside the individual rather than external.

Stage 4: Feelings and personal meanings are freely described as present objects owned by the self. . . . There is a beginning loosening of personal constructs. . . . There is some expression of self-responsibility for problems.

Stage 5: Many feelings are expressed in the moment of their occurrence and are thus experienced in the immediate present. These feelings are owned or accepted. . . . There is a questioning of the validity of many personal constructs. The person has a definite responsibility for the problems which exist in him.

Stage 6: Feelings previously denied are now experienced both with immediacy and *acceptance.*

Stage 7: The individual lives comfortably in the flowing process of his experiencing. New feelings are experienced with richness and immediacy, and this inner experiencing is a clear referent for behavior. Incongruence is minimal and temporary.

From Corsini, R. J. (ed.), *Current Psychotherapies,* Itasca, Illinois: Peacock Publishers, Inc. Copyright 1973 by Peacock Publishers, Inc. (Reprinted by permission.)

amount of psychological tension; he tends to make a more comfortable and more effective adjustment to school and to job; he meets new stress situations with an increased degree of inner calm, a calm which is reflected in less physiological upset . . . than would have been true if they had occurred prior to therapy. (Rogers, 1951, p. 186)

An Illustration of Client-Centered Therapy

Because client-centered therapy, like other phenomenological treatment approaches, focuses more upon processes than techniques, the preceding material may have left the reader aware of the principles which guide Rogerian therapy but somewhat unclear about how these principles are combined and translated into clinical practice. As already noted, films or tapes of Rogerian sessions provide excellent introductions to how the approach actually looks and sounds. Some extended case study transcripts are also available (e.g., Rogers, 1951, 1961). To provide just the briefest idea of what actually goes on in client-centered therapy, we present below some edited excerpts from Rogers's (1967) case of the "Silent Young Man," as described by Meador and Rogers (1973, pp. 139–144).[5]

The client in this case was a 28-year-old man who had been hospitalized as a "simple schizophrenic." During 11 previous months of therapy, "Jim" (a pseudonym) had made some progress, but was still quite withdrawn and inarticulate. Rather than giving up on this client as a "hopeless case," Rogers

[5]A tape recording of two complete interviews with this client is available for professional use from the American Academy of Psychotherapists, 6420 City Line Avenue, Philadelphia, PA. Its designation is the case of "Mr. VAC."

continued to adopt the therapeutic attitudes which he believed would ultimately bring about growth.

Therapist: I see there are some cigarettes here in the drawer. Hm? Yeah, it is hot out. (silence of 25 seconds)

Therapist: Do you look kind of angry this morning, or is that my imagination? (client shakes his head slightly) Not angry, huh? (silence of 1 minute, 26 seconds)

Therapist: Feel like letting me in on whatever is going on? (silence of 12 minutes, 52 seconds)

Therapist: I kind of feel like saying that "If it would be of any help at all I'd like to come in." On the other hand if it's something you'd rather—if you just feel more like being within yourself, why that's OK too—I guess another thing I'm saying, really, in saying that is, "I do care. I'm not just sitting here like a stick." (silence of 1 minute, 11 seconds)

Therapist: And I guess your silence is saying to me either you don't want to or can't come out right now and that's OK. So I won't pester you but I just want you to know, I'm here. (silence of 17 minutes, 41 seconds)

[After two more unanswered comments over the next minute or so, Rogers continues.]

Therapist: Maybe this morning you just wish I'd shut up—and maybe I should, but I just keep feeling I'd like to—I don't know, be in touch with you in some way.

(silence of 2 minutes, 21 seconds) [client yawns]

Therapist: Sounds discouraged or tired.

(silence of 41 seconds)

Client: [at last!] No. Just lousy.

Therapist: Everything's lousy, huh? You feel lousy? . . .

Client: No.

Therapist: No?

(silence of 20 seconds)

Client: No. I just ain't no good to nobody, never was, and never will be.

Therapist: Feeling that now, hm? That you're just no good to yourself, no good to anybody. Just that you're completely worthless, huh? . . .

Client: Yeah. That's what this guy I went to town with just the other day told me . . .

Therapist: I guess the meaning of that, if I get it right, is that here's somebody that—meant something to you and what does he think of you? Why, he's told you that he thinks you're no good at all. And that really knocks the props out from under you. [Jim weeps quietly] It just brings the tears.

Client: I don't care though.

Therapist: You tell yourself you don't care at all, but somehow I guess some part of you cares because some part of you weeps over it . . .

Client: I guess I always knew it.

Therapist: If I'm getting that right, it is that what makes it hurt worst of all is that when he tells you you're no good, well shucks, that's what you've always felt about yourself. Is that—the meaning of what you're saying? [Jim nods in agreement] . . . So that between his saying so and your perhaps feeling it underneath, you just feel about as no-good as anybody could feel.

[The client continues to cry and, after several more minutes of reflecting the sad, hopeless feelings being expressed, Rogers ends the interview. Three days later another session takes place. After some initial comments by the therapist, the client breaks in]:

Client: I'm gonna take off.

Therapist: You're going to take off? Really run away from here? . . . I know you don't like the place but it must be something special came up or something?

Client: I just want to run away and die.

Therapist: M-hm, M-hm, M-hm. It isn't even that you want to get away from here *to* something. You just want to leave here and go away and die in a corner, hm? . . . Can't help but wonder whether it's still true that some things this friend said to you—are those still part of the thing that makes you feel so awful?

Client: In general, yes.

[The next 30 minutes or so are taken up in further reflection of the client's negative feelings and in silences of up to 13 minutes]

Client: I might go today. Where, I don't know, but I don't care.

Therapist: Just feel your mind is made up and that you're going to leave. (silence of 53 seconds)

Client: That's why I want to go, 'cause I don't care what happens.

Therapist: M-hm, m-hm. That's why you want to go, because you really don't care about yourself. You just don't care *what* happens. And I guess I'd just like to say—I care about you. And I care what happens.

After a 30-second silence, the client bursts into tears and violent sobs. For the next 15 minutes or so, Rogers, (who soon becomes late for another appointment) reflects the intense emotions which pour forth.

According to Rogers, this is an important moment of therapeutic change. "Jim Brown, who sees himself as stubborn, bitter, mistreated, worthless, useless, hopeless, unloved, unlovable, *experiences* my caring. In that moment, his defensive shell cracks wide open, and can never again be quite the same" (Meador & Rogers, 1973, p. 145). The client in this case was able to leave the hospital after several more months of treatment and 8 years later reported to Rogers that he was happy, employed, and living on his own.[6]

Applications of the Client-Centered Approach

As is evident from the case illustration just presented, Rogers believes that his approach to treatment can be fruitfully applied to clients who display severe "psychotic" behaviors as well as to those labeled as "neurotics" or "personality disorders." It is also worth noting that, though Rogers began his clinical treatment work in one-to-one settings, his ideas and principles have more

---

[6]Rogers (1951) mentions another case in which the therapist and client said almost nothing to one another during months of sessions. Yet the experience of a genuine, caring relationship appeared to produce remarkable benefits.

recently been applied in group contexts of various kinds (e.g., Rogers, 1970). Indeed, most of Rogers's concepts have applications to nontherapy situations, including child-rearing, marital relations, education, and interpersonal interactions in general (see Rogers, 1961).

THE GESTALT THERAPY OF FRITZ PERLS

After Rogers' client-centered approach, the gestalt therapy of Friedrich S. (Fritz) Perls is probably the best known and most popular form of phenomenologically oriented treatment. The two approaches are similar in some ways. Like Rogers, Perls believed that human development depends upon self-awareness and, like client-centered therapy, gestalt therapy aims at clarifying and enhancing clients' awareness in order to free them to go on growing in their own unique, consciously guided ways. The methods through which the gestalt therapist works to achieve these goals differ markedly from the Rogerian mode, however. As we shall see, gestalt therapy requires a more active therapist and utilizes a set of more dramatic procedures. Before describing the process itself, we should take a brief look at the origins of Perls's approach.

Some Background on Gestalt Therapy

Friedrich (or Frederick) S. Perls was born in Berlin, Germany, in 1893. In the course of his extensive education he received both an M.D. (specializing in psychiatry) and a Ph.D. in psychology. His European *psychiatric* training was, as one might expect, strongly psychoanalytic; he studied at the Psychoanalytic Institutes in Berlin and Vienna. His *psychological* orientation, however, was that of the gestaltists. This meant that he had been influenced to think of the human organism as a unified whole, rather than just a fragmented set of warring components, and to focus upon active perceptual and organizational processes, not just instincts, as central to the development and guidance of human behavior (see Chapter 3).

Perls's educational background put him in a uniquely advantageous position to explore the implications of laboratory-based gestalt psychology for the improvement of clinical treatment procedures. This exploration occupied Perls from the 1940s until his death in 1970.

He described himself as a Wandering Jew and, indeed, he lived in many places. When Hitler came to power in Germany, Perls went first to Johannesburg, South Africa (where he established the South African Institute for Psychoanalysis), and then, in 1946, to New York. By this time Perls's ideas about therapy had reached the stage that he founded not another psychoanalytic institute, but the New York Institute for Gestalt Therapy. In the mid-1960s, Perls moved to Big Sur, California, where he became associate psychiatrist at the Esalen Institute, ". . . a vanguard cultural and educational center, where people met to experience and experiment with new trends in human relating" (Kempler, 1973, p. 252). Just before his death Perls moved to Vancouver, British Columbia (Canada) where he founded another institute for gestalt therapy.

Perls's discomfort with classical Freudian concepts first appeared in his book, *Ego, Hunger and Aggression: A Revision of Freud's Theory and Method* (1947). It was in this book that he initially focused upon the vital role played by *awareness* in the development and maintenance of "normal" human behavior, and he argued that the appearance of disordered behavior indicated that the psychological growth process was obstructed by defects, gaps, or distortions in awareness (see Chapter 3). These ideas ultimately led to the systematic formulation of an alternative approach to clinical treatment which Perls called gestalt therapy (Perls, 1969, 1970; Perls, Hefferline, & Goodman, 1951).

Perls noted that disturbances in awareness and the problems which accompany them take many forms, including the classic neurotic symptoms and defense mechanisms described by Freud and others. Like Adler and Sullivan, however, Perls appeared to focus upon these symptoms and defenses as manifested in interpersonal spheres. He noted, for example, that people who for various reasons find it uncomfortable to experience and express certain needs (such as for love) *directly* may develop manipulative strategies, games, or roles which are designed to satisfy those needs in *indirect* ways. The person may begin to devote more and more energy to the elaboration and maintenance of these games and roles (Adler would call them part of a maladaptive life-style), with the result that less and less energy is available for adaptive growth. Indeed, the person's growth process gets "hung up" or "stuck" as he or she seeks to cling to the problematic games by creating additional symptoms and defenses. The individual whose interactions with others are based upon seemingly constant illnesses or fears or aggressiveness or inadequacy provides a familiar illustration. Roles of this type tend to force other people to play along by being solicitous, loving, or whatever, but, because the others are being manipulated, the game soon becomes burdensome to them and may end in rejection. The client must then find someone else to "play with."

Perls pointed out that, to make matters worse, distorted or suppressed awareness often creates an impression that one is *not responsible* for one's problems. The blame is usually placed on other people ("my problem is my wife"), on environmental circumstances ("there are no interesting people in this city"), or on internal forces over which the client has no influence ("I can't control my anger"). This type of client is likely to look to the therapist as a person who can solve problems *for* him or her. A related observation emphasized by Perls is that most clients enter therapy ostensibly to understand themselves and solve their problems when, in fact, they really just want to play their neurotic games better. A common illustration of this phenomenon is provided by the man who wants to be taken care of (but cannot tolerate awareness of this need) and who finds nurturance indirectly by telling others of his lengthy struggle toward self-understanding through therapy.

The Goals of Gestalt Therapy

Gestalt therapists are oriented toward a few very basic goals in the course of treatment. Above all, like other phenomenologically oriented clinicians, the gestalt therapist seeks to reestablish the stalled process of client growth. This is achieved by helping clients (1) to become aware of those feelings, desires, and impulses which they have *disowned* but which are actually a part of them, and (2) to recognize those feelings, ideas, and values which they *think* are a genuine part of themselves but which, in fact, are borrowed or adopted from other people.

As these awarenesses are achieved, the client is encouraged to assimilate or "re-own" those genuine aspects of self that had been rejected and to reject those features that do not really belong. Ideally, when one assimilates and integrates all aspects of the personality (both the desirable and the not-so-desirable), one can be aware of and take responsibility for oneself as one really is, instead of being attached to and defensive of a partially phony, internally conflicted self-image.

For example, a person who really feels superior to others but has forced this feeling out of awareness in favor of a more socially acceptable air of humility will become aware of and express both sides of the conflict (i.e., "I'm great" versus "I shouldn't brag"). Once both sides or *poles* of this basic conflict are brought together to confront each other, the client may be better able to find some sort of resolution (e.g., "It's really OK to express my feelings of competence, but I need to take the feelings of others into account as well). As long as one side of the conflict is out of awareness, such resolution is impossible. According to Perls, when conflict resolutions begin to occur in the presence of full awareness of both poles, the person begins to grow again.

The Gestalt Therapy Approach

As was the case in client-centered therapy, the therapist-client relationship in gestalt therapy is ideally a coequal one involving mutual growth. As Kempler (1973, p. 266) put it, "the therapist is like a composing maestro facing an accomplished musician. The maestro expects that between them new and beautiful tunes will be created."

Focus on the Here-and-Now   Like other phenomenologists, Perls firmly believed that therapeutic progress can only be made by keeping the client in contact with her or his feelings as they occur in the immediate present, the "here-and-now." He expressed this belief in a conceptual equation where "Now = experience = awareness = reality" (Perls, 1970, p. 14). Any attempt on the part of the client to recount the past or anticipate the future is seen not only as resistant and obstructive of therapy goals, but as an escape from reality.

Further, instead of *reflecting* (as a Rogerian might) the client's nostalgia or desire to look to the future, a gestalt therapist will actively point out the avoidance and insist that it be terminated. An excellent example of this method was provided by Perls in his filmed interview with "Gloria" (Perls, 1965). At one point, Gloria says that what is happening in the interview reminds her of when she was a little girl. Perls immediately asks, *"Are* you a little girl?" to which Gloria answers, "Well, no, but it's the same feeling." Again Perls asks, *"Are* you a little girl?" Gloria says, "The feeling reminds me of it." Perls explodes: *"Are you a little girl?"* The client finally says, "No."

Keeping the client in touch with the immediate present serves a purpose beyond that of reducing avoidance of current feelings. It also helps the client to see that the past or the future may be important *in the present*. Talking *about* the past or the future in the abstract gets the client nowhere, according to Perls, but *experiencing* past feelings or fears of the future as they occur in the therapy session may be helpful. For example, consider this statement:

Client: My sister and I used to fight an awful lot when we were kids, but we seemed closer somehow then than we are now.

Instead of reflecting the feelings expressed here, the gestalt therapist would probably try to prevent the client from talking *about* his feelings as "things" that used to exist and get in touch instead with how he feels right now. To do this, the client might be asked to "talk" to his sister as if she were there and express his immediate feelings:

Therapist: Can you say this to your sister now?

Client: OK. I feel so far away from you now, Janie. I want to have that feeling of being in a family again.

Notice that by asking the client to "speak" directly to a person from the past, a general, intellectualized *report* of feeling becomes an immediate *present* feeling of which the client can be clearly aware.

The focus on the present is also evident in the language of gestalt therapy. Clients are usually required, for example, to speak in the present tense. A statement like "I wish I could have talked to you last night" is seen as less expressive of present feelings than "I really want to talk to you."

Handling Resistance   Perls, like Freud and others, realized that once a client finds a set of symptoms, games, and defenses that work, however imperfectly, to protect him or her from the pain of conflict and self-awareness, he or she will resist any efforts to break through or remove them. However, Perls believed that instead of viewing resistance only as an inanimate barrier to growth which the client must recognize and put aside, it is valuable for the client to explore the specific nature of the resistance.

To help the client do this, Perls used a technique which served him in other aspects of therapy as well. This technique is *role-playing* or part-taking. Thus, the client who displays or talks about resistance is asked to "become" that resistance in order to gain a clear, *experiential* awareness of what the resistance is doing *for* and *to* her or him. Polster and Polster (1973, pp. 53–54) present an idealized example of this technique. John, a member of a gestalt therapy group, finds it difficult to talk to another group member, Mary, because he says there is a "wall" between them. The therapist asks John to "play" the wall:

John: (as the wall) I am here to protect you against predatory women who will eat you alive if you open yourself up to them.[7]

Now the therapist asks John to "converse" with his resistance in order to

---

[7]Notice that, by "becoming" his resistance as it exists in the present, John experiences and expresses his feelings directly instead of talking *about* his difficulties on an abstract, intellectual level. Perls succinctly expressed his distrust of intellectual analysis as opposed to sensory awareness with the oft-quoted phrase "lose your mind and come to your senses."

fully experience both sides of the conflict which keeps him from relating easily to others in an intimate way:

John: (to the wall) Aren't you exaggerating? She looks pretty safe to me. In fact, she looks more scared than anything.

John: (as the wall) Sure she's scared. I'm responsible for that. I'm a very severe wall and I make a lot of people scared. That's how I want it and I have even affected you that way too. You're scared of me even though I'm really on your side.

John: (to the wall) I *am* scared of you and I even feel you inside me, like I have become like you. I feel my chest as though it were iron and I'm really getting mad about that.

John: (as the wall) Mad—at what? I'm your strength and you don't even know it. Feel how strong you are inside.

John: (to the wall) Sure I feel the strength but I also feel rigid when my chest feels like iron. I'd like to beat on you, knock you over and go over to Mary.

Here, the gestalt therapist urges the client to actually *do* what he *feels,* to "knock down" the wall and, in this situation at least, resolve the conflict in a growthful way.

Therapist: Beat on your iron.

John: (beats his chest and shouts) Get out of my way—Get *out* of my *way!* (silence of a few moments) My chest feels strong—but not like it's made of iron. (after another silence, John begins to cry and talks to Mary): I don't feel any wall between us anymore and I really want to talk to you.

Dealing with resistance in this way is just one example of a general gestalt therapy process in which the various sides of a conflict are brought together and expressed. Of course it is not always this easy for the client to become aware of feelings which are normally kept hidden. Where Freud used free association to help clients' self-exploration, Perls used a battery of other methods, several of which are described in the following sections.

Frustrating the Client   As noted earlier, Perls believed that most clients come to therapy hoping to feel better without really having to change or give up their maladaptive roles and games. Since he felt that allowing clients to continue using their customary styles in therapy would be a waste of everyone's time, Perls set out immediately to frustrate clients' efforts to relate to him as they normally do with others. Whether in individual or group therapy, the person with whom Perls worked at a given moment was on the "hot seat" in the sense that all attention was focused upon him or her, and anything that indicated symptoms, games, or resistance was pointed out and explored.

Assume, for example, that a client begins a first session with the statement "I've really been looking forward to having this session. I hope you can help me." Instead of reflecting this feeling or asking *why* the client feels this way, a gestalt therapist would probably focus on the manipulative aspect of the statement, which seems to contain the message, "I expect you to help me without my having to do much." Thus, the therapist might say "How do you think I could help you?" To this the client (somewhat taken aback) might respond "Well, I was hoping you could help me understand why I'm so unhappy." From here, the therapist would continue to frustrate the client's attempt to get her or him to take responsibility for solving the client's own problems and, in the process, would help the client to experience his real feelings in the situation:

Therapist: Tell me what you mean when you say "unhappy." (One major gestalt therapy principle, which is not unlike certain social-learning tenets, is to go from the general problem to its specific manifestations.)

Client: Oh, I don't know, it's just that I don't ever feel satisfied with myself. I never seem to be able to . . . I don't know—it's very complicated and hard for me to express.

Therapist: How old are you?

Client: Thirty-six.

Therapist: And as a 36-year-old person, you can't tell me what makes you unhappy?

Client: I wish I could, but I'm too confused about it myself.

Therapist: (who now infers that the client is "playing stupid" in order to avoid taking responsibility for or dealing with problems): Can you play me trying to help you? What would I say and what would I do?

Client: Well, you might say "Don't worry, I'll figure out what your problems are and help get you on the right track."

Therapist: OK, now say that to me, tell me how you expect me to do all this *for* you.

Client: OK, I see what you're saying. I guess I do hope you have some sort of magic pill or something.

At this point, the therapist might then repeat the request for a statement of the client's problems and, this time, might get a more mature answer.

Use of Nonverbal Cues Nonverbal behavior is an important source of raw material in gestalt therapy. If the therapist is to frustrate the client in such attempts to "play games" in treatment, she or he must be attentive to both what the client says *and* does. The nonverbal channel is seen as an especially useful carrier of obvious but subtle messages which often contradict the client's words. In a classic example, Perls (1965) recognizes that his client *says* she is frightened, but smiles at the same time. Perls calls her a "phony" (he argues that a frightened person does not smile), and, in the course of an angry retort, the client begins to be aware that her reported fear is part of an interpersonal game which helps get others to take care of her.

Here is another illustration:

Client: I wish I wasn't so nervous with people.

Therapist: Who are you nervous with?

Client: With everyone.

Therapist: With me, here, now?

Client: Yes, very.

Therapist: That's funny because you don't look nervous to me.
Client: (suddenly clasping his hands): Well I am!
Therapist: What are you doing with your hands?
Client: Nothing, I just clasped them together. It's just a gesture.
Therapist: Do the gesture again. (client reclasps his hands) And again, clasp them again, harder. (client clasps hands harder.) How does that feel?
Client: It feels tight, kind of constricted.
Therapist: Can you become that tightness or constriction? Can you get in touch with what that tightness might say to you?
Client: OK, ah, I'm tight. I'm holding everything together. I'm keeping the lid on you so that you don't let too much out.

The clasped hands made the therapist wonder what the gesture expressed. Instead of asking *why* the client clasped them, she pointed out *what* the client did. She then asked him to *concentrate* on the associated feelings by repeating and exaggerating the gesture. Once the feelings brought on by the gesture are expressed, the client is asked to identify with and elaborate on them. The result is that the client expresses a *defensive* feeling about being in therapy which had originally been described vaguely as "nervousness."

The Use of Dreams   In gestalt therapy, dreams are seen not merely as wish fulfillments, but as messages from the person to himself or herself. After recounting a dream, the client is encouraged to "read" the message it conveys by playing the part of some or all dream features and characters. In the process, Perls believed, the client may become aware of and assimilate disowned or otherwise inaccessible parts of the self. Here is an example of Perls's use of dream material:

Linda: I dreamed that I watch . . . a lake . . . drying up, and there is a small island in the middle of the lake, and a circle of . . . porpoises — they're like porpoises except that they can stand up, so they're like porpoises that are like people, and they're in a circle, sort of like a religious ceremony, and it's very sad — I feel very sad because they can breathe, they are sort of dancing around the circle, but the water, their element, is drying up. So it's like a dying—like watching a race of people, or a race of creatures, dying. And they are mostly females but a few of them have a small male organ, so there are a few males there, but they won't live long enough to reproduce, and their element is drying up. And there is one that is sitting over here near me and I'm talking to this porpoise and he has prickles on his tummy, sort of like a porcupine, and they don't seem to be a part of him. And I think that there's one good point about the water drying up, I think—well, at least at the bottom, when all the water dries up, there will probably be some sort of treasure there, because at the bottom of the lake there should be things that have fallen in, like coins or something, but I look carefully and all that I can find is an old license plate . . . That's the dream.

Perls: Will you please play the license plate?
Linda: I am an old license plate, thrown in the bottom of a lake. I have no use because I'm no value—although I'm not rusted—I'm outdated, so I can't be

used as a license plate . . . and I'm just thrown on the rubbish heap. That's what I did with a license plate, I threw it on a rubbish heap.

Perls: Well, how do you feel about this?

Linda: (quietly) I don't like it. I don't like being a license plate — useless.

Perls: Could you talk about this? That was such a long dream until you come to find a license plate; I'm sure this must be of great importance.

Linda: (sighs) Useless. Outdated . . . The use of a license plate is to allow — give a car permission to go . . . and I can't give anyone permission to do anything because I'm outdated . . . In California, they just paste a little—you buy a sticker—and stick it on the car, on the old license plate. (faint attempt at humor) So maybe someone could put me on their car and stick this sticker on me, I don't know . . .

Perls: OK, now play the lake.

Linda: I'm a lake . . . I'm drying up, and disappearing, soaking into the earth . . . (with a touch of surprise) *dying* . . . But when I soak into the earth, I become a part of the earth—so maybe I water the surrounding area, so . . . even in the lake, even in my bed, flowers can grow (sighs). New life can grow . . . from me (cries) . . .

Perls: You get the existential message?

Linda: Yes. (sadly, but with conviction) I can paint — I can create — I can create beauty. I can no longer reproduce, I'm like the porpoise — but I — I'm . . . I . . . keep wanting to say I'm food . . . I . . . as water becomes . . . I water the earth, and give life — growing things, the water — they need both the earth and water, and the . . . and the air and the sun, but as the water from the lake, I can play a part in something, and producing—feeding.

Perls: You see the contrast: On the surface, you find something some artifact — the license plate, the artificial you — but then when you go deeper, you find the apparent death of the lake is actually fertility . . .

Linda: And I don't need a license plate, or a permission, a license in order to . . .

Perls: (gently) Nature doesn't need a license plate to grow. You don't have to be useless, if you are organismically creative, which means if you are involved.

Linda: And I don't need permission to be creative . . . Thank you. (Perls, 1969, pp. 81–82)

Other Methods   The gestalt therapist uses a variety of other methods to help clients increase awareness and to promote "re-owning" of aliented aspects of personality. These are described in some detail by Levitsky and Perls (1970); we shall briefly mention a few of them here:

1   Use of Direct and Immediate Messages   Direct communication is encouraged as a means of helping the client take responsibility for his or her feelings. In a group treatment setting, the client who points to another client and says "she really makes me uncomfortable" would probably be asked to repeat the message directly to the person involved: "You make me uncomfortable." Similarly, "I" language is preferred over "it" language. A statement like "it makes me furious to hear that" contains a subtle message that "it" is responsible for the client's anger. A restatement (e.g., "I am angry at you") would probably be encouraged. Gossiping about people who are not present is prohibited. The assumption is that one evades responsibility for feelings and statements if their target is absent. Finally, clients are usually asked to convert indirect *questions* into direct, responsible *statements*. The message behind the question "Do you think I'll ever feel any better than I do now?" may actually be "I am terrified that I'll always be depressed and maybe kill myself." If so, it is seen as important for the client to be aware of and to express the fear.

   2   *Prohibition of Intellectual Discussion*   Just as the therapist tries to avoid asking abstract questions about the "why" of behavior (e.g., Why do you think you feel that way?"), the client in gestalt therapy is prevented from using elaborate intellectual analyses to avoid immediate, here-and-now awareness. The person who begins to expound a theory of a particular problem (e.g., "I really think all this goes back to a basic lack of self-confidence stemming from a time when I felt rejected by my parents") would probably be asked to identify with and "become" the nonconfident self in the present. Or, some nonverbal behavior which accompanied the theoretical analysis might be focused on by the therapist who might then request an exaggeration of the particular movement as a means of bringing its "message" into the foreground. In any case, clients would not be permitted to spin their wheels in intellectualized discussions *about* feelings.

   3   *Use of Internal Dialogues and Related Techniques*   We have already seen some ways in which clients in gestalt therapy are asked to "become" some of their characteristics and resistances. In many situations, especially group work, this technique is elaborated to include extended "conversations" not only between or among various "parts" of the person, but between the client and absent (or even dead) persons from the past with whom the client has "unfinished business." Among the most significant internal dialogues are those between the client's superego or conscience (called "topdog") and the part which is suppressed by "shoulds" and "oughts" (the "underdog"). Other related methods ask the client to "play the projection." Here, the assumption is that when one's disowned characteristics are projected onto other people (e.g., "She's so damned dependent!"), the best way to become aware of and re-own the feelings involved is to role-play. *Reversals* are also used to achieve similar kinds of awareness. Assume, for example, that a person vehemently denies feelings of tenderness toward others and conveys an image of coldness and self-sufficiency. This individual might be asked to play a warm, loving person who needs other people. In the process, the client may get in touch with exactly those feelings she or he has been suppressing.

An Illustration of Gestalt Therapy

The following edited excerpt from a gestalt group provides some idea of the way in which the various methods described above are integrated in practice. In this case the setting is not therapy per se, but a workshop run by Perls in which each group member was placed in turn on the "hot seat" (Perls, 1969).[8] The client, "Jane," had worked with Perls before and thus shows more familiarity with the method than would be expected of a new client; otherwise, the procedures are representative.

Jane: The dream I started on, the last time I worked, I never finished it, and I think the last part is as important as the first part. Where I left off, I was in the Tunnel of Love —

Perls: What are you picking on? (Jane has been scratching her leg)

Jane: Hmm . . . I'm just sitting here, for a minute, so I can really be here . . . Now I'm in the intermediate zone, and I'm — I'm thinking about two things: Should I work on the dream or should I work on the picking thing, because that's something I do a lot . . . I'll go back to the dream. [Jane tells about a dream and then begins to tell how anxious she is feeling right now]

Perls: Are you telling us a dream, or are you doing a job?

Jane: I'm telling a dream, but it's still — I'm not telling a dream.

Perls: Hm. Definitely not.

Jane: I can't say that I'm really aware of what I'm doing. Except physically. I'm aware of what's happening physically to me but — I don't really know what I'm doing.

Perls: I noticed one thing: When you come up on the hot seat, you stop playing the silly goose.

Jane: Hm. I get frightened when I'm up here.

Perls: You get dead.

Jane: . . . I'm wondering whether or not I'm dead. I notice that my legs are cold and my feet are cold. I feel — I feel strange . . . I notice that my attention is concentrated on that little matchbox on the floor.

Perls: OK. Have an encounter with the matchbox.

Jane: [to the matchbox] Right now I'm taking a break from looking at you . . . 'cause I don't know what's going on, and I don't know what I'm doing. I don't even know if I'm telling the truth.

Perls: What does the matchbook answer?

Jane: [as the matchbox] I don't care if you tell the truth or not. It doesn't matter to me. I'm just a matchbox.

Perls: Try this for size. Tell us, "I'm just a matchbox."

Jane: I'm just a matchbox and I feel silly saying that. I feel kind of dumb, being a matchbox . . . A little bit useful, not not very useful. There's a million like me. And you can look at me, and you can like me, and when I'm all used up, you can throw me away. I never liked being a matchbox . . . I don't know if that's the truth when I say I don't know what I'm doing. I know there's one part of me that knows what I'm doing . . . She's saying (with authority) well, *you*

---

[8]It is important to note that, although the person on the "hot seat" is the focus of attention, she or he is not isolated. In many cases, other group members also interact with the client and with the therapist (Polster & Polster, 1973).

know where you're at. You're playing dumb. You're playing stupid. You're doing this and you're doing that. . . . She's saying (briskly) now when you get in the chair, you have to be in the here-and-now, you have to do it *right,* you have to be turned on, you have to know everything—

Perls: "You have to do your job"

Jane: You have to do your job, and you have to do it *right.* And you have to—become totally self-actualized, and you have to get rid of all your hangups. . . .

[Now Jane spontaneously returns to being her frightened self again and talks to her demanding self]: You really make it hard for me. . . . You're really putting a lot of demands on me. . . . I don't know everything, and on top of that, I don't know what I'm doing half the time. . . .

Perls: So be your topdog again.

Jane: Is that —

Perls: Your topdog. That's the famous topdog. The righteous topdog. This is where the power is.

Jane: Yeah. Well—uh—I'm your topdog. You can't live without me. I'm the one that—I keep you noticed, Jane. If it weren't for me, nobody would notice you. [Jane now responds to "topdog"] Well, I don't want to be noticed, *you* do. . . . I don't really want to be noticed, as much as you do.

Perls: I would like you to attack the righteous side of that topdog.

Jane: Attack — the righteous side.

Perls: The topdog is always righteous. Topdog *knows* what you've got to do, has all the right to criticize, and so on.

Jane: Yeah. . . . You're a bitch! Like my mother. You know what's good for me. You make life hard for me. . . .

Perls: Now please don't change what your hands are doing, but tell us what's going on in your hands. . . . Let them talk to each other.

Jane: My left hand. I'm shaking, and I'm in a fist, straining forward . . . the fist is very tight, pushing my fingernails into my hand. It doesn't feel good, but I do it all the time. I feel tight.

Perls: And the right hand?

Jane: I'm holding you back around the wrist.

Perls: Tell it why you hold it back.

Jane: If I let you go you're gonna hit something. I don't know what you're gonna hit, but I have to—I have to hold you back 'cause you can't do that. Can't go around hitting things.

Perls: Now hit your topdog.

Jane: [gives short, harsh yells]

Perls: Now talk to your topdog. "Stop nagging—"

Jane: [yells at "topdog"] Leave me alone!

Perls: Again

Jane: Leave me alone!

Perls: Again

Jane: [screaming and crying] *Leave me alone!*

Perls: Again

Jane: (screams and cries) LEAVE ME ALONE! I DON'T HAVE TO DO WHAT YOU SAY! (still crying) I don't have to be that good! . . . I don't have to be in this chair! You make me! You make me come here! . . . I'd like to kill you.

Perls: Say this again.

Jane: I'd like to kill you.

Perls: Again

Jane: I'd like to *kill* you.

Perls: Can you squash it in your left hand?

Jane: It's as big as me . . . I'm strangling it. [Perls gives Jane a pillow which she strangles while making choking noises and crying]

Perls: OK. Relax, close your eyes (long silence). OK, come back to us.

[Later in the session, Perls asks Jane to turn her perfectionist "topdog" into an "underdog" and to talk down to it.]

Jane: [to her perfectionist "topdog"] . . . You don't have to do anything, you don't have to prove anything (cries). You're only twenty years old! You don't have to be the queen. . . .

Jane: [as her perfectionist "topdog"] OK, I understand that. I know that. I'm just in a *hurry*. I'm in a *big* hurry. . . . You have to keep hurrying and the days slip by and you think you're losing time, or something. I'm *much* too hard on you. I have to leave you alone.

Perls: . . . Let your topdog say "I'll be a bit more patient with you."

Jane: [as topdog] . . . I'll be a bit more patient with you.

Perls: Say this again.

Jane: It's very hard for me to be patient . . . But I'll try to be a bit more patient with you. . . . As I say that, I'm stomping my foot, and shaking my head.

Perls: OK. Say, "I *won't* be patient with you"

Jane: I won't be patient with you. [Perls asks Jane to repeat this and to take responsibility for the feeling by repeating the statement to several group members]

Perls: OK, how do you feel now?

Jane: OK

Perls: You understand, topdog and underdog are not yet together. But at least the conflict is clear, in the open, maybe a little less violent. (Perls, 1969, pp. 264–272)

Other detailed descriptions and case examples of gestalt therapy are available in Perls (1970), Polster and Polster (1973), and Rosenblatt (1975).

Applications of Gestalt Therapy

As was the case for Rogers, Perls saw his approach as valuable for use in one-to-one and group therapy with persons in various diagnostic categories (e.g., neurosis), but he also felt that it could be a useful route to increased awareness and improved functioning for people in general.

Perls believed that everyone is to some degree lacking in full awareness, and

Figure 11-2 Many sensitivity or growth groups engage in exercises such as this to foster mutual trust among members.

he recommended various individual and group exercises to enhance contact with oneself, other people, and various aspects of the inanimate environment (Perls, Hefferline, & Goodman, 1951). Many of these exercises have become a part of the wide array of sensitivity training groups, encounter groups, and personal growth groups which have achieved great popularity in recent years. Having group members really *look* at one another, close their eyes and focus attention on sensations coming from their bodies, enjoy the feelings of a backrub, listen to the emotions expressed in the sound of their own voices, or speak directly and intimately to one another are common examples of this type of experience.

This application of gestalt principles has been made not only in "temporary" groups formed specifically for awareness and growth purposes, but in more permanent aggregations as well. Coworkers, church congregations, extended family groups, neighbors, classmates, dormitory residents, and married couples can be given gestalt awareness experiences. An excellent summary of these applications is provided by Polster and Polster (1973, pp. 292–311). Many additional references are contained in Hatcher and Himmelstein's *Handbook of Gestalt Therapy* (1976).

OTHER PHENOMENOLOGICAL THERAPIES

Carl Rogers' and Fritz Perls' methods of treatment represent only two examples of the phenomenological approach to therapy. Other approaches are also compatible with the basic phenomenological orientation though some of them have not become treatment "packages" like those of Rogers or Perls. For example, many therapists blend psychodynamic or Rogerian or gestalt methods with concepts and principles stemming from humanistic or existential psychology (Maslow, 1967, 1968; May, 1969; May, Angel, & Ellenberger, 1958; see Chapter 3). The *logotherapy* of Viktor Frankl (1963, 1965, 1967) is based primarily upon existential philosophy and is oriented toward helping clients to (1) take responsibility for their feelings and actions, and (2) find meaning and purpose in their lives. Since Frankl believed that people can feel a lack of meaning and purpose without necessarily displaying neurotic or psychotic behaviors, he saw his approach as applicable to nonpatients as well as to persons who have been diagnostically labeled. The therapeutic procedures associated with humanistic and existential points of view are described in the sources cited above as well as in a recent introductory volume by Bugental (1978). See also Ford and Urban (1963) and Patterson (1973).

A phenomenologically oriented treatment approach which shares several features with social-learning theory is the *Fixed-Role Therapy* of George Kelly. On the basis of his personal-construct theory (Kelly, 1955; see Chapter 3) Kelly developed assessment and treatment methods aimed at helping clients to become aware of and, when necessary, change the subjective assumptions or expectations which they use to guide their behavior. Usually this means helping the client to adopt more flexible and elaborate constructs to replace the narrow, rigid ones which Kelly believed to be at the root of psychological disorders.

The clearly subjective, conscious orientation of Kelly's theory places it at least partially in the phenomenological "camp," but several facets of his methods are more at home elsewhere. Unlike most other phenomenologists who studiously avoid diagnostic procedures and often ignore a client's case history folder, Kelly advocated careful and systematic assessment of both the problems and the personal constructs characteristic of the client. He even advocated the use of certain psychological tests to help clarify the ways in which clients conceive of the world around them. Chief among these was Kelly's own Role Construct Repertory Test.

Another remarkable feature of Kelly's basically phenomenological treatment approach is that he went beyond the point of merely helping clients become aware of their maladaptive constructs or beliefs. Indeed, he encouraged them to experiment with specific alternative constructs. To assist in this enterprise, the therapist may ask the client to write a *fixed-role sketch,* a third-person account of what the client is really like and how he or she really feels. The client is then helped to restart personal growth by "temporarily" (for several weeks) role-playing the person described in the sketch. The role-playing takes place both in therapy sessions and in the "real world." During this period, the therapist treats the client as if she or he were the person in the sketch. Over time, the client may become comfortable with certain aspects of the experimentally adopted role and assimilate them. Other aspects may turn out to be foreign or unacceptable and will be dropped. Ideally, the final result will be behavior and guiding thoughts that are in line with how the client actually feels. For more details on Kelly's approach see Kelly (1955) or Patterson (1973).

AN EVALUATION OF PHENOMENOLOGICAL THERAPIES

Some evaluative comments about phenomenological *models* of clinical psychology were made in Chapter 3. Here, we shall focus primarily on the value and limitations of the clinical interventions that flow from those models. There is little doubt that phenomenological therapies and their nontherapy counterparts (e.g., sensitivity and personal growth groups) have had a significant impact. They provide a "third choice" which is welcomed by those who are not fully satisfied with the treatments offered by psychodynamic or social-learning models. This "third choice" is viewed as particularly attractive because its unabashedly positive, optimistic view of human beings generates faith in each client's ability to find meaning and self-actualization in life without having to exorcise unconscious, intrapsychic "demons" or to systematically extinguish bad habits or learn new skills. Phenomenological approaches are "upbeat." They do not dwell on pathology, but focus instead on growth and on what the client can *become*. This means that all individuals, whether or not they have specific problems, can presumably benefit from contact with one or more phenomenological growth experiences. Finally, the phenomenological emphasis upon the therapeutic *relationship* and a corresponding deemphasis on therapy *techniques* are appealing to many clinicians, especially those who feel uncomfortable if they see themselves trying to do things *to* their clients.

Nevertheless, phenomenological treatment approaches have come in for their share of criticism. Those who see problems and weaknesses in phenomenological therapies make the following points:

1 The language of phenomenology is often esoteric, complex, and generally unclear. This problem, already noted in Chapter 3 for the model itself, extends to writings about and the words used in many phenomenological therapies. Terms like B-values, Dasein, Eigenwelt, organismic experiencing, peak experiences, gestalt, self-concept, and the like may actually stand in the way of understanding the value of the treatments to which they apply. One client put it this way in a letter to Perls: "I tried reading your book, *Gestalt Therapy*, but I wish somebody . . . would write a book in very simple language . . . , explaining these same theories so that the average person . . . could maybe really get something more out of it" (Perls, 1970, p. 214). The extent of the problem is underscored by the fact that some writers have made fun of this therapy language without being too far from reality. Compare the following satire by Hoffman (1973, p. 76) with the direct quote from Kempler (1973) used in Chapter 3:

Client: Sorry I'm late today.
Therapist: Can you get more in touch with that sorrow?
Client: I hope it didn't inconvenience you.
Therapist: Let's focus on your capacity for choice rather than on my expectations.
Client: But I didn't mean to be late.

Therapist: I hear you, and I don't put it down. But where we need to be is the immanence of the I-thou relationship . . . emanating from the here-and-now, and from there into a consciousness of the tension between be-ing and non-be-ing, and eventually into the transcendence of be-ing itself, through to a cosmic awareness of the oceanic I-dentity of self and the space-time continuum.

Client: Gotcha.

There is another aspect of the language problem in phenomenological therapies as well. Proponents of these methods describe their goals as *humanistic,* and include among them things like client growth, creativity, fulfillment, joy, self-actualization, and individuality. Similarly, they describe the treatment context as a noncoercive, nonjudgmental, nondirective one in which client freedom is maximized. Critics argue that, while this may all be true (ideally, at least), these goals and contexts are not the sole property of phenomenology. Most psychodynamic and social-learning therapists would also see themselves as being basically oriented toward humanistic values and away from coercion and constraint. In fact, it would be difficult to find a therapist alive who does not believe in the *ideals* of phenomenological therapy even though her or his methods of reaching them differ.

2   Phenomenological treatment procedures are incomplete. It has often been argued that, by abandoning or deemphasizing clinical assessment and the client's history, phenomenological therapists may miss diagnostic signs or background facts (e.g., brain damage, biochemical problems, intellectual deficits, previous aggressive or suicidal incidents) that could be important to treatment planning and delivery. Trusting clients to know about or tell about these things is seen as naïve and potentially as dangerous as the abuses associated with traditional diagnosis.

It is also suggested that, while a good client-therapist relationship may be a *necessary* condition for effective treatment, it may not be a *sufficient* condition. The problems and circumstances of some clients are seen as beyond their ability to solve or change; they need more in the way of help than a genuine, empathic relationship.

There is also distrust of any therapy which relies so much on feeling and so little on reason and logic as do the phenomenological approaches. The phenomenological therapy relationship experience may produce an emotional "high," but there is concern among many observers that, without logic, planning, and the practice of new alternatives, client benefits may be temporary at best.

3   Phenomenological treatment procedures are vague and unrealistic. It has been pointed out that phenomenological methods are usually discussed as "processes" which are not clearly translated into specific therapist behaviors. Further, many writers question the processes themselves. For example, can a person ever achieve empathy, thus *really* knowing what it is like to be another person? Can any therapist *really* be nondirective and nonjudgmental? Nye (1975, p. 135) points out that "client-centered therapists, despite themselves, bring about changes in the client's behaviors through inadvertent, subtle reinforcements (for example, nodding their heads or changing their facial expressions when clients speak about 'interesting' things and remaining more passive when clients speak about 'uninteresting' things)."

4 Phenomenological treatments are actually rigid, not flexible. It has been argued that, by treating all clients in basically the same way on the assumption that each of them is troubled by the same general set of awareness-related problems, phenomenological therapists fall prey to the criticisms *they* have leveled at psychodynamic and social-learning therapies, namely, that the uniqueness of each client is not given sufficient attention. Indeed, social-learning therapists contend that their emphasis on careful assessment and on the design of special treatment programs tailored to each client's unique history is *more* humanistic than the phenomenological approach.

5 The beneficial effects of phenomenological treatments have not been firmly established. Most phenomenological therapists have maintained a vigorously antiscientific, even anti-intellectual stance toward the evaluation of their methods. Some of them view "data" as a four-letter word and insist that only the client and therapist can evaluate the therapy experience, and even then only in subjective terms, not in the language of science. This attitude has caused many observers to reject most phenomenological treatment as a serious approach to changing human behavior.

Some phenomenological theorists and therapists (notably Carl Rogers and his colleagues) have attempted to provide data on the *process* of their treatments, but the variables measured (e.g., accurate empathy) have tended to be heavily dependent upon subjective ratings and self-reports, both of which are seen as particularly vulnerable to bias and other threats to reliability and validity (Chinsky & Rappaport, 1970; Rappaport & Chinsky, 1972). Recent reviewers of research on therapist qualities in general noted that "the . . . variables most frequently selected by the researcher for study are, unfortunately, such simplistic, global concepts as to cause this field to suffer from possibly terminal vagueness" (Parloff, Waskow, & Wolfe, 1978, p. 273).

The same problems exist in interpreting research on the *outcome* of phenomenological treatments. The outcome data presented to substantiate the value of treatment tend to be based mainly upon various kinds of client self-reports. These may not be reliable or valid. After reviewing the results of phenomenological group therapy, Bednar and Kaul (1978, p. 792) note that "in spite of the apparent diversity of these [self-report] measures, it seems most appropriate to view [them]as reflecting a nonspecific factor of improvement based on more favorable subjective evaluations that may or may not be accompanied by observable behavioral changes."

The observation by some phenomenologists (e.g., Rogers) that their treatments result in a similar pattern of change from client to client has also been attacked by critics. They suggest that the pattern is due not to spontaneous growth, but to direct therapist influences such as modeling and reinforcement of certain client behaviors. In groups, clients may model for one another. A participant in a gestalt therapy group once raised this possibility with Perls: "Dr. Perls, . . . as you've been formulating and experiencing what has come out as gestalt therapy, I want to be reassured, I want to hear you say it, it seems like a process of discovery. Yet I think that people can arrange themselves to fit the expectations of the therapist, like, I sit here and watch person after person have a polarity, a conflict of forces, and I think I can do it too. But I don't know how spontaneous it would be, although I think I would feel spontaneous. You've experienced people over a long time; are we fitting you or have you discovered us?" (Perls, 1969, pp. 214–215). Perls's answer was "I don't know."

6 Phenomenological therapies can be dangerous under some circumstances. Because phenomenological approaches are so often applied in short-term group contexts which fall outside the range of formal therapy, many unscreened participants end up experimenting with growth experiences. And because the emphasis in phenomenology is upon feeling and experience, not reason and logic, the importance of the therapist's or "facilitator's" academic credentials and special training is sometimes deemphasized. The danger of permanent "psychotic breakdowns" and other disastrous consequences may not be as critical as some people fear, but phenomenological group experiences can indeed produce "casualties." While the definition of "casualty" is not entirely clear, available data indicate that from 0 to 8 percent of group participants may end up harmed in some sense by the experience. "Casualties" seem to occur most often among those who were relatively unstable to begin with, a fact which further emphasizes the danger of inadequate screening of group members (see Bednar & Kaul, 1978, for a review of process and outcome data from phenomenological groups).

7 Phenomenological approaches are applicable mainly to intelligent, introspective individuals. Despite the view that anyone can benefit from phenomenological growth experiences, it has been argued that these experiences may be helpful only to relatively well-integrated, functioning people. The value of phenomenological therapies for more severe behavior problems (e.g., "psychosis"), children, those under severe stress, and the retarded is suspected to be minimal.

Still, phenomenological methods do appear to have value. In our view, they provide an excellent set of *assessment* tools. Rogers' techniques are among the most productive interviewing procedures available and many gestalt exercises (e.g., dialogues, part-playing, and the like) can be productively used to help clients report on feelings that might otherwise require many interviews to reveal. Overall, we find ourselves in agreement with Korchin's (1976, p. 373) conclusion: "The ideas and methods of [phenomenological] psychotherapy are still in a formative period. . . . At this stage it is necessary to test and sharpen these ideas, in order to preserve the essential and discard the superficial."

Chapter 12

Community Psychology

- Organizing a community to demand improved public housing.
- Training volunteers to operate a "hotline" at a suicide prevention center.
- Increasing citizen participation in neighborhood problem solving.
- Teaching families how to reduce their energy consumption.
- Developing aftercare programs that enable formerly hospitalized mental patients to live in the community.
- Evaluating the effectiveness of new correctional techniques that attempt to divert offenders from the criminal justice system.
- Training paraprofessionals in the skills of crisis intervention, client advocacy, and problem solving.
- Assessing the impact of community mental health centers.

What do each of these activities share with one another? They are all examples of *community psychology,* a field closely related to traditional clinical psychology, but one which reflects somewhat different attitudes, objectives, techniques, and training.

Our purpose in this chapter is to acquaint you with community psychology: its history, its principles, its strengths, and its weaknesses. The often large differences between the clinician and the community psychologist which we shall describe are quite real, but one should also remember that clinical and community psychology are in many ways more alike than they are different. Each emphasizes a *psychological perspective* on human behavior. Each strives to apply this perspective in order to *change* human behavior and promote human welfare. And each champions the *scientific* study of human behavior.

The history of the mental health professions (psychology, psychiatry, social work, and psychiatric nursing) suggests that they have been transformed by three revolutions (Bellak, 1964; Hobbs, 1964). The term "revolution" implies that these changes possessed a dramatic, sudden, decisive quality and initiated approaches that were radically distinct from existing views of mental illness. In each of the mental health revolutions, the changes, especially with regard to treatment, were indeed dramatic and very controversial, although it is doubtful that they represented the total, clean break with each profession's past that we might expect of a bona fide revolution.

The first mental health revolution was advanced in 1793 by Philippe Pinel who unchained the inmates of the Bicêtre in Paris and advocated that the mentally ill be treated humanely and with the firm expectation that they could improve. This event marked the beginning of what has been termed the *moral era* of psychiatric treatment, a period spanning the first 70 years of the nineteenth century (see Chapter 2).

Sprafkin (1977) lists several characteristics of moral treatment. Prominent among these was the assumption that social and environmental disruption played a major role in causing mental disorders. Among the factors commonly thought to contribute to a pernicious environment were poverty, death of loved ones, and stress. Perhaps the most intriguing cause was excess "excitement from sea voyage" (Sprafkin, 1977, p. 63). Moral treatment also attempted to provide a benign treatment environment that was orderly, supportive, and consistently well disciplined. It cast the institution's staff into the role of a caring and concerned surrogate family for the patient. It emphasized the therapeutic virtues of hard work, religious worship, self-control, and the development of social skills and "good habits." Finally, moral treatment adopted an orientation that was more educational than medical or psychiatric but with a resolute optimism that mental disorders were curable.

Throughout the first half of the nineteenth century the important reforms of Pinel's moral era were extended by other mental health "muckrakers" such as William Tuke in England and Benjamin Rush in America. The moral era was quite short-lived (see Sprafkin, 1977, and Ullmann & Krasner, 1975, pp. 137–139 for discussions of the events that led to its decline), but most mental health historians recognize it as a movement that was unusually successful in treating major mental illness. In fact, as we shall discover later in this chapter, moral-era attitudes and techniques survive in many aspects of present-day community psychology.

The second revolution in mental health is attributed to Sigmund Freud's theories and to clinical demonstrations of the role of psychological factors in certain behavior disorders, particularly the neuroses (see Chapters 3 and 9).

Freud's work paved the way for psychotherapy to become a major treatment technique for psychiatric disorders. Like early breakthroughs in other fields, Freud's "talking cure" may now strike us as a simple, even obvious idea. However, at the end of the nineteenth century, the notion that mere conversations could be therapeutic stood as a radical departure from the increasing insistence that mental illness required medical interventions (see Chapter 2).

The third revolution in mental health is the focus of this chapter. It has been given a number of titles including community psychology, community mental health, and community psychiatry. While these terms share many common meanings, they are not synonymous and should not be used interchangeably. The primary topic of this chapter is *community psychology,* a broad-scale movement that attempts to apply psychological principles to the understanding of social problems and the creation of lasting social change. While no single definition of community psychology is entirely adequate, there is enough agreement on the essential uniqueness of this field to allow a few unifying concepts to be distilled from the welter of available definitions.

A prevalent belief of most community (and many clinical) psychologists is that the development of human behavior depends on interactions between people and their environments. This requires that efforts to alleviate social problems must entail change of *both* environmental events and individual behavioral competencies (Cowen, 1973). Although some community psychologists have attempted to change the social environment through political activism, most prefer to work "within the system" to develop interventions which focus on modification of both individual skills and the social systems within which such skills will be displayed.

In his recent comprehensive text on community psychology, Rappaport (1977) describes the importance of an *ecological* perspective for the field. This perspective emphasizes improving the fit between persons and environments by creating new social alternatives and developing personal resources, as opposed to eliminating the weaknesses of individuals or their communities. A similar affirmation of the ecological position is provided by Mann (1978), who describes community psychology as being devoted to strengthening the quality of community life either by improving social environments and resources or increasing personal competencies.

Other frequently cited definitions of community psychology are provided in Table 12-1.

Community Mental Health and Community Psychology: Basic Differences

Can community psychology be distinguished from community mental health? Should it be? The answer on both counts is "yes." Community mental health should be thought of as a subset of activities within community psychology primarily devoted to the delivery of mental health services to populations which historically have been underserved by mental health professionals. As such, community mental health is concerned most with *direct* services to consumers,

Table 12-1   Recent Definitions of Community Psychology

Source	Definition
Bennett, Anderson, Cooper, Hassal, Klein and Rosenblum (1966)	The study of general psychology processes that link social systems with individual behavior in complex interaction. Conceptual and experimental clarification of such linkages provide the basis for action programs directed toward improving individual, group, and social-system functioning.
Reiff (1968)	A field whose interventions are aimed at the social-system level in order to modify human behavior.
Bloom (1973)	The field of psychology that attempts to resolve social issues rather than individuals' troubles.
Sarason (1973)	The study of the psychological impact of proximal and distal communities, the evolution of communities, and the ways in which psychological knowledge can be brought to bear on the facilitation of adaptive social change.
Murrell (1973)	The field of psychology that studies the transactions between social-system networks, populations, and individuals; that develops and evaluates intervention methods which improve person-environment "fits"; that designs and evaluates new social systems, and from such knowledge and change seeks to enhance the psychological opportunities of the individual.
Zax and Specter (1974)	An approach to human behavior problems that emphasizes contributions to their development made by environmental forces as well as the potential contributions to be made toward their alleviation by the use of such forces.
Rappaport (1977)	A field which emphasizes an ecological perspective of interaction implying that the fit between persons and environments can be improved by creating new social alternatives and developing personal resources rather than eliminating the weaknesses of individuals or their communities.
Mann (1978)	A field concerned with participating in planning for social change, with organizing and implementing planned changes, with designing and conducting programs of service to provide for the human needs generated by social change, and with the development of community resources and processes to deal with the future implications of social changes.

while community psychology seeks broader social-system changes whose effects may radiate to individuals (Sarason, 1973).

The goals of community psychology relate to the community or subcommunity level (e.g., the creation or strengthening of social resources), while community mental health aims at achieving the most effective delivery of clinical services to needy persons. Bloom (1973) has contrasted community psychology's penchant for *social issues* with community mental health's attention to *individual troubles*. The former is a psychology *about* the community, the latter a psychology *in* the community (Mann, 1978).

Consider the following analogy from the world of sports. The relationship of community mental health to community psychology is a little like the association between the National League and major league baseball as a whole. The National League came first but was soon joined by the teams of the American League to form a larger structure. Like the National League, community mental health came first and was the financial impetus for what has become community psychology. Community mental health now exists as a major clinical component of its more comprehensive progeny, community psychology. More will be said of the relationship between these two fields in the sections that follow.

THE CULTIVATION OF COMMUNITY PSYCHOLOGY

Community psychology is a very young discipline. Although we will describe early factors that anticipate current practices, the proper focus of this section is a series of events and ideas beginning in the 1950s that culminated in the official birth of community psychology in 1965.

Early Contributions

Several developments early in the history of the mental health professions were antecedents to the ideology and practice of community psychology. We have already encountered one of these, moral treatment, whose emphasis on environmental determinants of disorder as well as its general reformist fervor are often considered inspirations for the community psychology movement. Other precursors are presented briefly below in a roughly chronological order.

1 The Advent of Clinical Psychology Community psychology is deeply embedded in clinical psychology. The vast majority of practicing community psychologists received their professional training in graduate clinical psychology training programs. Most actually functioned as clinical psychologists at some time during their careers. On occasion, many still do. Thus, the early history of clinical psychology is relevant to an analysis of community psychology. As Chapter 2 indicated, the first psychological clinic was started by Lightner Witmer at the University of Pennsylvania in 1896. The most important services of the first clinics were the diagnosis and treatment of children with a host of emotional and learning problems. Later clinics were more concerned with personality problems. Early clinical psychology was psychoeducational, and its emphasis on children reflected a belief that the treatment of early problems could prevent them from growing into major disabilities. In community psychology terms, this is called "secondary prevention."

2 The Mental Hygiene Movement In 1908 a former mental patient, Clifford Whittingham Beers, published *A Mind That Found Itself*. This moving book vividly described Beers's experiences as a hospitalized mental patient and called public attention to the deplorable conditions of mental institutions. The book had a significant and lasting impact on the mental health professions. It spurred several reforms in the treatment of the mentally ill, and led to the 1909

Clifford W. Beers (1876–1943) *(Photograph from* A Mind that Found Itself *by Clifford Whittingham Beers. Copyright 1907, 1917, 1921, 1923, 1931, 1932, 1934, 1935, 1937, 1939, 1940, 1942, 1944, 1948, 1953 by the American Foundation for Mental Hygiene, Inc. Reproduced by permission of Doubleday & Company, Inc.)*

founding of the National Committee for Mental Hygiene. Today, this organization is known as the National Association for Mental Health (NAMH) and is credited with initiating the *mental hygiene* and *child guidance* movements (the NAMH still publishes a professional journal entitled *Mental Hygiene*).

The mental hygienists professed a preference for promoting health rather than combating illness. Impressed by the success of public health's aggressive attack on contagious illnesses, they called for new preventive programs and public education efforts to "inoculate" people against mental illness. The status of the mental hygiene movement received a major boost when Beers succeeded in enlisting William James, America's leading psychologist, and Adolf Meyer, the foremost American psychiatrist of the day, as major spokesmen for his organization and its enlightened views on the treatment of mental disorders.

3   The Child Guidance Movement   The 1920s saw the continued growth of the child guidance movement, an evolutionary offspring of mental hygiene, which, as the name suggests, concentrated on the delivery of clinical services to children, especially those who were severely emotionally disturbed. The most famous child guidance clinic was the Juvenile Psychopathic Hospital opened by William Healy (a psychiatrist) and Grace Fernald (a psychologist) in 1909 in Chicago. The child guidance movement furthered the basic philosophy of the mental hygienists and solidified the concept of the *team approach* to treatment, an idea anticipated by Witmer's use of consultants from other professions. The "team" consisted of a psychiatrist who was in charge of treatment, a psychologist who was responsible for assessment, and a social worker who conducted social history interviews and sought to improve the social environment to which the patient would return.

4   World War I and World War II   Chapter 2 included a discussion of the extensive impact that World War I and World War II had on the profession of clinical psychology. Three aspects of that impact have clear relevance to community psychology. First, both wars, but particularly World War II, stimulated the growth of clinical psychology. The importance of this "psychology explosion" for community psychologists is apparent if we remember that most community psychologists were originally trained as clinical psychologists and that the financial support and national mandate for training clinicians were direct results of World War II.

Second, the two wars dramatically reshaped the nature of clinical psychology. Their combined effect was to make the profession more adult-oriented, more concerned with personality disorders and psychopathology, more enamored with psychotherapy as a treatment technique, and more often housed in institutional or hospital settings. These qualities contrast with the dominant features of clinical psychology during the first 15 years of the twentieth century. As we shall see (and as you may have already anticipated), the postwar attributes of clinical psychology have been severely criticized by those clinicians who became disenchanted with the profession's course. It was in the soil of this disenchantment that community psychology took root.

Finally, the two world wars strengthened a precedent in psychology that continues to the present day: It is a profession that is especially susceptible to the influence of the larger social and political events that occur outside it. Whether this is due to what Adler might have called the "social interest" of psychologists, a pervasive uncertainty within the profession about what its mission should be, or a persistent penchant for "trendy" relevance is not clear. What is clear is that, just as wars revolutionized the clinical psychology of Witmer, so did social and political changes in America during the last two decades nourish psychology's urge to "go community."

Recent Contributions

We are now at a point in history, the 1950s and 1960s, where a more concentrated array of influences come together to accelerate the development of community psychology. There is a particularly distinguishing feature of this time period: You have lived in it. Thus, you are probably familiar with many of its social events and are able to appreciate their effects on psychology.

Community psychology was a direct product of the mid-1960s, but it represents a culmination of developments which had been unfolding for the previous 10 to 15 years. One set of developments occurred mainly within the field of psychology, particularly clinical psychology, while the other involved extensive social and political changes taking place throughout America. Let us consider the professional factors first.

1 The Question of Psychotherapy's Effectiveness In 1952 Hans Eysenck, a British psychologist, published a review of several studies of traditional forms of psychotherapy with neurotic patients in which he concluded that the rate of recovery is virtually equivalent for those patients who receive therapy and those who do not. Specifically, Eysenck argued that the rate of "spontaneous remission" (i.e., improvement without any special treatment) was 72 percent over a 2-year period compared to an improvement rate of 44 percent for psychoanalysis and 64 percent for "eclectic" therapy. In later reviews, Eysenck (1961, 1966) evaluated several more studies and persisted in his pessimism, claiming that the additional data supported his initial conclusion and that the ineffectiveness of traditional therapy was not limited to neurotic patients.

Despite a host of criticisms aimed at Eysenck's concepts, thoroughness, fairness, and mathematical ability (e.g., Bergin, 1971; Luborsky, 1954; Strupp, 1963), his conclusions struck a responsive chord among many psychologists who quickly became skeptical about the positive effects of (mostly psychodynamic) psychotherapy. This belief has continued among many psychologists despite accumulating evidence that some forms of therapy often *do* make a difference and, in most cases, a positive one.

After carefully reanalyzing the data reviewed by Eysenck as well as over fifty more studies between 1952 and 1969, Bergin (1971) concluded that "psychotherapy on the average has modestly positive effects" (p. 228). Meltzoff and Kornreich (1970) reported that more than 80 percent of the studies evaluating psychotherapy's effectiveness yielded positive results. A recent review of 375 studies by Smith and Glass (1977) argued that the typical therapy recipient is better off than 75 percent of untreated individuals.

Nevertheless, these data have not entirely muted the clamor about psychotherapy's supposed ineffectiveness. Nor has the observation that the question of whether psychotherapy is effective is far too general to have much meaning (e.g., Paul, 1969a); it is somewhat akin to wondering whether food is good for you. The continuing controversy has caused many psychologists to become disenchanted with psychotherapy as an intervention technique, disillusioned with their profession for its emphasis on psychotherapy, and motivated to search for alternative ways of helping people change their lives. It is from these grounds that the practice of community psychology has developed.

2 The Question of Psychotherapy's Efficiency Even if some forms of psychotherapy are effective, many critics contended that it is still a very inefficient procedure. This inefficiency was thought to stem from many sources. First, as George Albee has often argued, there will never be enough trained professionals to offer one-to-one psychotherapy to all people who might need or want it. Albee (1968) is succinct: "We cannot produce a fraction of the medical and paramedical people the (illness model of mental disorder) demands" (p. 318).

A related objection is that psychotherapy's availability is restricted primarily to those people who can afford it or who already possess characteristics that clinicians favor. William Schofield (1964) coined the acronym YAVIS (Young-Attractive-Verbal-Intelligent-Successful) to describe the typical psychotherapy recipient (see also Goldstein, 1973). The unfortunate counterparts of this description are the HOUNDs (Homely-Old-Unsuccessful-Nonverbal-Dull), those who have the most pressing mental health needs but who are the least likely to demand or receive therapeutic services.

The problem of psychotherapy's inefficiency is compounded by the fact that many individuals prefer to take their troubles to someone other than a mental health professional. For example, Gurin, Veroff, and Feld (1960) found that more than two-thirds of the people they surveyed would seek the services of the clergy or family physician for a psychological problem rather than those of a mental health professional.

3 Devaluation of Psychological Assessment and Diagnosis Dissatisfaction with the practice of psychotherapy has been accompanied by a devaluation of the assessment functions with which psychologists have long been associated. Intelligence testing, personality assessment, and personnel selection have all been criticized on several grounds. As we have already seen in Chapters 4 and 6, the decline of psychological testing in recent years is the product of (1) research that challenges the reliability, and, particularly, the validity of many tests, (2) ethical concerns over the proper place of psychological tests in a democratic society and the possibility that tests will be misused or misinterpreted, and (3) evidence that tests and assessment practices in general are subject to many different kinds of bias.

While all of these criticisms have been recognized by most clinical psychologists, it is the last which has been the focus of many proponents of community psychology. To summarize their sentiment: Bias is everywhere. Diagnostic judgments, the nature of treatment given, and therapist attitudes

"*Yes, what is it? I'm very busy . . . .*"

Cartoon 12-1   There are several ways of handling the shortage of mental health personnel. This is not one of them. *(© 1972, Punch/Rothco.)*

have all been found to be influenced by clients' socioeconomic class (Haase, 1964; Hollingshead & Redlich, 1958; Lorion, 1974). Characteristics of mental health or illness also appear to depend on the sex of the person being rated (Broverman, Broverman, Clarkson, Rosenkrantz, & Vogel, 1970; but see Stricker, 1977). Finally, mental health professionals reveal a general tendency to perceive mental illness even in cases where there are very few indicators of any pathology (Temerlin, 1970). Added to these concerns is the contention that the very act of assessment or diagnosis can be damaging. Adverse consequences are thought to follow from a *self-fulfilling prophecy,* whereby predicting some behavior (e.g., aggression) increases the probability of that behavior actually occurring. The empirical evidence for this notion is quite scarce (Wilkins, 1977), but the fear that predictive labels will negatively influence patients, patients' friends, or professionals has led to a declining enthusiasm for psychological testing and diagnosis.

4   Dissatisfaction with the Medical Model   The major rallying point for critics of traditional clinical psychology over the past two decades has been their dissatisfaction with the so-called medical model which attempts to explain personal inadequacies and social breakdowns in terms of biological diseases and/or related psychological disturbances within individuals (see Chapter 3). Community psychology's objection to this concept is that it implies a benign environment by ignoring stress generated from sources as diverse as poor schooling, inadequate housing, political corruption, economic hardship, unemployment, racism, and nonresponsive social institutions.

Outside of psychology there were several forces which nurtured the development of community psychology. Three of these deserve special emphasis.

1 Social Activism The growth of social and political activism in this country during the 1960s was a force which dramatically affected almost all who experienced it. Psychologists were no exception. At a time when the effects of their treatments, their tests, and their science in general were being questioned, psychologists were understandably impressed with a social activism that produced results which were "bigger and quicker" than any of their own interventions. Great optimism prompted the (often harshly insistent) view that social progress could be achieved through direct social action, and psychologists wanted to be a part of it.

Rappaport (1977) identifies the civil rights movement, black separatist ideology, urban crises, the war on poverty, and the arrests and demonstrations of university students as separate but related events that produced the willingness and even enthusiasm of psychologists to expand their ideas of what the helping professions could do to promote social change.

2 Governmental Programs A second influence on community psychology came from the executive branch of the federal government. The Democratic administrations of presidents Kennedy and Johnson shared an emphasis on social reform grounded in a basic philosophy of domestic liberalism. There existed a spirit of both professionalism and commitment to realistic social improvement which contrasted with America's conservative stance in foreign affairs during the 1950s as well as with the slumbering domestic policies of the Eisenhower era (Halberstam, 1969). There was an escalation in the employment and status of social scientists, some of whom were given important responsibilities in the formation and direction of the "Great Society" programs. In the midst of this professional fervor, many psychologists learned about models of intervention which demonstrated greater breadth and impact than purely psychological approaches. As a result, psychologists began to aim at these larger targets of social reform and institutional change.

3 Legislation A final external force was exerted at the legislative level. Passage of the Mental Health Study Act in 1955 established the Joint Commission on Mental Health and Illness (JCMHI). The final report of this forty-five-member commission was released in 1961 under the title *Action for Mental Health*. This document is often considered the direct impetus for the community mental health and community psychology movements, because it recommended the construction of multiservice comprehensive care centers to serve the mental health needs of local communities (see Box 12-1 for a summary of other JCMHI recommendations).

The joint commission's final report was followed in 1963 by passage of the Community Mental Health Centers Act, also known as the Kennedy bill because

Box 12-1 A Summary of Recommendations Made by the Joint Commission on Mental Health and Illness in Its *Action for Mental Health*

1 A much larger proportion of total funds for mental health research should be invested in basic research as contrasted with applied research.

2 The Federal government should support the establishment of mental health research centers, or research institutues. These centers or institutes may operate in collaboration with educational institutions and training centers, or may be established independently.

3 . . . psychiatry and the allied mental health professions should adopt and practice a broad, liberal philosophy of what constitutes and who can do treatment within the framework of their hospitals, clinics, or other professional service agencies, particularly in relation to persons with psychoses or severe personality or character disorders that incapacitate them for work, family life, and everyday activity.

4 The mental health professions need to launch a national manpower recruitment and training program, expanding on and extending present efforts and seeking to stimulate the interest of American youth in mental health work as a career. This program should include all categories of mental health personnel.

5 Persons who are emotionally disturbed—that is to say, under psychological stress that they cannot tolerate—should have skilled attention and helpful counseling available to them in their community if the development of more serious mental breakdowns is to be prevented.

6 A national mental health program should recognize that major mental illness is the core problem and unfinished business of the mental health movement, and that the intensive treatment of patients with critical and prolonged mental breakdowns should have first call on fully trained members of the mental health professions.

7 Community mental health clinics serving both children and adults, operated as out-patient departments of general or mental hospitals, as part of State or regional systems for mental patient care, or as independent agencies, are a main line of defense in reducing the need of many persons with major mental illness for prolonged or repeated hospitalization. Therefore, a national mental health program should set as an objective one fully staffed, full-time mental health clinic available to each 50,000 of population.

8 No further State hospitals of more than 1,000 beds should be built, and not one patient should be added to any existing mental hospitals already housing 1,000 or more patients. It is further recommended that all existing State hospitals of more than 1,000 beds be gradually and progressively converted into centers for the long-term and combined care of chronic diseases, including mental illness. This conversion should be undertaken in the next ten years.

9 . . . aftercare and rehabilitation are essential parts of all service to mental patients, and the various methods of achieving rehabilitation should be integrated in all forms of services, among them day hospitals, night hospitals, aftercare clinics, public health nursing services, foster family care, convalescent nursing homes, rehabilitation centers, work services, and ex-patient groups.

10 A national mental health program should avoid the risk of false promise in "public education for better mental health" and focus on the more modest goal of disseminating such information about mental illness as the public needs and wants in order to recongize psychological forms of sickness and to arrive at an informed opinion in its responsibility toward the mentally ill.

11 Expenditures for public mental patient services should be doubled in the next five years—and tripled in the next ten.

From *Action for Mental Health* © 1961 by Basic Books, Inc., Publishers, New York. (Reprinted by permission.) For a complete list of the Joint Commission's recommendations, see pp.vii-xxiv of the report. For more recent, strongly prevention-oriented recommendations on national mental health policy, see the 1978 Report of the President's Commission on Mental Health.

of President John F. Kennedy's vigorous support for it. He regarded it as legislation that would create a national mental health program. This bill provided funds for the construction of a network of comprehensive mental health centers that would cover a service area of not less than 75,000 nor more than 200,000 people. The term "comprehensive care" was defined by this legislation to include ten types of services. Five of these services were considered *essential,* meaning that they were required for centers seeking federal funds; five other services were listed as *desirable,* indicating that they were important but not required for funding.

The five essential services are: inpatient care, partial hospitalization, outpatient treatment for adults and children, emergency services available on a 24-hour basis, and consultation and education programs. The five desirable services are: diagnostic services, social and vocational rehabilitation, precare and aftercare (including preadmission screening and home visits or halfway houses after discharge), training of mental health personnel, and research and evaluation of program effectiveness and the problems of mental illness.

Finally, in 1965, legislation was passed which actually mandated funds for the salaries of the personnel to be employed in these "comp care" centers. These so-called "staffing grants" were intended to provide staff funding for the first several years of operation, after which financial responsibility would be shifted to the individual states, health insurance, direct fees, and other sources.

The comprehensive care system continues to be an important ingredient in this country's mental health effort, although its role is probably not as prominent as was originally intended. On balance, the system should be considered a very modest but very expensive attainment. Its major achievement was that it, along with the development of antipsychotic drugs, promoted a drastic reduction of the patient population in mental institutions. It also "opened up" mental health services somewhat by including paraprofessional and nontraditionally trained personnel on treatment staffs and by offering community supervision or "after care" as an alternative to custodial confinement. A final noteworthy accomplishment was that mental health services were made available to people who had previously been chronically underserved by the mental health system.

One of the greatest limitations of the comprehensive care model has been financial. Since the late 1960s the federal government's commitment to mental health financing has weakened and become increasingly timid. As a consequence, by 1974 only 540 of the 2000 centers predicted to be operating by 1975 had been constructed. In addition, many of the centers in operation have suffered severe reductions in staff because the original federal staffing grants have run out and have not been renewed or replaced.

The community mental health movement has also been sharply criticized at a philosophical level. Many critics (e.g., Windle, Bass, & Taube, 1974) have argued that it has merely placed the old wine of the medical model in the new bottle of community centers while leaving intact the medical view and organization of mental health services. A second objection concerns program effectiveness, especially the fact that comprehensive care centers are not really

Box 12-2   The Nader Report

One measure of a movement's importance in our era is whether Ralph Nader has bothered to evaluate it. It may be small consolation to those evaluated, but the community mental health center (CMHC) movement achieved this level of notoriety when, in the summer of 1970, Nader's Center for Study of Responsive Law initiated an evaluation of the program. The subsequent report entitled *The Madness Establishment* (Chu and Trotter, 1974) was a wide-ranging indictment of the CMHC model.

Claiming that the plan "was vastly oversold (and) the original goals quickly perverted," the report charges that among a list of deficiencies, "NIMH feebly communicated the original intent of the program to state and local officials; failed to coordinate the location of the centers with other HEW health and social welfare efforts; made little attempt to train (or retrain) people for community work; avoided funding centers outside the narrow interests of the medical profession; did not engage consumers in the planning or operation of centers; and made only the most perfunctory evaluation of the program's performance. As a result, community mental health centers tend to involve only a renaming of conventional psychiatry, a collection of traditional clinical services that are in most cases not responsive to the needs of large segments of the community, and which often leave community people indifferent, sometimes antagonistic." (Chu & Trotter, 1974, pp. 202-203)

From Chu, F. D., & Trotter, S. *The Madness Establishment.* © 1974 by Viking Penguin, Inc. (Reprinted by permission.)

oriented toward *prevention* of human distress (Cowen, 1973). Another criticism has been that comprehensive care centers have not overcome the accessibility problem. Services are still not sought by persons who may be in need of them because of financial limitations, cultural barriers, geographic isolation, bureaucratic red tape, and the fear of being stigmatized. A related point stressed by almost all critics of the comprehensive care system is that sufficient community participation in the planning and direction of the centers has not occurred (Smith and Hobbs, 1966).

It may well be the case that the current pessimism surrounding comprehensive care centers is linked partly to the unrealistic optimism which greeted their creation 15 years ago. Great expectations run the risk of becoming great disappointments. But disappointments also have an educational value in that they sometimes point us in new and useful directions.

From this perspective, disappointments about the community mental health center model are not a wholly negative development because they have forced psychologists to rediscover and even extend the innovations that led to the modern community mental health movement. The remainder of this chapter will concentrate especially on the extensions, because they comprise an important part of community psychology.

Community Psychology's Formal Beginning

Now that the essential contributions have been identified, we are ready to announce the formal birth of community psychology. The birthdate was the spring of 1965. The place of birth was Swampscott, Massachusetts (a Boston suburb), where more than thirty psychologists, many already employed in community mental health centers, assembled to issue a call for community psychologists who would be "change agents, social system analysts, consultants in community affairs, and students generally of the whole man in relation to all his environments" (Bennett, 1965, p. 833). The community psychologist would be a *participant-conceptualizer:* someone who tries to change social conditions as much as understand them.

This conference stressed three other principles for the new profession. First, community psychology should not be limited to combating mental illness or disablement. Rather, it must work for "community well-being" and "furthering normal development" (Bennett, 1965). Second, community psychologists should assume responsibility for promoting community growth through planned social action and the scientific method. Finally, community psychology must be something broader, something more ambitious than community mental health which, as we have already seen, retains many of the trappings of the medical model.

Today, community psychology is in its adolescence and gives every impression of maturing into a full-fledged, independent discipline. Its accomplishments are recorded in several professional journals *(The American Journal of Community Psychology, The Community Mental Health Journal,* and *The Journal of Community Psychology).* It has been surveyed, explained, analyzed, and evaluated in a surge of special textbooks (e.g., Heller & Monahan, 1977; Mann, 1978; Murrell, 1973; Nietzel, Winett, MacDonald & Davidson, 1976; Rappaport, 1977; Zax & Specter, 1974). Since 1967 there has been a division of community psychology within the American Psychological Assocation, and several thousand psychologists are now members.

The training of community psychologists has also become an important activity of graduate psychology programs. In 1962 there was only one program offering an advanced degree (M.A. or Ph.D.) in community psychology and community mental health. In 1967 there were ten, and in 1974 there were twenty-one. By 1975, there were sixty-two graduate programs offering degrees in community psychology and community mental health (Meyer & Garrard, 1977). In order to consider current training needs, a National Conference on Training in Community Psychology was held in Austin, Texas, in April 1975, an appropriate commemoration of the Swampscott conference held just 10 years earlier.

PRINCIPLES OF COMMUNITY PSYCHOLOGY

In a paper that has had considerable impact on the thinking of community psychologists, Rappaport and Chinsky (1974) proposed that any model of mental health service can be divided into two basic components—a *conceptual component* and a *style of delivery component.* According to Rappaport (1977), the conceptual component is the model's fundamental theory of human behavior; it "dictates the empirical data base, theoretical notions and basic assumptions for understanding human behavior" (p. 72). The style of delivery component, on the other hand, "dictates how the service called for by the conceptual component will be offered to the target population" (Rappaport, 1977, pp. 72–73).

Community psychology can be analyzed from this perspective if we realize that it involves several essential components or principles, each of which can be organized under either the conceptual or style of delivery heading. It is important to remember that not every community psychologist will embrace each of these principles. However, when taken together, these ideas form the generally accepted nucleus of the field and serve to differentiate it from other examples of applied psychology, particularly clinical psychology. We shall address ourselves first to five principles which are related to the conceptual side of community psychology.

Conceptual Principles

1 Taking an Ecological Perspective This is ground already covered. You will remember from the definitions at the beginning of this chapter that the community psychologist believes that behavior cannot be explained solely through an analysis of individual factors. Change in the behavior of individuals may often need to be preceded by change in the functioning of social institutions. Even more than other psychologists, the community psychologist views social, environmental, and political factors as important determinants of behavior. Because problems in living are related to these broad-scale potential stresses, the community psychologist will often aim not so much for changes in individuals but for changes in the communities or subcommunities into which individuals must fit.

At a more practical level, the ecological perspective means that the psychologist must look for causes of behavior at several nonpsychological levels. For example, the child whose constant misbehavior in the classroom leads her to be labeled hyperactive may suffer some neurological impairment that is the basis of the problem. But the behavior may also be due to a classroom whose organization rewards underachievement, a curriculum whose subject matter is either too difficult or too easy for her level of development, or a peer culture that has been taught to devalue academic achievement. In a similar fashion, explanations at something other than the individual level of analysis could be offered for problems of delinquency and crime, alcoholism, unemployment, and drug abuse. In each case, the ecological perspective of the community psychologist directs attention to the role that social and environmental forces play in the development of human problems.

2 Seeking Social-System Change The type of change implied by the ecological perspective is often termed social-system-level change as distinguished from *person-oriented change*. Social-system changes are intended to make the important social institutions in our lives more responsive, more growth-enhancing. Changes in social systems can occur at a relatively low level, such as when one classroom in an entire school system begins to use a token economy to increase class participation. Social changes also can occur at a much higher level and actually involve the creation of an entirely new social institution, such as when a group of parents, dissatisfied with the quality of public education, begins its own alternative school.[1] Community psychologists have concentrated their efforts at social-system-level change in four areas: preschool and family care, the educational system, the criminal justice system, and, of course, the mental health system.

This is not to say that community psychologists never use person-oriented interventions. They do, often with the belief that they can be extremely successful (Cowen, 1973, 1977a), but their preference is for social-system-level changes when attainable, since these are thought to present the greatest opportunity to bring about important, durable changes in the lives of large numbers of people. There is also the belief that some social-system-oriented interventions can even prevent social and emotional problems rather than just remediate them.

3 Emphasizing Prevention The quest for prevention is the cardinal feature of community psychology. Prevention is community psychology's *summum bonum;* it is also, as we shall see, very rarely achieved.

Caplan (1964) identified three types of prevention: tertiary, secondary, and primary. The history of the mental health professions is actually a history of *tertiary prevention.* This type of prevention aims to minimize the severity of illness, reduce the short- and long-term consequences of the disorder, and contain the disturbance so that personal effectiveness is retained. Zax and Cowen (1972) argue that "tertiary prevention is prevention in name only" and is justified not because it eliminates dysfunction but because it is compatible with the "democratic-humanitarian goal of reducing human discomfort and providing maximal opportunity for all men to live effectively" (p. 453). Almost any form of treatment could lay claim to being tertiary prevention. However, the uniqueness of the term "prevention" is preserved only if we restrict its use to primary and early secondary interventions.

Secondary prevention aims for a reduction in the prevalence of illness through the coordinated efforts of early detection and rapid, effective intervention, or, as a cab driver was quoted as saying, "getting to people before they go nuts" (Schaar, 1978). For this reason, instruments that allow reliable and valid diagnosis as early in the course of a problem as possible are essential for secondary prevention. Secondary prevention programs are often directed at elementary school children because of the relationship between early school maladaptation and later adjustment problems and because of the belief that schools can be a vehicle for optimizing personal as well as educational growth.

An example of this approach is the Primary Mental Health Project (PMHP) of Cowen and his colleagues at the University of Rochester (Cowen, Dorr, Izzo, Madonia, & Trost, 1971). The PMHP uses quick-screening techniques to

---

[1]The reader interested in pursuing the issue of social-system-level change by community psychologists should consult Rappaport (1977, pp. 114–213).

identify primary schoolers who are having educational and behavioral problems. "At-risk" children are then seen by trained, nonprofessional child aides who assist the children to cope with their difficulties and build new skills. Outcome data on the PMHP suggest that the participants experience both behavioral and educational improvements (Cowen & Schochet, 1973). At the present time, the majority of preventive programs in community psychology occur at this secondary level.

Primary prevention involves the reduction and ultimate elimination of disorders by either modifying the pathogenic qualities of the environment or bolstering individuals' resources to the point where disorder will not occur. In theory, primary prevention can be accomplished by *social action,* where changes in community institutions are made in order to reduce problems, or through *interpersonal action,* in which the targets of change are important policy makers or other influential persons whose special status permits a "radiation" of any changes they might make. Urban renewal, job training, and some forms of specialized social welfare are examples of the first type of prevention. Family intervention, parent education, and the training of community care givers such as police or clergy are examples of prevention through interpersonal action.

4 Focus on Crisis Intervention   *Crisis intervention* is an example of a direct service which plays a prominent role in the work of many community psychologists. There are many types of crises which people face in their lives. There are the routine and predictable crises of development such as learning to walk, beginning school, and finding a job. Maturation also involves a series of psychological problems which must be resolved for optimal personality growth to occur. Several personality theorists (e.g., Erikson, 1963; Sullivan, 1953) have emphasized stages of psychological crisis to be mastered by the developing person. Other crises are less predictable and occur suddenly, before the person has had the benefit of preparation or advance planning. Serious illness, death of a loved one, serious economic setbacks, and natural disasters like fires or floods are examples of what is sometimes termed accidental crisis. A crisis is not always a negatively defined event. Certain life events such as a job promotion or a move to a new community may have a positive connotation for a person but still generate considerable stress and psychological threat (Holmes & Rahe, 1967).

In most cases, when individuals are confronted by a crisis, they are able to cope with and ultimately adapt to the demands of the situation. In some cases, however, adaptation and coping do not occur, and the crisis remains unsolved and seemingly insurmountable. Either because the person in question has limited resources for coping or because the problem is an especially intense and difficult one, some crises are not resolved. As a result the individual suffers emotional upset and disorganization, and if the crisis continues for a long time, serious personality disturbances may ensue.

Crisis intervention is a technique for helping persons deal effectively with apparently overwhelming problems at the time they are occurring. Interventions are usually intended for persons who otherwise would lack sufficient resources for dealing adequately with the crisis. There are, of course, many strategies of crisis intervention. In its most basic form, crisis intervention may take the form of a referral, in which the person is put into contact with appropriate resources. Intervention may consist of supportive listening, where the helper simply provides a sympathetic ear, or it may consist of techniques more specific to the needs of the crisis. Crisis intervention may focus on the individual involved in a crisis and attempt to help him or her understand what role he or she played in the creation of that particular crisis (Jacobsen, Strickler, & Maley, 1968).

Historically, there have been several precedents for the use of crisis intervention. Butcher and Maudal (1976) mention the short-term treatment of combat neurosis during World War II, the development of suicide prevention techniques, and the growth of "free clinics" in large, underserved metropolitan areas as important, early sources which contributed to the current crisis intervention movement.

Most commentators agree that the single most influential contribution to the practice of crisis intervention was the work of Erich Lindemann (1944) and his associate Gerald Caplan (1961). Lindemann's notions of crisis therapy were based on his work with relatives of victims of the tragic 1943 fire at the Coconut Grove, a Boston nightclub. Lindemann concluded that there were certain stages of grief through which persons must progress in order to adjust to the loss of the deceased person. He further demonstrated that grieving people could be helped in working through the essential stages of the bereavement process by therapy aimed specifically at the crisis itself, rather than at the person's general personality.

The goals of crisis intervention are usually more limited than those pursued in psychotherapy. Personality reconstruction and complete insight into the dynamics of adjustment difficulties are seldom achieved by crisis therapists. Butcher and Koss (1978) list the following objectives of crisis intervention as the most common ones: (1) relief of the client's primary symptoms as rapidly as possible, (2) prompt reestablishment of the client's previous emotional stability, and (3) development of the client's understanding of the current disturbance and its precipitating factors as well as an enhanced ability to cope with crises in the future. In some cases this last goal of increased coping ability is not as readily achieved as the first two objectives, primarily because of the brevity of treatment.

Just as crisis intervention can be distinguished from psychotherapy on the basis of its goals, these two forms of treatment can be contrasted by their different technical emphases. The most obvious difference involves time: crisis intervention is usually brief. In most cases treatment would not be expected to exceed 6 weeks. Accompanying these time limitations are important differences in the behavior of therapists. The crisis intervener is more likely than the "average" therapist to be directive and very active in sessions, to focus interest on the primary problem area, to be interested in the here-and-now rather than past reasons for the problem, and to offer direct advice, guidance, and information about alternative forms of desirable behavior. Because of the need for rapid decision making and rather intensive interaction, it is usually thought that effective crisis intervention requires highly experienced therapists (Butcher & Koss, 1978).

Like any form of therapy, crisis intervention regards assessment of the client's problem, strengths, weaknesses, and other personal characteristics to be an essential factor in successful treatment. A premium is placed on gathering this information as efficiently as possible, preferably in the initial session of crisis intervention. The development of a therapeutic relationship is considered as much a prerequisite for effective crisis intervention as for effective psychotherapy. Once again, however, a compromise must be struck between the evolution of this relationship and the limited time available for treatment. The delicacy of this compromise is one reason why therapist experience is so often considered an important factor in crisis intervention.

5 Promoting a "Psychological Sense of Community" Beyond solving immediate problems, the community psychologist is concerned with strengthening the ability of a community or subcommunity to plan and create its own change. This emphasis is reflected in what Sarason (1974) has called the "psychological sense of community":

> I have never met anyone—young or old, rich or poor, black or white, male or female, educated or not—to whom I have had any great difficulty explaining what I meant by the psychological sense of community. My explanation or language varied, of course, depending on whom I was talking with, but it never took long for them to comprehend that what I was getting at was the sense that one was part of a readily available, mutually supportive network of relationships upon which one could depend **and as** a result of which one did not experience sustained feelings of **loneliness that impel** one to actions or to adopting a style of living masking anxiety and **setting the** stage for later and more destructive anguish. It is not merely a matter of how many people one knows, or how many close friends one has, or even the number of loved ones—if they are scattered all over the country or world, if they are not part of the structure of one's everyday living, and if they are not available to one in a 'give and get' way, they can have little effect on one's immediate or daily sense of community. Indeed, for many people these treasured but only occasionally available relationships accentuate the lack of a feeling of community. . . . The community in which we live is a geo-political entity with which we feel little kinship. We may work in the community, pay taxes, and vote, but in no other respect feel a part of it. In fact, we may feel repelled by it because of the violence, crime, and conflict within it. We wish things were otherwise, but we feel impotent to do anything. We are aware that much money is being spent to repair our community, socially and physically, but the feeling persists that the seams of the community are not being tightened. We do not feel *needed* in our community and we rarely if ever seriously think about how we can contribute to the solution of its problems. We are busy during the day, tired at night, and seek recreation and entertainment on the weekends. And if we are parents, there are children who need our attention every day. Where is there time to engage in a community activity? What community activity? What do I have to contribute? Where am I *needed?* Our lives are

circumscribed spatially and psychologically, and it all seems so natural except for those poignant moments, quite frequent for many people, when we yearn to be part of a larger network of relationships that would give greater expression to our needs for intimacy, diversity, usefulness, and belongingness. The concept of the psychological sense of community is like that of hunger: neither is easy to define, but there is no mistaking it when an individual experiences the lack of a psychological sense of community, just as there is no mistaking what we think an individual experiences as a result of starvation. (p. 351–352)

Community psychologists create this sense of community by developing people's strengths rather than eliminating their weaknesses. The goal of increasing a community's competence and shared sense of purpose requires that community psychologists tolerate or even increase the positive diversity of the people they encounter. The ways in which a community insures its safety, educates its children, protects its environment, promotes its health, and establishes a sense of vitality in its citizens usually represent only a small portion of available means to desired ends. The truly successful community psychologist will help people create effective alternatives to existing social institutions by treating their cultural preferences and differences as assets rather than liabilities.

Style of Delivery
As noted earlier, a second way of defining a model of mental health service concerns the *style of service delivery*. Below are three important principles of delivery style from the perspective of community psychology.

1 Expansion of Professional Roles Clinical psychologists usually offer *direct services* to clients who, because they have some psychological complaint, are willing to pay for them. Community psychologists, on the other hand, are likely to emphasize *indirect services*. These are interventions which have no single "target" client, but which are expected to achieve benefits because the social-system changes they produce will *radiate* to the intended target groups. Another aspect of indirect service involves teaching subprofessionals to deliver many of the direct services formerly offered by professionals. This activity is, of course, in direct response to Albee's contention that there is not a sufficient number of professionals to meet the mental health needs of the population.

The shift from direct to indirect services is a key part of the expanded professional functions advocated by community psychologists. This role expansion has inspired new descriptions of psychologists: mental health consultant, the *un*professional, psychologist without a couch. Whatever the name, the meaning is consistent: Community psychologists try to amplify their impact through innovations in service delivery that involve something more than direct services.

Consultation is a very common activity for the community psychologist. Though certainly not the only psychological consultants (see Chapter 1), community psychologists typically have placed greater reliance on this function as a technique of intervention than have clinical psychologists (see Marrino &

Shore, 1975, or Woody, 1975, for a review of consultation activities within community psychology).

As noted in Chapter 1, professional consultation can take several forms (Caplan, 1963). The consultant may provide advice or assistance with the management of a particular professional case. This is called *case-oriented* or *client-centered consultation.* The consultant may also give advice concerning the administration of social service programs, a process known as *program-oriented,* or *program-centered consultation.* Or the consultant may influence the consultee's planning or delivery of mental health programs. This is known as *administrative consultation.*

Another example of expanding roles for community psychologists is the preparation of volunteers, paraprofessionals, and nonprofessionals for behavior change functions typically reserved for the professional. The passage of several pieces of antipoverty legislation within the past decade has created thousands of nonprofessional positions in community service agencies (Riessman, 1967). These include, among others, child care workers, mental health workers, self-help group leaders, peer counselors, and abortion counselors. The use of nonprofessionals in these roles is seen as having social advantages and ideological justifications. The "nonprofessional movement" creates meaningful careers for poor people, provides troubled people with help from persons with whom they share demographic characteristics, a cultural heritage, or strong political commitments, and provides a plentiful new source of workers necessary for adequate delivery of mental health services.

In many cases, helpers are drawn directly from the groups that will receive the services. These workers have been called *indigenous nonprofessionals,* and their cultural rootedness within a target group is considered one of their most fundamental assets. In other instances para- and nonprofessionals are drawn from groups with a high commitment to service but with a cheap price tag for their labor. College students and housewives are ubiquitous volunteers, and they have been used as classroom assistants (Alden, Rappaport, & Seidman, 1975), counselors for drug addict populations (Dwarshuis, Kolton, & Gorodezky, 1973), correctional agents in the criminal justice system (Twain, McGee, & Bennett, 1972), therapeutic aides for chronic mental patients (Holzberg, Knapp, & Turner, 1967; Rioch, Elkes, Flint, Usdansky, Newman, & Silber, 1963), and participants in community mental health centers and juvenile justice system programs (Bartles & Tyler, 1975; Davidson, Rappaport, Seidman, Berck, & Herring, 1975).

Community psychologists may also train relatives (Guerney, 1969), peers (Harris & Sherman, 1973), teachers (Meyers, 1975), and friends (Sulzer, 1965) to initiate behavior-change conditions or to maintain conditions that had been introduced during a professional intervention. This planned involvement of auxiliary personnel as treatment mediators has been a relatively popular recent feature, particularly in social-learning interventions.

2 Use of Activism Social action has been considered both an essential contribution and an unnecessary evil of community psychology. Next to prevention, social activism is considered the major dimension of an effective community psychology. Advocates of activist tactics claim that the professional's willingness to provoke, agitate, confront, and pressure is what accounts for a large measure of her or his effectiveness. Opponents of professional social action argue that such activity is incompatible with the objective observation and devotion to empiricism which are the behavioral scientist's defining characteristics.

In the present context, social activism refers to the use of *power* as a resource to accomplish social reform. Power may be economic, as when shareholders organize to influence the activities of major corporations. It may be political, as when lobbying accompanies any important piece of legislation or when attempts are made to get the "right" candidate elected to office. It may be the coercive power of civil (or not-so-civil) disobedience, as when people struggle to claim or assert their human rights.

Power also can be manipulated through publicity, and it is for this reason that community psychologists often try to cultivate media contacts in order to spread their influence through the printed word or the projected image. Finally, power resides in positions of leadership. Psychologists are increasingly seeking employment where they have access to the formation of social policy. Community psychologists like to be where the action is—a member of an urban planning team, a consultant to the city council, an advisor to legislators, a director of a citizen's advocate group, the head of a social service agency—these are all jobs with the potential to influence social change far beyond the individual level.

Not all community psychologists practice social activism, nor should they. Activism as a style of intervention requires special talents and temperaments. It also requires a degree of tolerance from the social environment. Activism should not be championed as its own objective. It is merely a style of intervening. While it can be very powerful, it should not dominate its practitioners.

These disclaimers aside, it would appear that a community psychology which is wedded to some types of activism will be more decisive and influential than would be the case without this dimension. The ideal is a profession which is as vigorous and creative in changing social conditions as it is in understanding them. While we have not yet fully accomplished either of these goals, it may be that the dual roles of "participant changer" and "conceptualizer" will require more than one type of community psychologist. Whether activism and conceptual clarity can be maintained best through single or multiple types of professionals, the objectives of the field must be to develop and use empirically verified principles of social change.

3 Use of Research as a Form of Intervention More than other psychologists, community psychologists are likely to view research as a technique of intervention, a way of producing change. This is particularly true in the case of *evaluation research,* which compares the effects of some new program or treatment against existing programs or against no intervention at all. In the event that an experimental procedure is associated with greater changes or benefits than alternative programs, the researcher has a basis for arguing that that procedure should be introduced on a more permanent basis.

Experimentation from this perspective is both a technique of demonstration and of persuasion. George Fairweather, a psychologist at Michigan State University, has coined the phrase *experimental social innovation* to describe research which, after demonstrating the relative superiority of a new program, can then be used to support that program's implementation.

Research as intervention is also exemplified by what is called *dissemination research*. This is experimentation designed to evaluate alternative methods of implementing those experimental programs which initial program evaluation research has shown to be successful. In the course of finding the most effective means of persuading other organizations or communities to adopt a given program, that program is, by necessity, adopted. The best example of dissemination research is represented by Fairweather's 5-year experimental project (Fairweather, Sanders, & Tornatzky, 1974), which evaluated the effectiveness of different approaches to persuading hundreds of mental hospitals to adopt an outpatient "lodge program" designed for chronic mental patients. The research investigated what techniques were most effective in actually activating the lodge program once a decision to adopt it had been made and explored the procedures the adoptees themselves used in spreading the lodge program to other mental health programs in their area.

EXAMPLES OF COMMUNITY PSYCHOLOGY

One of the best ways to understand community psychology is to examine just what it is that its typical practitioner does, so, in this section, we will present examples of the practice of community psychology. Many examples could have been chosen, such as interventions in the educational system, special preschool programs, day care, community organization, urban planning and development, the juvenile justice system, evaluation of social service agencies, community treatment of the chronically ill, and the training of non- and paraprofessional community workers. As the introductory section of this chapter indicated, the range of functions offered by a community psychologist is uncommonly broad.

Our focus will be upon how a community psychologist would confront some of the problems in the criminal justice system. Two of the most important areas of community psychologists' involvement in the criminal justice system are *deinstitutionalization* and *decriminalization*. Deinstitutionalization rests on two assumptions: first, that the restoration of offenders will be maximized to the extent that their institutional confinement is minimized and, second, that the preferred correctional settings are ones which possess the greatest similarity to the environments in which the adjustment of offenders should occur.

Probation is the most common deinstitutionalization procedure. The President's Commission on Law Enforcement and Administration of Justice (1967) reported that probation has become almost the standard sentence for first offenders. Some jurisdictions use it for as many as 70 percent of their felony convictions. But probation suffers from several problems, including case loads that are often three to four times as large as the recommended thirty-five offenders per probation officer (U.S. President's Commission, 1967). As a result, supervision of probationers is often only nominal. In lieu of adequate case management and supervision, probation officers must rely on strict aversive control of their clients, who often do not learn any new behavioral skills that could promote successful community adjustment.

Community psychologists have attempted to address some of these criticisms by developing new probation techniques which are based on social-learning principles. These procedures represent a welcome demonstration that psychologists can contribute to the goal of deinstitutionalization.

To date, the most comprehensive investigation of a social-learning approach to probation has been a well-controlled study by Polakow and Doctor (1974). The subjects were twenty-six adults (fifteen females, eleven males) who had served an average of 12.5 months on probation prior to the study. They had been transferred to the program because previous probation officers, using traditional case management procedures, had found them too difficult to work with. Most of the crimes for which these subjects had been convicted were drug related.

The new, experimental probation period consisted of three graduated contingency phases. In phase 1, the probationer earned a credit for weekly meetings with the probation officer. Accumulation of 8 credits allowed the participant to advance to stage 2, where points were earned for attending group meetings with other probationers. These group meetings were devoted to "experience sharing within the social context, discussion of problems, and support for positive self-correction of deviant behavior" (Polakow & Doctor, 1974, p. 65). Phase 2 lasted a minimum of 10 weeks.

Phase 3 required the participant to make a written, individualized contract with the probation officer that specified new behaviors which the probationer felt he or she needed to develop (e.g., obtaining employment, beginning new social activities). Contracts usually were confined to the one class of behavior which was considered to be the offender's most crucial deficit. Successful completion of contracted behaviors resulted in predetermined reductions in remaining probation time.

Polakow and Doctor (1974) compared participants' previous performance on traditional probation to that achieved during the contingency management period. Program evaluation focused on four outcomes: number of probation violations, number of new arrests, proportion of probation time during which the participant was employed, and attendance at scheduled probation meetings. The results for the first three measures are presented in Table 12-2 and clearly indicate the superior effectiveness of the contingency-based probation. Attendance at meetings also increased significantly during the contingency program. The arrest data are especially impressive, in light of the fact that no systematic contingencies were applied to the occurrence of illegal conduct, including drug usage.

Table 12-2   Probation Violations, Arrests, and Months Employed While on Regular Probation and Contingency Management

Dependent variable	Type of probation	Sex		Total	t diff
		M	F		
Mean number of probation viola-tions/year	Regular	1.43	2.05	1.75	5.05*
	Contingency	0.00	.26	.15	
Mean number of arrests while on probation	Regular	2.64	1.53	200	4.22*
	Contingency	.18	.13	.15	
Percentage of months em-ployed while on probation	Regular	51.9	38.6	44.6	3.30*
	Contingency	74.7	78.9	76.9	

*$p<.001$.

From Doctor, R., & Polakow, R. Proceedings of the 81st Annual Convention of the American Psychological Association. Copyright 1973 by the American Psychological Association. (Reprinted by permission.)

Results achieved during the contingency management program were also contrasted to outcomes produced by an intensive supervision program in which the probation officer was responsible for a reduced case load and thereby allowed more frequent contact with clients. The contingency management and intensive supervision case loads were matched in size and amount of time spent with each probationer. The mean ages of the two case loads were virtually equivalent. The outcome of this comparison was quite similar to that in Table 12-2. Contingency management probation was more effective than intensive probation in decreasing the mean number of probation violations and new arrests and in increasing the number of months employed. Contingency management probation has been applied to a number of other offenses including possession of dangerous drugs and child abuse.

Decriminalization involves a set of strategies intended to reverse the stigmatization that accompanies the criminal justice system's processing of accused and convicted persons. The movement of a criminal defendant through the justice system can be thought of as a series of procedures whereby the accused either exits from or is retained by the system. An exit point can be considered as any point of discretion where law enforcement, judicial, or correctional officials interrupt or terminate an individual's contact with the criminal justice system.

There are only five such exit points: (1) release on bail or some form of nonfinancial surety provides a temporary exit: (2) dismissal of charges; (3) acquittal; (4) reversal of conviction or sentence by a reviewing court; and (5) completion of a correctional sentence. Decriminalization can be thought of as a set of procedures for increasing the alternatives to existing exit points in the system. Community psychologists have placed special emphasis on creating early exits.

A popular type of decriminalization effort has been directed at the creation of alternatives to police arrest, the official procedure by which the operations of the criminal justice system are initiated. One type of problem in which police intervention often occurs is the family dispute or interpersonal crisis where an argument between civilians erupts into a violent confrontation. The "family disturbance call" is a dangerous activity for police. Bard (1971) cites data showing that 40 percent of on-duty police injuries occur while responding to this type of call.

Bard (1969, 1970; Bard & Berkowitz, 1967), a psychologist, was the first to develop a program by which a special group of New York City police officers (nine black and nine white volunteers) were trained to intervene in the typical family disturbance call without making an arrest. The training program focused on the development of interpersonal skills which would allow officers to intervene in the dispute in a manner that would minimize the possibility of civilian or police violence. Whenever possible the argument was quelled by crisis intervention techniques, and the disputants were referred to an appropriate social service agency for further assistance.

Methodological problems did not allow the comparison of the special officers' performance with that of nonparticipating police. However, none of the eighteen officers suffered any injuries as a result of their family crisis interventions. Another project (Driscoll, Meyer, & Schanie, 1973) included a follow-up assessment of families who had received assistance either from officers with special crisis training or untrained police. Citizens who had their call answered by trained officers evaluated their assistance significantly more favorably than those individuals whose calls were answered by regular police.

There are many other examples which show how a community psychologist might work within the criminal justice system. Bail reform, developing halfway houses, investigating the effects of certain parts of the criminal law, parole reform, and diverting offenders from the system itself are all important activities which community-oriented correctional psychologists have advocated.[2]

AN EVALUATION OF COMMUNITY PSYCHOLOGY

Community psychology has matured to the point that it can tolerate criticism, some of which comes from its own leaders. Critiques have been aimed at what community psychology has accomplished as well as what it has failed to accomplish. In this section we shall consider four of the most common complaints about the community psychology model.

---

[2]For detailed coverage of the special ethical and methodological dilemmas posed by these activities, see the Report of the Task Force on the Role of Psychology in the Criminal Justice System (1978).

Rhetoric versus Results   The most general criticism of community psychology is that its tenets are oversold and its accomplishments exaggerated. Community psychologists have been perceptive and prolific in pointing out what is wrong with both society and the mental health profession's efforts at correction, but they have been far less adept at coming up with a technology that produces specific, durable, social-system-oriented changes.

The rhetoric of the community psychology camp has not been matched by what should be the ultimate goal: results. Community psychologists are still stuck in the rut of arguing with clinicians about the ills of the medical model rather than getting on with the development of effective community interventions.

To illustrate this problem we surveyed the articles published in four recent issues of the *American Journal of Community Psychology*. Of the forty-two articles, only four described an original, applied intervention. The vast majority of the reports were concerned with the results of professional surveys, questionnaires, and other assessment instruments. Several articles were critical of the fact that community psychology lacked many concrete demonstrations of real accomplishment! Nowhere is this discrepancy between word and deed more apparent than in the case of primary prevention.

The Failure of Prevention   Community psychology's greatest failure is in the area where it sought its greatest success: primary prevention. In spite of all its clamor, impatience, good intentions, enthusiasm, and investments, community psychology can lay claim to precious few examples of effective primary prevention. After reviewing the history of nonaccomplishment in prevention, Emory Cowen, a community psychologist at the University of Rochester, concluded that

> . . . psychologists have done very little in true primary prevention. Measured by what we as psychologists have achieved, the concept is all aura and no substance. Although we agree overwhelmingly that "it's great," many of us cannot identify "it" in concrete form. The time has come to call our own bluff. We shall either continue, ostrich-like, to play word games that help us momentarily to feel righteous and avant-garde, or we must roll up our sleeves and start new, qualitatively different brands of programming and research. (1977b, p. 489)

Elsewhere, Cowen (1977a) has noted two main obstacles to primary prevention in mental health. First, most professionals are so unacquainted with actual examples of primary prevention that they are likely to confuse it with its secondary or even tertiary imitators. Cowen (1977b) has called this "definitional slippage": anything remotely resembling what one thinks primary prevention should be is mistakenly embraced as the "real thing."

The second obstacle is our fundamental lack of knowledge about *how* to prevent. We are often not certain about which independent variables most strongly influence human problems, and many of those about which we are certain may be so far from psychologists' areas of expertise that we are unable to do much about them.

Yet community psychologists are still working very hard at developing preventive techniques. Cowen (1977a) has nominated two areas that offer some promise. One is the *analysis and modification of social environments,* a type of social engineering in which classrooms, hospitals, day-care centers, recreational areas, and the like are organized in ways that enhance the development of the people they serve. The other is *competence building,* a strategy in which people are helped to build adaptive resources and skills early in life in order to prevent later maladjustments. Social skills training, cultural stimulation for disadvantaged youth, and promotion of academic achievement are all examples of this second approach.

It has been suggested that many social-learning-oriented techniques could serve as an intervention technology for community psychology. Nietzel, Winett, MacDonald and Davidson (1977) reviewed the effects of what they called *behavioral community psychology* on ten current community problems: education, juvenile justice, adult justice, drug abuse, alcoholism, community mental health, psychiatric patients, aging, unemployment, and environmental problems. In some cases, behavioral methods have produced a degree of preventive impact.

Overreach In addition to overstating its achievements, community psychology has been accused of losing sight of its appropriate and realistic objectives. For example, the idea that communities, not individuals, are the clients in need of modification has elicited a well-known critique from Warren Dunham, a sociologist. Dunham (1965) labeled the community movement the "newest therapeutic bandwagon," claiming that the new interest in the community is a compensation for the frustration that many clinicians have experienced in their unsuccessful attempts to treat chronic mental disorders such as the psychoses.

Like other critics, Dunham is skeptical about whether behavioral scientists are knowledgeable enough to heal whole communities:

What are the possible techniques that can be developed to treat the "collectivity"? Why do psychiatrists think that it is possible to treat the "collectivity" when there still exists a marked uncertainty with respect to the treatment and cure of the individual case? What causes the psychiatrist to think that if he advances certain techniques for treating the "collectivity," they will have community acceptance? If he begins to "treat" a group through discussions in order to develop personal insights, what assurances does he have that the results will be psychologically beneficial to the persons? Does the psychiatrist know how to organize a community along mentally hygienic lines and if he does, what evidence does he have that such an organization will be an improvement over the existing organization? In what institutional setting or in what cultural milieu would the psychiatrist expect to begin in order to move toward more healthy social relationships in the community? These are serious questions and I raise them with reference to the notion that the community is the patient. (Dunham, 1965, p. 306)

Ethical Objections Community psychology has evoked many ethical concerns. As with other criticisms, ethical issues have been raised by the field's proponents and opponents alike. A common fear is that community programs, particularly those aimed at prevention, may threaten individual freedoms and rights. Halleck (1969) has expressed concern that the community movement will result in an increasing encroachment on our privacy and right to live our lives the way we please. He fears the consequences of mental health professionals prescribing a "healthy" way of life for a community and then intervening to ensure that it becomes a reality.

There are at least two reasons why this particular fear may be somewhat exaggerated. First, Americans are notably resistant to controls and coercion. Our earnest mistrust of undue regulation from any source, whether it is political, military, or even medical, has been effective protection against the excesses of control suffered by other societies. At present, this quality appears sufficiently strong to prevent possible abuses by the overly zealous community psychologist.

Second, we must return to the issue of community psychology's record of accomplishment. As we have seen, outside the area of delivering traditional mental health services to larger segments of the population, the community movement has not produced the preventive programs or social-system-level changes it seeks. Community psychology's most pressing current ethical dilemma is not so much the threat of doing too much to communities as of doing too little.

A host of other ethical objections have been raised at one time or another about community psychology. Some critics fear that increasing the emphasis on prevention will distract professionals from offering the intensive treatment that severely disturbed clients require or that many types of clients prefer (Dunham, 1965). This is highly unlikely, especially since the mental health fields suffered from an insufficiency of professional personnel long before community psychology came along. In fact, as you will remember, one of the main motivations behind the community mental health movement was to bring more psychological services to greater numbers of people.

Other critics contend that there is some danger in the early identification and treatment associated with secondary prevention. By being too aggressive in finding "at-risk" persons, the psychologist may damage them with premature labels. Ullmann and Krasner (1975) warn that "case finding" should not turn into "case making."

Finally, there is the nagging uncertainty about exactly who it is in a community that decides the goals of community interventions. Is it the psychologist, the recipients of the program, the majority of the community, or only influential leaders? Community psychologists assure us that the aims of their interventions are directed by the people they serve. In a text on community psychology, Zax and Spector (1974) claim: "The notion of a community psychology would be impossible were it not for the fact that, because of the unity of social problems, need is felt for it at a grass roots level" (p. 325). This may be true, but as Korchin (1976) has argued, the notion of community participation is a complex ideal made all the more difficult by the frequent value conflicts between community residents and professional psychologists. Perlman (1977) has addressed this issue of autonomy versus manipulation in a consulting relationship. His advice on solving it is twofold: (1) organize community participation at the beginning of any program so that consumers can have an impact, and (2) remember that the ultimate focus of an intervention should be to help community members meet their own needs.

FINAL THOUGHTS

José Ortega y Gasset, the Spanish philosopher and statesman, claimed "a revolution only lasts 15 years, a period which coincides with the effectiveness of a generation." If this is true, the next few years will be a vital time for community psychology. Either it will falter and be remembered mainly as representing a period of upheaval in mental health which challenged and changed many of the functions of clinical psychologists, or it will extend itself through a new generation of psychologists who will develop and evaluate the programs of prevention and social-system-level change that have been promised. We prefer the latter fate and regard community psychology's first 15 years as the prelude to its more effective future.

Part Four

The Profession of Clinical Psychology

Chapter 13

Professional Issues in Clinical Psychology

If Lightner Witmer were to return from the dead for a review of the field he founded, we doubt he would recognize many modern clinicians as his professional colleagues. A few might match his original psychoeducational, child-oriented model and inspire a friendly and knowing nod of approval. But many others probably would require a special introduction to Witmer, who would probably be a bit bewildered by the clinicians who practice something so different from the clinical psychology of the early twentieth century.

Witmer would probably mutter to himself: "These people in private practice doing psychotherapy with adults must be psychiatrists. And this researcher studying biochemical factors in behavior disorder must be a physiological psychologist. What about these people making all the noise about community reform and development? They sound like politicians; probably Progressives, maybe Democrats. And those folks running growth and encounter groups—what would Wundt say?"

Having read the previous twelve chapters you no doubt sympathize with Witmer's confusion. Clinical psychology is an expanding profession which is becoming more and more difficult to summarize in a single volume. As we saw in Chapter 1, there is a long list of professional roles which clinicians now fill. However, no list could do full justice to the complexity of clinical psychology because it could not indicate either the multiple functions required by each of the job descriptions or the entirely new specialties within clinical psychology which will emerge in the years to come. Struck by an almost geometric growth in the number of clinicians, a proliferation of alternative roles, and an increasing specialization, commentators often struggle to find an apt description of clinical psychology's current status. A favorite summary is that clinical psychology is in "a transitional state."

Certainly this claim is not inaccurate, although it certainly is an understatement on at least two counts. First, it suggests that transition is a unique state, a novel era in an otherwise stable and tranquil history. This is, of course, not correct. One interesting feature of clinical psychology is that it has always been in constant transition. Witmer would not have had to wait until the seventies to be surprised by the changes in clinical psychology; he would have seen changes in the twenties, thirties, forties, fifties and sixties.

This state of flux has been a mixed blessing. On one hand, it has made clinical psychology a very exciting and challenging field with which to be associated. On the other hand, rapid transitions have prevented the profession from developing a "sound fund of tradition" (Guiora & Brandwin, 1968) which could serve as a common reference point for professional identity. It is a little like the child who is forced to become an adult before being an adolescent. Further, the growth and evolution of clinical psychology have been less matters of carefully planned development than of responsiveness to necessity, social demands, and financial opportunities for expansion (Shakow, 1978).

The words "transitional state" also tend to underestimate the current magnitude and pace of the changes in clinical psychology. The rate of transition has not been steady; it has been positively accelerating like an object falling through space. Each of the three decades since World War II has brought more extensive changes in the field than any preceding period.

Consider these three simple examples: (1) In 1947 there were 787 members of the APA's Division 12, the Division of Clinical Psychology. In 1964, there were 2883 members (Shakow, 1968). In 1978 the membership of Division 12 stood at 4337, approximately six times its size of 30 years ago. (2) In the first 50 years of clinical psychology there was only one major conference on professional training. It was held in 1949 in Boulder, Colorado. In the 30 years since Boulder, there have been four national training conferences and many smaller-scale conferences. (3) Early proposals for training in clinical psychology discouraged clinicians from entering private practice and only a handful of psychologists did so. A 1974 survey (Boneau & Cuca, 1974) revealed that 7.3 percent of doctoral-level APA members were in *full-time* private practice. Today almost 21 percent of APA doctoral-level health-care providers are *primarily* employed in private practice (Gottfredson & Dyer, 1978), and in their recent survey of Division 12 members, Garfield and Kurtz (1976) found that respondents spent approximately 25 percent of their professional time in the delivery of individual psychotherapy. These changes, along with many others related to the community mental health movement, health insurance, and society's demand for mental health services, suggest that it would be more accurate to portray clinical psychology as being not so much in transition as in an entirely new era.

The first era in the history of clinical psychology extended from its birth in 1896 to World War II (see Chapter 2). This was the time when clinical psychology appeared as a discipline, as a subfield of scientific psychology, and as a contributing member of the mental health team under the supervision of psychiatry. The 35 years since World War II have constituted clinical psychology's second era. During this period, the field's unique identity became established and expanded vigorously. This modern era has seen the field at least partly transformed from an academic discipline into a service profession. It has seen clinical psychology liberate itself from both the intolerant opposition of some members of nonclinical psychology and from the patronizing domination of psychiatry. It has been an era in which clinicians struggled for autonomy, got it, and became determined to retain it.

The professionalization and current status of clinical psychology are the topics of this last chapter. It is a story that has many subplots because, as we saw in Chapter 2, clinical psychology did not develop in an integrated or systematic way. Quite the contrary: the professionalization of clinical psychology is the result of progress on several different but overlapping fronts (Wolman, 1965). We will focus on five issues which we consider to be the most essential for understanding clinical psychology's struggle for professional recognition:

1 Professional Training.   What sort of training does one need to become a clinical psychologist, and what are the different options for obtaining this training?

2 Professional Regulation.   What are the mechanisms for ensuring that a clinical psychologist possesses certain minimum skills and meets minimum requirements to function professionally?

3 Professional Ethics.   What principles will guide clinicians in determining the ethical standards for their professional activities? How are matters of unethical behavior dealt with?

4 Professional Independence.   What should be the relationship between clinical psychology and other mental health professions? Should clinical psychology be a fully autonomous profession responsible for its own direction and supervision, or should it operate under the supervision of medicine, particularly psychiatry?

5 Perils of Professionalization.   Has the professionalization of clinical psychology been an asset or a detriment? Has the public benefited? Has the quality of clinical psychology improved?

PROFESSIONAL TRAINING

Throughout the first 4 decades of the twentieth century, advanced training for clinical psychologists made little progress. To the clinicians of that period, experience was not only the best teacher, it was practically the only teacher. Psychologists were increasingly involved in clinical work during this time, but their training for these activities was unstructured and unsystematic. Acquisition of the knowledge and experience necessary for competent clinical work was largely self-organized (Shakow, 1948).

A few steps toward greater formalization of clinical training were taken by the APA during the 1930s and early 1940s, but these were very cautious and virtually without effect. In 1931, a specially appointed APA Committee on Standards of Training for Clinical Psychologists was formed, and in 1935 this committee published a report which contained a number of recommendations for clinical training. The Psychology Department at Columbia University proposed a training curriculum for clinical psychologists in 1936 which involved 2 years of graduate work and a 1-year internship (Shakow, 1948). In 1938, Shakow cited the need for a year-long internship in the training of psychologists (Shakow, 1938). In 1943, a Committee on Training in Clinical Psychology released a report entitled "Proposed Program of Professional Training in Clinical Psychology," and 2 years later a report on graduate internship training in psychology was published.

Very little was accomplished with respect to the systematic training of clinical psychologists until the late 1940s, when the social needs brought about by World War II and the financial support provided by the Veterans Administration and the U.S. Public Health Service combined to offer psychology a unique opportunity for expansion, establishment, and esteem (see Blank & David, 1964).

The most influential psychologist in the development of clinical training programs was David Shakow, for many years the chief psychologist at Worcester State Hospital in Massachusetts and later an important figure at the National Institute of Mental Health. As early as 1942, Shakow saw the need for a 4-year doctoral-level training program in clinical psychology which included an internship during the third year (Shakow, 1942).

Shakow's foresight in this area attracted the attention of Carl Rogers, who was then president of the APA. Rogers asked Shakow to chair a Committee on Training in Clinical Psychology (CTCP) whose primary task was to formulate a recommended clinical training program. The committee, composed of six of the most distinguished clinicians of that era, prepared a report entitled "Recommended Graduate Training in Clinical Psychology." The report was presented to and accepted by the APA in September 1947 and was published that same year in the *American Psychologist*. The "Shakow report" set the pattern for clinical training and remains, with surprisingly few exceptions, a useful standard against which modern clinical programs can be evaluated.

You may remember that near the end of Chapter 2 we mentioned three important recommendations of the Shakow report on clinical training:

1 A clinical psychologist should be trained first and foremost as a psychologist.
2 Clinical training should be as rigorous as that for nonclinical areas of psychology.
3 Preparation of the clinical psychologist should be broad and directed

toward the "holy trinity" of research and professional goals: assessment, research, and therapy.

In addition to these objectives, several other general principles for graduate clinical programs were advocated in the Shakow report:

4 The core content of clinical training programs should involve study in six areas: general psychology, psychodynamics of behavior, diagnostic methods, research methods, related disciplines, and therapy.

5 The program should offer basic courses in principles as opposed to a large number of courses on special techniques.

6 Training should be organized around the integration of theory with practice: course work plus field work with persons representing both aspects of psychology. This emphasis on integrated training was a hallmark of Shakow's plan; mechanisms for integrating theory with practice are suggested in every one of his many articles on training.

7 Throughout the entire graduate program, the student should have contact with clinical material. "The student should from the first year be provided with opportunities for actual contact with human material in naturalistic, test and experimental situations in the setting of practicum, clerkship and internship" (Shakow, 1947, p. 544).

8 Opportunities should also be provided for contact with "normal" material, with persons who never establish clinical contacts.

9 The training atmosphere should encourage maturity and the continued growth of desirable personality characteristics.

10 The program should promote a sense of responsibility for patients and clients which in comparison with physicians is often deficient in psychologists.

11 There needs to be a systematic plan for the use of representatives of related disciplines to teach clinical trainees and for joint study with students in these related disciplines.

12 There must be an emphasis throughout the program on the research implications of clinical phenomena.

13 Trainees must also become sensitive to the social implications of their work. "They must acquire the ability to see beyond the responsibilities they owe the individual patient, to those they owe society" (Shakow, 1978, p. 151).

The Shakow report also suggested a possible year-by-year curriculum that would fulfill these criteria. This recommended schedule was not offered as a blueprint for training to which every university training program was expected to adhere but only as an illustrative model, one possible example of what an adequate clinical program could look like.

In this model, first-year clinical students would become acquainted with the systematic foundations and the core content of general psychology. They would also be trained in observational techniques. The second year would be devoted primarily to the experimental, diagnostic, and therapeutic content of clinical psychology. In addition to didactic material, students would acquire direct, practical experience with this material through practicum courses and clinical placements (or what Shakow called "clerkships").

The third year would be the internship, a year of intensive and extensive experience with clinical phenomena at an operational facility such as a hospital, clinic, or medical center. Here the student would have an opportunity to build a "mass of experience which gives concrete meaning to general principles" (Shakow, 1947, p. 551). Of all the components of an ideal training program, Shakow regarded the internship as the most essential. It was the component that engendered the student's sense of professional identity and immersed her or him in practical clinical experience.

Several objectives were to be met during the fourth year. The dissertation, perhaps begun in the third year, would be completed. The student would take a seminar on professional problems and ethics as well as seminars involving related disciplines. And the student would undergo a period of "self-evaluation." Self-evaluation usually meant being a patient in individual psychotherapy, preferably psychoanalysis, which would help the student uncover biases, attitudes, and personality problems that, if undetected, might interfere with later clinical work.

Most of today's clinical training programs are very much like Shakow's prototype. Perhaps the most obvious deviation is that it usually takes five rather than four years to complete the entire training sequence (the internship is usually taken in the fourth year). The major reasons for the extra year are that most programs now require their students to complete a master's thesis (usually in the second year), and some universities still retain some nonpsychology graduate requirements such as a foreign language. On the other hand, clinical students are now somewhat less likely to enter personal therapy than was the case 15 or 20 years ago.

While there are great variations in the curricula of APA-approved programs, the sample schedule of courses presented in Table 13-1 would be roughly equivalent to what you might encounter in most Ph.D. programs.

Finally, the Shakow report dealt with issues such as the best way to select graduate students, the undergraduate preparation for clinical graduate students, and the means by which professional growth and training could and should be continued after earning the Ph.D. (see Alexander, 1965, for a review of postgraduate training opportunities for clinical psychologists). The greatest impact of the report, however, was that it prescribed that special mix of scientific and professional preparation which has typified *most* clinical training programs ever since. This recipe for training (which we have already described as the scientist-professional model) was officially endorsed at clinical psychology's first major training conference held in Boulder, Colorado, in 1949 (Raimy, 1950).

The Boulder Conference

The Boulder Conference on Training in Clinical Psychology was convened with the financial support of the Veterans Administration and the U.S. Public Health Service which requested the APA to (1) name those universities that offered satisfactory training programs and (2) develop acceptable programs in universities that did not have them (Derner, 1965). The conference participants were drawn from university training programs and clinical practicum facilities.

The major result of Boulder was that its conferees endorsed the basic

Table 13-1   Sample Schedule of Ph.D. Program in Clinical Psychology

Fall Semester	Spring Semester
First year	

Psychological Statistics I
Introduction to Interviewing
Clinical Assessment I
Practicum in Assessment
History and Systems of Psychology
	Psychological Statistics II
	Clinical Assessment II
	Selected Proseminar (Social Psychology,
	  Developmental Psychology, Psychology
	  of Learning, Physiological Psychology)
	Theories and Research in Personality

Second year	

Psychopathology
Selected Proseminar (choose one
  from list above)
Systems of Psychotherapy
M.A. research
	Psychotherapy Practicum
	Clinical Seminar (Group Therapy, Behavior
	  Modification, Child and Family
	  Therapy, Community Psychology)
	M.A. research

Third year	

Psychotherapy Practicum
Clinical Seminar (choose one from
  list above)
Clinical Research Seminar (Research
  in Personality, Psychopathology
  Research, Research in Psychotherapy)
Advanced nonclinical seminar
	Advanced nonclinical seminar
	Clinical or nonclinical research seminar
	Psychotherapy Practicum

A written qualifying examination is to be taken during the third year of graduate work, but no later than the beginning of the fourth year. Only those students who have completed their M.A. thesis are permitted to register for the qualifying examination.

Fourth year	
Internship	
Fifth year	
Clinical or nonclinical research seminar Advanced nonclinical seminar Research on Dissertation	Same

recommendations of Shakow's committee and accepted the scientist-professional model of training. Clinical psychologists were expected to be equally proficient in research and professional practice and to have earned a Ph.D. in psychology from a university-based graduate program. A supervised, year-long internship would also be required. Shakow's plan became known as the *Boulder model.*

The Boulder conferees further agreed that some mechanism for monitoring, evaluating, and officially accrediting clinical training programs and internship facilities was necessary. As noted in Chapter 2, the APA formed an Education and Training Board whose Committee on Accreditation was charged with these tasks. Initially, all accreditation visits were made by members of the accreditation committee. However, by the late 1960s, the large number of clinical programs, and the need to accredit counseling and school psychology programs made this plan unworkable. At the present time, clinical training sites are visited by an APA accreditation team about every 5 years. The team consists of three psychologists (selected by the program from a list of potential visitors) who evaluate how well the program is meeting its own training goals and the standards of training set forth by the APA. The most recent revision of APA's criteria for accreditation was adopted in 1979.

The results of accreditation site visits are published each year in the APA's official journal, *The American Psychologist*. In 1979 there were 103 clinical training programs fully approved by the APA (see Box 13-1) and 136 fully-approved internships. In addition, there are many doctoral training programs that function without APA approval, either because the program has not requested a site visit or because approval has not been granted after an accreditation visit.

Box 13-1   APA-Approved Doctoral Programs in Clinical Psychology (1978)

In addition to the 103 fully-approved programs, there are six clinical programs that have received "provisional approval." This is a category for relatively new programs whose development shows promise or for programs that are innovative and consequently deviate from the usual accreditation criteria. For the institutions listed, the training programs are housed in the department of psychology unless otherwise indicated; the great majority of training programs still follow Shakow's recommendation that clinical students be trained in an environment that stresses general psychological knowledge.

Fully approved programs

Adelphi University, Institute of
  Advanced Psychological Studies
Alabama, University of
American University
Arizona State University
Arizona, University of
Arkansas, University of
Boston University
Bowling Green State University
Brigham Young University
California, University of (Berkeley)
California, University of
  (Los Angeles)
Case Western Reserve University
Catholic University of America
Cincinnati, University of
City University of New York (City
  College)
Clark University

Michigan State University
Michigan, University of
Minnesota, University of
Mississippi, University of
Missouri, University of
Montana, University of
Nebraska, University of
Nevada, University of
New Mexico, University of
New York University
North Carolina, University of
North Dakota, University of
North Texas State University
Northern Illinois University
Northwestern University Medical
  School, Department of Psychiatry
  and Behavioral Science
Ohio University
Oklahoma State University

Colorado, University of
Connecticut, University of
Delaware, University of
Denver, University of
Duke University
Emory University
Florida State University
Florida, University of
Fordham University
Fuller Theological Seminary
George Washington University
Georgia State University
Georgia, University of
Hawaii, University of
Houston, University of
Illinois, University of
Illinois, University of (Psy.D.
  Program)
Illinois, University of (Chicago
  Circle)
Indiana University
Iowa, University of
Kansas, University of
Kent State University
Kentucky, University of
Long Island University
Louisiana State University
Louisville, University of
Loyola University (Chicago)
Maine, University of
Manitoba, University of
Maryland, University of
Massachusetts, University of
McGill University
Memphis State University
Miami, University of (Florida)
Miami University (Ohio)
Oregon, University of

Pennsylvania State University
Pennsylvania, University of
Pittsburgh, University of
Purdue University, Department
  of Psychological Sciences
Rhode Island, University of
Rochester, University of
Rutgers—The State University
St. Louis University
South Carolina, University of
South Dakota, University of
South Florida, University of
Southern California, University of
Southern Illinois University
State University of New York at
  Buffalo
State University of New York at
  Stony Brook
Syracuse University
Teachers College, Columbia
  University
Temple University
Tennessee, University of
Texas, University of
Texas Tech University
Utah, University of
Vanderbilt University
Vermont, University of
Virginia Commonwealth University
Washington State University
Washington, University of
Washington University (St. Louis)
Waterloo, University of
Wayne State University
West Virginia University
Wisconsin, University of
Wyoming, University of
Yale University

Provisionally approved programs

Auburn University
Baylor University, Psy. D. Program
DePaul University
Missouri, University of (St. Louis)
Rutgers—The State University, Graduate
  School of Applied and Professional Psychology,
  Psy.D. Program
Yeshiva University

The Conferences at Stanford, Miami, and Chicago

Although the Boulder model and its two-fisted, scientist-professional Ph.D. remain the dominant training pattern in most programs, some clinicians have expressed discontent with it ever since 1949. There is clear evidence that this discontent has grown in recent years, and we have now reached a stage where there are two major alternatives to the Boulder model. We will describe each of these later; for now we need to examine the post-Boulder training conferences that set the stage for those alternatives.

1 Stanford   The Stanford conference was a 4-day affair held at Stanford University in 1955 (Strother, 1956). It posed no major threat to the continuation of the Boulder model and offered no significant new direction for clinical training, but it did anticipate some of the effects which the newly emerging community mental health movement would have on clinical psychology. It stressed the need to broaden the nature of training in order to prepare clinicians for the new professional roles which community mental health would offer.

2 Miami   The Miami Beach training conference was held in 1958 (Roe, Gustad, Moore, Ross, & Skodak, 1959). In the almost 10 years since Boulder, clinical psychology had undergone enough changes, expected and unexpected, to warrant some reevaluation of the scientist-professional model. Although questions were raised about the Ph.D., the conclusion was a conservative one: The Ph.D. program should be retained as the primary training vehicle, although departments were encouraged to develop programs that best suited their own resources and needs. Great emphasis was placed on the need for psychology to continue to train its graduates in the techniques of empirical research. The sentiment of this conference could thus be described as reflecting "tradition with flexibility." (See Lloyd & Newbrough, 1965, for more on the Stanford, Miami, and related conferences.)

3 Chicago   The 1965 Chicago Conference on the Professional Preparation of Clinical Psychologists broke two traditions. It was held in a city with a less than thrilling climate, and it was the first conference to seriously consider some alternative models of clinical training. An important theme of this conference was that, while the scientist-professional model should be continued, the potential value of a purely *professional* model of training should be appreciated.

The growing interest in a primarily professional model which stresses training for the delivery of clinical services stemmed from two sources. First, the need for psychological service providers was burgeoning due, in large part, to the expansion of the community mental health movement. Second, it was well known that only a very small percentage of psychologists, probably about 10 percent, account for the published research in psychology (see Table 1-1). In fact, the modal number of publications by doctoral-level clinicians is zero (Levy, 1962). Critics of the Boulder model argued that too much time was being spent training students for activities which, as professionals, they would never perform. At the same time, research-oriented departments of psychology were accepting increasing numbers of practice-oriented graduate students. The fit was often a bad one.

In place of the scientist-professional model, a professional program was proposed and described in the *Preconference Materials* (Zimet & Throne, 1965):

The distinctive feature of this pattern of doctoral training would be the effort to prepare a broadly trained psychological clinician prepared to intervene in a wide variety of settings for the purpose of fostering change and forestalling psychological problems. His training would include psychological science but would stress those areas in which clinical methods find their support. It would also include relevant material from related disciplines such as medicine and sociology. He would be introduced to a variety of diagnostic, remedial, and preventive procedures. His training would include analysis of the manner in which clinical methods are developed with the intent to make him a sophisticated evaluator of new methods developed in the future. Because he would not carry out a doctoral dissertation or learn foreign languages, he would have more time available for professional training and experience. Should he wish to develop the competence of a specialist in specified diagnostic, remedial, or preventive procedures he will need additional training—either on the job or in formal postdoctoral training programs.

We would expect a clinical psychologist trained in this manner to devote full time to professional practice oriented toward treatment, prevention, or both. He would use diagnostic instruments, carry out psychotherapy, engage in milieu therapy, use behavior therapy, consult in community mental health projects, work with groups, organizations, and communities—as the occasion demanded. He would, as far as his limited scientific training would permit, keep abreast of new methods as they developed and critically appraise them prior to adoption. He would contribute to the development of methods of practice by exchanging his professional experience with that of his colleagues. (pp. 21–22)

In the end, the conferees refused to endorse the explicitly professional model, preferring instead a rather open-ended scientist-professional plan that would not shortchange training for clinical activities. Training programs were urged to add faculty who were experienced clinicians involved in ongoing clinical work and also to broaden their criteria for acceptable research activities.

Diversity in training was encouraged by calling for pilot programs that would experiment with innovative ways of implementing the professional model. Special interest was focused on the first Psy.D. (Doctor of Psychology) program which was under development at the University of Illinois. The appropriate levels (doctoral and subdoctoral) and locations (department of psychology, medical center, independent professional school) of clinical training were also debated at Chicago.

The importance of the Chicago conference was that proposals for professional training models and subdoctoral programs, while not officially endorsed, were gaining credibility among clinical psychology's leadership. Innovation in doctoral training was supported by 90 percent of the conferees; 31 percent voted to wait to decide about the advisability of the Psy.D. until such programs had been tried and the quality of their students evaluated. Many of the ideas considered seriously for the first time at Chicago were adopted 8 years later by the participants at psychology's fifth and most recent training conference.

The Vail Conference

"Back to the resorts but not back to the basics" might summarize the National Conference on Levels and Patterns of Professional Training in Psychology held in the summer of 1973 in Vail, Colorado (Korman, 1976). Sponsored by a grant from the National Institute of Mental Health (NIMH), the Vail conference included 116 invited participants representing a wide range of psychological specialities, training orientations, graduate students, and minority-group psychologists. Vail was the most ambitious of the post-Boulder conferences. In only 5 days, the conference passed 150 resolutions, some of which introduced sweeping changes in the training of psychologists. These recommendations were organized around the following important themes (Korman, 1976).

1 Professional Training Models The conference officially recognized explicitly professional training programs as an acceptable model for those programs which defined their primary mission as the preparation of students for the delivery of basic clinical services. These "unambiguously professional" programs were to be given status equal to their more traditional scientist-professional counterparts. Professional programs could be housed in a number of settings including academic psychology departments, medical schools, or specially established professional schools.

When primary emphasis in graduate training was on the direct delivery and evaluation of professional services, the Psy.D. was seen as the appropriate degree. When primary emphasis was on the development of new knowledge in psychology, the Ph.D. would be preferred.

2 Levels of Training The conferees felt that priority should be given to programs that either provided multiple levels of training or demonstrated clear coordination with degree programs at varying levels. They felt that the concept of a *career ladder* should be replaced by the idea of a *career lattice,* an open-ended structure that would make possible upward professional mobility through continued, integrated training.

One of the boldest and most controversial of the Vail recommendations was that persons trained at the master's level should be considered to be professional psychologists. This sentiment was a reversal of the opinion of previous training conferences, and of the original Shakow report, all of which envisioned psychology as a doctoral-level profession. The Vail participants, on the other hand, felt that many of the services currently performed by doctoral psychologists could be performed with equal competence by personnel trained at the master's or submaster's level.[1]

As a consequence the conference called for the development of strong, professional master's programs and full APA membership for the master's-level individual. This initiative struck a responsive chord in many quarters, and soon several states had developed new M.A. training programs in clinical psychology. Today, master's level clinicians outnumber Ph.D.s in many of these states.

[1]The Vail conferees considered two types of submaster's programs: those that stressed academic psychology and those that emphasized training in applied skills. The latter type of program was to be offered in one of several ways: associate in arts (A.A.) and bachelor's degree programs as well as nondegree programs. The conference did not recommend that submaster's trainees be considered psychologists.

The M.A. proposal was certainly a dramatic one. It may also prove to have been short-lived, because the tide has once again turned against the master's degree as a recognized "degree of entry" for the professional psychologist. In 1977 the APA's Council of Representatives voted that the title "psychologist" should be reserved for those who have completed a *doctoral* training program. Part of this current trend is due to a recent reawakening of the traditional view of the clinical psychologist as someone whose preeminent contribution is not psychotherapy or diagnosis but empirical research, an activity for which a Ph.D. program is the best preparation.

The status of the master's-level clinician was also jeopardized by some ambivalence on the part of those Vail advocates who, while willing to endorse M.A.-trained persons as professionals, were unwilling to take the next logical step and recommend state certification or licensure for them. Another major obstacle to full professional standing and full psychological citizenship for the master's-level clinician has been a political one. Quite simply, the status of psychology as a profession vis-à-vis its frequent antagonist, psychiatry, is threatened by including the M.A. holder along with the Ph.D. psychologist. Professional autonomy for psychology is often seen as best preserved by defining psychology exclusively as a doctoral-level enterprise. This issue has gained increasing importance as the United States moves toward a system of national health insurance. Psychologists' claim of eligibility for reimbursement as private practitioners is strengthened by portraying clinical psychology as a profession of persons holding doctoral degrees (we shall return to this topic later).

3 Desirable Characteristics of Professional Training The Vail meeting was the most "activist" psychology training conference. It considered a myriad of issues related to the social obligations of psychology, affirmative action, racism and sexism, and the need for continuing professional development. Although those issues are beyond the scope of this chapter, the careful attention paid to them at Vail is another illustration that this conference, more than any of its predecessors, seriously challenged both the history and the future of professional psychology.

After five national training conferences, several smaller conferences, countless hours of discussion, contention, and argument among clinicians, educators, and students, what is the state of training in clinical psychology? That question allows no easy answer, although we feel we can give some general responses that are accurate. First, the scientist-professional model has proven to be a tough and durable competitor which is still the "champ" in terms of the number of programs professing it as their training philosophy. This model now comes in an increasing number of different packages. Many programs have increased the amount of time devoted to professional training in psychotherapy at the expense of courses in psychodiagnostics or general psychology. Others allow the internship to be satisfied in various ways such as part-time assignments that are spread out over a 2- or 3-year period. Several programs follow a special theoretical model (e.g., behavioral or psychoanalytic) which offers a relatively narrow approach to the field. Other programs emphasize a certain specialty such as child-clinical or community psychology.

In an effort to acquaint the prospective clinical student with the vast array of training possibilities, the APA annually publishes a book called *Graduate Study in Psychology,* which lists all graduate programs in psychology along with a brief description of entrance requirements and training features. In addition, almost all clinical programs have a special brochure which can be obtained by simply mailing a request for it. These brochures usually discuss in some detail the program's orientation, faculty interests, requirements, and means of financial support for students (see Appendix).

In addition to the strong and popular Boulder model, there are other training programs that depart markedly from the scientist-professional formulation. Two alternative models enjoy some measure of current popularity: the Psy.D. program and the professional school of psychology.[2]

The Doctor of Psychology (Psy.D.) Degree

The professional training model has a long history (Pottharst, 1976), but the first continuously functioning version was the Psy.D. program begun by the Department of Psychology at the University of Illinois (Urbana-Champaign) in 1968. The Psy.D. program is an attempt to provide students desiring careers in clinical service with training that is especially relevant to that goal. Emphasis is placed on acquiring the professional skills necessary for the delivery of competent psychological services. A master's thesis is not required, nor is a research-oriented dissertation, although a written, doctoral-level report of professional quality is a requirement for the Psy.D. candidate. The original Psy.D. curriculum was described as follows:

> There is no demand to decide the first year between research and service careers, because all students do the same things the first year. Their experiences will include a proseminar in general psychology, an introduction to clinical psychology, training in quantitative methods and research design, and courses in personality theory and behavior disorders.
>
> The second year all students will take a year-long sequence in behavior assessment, or psychodiagnostics, as we used to call it, as well as courses in social development and a didactic survey of approaches to clinical behavior modification. By this time, however, students will have to choose either to complete a master's thesis, which is required in the Ph.D. research program, or to take additional course work in preparation for a professional career. The courses for Doctor of Psychology candidates deal with basic medicine for clinical psychologists, community psychology, educational counseling, and the special education of exceptional children.
>
> In the third year the separation between programs grows wider, though there

---

[2] Another proposal that has been given some consideration is to train people not so much in one discipline (like clinical psychology or psychiatry) but mainly in the skills necessary for clinical work, particularly psychotherapy. This plan (Holt, 1969; Kubie, 1954) would in essence create a new profession and require a new degree (e.g., Doctor of Psychotherapy). It has not proven to be a very popular alternative because of a lack of resources and a belief that the concept of a profession of psychotherapy is too narrow.

still are common elements. All students will complete a two-semester practicum in clinical psychology, and all students will take two laboratory courses in clinical psychology, ordinarily in individual psychotherapy and in behavioral desensitization procedures. In this year, Ph.D. students must also complete four units of work in a minor field, while Doctor of Psychology students can enter additional clinical labs. This is where some very important clinical training will take place, and limitations of time and class size will restrict the labs almost exclusively to professionally oriented students. The laboratories, as we are planning them now, will offer continued training in individual treatment procedures (Ph.D. students only have time for one semester), operant methods with clinical populations, group therapy, community action, the assessment of brain dysfunction, clinical personality tests of the traditional kinds (Ph.D. students are rather lightly exposed to these in the required clinical assessment course), and two special education courses in the diagnosis and remediation of learning disabilities.

The fourth-year Ph.D. students will complete a dissertation, while Psy.D. students will complete an internship with varying proportions of experience in a local community clinic, zone centers for children and adults, and at least one more traditional hospital setting.

Graduates of the Ph.D. program who decide after all to learn more about professional clinical work can take a postdoctoral internship and be right where the products of Boulder-style programs have always been. Better yet, they can spend 2 years picking up the clinical labs they missed and completing an internship to meet requirements for the Doctor of Psychology degree. Doctors of Psychology who want to obtain Ph.D. degrees as well can complete the necessary research and language requirements in 2 additional years. (Peterson, 1968b, p. 513)

As you can see, the courses for Psy.D. and Ph.D. students were almost identical for the first 2 years of graduate study. The distinctly professional quality of the Psy.D. curriculum emerged toward the end of the second year and particularly in the third and fourth years.

As the program has evolved, a number of changes have occurred. For example, all formal course requirements are now concentrated in the first year. Five year-long clinical practica are required, but the selection of these courses is open to negotiation between the student and an advisor. The professional report is still required, and there has been an effort to differentiate this report from the Ph.D. dissertation. Peterson and Baron (1975) note: "The projects differ from traditional Ph.D. theses positively in that all are clearly relevant to professional services in some way and negatively in that none of them so far has offered the close design and extensive base of systematic data which most scholars would require of 'research' in our field" (p. 92).

The Psy.D. program at Illinois received APA accreditation in 1973. It is currently the only fully approved Psy.D. program, although the program at the Rutgers School of Applied and Professional Psychology has received provisional approval. Of course, the Psy.D. idea has not been received enthusiastically by all clinicians. Goldenberg (1973) summarizes some objections to the program:

(1) the Psy.D. program is likely to acquire second-class status in the eyes of faculty, students and the public; (2) the fact that support for the alternate doctorate comes

from the unlikely quarter of academic psychology is suspect as being perhaps a device for shunting aside the bothersome problem of professional training in clinical psychology; (3) the profession of clinical psychology is in a state of flux, with new roles and practices emerging, making this a particularly inappropriate time to create a new profession with activities that are only dimly foreseeable at present and whose present clinical skills may soon be obsolete; (4) two parallel programs, producing two different degrees, will tend to separate clinical practice from the rest of psychology even further, thus cutting the profession off from its scientific roots; (5) expert practitioners, necessary in a professional degree program, are likely to find it as difficult to be appointed and later promoted at the university as is the case now of competent clinical professors who do not publish research findings; and (6) future graduates of such programs are likely to be stigmatized because of their different degree and different training. (p. 85)

While in the past, arguments for and against the Psy.D. were based largely on the powers of persuasion, there are now some preliminary data by which the program can be evaluated. The dark fears and predictions of doom have not been borne out by these initial data which cover the 1968 to 1974 period and evaluate the first four graduates of the Illinois program (Peterson & Baron, 1975). A comparison of Psy.D. and Ph.D. students reveals virtually identical performance by the two groups in similar courses, on qualifying exams, and other required academic activities. Attrition rates are essentially equivalent. Psy.D. students have obtained highly rated professional jobs with little difficulty and with no apparent disadvantages stemming from the fact that their degree was new. Further, the program has survived several administrative changes, including the departure of some of the individuals most responsible for its introduction.

The Professional School

The professional school is a more recent and even more daring departure from the Ph.D. model of scientist-professional training. Unlike the Psy.D. concept at Illinois, the professional school of psychology abandons the traditional department of psychology as its organizational basis and forms its own autonomous context for professional training. This type of relocation is thought to free clinical psychology from the academic constraints of the university, to allow rewards for professional as well as or instead of scholarly achievements, and to provide students with faculty role models who are active, practicing clinicians.

Professional schools of psychology are often associated with a university (e.g., at Rutgers or Adelphi), but entirely independent units have also been established. Because they are not affiliated with an existing university, these schools are sometimes described as "freestanding" professional schools. The earliest example of a freestanding school was the California School of Professional Psychology founded under the auspices of the California Psychological Association in 1969. The school has four campuses (Los Angeles, San Francisco, San Diego, and Fresno) with approximately 800 students in the undergraduate, master's and doctoral programs. More than 250 Ph.D.'s had been awarded as of

1975 (Dörken & Cummings, 1977). In 1977 the Los Angeles and San Diego campuses filed application for APA accreditation as doctoral training programs in clinical psychology.

Most professional schools offer the Ph.D., though the Rutgers program offers the Psy.D. In spite of the California school's emphasis on service delivery, it does have a research component and, unlike Psy.D. programs, requires a dissertation. Several areas of specialization are offered at the school including psychotherapy and assessment, psychology of the schools, community psychology, applied developmental psychology, and child and family psychology.

One advantage of professional schools and one of the reasons for their popularity is the flexibility in curriculum which they provide. Dörken and Cummings (1977) list sixteen "educational innovations" of the California School of Professional Psychology which they feel have made the program a unique venture among graduate training programs (see Box 13-2).

It is not our purpose to examine the relative merits of the Psy.D. and the professional schools (for a comparison see Stricker, 1975). However, one point of contrast is quite clear: The professional school concept has proven to be the more popular of the two alternatives. At a time when Psy.D. programs have been started and then discontinued at various universities, professional schools continue to multiply. As of 1976 there were twenty-eight professional schools either in operation, soon to become operative, or under active consideration (Dörken & Cummings, 1977), and a National Association of Professional Schools of Psychology (NAPSP) has been formed with nine schools as charter members.

Whether this initial burst of enthusiasm for professional schools will be sustained or will fade into the background remains to be determined. At present, the most obvious hurdle is accreditation; without it the professional schools are unlikely to thrive. A second pressing problem is one shared by all training programs: financial support. The professional schools must demonstrate that they are capable of generating adequate funding on a continuing basis, not just for a 1- to 5-year pilot period. Apart from all the philosophical, intellectual, and scientific criteria, the relative certainty of financial support enjoyed by most universities is one of the most persuasive reasons why many clinical psychologists are unwilling to "liberate" themselves or their training programs from the traditional academic sanctuary.

PROFESSIONAL REGULATION

In the first decade of clinical psychology's professional era the dominant concern was graduate training, and the most important matters were curriculum development and program accreditation. In fact, Shakow (1965) referred to psychology's "breathless preoccupation" with training during the forties and fifties. Breathless or otherwise, clinicians discovered a new preoccupation during the sixties: regulation of psychological practice.

One major responsibility of a service profession like clinical psychology is

Box 13-2   Educational Innovations in a Professional School of Psychology

Dörken and Cummings (1977, pp. 136–137) listed the following unique features of the California School of Professional Psychology. Not all of these distinctions are typical of every professional school, but the list will give you some idea of the differences between training in the usual department of psychology and that which takes place in the professional school.

1   The singular focus is upon the training of professional psychologists.
2   All faculty are part-time and otherwise professionally active.
3   Students attend on a full-time (11-month, three-trimester) basis each academic year.
4   Faculty and students participate in all levels of CSPP governance.
5   There is no academic tenure. All faculty are hired on a contract basis with renewal subject to future curriculum requirements and instructional performance. Contracts range from 1 to 5 years, with the shorter terms for new faculty and the longer terms awarded to faculty of proven and continuing merit.
6   Each campus is small and limited to a maximum student enrollment of 250 graduate students.
7   Training is an educational contract in which the instruction, field experience and research are concurrent. All phases must be successfully completed in any year for advancement to the next.
8   All seven series in the curriculum are of equal importance: field experience, practice, and internship; theoretical and conceptual courses; the sociocultural context of human development; scientific investigation and methodology; professional skills; humanities and arts; and personal growth and psychotherapeutic experiences. These series cut across all specialty majors with the intent that the graduate will not only be professionally competent but also be an educated person. In addition, individualized study may be arranged.
9   At the graduate level, there is a strong base in social cultures (the Anglo, Jewish, Chicano, Black, and Oriental cultures—with native American studies under development).
10 There is continuing required personal growth (therapy) experience throughout graduate training.
11 Supervised field experience is undertaken concurrently with formal instruction at a minimum of 16 hours weekly each year, thus emphasizing experience-based career education.
12 Training is oriented toward a professional-scientist model, and although all legitimate research techniques are considered valid, the doctoral dissertation must be completed on time—no dissertation, no graduation, and no typical accumulation of ABDs (all but dissertation). Because the research is directed to a cogent professional problem, it is hoped that it will be the initiation of a career interest.
13 Standardized test scores are not part of the application process. Selection is based upon demonstrated intellectual potential, the applicant's biographical history, motivation for professional training, and personal qualifications.
14 No students are admitted without prior personal interview. For out-of-state applicants, an interview team is sent to major cities across the country. (CSPP conforms to national graduate student application deadlines.)
15 Courses are graded only on credit/incomplete/no credit bases. Together with the qualitative instructor's record, students are regularly apprised of their academic progress.
16 The school remains responsive to evolution within the profession, which in a broad sense "owns" the school. Violation of the professional standards of psychology is grounds for student suspension or expulsion.

the establishment of standards of competence which members of the profession must meet before they are authorized to practice. The ultimate purpose of such regulation is to protect the public from the unauthorized or incompetent practice of psychology by impostors, untrained persons, or psychologists who are unable to function at some minimum level of competence. Though some doubt the value of the regulation enterprise (e.g., Gross, 1978), psychology, like medicine and law, has developed its own system of professional regulation.

Certification and Licensure

The most important type of regulation takes the form of state laws that establish requirements for the practice of psychology and restrict the use of the term "psychologist" to persons with certain qualifications. This legislative regulation comes in two kinds of statutes: certification and licensure. In both cases the laws are introduced and passed at the state level because the Constitution delegates sovereignty over this type of regulation to the states. The actual legal basis for these laws rests in the right of the state to pass legislation that protects its citizens. Caveat emptor ("let the buyer beware") is thought to be insufficient protection when buyers are not well-enough informed about the services to know what to beware *of*.

A *certification* law restricts the use of the title "psychologist" or "certified psychologist" to people who have met requirements specified in the law. Certification protects the title of psychologist *only;* it does not regulate the actual practice of psychology. In several states a person may be a certified psychologist without having a doctoral degree.

Licensure, on the other hand, is a more restrictive type of statute. Licensure laws define the practice of psychology by specifying the services which the psychologist is authorized to offer the public. The requirements for licensure are more comprehensive than those for ceritification; a doctorate in psychology plus 1 or more years of experience are usually required before one is even allowed to take a licensure exam. In order to distinguish between certification and licensure, remember the following rule of thumb: A certification law would not prevent a nonpsychologist from doing the same things as a certified psychologist; it would only prevent the person from being called a psychologist. A licensure law on the other hand would prevent a nonpsychologist from using the term "psychologist," *and* it would also prohibit the person from offering any services which the average citizen would believe to be among the professional functions of a psychologist.

Several statutes combine certification and licensure provisions. The first paragraph of Kentucky's Statute 319 reads as follows:

> No person not licensed or certified as provided in KRS 319.005 to 319.131 shall engage in any practice which in the judgment of the board of examiners constitutes the practice of psychology as defined in KRS 319.010, and is against the public interest. No person shall use the title of "Psychologist" in this state without a license granted by said board of examiners and signed by each member thereof. No person not licensed as provided in KRS 319.005 to 319.131 shall hold himself out to the public by any title or description of services representing himself as a psychologist which incorporates the words "psychological, Psychologist," or "psychology"; except as such usage of title and/or description is authorized by the board. The use of the title "Psychologist" and the description of services cited above is authorized

to those who apply for and are granted certificates within two years after June 18, 1964 as long as they maintain such certificates.

Licensing laws are administered by a state board of psychology which is charged by the legislature with regulating the practice of psychology in that state. There are two major functions of any state board of psychology: (1) to determine the standards for admission to the profession and administer procedures for the selection and examination of candidates and (2) to regulate professional practice and conduct disciplinary proceedings involving violators of the professional standards set forth in the law.

Thus, a Ph.D. in clinical psychology does not allow the possessor to officially "hang out a shingle" and start to practice psychology. While the steps involved in becoming licensed differ somewhat from state to state, there is enough uniformity in the procedures of most states to offer a rough sketch of how the aspiring clinical psychologist would approach this task. Box 13-3 outlines the basic steps involved.

Connecticut was the first state to enact a psychology licensing law; Virginia, Kentucky and Ohio followed suit within 5 years (Carlson, 1978). Today, all fifty states, the District of Columbia, and several Canadian provinces have certification or licensure laws.

As more and more states passed certification or licensing statutes, a number of interstate problems began to emerge. It became obvious that there was a need for an organization to coordinate the activities of the state boards of psychology and to bring about some degree of uniformity in standards and procedures. To answer these needs, the American Association of State Psychology Boards (AASPB) was formed in 1961 at the sixty-ninth APA convention in New York City.

In addition to its coordinating efforts, the AASPB has developed a standardized, objective examination for use by the state boards in examining candidates for licensure. First released in 1964 and frequently revised since then, this Examination for Professional Practice in Psychology is sometimes called the "multistate," or "national," exam because it can be used by all jurisdictions as a part of their overall exam procedure (see Box 13-3). The AASPB also helped to develop a system of *reciprocity* which means that someone certified or licensed in one state can sometimes transfer that credential to some other jurisdiction.

In 1975 the first edition of the *National Register of Health Service Providers in Psychology* was published (Asher, 1975). The *Register* was intended as a listing of psychologists who possessed the necessary training and experience to be considered a "health service provider," defined as "a psychologist, certified/licensed at the independent practice level in his/her state who is duly trained and experienced in the delivery of direct, preventive, assessment, and therapeutic intervention services to the individual whose growth, adjustment or functioning is actually impaired or is demonstrably at high risk of impairment" (Asher, 1975, p. 1). The primary use of the *Register* will be to aid insurance companies and governmental agencies in identifying those psychologists who should be

Box 13-3   "So You Want to Be a Licensed Psychologist"

Imagine that you have just received your Ph.D. or Psy.D. from a clinical training program and are now interested in becoming a licensed or certified clinical psychologist. What are the steps you would have to take? Harrie Hess (1977) notes that the following sequence of hurdles will be encountered in obtaining licensure or certification in most states.

You must first request that the state board of psychology review and accept your credentials to determine your elegibility for examination. Their decision is based on several criteria:

1 **Administrative Requirements**   These do not involve matters of achievement as much as official status. For example, you must have reached a certain age, be a U.S. citizen, and have been a resident in the state for some minimum period. There is not too much to be done about these requirements; you either meet them or you do not. One bit of advice: Don't commit any felonies, engage in treason, or libel your governor. Those activities are judged to be indicative of poor moral character and, besides leaving a lasting smudge on your reputation, may leave you plenty of time to fantasize about licensure or certification while in prison.

2 **Education**   Almost all states require a doctoral degree in psychology from an appropriately accredited university (accreditation in this case refers not to APA approval but to accreditation of the entire university by a recognized accrediting agency). Official graduate and undergraduate transcripts are required.

3 **Experience**   This will usually amount to 1 or 2 years of supervised professional experience in a setting approved by the board. Some of the experience may have to be postdoctoral; letters of reference will be required from your supervisor(s).

If after scrutinizing your credentials the board feels you are elegible for examination, you will be so informed and invited for an exam. Here is what to expect:

1 **Examination Fee**   There is a charge for the examination. The tab for this event varies, but it is usually between $50 and $100.

2 **The Examination**   Many states will use the national exam. It contains about 150 to 200 objective items covering general psychology, (e.g., learning, social, developmental, motivation, and physiology), methodology, applications of psychology, and professional conduct and ethics. Since many candidates will want to practice a certain "specialty" like clinical, school, or industrial psychology, most boards also prepare essay examinations in these areas. You can also expect an oral examination by the board in which almost any material relevant to psychology is fair game.

3 **Reexamination**   If you should fail any part of the exam, you will probably be given another chance at that portion. Most boards feel that twice is enough, however; so if you fail the second time, it might be wise to reconsider the advantages of the family business.

In most states, you will be required to keep your license or certificate up-to-date only by paying a periodic renewal fee. However, some states have begun to require *continuing professional education* (CPE) as a condition for maintaining licensure or certification. Continuing professional education is usually provided in special postdoctoral institutes, seminars, or workshops conducted by some expert in a particular area. The purpose of this activity is to keep the practicing psychologist abreast of current developments and progress in important professional areas. In states requiring CPE, psychologists must be able to document their participation in a certain minimum number of CPE units of instruction. Although psychology has not yet developed its CPE plan to the level of professions like law or medicine, almost all psychologists agree that the future should and will see a definite strengthening of CPE requirements for their field.

considered eligible for reimbursement for delivering mental health services. Of the approximately 24,000 licensed or certified psychologists in the United States in 1975, about 7000 were listed in the first edition of the *Register*. Blue Cross/Blue Shield was the first major insurance carrier to use the *Register* to determine a psychologist's eligibility for reimbursement.

ABPP Certification

Another type of professional regulation exists in the form of certification by the American Board of Professional Psychology (ABPP), which until the late 1960s was known as the American Board of Examiners in Professional Psychology (ABEPP): hence the current phonetic abbreviation (pronounced ā.bĕp). The ABPP was founded in 1947 as a national organization that would certify the professional competence of psychologists. Its certification is signified by the award of a diploma in one of four areas: clinical psychology, counseling psychology, school psychology, or industrial psychology. There are now well over 2000 *diplomates,* the majority of them in the clinical area.

An ABPP diploma is usually considered more prestigious than state licensure, although it carries no greater legal authority. While licensure or certification is taken to signify at least a minimal level of competence, diplomate status is often interpreted as an endorsement of professional expertise, an indication that the person possesses a thorough and masterful knowledge of the field. The diplomate is usually considered a virtuoso, the "first fiddle" or "ace" of the staff. Despite this reputation, Schofield (1964) reported that, in a 1959 survey of diplomates, only 27 percent of the respondents reported direct material benefit as a result of their status.

The requirements for the ABPP diploma are more rigorous than those for licensure or certification. Five years of postdoctoral experience is a prerequisite to take the ABPP examination, which is conducted by a group of diplomates who observe the candidate dealing directly with clinical phenomena (e.g., giving a test or interacting with a psychotherapy client). Evaluation is concentrated on the candidate's knowledge and expertise in the areas of assessment, therapy, research, theory, and the ethics of psychological practice.

Other Forms of Legal Regulation

There has been an interesting by-product of psychology's increasing legal recognition: greater legal scrutiny. For example, the courts have historically been disinclined to pass judgment on what constitutes acceptable psychological treatment. More recently, this reluctance has given way to a greater willingness to evaluate the legality of both psychological and psychiatric care. It is apparent that courts are no longer willing to permit what they see as violations of clients' rights, despite the hazards inherent in the nonexpert evaluation of treatment methods.

A comprehensive review of the legal status of psychological treatments would far exceed our purpose here, but we will highlight three of the most frequently cited legal principles that have been used to challenge some forms of intervention. The first two (right to treatment and informed consent) are usually concerned with institutionalized persons such as mental patients or prison inmates. The third (privileged communication) is more often at issue with outpatient psychotherapy clients.

Right to Treatment   First suggested by Birnbaum (1960), the concept of the right to treatment for patients committed to psychiatric hospitals found legal support in the landmark *Rouse v. Cameron* (1966) decision. Subsequent cases have strengthened this doctrine through due process arguments (*Wyatt v. Stickney,* 1972; *Wyatt v. Aderholt,* 1974). Recently the Supreme Court concluded that a state cannot confine without treatment nondangerous individuals who can survive by themselves or with the help of others outside the institution (*Donaldson v. O'Connor,* 1975). Since *Rouse,* one federal court has expanded the right to treatment for the mentally ill to a right to rehabilitation for imprisoned offenders (*Holt v. Sarver,* 1970). Specifically, the *Holt* court held that the absence of affirmative rehabilitation programs where there are also conditions that militate against reform and rehabilitation may violate constitutional requirements.

Important aspects of the *Wyatt* decision included a ban on involuntary labor by patients unless compensated by the minimum wage and a requirement that the physical and psychological resources to which patients are entitled as constitutional rights be specified. The thrust of *Wyatt* is found in the directive that a patient is entitled to the "least restrictive conditions necessary to achieve the purposes of commitment."

The *Wyatt* case obviously has far-reaching implications for the legally acceptable reinforcers that can be used in hospital and (by implication) prison token economies (see *Clonce v. Richardson,* 1974). While based on the principle of reward, reinforcement programs require an initial state of deprivation to insure their motivational potency. *Wyatt* would require, however, the noncontingent availability of the following constitutionally protected rights:

1   payment of the minimum wage for therapeutic or nontherapeutic institutional work;
2   a right to privacy including a bed, closet, chair, and bedside table;
3   meals meeting minimum daily dietary requirements;
4   the right to visitors, religious services, and clean personal clothing;
5   recreational privileges (e.g., television in the day room); and
6   an open ward and ground privileges when clinically acceptable.

Understandably, psychologists have viewed *Wyatt* with some concern. Berwick and Morris's (1974, p. 436) comment is a typical one: "The field of law is beginning to step in and demand that mental patients get fair treatment; however, they may inadvertently be undermining attempts to establish adequate treatments." There is no doubt that *Wyatt* jeopardizes traditional token economies. At the same time, the decision is not incompatible with all possible behavior modification programs.

Wexler (1973) has recommended the contingent use of "idiosyncratic reinforcers," nonbasic items which certain patients particularly prefer (e.g., eating hard-boiled rather than soft-boiled eggs; watching *Kojak* rather than

Columbo). Token economies utilizing idiosyncratic reinforcers would probably be legally permissible because, by definition, idiosyncratic reinforcers are not the same as general rights. Another alternative (Wexler, 1974a) would be to continue to use the "*Wyatt* basics" as to-be-earned reinforcers but to require fully informed consent of all participants in the program (see below). One problem with this solution is that courts have held that informed consent to "drastic therapies" can be revoked at any time. This requirement would permit residents to convert contingent privileges into noncontingent rights whenever they wish, thereby depriving the program of its motivational impact.

Informed Consent   The claim that institutionalized persons have a right to treatment is complicated by the suggestion that they also may have a right to refuse it (Damich, 1974). Operationally, an individual's control over her or his treatment often takes the form of giving or withholding informed consent. Full informed consent involves several elements including full specifications of the nature of treatment, a description of its purpose, risks, and likely outcomes, advisement that consent may be terminated at any time without prejudice to the individual, and demonstration of a capacity to consent. Obtaining written informed consent is usually required for treatments of an experimental, intrusive, or aversive nature (e.g., psychosurgery: *Kaimowitz and Doe v. Department of Mental Health,* 1973, or apomorphine-based conditioning: *Knecht v. Gillman,* 1973).

At least one court (*Kaimowitz*) has concluded that the process of institutionalization affects an inmate's decision-making abilities to the extent that truly voluntary informed consent cannot be obtained from an involuntarily confined individual. The court claimed that neither knowledge of the process nor voluntary consent could be ensured with institutionalized persons and held that, in principle, participation in programs without necessary subject knowledge and voluntariness was coercive and therefore illegal.

As yet there is no legal doctrine allowing a patient to reject all rehabilitation or refuse all but the most preferred mode of treatment (Wexler, 1974a), but there is clear precedent that patients can disapprove methods which (1) violate their privacy (Spece, 1972), (2) are unduly drastic (Damich, 1974), or (3) are no more than cruel and unusual punishment (*Knecht v. Gillman*). Any extension of the reasoning of the *Kaimowitz* court could result in a doctrine that institutionalization robs the inmate of volitional decision making with respect to participation in less drastic treatments such as group therapy or token economies. Wexler (1974b) has commented on the irony of such a development: "If involuntary confinement itself creates coercion, administering any therapy to the patient violates his right *not* to be treated without consent—which obviously vitiates entirely the right *to* treatment" (p. 679). From the standpoint of the mental health profession, the problem might be mitigated by attempts to replace the consensual model of treatment with the more ethically appealing contract model (Schwitzgebel, 1974) or with a hierarchy of protections requiring differential levels of consent (Davison & Stuart, 1975).

Privileged Communication   Numerous state legislatures have passed laws that establish a general psychotherapist-client *privilege*. Privilege is a legal right imposed to protect the client from public disclosure of confidences by the therapist without the client's permission. In function, privilege is very much like confidentiality. The main difference is that confidentiality is an ethical obligation of a profession, not a legal requirement. The current proliferation of therapist-client privilege statutes is due mainly to the growing recognition that confidentiality of treatment is essential to the success of psychotherapy. Judge Edgerton of the U.S. Court of Appeals in the District of Columbia, quoting from Guttmacher and Weihofen's *Psychiatry and the Law,* emphasized the necessity of confidentiality for psychotherapy (*Taylor v. United States,* 1955):

> The psychiatric patient confides more utterly than anyone else in the world. He exposes to the therapist not only what his words directly express; he lays bare his entire self, his dreams, his fantasies, his sins, and his shame. Most patients who undergo psychotherapy know that this is what will be expected of them, and that they cannot get the help except on that condition. . . . It would be too much to expect them to do so if they knew that all they say—and all that the psychiatrist learns from what they say—may be revealed to the whole world from a witness stand. (p. 58)

Just as the law of some states recognizes this special sort of privilege, it recognizes several exceptions to it, the most common of which are: (1) where a psychologist and/or psychiatrist determine(s) that a client is in need of commitment to a hospital, (2) where a client has undergone a court-ordered examination and a judge has informed the client that his or her communications would not be privileged, and (3) where a patient introduces his or her mental condition as an element of a defense against a criminal conviction (Benthall-Nietzel, 1975).

Another area in which confidentiality is not legally required and in fact where violation of confidentiality may be legally mandated is where a client communicates to a therapist the intention to commit an unlawful or harmful act. This exception presents a real dilemma for the psychotherapist who, by the open and trusting character of the therapeutic relationship, may encourage expressions of violence or violent impulses from clients. The courts have held quite consistently that privilege does not apply where its use would conceal information that is necessary for public safety or the proper administration of justice (Benthall-Nietzel, 1975). This brings us to a practical question: Should a therapist who has heard a client threaten to harm another person be required to warn the intended victim, the victim's relatives, or the police of possible danger?

This question was raised in the now famous case of *Tarasoff v. Regents of University of California,* and the answer seems to be "yes." In the *Tarasoff* case, a couple sued the University of California, psychotherapists employed by the University, and the campus police to recover damages for the murder of their daughter (a UC coed) by a client of one of the psychotherapists. A lower court sustained the defendants' answers to the suit, but the Supreme Court reversed that decision.

Here are the facts of the case. The client, Poddar, told his psychotherapist, Dr. Lawrence Moore, of his intention to kill a young woman, Tatiana Tarasoff. The therapist informed his superior, Dr. Harvey Powelson, of this threat, and the campus police were called and requested in writing to confine Poddar. This they did, but shortly thereafter they released Poddar, concluding that he was rational and believing his promise that he would stay away from the Tarasoff's home. He didn't. After terminating his relationship with his therapist, Poddar killed Tatiana. He was later convicted of murder. No one had warned the woman or her parents of the threat. In fact, Powelson had asked the police to return Moore's letter and further ordered that all copies of the letter and Moore's therapy notes be destroyed and that Poddar not be confined.

In reaching its decision, the court weighed the importance of confidential therapy relationships against society's interest in protecting itself from dangerous persons. The balance was struck in favor of society's protection. The therapist's situation was analogized to that of a physician who would be held liable for a failure to warn persons threatened with a contagious disease.

PROFESSIONAL ETHICS

A code of ethics for any profession is a set of rules or principles which either encourages or forbids certain kinds of professional conduct. Ethics are normative statements; they are maxims for virtuousness. Ethical codes justify the selection of certain goals and patterns of behavior. All professions have developed ethical principles that suggest the proper way for the professional to behave toward the public they serve and toward each other. As psychology moved into its professional era, it needed to articulate the principles which could guide its members.

Psychology's first code of ethics was published in 1953 (APA, 1953). One of the unique features of this code was the manner by which it was developed. True to their empirical foundations, psychologists submitted to an APA committee a large number of "critical incidents" which involved some ethical dilemma that had actually occurred in a professional context. Using an inductive content analysis of this raw, real-life material, the committee distilled a comprehensive code to guide psychology in its early struggle with professional ethics. The original code was summarized into a set of general principles 6 years later (APA, 1959). After this version had been in use for 3 years, it was amended and formally adopted (APA, 1963). It served as the official ethical code until 1977, when it was again revised.

In 1967, the APA published its *Casebook on Ethical Standards of Psychologists*. It contains a restatement of the 1963 ethical principles as well as actual case material drawn from the discussions of the APA's Committee on Scientific and Professional Ethics and Conduct between 1959 and 1962. The facts of these case decisions have been disguised in order to protect the anonymity of both the innocent and the guilty. The *Casebook* (which is currently being updated) is intended to serve as a guide for how ethical principles are applied to real cases. It is the source which most psychologists study in order to educate themselves about the profession's ethical standards.

The 1977 code of ethics contains a preamble and nine principles covering all the primary areas of psychological activities: research, academic standards, therapy, testing, and diagnosis. All the principles are relevant to clinical psychologists in one way or another:

Preamble

Psychologists respect the dignity and worth of the individual and honor the preservation and protection of fundamental human rights. They are committed to increasing knowledge of human behavior and of people's understanding of themselves and others and to the utilization of such knowledge for the promotion of human welfare. While pursuing these endeavors, they make every effort to protect the welfare of those who seek their services or of any human being or animal that may be the object of study. They use their skills only for purposes consistent with these values and do not knowingly permit their misuse by others. While demanding for themselves freedom of inquiry and communication, psychologists accept the responsibility this freedom requires: competence, objectivity in the application of skills and concern for the best interests of clients, colleagues, and society in general. In the pursuit of these ideals, psychologists subscribe to principles in the following areas: 1. Responsibility, 2. Competence, 3. Moral and Legal Standards, 4. Public Statements, 5. Confidentiality, 6. Welfare of the Consumer, 7. Professional Relationships, 8. Utilization of Assessment Techniques, and 9. Pursuit of Research Activities.

Principle 1   Responsibility

In their commitment to the understanding of human behavior, psychologists value objectivity and integrity, and in providing services they maintain the highest standards of their profession. They accept responsibility for the consequences of their work and make every effort to insure that their services are used appropriately.

Principle 2   Competence

The maintenance of high standards of professional competence is a responsibility shared by all psychologists in the interest of the public and the profession as a whole. Psychologists recognize the boundaries of their competence and the limitations of their techniques and only provide services, use techniques, or offer opinions as professionals that meet recognized standards. Psychologists maintain knowledge of current scientific and professional information related to the services they render.

Principle 3   Moral and Legal Standards

Psychologists' moral, ethical and legal standards of behavior are a personal matter to the same degree as they are for any other citizen, except as these may compromise the fulfillment of their professional responsibilities, or reduce the trust in psychology or psychologists held by the general public. Regarding their own behavior, psychologists should be aware of the prevailing community standards and of the possible impact upon the quality of professional services provided by their conformity to or deviation from these standards. Psychologists are also aware of the possible impact of their public behavior upon the ability of colleagues to perform their professional duties.

Principle 4   Public Statements

Public statements, announcements of services, and promotional activities of psychologists serve the purpose of providing sufficient information to aid the consumer public in making informed judgments and choices. Psychologists represent accurately and objectively their professional qualifications, affiliations, and functions, as well as those of the institutions or organizations with which they or the statements may be associated. In public statements providing psychological information or professional opinions or providing information about the availability of psychological products and services, psychologists take full account of the limits and uncertainties of present psychological knowledge and techniques.

Principle 5   Confidentiality

Safeguarding information about an individual that has been obtained by the psychologist in the course of his teaching, practice, or investigation is a primary obligation of the psychologist. Such information is not communicated to others unless certain important conditions are met.

Principle 6   Welfare of the Consumer

Psychologists respect the integrity and protect the welfare of the people and groups with whom they work. When there is a conflict of interest between the client and the psychologist's employing institution, psychologists clarify the nature and direction of their loyalties and responsibilities and keep all parties informed of their commitments. Psychologists fully inform consumers as to the purpose and nature of an evaluative, treatment, educational or training procedure, and they freely acknowledge that clients, students, or participants in research have freedom of choice with regard to participation.

Principle 7   Professional Relationships

Psychologists act with due regard for the needs, special competencies and obligations of their colleagues in psychology and other professions. Psychologists respect the prerogatives and obligations of the institutions or organizations with which they are associated.

Principle 8   Utilization of Assessment Techniques

In the development, publication, and utilization of psychological assessment techniques, psychologists observe relevant APA standards. Persons examined have the right to know the results, the interpretations made, and, where appropriate, the original data on which final judgments were based. Test users avoid imparting unnecessary information which would compromise test security, but they provide requested information that explains the basis for decisions that may adversely affect that person or that person's dependents.

Principle 9   Pursuit of Research Activities

The decision to undertake research should rest upon a considered judgment by the individual psychologist about how best to contribute to psychological science and to human welfare. Psychologists carry out their investigations with respect for the people who participate and with concern for their dignity and welfare.

Box 13-4   An Example of an Ethical Dilemma

The following case history is drawn from the APA *Casebook* on ethical standards (1967, pp. 29–30). It deals with the difficult issue of a clinician's obligation to protect the welfare of a client on the one hand while remaining sensitive to the social interests inherent in criminal conduct on the other hand. It raises a somewhat different problem than the one involved in the *Tarasoff* case.

Case 6A

A fully trained clinical psychologist in private practice was referred a patient for psychotherapeutic treatment because of a "near nervous breakdown." The background of the patient revealed many stressful and traumatic circumstances. After a few visits the patient admitted to having committed murder, something which weighed heavily on his conscience. The psychologist wrote to the committee for advice, pointing out that no ethical principle fitted the case exactly, the closest being one dealing with situations in which knowledge and intent are revealed but in which an act has not yet been committed. The psychologist wrote further as follows:

> I find myself in a very uncomfortable position of not knowing whether accepting him in a treatment basis would be in effect condoning his act. It is possible to understand the internal pressures and the dynamics which led him to behave as he did. Nor am I sure when he says that he thinks he ought to make public what he has done and bear punishment for it that it is my responsibility to encourage this action. Theoretically I know that I should help him to clarify his own thinking to the point where he can take the course of action which he deems most suitable. However, as he himself states, not only is he involved, but the public knowledge of his act would have to be borne by his wife and daughters. From a psychotherapeutic point of view there is no doubt that this man is in intense psychic pain and regardless of what course he decides to follow I suppose that I could justify seeing him in a professional role in an attempt to make him more comfortable. Yet I do not find it possible to completely encapsulate his act. There is no indication that he is suspected of the act or that he would ever do it again.
>
> I am afraid that my own ethical values and social conscience are being intruded, and in a sense I suppose I am asking whether, in this case, they should not be. I do hope that I have outlined the situation clearly enough that your committee can help me to ascertain my ethical responsibilities as a psychologist.

Opinion

The committee felt the client should be accepted in therapy without condoning his act, but that the decision in such a case rested with the psychologist involved. In reaching such a decision, it is necessary to take into account responsibilities to both the profession and the community, in addition to recognizing the legal considerations as well. Since the laws in the different states vary with respect to privileged communication, the committee recommended as well that the psychologist confronted with such a question consult an attorney as to what his legal obligations might be under the particular circumstances.

Most clinicians believe in and are guided by the principles in this code. As exemplified by the case presented in Box 13-4, they take great pains to deal with complex and ethically ambiguous situations in accordance with the highest standards of professional conduct. On those relatively rare occasions when, as a fallible human being, a clinician or other psychologist makes an unwise choice and behaves in a questionable manner, she or he is subject to censure by local, state, and national bodies whose task it is to deal with violations of ethical practice.

Once a complaint of unethical behavior has been brought against an APA member and the appropriate committee has decided that the conduct in question was in fact unethical, the question of punishment must be confronted. The most severe APA sanction is to dismiss the offender from the association and inform the entire membership of this action. This penalty is embarrassing for most transgressors, humiliating for a few, but seldom devastating for any. In the case of extreme or repeated unethical conduct, a psychologist could be threatened with the loss of his or her license or certificate through action of the board of psychology in the state where the psychologist practices.

Research Ethics

Ethical principle 9 and its corollaries make the psychologist responsible for the welfare of research subjects, both animal and human. This direct statement on research ethics was quite clear in the 1963 code as well, but, because of the increasing public concern over violations of research subjects' human rights and new research regulations from the Department of Health, Education, and Welfare, the APA found it necessary to supplement its ethical standards with a special, more detailed set of principles covering research with human participants.

Once again the process of developing the principles was an empirical and participatory one. Psychologists supplied raw materials involving ethical problems encountered in their own research activities. An ad hoc Committee on Ethical Standards in Psychological Research assembled those data and from them drafted a set of principles which were presented to the APA membership in 1971. Following extensive discussion and suggestions by psychologists, the principles were revised and endorsed in final form in December of 1972. They were published with accompanying discussion and illustrative case material in *Ethical Principles in the Conduct of Research with Human Participants* (APA, 1973). The ten principles are:

> **Principle 1**   In planning a study the investigator has the personal responsibility to make careful evaluation of its ethical acceptability, taking into account these Principles for research with human beings. To the extent that this appraisal, weighing scientific and humane values, suggests a deviation from any Principle, the investigator incurs an increasingly serious obligation to seek ethical advice and to observe more stringent safeguards to protect the rights of the human research participant.
> **Principle 2**   Responsibility for the establishment and maintenance of acceptable ethical practice in research always remains with the individual investigator. The investigator is also responsible for the ethical treatment of research participants by collaborators, assistants, students, and employees, all of whom, however, incur parallel obligations.
> **Principle 3**   Ethical practice requires the investigator to inform the participant of all features of the research that reasonably might be expected to influence willingness to participate, and to explain all other aspects of the research about which the participant inquires. Failure to make full disclosure gives added emphasis to the investigator's responsibility to protect the welfare and dignity of the research participant.
> **Principle 4**   Openness and honesty are essential characteristics of the relationship between investigator and research participant. When the methodological requirements of a study necessitate concealment or deception, the investigator is required

to ensure the participant's understanding of the reasons for this action and to restore the quality of the relationship with the investigator.

Principle 5 Ethical research practice requires the investigator to respect the individual's freedom to decline to participate in research or to discontinue participation at any time. The obligation to protect this freedom requires special vigilance when the investigator is in a position of power over the participant. The decision to limit this freedom increases the investigator's responsibility to protect the participant's dignity and welfare.

Principle 6 Ethically acceptable research begins with the establishment of a clear and fair agreement between the investigator and the research participant that clarifies the responsibilities of each. The investigator has the obligation to honor all promises and commitments included in that agreement.

Principle 7 The ethical investigator protects participants from physical and mental discomfort, harm and danger. If the risk of such consequences exists, the investigator is required to inform the participant of that fact, secure consent before proceeding, and take all possible measures to minimize distress. A research procedure may not be used if it is likely to cause serious and lasting harm to participants.

Principle 8 After the data are collected, ethical practice requires the investigator to provide the participant with a full clarification of the nature of the study and to remove any misconceptions that may have arisen. Where scientific or humane values justify delaying or withholding information, the investigator acquires a special responsibility to assure that there are no damaging consequences for the participant.

Principle 9 Where research procedures may result in undesirable consequences for the participant, the investigator has the responsibility to detect and remove or correct these consequences, including, where relevant, long-term aftereffects.

Principle 10 Information obtained about the research participants during the course of an investigation is confidential. When the possibility exists that others may obtain access to such information, ethical research practice requires that this possibility, together with the plans for protecting confidentiality, be explained to the participants as a part of the procedure for obtaining informed consent.

These research principles continue to evoke heated discussions among psychologists because they are applied to questions which defy easy answers. For example, when is deception in research justified? How much information should participants be given about their research performance when that information may be threatening to their self-esteem? For how long after an experiment should researchers be held responsible for participants' welfare? It is comforting to know that in many instances, with or without codified ethics, most psychologists agree on what constitutes proper conduct by a researcher. But in those instances where honest and honorable psychologists might disagree on the ethical course of action, the guidance provided by the above principles is useful and necessary.

PROFESSIONAL INDEPENDENCE

The clinical psychologist finds it necessary or helpful to consult and collaborate with people from other professions in many aspects of clinical practice. Those professionals with whom clinical psychologists most often find themselves working include educators, attorneys, ministers, social workers, nurses, physicians and other types of psychologists.

For the most part, psychology's interprofessional relationships are healthy, profitable, and characterized by good will and respect. The most obvious sign of this harmony between professionals is the frequency of referrals made across groups. A teacher confronted with a child whose classroom misbehavior seems to be related to a serious emotional or family problem is likely to suggest that the family consult a psychologist. Psychologists, on the other hand, may encounter clients who may be in legal trouble and, rather than offer legal advice, will urge such clients to hire an attorney.

It is unfortunate that not all interprofessional relationships have been this serene. Psychologists have had a considerable degree of friction with physicians, particularly psychiatrists. In fact, one of clinical psychology's most lingering problems in its efforts at professionalization has been its usually wary, often stormy relationships with the medical profession. Garfield (1965) observes that, as early as 1917, psychiatrists were critical of psychologists, particularly "those who have termed themselves 'clinical psychologists'" and work in "so-called 'psychological clinics'" and provide "so-called expert testimony" ("Activities of Clinical Psychologists," 1917).

There have been two main sources of friction between clinical psychology and psychiatry. The first of these involved the independent practice of psychotherapy by psychologists (Hunt, 1965). More recently, the squabble has concentrated on psychologists' inclusion in insurance policies covering treatment for mental disorders. Although the two controversies are closely related, we should look at them individually in order to understand the basis and development of each.

Independent Practice of Psychotherapy   As long as psychologists confined themselves to research, consultation, and testing, physicians were content and did not interfere with these activities. Psychologists, by the same token, found no problem with the fact that physicians must be the authority on matters of physical disorder or organic treatments such as medication, electroconvulsive therapy, and surgery. Disagreement, when it came, centered on psychotherapy, which both professions offered to the public. As we saw in Chapter 2, when psychologists began to assert the right to engage in the independent practice of psychotherapy, psychiatrists objected and insisted that a psychotherapist must either be a physician or be under the supervision of a physician.

Sundberg, Tyler and Taplin (1973) provide a fair summary of the rationale for each position. First, from the psychiatrists' point of view:

> The treatment of human illness of all kinds traditionally and legally has been the responsibility of medical practitioners. Only the physician can be responsible for the diagnosis and treatment of mental illness. Physicians are experts on the functioning of the whole man, and it is always very difficult to disentangle the "mental" from the

"physical." The medical profession welcomes the appropriate utilization of the psychological skills of other professional groups as long as they are under the supervision of physicians. Furthermore, among physicians it is the psychiatrist who is particularly competent by training and experience to deal with mental illness. (p. 511)

Now the psychologists' response:

Psychologists by training and experience are qualified to deal with psychological problems, that is, problems that involve such processes as learning, motivation, personal development, and interpersonal relations. Granting psychiatric and medical responsibility for cases of organic disorder and psychosis, there remains over and above these a tremendous public need for psychological assistance. When psychologists have good training and experience, it is irrelevant and demeaning for them to be supervised by physicians regarding psychological matters. Moreover, many psychologists resent being excluded from the major American psychoanalytic associations, which through control by medical men in the early days restricted membership to those having the M.D. degree. This was done in spite of Freud's denial that medical training was important in psychoanalysis (Freud, 1950) and his defense of nonmedical colleagues. This restriction has been maintained in spite of the great contributions to psychoanalysis of distinguished nonmedical persons such as Anna Freud, Theodor Reik, Otto Rank, Erich Fromm, and Erik Erikson. (pp. 511–512)

One interesting historical footnote to this argument reveals that psychologists themselves were at one time opposed to practicing psychotherapy independently. This fact is often forgotten or overlooked by psychologists, but in 1949 the APA discouraged the practice of psychotherapy by psychologists who were not in collaboration with psychiatrists (Goldenberg, 1973). Listen to Shakow on this topic: "The leadership in therapy naturally rests in the hands of the psychiatrist because of his medical background, with its social and legally recognized responsibilities for treatment, and his major concern with this problem" (Shakow, 1948, p. 517).

History also reveals that, while psychologists reconsidered their position on the independent practice of psychotherapy (APA, 1958), psychiatrists did not. In fact, the American Medical Association (1954) adopted an official policy that psychotherapy was a medical procedure to be performed only by medically trained personnel. The basic strategy of the AMA in this battle was to oppose state legislation that would result in the certification and licensure of psychologists. As we have seen, this strategy was unsuccessful, a fact for which most clinical psychologists are very grateful. Today, in almost all parts of the country, clinicians are permitted by law to practice psychotherapy without interference from the medical establishment.

Indeed, to everyone's benefit, relations between psychologists and psychiatrists in many areas have improved considerably over the years. We seem to have entered a period of détente. Psychiatrists have increasingly come to accept psychologists as professionals and are less likely to treat them with the condescension that was so characteristic of earlier days. For their part, psychologists have shed some of their defensive armor and are not as prone to feel that they constantly must repel the assaults of psychiatric bullies. Both fields have been enhanced by the growing number of well-qualified persons who have entered the two professions, and mutual learning experiences are increasingly likely.

National Health Insurance Those psychiatrists who still oppose the practice of psychotherapy by psychologists usually do so quietly. However, the medical profession is not nearly as muted about its opposition to the inclusion of psychologists as health care providers eligible for reimbursement under any national health insurance plan. Here, the issue of psychology as a fully autonomous profession which can function without medical supervision is no longer merely a philosophical one; it now has clear economic implications.

The United States is the last of the industrialized countries which has not developed a national health insurance program. Although debate continues over the merits of private versus public insurance plans, it is virtually a foregone conclusion that within the next 5 years this country will have national health insurance. Thus the question is not *whether* there will be national health insurance, but what form will it take and what services will be reimbursable. A primary question is whether mental health services will be included.

Many members of Congress, viewing the high cost of Medicare, Medicaid, and the Civilian Health and Medical Program of the Uniformed Services (CHAMPUS), are concerned that including services for emotional and mental illness will make the system too expensive. Others are convinced that a truly comprehensive health plan must compensate services for emotional and mental illness. Advocates for including mental health services point to recent data showing that a *single session of psychotherapy* reduced subsequent utilization of medical resources by 60 percent among the recipients. There was about a 75 percent reduction in medical utilization among patients receiving two to eight sessions of psychotherapy (Cummings, 1977; see Olbrisch, 1977, for a review of additional data that support the conclusion that psychotherapy has a positive and cost-effective effect on physical health). Thus, the argument goes that, far from being economically disadvantageous, the cost of reimbursing psychotherapy services is likely to be more than offset by the savings in utilization of medical resources which would be realized.

The question of more parochial interest to psychologists and psychiatrists is what type of providers of mental health services will be eligible for insurance reimbursement (this is sometimes called "third-party payment").

There is no doubt that, like licensure in the fifties and sixties, inclusion in national health insurance is the emotional issue of the seventies for psychologists. Much of the proposed legislation dealing with national health insurance would provide reimbursement for mental health services provided by psychologists *only* when they are treating patients contacted through medical referral and

"Today, I'm not going to talk about my goddam mother. I'm going to talk about my goddam insurance company."

Cartoon 13-1   Drawing by Booth; © 1974, The New Yorker Magazine, Inc.

when they are under medical supervision. Most clinical psychologists regard this as an intolerable situation for a profession which aspires to full autonomy and propose instead what is termed "freedom-of-choice" legislation which would make services rendered by physicians or other *nonmedical* mental health professionals eligible for reimbursement.

It is worth noting that not all psychologists approve of psychology being included under health insurance benefits. Some, like Albee (1975), argue that reimbursing the cost of psychotherapy services by any profession through health insurance reinforces the incorrect belief that behavior problems are due to an illness and consequently directs resources away from needed social change and prevention programs (see Meltzer, 1975, for a similar discussion). Albee (1977) has also argued that, since it is the middle and upper classes that most frequently seek psychotherapy, the inclusion of this service under a federal insurance plan would require a regressive tax, a subsidy of the rich by the poor (see also Crowell, 1977).

The current status of psychologists' place in national health insurance is difficult to summarize because the situation is changing rapidly at both the state and federal levels. Crowell (1977) has reported that there are more than twenty national health insurance bills before Congress, each with different provisions for reimbursable services and providers. There is certainly a precedent for reimbursement of independent psychologist practitioners. Dörken's (1977) review revealed that "under disability, health insurance, and medical service plans, 24 states and the District of Columbia (including California, New York, Ohio, Michigan, and New Jersey), covering 60 percent of the population, had by December 1976 enacted statutes providing for direct access to and free choice of licensed/certified psychologists for covered benefits" (p. 273). The following additional recent developments have been of particular importance to clinical psychologists:

1 The Health Insurance Association of America approved a model Psychologist Direct Recognition bill intended to assist the other twenty-six states to secure freedom-of-choice legislation.
2 The Rehabilitation Act of 1973, PL 93-112, provides parity for licensed psychologists and physicians in both assessment and treatment services.
3 Services provided by clinical psychologists are covered under both the Federal Employee Health Benefits Act (PL 93-363) and the Federal Work Injuries Compensation Program (PL 94-212).
4 Licensed clinical psychologists with 2 years of supervised experience are recognized as *independent* health-care providers under CHAMPUS, the federal program that covers more than 6 million beneficiaries in all fifty states and the District of Columbia.

On the other hand, there are several important medical programs that do not recognize psychologists as independent health-care providers. Neither Medicare nor Medicaid includes psychologists as independent practitioners (Deleon, 1977), although there have been some recent proposals that would amend these programs to include psychologists. Nevertheless, according to Deleon (1977), "even a cursory review of the various national health insurance proposals, regardless of the philosophical or economic constituency whose interests they reflect, quickly indicates that there is very little enthusiasm for treating the nonphysician health care provider as an independent and autonomous professional. Practically every bill incorporates the language of our Medicare legislation, and under this act, psychological services are reimbursable only if they are under the direct supervision of a physician" (p. 267).

The medical profession has coined the term "medical psychotherapy" to refer to the type of mental health services that it feels should be eligible for compensation. This term is interpreted by psychology as a political maneuver intended to insure that physicians are identified as the appropriate providers of psychotherapeutic services. The counterargument by psychologists is that, in the vast majority of cases, there is nothing "medical" about psychotherapy.

Debate over the final form of national health insurance (NHI) is sure to continue for some time to come. And well it should, for whatever form it takes, health insurance will have a tremendous impact on the delivery and quality of mental health services in this country. For our part, we are impressed by the advantages of including psychologists in national health insurance and are convinced that there are no real advantages to be gained by excluding them. It is also important to recognize that one of psychology's most important contributions to a national system of health care would be to help evaluate the consequences of implementing the program itself. As evidence of this commitment to evaluative research, the APA established in 1976 a Task Force on Continuing Evaluation in National Health Insurance. This group published sixteen principles that it believed should guide the development of any health insurance legislation. The underlying sentiment of these principles was expressed in the introduction to the Task Force report in the April 1978 issue of the *American Psychologist:*

> The probable advent of NHI provides psychology and the other health professions with a remarkable opportunity to display professional maturity and leadership in also urging Congress to build into the NHI provisions for systematic evaluation of covered services and reimbursement only for effective treatments and programs. In the vast majority of cases, the only really ethical position lies in providing the public with effective services whose effectiveness is under systematic evaluation. It is unlikely that any health profession would in the long run lose by affirming its confidence in its ability to provide effective services, and the public could only gain. (p. 305)

PERILS OF PROFESSIONALIZATION

Have the first 3 decades of clinical psychology's professional era strengthened the field by making it into a better profession, or have they simply made it more like a guild which employs a proliferation of meaningless membership criteria? Has clinical psychology become a better profession by erecting standards of training, competence, and service, or is it merely a more closed profession? We shall consider such questions in these final pages.

The ultimate justification for the professionalization of any discipline is that the public will benefit from the standards that define and govern entry into the profession. Of course these restrictions will also benefit members of the profession in that they control the profession's size and reduce somewhat the possibilities of competition. There should be no objection to this latter function when it is a by-product of protecting the public from unqualified practitioners. The problem arises when the priorities of a profession are reversed, so that the promotion of its own members takes precedence over its obligation to the public.

As early as 1951, Fillmore Sanford, then the executive secretary of the APA, was aware of the perils of professionalization. In an effort to call psychology's full attention to its obligations as a profession, Sanford proposed a list of sixteen principles that should be considered "the criteria of a good profession" (Sanford, 1951, p. 667). He hoped that the sixteen criteria would serve as a guide for the development of psychology as a socially useful and responsive profession. Sandford's criteria of a good profession were:

1 A good profession is one that is motivated by a sense of social responsibility.

2 A good profession is one sufficiently perceptive of its place in society to guide continually its practices and policies so they conform to the best and changing interests of that society.

3 A good profession is one that is continually on guard lest it represent itself as able to render services that are beyond its demonstrable competence.

4 A good profession is one that is continually seeking to find its unique pattern of competence and that concentrates its efforts on the rendering of the unique service based on its pattern of competencies.

5 A good profession is one that devotes relatively little of its energy to "guild" functions, to the building of its own in-group strength, and relatively much of its energy to the serving of its social function.

6 The good profession is one that engages in rational and non-invidious relations with other professions having related or overlapping competencies and common purposes.

7 A good profession is one that devotes a proportion of its energies to the discovery of new knowledge.

8 The good profession is one in which there are good channels of communication between the discoverers of knowledge and the appliers of knowledge.

9 The good profession is one in which its discoverers of knowledge are not relegated to positions of second-rate status.

10 The good profession is one that is free of non-functional entrance requirements.

11 The good profession is one in which preparatory training is validly related to the ultimate function of the members of the profession.

12 A good profession is one in which the material benefits accruing to its members are proportional to social contributions.

13 The good profession is one whose members are socially and financially accessible to the public.

14 The good profession has a code of ethics designed primarily to protect the client and only secondarily to protect the members of the profession.

15 A good profession is one that facilitates the continuing education and training of all its members.

16 A good profession is one that is continually concerned with the validity of its techniques and procedures.

Sanford's statement remains timely. Although it was written in a prospective spirit as an idealistic vision of what psychology should strive for, it can be used retrospectively today as a yardstick against which one can measure what psychology has become.

The first two criteria deal with the need for psychologists to adjust to social needs and changes. At several points throughout this text, we have emphasized that clinical psychology has been especially responsive to the social and political events that have surrounded it. As we saw in Chapter 2, the growth of the profession itself was a reaction to social upheaval and virtually unprecedented human needs. In a similar fashion, the evolution of such disparate psychological activities as assessment, psychotherapy, community psychology, and social-learning interventions has roots in the fact that psychology has always been well-tuned to the current *Zeitgeist*.

Several criteria (i.e., 3, 4, 13, and 14) are concerned with the matter of professional ethics. Psychologists are justifiably proud of their code of ethics because it remains the only set of professional standards that was developed with explicitly empirical procedures. This pride has not fostered complacency, however, and the code continues to be revised and updated.

Three of the criteria (10, 11, and 15) involve issues of professional training, an area with which psychologists have been described as having a "breathless preoccupation." Clinical psychology has made a full commitment to the development of training programs that are most appropriate for the roles which clinicians are asked to fill. While value is still placed on the traditional Boulder model of training, it is valued in the context of constant experimentation with other systems of training intended to provide an adequate number of psychologists who concentrate on delivering clinical services. The one area which has lagged behind somewhat is continuing professional education (CPE). Progress is being made on this front, however, and we are confident that within the next 5 years a majority of states will be mandating CPE as a condition for the licensing of psychologists.

The sixth of Sanford's criteria is directly related to our recent discussion of interprofessional relationships. We are sure that this issue, especially as it relates to psychiatrists and clinical psychologists, will continue to be the focus of much attention. An adequate response to our sometimes troubled relations with psychiatry is likely to require a balancing act of some sort. On the one hand, clinicians must continue to search for new opportunities to collaborate and cooperate with *all* professions. At the same time, to be a first-rate profession, psychology must also be a free profession, unwilling to enter into any Faustian pact where the goodwill of the medical profession is purchased by acquiescence to its domination of psychology.

The greatest number of criteria discuss the priorities of the profession, the essential contributions which it should make to the public. There can be no doubt when reading this list that Sanford, like many psychologists before and after him, chose to affirm research and the advancement of new knowledge as psychology's primary activity. It is often argued that the creation of basic knowledge is the one function that separates the professional from the technician, who applies methods based on existing knowledge. This judgment may be most accurate for a new profession like clinical psychology, where "the fewer its techniques of demonstrable utility, the more of its resources it should devote to research" (Sanford, 1951, p. 669).

THE FUTURE OF CLINICAL PSYCHOLOGY

Finally, we have reached that point where authors are obliged to become seers who dazzle readers with a host of predictions about the future of their chosen profession. While we cannot completely resist the temptation of trying to tell the future, we hope to avoid the excesses of forecasting that can sometimes bedevil the incautious commentator. Our outlook on clinical psychology's future would emphasize the following points:

1 We are confident that the number of clinicians will continue to increase, although at a slower pace than has been true in recent years.

2 Accompanying this increase will be a broadening of the professional roles which clinicians will fill. We refer to this trend as "boundary stretching" and see a continuing tendency for psychologists to involve themselves in a great number of activities.

3 Clinical psychology will probably take on more of what has sometimes been called a "consumer orientation." This trend is already apparent in the large number of self-help groups that have been formed, the emphasis on professional accountability to clients, and the expectation that psychologists must develop their own standards as health service providers. The result of all these movements is that clinicians will constantly need to evaluate the effectiveness of their interventions. A recurring motif of a panel of prominent psychologists asked to speculate on psychology's future was that program evaluation would be an increasingly important and frequent activity of psychologists (Wertheimer, Barclay, Cook, Kiesler, Koch, Riegel, Rorer, Senders, Smith, & Sparling, 1978). The psychologist as researcher will always have a place in the future.

4 There appears to be considerable enthusiasm for developing innovative training programs that prepare psychologists for certain "specialty" areas like drug abuse and alcoholism, geriatrics, rural mental health, mental retardation, and community mental health. While we do not support the philosophy of "specialized" training in Ph.D. programs and are skeptical about the longevity of these efforts, they are almost certain to exert a significant influence on clinical training in the immediate future.

5 Tomorrow's growing emphasis on evaluation may be accompanied by some abandonment of a "brand name" approach to psychotherapy. As research indicates the effectiveness of behavior change techniques regardless of their theoretical origins, clinicians will probably find little advantage in identifying themselves as "behaviorists," "gestaltists," or "analysts." Some form of general systems theory may come to replace the narrower, pathology-oriented theories which most clinicians have embraced in the past, thereby leading to a further breakdown of psychotherapy "schools."

6 We doubt that there will be a steady progression in clinical psychology's general orientation toward intervention. It is more probable that, as Rappaport and Chinsky (1974) have observed, the philosophies and goals of intervention will move in cycles, stressing certain objectives in one era and rediscovering at another time the value of previous concepts. Current events provide the best illustration of this cyclical quality. The emphasis of the past 15 years has been on community mental health, an obvious reaction to the almost exclusive concern with the individual that typified the medical model of previous years. Now the pendulum is swinging back again; our attentions are turning inward. The current emphasis on personal autonomy, the pursuit of self-actualization and improvement, a renewed interest in spiritual life, and related trends all testify to the fact that efforts to enhance the growth of individuals have once again become a major goal of mental health professionals.

7 Psychologists will continue to work toward establishing the freedom of their profession. Organized psychology is likely to intensify its political efforts for the purpose of passing freedom-of-choice legislation. Individual clinical psychologists will need to keep abreast of the most modern techniques in psychotherapy so that they can continue to offer the public top-quality services. A vigorous program of continuing professional education may be one possible mechanism for achieving this end.

Of course, none of these projections tells us what clinical psychology should strive for and what it should avoid. For this wisdom we will rely on the ideas of a clinical psychologist who has given the question a career's worth of serious attention:

> Clinical psychology, after a long period spent as part of an academic discipline, is in the early stages of becoming a profession. It is going through the natural disturbances and difficulties which attend a growth process of this kind. However, if it selects its students carefully, for personality as well as intellect; if it trains thoroughly, in spirit as well as letter; if it trains broadly, recognizing that "specialists" . . . are not clinical psychologists; if it remains flexible about its training and encourages experimentation; if it does not become overwhelmed by immediate needs at the cost of important remoter goals; if it maintains its contact with its scientific background, remaining aware of the importance of theory as well as practice; if it remains modest in the face of the complexity of its problems, rather than becoming pretentious—in other words, if it finds good people and gives them good training—these disturbances and difficulties need not be of serious concern. Its future, both for itself as a profession and for society in the contribution it can make, is then assured. Fortunately, there are many reasons for believing that these are the prevailing aspirations in clinical psychology.

These words were written by David Shakow over 30 years ago (1948). They are as true today as they were then, and they provide sage advice for a profession whose accomplishments in the future should outshine the achievements of a distinguished past. We hope that this book may play a role in moving some of you to join in the creation of that future.

Appendix: Getting into Graduate School in Clinical Psychology

John P. Fiore, M.Ed.

Assistant Head for Undergraduate Affairs,

University of Illinois, Urbana-Champaign

As noted in Chapter 1, gaining admission to graduate training in clinical psychology is a highly competitive endeavor. Here are some questions and answers which are most relevant to the application enterprise.

GENERAL ISSUES

I Have Decided to Apply to Graduate School in Clinical Psychology. What Should I Do First?

In choosing graduate programs, you will want to make sure they provide the training and professional environment that will meet your needs. Therefore, you should clarify as much as possible your personal goals, objectives, and plans. Are you most interested in research, balanced training in clinical practice and research, or primarily in clinical practice? Are you interested in doctoral-level or master's-level programs? Do you have an interest in a specific client population? Do you have preferences related to types and/or locations of future employment? These are but a few of the questions you should be asking yourself before the application process begins. You will not have definitive answers for all possible questions, but you will have some, and these will probably indicate what is most important to you in choosing a graduate program.

Must I Apply to a Master's Degree Program and Complete it Before I Apply to a Doctoral Program?

There are different routes one can take to earn the doctorate in clinical psychology. A number of graduate programs provide master's degree training only. Many graduates from these programs terminate their formal education at the M.A.; others apply to doctoral programs.

Some graduate schools have separate training programs at the master's and doctoral levels and accept students for each. The master's program in these schools sometimes serves as a "feeder" to the doctoral program. However, each program is separate so that the student who does not enter the doctoral program will have completed training similar to that offered at "master's only" schools.

Another group of programs is designed to prepare doctoral-level clinicians only. They may award the master's degree after a minimum number of credits and a master's thesis have been completed, but it is important to recognize that these departments accept applications for the doctoral degree only.

If I Earn a Master's Degree, are my Chances for Then Being Admitted to a Doctoral Program Better or Worse?

Generally, the possession of a master's degree has little impact on the status of a student's application. Graduate schools are interested in the best candidates they can find. If your credentials are excellent, your chances for being admitted to a doctoral program are excellent. Some students who feel they need to improve their credentials may find master's degree work helpful in achieving that goal, but doctoral admission committees consider all academic work when making their decision. A mediocre undergraduate academic record is not automatically disregarded because it has been supplemented with a master's degree and good graduate school grades, but these graduate credentials can improve a student's chances for being seriously considered.

If I Chose to Terminate my Training After Earning a Master's Degree, Will my Opportunities for Doing Clinical Work be Limited?

Though there are many good clinical psychologists whose highest academic degree is the master's, the doctorate is still the standard of the profession. The following resolution was adopted by the American Psychological Association Council of Representatives.

The title "Professional Psychologist" has been used so widely and by persons with such a wide variety of training and experience that it does not provide the information the public deserves.

As a consequence, the APA takes the position and makes it a part of its policy that the use of the titles "Professional Psychologist," "School Psychologist," and "Industrial Psychologist" is reserved for those who have completed a doctoral training program in psychology in a university, college, or professional school of psychology that is APA or regionally accredited. In order to meet this standard, a transition period will be acknowledged for the use of the title "School Psychologist," so that ways may be sought to increase opportunities for doctoral training and to improve the level of the educational codes pertaining to the title.

The APA further takes the position and makes part of its policy that only those who have completed a doctoral training program in professional psychology in a university, college, or professional school of psychology that is APA or regionally accredited are qualified to independently provide unsupervised direct delivery of professional services including preventive, assessment, and therapeutic services. The exclusions mentioned above pertaining to school psychologists do not apply to the independent, unsupervised, direct delivery of professional services discussed in this paragraph.

Licensed or certified master's-level psychologists, having met earlier standards of the profession (i.e., were accorded grandmother/grandfather recognition) are to be regarded as comparably qualified through education, experience, examination, and the test of time, as are present and future doctoral psychologists, and shall be entitled under APA guidelines to include as part of their title the word "psychologist." (APA, 1978, p. vii)

Another fact which needs to be considered is that all states employ some form of licensing or certification for psychologists (see Chapter 13). Though requirements vary from state to state, an earned doctorate is a prerequisite in most of them. Before you decide to prepare for clinical work by earning a master's degree, be certain your career expectations can be met with this degree.

How Does One Identify "Good" Graduate Programs?

It is difficult to label graduate programs as "good" and "bad." The question to be answered is does a specific school and program fit a particular student's needs? A "research" versus "clinical" emphasis has already been discussed and can be ascertained for a specific program by corresponding with current graduate students and faculty at the particular school. If you can identify graduates of particular programs, ask them for their evaluation. Other things to consider include the size of the department and the program, the student/faculty ratio, opportunities for a variety of practicum experiences, the size and location of the campus and the community, the type and extent of department resources, and the particular philosophical school of thought which may be dominant in the program. Any of the above which is important to *you* should be considered when you attempt to identify the "good" programs.

One final caution concerns generalizing the quality of the department to the program. There are some psychology departments which are considered to be the best by many psychologists. Since your interest is in clinical psychology, do not assume that the clinical program is one of the best because the department is considered one of the best. Identify what is the best for *you* and judge each program against *your* criteria.

Are All Ph.D. Programs in Clinical Psychology Research-Oriented?

All Ph.D. programs in clinical psychology provide training in research as well as in clinical functions, but there are differences in emphasis from one institution to another. It is well worth your effort to learn of each program's emphasis when you are securing other information about the program. Note that programs which are *strictly* research-oriented make this fact clear in their information and refrain from using "clinical psychology" as a title (experimental psychopathology is a common substitute).

What Does American Psychological Association (APA) Accreditation of a Clinical Psychology Graduate Program Mean?

APA accreditation means the program has met a minimum standard of quality (see Chapter 13). The APA publication *Graduate Study in Psychology* explains:

Presently the APA accredits doctoral training programs in clinical, counseling, and school psychology only. Thus, departments that do not have such programs are not evaluated.

Furthermore, approval implies only that a program has voluntarily applied for examination by a knowledgeable group of individuals, that it has met a minimum level of acceptability for training in the speciality in question, and that it has been in operation long enough to have granted some doctorates in the speciality. There may be excellent departments that have not applied for accreditation or that have not had a doctoral program in clinical, counseling, or school psychology long enough to be eligible for approval. (APA, 1978, p. ix)

APPLICATION PROCEDURES

How Do I Get Initial Information About Graduate Schools?

There are several sources of information and you should use *all* of them. Some of the best informants are psychology faculty, especially those who are clinical psychologists. Preparing for courses, doing research, and keeping current for clinical practice requires careful review of new ideas and research as well as participation at professional meetings and workshops. This exposure to the field helps faculty know about various schools, training and research staff, the nature and philosophies of different programs, recent changes in the direction of certain departments, and other pertinent information. Though it is not reasonable to expect the faculty to know about all or even most doctoral programs, they will be able to provide you with good information about many of them.

Professional journals and related publications are information sources which are often overlooked. An excellent way to find programs that meet your needs is to use these sources to identify faculty who are studying topics and using approaches which interest you. A thorough search of the literature will very likely highlight programs which have several faculty with whom you might like to study. Find out where they are teaching by consulting the APA membership directory (most psychology departments have a recent edition).

Some colleges or undergraduate departments have a special advising staff for their students. The advisors or counselors may or may not be faculty, but if part of their job is to help with graduate school applications, you can benefit from their experience with former students. Even if this source of information does not exist at your school, all department offices receive pamphlets, notices, and general information brochures from many graduate psychology programs in the United States and Canada. Make full use of this information; it may answer some of your questions and inform you of new programs.

There are numerous books which list graduate schools and programs. The best of these for psychology is published by the American Psychological Association. It is called *Graduate Study in Psychology*. This book is revised annually and has over 600 pages of information, including application addresses, types of programs and degrees offered by each institution, size of faculty, financial aid information, tuition, degree requirements, admission requirements, average grades and entrance test scores for students admitted the previous year, comments about the program, and other valuable information. You may purchase a copy of this publication from the American Psychological Association, 1200 Seventeenth Street N.W., Washington, D.C. 20036. The cost of *Graduate Study in Psychology* for 1979–80 was $6.00.

Finally, your library should have catalogs from most, if not all, universities. Once you have identified clinical psychology programs which interest you, look at the graduate catalog for the university to get some idea of general university structure and requirements. If course descriptions are listed, you may be able to identify a particular program's emphasis.

How Many Potential Programs in Clinical Psychology Should be on my Initial List?

Your *initial* list should include as many programs as possible. The APA's *Graduate Study in Psychology* lists almost every clinical psychology program in the United States and Canada. As you use the various sources of information mentioned above and decide about location preferences, degree preferences, and the like, you will begin to systematically eliminate programs from your initial list. Once you have eliminated as many programs as possible by using the information you have compiled, you should write to each remaining program to request descriptions. This will allow you to continue to reduce the list on the basis of new information.

When Should I Write to Graduate Programs for Information?

You should request information in August and September, approximately a year before the projected admission date (e.g., September 1981 for Fall 1982 admission). Requesting material earlier than this sometimes gets you old information or places you on a waiting list until material is available. If you make a request too late, the material may not arrive in time for you to make effective use of it. Remember, you may have questions which arise from your reading of the material and you may wish to correspond with some departments before a final decision is made about whether or not to apply to them. This all requires time—give yourself plenty!

When Writing for Application Information, What Should I Ask for and What Format Should I Use?

At minimum, you should ask for information about the clinical psychology program, appropriate department and graduate school application forms, a graduate school program and course catalog, financial aid information, financial aid application forms, and a list of faculty and their research interests.

It is not necessary that your request for information be elaborate. A post card or form letter addressed to the department's graduate admission committee can be used, but be sure it includes a request for all the information you will need.

When Should I Apply?

Though department application deadlines vary, most are from February 1 through 15. A few come as early as December while others (mostly for master's degree programs) run as late as August. A safe rule of thumb is to use February 1 as a personal application deadline except for schools having earlier dates. Some schools which use later deadlines are often selecting students as applications are being processed. Therefore, it is to your advantage to submit your application to these schools early.

Submitting *very* early applications (September or October) is usually of no particular value since departments are not "tooled-up" for the admission process. Also, required test scores (to be discussed later) are not available this early in the school year.

How Many Programs Should I Apply to?

It is difficult to identify a specific number of applications which is appropriate for all students. I am reminded of two cases: One student applied to six schools and was admitted to all of them, while another applied to twenty-seven and was admitted to one. The general rule is apply to as many programs as you can reasonably afford. The larger the number of applications, the better your chances of being accepted.

Once you have decided on a final list of schools, ask yourself what you will do if you are not accepted by any of them. Perhaps at this point you may want to add one or two "safety valve" programs to fall back on. However, do not apply to programs which are really not acceptable to you. Such applications waste admission committee time, your time (and money) and may prevent a serious applicant from being admitted.

How Much Does Applying Cost?

Total testing costs can range from $13.00 to $40.00. Application fees usually vary from nothing to $25.00. Transcript costs (usually $1.00 each), additional test report fees, postage, and phone calls can add up very quickly. A total cost of $25.00 per application is about average.

QUALIFICATIONS AND CREDENTIALS

What Kinds of Courses and Experiences Will Help my Application?

Your undergraduate department will have designed a graduate preparatory major to meet your course needs. This will probably include a core program of introductory psychology, statistics, and experimental psychology (including a laboratory). These are the minimum requirements for most graduate programs, regardless of specialization area. In addition to these core courses and some breadth in psychology, Ph.D. programs often look for course work in mathematics, laboratory work in other sciences, and computer science courses. Remember, graduate programs are looking for the best students they can find, so a strong academic preparation is essential.

In addition to standard course work, independent research such as a bachelor's thesis and/or experience as an assistant to faculty who are involved in research is very helpful. This not only provides you with desired experience, but also allows faculty supervisors to observe your potential for scholarly endeavors and to include their evaluations and impressions in letters of recommendation.

Psychology departments will not expect you to enter their programs as a trained clinician, but they will look for evidence of experience in "helping relationships." Practica and relevant volunteer work will assist in establishing that your career decision is based in part on some firsthand knowledge of the field. Remember, impressions of what it is like to work in a field and actual working experiences are often very different. It is important that you know what you are getting into when you choose clinical psychology as a career.

What Grade Average is Necessary in Order to be Accepted?

Grade average requirements will vary across programs, degrees, and institutions. Some admissions committees will be concerned with a 4-year average, while others will consider the last 2 years only. For clinical psychology doctoral programs, a 3.5 grade average (on a 4-point system) is generally considered *minimum*. At highly competitive schools a 3.7 grade average may be more common, but other criteria are also taken into consideration. It is not unusual for a department to select a student with a 3.5 grade average over a student with a 4.0 grade average when other admissions data (test scores, research experience, course selection, and the like) are more in line with the program's goals, requirements, and orientation.

Generally, admission to master's degree programs is less competitive than for doctoral programs. Many master's programs have a minimum grade average requirement of B- (approximately 2.75), though the typical student admitted to such programs is likely to have a solid B (3.25) grade average.

What Testing is Involved in Applying to Graduate School?

Most graduate schools use standardized tests to assist them in evaluating applicants. The most common are the Graduate Record Examination (GRE) and the Miller Analogies Test (MAT).

The GRE Aptitude Test is described in the 1978–79 *GRE Information Bulletin* as follows:

> The GRE Aptitude Test measures general verbal, quantitative, and analytical abilities that are important for academic achievement. For the purpose of testing, aptitude is defined as developed abilities. The test not only reflects your abilities but necessarily reflects also the opportunity and effort that have contributed to the development of those abilities. The Aptitude Test, like other standardized tests, makes it possible to compare students with each other regardless of their individual backgrounds. A GRE score of 500, for example, has the same meaning whether earned by a student from a small, private liberal arts college or by a student at a large public university.
>
> To be as appropriate as possible to all examinees, who are characterized by wide-ranging interests, skills, and disciplines, the verbal section of the Aptitude Test must of necessity employ questions that draw from diverse areas of experience—from the activities of daily life and the domain of human relationships—and broad categories of academic interest such as the sciences, social studies, and humanities. The quantitative section assumes familiarity only with the arithmetic, plane geometry, and algebra that would have been learned in high school by most students. The questions in the analytical sections measure analytical skills required and developed in virtually all fields of study. No formal training in logic or methods or analysis is needed to do well on the analytical questions. Questions of various types and degrees of difficulty are kept in balance, and every attempt is made to avoid biases favoring any particular background or one sex over the other. (Educational Testing Service, 1978, p. 16)

The GRE Advanced Psychology Test is described in its 1978–79 information booklet as follows:

> The questions in the Advanced Psychology Test are drawn from courses of study most commonly offered within the broadly defined field of psychology. . . . Questions in the test often require the student to identify psychologists associated with particular theories or conclusions and to recall information from psychology courses. In addition, some questions require analyzing relationships, applying principles, drawing conclusions from experimental data, and evaluating experiments. Questions on the GRE Advanced Psychology Test are:
>
> **1** Experimental or natural science oriented, with questions distributed about equally among learning, physiological and comparative, and perception, and sensory psychology.
>
> **2** Social or social science oriented, with questions distributed about equally among personality, clinical and abnormal, developmental, and social psychology.
>
> **3** General, including historical and applied psychology, measurement, and statistics.
>
> A separate subscore is reported *for only the first two of these categories.* (p. 5)

The aptitude test is given in the morning on each testing date, while the advanced test is given in the afternoon. Each test requires about 3 hours.

The GRE Information Bulletin includes all application material and is available at most colleges and universities. You may also receive a copy by writing to:

Graduate Record Examinations
Educational Testing Service
Box 955
Princeton, New Jersey 08541

The basic fees for 1978–79 were $13.00 for the aptitude test and $13.00 for the advanced test.

The Miller Analogies Test (MAT) consists of one hundred very difficult verbal analogy items. Though the MAT is not as widely used as the GRE, a substantial number of programs require MAT scores. As with the GRE, testing is often available on college and university campuses. Further information about the MAT and testing locations can be obtained by writing to:

Psychological Corporation
304 East 45th Street
New York, New York 10017

Should I Take Both the GRE Aptitude Test and the GRE Advanced Test?

Since the Aptitude Test is generally required, there is no choice but to take it. As for the Advanced Test, your decision will be determined, in part, by your choice of schools. If you have decided on the graduate programs to which you will apply, the application information from these schools will indicate whether or not the Advanced Test is required. If you have not decided on a specific list of schools, you had better take both the Aptitude Test and the Advanced Test. If you wish to send only Aptitude Test results or only Advanced Test results to a particular school, Educational Testing Service will honor your request.

When Should I Take the Graduate Record Exam?

Most students choose to take the exam on the October test date in the fall of their senior year. The results of this test are usually in the mail to the student and to all schools designated by the student by the end of November.

There are six test dates scheduled each year. Educational Testing Service reports that it takes approximately 6 weeks to score tests and have the results in the mail. Therefore, the latest you can take the exam is on a scheduled date that is at least 6 weeks before the application deadline for a given institution. If February 1 is the deadline date, only October and December tests in the school year will meet the deadline.

When selecting test dates keep in mind that you are very likely to be taking both the Aptitude Test and the Advanced Test. Three hours of testing in the morning and three more hours in the afternoon can be tiring, so many students take the Aptitude Test on one test date and the Advanced Test on another.

Another consideration in selecting test dates is whether or not *you* wish to use the results in making decisions about where to apply. If you choose test dates that are sufficiently early, you will be able to look over your scores, consult advisors, and review resource material. For example, the APA's *Graduate Study in Psychology* lists average GRE scores for students admitted to specific schools. Students who apply to graduate programs without knowing their GRE scores are taking a chance. Scores at the 90th percentile permit application to a different set of schools than do scores at the 40th percentile. Being fully informed when you apply will save time and money, as well as increase your chances of being admitted to a clinical psychology program.

One test-scheduling strategy that has worked well for some students is to take the Aptitude Test in June, at the end of the junior year. The summer is then spent reviewing for the Advanced Test in Psychology which is taken in October of the senior year. This allows time for retaking tests if necessary and using the results for choosing schools.

Can I Study for the Tests?

There are several "how to prepare" books on the market. Generally, they provide a mathematics and vocabulary review, give tips on test taking, and provide sample GRE test items. The *GRE Information Bulletin* provides a sample GRE Aptitude Test. These sources can be helpful in familiarizing yourself with the types and forms of questions you are likely to encounter and can give you practice at pacing yourself during an examination.

One can review for the quantitative portion of the Aptitude Test, especially if you have been away from mathematics for a while. Brushing up on basic algebra and geometry will help you during the exam by reducing the time needed to recall how to solve particular problems. Students report that the quantitative portion of the test is not difficult but that it is fast paced. Know your basic math "cold," so you can work quickly and accurately.

Some of the sources frequently used by students in preparing for the GRE Aptitude Test include:

Brownstein, S., & Weiner, M. *Barron's How to Prepare for the Graduate Record Examination* (3rd ed.). Woodbury, New York: Barron's Educational Series, 1978.

Gruber, E. C., & Gruber, G. *The Graduate Record Examination Aptitude Test*. New York: Monarch Press, 1978.

Turner, D. R. *GRE* (4th ed.). New York: Arco, 1975.

As for the Advanced Test in psychology, remember that it covers all areas of psychology. Names, theories, and definitions are likely to be a part of the test, as are basic concepts. No one is expected to know about every area, so if you have not been exposed to certain aspects of psychology, you will no doubt have trouble with some questions. You can prepare for the Advanced Test in psychology by thoroughly reviewing a comprehensive text book in introductory psychology, such as:

Bourne, L. E., & Ekstrand, B. R. *Psychology: Its Principles and Meanings* (3rd ed.). Hinsdale, Illinois: The Dryden Press, 1979.

Hilgard, E. R., Atkinson, R. E., & Atkinson, R. L. *Introduction to Psychology* (7th ed.). New York: Harcourt, Brace, Jovanovich, 1979.

Zimbardo, P. G. *Psychology and Life* (10th ed.). Glenview, Illinois: Scott, Foresman, 1979.

Books covering history and systems in psychology will also be helpful in preparing for the exam. Some sources include:

Chaplin, J. P., & Krawiec, T. S. *Systems and Theories of Psychology*. New York: Holt, Rinehart, Winston, 1974.

Marx, M. H., & Hillix, W. S. *Systems and Theories in Psychology* (3rd ed.). New York: McGraw-Hill, 1979.

Other preparation sources for the GRE Advanced Test in psychology include:

Palmer, E. L. *Barron's How to Prepare for the Graduate Record Examination—Advanced Psychology Test.* New York: Barron's Educational Series, Inc., 1978.

Millman, S., & Nisbett, R. E. *Graduate Record Examination, Psychology Advanced Test* (2nd ed.). New York: Arco, 1977.

Preparation sources for the MAT include:

Gruber, G. K., & Gruber, E. G. *Preparation for the Miller's Analogies Test.* New York: Monarch Press, 1976.

Steinberg, R. J. *Barron's How to Prepare for the Miller's Analogies Test* (2nd ed.). New York: Barron's Educational Series, Inc., 1978.

Will I Need Letters of Recommendation for Graduate School Application? If so, How Many and from Whom?

Three letters of recommendation are usually required by the overwhelming majority of graduate programs in clinical psychology. At least two letters should be academic, i.e., from psychology faculty who are thoroughly familiar with your academic ability. If faculty from other disciplines can provide a better picture of your academic achievement and potential for graduate study, use them. The quality of the recommendation could be more important than whether or not the writer is a psychologist.

Letters from practicum or (relevant) job supervisors can also be helpful, since they help establish your success at working within the mental health field. Letters from "important people" such as senators, governors, and other political figures do not help your application. Generally, these say nothing more than "I've been asked to write . . ." and "please give this student full consideration." Such letters are likely to leave the impression that the student feels incapable of "making it" on his or her own. Unless the writer is in a position to judge the candidate's potential as a graduate student or a clinician, such "prestige" letters should not be submitted.

What Should I Know About Asking for Letters of Recommendation?

First, ask permission before you use someone's name as a reference. Many faculty will want to talk with you about your academic and career plans and objectives before agreeing to write a letter. Some will ask you to provide additional written information about yourself and may want to discuss this information with you. Be prepared to do this.

It is appropriate for you to provide faculty with information about yourself. Faculty with many students can easily forget individual students' work, when they took courses, and other details. Also, it is not unusual for faculty to know little about a student other than what has been observed in the classroom setting. General knowledge of the student's activities, accomplishments, and jobs can supplement classroom contacts in a way which enhances the tone and thrust of a reference letter.

Here is a list of information items you should provide faculty who are writing letters of reference for you:

1 Your full name.
2 Major, minor, curriculum, and specialization.
3 A computation of grade average in your major, in all college work, and in work since the end of the sophomore year.
4 A transcript of your college courses and grades.
5 A list of the psychology laboratory courses you have had.

6 A description of other research experiences, including comments on the full extent of your participation (include a copy of any major research papers).

7 A list of honor societies, clubs, and organizations to which you belong, along with comments on your participation (be sure to include positions of responsibility you held).

8 A brief discussion of jobs you have held and volunteer work you have done. Some students carry heavy work loads while being enrolled as full-time students in order to pay for their education. This type of information should be included.

9 An outline of your personal and professional plans and goals.

10 Any other information which it might be appropriate for this person to know as she or he writes a letter of recommendation.

Be sure to ask for letters and provide appropriate recommendation materials *early*. Remember, faculty often write letters for several students; give them plenty of time to prepare yours. To reduce the possibility of error and to speed the process:

1 Include a stamped, addressed envelope for each program for which a recommendation is being sent.

2 When forms are included, *your name* and other information which is not part of the formal recommendation should be *typed* in the appropriate space. *Do not hand blank forms to the recommender.*

3 Include a list of all the schools to which a recommendation is to be sent. Indicate which have forms to be completed and those that did not provide forms. This can later be used by the writer as a checklist against which actual references can be compared.

Will I be Able to See my Recommendation?

Letters of reference are not confidential unless you waive your right to see them. You are encouraged to consider doing so, however, since some readers feel that the recommendation is more likely to be a candid assessment if the writer knows the student will not see the letter. If you are concerned about what the letter might include, ask the writer if he or she can write a letter *supporting* your application.

Are Personal Interviews Required?

When interviews are part of the admissions procedure, they are likely to come only after the admission committee has considerably narrowed the number of applicants. Interviews are usually held on the school's campus, but, when a visit requires long-distance travel, a representative of the school may interview applicants at a location closer to their residences. Telephone interviews are sometimes used, but they are the exception rather than the rule. On the other hand, a student who has already been interviewed in person should be prepared for a follow-up telephone call. When final decisions are being made, the committee may want to ask some candidates a few more questions.

One bit of strategy used by one successful applicant might be considered. He kept information about the programs to which he had applied (e.g., who was on the faculty, particular emphases and strengths) along with notes about his interests and goals near his telephone. He felt that if he received a call, this preparation would reduce his anxiety about the conversation and help him organize his responses so that their emphasis would be appropriate for each institution. This also assured that he would include *all* the points he wanted to make so that he could avoid kicking himself later for not remembering to mention something important. He did receive a call and the strategy worked.

It is reasonable and appropriate for an applicant to visit various schools and talk with department representatives and graduate students about their programs. These conversations can be of assistance in deciding whether or not to apply or whether to accept an offer of admission. It is *not* desirable or appropriate to show up unannounced and expect department representatives to be available. Make an appointment ahead of time by calling the department chairperson and asking to meet with members of the clinical psychology program and with graduate students. Be prepared to outline in brief the nature of your questions, and have a number of alternate dates in mind before you call.

Are my College Transcripts Required?

Most programs will ask for a transcript of your college work from each institution at which you have studied. Transfer work summarized on the transcript from the last school you attended is not usually accepted—separate transcripts are required. You should call the schools you have attended to find out about transcript charges. Once that has been determined, send a letter to the director of student records at each school, enclosing a list of institutions to which a copy of your transcript is to be sent. Include a check to cover the cost.

FINANCIAL AID

What Kind of Financial Aid is Available for Graduate Study?

Financial aid comes in three forms: loans, grants, and work programs. The major sources of all financial aid are the universities themselves. This aid is, of course, limited to their own students. Other sources include guaranteed loan programs (many of which are sponsored by state governments) and national awards which are competitive and have specific criteria for application. These are awarded directly to the student for use at the school of her or his choice. One example of this type of aid is the Danforth graduate fellowship which provides support for 4 years. It is awarded to seniors who intend to obtain the highest degree in their fields and who have a serious interest in college teaching. Students applying to clinical programs with the intention of teaching in colleges or universities are eligible.

Since the availability of these national awards and loans changes regularly, you are encouraged to check for current information with the financial aid officer at your college or at the institution to which you are applying.

Since financial support is usually received through the program to which you are admitted, the aid information which you will receive with your application material is very important—read it carefully!

Loan programs exist on most campuses as a way of assisting students to invest in their own future. They usually carry a low interest rate with payments beginning after the student leaves graduate school.

Fellowships and scholarships are given on many campuses as outright grants to support and encourage very bright students with excellent potential. These are few in number and highly competitive in nature.

Assistantships come in two forms: research assistantships and teaching assistantships. Both are *jobs* in the university which require the graduate student to assist faculty in research projects or in teaching responsibilities (e.g., as discussion leaders, laboratory instructors, or paper graders). These usually require 10 to 20 hours of work each week.

Some programs have received grants from the federal government to provide *traineeships* in clinical psychology (see Chapters 2 and 13). As a result, there may be training grant funds available for a limited number of students at some institutions. Like fellowships, these are usually outright gifts, but do require that you carry a full academic load. They, too, are few in number and competition for them is keen.

Not all types of aid are offered at all schools. Be sure you understand what is potentially available at each school and at each level of graduate standing by carefully reading the financial aid information you receive.

Are There Assistantships Available from Departments Other Than the One to Which I Have Applied?

Assistantships of various types may be available on a campus. If you are accepted to a program with little or no financial aid, it is well worth your time to check on the availability of assistantships in other departments. For example, residence halls may hire graduate students to serve as counselors. Departments with large enrollments in undergraduate courses may have more teaching assistantships than graduate students in their programs and thus "import" assistants from related areas. Identify your skills and experiences and seek out jobs that fit them.

Do All Financial Aid Packages Involve About the Same Amount of Money?

Financial aid will vary from campus to campus and between departments on the same campus. For example, one school may give more money, but recipients are required to pay their own tuition. Others will give a smaller sum of money, but also pay tuition and fees. Some residence hall assistantships provide room and board only, others provide room, board, tuition and fees. If the amount of financial aid is an important factor in your selection of a graduate program, be sure you know both the amount you will receive and the costs you will incur before you make a final decision to accept or reject an offer of admission.

Are Separate References Required When Applying for Financial Aid?

Sometimes, separate application deadlines and reference letters are involved for financial aid consideration. Usually the letters of reference, when required, are copies of those used by departments in the admission process. The reference letters are usually used to assess the student's academic potential, not financial need. Read your application material carefully to determine just what is required in order to apply for financial aid, and remember that *deadlines for financial aid applications are sometimes earlier than deadlines for applying to clinical psychology graduate programs.*

OTHER IMPORTANT QUESTIONS

Are There Any Last-Minute Things I Need to Do When Applying?

Once your applications are sent out, you are encouraged to check with each department to which you have applied for the purpose of assuring that your application is complete. Each year, some applications are not considered because the students were unaware that they were incomplete. Some departments notify students when letters of reference or GRE scores are missing, but many do not. To eliminate this potential problem, ask each department to verify that your application is complete. Be sure to enclose a stamped, self-addressed envelope for their response. The following brief note and checklist provide examples of what might be sent.

Graduate Admissions Committee
Department of Psychology
University of Illinois
Champaign, Illinois 61820

To Whom It May Concern:

I have applied to your graduate program in clinical psychology. Since I am very interested in being accepted to your program, I would like to verify that my application file is complete. I have enclosed a checklist and a self-addressed, stamped envelope to assist you in providing me with that information. Thank you for your cooperation.

Sincerely,
Mary Smith

Date: _____   (PLEASE CHECK APPROPRIATE LINES)
                               Received

Application for Admission   _____
Application for Financial Aid   _____
GRE Aptitude Test Scores   _____
GRE Advanced Test Scores   _____
Miller Analogies Test Score   _____
Recommendation letters from:
  Professor Abigail Jones   _____
  Professor Herbert Long   _____
  Mr. Ben Wright   _____
Transcripts from:
  City Junior College   _____
  University of Colorado   _____
Are there other required materials which have not been received? _____
_____
_____

(Please return in enclosed stamped and addressed envelope.)

When I Am Admitted to a Program, How Long Will I Have to Make a Decision About Whether to Accept?

Most offers are made with a specific deadline for accepting or rejecting them. For doctoral programs, this is usually April 15. This date was adopted by the Council of Graduate Schools to protect students from being pressured to make decisions before having full information about their alternatives. The council's statement reads as follows:

Acceptance of an offer of a graduate scholarship, fellowship, traineeship, or graduate assistantship for the next academic year by an actual or prospective graduate student completes an agreement which both student and the graduate school expect to honor. In those instances in which the student indicates his/her acceptance prior to April 15 and subsequently desires to change his/her plans, he/she may submit in writing a resignation of his/her appointment at any time through April 15 in order to accept another scholarship, fellowship, traineeship, or graduate assistantship. However, an acceptance given or left in force after April 15 commits him/her not to accept another appointment without first obtaining formal release for the purpose. (APA, 1978, p. xi)

Obviously, if financial aid as described in this statement is not involved, the student is not under the same obligation. In such cases, however, courtesy dictates that you inform the department of your decision as soon as possible. This will be appreciated by the department and may provide space for another student. If you do not receive an acceptance letter in April, you may receive one later because space does become available as students decline offers.

REFERENCES

Abel, G.G. Assessment of sexual deviation in the male. In M. Hersen & A.S. Bellack (Eds.), *Behavioral assessment: A practical handbook*. Oxford: Pergamon Press, 1976, pp. 437–457.

Abel, G.G., Blanchard, E.B., Barlow, D.H., & Mavissakalian, M. Identifying specific erotic cues in sexual deviations by audiotaped descriptions. *Journal of Applied Behavior Analysis*, 1975, *8*, 247–260.

Abels, B.S., & Brandsma, J.M. *Therapy for couples*. San Francisco: Jossey-Bass Publishers, 1977.

Abood, L.G. A chemical approach to the problem of mental illness. In D. D. Jackson (Ed.), *The etiology of schizophrenia*. New York: Basic Books, 1960, pp. 91–119.

Abramowitz, S.I., Abramowitz, C.V., Jackson, C., & Gomes, B. The politics of clinical judgment: What nonliberal examiners infer about women who do not stifle themselves. *Journal of Consulting and Clinical Psychology*, 1973, *41*, 385–391.

Abramson, E., & Wunderlich, R.A. Anxiety, fear, and eating: A test of the psychosomatic concept of obesity. *Journal of Abnormal Psychology*, 1972, *79*, 317–321.

Ackerman, N.W. *The psychodynamics of family life*. New York: Basic Books, 1958.

Adams, H.E., Doster, J.A., & Calhoun, K.S. A psychologically based system of response classification. In A. R. Ciminero, K.S. Calhoun, and H. E. Adams (Eds.), *Handbook of behavioral assessment*. New York: Wiley, 1977, pp. 47–78.

Adler, A. *The practice and theory of individual psychology*. Paterson, N.J.: Littlefield, Adams, 1963.

Adler, A. *Problems of neurosis*. New York: Harper & Row, 1964.

Akutagawa, D.A. *A study in construct validity of the psycho-analytic concept of latent anxiety and a test of projection distance hypothesis*. Unpublished doctoral dissertation, University of Pittsburgh, 1956.

Albee, G.W. Conceptual models and manpower requirements in psychology. *American Psychologist*, 1968, *23*, 317–320.

Albee, G.W. The uncertain future of clinical psychology. *American Psychologist*, 1970, *25*, 1071–1080.

Albee, G.W. About Dr. Shakow, the March of Dimes, the triumph of truth, and angel food. *The Clinical Psychologist*, 1975, *29*, 9–10. (a)

Albee, G.W. To thine ownself be true. Comments on "insurance reimbursement." *American Psychologist*, 1975, *30*, 1156–1158. (b)

Albee, G.W. Does including psychotherapy in health insurance represent a subsidy to the rich from the poor? *American Psychologist*, 1977, *32*, 719–721.

Alberti, R.E., & Emmons, M.L. *Your perfect right: A guide to assertive behavior*. San Luis Obispo, Calif.: Impact Publishers, 1974.

Alden, L., Rappaport, J., & Seidman, E. College students as interventionists for primary grade children: A comparison of structured academic and companionship programs for children from low income families. *American Journal of Community Psychology*, 1975, *3*, 261–272.

Alexander, F. *The medical value of psychoanalysis*. New York: Norton, 1937.

Alexander, F. Psychoanalysis and psychotherapy. *Journal of the American Psychoanalytic Association*, 1954, *2*, 722–733.

Alexander, F.M. *Fundamentals of psychoanalysis*. New York: Norton, 1963.

Alexander, F.M. *Psychoanalysis and psychotherapy*. New York: Norton, 1956.

Alexander, F.M, & French, T.M. *Psychoanalytic therapy*. New York: Ronald Press Co., 1946.

Alexander, I.E. Postdoctoral training in clinical psychology. In B.B. Wolman (Ed.), *Handbook of Clinical Psychology*. New York: McGraw-Hill, 1965.

Alexander, J.F. Defensive and supportive communications in normal and deviant families. *Journal of Consulting and Clinical Psychology*, 1973, *40*, 223–232.

Alexander, J.F., & Parsons, B.V. Short-term behavioral intervention with delinquent families: Impact on family process and recidivism. *Journal of Abnormal Psychology*, 1973, *81*, 219–225.

Allen, G.J. The effectiveness of study counseling and desensitization in alleviating test anxiety in college students. *Journal of Abnormal Psychology*, 1971, 77, 282–289.

Allport, F.H. *Social psychology*. Cambridge, Mass.: Riverside Press, 1924.

Allport, G.W. The use of personal documents in psychological science. *Social Science Research Council Bulletin*, 1942, No. 49.

Allport, G.W. *Pattern and growth in personality*. New York: Holt, Rinehart, Winston, 1961.

Allport, G.W. *Letters from Jenny*. New York: Harcourt Brace, 1965.

Allport, G.W., & Vernon, C.E. *Study of values*. Boston: Houghton-Mifflin, 1931.

Allport, G.W., Vernon, C.E., and Lindzey, G. *Study of values* (revised manual). Boston: Houghton-Mifflin, 1970.

American Medical Association. Report of committee on mental health. *Journal of the American Medical Association*, 1954, *156*, 72.

American Psychiatric Association. *Diagnostic and statistical manual of mental disorders.* Washington, D.C.: American Psychiatric Association, 1968.

American Psychological Association. Recommended graduate training programs in clinical psychology. *American Psychologist*, 1947, *2*, 539–558.

American Psychological Association. *Ethical standards of psychologists.* Washington, D.C.: American Psychological Association, 1953.

American Psychological Association. Committee on Relations with Psychiatry, 1958 Annual Report. *American Psychologist*, 1958, *13*, 761–763.

American Psychological Association. Ethical standards of psychologists. *American Psychologist*, 1959, *14*, 279–282.

American Psychological Association. Ethical standards of psychologists. *American Psychologist*, 1963, *18*, 56–60.

American Psychological Association. *Casebook on ethical standards of psychologists.* Washington, D.C.: American Psychological Association, 1967.

American Psychological Association. *Ethical principles in the conduct of research with human participants.* Washington, D.C.: American Psychological Association, 1973.

American Psychological Association. *Standards for educational and psychological tests and manuals.* Washington, D.C.: American Psychological Association, 1974. (a)

American Psychological Association. *Standards for providers of psychological services.* Washington, D.C.: American Psychological Association, 1974. (b)

American Psychological Association. *Ethical standards of psychologists.* Washington, D.C.: American Psychological Association, 1977.

American Psychological Association. *Graduate study in psychology for 1979–1980* (12th ed.). Washington, D.C.: American Psychological Association, 1978. (a)

American Psychological Association. Task Force on Continuing Education in National Health Insurance. Continuing evaluation and accountability controls for a national health insurance program. *American Psychologist*, 1978, *33*, 305–313. (b)

Ames, L.B., Leonard, J., Métraux, R.W., & Walker, R.U. *Adolescent Rorschach responses: Developmental trends from ten to sixteen years.* New York: Hoeber-Harper, 1959.

Amrine, M. The 1965 congressional inquiry into testing: A commentary. *American Psychologist*, 1965, *20*, 859–870.

Anastasi, A. *Psychological testing* (3d ed.). New York: Macmillan, 1968.

Anastasi, A. *Psychological testing* (4th ed.). New York: Macmillan, 1976.

Andrews, T.G., & Dreese, M. Military utilization of psychologists during World War II. *American Psychologist*, 1948, *3*, 533–538.

Angle, H.V., Hay, L.R., Hay, W.M., & Ellinwood, E.H. Computer assisted behavioral assessment. In J.D. Cone & R.P. Hawkins (Eds.), *Behavioral assessment: New directions in clinical psychology.* New York: Bruner/Mazel, 1977, pp. 369–380.

Arbuckle, D.S. *Counseling: Philosophy, theory, and practice.* Boston: Allyn and Bacon, 1965.

Argyle, M., Trower, P., & Bryant, B. Explorations in the treatment of personality disorders and neuroses by social skills training. *British Journal of Medical Psychology*, 1974, *47*, 63–72.

Argyris, C. *Integrating the individual and the organization.* New York: Wiley, 1964.

Arkowitz, H., Lichtenstein, E., McGovern, K., & Hines, P. The behavioral assessment of social competence in males. *Behavior Therapy*, 1975, *6*, 3–13.

Arrington, R.E. *Interrelations in the behavior of young children*. New York: Columbia University Press, 1932.

Ash, P. The reliability of psychiatric diagnosis. *Journal of Abnormal and Social Psychology*, 1949, *44*, 272–276.

Ashem, B., & Donner, L. Covert sensitization with alcoholics: A controlled replication. *Behaviour Research and Therapy*, 1968, *6*, 7–12.

Asher, J. First edition of national register due; 7000 psychologists to be included. *APA Monitor*, May 1975, p. 1.

Association for the Advancement of Behavior Therapy. Ethical issues for human services. *AABT Newsletter*, 1977, *4*, 11.

Auger, T.J. Mental health terminology: A modern tower of Babel? *Journal of Community Psychology*, 1974, *2*, 113–116.

Auld, F., Jr., & Murray, E.J. Content-analysis studies of psychotherapy. *Psychological Bulletin*, 1955, *52*, 377–395.

Ayllon, T., & Azrin, N.H. The measurement and reinforcement of behavior of psychotics. *Journal of the Experimental Analysis of Behavior*, 1965, *8*, 357–383.

Ayllon, T. and Azrin, N.H. *The token economy: A motivational system for therapy and rehabilitation*. New York: Appleton-Century Crofts, 1968.

Baer, D.M., Wolf, M.M., and Risley, T.R. Some current dimensions of applied behavior analysis. *Journal of Applied Behavior Analysis*, 1968, *1*, 91–97.

Baier, D.E., & Dugan, R.E. Factors in sales success. *Journal of Applied Psychology*, 1957, *41*, 37–40.

Bales, R.F. *Interaction process analysis*. Cambridge: Addison-Wesley, 1950.

Ball, J.C. The reliability and validity of interview data obtained from 59 narcotic drug addicts. *American Journal of Sociology*, 1967, *72*, 650–654.

Bandura, A. *Principles of behavior modification*. New York: Holt, Rinehart, and Winston, 1969.

Bandura, A. Psychotherapy based upon modeling principles. In A.E. Bergin & S.L. Garfield (Eds.), *Handbook of psychotherapy and behavior change*. New York: Wiley, 1971, pp. 653–708.(a)

Bandura, A. *Social learning theory*. Morristown, N.J.: General Learning Press, 1971.(b)

Bandura, A. *Social learning theory*. Englewood Cliffs, N.J.: Prentice-Hall, 1977.(a)

Bandura, A. Self-efficacy: Toward a unifying theory of behavioral change. *Psychological Review*, 1977, *84*, 191–215.(b)

Bandura, A., Blanchard, E.B., & Ritter, B. The relative efficacy of desensitization and modeling approaches for inducing behavioral, affective, and attitudinal changes. *Journal of Personality and Social Psychology*, 1969, *13*, 173–199.

Bandura, A., Jeffery, R.W., & Wright, C.L. Efficacy of participant modeling as a function of response induction aids. *Journal of Abnormal Psychology*, 1974, *83*, 56–64.

Bandura, A., Ross, D., and Ross, S.A. Imitation of film-mediated aggressive models. *Journal of Abnormal and Social Psychology*, 1963, *66*, 3–11.

Bandura, A., & Walters, R.H. *Social learning and personality development*. New York: Holt, Rinehart, and Winston, 1963.

Bannister, D., Salmon, P., & Lieberman, D.M. Diagnosis-treatment relationships in psychiatry: A statistical analysis. *British Journal of Psychiatry*, 1964, *110*, 726–732.

Bard, M. Family intervention teams as a community mental health resource. *Journal of Criminal Law, Criminology, and Police Science*, 1969, *60*, 247–250.

Bard, M. *Training police as specialists in family crisis intervention.* Washington, D.C.: National Institute of Law Enforcement and Criminal Justice, U.S. Government Printing Office, 1970.

Bard, M. The role of law enforcement in the helping system. *Community Mental Health Journal,* 1971, *7,* 151–160.

Bard, M., & Berkowitz, B. Training police as specialists in family crisis intervention: A community psychology action program. *Community Mental Health Journal,* 1967, *3,* 315–317.

Barker, R.G. (Ed.). *The stream of behavior.* New York: Irvington Publishers, Inc., 1963.

Barker, R.G. *Ecological psychology.* Stanford: Stanford University Press, 1968.

Barker, R., Dembo, T., & Lewin, K. Frustration and regression: An experiment with young children. *University of Iowa Student Child Welfare,* 1941, *18,* No. 1.

Barker, R.G., & Wright, H.F. *One boy's day.* New York: Harper, 1951.

Barker, R.G., & Wright, H.F. *Midwest and its children: The psychological ecology of an American town.* New York: Row, Peterson, 1955.

Barlow, D.H. Assessment of sexual behavior. In A.R. Ciminero, K.S. Calhoun, & H.E. Adams (Eds.), *Handbook of behavioral assessment.* New York: John Wiley & Sons, 1977, pp. 461–508.

Barlow, D.H., Becker, J., Leitenberg, H., & Agras, W.S. Mechanical strain gauge recording of penile circumference change. *Journal of Applied Behavior Analysis,* 1970, *3,* 73–76.

Barnat, M.R. Student reactions to supervision: Guests for a contract. *Professional Psychology,* 1973, *4,* 17–22.

Barnett, H.G. *Being a Palauan.* New York: Holt, Rinehart & Winston, 1960.

Barrett, B. Reduction in rate of multiple tics by free-operant conditioning methods. *Journal of Nervous and Mental Disease,* 1962, *135,* 187–195.

Barrett, C.L. Systematic desensitization versus implosive therapy. *Journal of Abnormal Psychology,* 1969, *74,* 587–592.

Bartels, B.D., & Tyler, J.D. Paraprofessionals in the community mental health center. *Professional Psychology,* 1975, *6,* 442–452.

Barthell, C.N., & Holmes, D.S. High school yearbooks: A nonreactive measure of social isolation in graduates who later became schizophrenic. *Journal of Abnormal Psychology,* 1968, *73,* 313–316.

Bartlett, C.J., & Green, C.G. Clinical prediction: Does one sometimes know too much? *Journal of Counseling Psychology,* 1966, *13,* 267–270.

Barton, A. *Three worlds of therapy: An existential-phenomenological study of the therapies of Freud, Jung, and Rogers.* Palo Alto, Calif.: National Press Books, 1974.

Bass, B.M. The leaderless group discussion. *Psychological Bulletin,* 1954, *51,* 465–492.

Bateson, C., Jackson, D.D., Haley, J., & Weakland, J.H. Toward a theory of schizophrenia. *Behavioral Science,* 1956, *1,* 251–264.

Bayer, C.A. Self-monitoring and mild aversion treatment of trichotillomania. *Journal of Behavior Therapy and Experimental Psychiatry,* 1972, *3,* 139–141.

Bayley, N. Comparisons of mental and motor test scores for ages 1–15 months by sex, birth order, race, geographic location, and education of parents. *Child Development,* 1965, *36,* 379–411.

Beck, A.T. Cognitive therapy: Nature and relation to behavior therapy. *Behavior Therapy,* 1970, *1,* 184–200.

Beck, A.T. *Depression: Causes and treatment.* Philadelphia: University of Pennsylvania Press, 1972.

Beck, S.J. *Introduction to the Rorschach method.* Monograph No. 1. American Orthopsychiatric Association, 1937.

Bednar, R.L., & Kaul, T.J. Experiential group research: Current perspectives. In S.L. Garfield & A.E. Bergin (Eds.), *Handbook of psychotherapy and behavior change: An empirical analysis* (2d ed.). New York: John Wiley and Sons, 1978, 769–815.

Bednar, R.L., Melnick, J., & Kaul, T. Risk, responsibility, and structure: Ingredients for a conceptual framework for initiating group therapy. *Journal of Counseling Psychology,* 1974, *21,* 31–37.

Beers, C.W. *A mind that found itself* (5th ed.). New York: Doubleday, 1921, (originally published, 1908).

Begelman, C.A. Behavioral classification. In M. Hersen & A.S. Bellack (Eds.), *Behavioral assessment: A practical handbook.* New York: Pergamon Press, 1976.

Bell, J.E. *Family group therapy.* Public Health Monograph, *64,* Department of Health, Education and Welfare. Washington, D.C.: U.S. Government Printing Office, 1961.

Bellack, A.S., & Hersen, M. *Behavior modification.* Baltimore: Williams & Wilkins, 1977.

Bellack, A.S., & Schwartz, J.S. Assessment for self-control programs. In M. Hersen and A.S. Bellack (Eds.), *Behavioral assessment: A practical handbook.* New York: Pergamon Press, 1976, 111–142.

Bellak, L. (Ed.). *Handbook of community psychiatry and community mental health.* New York: Grune and Stratton, 1964.

Bellak, L. *A guide to the interpretation of the Thematic Apperception Test.* New York: Psychological Corporation, 1947.

Bellak, L., & Bellak, S. *Children's Apperception Test.* New York: CPS Company, 1952.

Bender, L.A. A visual motor Gestalt test and its clinical use. *American Orthopsychiatric Association,* Research Monographs, 1938, No. 3.

Bennett, C.C. Community psychology: Impressions of the Boston conference on the education of psychologists for community mental health. *American Psychologist,* 1965, *20,* 832–835.

Bennett, C.C. Anderson, L.S., Hassol, L., Klein, D., & Rosenblum, G. (Eds.). *Community psychology: A report of the Boston conference on the education of psychologists for community mental health.* Boston: Boston University and South Shore Mental Health Center, 1966.

Benney, M., Riesman, D., & Star, S.A. Age and sex in the interview. *American Journal of Sociology,* 1956, *62,* 143–152.

Bennis, W.G. *Changing organizations.* New York: McGraw-Hill, 1966.

Benthall-Nietzel, D. Physician-patient privilege and confidentiality. In *Report of Seminar on Law and Medicine,* Office of Continuing Legal Education, University of Kentucky College of Law, Lexington, Ky., 1975.

Benton, A.L. *Revised visual retention test: Manual.* New York: Psychological Corporation, 1963.

Berdie, R.F. The ad hoc committee on social impact of psychological assessment. *American Psychologist,* 1965, *20,* 143–146.

Berg, I.A. Response bias and personality: The deviation hypothesis. *Journal of Psychology,* 1955, *40,* 61–71.

Berg, I.A. The clinical interview and the case record. In I.A. Berg & L.A. Pennington (Eds.), *Clinical psychology* (3d ed.). New York: Ronald Press, 1966, pp.27–66.

Berg, I.A., & Adams, H.E. The experimental bases of personality assessment. In A.J. Bachrach (Ed.), *Experimental foundations of clinical psychology*. New York: Basic Books, 1962, 52–93.

Bergin, A.E. The evaluation of therapeutic outcomes. In A.E. Bergin & S.L. Garfield (Eds.), *Handbook of psychotherapy and behavior change: An empirical analysis*. New York: Wiley and Sons, Inc., 1971.

Bernardoni, L.C. A culture fair intelligence test for the ugh, no, and oo-la-la cultures. *Personnel and Guidance Journal*, 1964, *42*, 554–557.

Berne, E. *Transactional analysis in psychotherapy*. New York: Grove Press, 1961.

Berne, E. *Games people play*. New York: Grove Press, 1964.

Bernstein, D.A. Behavioral fear assessment: Anxiety or artifact? In H. Adams & P. Unikel (Eds.), *Issues and trends in behavior therapy*. Springfield: C.C. Thomas, 1973, 225–267.

Bernstein, D.A., & Beaty, W. The use of *in vivo* desensitization as part of a total therapeutic intervention. *Journal of Behavior Therapy and Experimental Psychiatry*, 1971, *2*, 259–265.

Bernstein, D.A., & Borkovec, T.D. *Progressive relaxation training*. Champaign, Ill. Research Press, 1973.

Bernstein, D.A., & Nietzel, M.T. Procedural variation in behavioral avoidance tests. *Journal of Consulting and Clinical Psychology*, 1973, *41*, 165–174.

Bernstein, D.A., & Nietzel, M.T. Demand characteristics in behavior modification: A natural history of a "nuisance." In M. Hersen, R.M. Eisler, & P.M. Miller (Eds.), *Progress in behavior modification* (Vol. 4). New York: Academic Press, 1977, 119–162.

Bernstein, D.A., & Paul, G.L. Some comments on therapy analogue research with small animal "phobias." *Journal of Behavior Therapy and Experimental Psychiatry*, 1971, *2*, 225–237.

Bernstein, L. The examiner as an inhibiting factor in clinical testing. *Journal of Consulting Psychology*, 1956, *20*, 287–290.

Bernstein, L., Bernstein, R.S., & Dana, R.H. *Interviewing: A guide for health professionals* (2d ed.). New York: Appleton-Century-Crofts, 1974.

Bersoff, D.N. Silk purses into sow's ears: The decline of psychological testing and a suggestion for its redemption. *American Psychologist*, 1973, *28*, 892–899.

Berwick, P., & Morris, L.A. Token economies: Are they doomed? *Professional Psychology*, 1974, *5*, 434–439.

Berzins, J.I. Therapist-patient matching. In A.S. Gurman & A.M. Razin (Eds.), *Effective psychotherapy: A handbook of research*. New York: Pergamon Press, 1977.

Best, J.A. Tailoring smoking withdrawal procedures to personality and motivational differences. *Journal of Consulting and Clinical Psychology*, 1975, *43*, 1–8.

Bieri, J., Atkins, A.L. Briar, S., Leaman, R.L., Miller, H., & Tripoldi, T. *Clinical and social judgment: The discrimination of behavioral information*. New York: Wiley, 1966.

Bijou, S.W., & Peterson, R.F. The psychological assessment of children: A functional analysis. In P. McReynolds (Ed.), *Advances in psychological assessment* (Vol. 2). Palo Alto, Calif.: Science and Behavioral Books, 1971, 63–78.

Bijou, S.W., Peterson, R.F., & Ault, M.H. A method to integrate descriptive and experimental field studies at the level of data and empirical concepts. *Journal of Applied Behavior Analysis*, 1968, *1*, 175–191.

Bijou, S.W., Peterson, R.F., Harris, F.R., Allen, K.E., & Johnston, M.S. Methodology for experimental studies of young children in natural settings. *The Psychological Record*, 1969, *19*, 177–210.

Binet, A., & Simon, T. Application des méthodes nouvelles au diagnostic du niveau intellectual chez des enfants normaux et anormaux d'hospice et d'ecole primaire. *L'Année Psychologique*, 1905, *11*, 245–336.

Binet, A., & Simon, T. [The development of intelligence in children.] (Elizabeth S. Fite, trans.). Vineland, N.J.: Training School, 1916.

Bingham, W.V.D., & Moore, B.V. *How to interview*. New York: Harper, 1924.

Bingham, W.V.D., Moore, B.V., & Gustad, J.W. *How to interview*. New York: Harper & Row, 1959.

Bion, W.R. The leaderless group project. *Bulletin of the Menninger Clinic*, 1946, *10*, 77–81.

Birnbaum, B.The right to treatment. *American Bar Association Journal*, 1960, *46*, 499.

Birnbaumer, N. Biofeedback training: A critical review of its clinical applications and some possible future directions. *European Journal of Behavioral Analysis and Modification*, 1977, *1*, 235–251.

Blake, B.G. The application of behaviour therapy to the treatment of alcoholism. *Behaviour Research and Therapy*, 1965, *3*, 75–85.

Blanchard, E.B., & Epstein, L.H. *A biofeedback primer*. Reading, Mass.: Addison-Wesley, 1978.

Blanck, G. Psychoanalytic technique. In B.B. Wolman (Ed.), *The therapist's handbook: Treatment methods of mental disorders*. New York: Van Nostrand Reinhold, 1976, 61–86.

Blank, L., & David, H.P. (Eds.). *Sourcebook for training in clinical psychology*. New York: Springer, 1964.

Bloom, B.L. The domain of community psychology. *American Journal of Community Psychology*, 1973, *1*, 8–11.

Bloomfield, H.H. Assertive training in an outpatient group of chronic schizophrenics: A preliminary report. *Behavior Therapy*, 1973, *4*, 277–281.

Blum, G. A study of the psychoanalytic theory of psychosexual development. *Genetic Psychology Monographs*, 1949, *39*, 3–99.

Bolgar, H. The case study method. In B.B. Wolman (Ed.), *Handbook of clinical psychology*. New York: McGraw-Hill, 1965, 28–39.

Boneau, A. Private practice pays handsomely. *APA Monitor*, May, 1974, 3.

Boneau, C.A., & Cuca, J.M. An overview of psychology's human resources: Characteristics and salaries from the 1972 APA survey. *American Psychologist*, 1974, *29*, 821–840.

Bonime, W. *The clinical use of dreams*. New York: Basic Books, 1962.

Bordin, E.S. Ambiguity as a therapeutic variable. *Journal of Consulting Psychology*, 1955, *19*, 9–15.

Borgatta, E.F. Analysis of social interaction: Actual role playing and projective. *Journal of Abnormal and Social Psychology*, 1955, *51*, 394–405.

Boring, E.G. *A history of experimental psychology* (2d ed.). New York: Appleton-Century-Crofts, 1950.

Borkovec, T.D., & O'Brien, G.T. Methodological and target behavior issues in analogue therapy outcome research. In M. Hersen, R.M. Eisler, and P.M. Miller (Eds.), *Progress in behavior modification*. New York: Academic Press, 1976, 133–172.

Borkovec, T.D., Stone, N.M., O'Brien, G.T., & Kaloupek, D.G. Evaluation of a clinically relevant target behavior for analogue outcome research. *Behavior Therapy*, 1974, *5*, 504–514.

Borkovec, T.D., Weerts, T.C., & Bernstein, D.A. Assessment of anxiety. In A.R. Ciminero, K.S. Calhoun, & H.E. Adams (Eds.), *Handbook of behavioral assessment*. New York: John Wiley & Sons, 1977, 367–428.

Borofsky, G.L. Issues in the diagnosis and classification of personality functioning. In A.I. Rabin (Ed.), *Clinical psychology: Issues of the seventies*. East Lansing, Mich.: Michigan State University Press, 1974, 24–48.

Boudin, H. Contingency contracting as a therapeutic tool in the deceleration of amphetamine use. *Behavior Therapy*, 1972, *3*, 604–608.

Bourne, L.E., and Ekstrand, B.R. *Psychology: Its principles and meanings* (2nd ed.). New York: Holt, Rinehart, Winston, 1976.

Braginsky, B.M., Braginsky, D.D., & Ring, K. *Methods of madness: The mental hospital as a last resort*. New York: Holt, Rinehart, Winston, 1969.

Braginsky, B.M., Grosse, M., & Ring, K. Controlling outcomes through impression management: An experimental study of the manipulative tactics of mental patients. *Journal of Consulting Psychology*, 1966, *30*, 295–300.

Bray, D.W., Campbell, R.J., & Grant, D.L. *Formative years in business: A long-term AT&T study of managerial lives*. New York: Wiley, 1974.

Brayfield, A.H. (Ed.). *American Psychologist special issue: Testing and public policy* (Vol. 20). Lancaster, Pa.: American Psychological Association, 1965.

Breger, L. Psychological testing: Treatment and research implications. *Journal of Consulting and Clinical Psychology*, 1968, *32*, 179–181.

Breger, L., & McGaugh, J.L. Critique and reformulation of "learning theory" approaches to psychotherapy and neurosis. *Psychological Bulletin*, 1965, *63*, 338–358.

Brehmer, B. Note on clinical judgment and the formal characteristics of clinical tasks. *Psychological Bulletin*, 1976, *83*, 778–782.

Brenner, C. *An elementary textbook of psychoanalysis*, New York: Anchor Books, 1974.

Breuer, J., and Freud, S. *Studies on hysteria*. New York: Avon Books, 1966.

Brill, A.A. *The basic writings of Sigmund Freud*. New York: Random House, 1938.

Brittain, H.L. A study in imagination. *Pedagogical Seminary and Journal of Genetic Psychology*, 1907, *14*, 137–207.

Broden, M., Hall, R.V., & Mitts, B. The effect of self-recording on the classroom behavior of two eighth-grade students. *Journal of Applied Behavior Analysis*, 1971, *4*, 191–199.

Brotemarkle, B.A. Fifty years of clinical psychology: Clinical psychology 1896–1946. *Journal of Consulting Psychology*, 1947, *11*, 1–4.

Broverman, I.K., Broverman, D.M., Clarkson, F.E., Rosenkrantz, P.S., & Vogel, S.R. Sex role stereotypes and clinical judgments of mental health. *Journal of Consulting and Clinical Psychology*, 1970, *34*, 1–7.

Brown, E. Assessment from a humanistic perspective. *Psychotherapy: Theory, Research, and Practice*, 1972, *9*, 103–106.

Brown, F. Clinical psychology. In A.M. Freedman & H.I. Kaplan (Eds.), *Diagnosing mental illness*. New York: Atheneum, 1972, 295–301.

Brown, R., & Herrnstein, R.J. *Psychology*. Boston: Little, Brown & Co., 1975.

Bruner, J.S., & Tagiuri, R. The perception of people. In G. Lindzey (Ed.), *Handbook of social psychology* (Vol. 2). Reading, Mass.: Addison-Wesley, 1954, 634–654.

Brunswick, E. *Systematic and representative design of psychological experiments with results in physical and social perception*. Berkeley: University of California Press, 1947.

Bryntwick, S., & Solyom, L. A brief treatment of elevator phobia. *Journal of Behavior Therapy and Experimental Psychiatry*, 1973, *4*, 355–356.

Buck, J.N. The H-T-P technique: A qualitative and quantitative scoring manual. *Journal of Clinical Psychology*, 1948, *4*, 319–396.

Bugental, D.E., Love, L.R., & Kaswan, J.W. Videotaped family interaction: Differences reflecting presence and type of child disturbance. *Journal of Abnormal Psychology*, 1972, *79*, 285–290.

Bugental, J.F.T. Humanistic psychology: A new break-through. *American Psychologist*, 1963, *18*, 563–567.

Bugental, J.F.T. *Psychotherapy and process: The fundamentals of an existential-humanistic approach*. Reading, Mass.: Addison-Wesley, 1978.

Bugental, J., & Zelen, S. Investigations into the "self-concept." I. The W-A-Y technique. *Journal of Personality*, 1950, *18*, 483–498.

Burchard, J.D. Systematic socialization: A programmed environment for the habilitation of antisocial retardates. *Psychological Record*, 1967, *17*, 461–476.

Burdock, E.I., & Hardesty, A.S. Psychological test for psychopathology. *Journal of Abnormal Psychology*, 1968, *73*, 62–69.

Burke, W.W. Organization development. *Professional Psychology*, 1973, *4*, 194–199.

Buros, O.K. (Ed.). *The 1940 mental measurements yearbook*. Highland Park, N.J.: Gryphon Press, 1938.

Buros, O.K. (Ed.). *Tests in print II*. Highland Park, N.J.: Gryphon Press, 1974.

Buros, O.K. (Ed.). *Personality tests and reviews II*. Highland Park, N.J.: Gryphon Press, 1975.

Buros, O.K. (Ed.). *The eighth mental measurements yearbook*. Highland Park, N.J.: Gryphon Press, 1978.

Busch, C.J., & Evans, I.M. The effectiveness of electric shock and foul odor as unconditioned stimuli in classical aversive conditioning. *Behaviour Research and Therapy*, 1977, *15*, 167–176.

Bushell, D., Wrobel, P.A., & Michaelis, M.L. Applying "group" contingencies to the classroom study behavior of preschool children. *Journal of Applied Behavior Analysis*, 1968, *1*, 55–61.

Butcher, J.N. Personality assessment: Problems and perspectives. In J.N. Butcher (Ed.), *Objective personality assessment*. New York: Academic Press, 1972, 1–20.

Caligor, L. The detection of paranoid trends by the eight card redrawing test (8 CRT). *Journal of Clinical Psychology*, 1952, *8*, 397–401.

Campbell, D.T., & Fiske, D.W. Convergent and discriminant validation by the multitrait-multimethod matrix. *Psychological Bulletin*, 1959, *56*, 81–105.

Campbell, D.T., & Stanley, J.C. *Experimental and quasi-experimental designs for research*. Chicago: Rand-McNally, 1963.

Cannell, C.F., & Kahn, R.L. Interviewing. In G. Lindzey & E. Aronson (Eds.), *Handbook of social psychology* (2d ed.) (Vol. 2). Reading, Mass.: Addison-Wesley, 1968, 526–595.

Cantril, H. *Gauging public opinion*. Princeton, N.J.: University Press, 1944.

Caplan, G. *An approach to community mental health*. New York: Grune & Stratton, 1961.

Caplan, G. Types of mental health consultation. *American Journal of Orthopsychiatry*, 1963, *33*, 470–481.

Caplan, G. *Principles of preventive psychiatry*. New York: Basic Books, 1964.

Caplan, G. *The theory and practice of mental health consultation*. New York: Basic Books, 1970.

Carkhuff, R.R., Barnett, W.Y., Jr., & McCall, J.N. *The counselor's handbook: Scale and profile interpretations of the MMPI*. Urbana, Ill.: R.W. Parkinson & Associates, 1965.

Carlson, H.S. The AASPB Story: The beginnings and first 16 years of the American Association of State Psychology Boards, 1961–1977. *American Psychologist*, 1978, *33*, 486–495.

Carpenter, J.C. Intrasubject and subject-agent effects in ESP experiments. In B.B. Wolman (Ed.), *Handbook of parapsychology*. New York: Van Nostrand Reinhold, 1977, 202–272.

Cartwright, R.A. A comparison of the response to psychoanalytic and client-centered therapy. In L.A. Gottschalk & A.H. Auerbach (Eds.), *Methods of research in psychotherapy*. New York: Appleton-Century-Crofts, 1966, 517–529.

Cataldo, M.F., & Risley, T.R. Evaluation of living environments: The MANIFEST description of ward activities. In P.O. Davidson, F.W. Clark, L.A. Hamerlynck (Eds.), *Evaluation of behavioral programs in community, residential and school settings*. Champaign, Ill.: Research Press, 1974, 201–222.

Cattell, R.B. A culture-free intelligence test. *Journal of Educational Psychology*, 1940, *31*, 161–179.

Cattell, R.B. *The scientific analysis of personality*. Baltimore: Penguin Books, 1965.

Cattell, R.B., & Eber, H.W. *Manual for forms A and B of the sixteen personality factor questionnaire*. Institute for Personality and Ability Testing, Champaign, Ill. 1962.

Cautela, J.R. Treatment of compulsive behavior by covert sensitization. *Psychological Record*, 1966, *86*, 33–41.

Cautela, J.R. *Behavior analysis forms for clinical intervention*. Champaign, Ill.: Research Press, 1977.

Cautela, J.R., & Kastenbaum, R.A. A reinforcement survey schedule for use in therapy, training, and research. *Psychological Reports*, 1967, *20*, 1115–1130.

Cautela, J.R., & Rosenstiel, A.K. Use of covert sensitization in treatment of drug abuse. *The International Journal of the Addictions*, 1975, *10*, 277–303.

Cavior, N., & Marabotto, C. Monitoring verbal behaviors in dyadic interactions. *Journal of Consulting and Clinical Psychology*, 1976, *44*, 68–76.

Chapman, L.J. Studies of psychodiagnostic errors of observation as a contribution toward a non-dynamic psychopathology of everyday life. In H.E. Adams and W.K. Boardman (Eds.), *Advances in experimental clinical psychology*. New York: Pergamon, 1971, 123–163.

Chapman, L.J., & Chapman, J.P. The genesis of popular but erroneous psychodiagnostic observations. *Journal of Abnormal Psychology*, 1967, *72*, 193–204.

Chasen, B.G., & Weinberg, S.L. Diagnostic sex-role bias: How can we measure it? *Journal of Personality Assessment*, 1974, *39*, 620–629.

Chess, S., Thomas, A., & Birch, H.G. Distortions in developmental reporting made by parents of behaviorally disturbed children. *Journal of the American Academy of Child Psychiatry*, 1966, *5*, 226–231.

Chinsky, J.M., & Rappaport, J. Brief critique of meaning and reliability of "accurate empathy" ratings. *Psychological Bulletin*, 1970, *73*, 379–382.

Christophersen, E.R., Arnold, C.M., Hill, D.W., & Quilitch, H.R. The home point system: Token reinforcement procedures for application by parents of children with behavior problems. *Journal of Applied Behavior Analysis,* 1972, 5, 485–497.

Chu, F.D., & Trotter, S. *The madness establishment: Ralph Nader's study group report on the National Institute of Mental Health.* New York: Grossman, 1974.

Chun, Ki-Taek, Cobb, S., & French, J.R.R., Jr. *Measures for psychological assessment: A guide to 3000 original sources and their applications.* Ann Arbor, Mich.: Institute of Social Research, 1975.

Ciminero, A.R. Behavioral assessment: An overview. In A.R. Ciminero, K.S. Calhoun, & H.E. Adams (Eds.), *Handbook of behavioral assessment.* New York: Wiley, 1977, 3–13.

Ciminero, A.R., Calhoun, K.S., & Adams, H.E. *Handbook of behavioral assessment.* New York: Wiley, 1977.

Ciminero, A.R., Nelson, R.O., & Lipinski, D.P. Self-monitoring procedures. In A.R. Ciminero, K.S. Calhoun, & H.E. Adams (Eds.), *Handbook of behavioral assessment.* New York: John Wiley & Sons, 1977, 195–232.

Clement, P.W. Parents, peers, and child patients make the best therapists. In G.J. Williams & S. Gordon (Eds.), *Clinical child psychology: Current practices and future perspectives.* New York: Behavioral Publications, 1974, 81–97.

Clement, P.W., & Richard, R.C. Children's reinforcement survey. Unpublished manuscript, Fuller Theological Seminary, Pasadena, Calif., 1970.

Cline, V.B., & Richards, J.M., Jr. The generality of accuracy of interpersonal perception. *Journal of Abnormal and Social Psychology,* 1961, *62,* 446–449.

Clonce v. Richardson, 379 F. Supp. 338 (W.D., Mo., 1974).

Cohen, H.L. Educational therapy: The design of learning environments. *Research in Psychotherapy,* 1968, *3,* 21–58.

Cohen, H.L. Programming alternatives to punishment: The design of competence through consequences. In S.W. Bijou & E. Ribes-Inesta (Eds.), *Behavior modification: Issues and extensions.* New York: Academic Press, 1972, 63–84.

Cohen, H.L., & Filipzak, J. *A new learning environment.* San Francisco: Jossey-Bass, 1971.

Cole, J.K., & Magnussen, M.G. Where the action is. *Journal of Consulting Psychology,* 1966, *30,* 539–543.

Colmen, J.G., Kaplan, S.J., & Boulger, J.R. Selection and selecting research in the Peace Corps. Peace Corps Research Note No. 7, August, 1964.

Colson, C.E. Olfactory aversion therapy for homosexual behavior. *Journal of Behavior Therapy and Experimental Psychiatry,* 1972, *3,* 185–187.

Committee on Training and Clinical Psychology. Recommended graduate training program in clinical psychology. *American Psychologist,* 1947, *2,* 539–558.

Comrey, A.L., Backer, E., & Glaser, E.M. *A sourcebook for mental health measures.* Los Angeles: Human Interaction Research Institute, 1973.

Cone, J.D. The relevance of reliability and validity for behavioral assessment. *Behavior Therapy,* 1977, *8,* 411–426.

Cone, J.D., & Hawkins, R.P. (Eds.). *Behavioral assessment: New directions in clinical psychology.* New York: Bruner-Mazel, 1977.

Cook, D.W. The scientist professional: Can psychology carry it off? *The Canadian Psychologist,* 1965, *6a,* 93–109.

Cook, T.D., & Campbell, D.T. *Quasi-experimentation: Design and analysis issues for field settings.* Chicago: Rand-McNally, 1979.

Cooper, A., Furst, J.D., & Bridger, W.H. A brief commentary on the usefulness of studying fears of snakes. *Journal of Abnormal Psychology*, 1969, *74*, 413–414.

Cooper, J.O. *Measurement and analysis of behavioral techniques*. Columbus, Ohio: Charles E. Merrill, 1974.

Corsini, R.J. *Current psychotherapies*. Itasca, Ill.: Peacock, 1973.

Covner, B.J. Studies in phonographic recordings of verbal material. III. The completeness and accuracy of counseling interview reports. *Journal of General Psychology*, 1944, *30*, 181–203.

Covner, B.J. Studies in phonographic recordings. I. The use of phonographic recordings in counseling practice and research. *Journal of Consulting Psychology*, 1972, *6*, 105–113.

Cowen, E.L. The experimental analogue: An approach to research in psychotherapy. *Psychological Reports*, 1961, *8*, 9–10.

Cowen, E.L. Social and community intervention. *Annual Review of Psychology*, 1973, *24*, 423–472.

Cowen, E.L. Baby steps toward primary prevention. *American Journal of Community Psychology*, 1977, *5*, 1–22. (a)

Cowen, E.L. Psychologists in primary prevention: Blowing the cover story. An editorial. *American Journal of Community Psychology*, 1977, *5*, 481–490. (b)

Cowen, E.L., Dorr, D., Izzo, L.D., Madonia, A.J., & Trost, M.A. The primary mental health project: A new way of conceptualizing and delivering school mental health services. *Psychology in the Schools*, 1971, *5*, 216–225.

Cowen, E.L., & Schochet, B.B. Referral and outcome differences between terminating and nonterminating children seen by nonprofessionals in a school mental health project. *American Journal of Community Psychology*, 1973, *1*, 103–112.

Craighead, W.E., Kazdin, A.E., & Mahoney, M.J. *Behavior modification: Principles, issues, and applications*. Boston: Houghton Mifflin, 1976.

Craik, K.H. The assessment of places. In P. McReynolds (Ed.), *Advances in psychological assessment* (Vol. 2). Palo Alto, Calif.: Science and Behavior Books, 1971, 40–62.

Craik, K.H. Environmental psychology. In P.H. Mussen and M. Rosenzweig (Eds.), *Annual review of psychology*, Palo Alto, Calif.: Annual Review, Inc., 1973, 403–422.

Cronbach, L.J. Response sets and test validity. *Educational and psychological measurement*, 1946, *6*, 475–494.

Cronbach, L.J. Two disciplines of scientific psychology. *American Psychologist*, 1957, *12*, 671–684.

Cronbach, L.J. *Essentials of psychological testing* (2d ed.). New York: Harper & Row, 1960.

Cronbach, L.J. *Essentials of psychological testing* (3d ed.). New York: Harper & Row, 1970.

Cronbach, L.J. Five decades of public controversy over mental testing. *American Psychologist*, 1975, *30*, 1–14.

Cronbach, L.J., & Gleser, G.C. *Psychological tests and personnel decisions* (2d ed.). Urbana, Ill.: University of Illinois Press, 1965.

Cronbach, L.J., Gleser, G.C., Nanda, H., & Rajaratnam, N. *The dependability of behavioral measurements*. New York: Wiley, 1972.

Cronbach, L.J., & Meehl, P.E. Construct validity in psychology tests. *Psychological Bulletin*, 1955, *52*, 281–302.

Crow, W.J. The effect of training upon accuracy and variability in interpersonal perception. *Journal of Abnormal and Social Psychology*, 1957, *55*, 355–359.

Crow, W.J., and Hammond, K.R. The generality of accuracy and response sets in interpersonal perception. *Journal of Abnormal and Social Psychology*, 1957, *54*, 384–390.

Crowell, E. Redistributive aspects of psychotherapy's inclusion in national health insurance: A summary. *American Psychologist*, 1977, *32*, 731–737.

Cuca, J. Clinicians compose 36 percent of APA. *APA Monitor*, January 1975, 4.(a)

Cuca, J. Survey shows deteriorating job market for new doctoral psychologists. *APA Monitor*, November 1975, 11.(b)

Cummings, N.A. The anatomy of psychotherapy under national health insurance. *American Psychologist*, 1977, *32*, 711–718.

Cutter, F., & Farberow, N.L. The consensus Rorschach. In B. Klopfer, M.M. Meyer, & F.B. Brawer (Eds.), *Developments in the Rorschach technique. III. Aspects of personality structure*. Harcourt, Brace, Jovanovich, 1970, 209–262.

Dahlstrom, W.G., Welsh, G.S., & Dahlstrom, L.E. *An MMPI handbook, Vol. 1, Clinical interpretation* (Rev. ed.). Minneapolis: University of Minnesota, 1972.

Dailey, C.A. The effects of premature conclusions upon the acquisition of understanding a person. *Journal of Psychology*, 1952, *33*, 133–152.

Dailey, C.A. The practical utility of the clinical report. *Journal of Consulting Psychology*, 1953, *17*, 297–302.

Damich, E. The right against treatment: Behavior modification and the involuntarily committed. *Catholic University Law Review*, 1974, *23*, 774–787.

Dana, R.H. The perceptual organization TAT score, number, order, and frequency. *Journal of Projective Techniques*, 1959, *23*, 307–310.

Dana, R.H., & Leech, S. Existential assessment. *Journal of Personality Assessment*, 1974, *38*, 428–435.

David, H.P. A Szondi Test bibliography, 1939–1953. *Journal of Projective Techniques*, 1954, *18*, 17–32.

Davidson, W.S. Studies of aversive conditioning for alcoholics: A critical review of theory and research methodology. *Psychological Bulletin*, 1974, *81*, 571–581.

Davidson, W.S., Rappaport, J., Seidman, E., Berck, D., & Herring, J. The diversion of juvenile delinquents: An experimental examination. Unpublished manuscript, University of Illinois at Urbana-Champaign, 1975.

Davis, J.D. *The interview as arena*. Stanford, Calif.: Stanford University Press, 1971.

Davison, G.C., & Neale, J.M. *Abnormal psychology: An experimental clinical approach*. New York: Wiley, 1974.

Davison, G.C., & Stuart, R.B. Behavior therapy and civil liberties. *American Psychologist*, 1975, *30*, 755–763.

Davison, G.C., & Wilson, G.T. Processes of fear reduction in systematic desensitization: Cognitive and social reinforcement factors in humans. *Behavior Therapy*, 1973, *4*, 1–21.

Dawe, H.C. An analysis of two-hundred quarrels of pre-school children. *Child Development*, 1934, *5*, 139–157.

DeLeon, P.H. Implications of national health policies for professional psychology. *Professional Psychology*, 1977, *8*, 263–268.

Delfini, L.F., Bernal, M.E., & Rosen, P.M. A comparison of normal and deviant boys in their homes. In E.J. Mash, L.A. Hamerlynck, and L.C. Handy (Eds.), *Behavior modification and families*. New York: Brunner Mazel, 1976, 228–248.

Delprato, D.J. Face validity of test and acceptance of generalized personality descriptions. *Journal of Personality Assessment*, 1975, *39*, 345–348.

DeMoor, W. Systematic desensitization versus prolonged high intensity stimulation (flooding). *Journal of Behavior Therapy and Experimental Psychiatry*, 1970, *1*, 45–52.

Dennis, W. *Readings in the history of psychology*. New York: Appleton-Century-Crofts, 1948.

Derner, G.F. Graduate education in clinical psychology. In B.B.Wolman (Ed.), *Handbook of clinical psychology*. New York. McGraw-Hill, 1965.

Deutsch, F., & Murphy, W.F. *The clinical interview*. New York: International Universities Press, 1955.

Deysach, R.E., Hiers, T.G., & Ross, A.W. Situational determinants of performance on the Rotter internal-external locus of control scale. *Journal of Consulting and Clinical Psychology*, 1976, *44*, 303.

Dickson, C.R. Role of assessment in behavior therapy. In P. McReynolds (Ed.), *Advances in psychological assessment* (Vol. 3). San Francisco: Jossey-Bass, 1975, 341–388.

DiGiuseppe, R.A., & Miller, N.J. A review of outcome studies on rational-emotive therapy. In A. Ellis & R. Grieger (Eds.), *Handbook of rational-emotive therapy*. New York: Springer, 1977, 72–95.

Dillehay, R.C. On the irrelevance of the classical negative evidence concerning the effect of attitudes on behavior. *American Psychologist*, 1973, *28*, 887–891.

DiMascio, A., Boyd, R.W., Greenblatt, M., & Solomon, H.C. The psychiatric interview: A sociophysiologic study. *Diseases of the Nervous System*, 1955, *16*, 2–7.

DiNardo, P.A. Social class and diagnostic suggestion as variables in clinical judgment. *Journal of Consulting and Clinical Psychology*, 1975, *43*, 363–368.

Dirks, S.J., & Kuldau, J.M. Validity of self-report by psychiatric patients of employment earnings and hospitalization. *Journal of Consulting and Clinical Psychology*, 1974, *42*, 738.

Doctor, R., & Polakow, R. A behavior modification program for adult probationers. *Proceedings of the 81st Annual Convention of the American Psychological Association*. Washington, D.C.: APA, 1973.

Doering, C.R., & Raymond, A.F. Additional note on reliability. In *Schizophrenia: Statistical studies from the Boston Psychopathic Hospital* (1925–1934), No. 6, 1935.

Dollard, J., & Miller, N.E. *Personality and psychotherapy: An analysis in terms of learning, thinking, and culture*. New York: McGraw-Hill, 1950.

Dollin, A., & Reznikoff, M. Diagnostic referral questions in psychological testing. *Psychological Reports*, 1966, *19*, 610.

Dörken, H. CHAMPUS ten-state claim experience for mental disorder: Fiscal year 1975. *American Psychologist*, 1977, *32*, 697–710.

Dörken, H., Cummings, N.A. A school of psychology as innovation in professional education: The California School of Professional Psychology. *Professional Psychology*, 1977, *8*, 129–148.

Drake, L.E., & Oetting, E.R. *An MMPI codebook for counselors*. Minneapolis: University of Minnesota Press, 1959.

Dreikurs, R. The meaning of dreams. *Chicago Medical School Quarterly*, 1944, *3*, 4–6, 25–26.

Dreikurs, R. The psychological interview in medicine. *American Journal of Individual Psychology*, 1954, *10*, 99–122.

Driscoll, J.M., Meyer, R.G., & Schanie, C.S. Training in family crisis intervention. *Journal of Applied Behavioral Science*, 1973, *9*, 62–82.

DuBois, P.H. *A history of psychological testing*. Boston: Allyn and Bacon, 1970.

Dunham, H.W. Community psychiatry: The newest therapeutic bandwagon. *Archives of General Psychiatry*, 1965, *12*, 303–313.

Dunnette, M.D. (Ed.). *Handbook of industrial and organizational psychology*. Chicago: Rand McNally, 1976.

Dwarshuis, L., Kolton, M., & Gorodezky, M. Role of volunteers in innovative drug treatment programs. *Proceedings of the 81st Convention of the American Psychological Association*. Washington, D.C.: American Psychological Association, 1973.

D'Zurilla, T.J., Wilson, G.T., & Nelson, R.O. A preliminary study of the effectiveness of graduated prolonged exposure in the treatment of irrational fear. *Behavior Therapy*, 1973, *4*, 672–685.

Edelstein, B.A., & Eisler, R.M. Effects of modeling and modeling with instructions and feedback on the behavioral components of social skills. *Behavior Therapy*, 1976, 7, 382–389.

Educational Testing Service. *A description of the advanced psychology test*, 1977–79. Princeton, N.J.: Educational Testing Service, 1977.

Educational Testing Service. *GRE information bulletin*. Princeton, N.J.: Educational Testing Service, 1978.

Edwards, A.L. *The social desirability variable in personality assessment and research*. New York: Dryden, 1957.

Edwards, A.L. *Edwards personal preference schedule*. New York: Psychological Corporation, 1959.

Edwards, A.L. *The measurement of personality traits by scales and inventories*. New York: Holt, Rinehart, Winston, 1970.

Eells, K., Davis, A., Havinghurst, R.J., Herrick, V.E., & Tyler, R.W. *Intelligence and cultural differences*. Chicago: University of Chicago Press, 1951.

Einhorn, H.J., & Hogarth, R.M. Confidence in judgment: Persistence of the illusion of validity. *Psychological Review*, 1978, *85*, 395–416.

Eisler, R.M., Hersen, M., Miller, P.M., & Blanchard, E.B. Situational determinants of assertive behaviors. *Journal of Consulting and Clinical Psychology*, 1975, *43*, 330–340.

Eisler, R.M., Miller, P.M., & Hersen, M. Components of assertive behavior. *Journal of Clinical Psychology*, 1973, *29*, 295–299.

Elizur, A. Content analysis of the Rorschach with regard to anxiety and hostility. *Journal of Projective Techniques*, 1949, *13*, 247–284.

Elkins, R. Aversion therapy for alcoholism: Chemical, electrical, or verbal imagery. *The International Journal of the Addictions*, 1975, *10*, 157–209.

Ellis, A. *Reason and emotion in psychotherapy*. New York: Lyle Stuart, Inc., 1962.

Ellis, A. Rational-emotive therapy. In R. Corsini (Ed.), *Current psychotherapies*. Itasca, Ill.: F.E. Peacock Publishers, 1973.

Ellis, A. Research data supporting the clinical and personality hypotheses of RET and other cognitive-behavior therapies. In A. Ellis and R. Grieger (Eds.), *Handbook of rational-emotive therapy*. New York: Springer, 1977, 35–71.

Ellis, A., & Grieger, R. (Ed.). *Handbook of rational-emotive therapy*. New York: Springer, 1977.

Endler, N.S., Hunt, J.McV., & Rosenstein, A.J. An S-R inventory of anxiousness. *Psychological Monographs*, 1962, *76*, 1–33.

Englemann, S. The effectiveness of direct verbal instruction on IQ performance and achievement in reading and arithmetic. In R. Ulrich, T. Stachnik, & J. Mabry (Eds.), *Control of human behavior* (Vol. 3). Glenview, Ill.: Scott, Foresman, 1974, 69–84.

English, H.B. Three cases of the conditioned fear response. *Journal of Abnormal and Social Psychology*, 1929, *24*, 221–225.

English, H.B., & English, A.C. *A comprehensive dictionary of psychological and psychoanalytic terms*. New York: Longmans, Green, 1958.

Epstein, L.H. Psychophysiological measurement in assessment. In M. Hersen & A.S. Bellack (Eds.), *Behavioral assessment: A practical handbook*. Oxford: Pergamon Press, 1976, 207–232.

Epstein, L.H., & LaPorte, R.E. Behavioral epidemiology. *Behavior Therapist*, 1978, *1*, 3–5.

Epstein, L.H., Miller, P.M., & Webster, J.S. The effects of reinforcing concurrent behavior on self-monitoring. *Behavior Therapy*, 1976, 7, 89–95.

Erikson, E.H. Ego development and historical change. *The psychoanalytic study of the child* (Vol. 2), New York: International Universities Press, 1946, 359–396.

Erikson, E.H. Identity and the life cycle. *Psychological Issues*, 1959, *1* 18–164.

Erikson, E.H. *Childhood and society* (Rev. ed.). New York: Norton, 1963.

Erlich, J., & Reisman, D. Age and authority in the interview. *Public Opinion Quarterly*, 1961, *25*, 39–56.

Eron, L.D. A normative study of the thematic apperception test. *Psychological Monographs*, 1950, *64*(9).

Ervin, S.J., Jr. Why senate hearings on psychological tests. *American Psychologist*, 1965, *20*, 879–880.

Evans, E.C. Physiognomics in the ancient world. *Transactions of the American Philosophical Association*, 1969, Vol. 59, Part 5.

Evans, I.M. Theoretical and experimental aspects of the behaviour modification approach to autistic children. In M. Rutter (Ed.), *Infantile autism: Concepts, characteristics and treatment*. Edinburgh: Churchill Livingstone, 1971.

Evans, I.M., & Nelson, R.O. Assessment of child behavior problems. In A.R. Ciminero, K.S. Calhoun, & H.E. Adams (Eds.). *Handbook of behavioral assessment,* New York: John Wiley & Sons, Inc., 1977, 603–610.

Exner, J.E. The self-focus sentence completion: A study of egocentricity. *Journal of Personality Assessment*, 1973, *37*, 437–455.

Exner, J.E. *The Rorschach: A comprehensive system*. New York: Wiley, 1974.

Exner, J.E., Jr. Projective techniques. In I.B. Weiner (Ed.), *Clinical methods in psychology*. New York: Wiley, 1976, 61–121.

Eyberg, S.M., & Johnson, S.M. Multiple assessment of behavior modification with families: Effects of contingency contracting and order of treated problems. *Journal of Consulting and Clinical Psychology*, 1974, *42*, 594–606.

Eysenck, H.J. The effects of psychotherapy: An evaluation. *Journal of Consulting Psychology*, 1952, *16*, 319–324.

Eysenck, H.J. Learning theory and behaviour therapy. *Journal of Mental Science*, 1959, *105*, 61–75.

Eysenck, H.J. (Ed.). *Behaviour therapy and the neuroses: Readings in modern methods of treatment derived from learning theory*. New York: Pergamon Press, 1960.

Eysenck, H.J. The effects of psychotherapy. In H.J. Eysenck (Ed.), *Handbook of abnormal psychology*. New York: Basic Books, 1961.

Eysenck, H.J. *Experiments in behavior therapy*. Oxford: Pergamon Press, 1964.

Eysenck, H.J. *The effects of psychotherapy*. New York: International Science Press, 1966.

Eysenck, H.J., & Rachman, S. *The causes and cures of neurosis*. San Diego, Calif.: Knapp, 1965.

Fairweather, G.W. *Methods of experimental social innovation*. New York: Wiley, 1967.

Fairweather, G.W., Sanders, D.H., & Tornatzky, L.G. *Creating change in mental health organizations*. New York: Pergamon Press, 1974.

Fancher, R.E. *Psychoanalytic psychology: The development of Freud's thought*. New York: W.W. Norton, 1973.

Farina, A., Arenberg, D., & Guskin, S. A scale for measuring minimal social behavior. *Journal of Consulting Psychology*, 1957, *21*, 265–268.

Fast, J. *Body language*. New York: M. Evans, 1970.

Feldman, S.S. *Mannerisms of speech and gestures in everyday life*. New York: International Universities Press, 1959.

Fenichel, O. *Problems of psychoanalytic technique*. New York: Norton, 1941.

Fenlason, A.F. *Essentials in interviewing*. New York: Harper & Row, 1952.

Fensterheim, H. The initial interview. In A.A. Lazarus (Ed.), *Clinical behavior therapy*. New York: Bruner/Mazel, 1972, 22–40.

Ferster, C.B. Classification of behavioral pathology. In L. Krasner & L.P. Ullmann (Eds.), *Research in behavior modification*. New York: Holt, Rinehart, Winston, 1965, 9–26.

Ferster, C.B., & Perrott, M.C. *Behavior principles*. New York: Appleton-Century-Crofts, 1968.

Festinger, L., Riecken, H.W., and Schachter, S. *When prophecy fails*. Minneapolis: University of Minnesota Press, 1956.

Fidler, D.S., & Kleinknecht, R.E. Randomized response versus direct questioning: Two data-collection methods for sensitive information. *Psychological Bulletin*, 1977, *84*, 1045–1049.

Fiedler, F.E. A comparison of therapeutic relationships in psychoanalytic, nondirective, and Adlerian therapy. *Journal of Consulting Psychology*, 1950, *14*, 436–445.

Filer, R.N. The clinician's personality and his case reports. *American Psychologist*, 1952, *7*, 336.

Fine, R. *The healing of the mind: The technique of psychoanalytic psychotherapy*. New York: David McKay, 1971.

Fine, R. Psychoanalysis. In R. Corsini (Ed.), *Current psychotherapies*. Itasca, Ill.: F.E. Peacock, 1973.

Fischer, C.T. The testee as co-evaluator. *Journal of Counseling Psychology*, 1970, *17*, 70–76.

Fish, J.M. *Placebo therapy*. San Francisco: Jossey-Bass Publishers, 1973.

Fisher, S., & Fisher, R. Test of certain assumptions regarding figure drawing analysis. *Journal of Abnormal and Social Psychology*, 1950, *45*, 727–732.

Fisher, S., & Greenberg, R.P. *The scientific credibility of Freud's theories and therapy*. New York: Basic Books, 1977.

Fiske, D.W. *Strategies for personality research*. San Francisco: Jossey-Bass, 1978.

Flanagan, J.C. The critical incident technique. *Psychological Bulletin*, 1954, *51*, 327–358.

Flanagan, J.C., & Schmid, F.W. The critical incident approach to the study of psychopathology. *Journal of Clinical Psychology*, 1959, *15*, 136–139.

Ford, D.H., & Urban, H.B. *Systems of psychotherapy: A comparative study*. New York: John Wiley and Sons, 1963.

Forer, B.R. The fallacy of personal validations: A classroom demonstration of gullibility. *Journal of Abnormal and Social Psychology*, 1949, *44*, 118–123.

Forer, B.R. A structured sentence completion test. *Journal of Projective Techniques*, 1950, *14*, 15–29.

Foster, A. Writing psychological reports. *Journal of Clinical Psychology*, 1951, *7*, 195.

Fowler, R.D., Jr. Automated interpretation of personality test data. In J.N. Butcher (Ed.), *MMPI: Research developments and clinical applications*. New York: McGraw-Hill, 1969, 105–126.'

Fox, V. The effects of counseling on adjustment in prison. *Social Forces*, 1954, *32*, 285–289.

Frank, G. Measures of intelligence and conceptual thinking. In I.B. Weiner (Ed.), *Clinical methods in psychology*. New York: Wiley, 1976, 123–186.

Frank, J.D. Some determinants, manifestations, and effects of cohesiveness in therapy groups. *International Journal of Group Psychotherapy*, 1957, 7, 53–63.

Frank, J.D. *Persuasion and healing* (Rev. ed.). Baltimore: The Johns Hopkins University Press, 1973.

Frank, L.K. Projective methods for the study of personality. *Journal of Psychology*, 1939, *8*, 343–389.

Franks, C.M. (Ed.). *Conditioning techniques in clinical practice and research*. New York: Springer, 1964.

Franks, C.M. Forward. In E.J. Mash & L.G. Terdal (Eds.), *Behavior therapy assessment*. New York: Springer, 1976, XI–XIII.

Fredericksen, L.W., Jenkins, J.O., Foy, D.W., & Eisler, R.M. Social skills training in the modifications of abusive verbal outbursts in adults. *Journal of Applied Behavior Analysis*, 1976, *9*, 117–125.

Frederiksen, L.W., Miller, P.M., & Peterson, G.L. Topographical components of smoking behavior. *Addictive Behaviors*, 1977, *2*, 55–61.

Frederiksen, N. Toward a taxonomy of situations. *American Psychologist*, 1972, *27*, 114–123.

Freud, A. *The ego and mechanisms of defense*. New York: International Universities Press, 1946.

Freud, S. *On the psychopathology of everyday life*. New York: Macmillan, 1914.

Freud, S. [*An outline of psychoanalysis*], (J. Strachey, trans.). New York: W.W. Norton, 1949.

Freud, S. The interpretation of dreams (1900). In J. Strachey (Ed.), *The standard edition of the complete psychological works of Sigmund Freud*. London: Hogarth Press, 1953–1964.(a)

Freud, S. Jokes and their relation to the unconscious (1905). In the *Standard edition of the complete psychological works of Sigmund Freud* (Vol. 8). London: Hogarth Press, 1953–1964.(b)

Freud, S. *The standard edition of the complete psychological works of Sigmund Freud* (24 vols.). London: Hogarth Press, 1953–1964.(c)

Freud, S. Remembering, repeating, and working through. In J. Strachey (Ed.), *The standard edition of the complete psychological works of Sigmund Freud*.(Vol. 12), London: Hogarth, 1958, 145–156.

Freud, S. Further recommendations in the technique of psychoanalysis. *Zeitschrift*, BD. I, 1913. Reprinted in S. Freud, *Therapy and technique*. New York: Collier Books, 1963.(a)

Freud, S. Recommendations for physicians on the psychoanalytic method of treatment. *Zentralblatt*, BD. II., 1912. Reprinted in S. Freud, *Therapy and technique*. New York: Collier Books, 1963.(b)

Freud, S. Further recommendations in the technique of psychoanalysis. *Zeitschrift*, BD. III, 1915. Reprinted in S. Freud, *Therapy and technique*. New York: Collier Books, 1963.(c)

Freud, S. *On psychotherapy*. Lecture delivered before the College of Physicians in Vienna, December 12, 1904. Reprinted in S. Freud, *Therapy and technique*. New York: Collier Books, 1963.(d)

Friedman, H. Perceptual regression in schizophrenia: An hypothesis suggested by use of the Rorschach test. *Journal of Projective Techniques*, 1953, *17*, 171–185.

Fulkerson, S.C., & Barry, J.R. Methodology and research on the prognostic use of psychological tests. *Psychological Bulletin*, 1961, *58*, 177–204.

Fuller, P.R. Operant conditioning of a vegetative human organism. *American Journal of Psychology*, 1949, *62*, 587–590.

Galton, F. Psychometric experiments. *Brain*, 1879, *2*, 149–162.

Galton, F. Inquiries into human faculty and its development. In W. Dennis (Ed.), *Readings in the history of psychology*. New York: Appleton-Century-Crofts, 1948, 277–289.

Ganzer, V.J. & Sarason, I.G. Interrelationships among hostility, experimental conditions, and verbal behavior. *Journal of Abnormal and Social Psychology*, 1964, *68*, 79–84.

Garfield, S.L. Historical introduction. In B.B. Wolman (Ed.), *Handbook of clinical psychology*. New York: McGraw-Hill, 1965, 125–140.

Garfield, S.L. Clinical psychology and the search for identity. *American Psychologist*, 1966, *21*, 353–362.

Garfield, S. *Clinical psychology: The study of personality and behavior*. Chicago: Aldine, 1974.

Garfield, S.L., & Bergin, A.E. (Eds.). *Handbook of psychotherapy and behavior change* (2d ed.). New York: John Wiley and Sons, 1978.

Garfield, S.L., & Kurtz, R. A survey of clinical psychologists: Characteristics, activities and orientations. *The Clinical Psychologist*, 1974, *28*, 7–10.

Garfield, S.L., & Kurtz, R. Clinical psychologists in the 1970s. *American Psychologist*, 1976, *31*, 1–9.

Garfield, S.L., & Kurtz, R. A study of eclectic views. *Journal of Consulting and Clinical Psychology*, 1977, *45*, 78–83.

Garner, A.M., & Smith, G.M. An experimental videotape technique for evaluating trainee approaches to clinical judging. *Journal of Consulting and Clinical Psychology*, 1976, *44*, 945–950.

Garner, H.H. *Psychotherapy*. St. Louis: W. H. Green, 1970.

Garrett, A. *Interviewing: Its principles and methods*. New York: Family Welfare Association of America, 1942.

Gaul, D.J., Craighead, W.E., & Mahoney, M.J. Relationship between eating rates and obesity. *Journal of Consulting and Clinical Psychology*, 1975, *43*, 123–125.

Geer, J.H. Phobia treated by reciprocal inhibition. *Journal of Abnormal and Social Psychology*, 1964, *69*, 642–645.

Geer, J.H. The development of a scale to measure fear. *Behaviour Research and Therapy*, 1965, *3*, 45–53.

Geer, J.H. Sexual functioning: Some data and speculations on psychophysiological assessment. In J.D. Cone & R.P. Hawkins (Eds.), *Behavioral assessment: New directions in clinical psychology*. New York: Brunner/Mazel, 1977, 196–209.

Gelinas, D.J. The psychotherapy supervisor's dilemma: Problematic client-therapist interaction patterns. Paper presented at the meeting of the American Psychological Association, Washington, D.C., September 1976.

Gentile, J.R., Roden, A.H., & Klein, R.D. An analysis of variance model for the intrasubject replication design. *Journal of Applied Behavior Analysis*, 1972, *5*, 193–198.

Gesell, A., & Amatroda, C.S. *Developmental diagnosis* (2d ed.) New York: Hoeber-Harper, 1947.

Gilberstadt, H., & Duker, J. *A handbook for clinical and actuarial MMPI interpretation*. Philadelphia: Saunders, 1965.

Gill, M., Newman, R., Redlich, F.C., & Sommers, M. *The initial interview in psychiatric practice*. New York: International Universities Press, 1954.

Glasgow, R., & Arkowitz, H. The behavioral assessment of male and female social competence in dyadic heterosecual interactions. *Behavior Therapy*1975, *4*, 488–499.

Glass, G.V., Wilson, V.L., & Gottman, J.M. *Time series analysis in the behavioral sciences*. Boulder, Colo.: Laboratory of Education Research, University of Colorado, 1973.

Goffman, E. The presentation of self in everyday life. Garden City, NY: Doubleday, 1959.

Goffman, E. *Asylums*. New York: Doubleday, 1961.

Goldberg, L.R. The effectiveness of clinicians' judgments: The diagnosis of organic brain damage from the Bender-Gestalt test. *Journal of Consulting Psychology*, 1959, *23*, 25–33.

Goldberg, L.R. Diagnosticians vs. diagnostic signs: The diagnosis of psychosis vs. neurosis from the MMPI. *Psychological Monographs*, 1965, *79*(9, Whole No. 602).

Goldberg, L.R. Simple models or simple processes? Some research on clinical judgments. *American Psychologist*, 1968, *23*, 483–496. (a)

Goldberg, L.R. Seer over sign: The first "good" example? *Journal of Experimental Research in Personality*, 1968, *3*, 168–171. (b)

Goldberg, L.R. Man versus model of man: A rationale plus evidence for a method of improving on clinical inferences. *Psychological Bulletin*, 1970, *73*, 422–432.

Goldberg, L.R. Objective diagnostic tests and measures. *Annual Review of Psychology*, 1974, *25*, 343–366.

Goldberg, L.R., & Werts, C.E. The reliability of clinicians' judgments: A multitrait-multimethod approach. *Journal of Consulting Psychology*, 1966, *30*, 199–206.

Goldberg, P.A. A review of sentence completion methods in personality assessment. *Journal of Projective Techniques and Personality Assessment*, 1965, *29*, 12–45.

Golden, M. Some effects of combining psychological tests on clinical inferences. *Journal of Consulting Psychology, 1964, 28, 440–446.*

Goldenberg, H. *Contemporary clinical psychology*. Monterey, Calif.: Brooks/Cole, 1973.

Goldfried, M.R. Behavioral assessment. In I.B. Weiner (Ed.), *Clinical methods in psychology*. New York: John Wiley & Sons, 1976, 281–330.

Goldfried, M.R., & Davison, G.C. *Clinical behavior therapy*. New York: Holt, Rinehart, Winston, 1976.

Goldfried, M.R., Decenteceo, E.T., & Weinberg, L. Systematic rational restructuring as a self control technique. *Behavior Therapy*, 1974, *5*, 247–254.

Goldfried, M.R., & D'Zurilla, T.J. A behavior-analytic model for assessing competence. In C.D. Spielberger (Ed.), *Current topics in clinical and community psychology*, (Vol. 1). New York: Academic Press, 1969, 151–196.

Goldfried, M.R., & Kent, R.N. Traditional versus behavioral personality assessment: A comparison of methodological and theoretical assumptions. *Psychological Bulletin*, 1972, *77*, 409–420.

Goldfried, M.R., & Linehan, M.M. Basic issues in behavioral assessment. In A.R. Ciminero, K.S. Calhoun, & H.E. Adams (Eds.), *Handbook of behavioral assessment*. New York: Wiley, 1977, 15–46.

Goldfried, M.R., & Sprafkin, J.N. *Behavioral personality assessment*. Morristown, N.J.: General Learning Press, 1974.

Goldfried, M.R., Stricker, G., & Weiner, I.B. *Rorschach handbook of clinical and research applications*. Englewood Cliffs, N.J.: Prentice-Hall, 1971.

Goldiamond, I. Self control procedures in personal behavior problems. *Psychological Reports*, 1965, *17*, 851–868.

Golding, S.L., & Rorer, L.G. Illusory correlation and subjective judgment. *Journal of Abnormal Psychology*, 1972, *80*, 249–260.

Goldman, B.A., & Busch, J.C. (Eds.). *Directory of unpublished experimental mental measures* (Vol. 2). New York: Human Sciences Press, 1978.

Goldman, B.A., & Saunders, J.L. (Eds.). *Directory of unpublished experimental measures* (Vol. 1). New York: Human Sciences Press, 1974.

Goldschmid, M.L., Stein, D.D., Weissman, H.N., & Sorrels, J. A survey of the training and practices of clinical psychologists. *The Clinical Psychologist*, 1969, *22*, 89–94, 107.

Goldsmith, J.B. Systematic development and evaluation of a behavioral program for training psychiatric inpatients in interpersonal skills. Unpublished doctoral dissertation, University of Wisconsin, 1973.

Goldsmith, J.B., & McFall, R.M. Development and evaluation of an interpersonal skill-training program for psychiatric inpatients. *Journal of Abnormal Psychology*, 1975, *84*, 51–58.

Goldstein, A.J., & Chambless, D.L. A reanalysis of agoraphobia. *Behavior Therapy*, 1978, *9*, 47–59.

Goldstein, A.P. *Psychotherapeutic attraction*. New York: Pergamon Press, 1971.

Goldstein, A.P. Behavior therapy. In R. Corsini (Ed.), *Current psychotherapies*. Itaska, Ill.: F.E. Peacock Publishers, Inc., 1973. (a)

Goldstein, A.P. *Structured learning therapy: Toward a psychotherapy for the poor*. New York: Academic Press, 1973. (b)

Goldstein, A.P. Relationship-enhancement methods. In F.H. Kanfer & A.P. Goldstein (Eds.), *Helping people change*. New York: Pergamon Press, 1976, 15–49.

Goldstein, A.P., Martens, J., Hubben, J., VanBelle, H.A., Schaaf, W., Wiersma, H., Goedhart, A. The use of modeling to increase independent behavior. *Behaviour Research and Therapy*, 1973, *11*, 31–42.

Goldstein, K., & Scheerer, M. Abstract and concrete behavior: An experimental study with special tests. *Psychological Monographs*, 1941, *53*(239), 151.

Goodenough, F.L. *Mental testing*. New York: Rinehart, 1949.

Goodman, E.S., & Maultsby, M.C. *Emotional well being through rational behavior training*. Springfield, Ill.: Charles C. Thomas, 1974.

Gorden, R.L. *Interviewing: Strategy, techniques, and tactics*. Homewood, Ill.: Dorsey Press, 1969.

Gottfredson, G.D., & Dyer, S.E. Health service providers in psychology. *American Psychologist*, 1978, *33*, 314–338.

Gottman, J. Couples interaction scoring system (CISS): Instructions for use of CISS.

Unpublished manuscript, Indiana University, 1974.

Gottman, J., & Markman, H.J. Experimental designs in psychotherapy research. In S. Garfield & A. Bergin (Eds.), *Handbook of psychotherapy and behavior change* (2d ed.). New York: John Wiley & Sons, 1978, 12–62.

Gottman, J., Markman, H., & Notarius, C. The topography of marital conflict: A sequential analysis of verbal and nonverbal behavior. *Journal of Marriage and the Family*, 1977, *39*, 461–477.

Gough, H.G. *California psychological inventory: Manual.* Palo Alto, Calif.: Consulting Psychologists Press, 1957 (Rev. 1964).

Gough, H.G. Clinical versus statistical prediction in psychology. In L. Postman (Ed.), *Psychology in the making.* New York: Knopf, 1962, 526–584.

Gough, H.G., & Sandhu, H.S. Validation of the CPI socialization scale in India. *Journal of Abnormal and Social Psychology*, 1964, *68*, 544–547.

Gough, H.G., Wenk, E.A., & Rozynko, V.V. Parole outcome as predicted from the CPI, the MMPI, and a base expectancy table. *Journal of Abnormal Psychology*, 1965, *70*, 432–441.

Graham, F.K., & Kendall, B.S. Memory-for-designs test: Revised general manual. *Perceptual and Motor Skills*, 1960, *11*, 147–188.

Grantham, R.J. Effects of counselor sex, race, and language style on black students in initial interviews. *Journal of Counseling Psychology*, 1973, *20*, 553–559.

Grayson, H.M., & Tolman, R.S. A semantic study of concepts of clinical psychologists and psychiatrists. *Journal of Abnormal and Social Psychology*, 1950, *45*, 216–231.

Greenblatt, M. Discussion of papers by Saslow, Matarazzo, & Lacey. In E.A. Rubinstein & M.B. Parloff (Eds.), *Research in psychotherapy* (Vol. 1). Washington, D.C.: American Psychological Association, 1959, 209–220.

Greene, R.L. Student acceptance of generalized personality interpretations: A reexamination. *Journal of Consulting and Clinical Psychology*, 1977, *45*, 965–966.

Greenson, R.R. *The technique and practice of psychoanalysis.* New York: International Universities Press, 1967.

Greenspoon, J. Verbal conditioning and clinical psychology. In A.J. Bachrach (Ed.), *Experimental foundations of clinical psychology.* New York: Basic Books, 1962, 510–553.

Greenwald, H. (Ed.), *Great cases in psychoanalysis.* New York: Ballantine Books, 1959.

Greist, J.H., Klein, M.H., & Van Cura, L.J. A computer interview for psychiatric patient target symptoms. *Archives of General Psychiatry*, 1973, *29*, 247–254.

Gross, S.J. The myth of professional licensing. *American Psychologist*, 1978, *33*, 1009–1016.

Grossberg, J.M., & Grant, B.F. Clinical psychophysics: Applications of ratio scaling and signal detection methods to research on pain, fear, drugs, and medical decision making. *Psychological Bulletin*, 1978, *85*, 1154–1176.

Grotjahn, M. *Beyond laughter: Humor and the subconscious.* New York: McGraw-Hill, 1957.

Guerney, B.G. (Ed.). *Psychotherapeutic agents: New roles for nonprofessionals, parents, and teachers.* New York: Holt, Rinehart, & Winston, 1969.

Guiora, A.Z., & Brandwin, M.A. *Perspectives in clinical psychology.* Princeton, N.J.: D. Van Nostrand Co., Inc., 1968.

Guntrip, H. *Psychoanalytic theory, therapy, and the self.* New York: Basic Books, 1973.

Gurin, G., Veroff, J., & Feld, S. *Americans view their mental health.* New York: Basic Books, 1960.

Gurman, A.S., & Kniskern, D.P. Research on marital and family therapy: Progress, perspectives, and prospects. In S.L. Garfield & A.E. Bergin (Eds.), *Handbook of psychotherapy and behavior change* (2d ed.). New York: John Wiley & Sons, 1978.

Gurman, A.S., & Razin, A.M. *Effective psychotherapy: A handbook of research*. New York: Pergamon Press, 1977.

Guthrie, E.R. *The psychology of learning*. New York: Harper & Row, 1935.

Gutride, M.E., Goldstein, A.P., & Hunter, G.F. The use of modeling and role playing to increase social interaction among asocial psychiatric patients. *Journal of Consulting and Clinical Psychology*, 1973, *40*, 408–415.

Haase, W. The role of socioeconomic class in examiner bias. In F. Riessman, J. Cohen, & A. Pearl (Eds.), *Mental health of the poor*. New York: Free Press, 1964.

Hagen, R.L., Craighead, W.E., & Paul, G.L. Staff reactivity to evaluative behavioral observations. *Behavior Therapy*, 1975, *6*, 201–205.

Halberstam, D. *The best and the brightest*. New York: Random House, 1969.

Haley, J. *Changing families: A family therapy reader*. New York: Grune and Stratton, 1971.

Hall, C.S. *The meaning of dreams*. New York: Harper & Row, 1953.

Hall, C.S., & Lindzey, G. *Theories of personality* (2d ed.). New York: Wiley, 1970.

Hall, R.V., Axelrod, S., Tyler, L., Grief, E., Jones, F.C., & Robertson, R. Modification of behavior problems in the home with a parent as observer and experimenter. *Journal of Applied Behavior Analysis*, 1972, *5*, 53–64.

Hall, R.V., Fox, R., Willard, D., Goldsmith, L., Emerson, M., Owen, M., Davis, F., & Porcia, E. The teacher as observer and experimenter in the modification of disputing and talking-out behaviors. *Journal of Applied Behavior Analysis*, 1971, *4*, 141–149.

Halleck, S.L. Community psychiatry: Some troubling questions. In L.M. Roberts, S.L. Halleck, & M.B. Loeb (Eds.), *Community psychiatry*. Garden City, N.Y.: Doubleday, Anchor Books, 1969.

Hallenstein, C.B. Ethical problems of psychological jargon. *Professional Psychology*, 1978, *9*, 111–116.

Hammer, E.F. Projective drawings. In A.I. Rabin (Ed.), *Projective techniques in personality assessment*. New York: Springer, 1968, 366–393.

Hammer, E., & Piotrowski, Z.A. Hostility as a factor in the clinician's personality as it affects his interpretation of projective drawings (H-T-P). *Journal of Projective Techniques*, 1953, *17*, 210–216.

Hammond, K.R., & Allen, J.M. *Writing clinical reports*. Englewood Cliffs, N.J: Prentice-Hall, 1953.

Handler, L. Psychotherapy, assessment, and clinical research: Parallels and similarities. In A.I. Rabin (Ed.), *Clinical psychology: Issues of the seventies*. East Lansing, Mich.: Michigan State University Press, 1974, 49–62.

Hanks, L.M., Jr. Prediction from case material to personality data. *New York Archives of Psychology*, 1936, *29*, No. 207.

Harmatz, M.G., Mendelsohn, R., & Glassman, M.L. *Behavioral observations in the study of schizophrenia*. Paper presented at the 81st Annual Meeting of the American Psychological Association, Montreal, Quebec, Canada, August 1973.

Harper, R.A. *Psychoanalysis and psychotherapy: Thirty-six systems*. Englewood Cliffs, N.J.: Prentice-Hall, Inc., 1959.

Harper, R.G., Wiens, A.N., & Matarazzo, J.D. *Nonverbal communication: The state of the art*. New York: Wiley, 1978.

Harris, V.W., & Sherman, J.A. Effects of peer tutoring and consequences on the math performance of elementary classroom students. *Journal of Applied Behavior Analysis*, 1973, *6*, 587–598.

Harrison, R. Thematic apperceptive methods. In B.B. Wolman (Ed.), *Handbook of clinical psychology*. New York: McGraw-Hill, 1965, 562–620.

Harrower, M.R. *Psychodiagnostic inkblots*. New York: Grune & Stratton, 1945.

Harrower, M. *The practice of clinical psychology*. Springfield, Ill.: Charles C. Thomas, 1961.

Harrower, M. Clinical psychologists at work. In B.B. Wolman (Ed.), *Handbook of clinical psychology*. New York: McGraw-Hill, 1965, 1443–1458. (a)

Harrower, M. Differential diagnosis. In B.B. Wolman (Ed.), *Handbook of clinical psychology*. New York: McGraw-Hill, 1965, 381–402. (b)

Harrower, M.R., & Steiner, M. *Large scale Rorschach techniques*. Springfield, Ill.: Charles C. Thomas, 1945.

Hartlage, L., Freeman, W., Horine, L., & Walton, C. Decisional utility of psychological reports. *Journal of Clinical Psychology*, 1968, *24*, 481–483.

Hartmann, D.P. Forcing square pegs into round holes: Some comments on "An analysis of variance model for the intrasubject replication design." *Journal of Applied Behavior Analysis*, 1974, *7*, 635–638.

Hartmann, D.P. Considerations in the choice of interobserver reliability estimates. *Journal of Applied Behavior Analysis*, 1977, *10*, 103–116.

Hartmann, H. Psychoanalysis and the concept of health. *International Journal of Psychoanalysis*, 1939, *20*, 308–321.

Hartmann, H. *Ego psychology and the problem of adaptation*. New York: International Universities Press, 1958.

Hartshorne, H., & May, M.A. *Studies in deceit*. New York: Macmillan, 1928.

Hatcher, C., & Himmelstein, P. (Eds.). *The handbook of Gestalt therapy*. New York: Jason Aronson, 1976.

Hathaway, S.R. A study of human behavior: the clinical psychologist. *American Psychologist*, 1958, *13*, 255–265.

Hathaway, S.R., & Meehl, P.E. *An atlas for the clinical use of the MMPI*. Minneapolis: University of Minnesota Press, 1951.

Hawkins, R.P. Who decided that was the problem? Two stages of responsibility for applied behavior analysis. In W.S. Wood (Ed.), *Issues in evaluating behavior modification*. Champaign, Ill.: Research Press, 1975, 195–214.

Hawkins, R.P., & Dobes, R.W. Behavioral definitions in applied behavior analysis: Explicit or implicit. In B.C. Etzel, J.M. LeBlanc, & D.M. Baer (Eds.), *New developments in behavioral research: Theory, method and application. In honor of Sidney W. Bijou*. Hillsdale, N.J.: Lawrence Erlbaum Assoc., 1977, 167–188.

Haynes, J.R., & Sells, S.B. Assessment of organic brain damage by psychological tests. *Psychological Bulletin*, 1963, *60*, 316–325.

Haynes, S.N. *Principles of behavioral assessment*. New York: Gardner Press, 1978.

Heath, J.R., & Wilson, H.J. Forces and rates observed during in vivo toothbrushing. *Biomedical Engineering*, 1974, *9*, 61–64.

Heitler, J.B. Preparatory techniques in initiating expressive psychotherapy with lower-class, unsophisticated patients. *Psychological Bulletin*, 1976, *83*, 339–352.

Heller, K. Laboratory interview research as analogue to treatment. In A.E. Bergin & S.L. Garfield (Eds.), *Handbook of psychotherapy and behavior change*. New York: Wiley, 1971, 126–153.

Heller, K. Interview structure and interviewer style in initial interviews. In A.W. Siegman & B. Pope (Eds.), *Studies in dyadic communication*. New York: Pergamon Press, 1972, 9–28.

Heller, K., Davis, J.D., and Myers, R.A. The effects of interviewer style in a standardized interview. *Journal of Consulting Psychology*, 1966, *30*, 501–508.

Heller, K., & Monahan, J. *Psychology and community change*. Homewood, Ill.: Dorsey Press, 1977.

Heller, K., Myers, R.A., & Kline, L.V. Interviewer behavior as a function of standardized client roles. *Journal of Consulting Psychology*, 1963, *27*, 117–122.

Hendriks, A.F.C.J. *Reported versus observed deviancy*. Unpublished manuscript, University of Nijmegen, Netherlands, 1972.

Henry, W.E. *The analysis of fantasy: The thematic apperception technique in the study of personality*. New York: Wiley, 1956.

Herron, R.E., & Ramsden, R.W. A telepedometer for the remote measurement of human locomotor activity. *Psychophysiology*, 1967, *4*, 112–115.

Hersen, M. Historical perspectives in behavioral assessment. In M. Hersen & A.S. Bellack (Eds.), *Behavioral assessment*. New York: Pergamon Press, 1976, 3–22.

Hersen, M., & Bellack, A.S. (Eds.). *Behavioral assessment*. New York: Pergamon Press, 1976.

Hersen, M., & Bellack, A.S. Assessment of social skills. In A.R. Ciminero, K.S. Calhoun, & H.E. Adams (Eds.), *Handbook of behavioral assessment*. New York: John Wiley & Sons, 1977, 509–554.

Hersen, M., Eisler, R., & Miller, P. An experimental analysis of generalization in assertive training. *Behaviour Research and Therapy*, 1974, *12*, 295–310.

Hess, H. Entry requirements for professional practice of psychology. *American Psychologist*, 1977 *32*, 365–368.

Heyns, R., & Lippitt, R. Systematic observational techniques. In G. Lindzey, (Ed.), *Handbook of social psychology* (Vol. 1). Cambridge, Mass.: Addison-Wesley, 1954, 370–404.

Hilgard, E.R. Pain as a puzzle for psychology and physiology. *American Psychologist*, 1969, *24*, 103–114.

Hilgard, E.R. (Ed.). *American psychology in historical perspective, 1892–1977*. Washington, D.C.: American Psychological Association, 1978.

Hilgard, E.R., Atkinson, R.C., & Atkinson, R.L. *Introduction to psychology* (7th ed.). New York: Harcourt, Brace, Jovanovich, 1979.

Hobbs, N. Mental health's third revolution. *American Journal of Orthopsychiatry*, 1964, *34*, 822–833.

Hoch, E.L. Psychology today: Conceptions and misconceptions. *The profession of psychology*. New York: Holt, Rinehart, Winston, 1962.

Hoch, E.L. *Experimental contributions to clinical psychology*. Belmont, Calif.: Brooks/ Cole, 1971.

Hoffman, B. *The tyranny of testing*. New York: Crowell-Collier, 1962.

Hoffman, P.J. The paramorphic representation of clinical judgment. *Psychological Bulletin*, 1960, *57*, 116–131.

Hoffman, R.S. The varieties of psychotherapeutic experience. *Journal of Irreproducible Results*, 1973, *19*, 76–77.

Hogan, R.A. The implosive technique. *Behaviour Research and Therapy*, 1968, *6*, 423–431.

Holland, G.A. Transactional analysis. In R. Corsini (Ed.), *Current psychotherapies*. Itasca, Ill.: F.E. Peacock Publishers, Inc. 1973.

Holland, J.G., & Skinner, B.F. *The analysis of behavior: A program for self instruction.* New York: McGraw-Hill, 1961.

Hollingshead, A.B., & Redlich, F.C. *Social class and mental illness.* New York; Wiley, 1958.

Holsopple, J.Q., & Miale, F.R. *Sentence completion: A projective method for the study of personality.* Springfield, Ill.: Charles C. Thomas, 1954.

Holt, R.R. Formal aspects of the TAT: A neglected resource. *Journal of Projective Techniques,* 1958, *22,* 163–172.

Holt, R.R. Kubie's dream and its impact upon reality. Psychotherapy as an autonomous profession. *Journal of Nervous and Mental Disease,* 1969, *149,* 186–207.

Holt, R.R. *Assessing personality.* New York: Harcourt, Brace, Jovanovich, 1971.

Holt, R.R. *Methods in clinical psychology: Projective assessment* (Vol. 1). New York: Plenum Press, 1978.

Holt, R.R., & Luborsky, L. *Personality patterns of psychiatrists: A study of methods for selecting residents* (Vol. 1). New York: Basic Books, 1958.

Holt v. Sarver, 309F. Supp. 362 (E.D. Ark. 1970).

Holtzman, W.H., Thorpe, J.S., Swartz, J.D., & Herron, E.W. *Inkblot perception and personality.* Austin: University of Texas Press, 1961.

Holzberg, J.D., Knapp, R.H., & Turner, J.L. College students as companions for the mentally ill. In E.L. Cowen, E.A. Gardner, & M. Zax (Eds.), *Emergent approaches to mental health problems.* New York: Appleton-Century-Crofts, 1967.

Honigfeld, G., Gillis, R., & Klett, J. NOSIE 30: A treatment sensitive ward behavior scale. *Psychological Reports,* 1966, *19,* 180–182.

Hsu, J.J. Electroconditioning therapy of alcoholics. A preliminary report. *Quarterly Journal of Studies on Alcohol,* 1965, *26,* 449–459.

Hull, C.L. *Principles of behavior.* New York: Appleton, 1943.

Hunt, W.A. *The clinical psychologist.* Springfield, Ill.: Charles C. Thomas, 1956.

Hunt, W.A. Relations with other professions. In B.B. Wolman (Ed.), *Handbook of clinical psychology.* New York: McGraw-Hill, 1965.

Hunt, W.A., & Jones, N.F. The experimental investigation of clinical judgment. In A.J. Bachrach (Ed.), *Experimental foundations of clinical psychology.* New York: Basic Books, 1962, 26–51.

Hutt, C., & Hutt, S.J. Stereotypy, arousal and autism. *Human Development,* 1968, *11,* 277–286.

Hutt, C., & Ounsted, C. The biological significance of gaze aversion with particular reference to the syndrome of infantile autism. *Behavioral Science,* 1966, *11,* 346–356.

Hutt, S.J., & Hutt, C. (Eds.), *Behavior studies in psychiatry.* Oxford: Pergamon, 1970.

Hyman, H.H., Cobb, W.J., Feldman, J.J., Hart, C.W., & Stember, G.H. *Interviewing in social research.* Chicago: University of Chicago Press, 1954.

Institute of Personality Assessment and Research. *Annual report: 1969–1970.* Berkeley, Calif.: University of California, 1970.

Ittleson, W., Rivlin, L., & Proshansky, H.M. The use of behavioral maps in environmental psychology. In H. Proshansky, W. Ittleson, & L. Rivlin (Eds.), *Environmental psychology: Man and his physical setting.* New York: Holt, Rinehart, & Winston, 1970, 658–668.

Jackson, B. Treatment of depression by self-reinforcement. *Behavior Therapy,* 1972, *3,* 298–307.

Jackson, D.N. *Personality research form manual.* Goshen, N.Y.: Research Psychologists Press, 1967.

Jackson, D.N., & Messick, S. Content and style in personality assessment. *Psychological Bulletin*, 1958, *55*, 243–252.

Jackson, D.N., & Messick, S. Acquiesence and desirability as response determinants on the MMPI. *Educational and Psychological Measurement*, 1961, *21*, 771–790.

Jacobson, A., Kales, A., Lehmann, D., & Zweizig, J.R. Somnambulism: All night electroencephalographic studies. *Science*, 1965, *148*, 975–977.

Jacobson, E. *Progressive relaxation*. Chicago: University of Chicago Press, 1938.

Johnson, M.L. Seeing's believing. *New Biology*, 1953, *15*, 60–80.

Johnson, S.M., & Bolstad, O.D. Methodological issues in naturalistic observation: Some problems and solutions for field research. In L.A. Hamerlynck, L.C. Handy, & E.J. Mash (Eds.), *Behavior change: Methodology, concepts, and practice*. Champaign, Ill.: Research Press, 1973, 7–67.

Johnson, S.M., & Lobitz, G.K. Parental manipulation of child behavior in home observations. *Journal of Applied Behavior Analysis*, 1974, *7*, 23–32.

Joint Commission on Mental Illness and Health. *Action for mental health*. New York: Basic Books, 1961.

Jones, E. *The life and work of Sigmund Freud* (Vols. 1, 2, and 3). New York: Basic Books, 1953, 1955, 1957.

Jones, E.E., & Nisbett, R.E. *The actor and the observer: Divergent perceptions of the causes of behavior*. New York: General Learning Press, 1971.

Jones, H.E. et al. *Development in adolescence*. New York: Appleton-Century, 1943.

Jones, M.C. A laboratory study of fear: The case of Peter. *Pedagogical Seminary and Journal of Genetic Psychology*, 1924, *31*, 308–315. (a)

Jones, M.C. The elimination of childrens' fears. *Journal of Experimental Psychology*, 1924, *7*, 382–380. (b)

Jones, R.R., Reid, J.B., & Patterson, G.R. Naturalistic observation in clinical assessment. In P. McReynolds (Ed.), *Advances in psychological assessment* (Vol. 3). San Francisco: Jossey-Bass, Inc., 1975, 42–95.

Jourard, S.M. The effects of experimenters' self-disclosure on subjects' behavior. In C.D. Spielberger (Ed.), *Current topics in clinical and community psychology*. New York: Academic Press, 1969, 109–150.

Jung, C.G. The association method. *American Journal of Psychology*, 1910, *21*, 219–269.

Jurjevich, R.M. *The hoax of Freudism*. Philadelphia: Dorrence & Co., 1974.

Kagan, J. The measurement of overt aggression from fantasy. *Journal of Abnormal and Social Psychology*, 1956, *52*, 390–393.

Kagan, N. Influencing human interaction—Eleven years with IPR. In B.A. Jacobs, R.K. Buschman, R.F. Dency, D.T. Schaeffer, & J. Stieber (Eds.), *Counselor training*. Arlington, Va.: National Drug Abuse Training Center, 1974, 329–346.

Kahn, R.L., & Cannell, C.F. *The dynamics of interviewing: Theory, technique, and cases*. New York: Wiley, 1957.

Kahn, T.C. Personality projection on culturally structured symbols. *Journal of Projective Techniques*, 1955, *19*, 431–442.

Kaimowitz and Doe v. Department of Mental Health for the State of Michigan, C.A. 73-19434-AW (Cir. Court of Wayne, Mich., July 10, 1973).

Kallman, W.M., & Feuerstein, M. Psychophysiological procedures. In A.R. Ciminero, K.S. Calhoun, & H.E. Adams (Eds.), *Handbook of behavioral assessment*. New York: John Wiley & Sons, 1977, 329–364.

Kanfer, F.H. Vicarious human reinforcements: A glimpse into the black box. In L.

Krasner and L.P. Ullmann (Eds.), *Research in behavior modification*. New York: Holt, Rinehart, Winston, 1965, 244–267.

Kanfer, F.H. Verbal conditioning: A review of its current status. In T.R. Dixon & D.L. Horton (Eds.), *Verbal behavior and general behavior theory*. Englewood Cliffs, N.J.: Prentice-Hall, 1968, 245–290.

Kanfer, F.H. Self management methods. In F.H. Kanfer and A.P. Goldstein (Eds.), *Helping people change: A textbook of methods*. New York: Pergamon Press, 1975, 309–355.

Kanfer, F.H., & Karoly, P. Self-control: A behavioristic excursion into the lion's den. *Behavior Therapy*, 1972, *3*, 398–416.

Kanfer, F.H., & McBrearty, J.F. Minimal social reinforcement and interview content. *Journal of Clinical Psychology*, 1962, *18*, 210–215.

Kanfer, F.H., & Saslow, G. Behavioral diagnosis. In C.M. Franks (Ed.), *Behavior therapy: Appraisal and status*. New York: McGraw-Hill, 1969, 417–444.

Kaplan, A. *The conduct of inquiry*. San Francisco: Chandler, 1964.

Karoly, P. Ethical considerations in the application of self-control techniques. *Journal of Abnormal Psychology*, 1975, *84*, 175–177.

Karst, T.O., & Trexler, L.D. Initial study using fixed-role and rational-emotive therapy in treating public speaking anxiety. *Journal of Consulting and Clinical Psychology*, 1970, *34*, 360–366.

Kass, R.E., & O'Leary, K.D. The effects of observer bias in field-experimental settings. Paper presented at a symposium on behavior analysis in education, University of Kansas, Lawrence, Kan., April 1970.

Katz, D. Do interviewers bias poll results? *Public Opinion Quarterly*, 1942, *6*, 248–268.

Katz, R.C., & Zlutnick, S. (Eds.). *Behavior therapy and health care: Principles and applications*. New York: Pergamon Press, 1975.

Kaul, T., & Bednar, R.L. Conceptualizing group research: A preliminary analysis. *Journal of Small Group Behavior*, 1978, *9*, 173–191.

Kavanagh, D., & Zandler, H.A. A versatile recording system for studies of mastication. *Medical Electronics Biological Engineering*, 1965, *3*, 291–300.

Kazdin, A.E. Covert modeling and reduction of avoidance behavior. *Journal of Abnormal Psychology*, 1973, *81*, 87–95.

Kazdin, A.E. Effects of covert modeling and model reinforcement on assertive behavior. *Journal of Abnormal Psychology*, 1974, *83*, 240–252. (a)

Kazdin, A.E. Self-monitoring and behavior change. In M.J. Mahoney & C.E. Thoresen (Eds.), *Self-control: Power to the person*. Monterey, Calif.: Brooks-Cole, 1974, 218–246. (b)

Kazdin, A.E. *History of behavior modification: Experimental foundations of contemporary research*. Baltimore: University Park Press, 1978. (a)

Kazdin, A.E. Evaluating the generality of findings in analogue therapy research. *Journal of Consulting and Clinical Psychology*, 1978, *46*, 673–686. (b)

Kazdin, A.E., & Bootzin, R.R. The token economy: An evaluative review. *Journal of Applied Behavior Analysis*, 1972, *5*, 343–372.

Kazdin, A.E., & Klock, J. The effect of nonverbal teacher approval on student attentive behavior. *Journal of Applied Behavior Analysis*, 1973, *6*, 643–654.

Kazdin, A.E., & Kopel, S.A. On resolving ambiguities of the multiple baseline design: Problems and recommendations. *Behavior Therapy*, 1975, *6*, 601–608.

Kazdin, A.E., & Wilcoxon, L.A. Systematic desensitization and nonspecific treatment effects: A methodological evaluation. *Psychological Bulletin*, 1976, *83*, 729–758.

Keefe, F.J., Kopel, S.A., & Gordon, S.B. *A practical guide to behavioral assessment.* New York: Springer, 1978.

Keeley, S.M., Shemberg, K.M., & Carbonell, J. Operant clinical intervention: Behavior management or beyond? Where are the data? *Behavior Therapy*, 1976, *7*, 292–305.

Keller, F.S. A personal course in psychology. In R. Ulrich, T. Stachnik, & J. Mabry (Eds.), *Control of human behavior*. Glenview, Ill.: Scott, Foresman, 1966, 91–93.

Kelly, E.L. Clinical psychology—1960: A report of survey findings. *Newsletter, Division of Clinical Psychology of APA*, 1961, *14*, 1–11.

Kelly, E.L. Clinical psychology: The postwar decade. In I.N. Mensh (Ed.), *Clinical psychology: Science and profession*. New York: Macmillan, 1966, 104–121.

Kelly, E., & Fiske, D.W. *The prediction of performance in clinical psychology*. Ann Arbor, Mich. : University of Michigan Press, 1951.

Kelly, G.A. *The psychology of personal constructs*. New York: Norton, 1955.

Kelly, G.A. The theory and technique of assessment. In P.R. Farnsworth & Q. McNemar (Eds.), *Annual review of psychology* (Vol. 9). Palo Alto, Calif.: Annual Reviews, Inc., 1958, 323–352.

Kempler, W. Gestalt therapy. In R. Corsini (Ed.), *Current psychotherapies*. Itasca, Ill.: Peacock, 1973, 251–286.

Kennedy, J.L., & Uphoff, H.F. Experiments on the nature of extra-sensory perception: III. The recording error criticism of extra-chance scores. *Journal of Parapsychology*, 1939, *3*, 226–245.

Kent, R.N., & Foster, S.L. Direct observational procedures: Methodological issues in naturalistic settings. In A.R. Ciminero, K.S. Calhoun, & H.E. Adams (Eds.), *Handbook of behavioral assessment*. New York: John Wiley & Sons, 1977, 279–328.

Kent, R.N., O'Leary, K.D., Diament, C., & Dietz, A. Expectation biases in observational evaluation of therapeutic change. *Journal of Consulting and Clinical Psychology*, 1974, *42*, 774–781.

Kernberg, O. *Object relations, theory and clinical psychoanalysis*. New York: Jason Aronson, 1976.

Kessler, M., & Gomberg, C. Observations of barroom drinking: Methodology and preliminary results. *Quarterly Journal of Studies on Alcohol*, 1974, *35*, 1392–1396.

Kiesler, D.J. Experimental designs in psychotherapy research. In A.E. Bergin and S.L. Garfield (Eds.), *Handbook of psychotherapy and behavior change*. New York: Wiley & Sons, 1971.

Klein, M. *The psychoanalysis of children*. New York: Grove Press, 1960.

Klein, M., Dittman, A.T., Parloff, M.B., & Gill, M.M. Behavior therapy: Observations and reflections. *Journal of Consulting and Clinical Psychology*, 1969, *33*, 259–266.

Kleinknecht, R.A., & Bernstein, D.A. Assessment of dental fear. *Behavior Therapy*, 1978, *9*, 626–634.

Kleinmuntz, B. MMPI decision rules for the identification of college maladjustment: A digital computer approach. *Psychological Monographs*, 1963, *77*(14, Whole No. 477).

Klopfer, B., & Kelley, D.M. The technique of the Rorschach performance. *Rorschach Research Exchange*, 1937, *2*, 1–14.

Klopfer, B., & Kelley, D.M. *The Rorschach technique*. New York: Harcourt, Brace, & World, 1942.

Klopfer, W.G. *The psychological report*. New York: Grune & Stratton, 1960.

Kluckhohn, C. The influence of psychiatry on anthropology in America during the last 100 years. In J.K. Hall, G. Zilboorg, and H.A. Bunker (Eds.), *One hundred years of American psychiatry*. New York: Columbia University Press, 1944.

Knecht v. Gillman, 488F 2nd 1136–1137 (8th Cir. 1973).

Koffka, K. *Principles of Gestalt psychology*. New York: Harcourt, Brace, 1935.

Kohler, W. *The mentality of apes*. New York: Harcourt, Brace, 1925.

Kohut, H. *The analysis of self*. New York: International Universities Press, 1971.

Kopell, B.S., & Rosenbloom, M.J. Scalp-recorded potential correlates of psychological phenomena in man. In P. McReynolds (Ed.), *Advances in psychological assessment* (Vol. 3). San Francisco: Jossey-Bass, 1975, 433–476.

Korchin, S.J. *Modern clinical psychology: Principles of intervention in the clinic and community*. New York: Basic Books, Inc., 1976.

Korman, M. National conference on levels and patterns of professional training in psychology: The major themes. *American Psychologist*, 1974, *29*, 441–449.

Korman, M. (Ed.). *Levels and patterns of professional training in psychology*. Washington, D.C.: American Psychological Association, 1976.

Korsch, B.M., & Negrete, V.F. Doctor-patient communication. *Scientific American*, 1972, *227*, 66–74.

Kostlan, A. A method for the empirical study of psychodiagnosis. *Journal of Consulting Psychology*, 1954, *18*, 83–88.

Kotchen, T. Existential mental health: An empirical approach. *Journal of Individual Psychology*, 1960, *16*, 174–181.

Krasner, L. Studies of the conditioning of verbal behavior. *Psychological Bulletin*, 1958, *55*, 148–171.

Krasner, L. Verbal conditioning and psychotherapy. In L. Krasner & L.P. Ullmann (Eds.), *Research in behavior modification*. New York: Holt, Rinehart, & Winston, 1965, 211–228.

Krasner, L. Behavior therapy. In P.H. Mussen (Ed.), *Annual Review of Psychology* (Vol. 22). Palo Alto, Calif.: Annual Reviews, 1971.

Krasner, L. The future and past in the behaviorism-humanism dialogue. *American Psychologist*, 1978, *33*, 799–804.

Krasner, L., & Ullmann, L.P. (Eds.). *Research in behavior modification: New developments and implications*. New York: Holt, Rinehart, & Winston, 1965.

Krasner, L., & Ullmann, L.P. *Behavior influence and personality*. New York: Holt, Rinehart, & Winston, Inc., 1973.

Krech, D., Crutchfield, R.S., & Ballachey, E.L. *Individual in society*. New York: McGraw-Hill, 1962.

Kremers, J. *Scientific psychology and naive psychology*. Nijmegen, Netherlands: Drukkerij Gebr. Janssen N.V., 1960.

Kubany, E.S., & Sloggett, B.B. Coding procedure for teachers. *Journal of Applied Behavior Analysis*, 1973, *6*, 339–344.

Kubie, L.S. The pros and cons of a new profession: A doctorate in medical psychology. *Texas Reports on Biology and Medicine*, 1954, *12*, 125–170.

Kupfer, D.J., Detre, T.P., Foster, F.G., Tucker, G.J., & Delgado, J. The application of Delgado's telemetric mobility recorder for human studies. *Behavioral Biology*, 1972, *7*, 585–590.

Kutash, S.B. Modified psychoanalytic therapies. In B.B. Wolman (Ed.), *The therapist's handbook*. New York: Van Nostrand Reinhold, 1976, 87–116.

L'Abate, L. *Principles of clinical psychology*. New York: Grune & Stratton, 1964.

L'Abate, L. Introduction. In L. L'Abate (Ed.), *Models of clinical psychology*. Research paper number 22. Atlanta, Ga.: Georgia State College, 1969.

Lader, M.H., & Mathews, A.M. A physiological model of phobic anxiety and desensitization. *Behaviour Research and Therapy*, 1968, *6*, 411–421.

Laing, R.D. *The politics of experience.* New York: Pantheon, 1967.

Lambert, N.M., Cox, H.W., & Hartsough, C.S. The observability of intellectual functioning of first graders. *Psychology in the Schools,* 1970, *7,* 74–85.

Lang, P.J. Fear reduction and fear behavior: Problems in treating a construct. In J.M. Shlien (Ed.), *Research in psychotherapy* (Vol. 3). Washington, D.C.: American Psychological Association, 1968, 90–102.

Lang, P.J. The application of psychophysiological methods to the study of psychotherapy and behavior modification. In A.E. Bergin & S.L. Garfield (Eds.), *Handbook of psychotherapy and behavior change: An empirical analysis.* New York: Wiley, 1971, 75–125.

Lang, P.J. Research on the specificity of feedback training: Implication for the use of biofeedback in the treatment of anxiety and fear. In J. Beatty & H. Legewie (Eds.), *Biofeedback and behavior,* Proceedings of the NHTO Symposium on Biofeedback & Behavior, Munich, July 1976. New York: Plenum Press, 1977.

Lang, P.J., & Lazovik, A.D. Experimental desensitization of a phobia. *Journal of Abnormal and Social Psychology,* 1963, *66,* 519–525.

LangeA.J.,& Jakubowski, P. *Responsible assertive training.* Champaign, Ill.: Research Press, 1976.

Lanyon, R.I. Measurement of social competence in college males. *Journal of Consulting Psychology,* 1967, *31,* 495–498.

Lanyon, R.I., & Goodstein, L.D. *Personality assessment.* New York: Wiley, 1971.

LaPiere, R.T. Attitudes vs. actions. *Social Forces,* 1934, *13,* 230–237.

Lapouse, R., & Monk, M.A, An epidemiologic study of behavior characteristics in children. *American Journal of Public Health,* 1958, *48,* 1134–1144.

Lavigueur, H., Peterson, R.A., Sheese, J.G., & Peterson, L.W. Behavioral treatment in the home: Effects on an untreated sibling and long-term follow-up. *Behavior Therapy,* 1973, *4,* 431–441.

Lawlis, G.F. Response styles of a patient population on the Fear Survey Schedule. *Behaviour Research and Therapy,* 1971, *9,* 95–102.

Lazarus, A.A. New methods in psychotherapy: A case study. *South African Medical Journal,* 1958, *32,* 660–664.

Lazarus, A.A. Group therapy of phobic disorders by systematic desensitization. *Journal of Abnormal and Social Psychology,* 1961, *63,* 504–510.

Lazarus, A.A. *Behavior therapy and beyond.* New York: McGraw-Hill, 1971.

Lazarus, A.A. Multimodel behavior therapy: Treating the "basic id." *Journal of Nervous and Mental Disease,* 1973, *156,* 504–510.

Lazarus, R.S. Cognitive and personality factors underlying threat and coping. In M.H. Appley & R. Trumball (Eds.), *Psychological stress: Issues in research.* New York: Appleton-Century-Crofts, 1967, 151–169.

Leary, T., & Gill, M. The dimensions and a measure of the process of psychotherapy: A system for the analysis of the content of clinical evaluations and patient-therapist verbalizations. In E.A. Rubinstein & M.B. Parloff (Eds.), *Research in psychotherapy* (Vol. 1). Washington, D.C.: American Psychological Association, 1959, 62–95.

LeBow, M.D., Goldberg, P.S., & Collins, A. A methodology for investigating differences in eating between obese and nonobese persons. *Behavior Therapy,* 1976, *7,* 707–709.

LeBow, M.D., Goldberg, P.S., & Collins, A. Eating behavior of overweight and nonoverweight persons in the natural environment. *Journal of Consulting and Clinical Psychology,* 1977, *45,* 1204–1205.

Lederer, W.J., & Jackson, D.D. *The mirages of marriage*. New York: Norton, 1968.

Ledvinka, J. Race of interviewer and the language elaboration of black interviewees. *Journal of Social Issues*, 1971, *27*, 185–197.

Ledwidge, B. Cognitive behavior modification: A step in the wrong direction? *Psychological Bulletin*, 1978, *85*, 353–375.

Lee, S.D., & Temerlin, M.K. Social class, diagnosis, and prognosis for psychotherapy. *Psychotherapy: Theory, Research, and Practice*, 1970, *7*, 181–185.

Lehner, G.F. Defining psychotherapy. *American Psychologist*, 1952, *7*, 547.

Leitenberg, H. (Ed.). *Handbook of behavior modification and behavior therapy*. Englewood Cliffs, N.J.: Prentice-Hall, 1976.

Leitenberg, H., Agras, W.S., Barlow, D.H., & Oliveau, D.C. Contribution of selective positive reinforcement and therapeutic instructions to systematic desensitization therapy. *Journal of Abnormal Psychology*, 1969, *74*, 113–118.

Leiter, R.G. The Leiter International Performance Scale. *University of Hawaii Bulletin*, 1936, *15* (7, Serial No. 13).

Lennard, H.L., & Bernstein, A. *The anatomy of psychotherapy: Systems of communication and expectation*. New York: Columbia University Press, 1960.

Levenberg, S.B. Professional training, psychodiagnostic skill, and kinetic family drawings. *Journal of Personality Assessment*, 1975, *39*, 389–393.

Levinson, H. The clinical psychologist as organizational diagnostician. *Professional Psychology*, 1972, *3*, 34–40.

Levis, D.J. The phobic test apparatus: An objective measure of human avoidance behavior to small objects. *Behaviour Research and Therapy*, 1969, *7*, 309–315.

Levy, L.H. The skew in clinical psychology. *American Psychologist*, 1962, *17*, 244–249.

Levy, L.H. *Psychological interpretation*. New York: Holt, Rinehart, & Winston, 1963.

Lewandowski, D.G., & Sarcuzzo, D.P. The decline of psychological testing. *Professional Psychology*, 1976, *7*, 177–184.

Lewinsohn, P.M., Nichols, R.C., Pulos, L., Lomont, J.F., Nickel, H. J., & Siskind, G. The reliability and validity of quantified judgments from psychological tests. *Journal of Clinical Psychology*, 1963, *19* 64–73.

Lewinsohn, P.M., & Shaffer, M. Use of home observations as an integral part of the treatment of depression: Preliminary report and case studies. *Journal of Consulting & Clinical Psychology*, 1971, *37*, 87–94.

Lewittes, D.J., Moselle, J.A., & Simmons, W.L. Sex role bias in clinical judgments based on Rorschach interpretations. *Proceedings of the 81st Annual Convention of the American Psychological Association*, 1973, *8*, 497–498.

Libby, W. The imagination of adolescents. *American Journal of Psychology*, 1908, *19*, 249–252.

Liberman, R.P. Behavioral approaches to family and couples therapy. *American Journal of Orthopsychiatry*, 1970, *40*, 106–118.

Liberman, R.P., DeRisi, W.J., King, L.W., Eckman, T.A., & Wood, D. Behavioral measurement in a community mental health center. In P.O. Davidson, F.W. Clark, & L.A. Hamerlynck (Eds.), *Evaluation of behavioral programs*. Champaign, Ill.: Research Press, 1974, 103–139.

Libet, J.M., & Lewinsohn, P.M. Concept of social skill with special reference to the behavior of depressed persons. *Journal of Consulting and Clinical Psychology*, 1973, *40*, 304–312.

Lick, J.R. The effects of pretreatment demand characteristics on verbally reported fear. *Behavior Therapy*, 1977, *8*, 727–730.

Lidz, R.W., & Lidz, T. The family environment of schizophrenic patients. *American Journal of Psychiatry*, 1949, *106*, 332–345.

Liebert, R.M., & Spiegler, M.D. *Personality* (2d ed.). Homewood, Ill.: Dorsey Press, 1974.

Liebert, R.M., & Spiegler, M.D. *Personality: Strategies and issues* (3d ed.). Homewood, Ill.: 1978.

Lindesmith, A.R., and Strauss, A. A critique of culture-personality writings. *American Sociological Review*, 1950, *15*, 587–600.

Lindner, R. *The fifty minute hour*. New York: Rinehart, 1954.

Lindner, R. The girl who couldn't stop eating. In H. Greenwald (Ed.), *Great cases in psychoanalysis*. New York: Ballantine, 1959, 107–151.

Lindsley, O.R., Skinner, B.F., & Solomon, H.C. *Studies in behavior therapy. Status report 1*. Waltham, Mass.: Metropolitan State Hospital, 1953.

Lindzey, G. The thematic apperception test: Interpretive assumptions and related empirical evidence. *Psychological Bulletin*, 1952, *49*, 1–25.

Lindzey, G. On the classification of projective techniques. *Psychological Bulletin*, 1959, *56*, 158–68.

Lindzey, G. *Projective techniques and cross-cultural research*. New York: Appleton-Century-Crofts, 1961.

Lindzey, G., Bradford, J., Tejessy, C., & Davids, A. Thematic apperception test: An interpretive lexicon. *Journal of Clinical Psychology Monograph Supplement*, 1959, No. 12.

Linehan, M.M. Issues in behavioral interviewing. In J.D. Cone & R.P. Hawkins (Eds.), *Behavioral assessment: New directions in clinical psychology*. New York: Bruner/Mazel, 1977, 30–51.

Lipinski, D.P., Black, J.L., Nelson, R.O., & Ciminero, A.R. The influence of motivational variables on the reactivity and reliability of self-recording. *Journal of Consulting and Clinical Psychology*, 1975, *43*, 637–646.

Little, K.B., & Shneidman, E.S. Congruences among interpretations of psychological test and anamnestic data. *Psychological Monographs*, 1959, *73* (Whole No. 476).

Little, L.M., & Curran, J.P. Covert sensitization: A clinical procedure in need of some explanation. *Psychological Bulletin*, 1978, *85*, 513–531.

Lloyd, D., & Newbrough, J.R. Previous conferences on graduate education in psychology: A summary and review. In C.N. Zimet & F.M. Thorne (Eds.), *Preconference materials*. Washington, D.C.: American Psychological Assoc., 1965, 1–15.

Loevinger, J. Measurement in clinical psychology. In B.B. Wolman (Ed.), *Handbook of clinical psychology*. New York: McGraw-Hill, 1965, 78–94.

Lopez, F.M., Jr. *Evaluating executive decision making*. New York: American Management Association, 1966.

Lorion, R.P. Patient and therapist variables in the treatment of low income patients. *Psychological Bulletin*, 1974, *81*, 344–354.

Lorr, M., Klett, J., McNair, D.M., & Lasky, J.J. *Manual. Inpatient multidimensional psychiatric scale*. Veterans Administration, 1962.

Lubin, B.L. Adjective checklists for measurement of depression. *Archives of General Psychiatry*, 1965, *12*, 57–62.

Lubin, B., & Lubin, A.W. Patterns of psychological services in the U.S.: 1959–1969. *Professional Psychology*, 1972, *3*, 63–67.

Lubin, B., Wallis, R.R., & Paine, C. Patterns of psychological test usage in the United

States: 1935–1969. *Professional Psychology*, 1971, *2*, 70–74.

Luborsky, L. A note on Eysenck's article, "The effects of psychotherapy: An evaluation." *British Journal of Psychology*, 1954, *45*, 129–131.

Luborsky, L., & Spence, D.P. Quantitative research on psychoanalytic therapy. In S.L. Garfield & A.E. Bergin (Eds.), *Handbook of psychotherapy and behavior change* (2d ed). New York: Wiley, 1978, 331–368.

Lucero, R.J., & Meyer, B.T. A behavior rating scale suitable for use in mental hospitals. *Journal of Clinical Psychology*, 1951, *7*, 250–254.

Ludwig, A.O., & Ranson, S.W. A statistical follow-up of effectiveness of treatment of combat-induced casualties: Returns to full combat duty. *Military Surgeon*, 1947, *100*, 51–62.

Lushene, R.E., O'Neil, H.F., & Dunn, T. Equivalent validity of a completely computerized MMPI. *Journal of Personality Assessment*, 1974, *38*, 353–361.

MacDonald, M.L. Measuring assertion: A model and method. *Behavior Therapy*, 1978, *9*, 889–899.

MacDonald, M., & Bernstein, D.A. Treatment of a spider phobia with *in vivo* and imaginal desensitization. *Journal of Behavior Therapy and Experimental Psychiatry*, 1974, *5*, 47–52.

MacDonald, M.L., Lindquist, C.V., Kramer, J.A., McGrath, R.A., & Rhyne, L.L. Social skills training: The effects of behavior rehearsal in groups on dating skills. *Journal of Counseling Psychology*, 1975, *22*, 224–230.

Machover, K. *Personality projection in the drawing of the human figure.* Springfield, Ill.: Thomas, 1949.

MacPhillamy, D.J., & Lewinsohn, P.M. Measuring reinforcing events. *Proceedings of the 80th Annual Convention, American Psychological Association*, 1972.

Magaret, A. Clinical methods: Psychodiagnostics. *Annual Review of Psychology*, 1952, *3*, 283–320.

Mahl, G.F. Exploring emotional states by content analysis. In I. Pool (Ed.), *Trends in content analysis*. Urbana, Ill.: University of Illinois Press, 1959, 89–130.

Mahoney, K. Count on it: A simple self-monitoring device. *Behavior Therapy*, 1974, *5*, 701–703.

Mahoney, M.J. The self-management of covert behavior: A case study. *Behavior Therapy*, 1971, *2*, 575–578.

Mahoney, M.J. *Cognition and behavior modification*. Cambridge, Mass.: Ballinger, 1974. (a)

Mahoney, M.J. Self-reward and self-monitoring techniques for weight control. *Behavior Therapy*, 1974, *5*, 48–57. (b)

Mahoney, M.J. *Scientist as subject: The psychological imperative.* Cambridge, Mass.: Ballinger, 1976.

Mahoney, M.J. Experimental methods in outcome evaluation. *Journal of Consulting and Clinical Psychology*, 1978, *46*, 660–672.

Mahoney, M.J., & Thoresen, C.E. *Self-control: Power to the person.* Monterey, Calif.: Brooks-Cole, 1974.

Mahrer, A.R. (Ed.). *New approaches to personality classification*, New York: Columbia University Press, 1970.

Malmo, R.B., Shagass, C., & Davis, F.H. Symptom specificity and bodily reactions during psychiatric interview. *Psychosomatic Medicine*, 1950, *12*, 362–376.

Maloney, M.P., & Ward, M.P. *Psychological assessment: A conceptual approach.* New York: Oxford University Press, 1976.

Mann, P.A. *Community psychology: Concepts and applications*. New York: The Free Press, 1978.

Mannino, F.V., & Shore, M.F. The effects of consultation: A review of empirical studies. *American Journal of Community Psychology*, 1975, *3*, 1–21.

Marcia, J.E., Rubin, B.M., & Efran, J.S. Systematic desensitization: Expectancy change or counter conditioning. *Journal of Abnormal Psychology*, 1969, *74*, 382–387.

Marks, P.A., & Seeman, W. *The actuarial description of abnormal personality*. Baltimore: Williams and Wilkins, 1963.

Marx, M.H., & Hillix, W.A. *Systems and theories in psychology* (3d ed.) New York: McGraw-Hill, 1979.

Mash, E.J., & McElwee, J.D. Situational effects on observer accuracy: Behavior predictability, prior experience, and complexity of coding categories. *Child Development*, 1974, *45*, 367–377.

Mash, E.J., & Terdal, L.G. (Eds.). *Behavior therapy assessment*. New York: Springer, 1976.

Mash, E.J., Terdal, L., & Anderson, K. The response-class matrix: A procedure for recording parent-child interactions. *Journal of Consulting and Clinical Psychology*, 1973, *40*, 163–164.

Masling, J. The influence of situational and interpersonal variables in projective testing. *Psychological Bulletin*, 1960, *57*, 65–68.

Masling, J. Role-related behavior of the subject and psychologist and its effect upon psychological data. In D. Levine (Ed.), *Nebraska symposium on motivation, 1966*. Lincoln, Neb.: University of Nebraska Press, 1966, 67–103.

Maslow, A.H. *Motivation and personality*. New York: Harpers, 1954.

Maslow, A.H. *Toward a psychology of being*. Princeton, N.J.: D. Van Nostrand, 1962.

Maslow, A.H. Self-actualization and beyond. In J.F.T. Bugental (Ed.), *Challenges of humanistic psychology*. New York: McGraw-Hill, 1967.

Maslow, A.H. *Toward a psychology of being* (2d ed.). New York: Van Nostrand Reinhold, 1968.

Maslow, A.H. *The farther reaches of human nature*. New York: Viking Press, 1971.

Masserman, J.H. *Behavior and neurosis: An experimental psycho-analytic approach to psychobiologic principles*. Chicago: University of Chicago Press, 1943.

Matarazzo, J.D. Prescribed behavior therapy: Suggestions from interview research. In A.J. Bachrach (Ed.), *Experimental foundations of clinical psychology*. New York: Basic Books, 1962, 471–509.

Matarazzo, J.D. The interview. In B.B. Wolman (Ed.), *Handbook of clinical psychology*. New York: McGraw-Hill, 1965, 403–450.

Matarazzo, J.D. Higher education, professional accreditation, and licensure. *American Psychologist*, 1977, *32*, 856–859.

Matarazzo, J.D., Weins, A.D., Saslow, G., Dunham, R.M., & Voas, R. B. Speech durations of astronaut and ground communicator, *Science*, 1964, *143*, 148–150.

Matarazzo, J.D., Weitman, M., Saslow, G., & Weins, A.N. Interviewer influence on durations of interviewee speech, *Journal of Verbal Learning and Verbal Behavior*, 1963, *1*, 451–458.

Matarazzo, J.D., & Wiens, A.N. *The interview: Research on its anatomy and structure*. Chicago: Aldine-Atherton, 1972.

May, R. The origins and significance of the existential movement in psychology. In R. May, E. Angel, & H.F. Ellenberger (Eds.), *Existence: A new dimension in psychiatry and psychology*. New York: Basic Books, 1958, 3–36.

May, R. *Love and will*. New York: Norton, 1969.

May, R., Angel, E., and Ellenberger, H.F. (Eds.), *Existence: A new dimension in psychiatry and psychology*. New York: Basic Books, 1958.

Mayman, M. Bibliography on clinical training, 1955–1963. In L. Blank & H.P. David (Eds.), *Sourcebook for training in clinical psychology*. New York: Springer, 1964.

McArthur, C.C. Clinical vs. statistical prediction. *Proceedings of the 1955 Invitational Conference on Testing Problems*. Princeton, N.J.: Educational Testing Service, 1956, 99–106.

McClelland, D.C., Atkinson, J.W., Clark, R.A., & Lowell, E.L. *The achievement motive*. New York: Appleton-Century-Crofts, 1953.

McCoy, S.A. Clinical judgments of normal childhood behavior. *Journal of Consulting and Clinical Psychology*, 1976, *44*, 710–714.

McFall, R.M. Effects of self-monitoring on normal smoking behavior. *Journal of Consulting and Clinical Psychology*, 1970, *35*, 135–142.

McFall, R.M. Parameters of self-monitoring. In R.B. Stuart (Ed.), *Behavioral self-management: Strategies, techniques, and outcome*. New York: Brunner/Mazel, 1977, 196–214.

McFall, R.M., & Hammen, C.L. Motivation, structure, and self-monitoring: Role of nonspecific factors in smoking reduction. *Journal of Consulting and Clinical Psychology*, 1971, *37*, 80–86.

McFall, R.M., & Lillesand, D.B. Behavior rehearsal with modeling and coaching in assertion training. *Journal of Abnormal Psychology*, 1971, *77*, 313–323.

McFall, R.M., & Marston, A.R. An experimental investigation of behavioral rehearsal and assertive training. *Journal of Abnormal Psychology*, 1970, *76*, 295–303.

McFall, R.M., & Twentyman, C.T. Four experiments on the relative contributions of rehearsal, modeling, and coaching to assertion training. *Journal of Abnormal Psychology*, 1973, *81*, 199–218.

McNamara, J.R. The use of self-monitoring techniques to treat nail biting. *Behaviour Research and Therapy*, 1972, *10*, 193–194.

McReynolds, P. Historical antecedents of personality assessment. In P. McReynolds (Ed.), *Advances in psychological assessment* (Vol. 3). San Francisco: Jossey-Bass, 1975, 477–532.

McReynolds, P., Ballachey, E.L., & Ferguson, J.T. Development and evaluation of a behavioral scale for appraising the adjustment of hospitalized patients. *American Psychologist*, 1952, *7*, 340.

McSweeny, A.J. Including psychotherapy in national health insurance: Insurance guidelines and other proposal solutions. *American Psychologist*, 1977, *32*, 722–730.

Mead, M. *Coming of age in Samoa*. New York: Morrow, 1928.

Mead, M. *From the South Seas*. New York: Morrow, 1939.

Meador, B.D., & Rogers, C.R. Client-centered therapy. In R. Corsini (Ed.), *Current psychotherapies*. Itasca, Ill.: F.E. Peacock, 1973, 119–165.

Mednick, S.A., & Shaffer, J.B.P. Mothers' retrospective reports in child-rearing research. *American Journal of Orthopsychiatry*, 1963, *33*, 457–461.

Meehl, P.E. *Clinical versus statistical prediction*. Minneapolis: University of Minnesota Press, 1954.

Meehl, P.E. Wanted—A good cookbook. *American Psychologist*, 1956, *11*, 263–272.

Meehl, P.E. When shall we use our heads instead of the formula? *Journal of Counseling Psychology*, 1957, *4*, 268–273.

Meehl, P.E. The cognitive activity of the clinician. *American Psychologist*, 1960, *15*, 19–27.

Meehl, P.E. Seer over sign: The first good example. *Journal of Experimental Research in Personality*, 1965, *1*, 27–32.

Meehl, P.E. Reactions, reflections, projections. In J.N. Butcher (Ed.), *Objective personality assessment*. New York: Academic Press, 1972, 131–189.

Mehlman, B. The reliability of psychiatric diagnosis. *Journal of Abnormal and Social Psychology*, 1952, *47*, 577–578.

Meichenbaum, D.H. Examination of model characteristics in reducing avoidance behavior. *Journal of Personality and Social Psychology*, 1971, *17*, 298–307.

Meichenbaum, D. Cognitive modification of test anxious college students. *Journal of Consulting and Clinical Psychology*, 1972, *39*, 370–380.

Meichenbaum, D.H. Self instruction methods. In F.H. Kanfer and A.P. Goldstein (Eds.), *Helping people change*. New York: Pergamon Press, 1974.

Meichenbaum, D. *Cognitive behavior modification*. Morristown, N.J.: General Learning Press, 1974.

Meichenbaum, D. A cognitive-behavior modification approach to assessment. In M. Hersen & A.S. Bellack (Eds.), *Behavioral assessment: A practical handbook*. New York: Pergamon Press, 1976, 143–171.

Meichenbaum, D.H., Gilmore, J.B., & Fedoravicius, A. Group insight vs. group desensitization in treating speech anxiety. *Journal of Consulting and Clinical Psychology*, 1971, *36*, 410–421.

Melnick, J. A comparison of replication techniques in the modification of minimal dating behavior. *Journal of Abnormal Psychology*, 1973, *81*, 51–59.

Melton, A.W. (Ed.). *Apparatus tests*. Washington: Government Printing Office, 1947,

Meltzer, M.L. Insurance reimbursement: A mixed blessing. *American Psychologist*, 1975, *30*, 1150–1156.

Meltzoff, J., & Kornreich, M. *Research in psychotherapy*. New York: Atherton Press, Inc., 1970.

Mendel, W.M., & Rapport, S. Determinants of the decision for psychiatric hospitalization. *Archives of General Psychiatry*, 1969, *20*, 321–328.

Menninger, K. *A manual for psychiatric case study*. New York: Grune & Stratton, 1952.

Menninger, K. *The theory of psychoanalytic technique*. New York: Basic Books, 1958.

Mercatoris, M., & Craighead, W.E. The effects of non-participant observation on teacher and pupil classroom behavior. *Journal of Educational Psychology*, 1974, *66*, 512–519.

Merrill, M.A. The significance of IQ's on the revised Stanford-Binet scales. *Journal of Educational Psychology*, 1938, *29*, 641–651.

Meyer, M.L., & Gerrard, M. Graduate training in community psychology. *American Journal of Community Psychology*, 1977, *5*, 155–164.

Meyer, V., Liddell, A., & Lyons, M. Behavioral interviews. In A.R. Ciminero, K.S. Calhoun, & H.E. Adams (Eds.), *Handbook of behavioral assessment*. New York: Wiley, 1977, 117–152.

Meyers, J. Consultee centered consultation with a teacher as a technique in behavior management. *American Journal of Community Psychology*, 1975, *3*, 111–122.

Miklich, D.R. Radio telemetry in clinical psychology and related areas. *American Psychologist*, 1975, *30*, 419–425.

Miller, B.V., & Bernstein, D.A. Instructional demand in a behavioral avoidance test for claustrophobic fear. *Journal of Abnormal Psychology*, 1972, *80*, 206–210.

Miller, J.G. The nature of living systems. *Behavioral Science*, 1971, *16*, 277–301.

Miller, L.K., & Miller, O. Reinforcing self help group activities of welfare recipients. *Journal of Applied Behavior Analysis*, 1970, *3*, 57–64.

Miller, N.E. Learnable drives and rewards. In S.S. Stevens (Ed.), *Handbook of experimental psychology*. New York: Wiley, 1951, 435–472.

Miller, N.E. Learning of visceral and glandular responses. *Science*, 1969, *163*, 434–445.

Miller, N.E., & Dollard, J. *Social learning and imitation*. New Haven, Conn.: Yale University Press, 1941.

Miller, P.M., Becker, J.V., Foy, D.W., & Wooten, L.S. Instructional control of the components of alcoholic dringing behavior. *Behavior Therapy*, 1974, *7*, 472–480.

Miller, P.M., Hersen, M., Eisler, R.M., & Hilsman, G. Effects of social stress on operant drinking of alcoholics and social drinkers. *Behaviour Research and Therapy*, 1974, *12*, 67–72.

Mills, R.B., McDevitt, R.J., & Tonkin, S. Situational tests in metropolitan police recruit selection. *Journal of Criminal Law, Criminology, and Police Science*, 1966, *57*, 99–106.

Mintz, S. Survey of student therapists' attitudes toward psychodiagnostic reports. *Journal of Consulting and Clinical Psychology*, 1968, *32*, 500.

Mischel, W. *Personality and assessment*. New York: Wiley, 1968.

Mischel, W. *Introduction to personality*. New York: Holt, Rinehart, Winston, 1971.

Mischel, W. Toward a cognitive social learning reconceptualization of personality. *Psychological Review*, 1973, *80*, 252–283.

Moos, R.H. Behavioral effects of being observed: Reactions to a wireless radio transmitter. *Journal of Consulting & Clinical Psychology*, 1968, *32*, 383–388.

Moos, R.H. Assessment and impact of social climate. In P. McReynolds (Ed.), *Advances in psychological assessment* (Vol. 3). San Francisco: Jossey-Bass, 1975, 8–41.

Moreno, J.L. *Psychodrama*. New York: Beacon House, 1946.

Morgan, C.L. *Habit and instinct*. London: E. Arnold, 1896.

Morgan, C., & Murray, H.A. A method for investigating phantasies: The thematic apperception test. *Archives of Neurology and Psychiatry*, 1935, *34*, 289–306.

Morgan, H., & Cogger, J. *The interviewer's manual*. New York: Psychological Corporation, 1972.

Morganstern, K.P. Behavioral interviewing: The initial stages of assessment. In M. Hersen & A.S. Bellack (Eds.), *Behavioral assessment*. New York: Pergamon Press, 1976, 51–76.

Morris, C. *The open self*. New York: Prentice-Hall, 1948.

Morris, D. *Manwatching: A field guide to human behavior*. New York: Harry N. Abrams, Inc., 1977.

Mosak, H.H., & Dreikurs, R. Adlerian psychotherapy. In R. Corsini (Ed.), *Current psychotherapies*. Itasca, Ill.: Peacock Press, 1973, 35–83.

Mosak, H.H., & Gushurst, R.S. Some therapeutic uses of psychologic testing. *American Journal of Psychotherapy*, 1972, *26*, 539–546.

Moustakas, C.E., Sigel, I.E., & Schalock, H.D. An objective method for the measurement and analysis of child-adult interaction. *Child Development*, 1956, *27*, 109–134.

Mowrer, O.H. A stimulus response analysis of anxiety and its role as a reinforcing agent. *Psychological Review*, 1939, *46*, 553–565.

Mowrer, O.H. *Learning theory and personality dynamics*. New York: Ronald Press, 1950.

Mowrer, O.H. *Learning theory and behavior*. New York: Wiley, 1960.

Mullahy, P. Non-Freudian analytic theories. In B.B. Wolman (Ed.), *Handbook of clinical psychology*. New York: McGraw-Hill, 1965, 341–377.

Munroe, R. *Schools of psychoanalytic thought*. New York: Dryden Press, 1955.

Murray, H.A. *Explorations in personality*. Fairlawn, N.J.: Oxford, 1938.

Murray, H.A. *Thematic apperception test*. Cambridge: Harvard University Press, 1943.

Murrell, S.A. *Community psychology and social systems*. New York: Behavioral Publications, 1973.

Murstein, B.I. *Theory and research in projective techniques (emphasizing the TAT)*. New York: Wiley, 1963.

Murstein, B.I. Assumptions, adaptation level, and projective techniques. In B.I. Murstein (Ed.), *Handbook of projective techniques*. New York: Basic Books, 1965, 49–69.

Murstein, B. Normative written TAT responses for a college sample. *Journal of Personality Assessment*, 1972, *36*, 109–147.

Mussen, P.H., & Scodel, A. The effects of sexual stimulation under varying conditions on TAT sexual responsiveness. *Journal of Consulting Psychology*, 1955, *19*, 90.

Napoli, P.J. Interpretative aspects of finger painting. *Journal of Psychology*, 1947, *23*, 93–132.

Nathan, P.E. *Cues, decisions and diagnoses*. New York: Academic Press, 1967.

Nay, W.R. *Behavioral intervention*. New York: Gardner Press, 1976.

Nay, W.R. *Multimethod clinical assessment*. New York: Gardner Press, 1979.

Nelson, R.O. Assessment and therapeutic functions of self-monitoring. In M. Hersen, R.M. Eisler, & P.M. Miller (Eds.), *Progress in behavior modification*. New York: Academic Press, 1977, 264–308.

Nettler, G. Test burning in Texas. *American Psychologist*, 1959, *14*, 682–683.

Neuringer, C. (Ed.). *Psychological assessment of suicidal risk*. Springfield, Ill.: Charles C. Thomas, 1974.

Newman, E. *Strictly speaking*. New York: Warner, 1974.

Nietzel, M.T., & Bernstein, D.A. The effects of instructionally-mediated demand upon the behavioral assessment of assertiveness. *Journal of Consulting and Clinical Psychology*, 1976, *44*, 500.

Nietzel, M.T., Martorano, R., & Melnick, J. The effects of covert modeling with and without reply training on the development and generalization of assertive responses. *Behavior Therapy*, 1977, *8*, 183–192.

Nietzel, M.T., & Moore, D. Generalization and maintenance effects of social learning therapies for drug abuse: Indications of neglected criteria. *Drug Forum*. in press.

Nietzel, M.T., Winett, R.A., MacDonald, M.L., & Davidson, W.S. *Behavioral approaches to community psychology*, New York: Pergamon Press, 1977.

Nisbett, R.E. Taste, deprivation, and weight determinants of eating behavior. *Journal of Personality & Social Psychology*, 1968, *10*, 107–116.

Norman, W.T. Psychometric considerations for a revision of the MMPI. In J.N. Butcher (Ed.), *Objective personality assessment: Changing perspectives*. New York: Academic Press, 1972, 59–83.

Nye, R.D. *Three views of man: Perspectives from Sigmund Freud, B.F. Skinner, and Carl Rogers*. Monterey, Calif.: Brooks/Cole, 1975.

Nyman, L. Some odds on getting into Ph.D. programs in clinical psychology and counseling psychology. *American Psychologist*, 1973, *28*, 934–935.

O'Brien, J.S., Raynes, A.E., & Patch, V.D. Treatment of heroin addiction with aversion therapy, relaxation training, and systematic desensitization. *Behaviour Research and Therapy*, 1972, *10*, 77–80.

O'Conner v. Donaldson, 422 U.S. 563 (1975).

O'Dell, J.W. P.T. Barnum explores the computer. *Journal of Consulting and Clinical Psychology*, 1972, *38*, 270–273.

Office of Strategic Services Assessment Staff. *Assessment of men*. New York: Rinehart, 1948.

Olbrisch, M.E. Psychotherapeutic interventions in physical health: Effectiveness and economic efficiency. *American Psychologist*, 1977, *32*, 761–777.

Oldfield, R.C. *The psychology of the interview*. London: Methuen, 1941.

O'Leary, K.D., & Becker, W.C. Behavior modification of an adjustment class: A token reinforcement program. *Exceptional Children*, 1967, *33*, 637–642.

O'Leary, K.D., Becker, W.C., Evans, M.B., & Saudargas, R.A. A token reinforcement program in a public school: A replication and systematic analysis. *Journal of Applied Behavior Analysis*, 1969, *2*, 3–13.

O'Leary, K.D., & Kent, R. Behavior modification for social action: Research tactics and problems. In L.A. Hamerlynck, L.C. Handy, & E.J. Mash (Eds.), *Behavior change: Methodology, concepts, and practice*. Champaign, Ill.: Research Press, 1973, 69–96.

O'Leary, K.D., Kent, R.N., & Kanowitz, J. Shaping data collection congruent with experimental hypotheses. *Journal of Applied Behavior Analysis*, 1975, *8*, 43–51.

O'Leary, K.D., & O'Leary, S.G. (Eds.). *Classroom management*. Elmsford, N.Y.: Pergamon Press, 1972.

O'Leary, K.D., & Wilson, G.T. *Behavior therapy: Application and outcome*. Englewood Cliffs, N.J.: Prentice-Hall, 1975.

Olive, H. Psychoanalysts' opinions of psychologists' reports: 1952 and 1970. *Journal of Clinical Psychology*, 1972, *28*, 50–54.

Orbach, C.E., & Tallent, N. Modification of perceived body and body concepts following the construction of a colostomy. *Archives of General Psychiatry*, 1965, *12*, 126–135.

Orne, M. On the social psychology of the psychological experiment: With particular reference to demand characteristics and their implications. *American Psychologist*, 1962, *17*, 776–783.

Orne, M.T., & Scheibe, K.E. The contribution of nondeprivation factors in the production of sensory deprivation effects: The psychology of the panic button. *Journal of Abnormal and Social Psychology*, 1964, *68*, 3–12.

Orne, M.T., & Wender, P. Anticipatory socialization for psychotherapy: Method and rationale. *American Journal of Psychiatry*, 1968, *124*, 88–98.

O'Rourke, J.F. Field and laboratory: The decision-making behavior of family groups in two experimental conditions. *Sociometry*, 1963, *26*, 422–435.

Osborne, J.G. Free-time as a reinforcer in the management of a classroom behavior. *Journal of Applied Behavior Analysis*, 1969, *2*, 113–118.

Oskamp, S. Overconfidence in case-study judgments. *Journal of Consulting Psychology*, 1965, *29*, 261–265.

Oskamp, S. Clinical judgments from the MMPI: Simple or complex? *Journal of Clinical Psychology*, 1967, *23*, 411–415.

Owens, W.A., & Henry, E.R. *Biographical data in industrial psychology: A review and evaluation*. Greensboro, N.C.: Creativity Research Institute, The Richardson Foundation, 1966.

Palmer, J.O. *The psychological assessment of children*. New York: Wiley, 1970.

Parloff, M.B., Waskow, I.E., & Wolfe, B.E. Research on therapist variables in relation to process and outcome. In S.L. Garfield and A.E. Bergin (Eds.), *Handbook of psychotherapy and behavior change*. New York: Wiley, 1978, 233–282.

Pasamanick, B., Dinitz, S., & Lefton, M. Psychiatric orientation and its relation to diagnosis and treatment in a mental hospital. *American Journal of Psychiatry*, 1959, *116*, 127–132.

Patterson, G.R. *Families: Applications of social learning to family life*. Champaign, Ill.: Research Press, 1971.

Patterson, G.R., Cobb, J.A., & Ray, R. A social engineering technology for retraining the families of aggressive boys. In H.E. Adams & I.P. Unikel (Eds.), *Issues and trends in behavior therapy*, Springfield, Ill.: Thomas, 1973, 139–224.

Patterson, G.R., Ray, R.S., Shaw, D.A., & Cobb, J.A. *Manual for coding of family interactions*, 1969 (Document No. 01234). Available from ASIS/NAPS, c/o Microfiche Publications, 305 East 46th St., New York, N.Y., 10017.

Patuxent Institution. *Maryland's defective delinquency statute: A progress report*. Maryland Department of Public Safety and Corrections, 1973.

Paul, G.L. *Insight versus desensitization in psychotherapy: An experiment in anxiety reduction*. Stanford, Calif.: Stanford University Press, 1966.

Paul, G.L. Behavior modification research: Design and tactics. In C.M. Franks (Ed.), *Behavior therapy: Appraisal and status*. New York: McGraw-Hill, 1969, 29–62. (a)

Paul, G.L. Outcome of systematic desensitization, II. In C. Franks (Ed.), *Behavior therapy: Appraisal and status*. New York: McGraw Hill, 1969. (b)

Paul, G.L., & Lentz, R.J. *Psychosocial treatment of chronic mental patients: Milieu versus social-learning programs*. Cambridge, Mass.: Harvard University Press, 1977.

Pavlov, I.P. *Conditioned reflexes*. New York: Oxford University Press, 1927.

Peck, C.P., & Ash, E. Training in the Veterans Administration. In L. Blank & H.P. David (Eds.), *Sourcebook for training in clinical psychology*. New York: Springer, 1964, 61–81.

Penrose, L.S., & Raven, J.C. A new series of perceptual tests. *British Journal of Medical Psychology*, 1936, *16*, 97–104.

Perlman, B. Ethical concerns in community mental health. *American Journal of Community Psychology*, 1977, *5*, 45–58.

Perloff, R. Anwar: Menachem:: Dick: Nick. *APA Monitor*, 1978, *9* (1), 14.

Perls, F.S. *Ego, hunger, and aggression*. New York: Random House, 1947.

Perls, F.S. Gestalt therapy, Film no. 2. In Everett Shostrom (Ed.), *Three approaches to psychotherapy*. (Three 16 mm color motion pictures.) Santa Ana, Calif.: Psychological Films, 1965.

Perls, F.S. *Gestalt therapy verbatim*. Lafayette, Calif.: Real People Press, 1969.

Perls, F.S. Four lectures. In J. Fagan & I.L. Shepherd (Eds.), *Gestalt therapy now*. Palo Alto, Calif.: Science and Behavior Books, 1970, 14–38.

Perls, F.S., Hefferline, R.F., & Goodman, P. *Gestalt therapy*. New York: Julian Press, 1951.

Peterson, D.R. *The clinical study of social behavior*. New York: Appleton-Century-Crofts, 1968. (a)

Peterson, D.R. The doctor of psychology program at the University of Illinois. *American Psychologist*, 1968, *23*, 511–516. (b)

Peterson, D.R. Is psychology a profession? *American Psychologist*, 1976, *31* 576–581.

Peterson, D.R., & Baron, A. Status of the University of Illinois doctor of psychology program, 1974. *Professional Psychology*, 1975, *6*, 88–95.

Petzelt, J.T., & Craddick, R. Present meaning of assessment in psychology. *Professional Psychology*, 1978, *9*, 587–591.

Phillips, E.L. *Counseling and psychotherapy: A behavioral approach*. New York: Wiley, 1977.

Phillips, L. *Human adaptation and its failures*. New York: Academic Press, 1968.

Piaget, J. *The psychology of intelligence*. London: Kegan Paul, 1947.

Pinneau, S.R., & Milton, A. The ecological validity of the self report. *Journal of Genetic Psychology*, 1958, *93*, 249–276.

Piotrowski, Z. Digital computer interpretation of ink-blot test data. *Psychiatric Quarterly*, 1964, *38*, 1–26.

Pitrowski, Z. Psychological testing of intelligence and personality. In A.M. Freedman & H.I. Kaplan (Eds.), *Diagnosing mental illness: Evaluation in psychiatry and psychology*. New York: Atheneum, 1972, 41–85.

Pittenger, R.E., Hockett, C.F., & Danehy, J.J. *The first five minutes: A sample of microscopic interview analyses*. Ithaca, N.Y.: Paul Martineau, 1960.

Polakow, R., & Doctor, R. A behavioral modification program for adult drug offenders. *Journal of Research in Crime and Delinquency*, 1974, *11*, 63–69.

Polansky, N., Freeman, W., Horowitz, M., Irwin, L., Papanis, N., Rappaport, D., & Whaley, F. Problems of interpersonal relations in research on groups. *Human Relations*, 1949, *2*, 281–291.

Polster, E., & Polster, M. *Gestalt therapy integrated: Contours of theory and practice*. New York: Brunner/Mazel, 1973.

Pomeranz, D.M., & Goldfried, M.R. An intake report outline for behavior modification. *Psychological Reports*, 1970, *26*, 447–450.

Pomerleau, O.F., & Brady, J.P. (Eds.). *Behavioral medicine: Theory and practice*. Baltimore: Williams & Wilkins, 1979.

Pomerleau, O.F., & Pomerleau, C.S. *Break the smoking habit*. Champaign, Ill.: Research Press, 1977.

Pope, B., & Siegman, A.W. Interviewer warmth in relation to interviewee verbal behavior. *Journal of Consulting and Clinical Psychology*, 1978, *32*, 588–595.

Porter, E.H., Jr. The development and evaluation of a measure of counseling interview procedures. *Educational and Psychological Measurement*, 1943, *3*, 105–126, 215–238.

Potash, H.M. Supervision as personal growth. In A.I. Rabin (Ed.), *Clinical psychology: Issues of the seventies*. East Lansing: Michigan State University Press, 1974, 180–189.

Potkay, C.R. The role of personal history data in clinical judgment: A selective focus. *Journal of Personality Assessment*, 1973, *37*, 203–213.

Pottharst, K.E. A brief history of the professional model of training. In M. Korman (Ed.), *Levels and patterns of professional training in psychology*. Washington, D.C.: American Psychological Association, 1976, 33–40.

Purcell, K., & Brady, K. Adaptation to the invasion of privacy: Monitoring behavior with a miniature radio transmitter. *Merrill-Palmer Quarterly of Behavior and Development*, 1966, *12*, 242–254.

Rabin, A.I. (Ed.). *Clinical psychology: Issues of the seventies*. East Lansing: Michigan State University Press, 1974.

Rabin, A.I., & Haworth, M.R. (Eds.). *Projective techniques with children*. New York: Grune & Stratton, 1960.

Raimy, V.C. *Training in clinical psychology*. New York: Prentice-Hall, 1950.

Raines, G.N., & Rohrer, J.H. The operational matrix of psychiatric practice, I.

Consistency and variability in interview impressions of different psychiatrists. *American Journal of Psychiatry*, 1955, *111*, 721–733.

Raines, G.N., & Rohrer, J.H. The operational matrix of psychiatric practice, II. Variability in psychiatric impressions and the projection hypotheses. *American Journal of Psychiatry*, 1960, *117*, 133–139.

Rapaport, D. *Organization and pathology of thought*. New York: Columbia University Press, 1951.

Rapaport, D., Gill, M.M., & Shafer, R. *Diagnostic psychological testing* (Vol. 1). Chicago: Yearbook, 1945.

Rapaport, D., Gill, M.M., & Shafer, R. *Diagnostic psychological testing* (Vol. 2). Chicago: Yearbook, 1946.

Rapp, D.W. Detection of observer bias in the written record. Unpublished manuscript, University of Georgia, 1965.

Rappaport, J. *Community psychology: Values, research and action*. New York: Holt, Rinehart, & Winston, 1977.

Rappaport, J., & Chinsky, J.M. Accurate empathy: Confusion of a construct. *Psychological Bulletin*, 1972, *77*, 400–404.

Rappaport, J., & Chinsky, J.M. Models for delivery of services from a historical and conceptual perspective. *Professional Psychology*, 1974, *5*, 42–50.

Raven, J.C. Standardization of progressive matrices, 1938. *British Journal of Medical Psychology*, 1941, *19*, 137–150.

Raymond, M.J. Case of fetishism treated by aversion therapy. *British Medical Journal*, 1956, *2*, 854–857.

Redd, W.H., Porterfield, A.L., & Andersen, B.L. *Behavior modification: Behavioral approaches to human problems*. New York: Random House, 1979.

Rehm, L.P., & Marston, A.R. Reduction of social anxiety through modification of self-reinforcement: An instigation therapy technique. *Journal of Consulting and Clinical Psychology*, 1968, *32*, 565–574.

Reid, J.B. Reliability assessment of observation data: A possible methodological problem. *Child Development*, 1970, *41*, 1143–1150.

Reiff, R.R. Social intervention and the problem of psychological analysis. *American Psychologist*, 1968, *23*, 524–530.

Reik, T. *Listening with the third ear*. New York: Farrar, Straus, & Giroux, 1948.

Reimringer, M.J., Morgan, F., & Bramwell, P. Succinylcholine as a modifier of acting out behavior. *Clinical Medicine*, July 1970, *28–29*.

Reisman, J.M. *The development of clinical psychology*. New York: Appleton-Century-Crofts, 1966.

Report of the Task Force on the Role of Psychology in the Criminal Justice System. *American Psychologist*, 1978, *33*, 1099, 1113.

Report to the President from the President's Commission on Mental Health (Vol. 1). Washington, D.C.: U.S. Government Printing Office, 1978.

Reynolds, W.M. Psychological tests: Clinical usage versus psychometric quality. *Professional Psychology*, 1979, *10*, 324–329.

Rice, S.A. Contagious bias in the interview: A methodological note. *American Journal of Sociology*, 1929, *35*, 420–423.

Richardson, S.A., Dohrenwend, B.S., & Klein, D. *Interviewing: Its forms and functions*. New York: Basic Books, 1965.

Reissman, F. Strategies and suggestions for training nonprofessionals. *Community Mental Health Journal*, 1967, *3*, 103–110.

Rieu, E.V. (Trans.). *Homer: The Iliad*. Hammondsworth, Middlesex: Penguin, 1950.

Rimm, D.C., & Masters, J.C. *Behavior therapy: Techniques and empirical findings* (2d ed.). New York: Academic Press, 1979.

Rioch, M.J., Coulter, W.R., & Weinberger, D.M. *Dialogues for therapists: Dynamics of learning and supervision*. San Francisco: Jossey-Bass, 1976.

Rioch, M.J., Elkes, C., Flint, A.A., Usdansky, B.S., Newman, R.G., & Silber, E. NIMH pilot study in training of mental health counselors. *American Journal of Orthopsychiatry*, 1963, *33*, 678–689.

Ritter, B. The use of contact desensitization, demonstration-plus-participation and demonstration-alone in the treatment of acrophobia. *Behaviour Research and Therapy*, 1970, *7*, 157–164.

Robbins, L.C. The accuracy of parental recall of child development and of child rearing practices. *Journal of Abnormal and Social Psychology*, 1963, *66*, 261–270.

Robinson, J.T., & Cohen, L.D. Individual bias in psychological reports. *Journal of Clinical Psychology*, 1954, *10*, 333–336.

Rodgers, D.A. Minnesota Multiphasic Personality Inventory. In O.K. Buros (Ed.), *The seventh mental measurements yearbook* (Vol. 1). Highland Park, N.J.: The Gryphon Press, 1972, 245–250.

Roe, A., Gustad, J.W., Moore, B.V., Ross, S., & Skodak, M. (Eds.). *Graduate education in psychology*. Washington, D.C.: American Psychological Association, 1959.

Rogers, C.R. *The clinical treatment of the problem child*. Boston: Houghton Mifflin, 1939.

Rogers, C.R. *Counseling and psychotherapy*. Boston: Houghton Mifflin, 1942.

Rogers, C.R. *Client-centered therapy*. Boston: Houghton Mifflin, 1951.

Rogers, C.R. *Psychotherapy and personality change*. Chicago: University of Chicago Press, 1954.

Rogers, C.R. A theory of therapy, personality, and interpersonal relationships, as developed in the client-centered framework. In S. Koch, (Ed.), *Psychology: A study of a science, Vol. III, Formulations of the person and the social context*. New York: McGraw-Hill, 1959, 184–256.

Rogers, C.R. *On becoming a person*. Boston: Houghton-Mifflin, 1961.

Rogers, C.R. Client-centered therapy, Film no. 1. In Everett Shostrom (Ed.), *Three approaches to psychotherapy*. (Three 16 mm. color motion pictures.) Santa Ana, Calif.: Psychological Films, 1965.

Rogers, C.R. (Ed.). *The therapeutic relationship and its impact: A study of psychotherapy with schizophrenics*. With E.T. Gendlin, D.J. Kiesler, and C. Louax. Madison, Wis.: University of Wisconsin Press, 1967.

Rogers, C.R. *Freedom to learn*. Columbus, Ohio: Merrill, 1969.

Rogers, C.R. *Carl Rogers on encounter groups*. New York: Harper & Row, 1970.

Rogers, C.R. Remarks on the future of client-centered therapy. In D.A. Wexler & L.N. Rice (Eds.), *Innovations in client-centered therapy*. New York: Wiley, 1974, 7–13.

Romanczyk, R.G., Kent, R.N., Diament, C., & O'Leary, K.D. Measuring the reliability of observational data: A reactive process. *Journal of Applied Behavior Analysis*, 1973, *6*, 175–184.

Rorer, L.G. The great response style myth. *Psychological Bulletin*, 1965, *63*, 129–156.

Rosen, A. Detection of suicidal patients: An example of some limitations in the prediction of infrequent events. *Journal of Consulting Psychology*, 1954, *18*, 397–403.

Rosen, G.M. Is it really necessary to use mildly phobic analogue subjects? *Behavior Therapy*, 1975, *6*, 68–71.

Rosen, R.C., & Kopel, S.A. Penile plethysmography and biofeedback in the treatment of a transvestite-exhibitionist. *Journal of Consulting and Clinical Psychology*, 1977, *45*, 908–916.

Rosenblatt, D. *Opening doors: What happens in Gestalt therapy*. New York: Harper & Row, 1975.

Rosenthal, H.R. The final dream: A criterion for the termination of therapy. In A. Adler & D. Deutsch (Eds.), *Essays in individual psychology*. New York: Grove Press, 1959, 400–409.

Rosenthal, R. *Experimenter effects in behavioral research*. New York: Appleton-Century-Crofts, 1966.

Rosenthal, R., & Jacobsen, L. *Pygmalion in the classroom: Teacher expectations and pupils' intellectual development*. New York: Holt, Rinehart & Winston, 1968.

Rosenthal, T.L. Modeling therapies. In M. Hersen, R.M. Eisler, & P.M. Miller (Eds.), *Progress in behavior modification* (Vol. 2). New York: Academic Press, 1976, 53–97.

Rosenwald, G.C. Psychodiagnosis and its discontents: A contribution to the understanding of professional identity and compromise. *Psychiatry*, 1963, *26*, 222–240.

Rosenzweig, S. Apperceptive norms for the Thematic Apperception Test. I. The problem of norms in projective methods. *Journal of Personality*, 1949, *17*, 475–482.

Rosenzweig, S., & Fleming, E.E. Apperceptive norms for the Thematic Apperception Test. II. An empirical investigation. *Journal of Personality*, 1949, *17*, 483–503.

Rotter, J.B. *Social learning and clinical psychology*. Englewood Cliffs, N.J.: Prentice-Hall, 1954.

Rotter, J.B. *Clinical psychology* (2d ed.). Englewood Cliffs, N.J.: Prentice-Hall, 1971.

Rotter, J.B., & Rafferty, J.E. *The Rotter Incomplete Sentences Test*. New York: Psychological Corporation, 1950.

Rotter, J.B., & Wickens, D.D. The consistency and generality of ratings of "social aggressiveness" made from observation of role playing situations. *Journal of Consulting Psychology*, 1948, *12*, 234–239.

Rouse v. Cameron, 373 F 2nd 451, 452 (D.C. Cir. 1966).

Routh, D.K., & King, K.M. Social class bias in clinical judgment. *Journal of Consulting and Clinical Psychology*, 1972, *38*, 202–207.

Rugh, J.D. A telemetry system for measuring chewing behavior in humans. *Behavior Research Methods and Instrumentation*, 1971, *3*, 73–77.

Rugh, J.D., & Schwitzgebel, R.L. Instrumentation for behavioral assessment. In A.R. Ciminero, K.S. Calhoun, & H.E. Adams (Eds.), *Handbook of behavioral assessment*. New York: John Wiley & Sons, 1977, 79–113.

Rutner, I.T. The modification of smoking behavior through techniques of self-control. Unpublished masters thesis, Wichita State University, 1967.

Rutner, I.T., & Pear, J.J. An observational methodology for investigating phobic behavior: Preliminary report. *Behavior Therapy*, 1972, *3*, 437–440.

Sacks, J.M., & Levy, S. The sentence completion test. In L.E. Abt & L. Bellak (Eds.), *Projective psychology*, New York: Knopf, 1950, 357–402.

Sahakian, W.S. *Psychology of personality: Readings in theory* (2d ed). Chicago: Rand-McNally, 1974.

Salter, A. *Conditioned reflex therapy: The direct approach to the reconstruction of personality*. New York: Creative Age Press, 1949.

Salzinger, K. Experimental manipulation of verbal behavior: A review. *Journal of Genetic Psychology*, 1959, *61*, 65–95.

Samph, T. The role of the observer and his effects on teacher classroom behavior. *Occasional Papers,* 1969, No. 2, Oakland Schools, Pontiac, Mich.

Sands, W.L. Psychiatric history and mental status. In A.M. Freedman & H.I. Kaplan (Eds.), *Diagnosing mental illness*. New York: Athenum, 1972, 20–40.

Sanford, F.H. Annual report of the executive secretary. *American Psychologist*, 1951, *6*, 664–670.

Santostefano, S. Performance testing of personality. *Merrill-Palmer Quarterly*, 1962, *8*, 83–97.

Santostefano, S. Miniature situations and methodological problems in parent-child interaction research. *Merrill-Palmer Quarterly*, 1968, *14*, 285–312.

Sarason, I.G. The evolution of community psychology. *American Journal of Community Psychology*, 1973, *1*, 91–97.

Sarason, I.G. *Abnormal psychology* (2d ed.) Englewood Cliffs, N.J.: Prentice-Hall, 1976.

Sarason, S.B. *The clinical interaction, with special reference to the Rorschach*. New York: Harper, 1954.

Sarason, S.B. *The psychological sense of community: Prospects for community psychology*. San Francisco: Jossey-Bass Publishers, 1974.

Sarbin, T.R., Taft, R., & Bailey, D.E. *Clinical inference and cognitive theory*. New York: Holt, Rinehart, Winston, 1960.

Sashkin, M. Organizational development practices. *Professional Psychology*, 1973, *4*, 187–193.

Saslow, G., & Matarazzo, J.D. A technique for studying changes in interview behavior. In E.A. Rubinstein & M.B. Parloff (Eds.), *Research in psychotherapy* (Vol. 1). Washington, D.C.: American Psychological Association, 1959, 125–159.

Satir, V. *Conjoint family therapy* (Rev. ed.). Palo Alto, Calif.: Science and Behavior Books, 1967.

Sattler, J.M., & Theye, R. Procedural, situational, and interpersonal variables in individual intelligence testing. *Psychological Bulletin*, 1967, *68*, 347–360.

Saul, L.J. The psychoanalytic diagnostic interview. *Psychoanalytic Quarterly*, 1957, *26*, 76–90.

Sawyer, J. Measurement *and* prediction, clinical *and* statistical. *Psychological Bulletin*, 1966, *66*, 178–200.

Schaar, K. Vermont: Getting through the adult years. *APA Monitor*, 1978, *9*, 7.

Schachter, S., & Gross, L.P. Manipulated time and eating behavior. *Journal of Personality and Social Psychology*, 1968, *10*, 98–106.

Schaefer, H.H., & Martin, P.L. *Behavior therapy* (2d ed.). New York: McGraw-Hill, 1975.

Scheff, T.J. *Being mentally ill*. Chicago: Aldine, 1966.

Schmidt, H.O., & Fonda, C.P. The reliability of psychiatric diagnosis: A new look. *Journal of Abnormal and Social Psychology*, 1956, *52*, 262–267.

Schofield, W. Standards for clinical psychology: Origins and evaluation. In L. Blank and H.P. David (Eds.), *Sourcebook for training in clinical psychology. New York: Springer, 1964. (a)*

Schofield, W. *Psychotherapy: The purchase of friendship*. Englewood Cliffs, N.J.: Prentice Hall, 1964. (b)

Schroeder, S.R. Automated transduction of sheltered workshop behaviors. *Journal of Applied Behavior Analysis*, 1972, *5*, 523–525.

Schuller, D.Y., & McNamara, J.R. *Expectancy factors in behavioral observation.* Unpublished manuscript, 1975.

Schulmann, J.L., & Reisman, J. An objective measurement of hyperactivity. *American Journal of Mental Deficiency*, 1959, *64*, 455–456.

Schwartz, R.M., & Gottman, J. Toward a task analysis of assertive behavior. *Journal of Consulting and Clinical Psychology*, 1976, *44*, 910–920.

Schwitzgebel, R.K. *A contractual model for the protection of prisoners' rights.* Paper presented at the 82nd Annual Convention of the American Psychological Association, New Orleans, 1974.

Schwitzgebel, R.K., & Kolb, D.A. Inducing behavior change in adolescent delinquents. *Behaviour Research & Therapy*, 1964, *1*, 297–304.

Schwitzgebel, R.K., and Kolb, D.A. *Changing human behavior.* New York: McGraw-Hill, 1974.

Scott, R.D., & Johnson, ·R.W. Use of the weighted application blank in selecting unskilled employees. *Journal of Applied Psychology*, 1967, *51, 393–395.*

Sechrest, L.B. Incremental validity: A recommendation. *Educational and Psychological Measurement*, 1963, *23*, 153–158.

Seeman, J.A. A study of the process of nondirective therapy. *Journal of Consulting Psychology*, 1949, *13*, 157–168.

Seeman, J.A. On supervising student research. *American Psychologist*, 1973, *28*, 900–906.

Serber, M. Shame aversion therapy with and without heterosexual retraining. In R.D. Rubin, H. Fensterheim, J.D. Henderson, & L.P. Ullmann (Eds.), *Advances in behavior therapy.* New York: Academic Press, 1972, 115–119.

Shadel, C.A. Aversion treatment of alcohol addiction. *Quarterly Journal of Studies of Alcohol*, 1944, *5*, 216–228.

Shaffer, G.W., & Lazarus, R.S. *Fundamental concepts in clinical psychology.* New York: McGraw-Hill, 1952.

Shakow, D. An internship year for psychologists (with special reference to psychiatric hospitals). *Journal of Consulting Psychology*, 1938, *2*, 73–76.

Shakow, D. The training of the clinical psychologist. *Journal of Consulting Psychology*, 1942, *6*, 277–288.

Shakow, D. Recommended graduate training program in clinical psychology. *American Psychologist*, 1947, *2*, 539–558.

Shakow, D. Clinical psychology: An evaluation. In L.G. Lowrey & V. Sloane (Eds.), *Orthopsychiatry, 1923–1948: Retrospect and prospect.* New York: American Orthopsychiatric Association, Inc., 1948.

Shakow, D. Seventeen years later: Clinical psychology in the light of the 1947 CTCP report. *American Psychologist*, 1965, *20*, 353–362.

Shakow, D. Clinical psychology. In D.L. Sills (Ed.), *International encyclopedia of the social sciences.* London: Collier Macmillan, 1968.

Shakow, D. *Clinical psychology as science and profession.* Chicago: Aldine, 1969.

Shakow, D. What *is* clinical psychology? *The Clinical Psychologist*, 1975, *29*, 6–8.

Shakow, D. Clinical psychology seen some 50 years later. *American Psychologist*, 1978, *33*, 148–158.

Shannon, D., & Weaver, W. *The mathematical theory of communication.* Urbana, Ill.: University of Illinois Press, 1949.

Shapiro, A.K. Placebo effects in medicine, psychotherapy, and psychoanalysis. In A.E.

Bergin & S.L. Garfield (Eds.), *Handbook of psychotherapy and behavior change: An empirical analysis*. New York: John Wiley & Sons, Inc., 1971.

Shemberg, K., & Keeley, S. Psychodiagnostic training in the academic setting: Past and present. *Journal of Consulting and Clinical Psychology*, 1970, *34*, 205–211.

Sherman, M., Trief, P., & Sprafkin, R. Impression management in the psychiatric interview: Quality, style, and individual differences. *Journal of Consulting and Clinical Psychology*, 1975, *43, 867–871.*

Shneidman, E.S. *The make-a-picture-story test*. New York: Psychological Corporation, 1949.

Shneidman, E.S. *Thematic test analysis*. New York: Grune & Stratton, 1951.

Shneidman, E.S. Projective techniques. In B.B. Wolman (Ed.), *Handbook of clinical psychology*. New York: McGraw-Hill, 1965, 498–521.

Shostrom, E.L. *Personal orientation inventory: An inventory for the measurement of self-actualization*. San Diego, Calif.: Educational and Industrial Testing Service, 1968.

Siegel, L., & Sameroff, A. Monitoring system for infant movement, vocalization and nurse interaction. *Behavior Research Methods and Instrumentation*, 1971, *3*, 305–306.

Siegman, A.W. Do interviewer mm-hmm's reinforce interviewee verbal productivity? *Proceedings of the 80th Annual Convention of the American Psychological Association*, 1972, *7*, 323–324.

Siegman, A.W. The gain-loss principle and interpersonal attraction in the interview. *Proceedings of the Division of Personality and Social Psychology*, 1974, 83–85.

Siegman, A.W. Do noncontingent interviewer mm-hmm's facilitate interviewee productivity? *Journal of Consulting and Clinical Psychology*, 1976, *44*(2) 171–182.

Sines, J.O. Actuarial methods in personality assessment. In B.A. Maher (Ed.), *Progress in experimental personality research* (Vol. 3). New York: Academic Press, 1966, 133–193.

Sines, L.K. The relative contribution of four kinds of data to accuracy in personality assessment. *Journal of Consulting Psychology*, 1959, *23*, 483–492.

Sintchak, G., & Geer, J. A vaginal plethysmograph system. *Psychophysiology*, 1975, *12*, 113–115.

Siskind, G. Fifteen years later: A replication of "A semantic study of concepts of clinical psychologists and psychiatrists." *Journal of Psychology*, 1967, *65*, 37–7.

Skinner, B.F. *Verbal behavior*. Cambridge, Mass.: Harvard University Press, 1948.

Skinner, B.F. *Science and human behavior*. New York: MacMillan, 1953.

Skinner, B.F. *Verbal behavior*. New York: Appleton-Century-Crofts, 1957.

Skinner, B.F. *Beyond freedom and dignity*. New York: Knopf, 1971.

Slack, C.W. Experimenter-subject psychotherapy: A new method of introducing intensive office treatment for unreachable cases. *Mental Hygiene*, 1960, *44*, 238–256.

Slack, W.V., & VanCura, L.J. Patient reaction to computer-based medical interviewing. *Computers and Biomedical Research*, 1968, *1*, 527–531.

Smith, H. A comparison of interview and observation measures of mother behavior. *Journal of Abnormal and Social Psychology*, 1958, *57*, 278–282.

Smith, M.B., & Hobbs, N. The community and the community mental health center. *American Psychologist*, 1966, *21*, 499–509.

Smith, M.L., & Glass, G.V. Meta-analysis of psychotherapy outcome studies. *American Psychologist*, 1977, *32*, 752–760.

Smith, R.E., Diener, E., & Beaman, A. Demand characteristics and the behavioral avoidance measures of fear in behavior therapy analogue research. *Behavior Therapy*, 1974, *5*, 172–182.

Snyder, C.R. Acceptance of personality interpretations as a function of assessment procedures. *Journal of Consulting and Clinical Psychology*, 1974, *42*, 150.

Snyder, C.R., & Larson, G.R. A further look at student acceptance of general personality interpretations. *Journal of Consulting and Clinical Psychology*, 1972, *38*, 384–388.

Snyder, C.R., Shenkel, R.J., & Lowry, C.R. Acceptance of personality interpretations: The "Barnum effect" and beyond. *Journal of Consulting and Clinical Psychology*, 1977, *45*, 104–114.

Snyder, W.V. (Ed.). *Group report of a program of research in psychotherapy*. State College, Penn.: Department of Psychology, Pennsylvania State University, 1953.

Snyder, W.V. Client-centered therapy. In L.A. Pennington & I.A. Berg (Eds.), *An introduction to clinical psychology*. New York: Ronald, 1954, 529–556.

Snyder, W.V. An investigation of the nature of nondirective psychotherapy. *Journal of General Psychology*, 1945, *33*, 193–232.

Sobell, L.C., & Sobell, M.B. Outpatient alcoholics give valid self-reports. *Journal of Nervous and Mental Disease*, 1975, *161*, 32–42.

Sobell, M.B., Schaefer, H.H., & Mills, K.C. Differences in baseline drinking behavior between alcoholics and normal drinkers. *Behaviour Research and Therapy*, 1972, *10*, 257–267.

Sobell, M.B., Sobell, L.C., & Samuels, F.H. Validity of alcohol-related arrests by alcoholics. *Quarterly Journal of Studies on Alcohol*, 1974, *35*, 276–280.

Sollod, R.N. Carl Rogers and the origins of client-centered therapy. *Professional Psychology*, 1978, *9*, 93–104.

Solomon, R.L., Kamin, L.J., & Wynne, L.C. Traumatic avoidance learning: The outcomes of several extinction procedures with dogs. *Journal of Abnormal and Social Psychology*, 1953, *48*, 291–302.

Soskin, W.F. Bias in postdiction from projective tests. *Journal of Abnormal and Social Psychology*, 1954, *49*, 69–74.

Soskin, W., & John, V.P. The study of spontaneous talk. In R. Barker (Ed.), *The stream of behavior*. New York: Appleton-Century-Crofts, 1963, 228–281.

Spanos, N.P. Witchcraft in histories of psychiatry: A critical analysis and an alternative conceptualization. *Psychological Bulletin*, 1978, *85*, 417–439.

Spece, R. Conditioning and other techniques used to "treat?," "rehabilitate?," "demolish?" prisoners and mental patients. *Southern California Law Review*, 1972, *45*, 616–684.

Spence, K.W. *Behavior theory and conditioning*. New Haven, Conn.: Yale University Press, 1956.

Spielberger, C.D., Gorsuch, R.L., & Lushene, R.E. *The state-trait anxiety inventory (STAI) test manual for form X*. Palo Alto, Calif.: Consulting Psychologists Press, 1970.

Spitzer, R.L., Endicott, J., Fleiss, J.L., & Cohen, J. The psychiatric status schedule. *Archives of General Psychiatry*, 1970, *23*, 41–55.

Spitzer, R.L., Fleiss, J.L., Burdock, E.I., & Hardesty, A.S. The mental status schedule: Rationale, reliability, and validity. *Comprehensive Psychiatry*, 1964, *5*, 384–394.

Sprafkin, R.P. The rebirth of moral treatment. *Professional Psychology*, 1977, *8*, 161–169.

Stagner, R. The gullibility of personnel managers. *Personnel Psychology*, 1958, *11*, 347–352.

Stampfl, T.G., & Levis, D.J. *Implosive therapy: Theory and technique*. Morristown, N.J.: General Learning Press, 1973.

Stanton, H.R., & Litwak, E. Toward the development of a short form test of interpersonal competence. *American Sociological Review*, 1955, *20*, 668–674.

Stein, M.U. The use of sentence completion test for the diagnosis of personality. *Journal of Clinical Psychology*, 1947, *3*, 46–56.

Stevenson, I., & Sheppe, W.M., Jr. The psychiatric examination. In S. Arieti (Ed.), *American handbook of psychiatry* (Vol. 1). New York: Basic Books, 1959, 215–234.

Stewart, D.J., & Patterson, M.L. Eliciting effects of verbal and nonverbal cues on projective test responses. *Journal of Consulting and Clinical Psychology*, 1973, *41*, 74–77.

Stone, D.R. A recorded auditory apperception test as a new projective technique. *Journal of Psychology*, 1950, *29*, 349–353.

Stricker, G. On professional schools and professional degrees. *American Psychologist*, 1975, *30*, 1062–1066.

Stricker, G. Implications of research for psychotherapeutic treatment of women. *American Psychologist*, 1977, *32*, 14–22.

Strother, C.R. *Psychology and mental health*. Washington, D.C.: American Psychological Association, 1956.

Strupp, H.H. *Psychotherapists in action: Explorations of the therapist's contribution to the treatment process*. New York: Grune & Stratton, 1960.

Strupp, H.H. The outcome problem in psychotherapy revisited. *Psychotherapy*, 1963, *1*, 1–13.

Strupp, H.H. Freudian analysis today. *Psychology Today*, 1972, *6*(2), 33–40.

Strupp, H.H., & Hadley, S. A tripartite model of mental health and therapeutic outcomes. *American Psychologist*, 1977, *32*, 197–196.

Stuart, R.B. *Guide to client-therapist treatment contract*. Champaign, Ill.: Research Press, 1975.

Stuart, R.B., & Davis, B. *Slim chance in a fat world*. Champaign, Ill.: Research Press, 1972.

Stuart, R.B., & Stuart, F. *Marital pre-counseling inventory*. Champaign, Ill.: Research Press, 1972.

Stuart, R.B., & Stuart, F. *Pre-marital counseling inventory*. Champaign, IL: Research Press, 1975.

Sullivan, H.S. *The interpersonal theory of psychiatry*. New York: Norton, 1953.

Sullivan, H.S. *The psychiatric interview*. New York: Norton, 1954.

Sulzer, E. Behavior modification in adult psychiatric patients. In L.P. Ullmann & L. Krasner (Eds.), *Case studies in behavior modification*. New York: Holt, Rinehart, & Winston, 1965.

Sundberg, N.D. The acceptability of "fake" versus "bona fide" personality test interpretations. *Journal of Abnormal and Social Psychology*, 1955, *50*, 145–147.

Sundberg, N.D. The practice of psychological testing in clinical services in the United States. *American Psychologist*, 1961, *16*, 79–83.

Sundberg, N.D. *Assessment of persons*. Englewood Cliffs, N.J.: Prentice-Hall, 1977.

Sundberg, N.D., & Tyler, L.E. *Clinical psychology: An introduction to research and practice*. New York: Appleton-Century-Crofts, 1962.

Sundberg, N.D., Tyler, L.E., & Taplin, J.R. *Clinical psychology: Expanding horizons* (2d ed.), Englewood Cliffs, N.J.: Prentice-Hall, Inc., 1973.

Surratt, P.O., Ulrich, R.E., & Hawkins, R.P. An elementary student as a behavioral engineer. *Journal of Applied Behavior Analysis*, 1969, *2*, 85–92.

Szasz, T.S. The myth of mental illness. *American Psychologist*, 1960, *15*, 113–118.

Szasz, T.S. The psychiatric classification of behavior: A strategy of personal constraint. In L.D. Eron (Ed.), *The classification of behavior disorders*. Chicago: Aldine, 1966.

Szondi, L., Moser, U., & Webb, M.W. *The Szondi test in diagnosis, prognosis and treatment*. Philadelphia: Lippincott, 1959.

Taft, J. *The dynamics of therapy in a controlled relationship*. New York: Harper, 1951.

Taft, R. The ability to judge people. *Psychological Bulletin*, 1955, *52*, 1–23.

Tallent, N. An approach to the improvement of clinical psychological reports. *Journal of Clinical Psychology*, 1956, *12*, 103–109.

Tallent, N. On individualizing the psychologist's clinical evaluation. *Journal of Clinical Psychology*, 1958, *14*, 243–244.

Tallent, N. *Psychological report writing*. Englewood Cliffs, N.J.: Prentice-Hall, 1976.

Tallent, N., & Reiss, W.J. Multidisciplinary views on the preparation of written, psychological reports, III. The trouble with psychological reports. *Journal of Clinical Psychology*, 1959, *15*, 444–446.

Taplin, P.S., & Reid, J.B. Effects of instructional set and experimenter influence on observer reliability. *Child Development*, 1973, *44*, 547–554.

Tarasoff v. Regents of the University of California, sup. 131 Cal. Rptr. 14 (1976).

Tarde, G. *The laws of imitation*. New York: Holt, 1903.

Tarler-Benlolo, L., & Love, W.A. A sexual phobia treated with macadamia nuts. *Journal of Behavior Therapy and Experimental Psychiatry*, 1977, *8,* 113–114.

Tasto, D.L., Hickson, R., & Rubin, S.E. Scaled profile analysis of fear survey schedule factors. *Behavior Therapy*, 1971, *2*, 543–549.

Taylor, J.A. A personality scale of manifest anxiety. *Journal of Abnormal and Social Psychology*, 1953, *48*, 285–290.

Taylor v. United States, 95 U.S. App. O.C. 373, 222 F.2d 398, 401 (1955).

Temerlin, M.K. Suggestion effects in psychiatric diagnosis. *Journal of Nervous and Mental Disease*, 1968, *147*, 349–353.

Temerlin, M.K. Diagnostic bias in community mental health. *Community Mental Health Journal*, 1970, *6*, 110–117.

Teuber, H.L., & Powers, E. Evaluating therapy in a delinquency prevention program. *Research Publications of the Association for Research in Nervous and Mental Disease*, 1951, *31*, 138–147.

Tevekhov,Y. A system for the study of man's equilibrium. *Biomedical Engineering*, 1974, *9*, 478–480.

Thackray, R.I., & Orne, M.T. Effects of the type of stimulus employed and the level of subject awareness on the detection of deception. *Journal of Applied Psychology*, 1968, *52*, 234–239.

Tharp, R.G., & Wetzel, R.J. *Behavior modification in the natural environment*. New York: Academic Press, 1969.

Thomas, D.R., Becker, W.C., & Armstrong, M. Production and elimination of disruptive classroom behavior by systematically varying teacher's behavior. *Journal of Applied Behavior Analysis*, 1968, *1*, 35–45.

Thomas, D.S. *Some new techniques for studying social behavior*. New York: Columbia University, 1929.

Thomas, D.S., Loomis, A.M., & Arrington, R.E. *Observational studies of social behavior* (Vol. 1). Yale University: Institute of Human Relations, 1933.

Thomas, E.J. Bias of therapist influence in behavioral assessment. *Journal of Behavior Therapy and Experimental Psychiatry*, 1973, *4*, 107–111.

Thompson, T., & Grabowski, J. (Eds.). *Behavior modification of the mentally retarded.* New York: Oxford University Press, 1972.

Thoresen, C.E., & Mahoney, M.J. *Behavioral self control.* New York: Holt, Rinehart & Winston, 1974.

Thorndike, E.L. *Animal intelligence.* New York: MacMillan, 1911.

Thorndike, E.L., Terman, L.M., Freeman, F.N., Colvin, S.S., Pintner, R., Ruml, B., Pressey, S.L., Henmon, A.C., Peterson, J., Thurstone, L.L., Woodrow, H., Dearborn, W.F., & Haggerty, M.E. Intelligence and its measurement: A symposium. *Journal of Educational Psychology*, 1921, *12*, 123–147, 195–216.

Thorne, F.C. Theoretical foundations of directive psychotherapy. *Current Trends in Clinical Research*, 1948, *49*, 867–928.

Thorne, F.C. *Integrative psychology.* Brandon, V.: Clinical Psychology Publishing Co., 1967.

Thorne, F.C. Value factors in clinical judgment. *Journal of Clinical Psychology*, 1969, *25*, 231.

Thorne, F.C. Clinical judgment. In R.H. Woody & J.D. Woody (Eds.), *Clinical assessment in counseling and psychotherapy.* Englewood Cliffs, N.J.: Prentice-Hall, 1972, 30–85.

Thorne, F.C. Eclectic psychotherapy. In R. Corsini (Ed.), *Current psychotherapies.* Itasca, Ill.: F.E. Peacock Publishers, Inc., 1973.

Tiffin, J., Parker, B.J., & Haberstat, R.W. The analysis of personnel data in relation to turnover on a factory job. *Journal of Applied Psychology*, 1974, *31*, 615–616.

Time. Beating the devil. February 7, 1969, 30.

Toepfer, C., Reuter, J., & Maurer, C. Design and evaluation of an obedience training program for mothers of preschool children. *Journal of Consulting and Clinical Psychology*, 1972, *39*, 194–198.

Tomkins, S.S. *The Tomkins-Horn Picture Arrangement Test.* New York: Springer, 1957.

Trexler, L.D., & Karst, T.O. Rational-emotive therapy, placebo, and no treatment effects on public speaking anxiety. *Journal of Abnormal Psychology*, 1972, *79*, 60–67.

Tryon, R.C. Psychology in flux: The academic-professional bipolarity. *American Psychologist*, 1963, *18*, 134–43.

Tryon, W.W. A system of behavioral diagnosis. *Professional Psychology*, 1976, *7*, 495–506.

Twain, D., McGee, R., & Bennett, L.A. Functional areas of psychological activity. In S.L. Brodsky (Ed.), *Psychologists in the criminal justice system.* Urbana, Ill.: University of Illinois Press, 1973.

Twentyman, C.T., & McFall, R.M. Behavioral training of social skills in shy males. *Journal of Consulting and Clinical Psychology, 1975, 43*, 394–395. University of Illinois Press, 1973.

Ullmann, L.P. Behavioral community psychology: Implications, opportunities, and responsibilities. Forward to M.T. Nietzel, R.A. Winett, M.L. MacDonald, W.S. Davidson, *Behavioral approaches to community psychology.* New York: Pergamon Press, 1977.

Ullmann, L.P., & Hunrichs, W.A. The role of anxiety in psychodiagnosis: Replication and extension. *Journal of Clinical Psychology*, 1958, *14*, 276–279.

Ullmann, L.P., & Krasner, L. (Eds.) *Case studies in behavior modification.* New York: Holt, Rinehart, and Winston, 1965.

Ullmann, L.P., & Krasner, L. *A psychological approach to abnormal behavior.* Englewood Cliffs, N.J.: Prentice-Hall, 1969.

Ullmann, L.P., & Krasner, L. *A psychological approach to abnormal behavior.* Englewood Cliffs, N.J.: Prentice-Hall, 1975.

Ulrich, R.E., Stachnik, T.J., & Stainton, N.R. Student acceptance of generalized personality interpretations. *Psychological Reports*, 1963, *13*, 831–834.

Underwood, B.J. *Psychological research.* New York: Appleton-Century-Crofts, 1957.

U.S. President's Commission. *The challenge of crime in a free society: A report by the president's commission on law enforcement and administration of justice.* Washington, D.C.: U.S. Government Printing Office, 1967.

Van Lennep, D.J. The Four-Picture Test. In H.H. Anderson and G.L. Anderson (Eds.), *An introduction to projective techniques.* Englewood Cliffs, N.J.: Prentice-Hall, 1951.

Vaughn, C.L., & Reynolds, W.A. Reliability of personal interview data. *Journal of Applied Psychology*, 1951, *35*, 61–63.

Verny, T.R. *Inside groups: A practical guide to encounter groups and group therapy.* New York: McGraw-Hill, 1974.

Vietze, P., Foster, M., & Friedman, S. A portable system for studying head movements in infants in relation to contingent and noncontingent sensory stimulation. *Behavior Research, Methods and Instrumentation*, 1974, *6*, 338–340.

Wachtel, P.L. *Psychoanalysis and behavior therapy.* New York: Basic Books, 1977.

Wade, T.C., & Baker, T.B. Opinions and use of psychological tests: A survey of clinical psychologists. *American Psychologist*, 1977, *32*, 874–882.

Wahler, R.G., & Leske, G. *Accurate and inaccurate observer summary reports.* Unpublished manuscript, University of Tennessee, 1972.

Wahler, R.G., Winkel, G.H., Peterson, R.F., & Morrison, D.C. Mothers as behavior therapists for their own children. *Behaviour Research and Therapy*, 1965, *3*, 113–134.

Walker, R.G. A comparison of clinical manifestations of hostility with Rorschach and MAPS performance. *Journal of Projective Techniques*, 1951, *15*, 444–460.

Walker, R.S., & Walsh, J.A. As others see us? The Medieval Multi-Purpose Inquiry. *Perceptual and Motor Skills*, 1969, *28*, 414.

Wallace, J. An abilities conception of personality: Some implications for personality measurement. *American Psychologist*, 1966, *21*, 132–138.

Wallace, J. What units shall we employ? Allport's question revisited. *Journal of Consulting Psychology*, 1967, *31*, 56–64.

Wallen, R.W. *Clinical psychology: The study of persons.* New York: McGraw-Hill, 1956.

Waller, R.G., & Leske, G. Accurate and inaccurate observer summary reports. *Journal of Nervous and Mental Disease*, 1973, *156*, 386–394.

Wallerstein, R.S., & Sampson, H. Issues in research in the psychoanalytic process. *International Journal of Psychoanalysis*, 1971, *52*, 11–50.

Walls, R.T., Werner, T.J., Bacon, A., & Zane, T. Behavior checklists. In J.D. Cone & R.P. Hawkins (Eds.), *Behavioral assessment: New directions in clinical psychology.* New York: Brunner/Mazel, 1977, 77–146.

Walsh, W.B. Validity of self-report. *Journal of Counseling Psychology*, 1967, *14*, 18–23.

Walter, H.I., & Gilmore, S.K. Placebo versus social learning effects in parent training procedures designed to alter the behavior of aggressive boys. *Behavior Therapy*, 1973, *4*, 361–377.

Wandersman, A., Poppen, P., & Ricks, D. *Humanism and behaviorism: Dialogue and growth.* New York: Pergamon Press, 1976.

Watley, D.J. Feedback training and improvement of clinical forecasting. *Journal of Counseling Psychology*, 1968, *15*, 167–171.

Watson, D.L., & Tharp, R.G. *Self-directed behavior: Self-modification for personal adjustment*. Monterey, Calif.:Brooks-Cole, 1972.

Watson, J.B. Psychology as the behaviorist views it. *Psychological Review*, 1913, *20*, 158–177.

Watson, J.B. *Psychology from the standpoint of a behaviorist*. Philadelphia: J.D. Lippincott, 1919.

Watson, J.B. *Behaviorism*. New York: Norton, 1924.

Watson, J.B. *Behaviorism*. New York: Norton, 1930 (Rev. ed.).

Watson, J.B., & Rayner, R. Conditioned emotional reactions. *Journal of Experimental Psychology*, 1920, *3*, 1–14.

Watson, R.I. *The clinical method in psychology*. New York: Harper, 1951.

Watson, R.I. A brief history of clinical psychology. *Psychological Bulletin*, 1953, *50*, 321–346.

Watson, R.I. *The great psychologists from Aristotle to Freud*. Philadelphia: Lippincott, 1963.

Webb, E., Campbell, D.T., Schwartz, R.D., & Sechrest, L.B. *Unobtrusive measures: Nonreactive research in the social sciences*. Chicago: Rand-McNally, 1966.

Weick, K.E. Systematic observational methods. In G. Lindzey & E. Aronson (Eds.), *Handbook of social psychology* (Vol. 2) (2d ed.). Reading, Mass.: Addison-Wesley, 1968, 357–451.

Weinman, B., Gelbart, P., Wallace, M., & Post, M. Inducing assertive behavior in chronic schizophrenics: A comparison of socio-environmental, desensitization, and relaxation therapies. *Journal of Consulting and Clinical Psychology*, 1972, *39*, 246–252.

Weiss, R.L., & Margolin, G. Assessment of marital conflict and accord. In A.R. Ciminero, K.S. Calhoun, & H.E. Adams (Eds.), *Handbook of behavioral assessment*. New York: John Wiley, 1977, 555–602.

Weiss, T., & Engel, B.T. Operant conditioning of heart rate in patients with premature ventricular contractions. *Psychosomatic Medicine*, 1971, *33*, 301–321.

Wellner, A.M. Survey of psychology services in state mental hospitals. *American Psychologist*, 1968, *23*, 377–380.

Wells, F.L., & Ruesch, J. *Mental examiners' handbook* (2d ed.). New York: Psychological Corporation, 1945.

Wenar, C., & Coulter, J.B. A reliability study of developmental histories. *Child Development*, 1962, *33*, 453–462.

Wernick, R. *They've got your number*. New York: Norton, 1956.

Werry, J.S., & Quay, H.C. Observing the classroom behavior of elementary school children. *Exceptional Children*, 1969, *35*, 461–476.

Wertheimer, M. Studies in the theory of Gestalt psychology. *Psychological Forschung*, 1923, *4*, 300–350.

Wertheimer, M., Barclay, A.G., Cook, S.W., Kiesler, C.A., Koch, S., Riegel, K.F., Rorer, L.G., Senders, V.L., Smith, M.D., & Sperling, S.E. Psychology and the future. *American Psychologist*, 1978, *33*, 631–647.

Wexler, D.B. Token and taboo: Behavior modification, token economics and the law. *California Law Review*, 1973, *61*, 81–109.

Wexler, D.B. Of rights and reinforcer. *San Diego Law Review*, 1974, *11*, 957–971. (a)

Wexler, D.B. Mental health law and the movement toward voluntary treatment. *California Law Review*, 1974, *62*, 671–692. (b)

Wheeler, D.R. Imaginal productivity tests: Beta inkblot test. In H.A. Murray (Ed.), *Explorations in Personality*. New York: Oxford University Press, 1938, 111–150.

Wheeler, W.M. An analysis of Rorschach indices of male homosexuality. *Journal of Projective Techniques*, 1949, *13*, 97–126.

White, B.L., & Watts, J.C. (Eds.). *Experience and environment: Major influences on the development of the young child* (Vol. 1). Englewood Cliffs, N.J.: Prentice-Hall, 1973.

White, R.A. The influence of the experimenter motivation, attitudes and methods of handling subjects in Psi test results. In B.B. Wolman (Ed.), *Handbook of parapsychology*, New York: Van Nostrand Reinhold, 1977, 273–301.

White, R.F., & Watt, N.F. *The abnormal personality* (4th ed.). New York: Ronald Press, 1973.

Whitehorn, J.C. Guide to interviewing and clinical personality study. *Archives of Neurology and Psychiatry*, 1944, *52*, 197–216.

Wicker, A.W. Attitudes versus actions: The relationship of verbal and overt behavioral responses to attitude objects *Journal of Social Issues*, 1969, *25*, 41–78.

Wiens, A.N. The assessment interview. In I.B. Weiner (Ed.), *Clinical methods in psychology*. New York: Wiley, 1976, 3–60.

Wiggins, J.S. *Personality and prediction: Principles of personality assessment*. Reading, Mass.: Addison-Wesley, 1973.

Wildman, B.G., & Erickson, M.T. Methodological problems in behavioral observation. In J.D. Cone & R.P. Hawkins (Eds.), *Behavioral assessment: New directions in clinical psychology*. New York: Brunner/Mazel, 1977, 255–273.

Wilkins, W. Desensitization: Social and cognitive factors underlying the effectiveness of Wolpe's procedure. *Psychological Bulletin*, 1971, *76*, 311–317.

Wilkins, W. Expectancy of therapeutic gain: An empirical and conceptual critique. *Journal of Consulting and Clinical Psychology*, 1973, *40*, 69–77.

Wilkins, W. Self-fulfilling prophecy: Is there a phenomenon to explain? *Psychological Bulletin*, 1977, *584*, 55–56.

Williams, R.B., & Gentry, W.D. *Behavioral approaches to medical treatment*. Cambridge, Mass.: Ballinger, 1977.

Williams, R.J., & Brown, R.A. Differences in baseline drinking behavior between New Zealand alcoholics and normal drinkers. *Behaviour Research and Therapy*, 1974, *12*, 287–294.

Williams, T.R. *Field methods in the study of culture*. New York: Holt, Rinehart, & Winston, 1967.

Willis, J., & Giles, D. Behaviorism in the twentieth century: What we have here is a failure to communicate. *Behavior Therapy*, 1978, *9*, 15–27.

Willis, T.A., Weiss, R.L., & Patterson, G.R. A behavioral analysis of the determinants of marital satisfaction. *Journal of Consulting and Clinical Psychology*, 1974, *42*, 802–811.

Wilson, G.T. On the much discussed term "behavior therapy." *Behavior Therapy*, 1978, *9*, 89–98.

Wilson, G.T., & Davison, G.C. Aversion techniques in behavior therapy: Some theoretical and methodological considerations. *Journal of Consulting and Clinical Psychology*, 1969, *33*, 327–329.

Wilson, G.T., & Davison, G.C. Processes of fear reduction in systematic desensitization: Animal studies. *Psychological Bulletin*, 1971, *76*, 1–14.

Wilson, M.L., & Rappaport, J. Personal self-disclosure: Expectancy and situational effects. *Journal of Consulting and Clinical Psychology*, 1974, *42*, 901–908.

Windle, C., Bass, R.D., & Taube, C.A. PR aside: Initial results from NIMH service program evaluation studies. *American Journal of Community Psychology*, 1974, *2*, 311–327.

Wing, J.K., Cooper, J.E., & Sartorius, N. *The measurement and classification of psychiatric symptoms*. London: Cambridge University Press, 1974.

Wittenborn, J.R. *The Wittenborn Psychiatric Rating Scales*. New York: The Psychological Corporation, 1955.

Wolberg, L.R. *The technique of psychotherapy* (2d ed). New York: Grune & Stratton, 1967.

Wolf, G.A. *Collecting data from patients*. Baltimore: University Park Press, 1977.

Wolman, B.B. (Ed.). *Handbook of clinical psychology*. New York: McGraw-Hill, 1965.

Wolpe, J. *Psychotherapy by reciprocal inhibition*. Stanford, Calif.: Stanford University Press, 1958.

Wolpe, J. *The practice of behavior therapy*. New York: Pergamon, 1969.

Wolpe, J. *The practice of behavior therapy* (2d ed.). New York: Pergamon, 1973.

Wolpe, J., & Lang, P.J. A fear survey schedule for use in behavior therapy. *Behaviour Research and Therapy*, 1964, *2*, 27–30.

Wolpe, J., & Lang, P.J. *Fear Survey Schedule*. San Diego, Calif.: Educational and Industrial Testing Service, 1969.

Wolpe, J., & Lazarus, A.A. *Behavior therapy techniques: A guide to the treatment of neuroses*. New York: Pergamon Press, 1966.

Woltmann, A.G. The use of puppetry as a projective method in therapy. In H.H. Anderson & G.L. Anderson (Eds.), *An introduction to projective techniques*. Englewood Cliffs, N.J.: Prentice-Hall, 1951, 606–638.

Woods, J.P. Careers: New models, new roles, new work. *APA Monitor*, January, 1976, 6–7.

Woody, R.H. Process and behavioral consultation. *American Journal of Community Psychology*, 1975, *3*, 277–286.

Wright, H.F. Observational child study. In P.E. Mussen (Ed.), *Handbook of research methods in clinical development*. New York: Wiley, 1960, 71–139.

Wright, H.F. *Recording and analyzing child behavior: With ecological data from an American town*. New York: Harper & Row, 1967.

Wroblewski, P.F., Jacob, T., & Rehm, L.P. The contribution of relaxation to symbolic modeling in the modification of dental fears. *Behaviour Research and Therapy*, 1977, *15*, 113–114.

Wyatt, F. What is clinical psychology? In A.Z. Guiora & M.A. Brandwin (Eds.), *Perspectives in clinical psychology*. Princeton, N.J.: VanNostrand, 1968, 222–238.

Wyatt v. Aderholt, 503 F2d 1305 (5th cir. 1974).

Wyatt v. Stickney, 344 F Supp. 373, 380 (N.D. Alabama, 1972).

Yalom, I. *The theory and practice of group psychotherapy*. New York: Basic Books, 1975.

Yang, R.K., & Bell, R.Q. Assessment of infants. In P. McReynolds (Ed.), *Advances in psychological assessment* (Vol. 3). San Francisco: Jossey–Bass, 1975, 137–185.

Yarrow, M.R., Campbell, J.D., & Burton, R.V. *Child-rearing: An inquiry into research and methods*. San Francisco: Jossey-Bass, 1968.

Yarrow, M.R., Campbell, J.D., & Burton, R.V. Recollections of childhood: A study of the retrospective method. *Monographs of the Society for Research in Child Development*, 1970, *35* (5, No. 138).

Yates, A.J. *Behavior therapy*. New York: Wiley & Sons, 1970.

Zax, M., & Cowen, E.L. *Abnormal psychology: Changing conceptions*. New York: Holt, Rinehart, & Winston, 1972.

Zax, M., & Specter, G.A. *An introduction to community psychology*. New York: John Wiley & Sons, 1974.

Zegiob, L.E., Arnold, S., & Forehand, R. An examination of observer effects in parent-child interactions. *Child Development*, 1975, *46*, 509–512.

Zetzel, E.R. An approach to the relation between concept and content in psychoanalytic theory. *The Psychoanalytic Study of the Child*, 1956, *11*, 99–121.

Zigler, E., & Phillips, L. Social effectiveness and symptomatic behaviors. *Journal of Abnormal and Social Psychology*, 1960, *61*, 231–238.

Zilboorg, G., & Henry, G.W. *A history of medical psychology*. New York: W.W. Norton, 1941.

Zimet, C.N., & Throne, F.M. *Preconference materials*. Conference on the Professional Preparation of Clinical Psychologists. Washington, D.C.: American Psychological Association, 1965.

Zubin, J. The role of models in clinical psychology. In L. L'Abate (Ed.), *Models of clinical psychology*. Research paper number 22. Atlanta, Ga.: Georgia State College, 1969, 5–12.

Zubin, J., Eron, L.D., & Schumer, F. *An experimental approach to projective techniques*. New York: John Wiley & Sons, 1965.

Zuckerman, M. Physiological measures of sexual arousal in the human. *Psychological Bulletin*, 1971, *75*, 297–329.

Zuckerman, M., & Lubin, B. *Manual for the multiple affect adjective checklist*. San Diego, Calif.: Educational and Industrial Testing Service, 1965.

ADDITIONAL REFERENCES

Barker, R.G., Schoggen, M.F., & Barker, L.S. Hemerography of Mary Ennis. In A. Burton & R.E. Harris (Eds.), *Clinical studies of personality*. New York: Harper & Row, 1955, 768–808.

Bellak, L. *The thematic apperception test and children's apperception test in clinical use*. New York: Grune & Stratton, 1954.

Butcher, J.N., & Koss, M.P. Research on brief and crisis-oriented psychotherapies. In S.L. Garfield & A.E. Bergin (Eds.), *Handbook of psychotherapy and behavior change: An empirical analysis* (2d ed.). New York: John Wiley & Sons, Inc., 1971.

Cautela, J.R., & Upper, D. The behavioral inventory battery: The use of self-report measures in behavioral analysis and therapy. In M. Hersen & A. Bellack (Eds.), *Behavioral assessment: A practical handbook*. New York: Pergamon Press, 1976, 77–110.

Cohen, E., Motto, J.A., & Seiden, R.H. An instrument for evaluating suicide potential: A preliminary study. *American Journal of Psychiatry*, 1966, *122*, 886–891.

Frankl, V. *Man's search for meaning*. New York: Washington Square Press, 1963.

Frankl, V. *The doctor and the soul.* New York: Knopf, 1965.

Frankl, V. Psychotherapy and existentialism: Selected papers on logotherapy. New York: Washington Square Press, 1967.

Greenspoon, J., & Gersten, C.D. A new look at psychological testing: Psychological testing from the standpoint of a behaviorist. *American Psychologist,* 1967, *22,* 848–853.

Gross, M.L. *The brain watchers.* New York: Random House, 1962.

Guilford, J.P., & Zimmerman, W.S. *The Guilford-Zimmerman temperament survey: Manual of instructions and interpretations.* Beverly Hills, Calif.: Sheridan Supply Co., 1949.

Kent, G.H., & Rosanoff, A.J. A study of association in insanity. *American Journal of Insanity,* 1910, *67,* 37–96, 317–390.

Levitsky, A., & Perls, F.S. The rules and games of gestalt therapy. In J. Fagan & I.L. Shephers (Eds.), *Gestalt therapy now.* Palo Alto, Calif.: Science and Behavior Books, 1970, 29.

Lindemann, E. Symptomology and management of acute grief. *American Journal of Psychology,* 1944, *101,* 141–148.

Matarazzo, J.D., Wiens, A.N., Matarazzo, R.G., & Saslow, G. Speech and silence behavior in clinical psychotherapy and its laboratory correlates. In J.M. Shlien (Ed.), *Research in psychotherapy.* Washington, D.C.: American Psychological Association, 1968.

Patterson, C.H. *Theories of counseling and psychotherapy* (2d ed.). New York: Harper & Row, 1973.

Payne, A.F. *Sentence completions.* New York: New York Guidance Clinic, 1928.

Pope, B., Nudler, S., Vonkorff, M.R., & McGhec, J.P. The experienced professional interviewer versus the complete novice. *Journal of Consulting and Clinical Psychology,* 1974, *42,* 680–690.

Rathus, S.A. A 30-item schedule for assessing assertive behavior. *Behavior therapy,* 1973, *4,* 398–406.

Raush, H.L., & Bordin, E.S. Warmth in personality development and in psychotherapy. *Psychiatry,* 1957, *20,* 351–363.

Reynolds, G.S. *A primer of operant conditioning.* Glenview, Ill.: Scott, Foresman, 1968.

Richardson, F.C., & Tasto, D.L. Development of factor analysis of a social anxiety inventory. *Behavior therapy,* 1976, *7,* 453–462.

Sacks, J.M., and Levy, S. The sentence completion test. In L.E. Abt & L. Bellak (Eds.), *Projective psychology.* New York: Knopf, 1950, 357–402.

Storrow, H.A. *Introduction to scientific psychiatry: A behavioral approach to diagnosis and treatment.* New York: Appleton-Century-Crofts, 1967.

Tendler, A.D. A preliminary report on a test for emotional insight. *Journal of Applied Psychology,* 1930, *14,* 123–136.

Watson, D., & Friend, R. Measurement of social-evaluative anxiety. *Journal of Consulting and Clinical Psychology,* 1969, *33,* 448–457.

Webb, J.T. Regional and sex differences in MMPI scale high-point frequencies of psychiatric patients. *Journal of Clinical Psychology,* 1971, *27,* 483–486.

Weiss, J.H. The effect of professional training and amount and accuracy of information on behavioral prediction. *Journal of Consulting Psychology,* 1963, *27,* 257–262.

Williams, R.L. The Black Intelligence Test of Cultural Homogeneity (BITCH)—100: A culture-specific test. Paper presented at the American Psychological Association meeting. Honolulu, September 1972.

Name Index

Subject Index